The Scottish Law of
DEBT

The Scottish Law of
DEBT

W. A. WILSON, M.A., LL.B.
*Lord President Reid Professor of Law,
University of Edinburgh*

SECOND EDITION

W. GREEN/Sweet & Maxwell
EDINBURGH
1991

First published in 1982
Second edition 1991

© 1991
W. A. Wilson

ISBN 0 414 00937 1

A catalogue record for this
book is available from
the British Library

Printed in Great Britain by
Hartnolls

PREFACE TO SECOND EDITION

THE new legislation on bankruptcy, corporate insolvency and diligence has required the rewriting of much of the text. The object has again been to state the position of the creditor in a general way and not to produce a detailed and comprehensive treatise on the law of diligence and insolvency. One notes that on two matters—the effect of attachment of the floating charge and the prescription of cautionary obligations—the Inner House, no doubt proceeding by some higher corniche, has reached the same result as was suggested in the last edition.

Since the last edition the literature in the field has expanded substantially and I have derived much benefit from reading Maher and Cusine on *Diligence*, McBryde on *Bankruptcy* and St Clair and Drummond Young on *Corporate Insolvency*. I also found very useful Mr Fayyad Algudah's LL.M. dissertation on the administration procedure.

I am again indebted to many of my university colleagues, particularly Mr George Gretton and Mr Kenneth Reid, for help given in various ways, to Ms Jane Mair for compiling the tables and index and to the staff of W. Green for their tolerance and efficiency in the production of the book. I have attempted to state the law as at 30th September 1990.

Edinburgh,   W.A.W.
1 June 1991

CONTENTS

	PAGE
Preface to Second Edition	v
Table of Cases	ix
Table of Statutes	xlv
Abbreviations	lxxiii
Principal Works Cited	lxxiv

1. THE NATURE OF DEBT	1
2. COMMON DEBTS	15
3. THE CONSUMER CREDIT ACT	27
4. CREDIT TRANSACTIONS	49
5. BONDS AND BILLS	60
6. CHEQUES	78
7. SECURITIES: CORPOREAL MOVEABLES	89
8. SECURITIES: OTHER PROPERTY	99
9. SECURITIES GRANTED BY A COMPANY	106
10. CAUTIONARY OBLIGATIONS	123
11. RECOVERY OF DEBTS	128
12. PAYMENT	147
13. COMPENSATION AND RETENTION	157
14. OTHER DEFENCES	167
15. DILIGENCE	175
16. POINDING	182
17. ARRESTMENT	191
18. DILIGENCES AGAINST EARNINGS	205
19. OTHER DILIGENCE	215
20. SEQUESTRATION	221
21. SEQUESTRATION: THE ESTATE	229
22. ANTECEDENT TRANSACTIONS	237
23. THE CLAIM	245
24. ALTERNATIVES TO SEQUESTRATION	255
25. LIQUIDATION	259
26. VOLUNTARY ARRANGEMENTS AND ADMINISTRATION ORDERS	273
27. ASSIGNATION OF DEBTS	283
28. JOINT AND SEVERAL OBLIGATIONS	290
29. DEATH	295
30. SPECIAL PARTIES	307
Index	321

TABLE OF CASES

	PARA
A. v. B. (1618) Mor.2771	17.11
—— v. —— (1747) Mor.2648	13.7
—— v. B.C.& Co. (1956) 72 Sh.Ct.Rep.29	4.5
A.B. & Co. v. C.D. (1909) 25 Sh.Ct.Rep.106	11.1
A.R.V. Aviation Ltd., Re [1989] B.C.L.C.664	26.8
Abbey National Building Society v. Strang, 1981 S.L.T.(Sh.Ct.)4	17.6
Abel v. Watt (1883) 11 R.149	20.7
Aberdeen, Earl of v. Merchiston's Crs. (1729) Mor.867	27.3
Aberdeen Town and County Bank v. Davidson (1885) 1 Sh.Ct.Rep.212	5.26
Adair v. Cunningham (1887) 4 Sh.Ct.Rep.51	5.3
Adam v. Anderson (1837) 15 S.1225	17.2
—— v. Macdougall (1831) 9 S.570	12.13
—— v. McRobbie (1845) 7 D. 276	21.1
—— v. Sutherland (1863) 2 M.6	7.12
Adam & Winchester v. White's Tr. (1884) 11 R.863	23.1
Adam Cochran & Co. v. Conn, 1989 S.L.T.(Sh.Ct.)27	11.5
Adam's Trs. v. Burns (1939) 55 Sh.Ct.Rep.196	4.6
Adamson v. McMitchell (1624) Mor. 859	27.4
Advocate, Lord, v. Blairwest Investments Ltd., (Sh.Ct.) 1989 S.C.L.R.352	25.2
—— v. Galloway (1884) 11 R.541	6.15
—— v. Hepburn, 1990 G.W.D.3-143	14.4
—— v. Huron and Erie Loan and Savings Co., 1911 S.C.612	30.20
—— v. Macfarlane's Trs. (1893) 31 S.L.R. 357	29.2
—— v. McInnes Textiles Ltd., 1978 S.L.T.(Notes)84	25.7
—— v. Royal Bank of Scotland, 1977 S.C.155	16.13, 17.12, 17.13, 17.14
Advocates, Faculty of, v. Dickson (1718) Mor.866	27.4
Agnew v. Ferguson (1903) 5 F.879	1.6, 12.7
—— v. Norwest Construction Co., 1935 S.C.771	17.3
"Aifanourios", The, 1980 S.C.346	11.10
Ainslie v. McGowan, 1974 S.L.T.(Sh.Ct.)19	4.3
Air Ecosse Ltd. v. Civil Aviation Authority, 1987 S.L.T.751	26.5
Airdrie, Provost of, v. French (1915) 31 Sh.Ct.Rep.189	5.3
Aitchison v. McDonald, 1911 S.C.174	30.16
Aitken v. Kyd (1890) 28 S.L.R.115	20.6
Aitken & Co. v. Pyper (1900) 38 S.L.R.74	10.1
Aitken's Trs. v. Bank of Scotland, 1944 S.C.270	10.3, 28.7
Akrokerri (Atlantic) Mines Ltd. v. Economic Bank [1904] 2 K.B.465	6.11
Alan (W.J.) & Co. Ltd. v. El Nasr Export and Import Co. [1972] 2 Q.B.189	12.3
Alexander v. Campbell's Trs. (1903) 5 F. 634	1.9, 11.1
—— v. McLay (1826) 4 S.439	16.2
—— v. Scott (1827) 6 S.150	28.1
Alison v. Duncan (1711) Mor. 2657	27.5
Allan v. Allan & Co. (1831) 9 S.519	12.5
—— v. Murray (1894) 10 Sh.Ct.Rep.103	21.7
—— v. Ormiston (1817) Hume 477	4.6
—— v. Williamson (1741) Elchies' Heritable No. 12	29.2
Allan & Son v. Brown and Lightbody (1890) 6 Sh.Ct.Rep.278	27.1
Allan, Buckley Allan & Milne v. Pattison (1893) 21 R.195	10.3
Allan (James) & Sons (Contractors) Ltd. v. Gourlay, 1956 S.L.T.(Sh.Ct.)77	13.2
Allan (Robert) and Partners v. McKinstray, 1975 S.L.T.(Sh.Ct.)63	2.9
Allan's Exr. v. Union Bank of Scotland Ltd., 1909 S.C.206	17.3
Allan's Trs. v. Lord Advocate, 1971 S.C.(H.L.)45	7.3
Allchin v. South Shields Corporation [1943] 25 T.C.445	12.7
Allen v. McCombie's Trs., 1909 S.C.710	28.1
Allen (David) & Sons Billposting Ltd. v. Bruce, 1933 S.C.253	12.7
Aluminium Industrie B.V. v. Romalpa Ltd. [1976] 1 W.L.R.676	2.3
Alvis v. Harrison, 1989 S.L.T.746	11.14

Table of Cases

Ambassadors (Bournemouth), Re (1961) 105 S.J. 969 .... 9.12
American Mortgage Co. of Scotland Ltd. v. Sidway, 1908 S.C. 500 .... 1.11, 17.3
Anderson v. Buchanan (1848) 11 D. 270 .... 16.2
—— v. Croall & Sons Ltd. (1903) 6 F.153 .... 30.2
—— v. Dayton (1884) 21 S.L.R.787 .... 10.1, 28.2
—— v. Dow (1907) 23 Sh.Ct.Rep.51 .... 2.10
—— v. Forth Marine Insurance Co. (1845) 7 D.268 .... 12.14
—— v. McCall (1866) 4 M.765 .... 7.3
—— v. Mackinnon (1876) 3 R.608 .... 13.10, 23.9, 28.2
—— v. North of Scotland Bank (1901) 4 F.49 .... 6.15, 13.4
—— v. Schaw (1739) Mor.2646 .... 13.7
—— v. Scottish N.E. Rlwy. Co. (1867) 3 S.L.R.270 .... 17.2
—— v. Stewart (1831) 10 S.49 .... 29.7
—— v. Western Bank (1859) 21 D.230 .... 22.5
Anderson (Gordon) (Plant) Ltd. v. Campsie Construction Ltd., 1977 S.L.T.7 ..... 17.14, 30.19
Anderson's Tr. v. Fleming (1871) 9 M.718 .... 7.8, 22.7
—— v. Sommerville & Co. (1899) 36 S.L.R.833 .... 8.1, 22.6
Anderson's Trs. v. Webster (1883) 11 R.35 .... 6.14
Anglo-Austrian Printing and Publishing Union, Re [1895] 2 Ch.891 .... 9.18
Angus' Tr. v. Angus (1901) 4 F.181 .... 22.6
Annand's Trs. v. Annand (1869) 7 M.526 .... 4.2
Anstruther v. Wilkie (1856) 18 D.405 .... 2.8
Antermony Coal Co. v. Wingate (1866) 4 M.1017 .... 30.10
Apollo Leasing Ltd. v. Scott, 1984 S.L.T.(Sh.Ct.)90 .... 3.3
Arab Bank Ltd. v. Ross [1952] 2 Q.B.216 .... 5.9
Archivent Sales & Development Ltd. v. Strathclyde Regional Council, 1985 S.L.T.154 .... 2.3
Armia Ltd. v. Daejan Developments Ltd., 1979 S.C.(H.L.)56 .... 2.11
Armour v. Duff, 1912 S.C.120 .... 30.2
Armour v. Thyssen Edelstahlwerke A.G., 1990 S.L.T.891 .... 2.3
Armour & Melvin v. Mitchell, 1934 S.C.94 .... 13.1, 13.2
Armour and Mycroft, Petrs., 1983 S.L.T.453 .... 9.15
Armstrong v. Wilson (1842) 4 D.1347 .... 19.6
Arnott's Trs. v. Forbes (1881) 9 R.89 .... 27.7
Arrow Chemicals Ltd. v. Guild, 1978 S.L.T.206 .... 28.5
Arthur (1903) 10 S.L.T.550 .... 29.11
Asphaltic Limestone Co. v. Corporation of Glasgow, 1907 S.C.463 .... 13.4, 13.10
Associated Portland Cement Manufacturers Ltd. v. McInally, 1970 S.L.T.(Sh.Ct.)9 .... 11.13
Athena, The (1921) 8 LL.L.Rep.482 .... 7.5
Athya v. Clydesdale Bank (1881) 18 S.L.R.287 .... 24.2
Atlantic Computers plc, Re [1990] 6 I.L.&P.66 .... 26.8, 26.11
Atlantic Engine Co. (1920) Ltd. v. Lord Advocate, 1955 S.L.T.17 .... 13.8
Auchteroni & Co. v. Midland Bank Ltd. [1928] 2 K.B.294 .... 6.12
Avery v. Cantilever Shoe Co. Ltd., 1942 S.C.469 .... 11.13
Ayerst v. C. & K. (Construction) Ltd. [1976] A.C. 167 .... 25.7
Ayres v. Moore [1940] 1 K.B.278 .... 5.16
Ayton v. Romanes (1895) 3 S.L.T.203 .... 27.3, 27.4

B.O.C.M. SILCOCK LTD. v. Hunter, 1976 S.L.T.217 .... 10.1
Baillie v. McIntosh (1753) Mor.2680 .... 13.6
—— v. Wilson (1840) 2 D.495 .... 17.3
Baines and Tait v. Compagnie Generale des Mines d'Asphalte (1879) 6 R.846 ..... 11.9
Baird v. Baird, 1910 1 S.L.T.95 .... 11.9
Baird & Brown v. Stirrat's Tr. (1872) 10 M.414 .... 23.5
Baird's Trs. v. Baird & Co. (1877) 4 R.1005 .... 1.6
Baker, Re [1954] 1 W.L.R.1144 .... 25.12
Baker v. Lipton (1899) 15 T.L.R.435 .... 12.1
Balfour v. Baird & Sons, 1959 S.C.64 .... 28.5
—— v. Smith and Logan (1877) 4 R.454 .... 1.6
Balfour Melville v. Duncan (1903) 5 F.1079 .... 1.6

Table of Cases

Ballachulish Slate Quarries v. Menzies (1908) 45 S.L.R.667	27.1
Ballantyne v. Barr (1867) 5 M.330	20.6
Ballantyne's Trs. v. Ballantyne's Trs., 1941 S.C.35	29.5
Ballenden (Lord), Crs. of, v. Countess of Dalhousie (1707) Mor.865	27.4
Balmerino, Lord, v. Dick's Crs. (1664) Mor.2681	13.6
Bank of Baroda v. Punjab National Bank [1944] A.C.176	6.1
Bank of England v. Vagliano Brothers [1891] A.C.107	6.12
Bank of Scotland v. Baird (Sh.Ct.) 1987 S.C.L.R.18	13.2
—— v. Davis, 1982 S.L.T.20	11.7
—— v. W. & G. Fergusson (1898) 1 F.96	14.7
—— v. Hutchison Main & Co. Ltd. (Liqrs.), 1914 S.C.(H.L.)1	8.1, 21.2, 25.1, 25.7
—— v. Lamont & Co. (1889) 16 R.769	5.25
—— v. Logie, 1986 S.L.T.(Sh.Ct.)47	11.7
—— v. Mackay, 1991 S.L.T.163	20.3
—— v. MacLeod, 1986 S.L.T. 504	10.3
—— v. McNeill, 1977 S.L.T.(Sh.Ct.)2	30.2
—— v. Reid (1886) 2 Sh.Ct.Rep.376	6.9
—— v. Robertson (1870) 8 M.391	6.15
—— v. Rorie (1908) 16 S.L.T.21	30.2
—— v. Seitz, 1989 S.L.T.641; 1990 S.L.T.584	12.4
—— v. Stewart & Ross, 7 February 1811, F.C.	22.8
Bank of Scotland, Petrs., 1988 S.L.T.690	25.8
Banks v. D.R.G. plc, 1988 S.L.T.825	11.14, 11.19
Bankhardt's Trs. v. Scottish Amicable Life Assurance Society (1871) 9 M.443	17.3
Banque de l'Indochine et de Suez S.A. v. Euroseas Group Finance Co. Ltd. [1981] 3 All E.R.198	5.14
Banque Indo Suez v. Maritime Co. Overseas Inc., 1984 S.C.120	7.5
Barbor v. Middleton, 1988 S.C.L.R.178	25.9
Barclay v. Chief Constable, Northern Constabulary, 1986 S.L.T.562	14.7
—— v. Clerk (1683) Mor.2641	13.7
Barclay Curle & Co. Ltd. v. Sir James Laing & Sons Ltd., 1908 S.C.82	11.10
Barclays Bank v. Astley Industrial Trust Ltd. [1970] 2 Q.B. 527	6.4, 6.13
—— v. Bank of England [1985] 1 All E.R.385	6.1
—— v. Lawton's Trs., 1928 S.L.T.298	29.6
—— v. McGreish, 1983 S.L.T.344	29.5
Barlass v. Barlass's Trs., 1916 S.C.741	29.6
Barnet v. Duncan (1831) 10 S.128	29.3
Barnett v. Colvill (1840) 2 D.337	12.8
Barnton Hotel Co. v. Cook (1899) 1 F.1190	7.7
Barr & Shearer v. Cooper (1875) 2 R.(H.L.)14	7.7
Barstow v. Inglis (1857) 20 D.230	6.15
Batey (William) (Exports) Ltd. v. Kent, 1987 S.L.T.557	11.10
Baynes v. Graham (1796) Mor.2904	17.9
Beard v. Beveridge, Herd and Sandilands, W.S., 1990 S.L.T.609	14.9
Beaton v. Wilkie (1927) 43 Sh.Ct.Rep.193	10.1
Beattie & Son v. Pratt (1880) 7 R.1171	11.10, 17.15
Bechuanaland Exploration Co. v. London Trading Bank Ltd. [1898] 2 Q.B.658	5.2
Beith v. Mackenzie (1875) 3 R.185	29.6
Beith (Alexander) Ltd. v. Allen, 1961 S.L.T.(Notes)80	5.21, 6.13
Belhaven Engineering & Motors Ltd. v. Reid (1910) 26 Sh.Ct.Rep.234	12.13
Belk v. Best [1942] 1 Ch.77	12.7
Bell v. Andrews (1885) 12 R.961	7.12
—— v. Bell (1897) 4 S.L.T.214	5.27
—— v. Cadell (1831) 10 S.100	1.7
—— v. Thomson (1867) 6 M.64	1.6
—— v. Willison (1831) 9 S.266	29.7
Bell Brothers (H.P.) Ltd. v. Aitken, 1939 S.C.577	1.6, 2.6
Bell, Rannie & Co. v. Smith (1885) 22 S.L.R. 597	16.2
Bell's Sports Centre (Perth) Ltd. v. William Briggs & Sons Ltd., 1971 S.L.T.(Notes)48	11.7
Bell's Tr. v. Bell (1884) 12 R.85	29.10
"Ben Gairn", The, 1979 S.C.98	1.6

Bendy Brothers Ltd. v. McAlister (1910) 26 Sh.Ct.Rep.152	16.11
Benhar Coal Co. v. Turnbull (1883) 10 R.558	17.12
Benjedward's Crs. (1753) Mor.743	17.2
Bennett v. Inverest Paper Co. (1891) 18 R.975	30.1, 30.2
Bentley v. MacFarlane, 1964 S.C.76	27.6
Bermans & Nathans Ltd. v. Weibye, 1983 S.C.67	7.10
Bertram v. McIntyre (1934) 50 Sh.Ct.Rep.194	6.14
Bethune v. Morgan (1874) 2 R.186	29.5
Binning v. Macdoual (1738) Mor.736	17.6
Binstock (J.E.), Miller & Co. v. E. Coia & Co. Ltd. (1957) 73 Sh.Ct.Rep.178	13.2, 27.7
Bishop v. Bryce, 1910 S.C.426	6.14
Black v. Gibb, 1940 S.C.24	6.14
—— v. Scott (1830) 8 S.367	17.6
Blacks v. Girdwood (1885) 13 R.243	30.8
Blackwood & Tinto Ltd. v. Gascoines Ltd., 1950 S.L.T.(Sh.Ct.)5	30.3
Blair v. North British and Mercantile Insurance Co. (1889) 16 R.325	20.6
Blair Iron Co. v. Alison (1855) 18 D.(H.L.)49; 6 W.&S.56	13.5
Blair's Trs. v. Payne (1884) 12 R.104	11.7
Blincow's Tr. v. Allan & Co. (1828) 7 S.124; (1833) 7 W.&S.26	22.6
Blum v. O.C.P. Repartition SA [1988] B.C.L.C.170	5.14
Blyth Dry Docks & Shipbuilding Co. Ltd. v. Commissioners for Port of Calcutta, 1972 S.L.T.(Notes)7	27.6
Bob Gray (Access) Ltd. v. T.M. Standard Scaffolding Ltd., 1987 S.C.L.R.720	22.9
Boak v. Megget (1844) 6 D.662	7.3
Boland v. White Cross Insurance Association, 1926 S.C.1066	1.11, 17.3, 17.8
Boland (T.) & Co. Ltd. v. Dundas's Trs., 1975 S.L.T.(Notes)80	2.11
Bolden v. Ferguson (1863) 1 M.522	22.1
Bonar v. Liddell (1841) 3 D.830	30.1
Bond Worth Ltd., Re [1980] Ch.228	2.3
Bondina Ltd. v. Rollaway Shower Blinds Ltd. [1986] 1 W.L.R.517	5.14
Booth v. Booth [1922] 1 K.B.66	12.7
Borden (U.K.) Ltd. v. Scottish Timber Products Ltd. [1981] Ch.25	2.3
Borland v. Lochwinnoch Golf Club, 1986 S.L.T.(Sh.Ct.)13	30.16
Borthwick v. Bremner (1833) 12 S.121	7.7
—— v. Scottish Widows' Fund (1864) 2 M.595	13.10
Bosco Design Services Ltd. v. Plastic Sealant Services Ltd., 1979 S.C.189	2.11
Bouboulis v. Mann Macneal & Co., 1926 S.C.637	25.3
Bowe and Christie v. Hutchison (1868) 6 M.642	6.14
Bowmaker (Commercial) Ltd. v. Dunnigan, 1976 S.L.T.(Sh.Ct.)54	2.6
Boyd v. Millar, 1934 S.N.7	4.3
—— v. Turnbull & Findlay, 1911 S.C.1006	7.11
Boyle (John S.) Ltd. v. Boyle's Trs., 1949 S.L.T.(Notes)45	4.2
Braby (Frederic) & Co. Ltd. v. Edwin Danks & Co. (Oldbury) Ltd. (1907) 15 S.L.T.161	17.4
Bradford Old Bank Ltd. v. Sutcliffe [1918] 2 K.B.833	12.5
Bradley v. Scott, 1966 S.L.T.(Sh.Ct.)25	2.11
Brand v. Allan (1913) 29 Sh.Ct.Rep.76	4.5
—— v. Kent (1892) 20 R.29	11.10
Brandao v. Barnett (1846) 12 Cl.&F.787	7.10
Brash v. Brash, 1966 S.L.T.157; 1966 S.C.56	11.10, 17.2
Breadalbane's Trs. v. Jamieson (1873) 11 M.912	29.10
Brebner v. Henderson, 1925 S.C.643	5.14
Brember v. Rutherford (1901) 4 F.62	30.9
Brett v. Williamson, 1980 S.L.T.(Sh.Ct.)56	2.9
Bridge v. Campbell Discount Co. Ltd. [1962] A.C.600	1.6
—— v. South Portland St. Synagogue, 1907 S.C.1351	30.16
Bridges v. Ewing (1836) 15 S.8	17.4
Bright v. Low, 1940 S.C.280	11.14
Brightlife, Re [1987] Ch.200	9.1
Britannia Steamship Insurance Association Ltd. v. Duff, 1909 S.C.1261	10.1
British Airport plc v. Powdrill [1990] 2 W.L.R.1362	26.5, 26.8
British Airways v. Parish [1979] 2 Lloyd's Rep. 361	5.14

Table of Cases

British Bata Shoe Co. Ltd. *v.* Double M. Shah Ltd., 1981 S.L.T.(Notes)5; 1980
    S.C.311 .... 12.11, 12.6
British Gas plc *v.* Darling, 1990 S.L.T.(Sh.Ct.)53 .... 11.15
British General Insurance Co. *v.* Borthwick (1924) 40 Sh.Ct.Rep.198 .... 20.2
British Hydro-Carbon Chemicals Ltd. and British Transport Commission, *Petrs.*,
    1961 S.L.T.280 .... 1.6
British Linen Co. *v.* Carruthers and Fergusson (1883) 10 R.923 .... 6.7, 6.10
—— *v.* Cowan (1906) 8 F.704 .... 5.10, 5.21
—— *v.* Esplin (1849) 11 D.1104 .... 12.13
—— *v.* Gourlay (1877) 4 R.651 .... 23.4
—— *v.* Kansas Investment Co. Ltd. (1895) 3 S.L.T.138 .... 17.3
—— *v.* Monteith (1858) 20 D.557 .... 10.3
—— *v.* Rainey's Tr. (1885) 12 R.825 .... 27.2, 27.9
—— *v.* Thomson (1853) 15 D.314 .... 12.14
British Marine Mutual Insurance Association Ltd. *v.* Adamson (1932) 48
    Sh.Ct.Rep.3 .... 23.4
British Motor Body Co. Ltd. *v.* Thomas Shaw (Dundee) Ltd., 1914 S.C.922 ... 13.2, 13.9
British Oxygen Co. *v.* South West Scotland Electricity Board, 1958 S.C.53 .... 1.6
British Railways Board *v.* Birrell, 1971 S.L.T.(Notes)17 .... 2.11
—— *v.* Glasgow Corporation, 1976 S.C.224 .... 1.6
—— *v.* Ross and Cromarty County Council, 1974 S.C.27 .... 1.6, 11.7
—— *v.* Strathclyde Regional Council, 1980 S.L.T.63; 1981 S.C.90 .... 14.7
Broddelius *v.* Grischotti (1887) 14 R.536 .... 5.23
Brook *v.* Hook (1871) L.R. 6 Ex.89 .... 5.10, 5.21
Brooke *v.* Price [1917] A.C.115 .... 12.7
Brown *v.* Brecknell, Munro & Rogers (1928) Ltd. (1938) 54 Sh.Ct.Rep.254 .... 2.6
—— *v.* Carron Co. (1898) 6 S.L.T.231 .... 2.2
—— *v.* Duff's Tr. (1850) 13 D.149 .... 17.2
—— *v.* Elies (1686) Mor.2566 .... 13.5
—— *v.* Hunter-Arundell's Trs. (1899) 15 Sh.Ct.Rep.281 .... 21.8
—— *v.* Nisbet & Co. Ltd. (1941) 57 Sh.Ct.Rep.202 .... 2.9
—— *v.* Sutherland (1875) 2 R.615 .... 1.8, 5.14
—— *v.* Wallace (1894) 10 Sh.Ct.Rep.142 .... 29.6
Browne's Tr. *v.* Anderson (1901) 4 F.305 .... 27.3, 27.4
Brownlee *v.* Robb, 1907 S.C.1302 .... 27.2, 27.5
Brownlie, Watson & Beckett *v.* Caledonian Rlwy. Co., 1907 S.C.617 .... 2.7
Bruce *v.* Calder (1904) 20 Sh.Ct.Rep.288 .... 4.5
—— *v.* Scottish Amicable Life Assurance Society, 1907 S.C.637 .... 28.3
Bruce (W. & A.S.) *v.* Ewans, 1986 S.L.T.(Sh.Ct.)20 .... 2.8
Brugh *v.* Gray (1717) Mor.1125 .... 22.8
Brunton *v.* Bone (1858) 1 S.L.J.58 .... 6.14
Bryan *v.* Butters Bros. & Co. (1892) 19 R.490 .... 4.5
Bryson & Co. Ltd. *v.* Glasgow Civil Service & Mercantile Guild (1916) 32
    Sh.Ct.Rep.23 .... 30.16
Buchan, Earl of, *v.* His Creditors (1835) 13 S.1112 .... 17.3
Buchanan *v.* Cameron, 1973 S.C.285 .... 11.7
—— *v.* Main (1900) 3 F.215 .... 10.1, 10.3, 12.5, 28.2
—— *v.* Royal Bank (1842) 5 D.211 .... 29.3
—— *v.* Stewart (1874) 2 R.78 .... 1.6
Buchanan & Carswell *v.* Eugene Ltd., 1936 S.C.160 .... 1.6
Buie *v.* Gordon (1827) 5 S.464; (1831) 9 S.923 .... 30.21
Bunten *v.* Hart (1902) 9 S.L.T.476 .... 11.7
Burnett *v.* Westminster Bank [1966] 1 Q.B.742 .... 6.2
Burns *v.* Burn (1879) 7 R.355 .... 11.10
—— *v.* ——, 1964 S.L.T.(Sh.Ct.)21 .... 4.5
—— *v.* Garscadden (1901) 8 S.L.T.321 .... 2.11
—— *v.* Gillies (1906) 8 F.460 .... 17.6
—— *v.* Martin (1887) 14 R.(H.L.)20 .... 28.1
—— *v.* Monro (1844) 6 D.1352 .... 17.8
Burrell *v.* Burrell's Trs., 1916 S.C.729 .... 13.4
Burt *v.* Bell (1861) 24 D.13 .... 13.1
—— *v.* Laing, 1925 S.C.181 .... 12.11

Table of Cases

Busby Spinning Co. Ltd. *v.* BMK Ltd., 1988 S.L.T.246 .... 13.10
Butler *v.* Butler [1961] P.33 .... 12.7
Buttercase & Geddie's Tr. *v.* Geddie (1897) 24 R.1128 .... 24.2
Byng *v.* Campbell (1893) 1 S.L.T.371 .... 17.4

C.I.R. *v.* Hartley (1956) 36 T.C.348 .... 12.7
Cadzow Finance Co. Ltd. *v.* Fleming, 1985 S.L.T.(Sh.Ct.)37 .... 11.19
Cairney *v.* Macgregor's Trs., 1916 1 S.L.T.357 .... 5.27
Calder & Co. *v.* Cruikshank's Tr. (1889) 17 R.74 .... 10.3
Caldwell *v.* Hamilton, 1919 S.C.(H.L.)100 .... 17.3, 20.1
Caledonian Insurance Co. *v.* Beattie (1898) 5 S.L.T.349 .... 27.2
Caledonian Rlwy. Co. *v.* Colt (1860) 3 Macq.833 .... 1.6
California Redwood Co. *v.* Merchant Banking Co. of London (1886) 13 R.1202 ... 25.5
Callum *v.* Ferrier (1825) 1 W.&.S.399 .... 7.7
Cameron *v.* Panton's Trs. (1891) 18 R.728 .... 12.10
Campbell *v.* Carphin, 1925 S.L.T.(Sh.Ct.)30 .... 13.10
—— *v.* Farquhar (1724) Mor.14626 .... 28.1
—— *v.* Little (1823) 2 S.484 .... 13.10
—— *v.* McCutcheon, 1963 S.C.505 .... 2.11
—— *v.* McKellar, 1926 S.L.T.(Sh.Ct.)82 .... 15.5
—— *v.* Napier (1678) Mor. 5035 .... 12.13
—— *v.* Watson's Tr. (1898) 25 R.690 .... 17.6
Campbell & Beck *v.* Macfarlane (1862) 24 D.1097 .... 24.2
Campbell (J. & W.) & Co. (1899) 6 S.L.T.406 .... 29.6
Campbell's J.F. *v.* National Bank, 1944 S.C.495 .... 29.11
Campbell's Tr. *v.* De Lisle's Exrs. (1870) 9 M.252 .... 19.3
Campbell's Trs. *v.* Campbell's Trs., 1950 S.C.48 .... 14.5
—— *v.* Whyte (1884) 11 R.1078 .... 27.5
Campos *v.* Kentucky & Indiana Terminal Railroad Co. [1962] 2 Lloyd's Rep. 459 .. 1.4
Cant *v.* Eagle Star Insurance Co., 1937 S.L.T.444 .... 17.8
Cantiere San Rocco *v.* Clyde Shipbuilding and Engineering Co., 1923 S.C.(H.L.)105 .... 1.6
Cardno & Darling *v.* Steuart (1869) 7 M.1026 .... 11.7
Carlton *v.* Miller, 1978 S.L.T.(Sh.Ct.)36 .... 16.8
Carmichael *v.* Caledonian Rlwy. Co. (1870) 8 M.(H.L.)119 .... 11.7
—— *v.* Carmichael (1719) Mor.2677 .... 13.6
—— *v.* Carmichael's Exrx., 1920 S.C.(H.L.)195 .... 24.2
Carmichael's Tr. *v.* Carmichael, 1929 S.C.265 .... 4.5
Carnoway *v.* Ewing (1611) Mor.14988 .... 19.5
Carntyne Motors *v.* Curran, 1958 S.L.T.(Sh.Ct.)6 .... 7.8
Carr *v.* L.A., 1990 S.L.T.225 .... 11.19
Carrigan *v.* Duncan, 1971 S.L.T.(Sh.Ct.)33 .... 28.5
Carron Co. *v.* Currie & Co. (1896) 33 S.L.R.578 .... 17.6
Carter *v.* Johnstone (1886) 13 R.698 .... 22.5, 22.6
—— *v.* McIntosh (1862) 24 D.925 .... 27.1, 27.2, 27.4
Cassells *v.* Stewart (1879) 6 R.936 .... 17.3
Castle Phillips Finance Ltd. *v.* Williams [1986] C.C.L.R.13 .... 3.2
Cathcart *v.* Moodie (1804) Mor. "Heir & Executor" App. 1 No.2 .... 29.6
Cauvin *v.* Robertson (1783) Mor.2581 .... 13.4
Central Motor Engineering Co. *v.* Galbraith, 1918 S.C.755 .... 30.13
Centrebind Ltd., *Re* [1966] 3 All E.R. 889 .... 25.14
Chafer (J.W.) (Scotland) Ltd. *v.* Hope, 1963 S.L.T.(Notes)11 .... 13.9
Chamber's J.F. *v.* Vertue (1893) 20 R.257 .... 27.5
Chambers' Trs. *v.* Smith (1878) 5 R.(H.L.)151 .... 17.3
Channel Airways *v.* Manchester Corporation [1974] 1 Lloyd's Rep. 456 .... 7.6
Charge Card Services Ltd., *Re* [1987] Ch.150; [1989] Ch.497 .... 12.3
Chiesley *v.* His Sisters (1704) Mor.5531 .... 29.2
Christie *v.* Birrells, 1910 S.C.986 .... 13.2
—— *v.* Keith (1838) 16 S.1224 .... 13.10, 30.12
—— *v.* Matheson (1871) 10 M.9 .... 11.7
—— *v.* Ruxton (1862) 24 D.1182 .... 8.1
Christie's Trs. *v.* Muirhead (1870) 8 M.461 .... 4.5

Table of Cases

Christison v. Knowles (1901) 3 F.480	14.5
Chrystal v. Chrystal (1900) 2 F.373	12.11
Chrystal's Tr. v. Chrystal, 1912 S.C.1003	22.10
City of Edinburgh Brewery Co. v. Gibson's Tr. (1869) 7 M.886	2.4
City of Glasgow District Council v. Excess Insurance Co. Ltd., 1986 S.L.T.585	10.2
—— v. Excess Insurance Co. Ltd. (No. 2), 1990 S.L.T.225	10.2
—— v. Morrison McChlery & Co., 1985 S.C. 52	1.6
Clan Line Steamers Ltd. v. Earl of Douglas Steamship Co. Ltd., 1913 S.C.967	17.16
Clan Steam Trawling Co. Ltd. v. Aberdeen Steam Trawling and Fishing Co. Ltd., 1908 S.C. 651	1.6
Clancey v. Dixon's Ironworks Ltd., 1955 S.L.T.36	11.7
Claremont's Trs. v. Claremont (1896) 4 S.L.T.144	27.1
Clark v. Scottish Amicable Insurance Co. (1922) 38 Sh.Ct.Rep.170	17.3
—— v. Scottish Amicable Life Assurance Society, 1922 S.L.T.(Sh.Ct.)88	17.8
—— v. West Calder Oil Co. (1882) 9 R.1017	7.3, 25.1, 25.7
Clark & Macdonald v. Schulze (1902) 4 F.448	12.6
Clark & Rose Ltd. v. Mentiplay, 1989 S.L.T.(Sh.Ct.)66	11.19
Clark Taylor & Co. Ltd. v. Quality Site Development (Edinburgh) Ltd., 1981 S.C.111	2.3, 21.2
Clark's Exrx. v. Brown, 1935 S.C.110	4.5
Clarkson v. Johnston (1934) 50 Sh.Ct.Rep.318	4.5
Claydon v. Bradley [1987] 1 W.L.R.521	5.27
Clayton v. Lowthian (1826) 2 W.&S.40	29.10
Cleghorn v. Yorston (1707) Mor.14624	28.1
Cleland v. Stevenson (1669) Mor.2682	13.6
Clelland v. Baillie (1845) 7 D.461	29.6
Cleveleys Investment Trust Co. v. Inland Revenue, 1971 S.C.233	7.1
Clipper Shipping Co. Ltd. v. San Vincente Partners, 1989 S.L.T. 204	11.10
Cloberhill v. Ladyland (1631) Mor.14623	28.1
Clyde Air Extraction Ltd. v. Helmville Ltd., 1964 S.L.T.(Sh.Ct.)49	2.7
Clydesdale & North of Scotland Bank Ltd. v. Diamond (1963) 79 Sh.Ct.Rep.145	5.16
Clydesdale Bank v. D. & H. Cohen, 1943 S.C.244	10.1
—— v. Liqrs. of James Allan Senior & Son, 1926 S.C.235	5.19, 6.13, 23.4
—— v. McIntyre, 1909 S.C.1405	23.4
—— v. Morison's Tr., 1982 S.C.26	30.13
—— v. Paul (1877) 4 R.626	6.13
—— v. Royal Bank (1876) 3 R.586	6.13
—— v. Walker & Bain, 1926 S.C.72	7.5
Coats v. Glasgow Corporation (1912) 28 Sh.Ct.Rep.38	12.1
—— v. Union Bank of Scotland, 1928 S.C.711; 1929 S.C.(H.L.)114	5.22, 28.1
Cobham v. Minter, 1986 S.L.T.336	27.6
Cohen (George), Sons & Co. Ltd. v. Jamieson & Paterson, 1963 S.L.T.35	2.5
Coldunell Ltd. v. Gallon [1986] Q.B.1184	3.2
Cole-Hamilton v. Boyd, 1963 S.C.(H.L.)1	27.1, 28.6, 28.8
Coles, Petr., 1951 S.C.608	27.1
Colonial Mutual Life Assurance Society Ltd. v. Brown, 1911 1 S.L.T.158	11.5
Colquhoun's Tr. v. Campbell's Trs. (1902) 4 F.739	21.4
Columbian Fireproofing Co. Ltd., Re [1910] 2 Ch.120	9.12
Comex Houlder Diving Ltd. v. Colne Fishing Co. Ltd., 1987 S.L.T.442	1.6, 1.9, 28.6
Commercial Aluminium Windows Ltd. v. Cumbernauld Development Corporation, 1987 S.L.T.(Sh.Ct.)91	17.13
Commercial Bank of Scotland v. Biggar, 1958 S.L.T.(Notes)46	1.6
—— v. Eagle Star Insurance Co. Ltd., 1950 S.L.T.(Notes)30	17.3
—— v. Fraser Ross & Co. Ltd. (1906) 22 Sh.Ct.Rep.169	5.13
—— v. Henderson (1897) 13 Sh.Ct.Rep.136	6.2
—— v. Lanark Oil Co. Ltd. (1886) 14 R.147	25.3
—— v. Lyon (1909) 25 Sh.Ct.Rep.312	6.10
—— v. Rhind (1860) 3 Macq.643	12.14
—— v. Tod's Tr. (1895) 33 S.L.R.161	30.13
—— v. Turner (1944) 60 Sh.Ct.Rep.95	12.5
Commerzbank Aktiengesellschaft v. Large, 1977 S.C.375	1.5
Company, A, Re [1986] B.C.L.C.261	25.2

Company (No. 003729 of 1982), *Re* [1984] 1 W.L.R. 1090 ...... 25.3
Company (No. 00175 of 1987), *Re* [1987] B.C.L.C.467 ...... 26.3
Conacher v. Conacher (1857) 20 D.252 ...... 11.13
Connal & Co. v. Loder (1868) 6 M.1095 ...... 5.2
Connochie v. British Linen Bank (1943) 59 Sh.Ct.Rep.44 ...... 12.14
Constant v. Kincaid & Co. (1902) 4 F.901 ...... 27.1
Consumer and Industrial Press Ltd., *Re* [1988] B.C.L.C.177 ...... 26.4
Cook's Tr., *Petr.*, 1985 S.L.T.33 ...... 21.1
Corbet v. Hamilton (1707) Mor. 2642 ...... 13.7
Cord v. Gormley, 1971 S.L.T.(Sh.Ct.)19 ...... 2.11
Cormack v. Anderson (1829) 7 S.868 ...... 21.15
Cornish Manures Ltd., *Re* [1967] 1 W.L.R.807 ...... 25.14
Corvi v. Ellis, 1969 S.L.T.350 ...... 28.5, 28.6
Cory Brothers & Co. Ltd. v. Owners of "Mecca", L.R. [1897] A.C.286 ...... 12.5
Couper's Trs. v. National Bank (1889) 16 R.412 ...... 12.14
Coutts' Tr. and Doe v. Webster (1886) 13 R.1112 ...... 22.6
Cowan v. Gowans (1878) 5 R.581 ...... 13.6, 13.10
—— v. Shaw (1878) 5 R. 680 ...... 13.6
Cowbrough v. Robertson (1879) 6 R.1301 ...... 4.6
Cowdenbeath Coal Co. Ltd. v. Clydesdale Bank Ltd. (1895) 22 R.682 ...... 22.8
Cox v. Tait (1843) 5 D.1283 ...... 14.1
Craig v. Hunter & Son (1905) 13 S.L.T.525 ...... 22.6
—— v. Iona Hotels Ltd., 1988 S.C.L.R.130 ...... 25.2, 25.3
Craig & Co. v. Blackater, 1923 S.C.472 ...... 30.2
Craig & Rose Ltd. v. Lamarra, 1975 S.C.316 ...... 12.11
Craik v. Glasgow Taxicab Co. Ltd. (1911) 27 Sh.Ct.Rep.157 ...... 2.9
Cranstoun v. Bontine (1830) 8 S.425; (1832) 6 W.&S.79 ...... 22.8
Crawford v. Bennet (1827) 2 W.&S.608 ...... 12.14
—— v. Black (1829) 8 S.158 ...... 15.1
—— v. Hutton (1680) Mor.11832 ...... 29.7
Crear v. Morrison (1882) 9 R.890 ...... 1.10
Creative Press v. Harman [1973] I.R.313 ...... 5.27
Credit Lyonnais v. George Stevenson & Co. Ltd. (1901) 9 S.L.T.93 ...... 1.6
Crerar v. Bank of Scotland, 1921 S.C.736; 1922 S.C.(H.L.)137 ...... 8.1
—— v. Dow (1906) 22 Sh.Ct.Rep.311 ...... 24.2
Crichton's Tr. v. Stewart (1866) 4 M.689 ...... 23.1
Critchley v. Campbell (1884) 11 R.475 ...... 11.13
Crittal Warmlife Ltd. v. Flaherty, 1988 G.W.D.22-930 ...... 20.8
Croall & Croall v. Sharp (1954) 70 Sh.Ct.Rep.129 ...... 13.2
Crockart's Tr. v. Hay & Co. Ltd., 1913 S.C.509 ...... 7.10, 22.7
Crofts v. Stewart's Trs., 1927 S.C.(H.L.)65 ...... 2.11
Cromarty Leasing Ltd. v. Turnbull, 1988 S.L.T.(Sh.Ct.)62 ...... 30.16
Crombie v. British Transport Commission, 1961 S.L.T.115 ...... 11.1, 11.13
Crosbie's Trs. v. Wright (1880) 7 R.823 ...... 6.15
Croshaw v. Pritchard and Renwick (1899) 16 T.L.R. 45 ...... 2.9
Croskery v. Gilmour's Trs. (1890) 17 R.697 ...... 28.1, 28.5
Crouch v. Credit Foncier of England Ltd. (1873) 8 Q.B.D.374 ...... 5.2
Crown Estate Commissioners v. Liqrs. of Highland Engineering Ltd., 1975 S.L.T.58 ...... 25.7
Cullen v. Buchanan (1862) 24 D.1280 ...... 11.10
Cumbernauld Development Corporation v. Mustone Ltd., 1983 S.L.T.(Sh.Ct.)55 ...... 9.11
Cumming v. Stewart, 1928 S.C.709 ...... 29.3
Cuningham v. Home (1760) Mor.747 ...... 17.2
Cuninghame v. Walkinshaw Oil Co. Ltd. (1886) 14 R.87 ...... 25.3
Cunningham-Jardine v. Cunningham-Jardine's Trs., 1979 S.L.T.298 ...... 11.4
Cunninghame v. Boswell (1868) 6 M.890 ...... 11.7
Cuninghame Stevenson & Co. v. Wilson, 17 January 1809, F.C. 13.7
Cust v. Garbet & Co. (1775) Mor.2795 ...... 29.7
Customs and Excise Commissioner v. Diners Club Ltd. [1989] 1 W.L.R.1196 ...... 12.3
Cuthbert v. Cuthbert's Trs., 1908 S.C.967 ...... 27.1
Cuthbertson v. Paterson, 1968 S.L.T.(Sh.Ct.)21 ...... 4.2
Cuthill v. Strachan (1894) 21 R.549 ...... 12.5

Table of Cases

DALBLAIR MOTORS LTD. *v.* J. Forrest & Son (Ayr) Ltd. (1954) 70 Sh.Ct.Rep.107 ...	2.9
Dalmellington Iron Co. *v.* Glasgow and South-Western Rlwy. Co. (1889) 16 R.523	1.6
Dalrymple's Trs. *v.* Lancashire Trust Corporation (1894) 2 S.L.T.79	11.9
Darling *v.* Wilson's Tr. (1887) 15 R.180	7.3
Darlington *v.* Gray (1836) 15 S.197	28.1
Davidson *v.* Balcanqual (1629) Mor.2773	17.11
—— *v.* Davidson's Trs., 1952 S.L.T.(Notes)3	11.4
—— *v.* Murray (1784) Mor.761	17.4
—— *v.* Union Bank of Scotland (1881) 19 S.L.R. 15	24.2
Davidson & Syme, W.S. *v.* Booth, 1972 S.L.T.122	2.8
Davidson Pirie & Co. *v.* Dihle's Reps. (1900) 2 F.640	29.8
Davies *v.* Hunter, 1934 S.C.10	12.12
Davis *v.* Directloans Ltd. [1986] 2 All E.R.783	3.2
Dawson *v.* Cullen (1825) 4 S.39	16.2
—— *v.* Lauder (1840) 2 D.525	22.7
Day *v.* McLea (1889) 22 Q.B.D.610	11.2
Dean Warwick Ltd. *v.* Borthwick, 1983 S.L.T.533	11.7
Deeley *v.* Lloyds Bank Ltd. [1912] A.C.756	12.5
Delaney *v.* Stirling (1892) 20 R.506	28.7, 28.8
Dempster (R. & J.) Ltd. *v.* Motherwell Bridge and Engineering Co. Ltd., 1964 S.L.T.353	11.7
Denholm Young (E. & A.) & Co. *v.* MacElwee (1918) 34 Sh.Ct.Rep.193	17.2
Destone Fabrics Ltd., *Re* [1941] Ch. 319	9.12
Devaynes *v.* Noble (1816) 1 Mer.572	12.5
Devos Gebroeder (N.V.) *v.* Sunderland Sportswear Ltd., 1989 S.L.T.382; 1990 S.L.T.473	14.5, 14.7
Dick *v.* Dick, 1950 S.L.T.(Notes)44	5.27
Dick & Stevenson *v.* Woodside Steel & Iron Co. (1888) 16 R.242	13.9
Dick's Exrx. *v.* Dick, 1964 S.L.T.(Sh.Ct.)41	4.2
Dickie *v.* Singh, 1974 S.L.T.129	5.27
Dickson *v.* Barbour (1828) 6 S.856	29.7
—— *v.* Blair (1871) 10 M.41	4.6
—— *v.* Clydesdale Bank, 18 December 1936, *unreported*	12.14
—— *v.* ——, 1937 S.L.T.585	6.6
—— *v.* Halbert (1854) 16 D.586	12.13
—— *v.* National Bank, 1917 S.C.(H.L.)50	6.15
—— *v.* Nicholson (1885) 17 D.1011	7.7
—— *v.* Trotter (1776) Mor.873	27.4
—— *v.* United Dominions Trust Ltd., 1988 S.L.T.19	21.10
Dickson's Trs. *v.* Dickson's Trs., 1930 S.L.T.226	12.13
Dillon *v.* Napier, Shanks & Bell (1893) 20 S.L.R.685	28.5, 28.8
Dinwoodie's Exrx. *v.* Carruther's Exr. (1895) 23 R.234	29.5
Dixon *v.* Bovill (1856) 3 Macq.1	5.2
—— *v.* Cowan (1828) 7 S.132	22.6
Dobell, Beckett & Co. *v.* Neilson (1904) 7 F.281	7.3
Dobie *v.* Mitchell (1854) 17 D.97	22.1
Dobson *v.* Christie (1835) 13 S.582	13.4
Docherty *v.* Royal Bank, 1962 S.L.T.(Notes)102	12.14
Dods *v.* Welsh (1904) 12 S.L.T.110	22.5
Doig *v.* Lawrie (1903) 5 F.295	10.3
Donaldson *v.* Kennedy (1833) 11 S.740	12.6
—— *v.* Ord (1855) 17 D.1053	17.8, 27.3
Dormer *v.* Melville Dundas & Whitson Ltd., 1990 S.L.T.186	28.6
Dougal *v.* Gordon (1795) Mor.851	27.4
Dougall *v.* Lornie (1899) 1 F.1187	12.5
Doughty *v.* Wells (1906) 14 S.L.T.299	24.2
Douglas *v.* Douglas's Trs. (1867) 5 M.827	11.7
—— *v.* Gibson-Craig (1832) 10 S.647	22.5
—— *v.* Hogarth (1901) 4 F.148	28.5, 28.8
—— *v.* Jones (1831) 9 S.856	11.9
Douglas Gardiner & Mill *v.* Mackintosh's Trs., 1916 S.C.125	17.3
Douglas Griggs Engineering Ltd., *Re* [1963] Ch.19	25.3

Douglas Milne Ltd. *v.* Borders Regional Council, 1990 G.W.D.8-445 .... 14.7
Doune, Lord, *v.* John Dye & Son Ltd., 1972 S.L.T.(Sh.Ct.)30 .... 11.2
Dow *v.* Pennell's Tr., 1929 S.L.T.674 .... 23.1
Dow & Co. *v.* Union Bank (1875) 2 R.459 .... 17.12, 23.4
Downie *v.* Saunder's Trs. (1898) 6 S.L.T.134 .... 5.7
Dresdner Bank *v.* Wolfson & Sons Ltd. (1928) 44 Sh.Ct.Rep.262 .... 5.13
Drew *v.* Drew (1855) 17 D.559 .... 13.5
—— *v.* —— (1870) 9 M.163 .... 13.8, 17.3, 27.1
Drughorn Ltd. *v.* Rederiaktiebolaget Transatlantic [1919] A.C.203 .... 30.1
Drummond *v.* Ewing (1752) Elchies' Heritable No.16 .... 29.2
—— *v.* Muirhead & Guthrie Smith (1900) 2 F.585 .... 7.11
Drybrough & Co. Ltd. *v.* Roy (1903) 5 F.665 .... 5.19
Dryburgh *v.* Gordon (1896) 24 R.1 .... 19.3
—— *v.* Macpherson, 1944 S.L.T.116 .... 4.5
Dryburgh & Co. Ltd., *Petrs.*, (Sh.Ct.) 1989 S.C.L.R.279 .... 20.3
Dudgeon *v.* Reid (1829) 7 S.729 .... 14.2
Duff *v.* Wood (1858) 20 D.1231 .... 11.10
Dunbarton County Council *v.* George W. Sellars & Sons Ltd., 1973 S.L.T.(Sh.Ct.)67 .... 21.2
Duncan *v.* Forbes (1878) 15 S.L.R.371 .... 1.6
—— *v.* Motherwell Bridge & Engineering Co., 1952 S.C.131 .... 1.6
—— *v.* River Clyde Trs. (1851) 13 D.518; (1853) 25 Sc.Jur.331 .... 12.6
Duncan, Galloway & Co. *v.* Duncan, Falconer & Co., 1913 S.C.265 .... 1.6
Duncan's Trs. *v.* Shand (1873) 11 M.254 .... 4.5
Dundee Corporation *v.* Marr, 1971 S.C.96 .... 7.12
Dundee Masters and Seamen *v.* Cockerill (1869) 8 M.278 .... 1.6
Dundee Police Commissioners *v.* Straton (1884) 11 R.586 .... 28.1
Dunfermline District Council *v.* Blyth & Blyth Associates, 1985 S.L.T.345 .... 14.5
Dunipace, Laird of, *v.* Sandis (1624) Mor.859 .... 27.4
Dunlop *v.* McGowans, 1980 S.C.(H.L.)73 .... 14.5, 14.6
—— *v.* Spiers (1776) Mor.14610; (1777) (H.L.) Mor. s.v. "Society" App.No.2 .... 30.13
—— *v.* Weir (1823) 2 S.167 .... 17.2
Dunn *v.* Britannic Assurance Co. Ltd., 1932 S.L.T.244 .... 29.11
Dunn & Co. *v.* Anderston Foundry Co. Ltd. (1894) 21 R.880 .... 11.7
Dunn's Tr. *v.* Hardy (1896) 23 R.621 .... 4.5
Durham Fancy Goods Ltd. *v.* Michael Jackson (Fancy Goods) Ltd. [1968] 2 Q.B.839 .... 5.14
Durie's Trs. *v.* Ayton (1894) 22 R.34 .... 11.7
Duthie (Arthur) & Co. Ltd. *v.* Merson & Gerry, 1947 S.C.43 .... 2.7, 11.2
Dyce *v.* Paterson (1846) 9 D.310 .... 4.6
Dynamics Corporation of America, *Re* [1973] 1 W.L.R.63 .... 25.3, 30.19

EAGLEHILL LTD. *v.* J. Needham Ltd. [1973] A.C.992 .... 5.26
Eastern Capital Futures Ltd., *Re* [1989] B.C.L.C.371 .... 25.7
Edelstein *v.* Schuler & Co. [1902] 2 K.B.144 .... 5.2
Edinburgh Albert Buildings Co. *v.* General Guarantee Corporation, 1917 S.C.239 . 7.12
Edinburgh and District Tramways Co. Ltd. *v.* Courtenay, 1909 S.C.99 .... 1.6
Edinburgh Life Assurance Co. *v.* Balderston, 1909 2 S.L.T.323 .... 1.6
Edmond *v.* Dingwall's Trs. (1860) 23 D.21 .... 24.2
—— *v.* Gordon (1858) 3 Macq.116 .... 1.1, 27.4
Edward *v.* Fyfe (1823) 2 S.431 .... 12.9
Elders *v.* Allen (1833) 11 S.902 .... 16.2
Electric Construction Co. *v.* Hurry & Young (1897) 24 R.312 .... 2.5
Ell Bros. *v.* Sneddon (1929) 45 Sh.Ct.Rep.351 .... 12.6
Ellerman Lines Ltd. *v.* Clyde Navigation Trustees, 1909 S.C.690 .... 28.5
Elliott *v.* Bax-Ironside [1925] 2 K.B.301 .... 5.14
—— *v.* Director General of Fair Trading [1980] 1 W.L.R.977 .... 4.13
—— *v.* Elliots (1711) Mor.2658 .... 13.4
Elmslie *v.* Hunter (1936) 52 Sh.Ct.Rep.181 .... 17.2
Elphingston *v.* Ord (1624) Mor.858 .... 27.4
Emslie *v.* Tognarelli's Exrs., 1967 S.L.T.(Notes)66 .... 29.6, 29.8, 29.11

Enever v. Craig, 1913 2 S.L.T.30	5.8
Engdiv Ltd. v. G. Percy Trentham Ltd., 1990 S.L.T.617	28.6
Equitable Loan Company of Scotland Ltd. v. Storie, 1972 S.L.T.(Notes)20	2.11
Erskine (1710) Mor.14997	19.5
Erskine (James) v. Weibye, 1976 S.L.T.(Sh.Ct.)14	2.9
Eshun v. Moorgate Mercantile Co. Ltd. [1971] 1 W.L.R.722	3.16
Esso Petroleum Co. Ltd. v. Hall Russell & Co. Ltd., 1988 S.L.T.874	1.6
Eunson v. Johnson & Greig, 1940 S.C.49	2.7
Evans v. Pinchere (1907) 23 Sh.Ct.Rep.111	17.2
—— v. Stool (1885) 12 R.1295	29.5
Ewart v. Latta (1865) 3 M.(H.L.)36	10.1, 28.3
Ewing & Co v. McClelland (1860) 22 D.1347	30.9
Exchange Loan Co. v. McAweeny (1907) 24 Sh.Ct.Rep.217	5.19
Exchange Telegraph Co. Ltd. v. Giulianotti, 1959 S.L.T.293	1.6
Export Credits Guarantee Department v. Turner, 1981 S.L.T. 286	2.3, 21.2
Fair v. Hunter (1861) 24 D.1	1.1
Fairbairn v. Fairbairn (1868) 6 M.640	4.5
Falconer v. Dalrymple (1870) 9 M.212	12.6
Falkirk Magistrates v. Lundie (1892) 8 Sh.Ct.Rep.272	1.11
Family Endowment Society, Re (1870) L.R. 5 Ch.118	14.2
Farquhar v. McKain (1638) Mor.2282	28.1
Farrans (Construction) Ltd. v. Dunfermline District Council, 1988 S.L.T.466	11.7
Feist v. Societé Intercommunale Belge D'Electricité [1934] A.C.161	1.4
Feld British Agencies Ltd. v. Jas. Pringle Ltd., 1961 S.L.T.123	13.2
Ferenze Spinning Co. v. Wallace (1858) 1 Scot. Law Journal 93	6.14
Ferguson v. Bothwell (1882) 9 R.687	11.5, 16.10
—— v. Douglas (1796) 3 Pat.App.503	5.23
—— v. Ferguson (1899) 15 Sh.Ct.Rep.20	29.5
—— v. Muir (1711) Mor.2659	13.4
Ferguson and Stuart v. Grant (1856) 18 D.536	7.11
Ferrier v. British Linen Co., 20 November 1807, F.C.	13.4
—— v. Crockhart, 1937 S.L.T.205	29.8
Field v. R.H. Thomson & Co. (1902) 10 S.L.T.261	4.5
Field & Allan v. Gordon (1872) 11 M.132	13.9
Financings Ltd. v. Baldock [1963] 2 Q.B.104	2.6
Findlay v. Waddell, 1910 S.C.670	7.9
Findlay Bannatyne & Co.'s Assignee v. Donaldson (1864) 2 M.(H.L.)86	11.7
Findlay's Trs. v. Shanks, 1930 S.L.T.(Sh.Ct.)32	11.6
Fingland & Mitchell v. Howie, 1926 S.C.319	13.2
Finlay (James) Corporation Ltd. v. McCormack, 1986 S.L.T.106	20.3
Fisher v. Raven [1964] A.C.210	3.1
—— v. Stewart (1828) 7 S.97	19.5
Fixby Engineering Co. Ltd. v. Auchlochan Sand and Gravel Co. Ltd., 1974 S.L.T.(Sh.Ct.)58	2.9
Flanagan v. Dempster Moore & Co., 1928 S.C.308	11.14
Fleming v. Gemmill, 1908 S.C.340	28.1
—— v. Imrie (1868) 6 M.363	14.3
—— v. Thomson (1826) 2 W.&S. 277	10.4
—— v. Yeaman (1884) 9 App.Cas.966	1.11, 20.2
Fleming's Trs. v. McHardy (1892) 19 R.542	24.2
Flensburg Steam Shipping Co. v. Seligmann (1871) 9 M.1011	11.7
Fletcher v. Young, 1936 S.L.T. 572	12.7, 17.8
Flett v. Mustard, 1936 S.C.269	24.2
Flowerdew v. Buchan (1835) 13 S.615	27.1
Flynn v. Scott, 1949 S.C.442	2.4
Forbes v. Brebner (1751) Mor.1128	22.6
—— v. Forbes (1869) 8 M.85	4.1, 11.7
—— v. House of Clydesdale Ltd., 1988 S.L.T.594	14.6
—— v. Pitsligo (1628) Mor.12479	4.6
—— v. Whyte (1890) 18 R.182	1.11
Forbes Smith (D.) & Johnston v. Kaye, 1975 S.L.T.(Sh.Ct.)33	30.10

Table of Cases

Ford's Trs. v. Ford, 1940 S.C.426 .... 29.5
Forrest v. Forrest (1863) 1 M.806 .... 29.8
—— v. Scottish County Investment Co., 1916 S.C.(H.L.)28 .... 2.10
Forsyth v. Hare & Co. (1834) 13 S.42 .... 30.10
Forth & Clyde Construction Co. Ltd. v. Trinity Timber & Plywood Co. Ltd., 1984 S.C.1 .... 8.6, 9.11, 9.18, 9.19
Fortune v. Young, 1918 S.C.1 .... 10.1, 30.6
Forward Trust Ltd. v. Whymark [1989] 3 All E.R.915 .... 3.16
Fowler v. Brown, 1916 S.C.597 .... 13.7, 16.15
Fox v. Anderson (1849) 11 D.1194 .... 14.2
Foxhall & Gyle (Nurseries) Ltd., Petrs., 1978 S.L.T(Notes)29 .... 25.3
Franco-British Electrical Co. v. Jean Dougall Macdonald Ltd. (1949) 65 Sh.Ct.Rep.82 .... 2.10
Fraser v. Bannerman (1853) 15 D.756 .... 19.6
—— v. J. Morton Wilson Ltd., 1965 S.L.T.(Notes)85 .... 11.7
Fraser-Johnston Engineering Co. v. Jeffs, 1920 S.C.222 .... 11.8
Fraser's Exrx. v. Wallace's Trs. (1893) 20 R.374 .... 11.5
French v. Earl of Galloway (1730) Mor.14706 .... 28.1
Frimokar (U.K.) Ltd. v. Mobile Technical Plant (International) Ltd., 1990 S.L.T.180 .... 2.5
Fritz's Agency Ltd. v. Moss' Empires Ltd. (1922) 38 Sh.Ct.Rep.124 .... 17.3
Fulton Clyde Ltd. v. J.F. McCallum & Co. Ltd., 1960 S.L.T.253; 1960 S.C.78 .. 13.2, 13.9
Furmston, Petr., 1987 S.L.T.(Sh.Ct.)10 .... 25.3
Fyfe v. Crondace Ltd., 1986 S.L.T.528 .... 14.6

G. & A. (Hotels) Ltd. v. T.H.B. Marketing Services Ltd., 1983 S.L.T.497 .. 13.10, 25.5
G. & C. Finance Corporation Ltd. v. Brown, 1961 S.L.T.408 .... 7.3, 21.7
Gairdner v. Milne and Co. (1858) 20 D.565 .... 7.7, 14.1
Galashiels Provident Building Society v. Newlands (1893) 20 R.821 .... 12.7, 12.13
Galbraith v. Campbell's Trs. (1885) 22 S.L.R.602 .... 15.5
—— v. Cuthbertson (1866) 4 M.295 .... 4.6
Gall v. Murdoch (1821) 1 S.77 .... 13.4
Gallemos Ltd. (In Receivership) v. Barratt (Falkirk) Ltd., 1990 S.L.T.98 ..... 27.2, 27.3
Galletly's Trs. v. Lord Advocate (1880) 8 R.74 .... 29.5
Gallie v. Lockhart (1840) 2 D.445 .... 29.3
Galloway v. Galloway (1799) Mor. 11122 .... 13.6
—— v. MacKinnon (1936) 52 Sh.Ct.Rep.135 .... 13.7, 29.6
Gamage (A.W.) Ltd. v. Charlesworth's Tr., 1910 S.C.257 .... 2.2, 21.7
Garden Haig Scott & Wallace v. Stevenson's Tr., 1962 S.C.51 .... 7.11
Gardiner v. Stewart's Trs., 1908 S.C.985 .... 29.5
Garpel Haematite Co., Liqr. of the, v. Andrew (1866) 4 M.617 .... 7.11
Garscadden v. Ardrossan Dry Dock Co. Ltd., 1910 S.C.178 .... 7.8, 13.9
Gartside v. I.R.C. [1968] A.C.553 .... 1.11
Gatoil International Inc. v. Arkwright-Boston Manufacturers Mutual Insurance Co., 1985 S.L.T.68 .... 11.10
Gatty v. Maclaine, 1921 S.C.(H.L.)1 .... 4.1
Gavin's Tr. v. Fraser, 1920 S.C.674 .... 7.3
Gemmell v. Annandale & Son Ltd. (1899) 36 S.L.R.658 .... 12.6
George Hotel (Glasgow) Ltd. v. Prestwick Hotels Ltd., 1961 S.L.T.(Sh.Ct.)61 .... 11.13
Georgia Pacific Corporation v. Evalend Shipping Co. S.A., 1988 S.L.T.683 ...... 7.7
Gibb v. Brock, 12 May 1838, F.C. 13.10
—— v. Lombank Scotland Ltd., 1962 S.L.T.288 .... 6.2
Gibson v. Carson, 1980 S.C.356 .... 14.8
—— v. Forbes (1833) 11 S.916 .... 7.3
—— v. Hunter Home Designs Ltd., 1976 S.C.23 .... 21.15, 25.7
—— v. May (1841) 3 D.974 .... 24.2
Gibson and Stewart v. Brown & Co. (1876) 3 R.328 .... 7.8, 13.9
Gibson's Trs. v. Galloway (1896) 23 R.414 .... 5.19
Gilbey Vintners Scotland Ltd. v. Perry, 1978 S.L.T.(Sh.Ct.)48 .... 11.2
Gilchrist v. Paton, 1979 S.C.380 .... 2.11
Gill v. Gill, 1907 S.C.532 .... 4.5
—— v. ——, 1938 S.C.65 .... 29.5
Gillies v. Bow, 1877, Guthrie's Select Cases I, 196 .... 17.15

Gilmour v. Finnie (1832) 11 S.193	28.2
—— v. Gilmours (1873) 11 M.853	24.2
Gilmour (James) (Crossford) Ltd. v. John Williams (Wishaw) Ltd., 1970 S.L.T.(Sh.Ct.)6	17.12
Gilmour Shaw & Co's Tr. v. Learmonth, 1972 S.C.137	22.1
Gladstone v. McCallum (1896) 23 R.783	7.7
Glasgow Corporation v. Lord Advocate, 1959 S.C.203	1.6
Glasgow, Executive Council for the City of, v. T. Sutherland Henderson Ltd., 1955 S.L.T.(Sh.Ct.)33	27.2
Glasgow Gas Light Co. v. Barony Parish of Glasgow (1868) 6 M.406	11.7
Glasgow Pavilion Ltd. v. Motherwell (1903) 6 F.116	12.1, 12.2
Glen v. Gilbey Vintners Ltd., 1986 S.L.T.553	2.4
Glen Music Co. Ltd. v. City of Glasgow District Council, 1983 S.L.T.(Sh.Ct.)26	11.10
Glendinning v. Hope & Co. (1878) 5 R.770	7.10
Glickman v. Linda, 1950 S.C.18	6.1
Gomba Holdings Ltd. v. Minories Finance Ltd. [1987] B.C.L.C.115	9.15
Gordon v. Brock (1838) 1 D.1	22.6
—— v. Johnston's Heirs (1703) Mor.11408	12.9
—— v. Kerr (1898) 25 R.570	5.27
—— v. McCubbin (1851) 13 D.1154	1.11
—— v. Trotter (1833) 11 S.696	12.14
Gorrie's Tr. v. Gorrie (1890) 17 R.1051	22.1
Gourlay v. Clydesdale Bank Ltd. (1900) 7 S.L.T.473	12.5
—— v. Mackie (1887) 14 R.403	8.1
Govan Old Victualling Society Ltd. v. Wagstaff (1907) 44 S.L.R.295	11.4
Gow v. McDonald (1827) 5 S.472	4.6
Gow's Exrs. v. Sim (1866) 4 M.578	4.4, 4.6
Gracie v. Gracie, 1910 S.C.899	17.6
Graeme v. Murray (1738) Mor.3141	29.7
Graeme's Tr. v. Giersberg (1888) 15 R.691	27.5
Graham v. Gordon (1843) 5 D.1207	1.9
—— v. Graham, 1955 S.L.T.(Notes)15	11.14
—— v. Macfarlane & Co. (1869) 7 M.640	17.6
Graham & Co. v. Raeburn & Verel (1895) 23 R.84	7.1
Graham's Trs. v. Gillies, 1956 S.C.437	6.15
Grand Empire Theatres, Liqr. of, v. Snodgrass, 1932 S.C.(H.L.)73	7.11
Grandison's Trs. v. Jardine (1895) 22 R.925	11.7
Granor Finance Ltd. v. Liqr. of Eastore Ltd., 1974 S.L.T.296	2.6
Grant v. Gray (1828) 6 S.489	27.5
—— v. McAlister (1948) 64 Sh.Ct.Rep.261	13.2
—— v. Maclean (1757) Mor.11402	12.10
Grant's Exrx. v. Grant, 1922 S.L.T.156	4.3
Grant's Trs. v. McDonald, 1939 S.C.448	6.15
Grant Melrose & Tennent Ltd. v. W. & G. DuCros Ltd. (1927) 43 Sh.Ct.Rep.347	11.9
Gray v. Bain (1954) 70 Sh.Ct.Rep.65	6.14
—— v. Graham (1855) 2 Macq. 435	7.7, 7.11
—— v. Johnston, 1928 S.C.659	1.6
—— v. Munro (1829) 8 S.221	4.4
—— v. Reid (1699) Mor.11399	12.10
Gray & Son Ltd. v. Stern, 1953 S.L.T.(Sh.Ct.)34	2.10
Gray's Inn Construction Co., Re [1980] 1 W.L.R.711	25.5., 25.7
Gray's Trs. v. Benhar Coal Co. Ltd. (1881) 9 R.225	25.1, 25.7
—— v. Royal Bank of Scotland (1895) 23 R.199	13.4
Great Western Rlwy. Co. v. London & County Banking Co. Ltd. [1901] A.C.414	6.11
Greater Glasgow Health Board v. Baxter Clark & Paul, 1990 G.W.D.12-625	14.8
Green v. Miller's Debt Recovery Services, 1954 S.L.T.(Sh.Ct.)26	17.8
Green (F.W.) & Co. Ltd. v. Brown & Gracie Ltd., 1960 S.L.T.(Notes)43	11.7
Greenock Banking Co. v. Smith (1844) 6 D.1340	12.13
Greenock Harbour Trs. v. Glasgow & South Western Rlwy. Co., 1909 S.C.(H.L.)49	11.7
Greenwood v. Martins' Bank Ltd. [1933] A.C.51	5.10, 5.21
—— v. Mundle, 1957 S.L.T.(Notes)15	16.15

Table of Cases

Greig v. Christie (1837) 16 S.242 .... 17.3
Grewar v. Cross (1904) 12 S.L.T.84 .... 13.9
"Grey Dolphin", The, 1982 S.C.5 .... 17.16
Griffith's Trs. v. Griffiths, 1912 S.C.626 .... 29.6
Grigor Allan v. Urquhart (1887) 15 R.56 .... 27.3, 27.4
Grindall v. John Mitchell (Grangemouth) Ltd., 1987 S.L.T.137 .... 21.10
Grunwald v. Hughes, 1964 S.L.T.94 .... 28.5
Guild v. Orr Ewing & Co. (1858) 20 D.392 .... 22.6
Gunn v. Hunter (1886) 13 R.573 .... 11.13
Guthrie v. McKimmie's Tr., 1952 S.L.T.(Sh.Ct.)49 .... 11.4
—— v. Morren (1939) 55 Sh.Ct.Rep.172 .... 17.4

H.M.V. Fields Properties Ltd. v. Skirt 'n' Slack Centre of London Ltd., 1987 S.L.T.2 .... 11.7
Haddington, Countess of, v. Richardson (1822) 1 S.362 .... 11.10
Haddon's Exrx. v. Scottish Milk Marketing Board, 1938 S.C.168 .... 11.7
Haggarty v. Scottish Transport and General Workers Union, 1955 S.C.109 .... 1.6
Haig and Others v. Lord Advocate, 1976 S.L.T.(Notes)16 .... 25.1, 25.2
Haldane v. Speirs (1872) 10 M.537 .... 4.5, 6.14, 12.16
Haldane's Trs. v. Murphy (1881) 9 R.269 .... 1.12
Halifax Building Society v. Smith, 1985 S.L.T.(Sh.Ct.)25 .... 19.3
Hall (William) (Contractors) Ltd., Re [1967] 1 W.L.R.948 .... 25.12
Hamilton v. Cuthbertson (1841) 3 D.494 .... 23.6
—— v. Duke of Montrose (1906) 8 F.1026 .... 2.4
—— v. Kinnear & Sons (1825) 4 S.102 .... 19.6
—— v. Western Bank of Scotland (1856) 19 D.152 .... 7.3
Hamilton & Co. v. Freeth (1889) 16 R.1022 .... 10.1, 28.2
Hamilton's Exr. v. Bank of Scotland, 1913 S.C.743 .... 10.3
Hamilton Leasing Ltd. v. Clark, 1974 S.L.T.(Sh.Ct.)95 .... 28.1
Handren v. Scottish Construction Co. Ltd., 1967 S.L.T.(Notes)21 .... 11.7
Hannay & Sons' Tr. v. Armstrong & Co. (1875) 2 R.399; (1877) 4 R.(H.L.)43 .... 13.10
Harper v. Connor's Trs. (1927) 43 Sh.Ct.Rep.138 .... 29.6
—— v. Faulds (1791) Mor.2666 .... 7.10
Harris Simons Constructions Ltd., Re [1989] 1 W.L.R.368 .... 26.4
Harvest Lane Bodies Ltd., Re [1969] 1 Ch.457 .... 25.15
Harvey v. McAdie (1888) 4 Sh.Ct.Rep.254 .... 15.5
Harvey Brand & Co. v. Buchanan Hamilton & Co.'s Tr. (1886) 4 M.1128 .... 13.4
Harvey's Yoker Distillery v. Singleton (1901) 8 S.L.T.369 .... 17.11
Harvie's Trs. v. Bank of Scotland (1885) 12 R.1141 .... 10.1, 23.7
Haughhead Coal Co. v. Gallocher (1903) 11 S.L.T.156 .... 12.4, 16.15
Hawking v. Hafton House Ltd., 1990 G.W.D.6-333 .... 17.14
Hay v. Crawford (1712) Mor.2571 .... 13.4
—— v. Torbet, 1908 S.C.781 .... 12.5
Hay & Kyd v. Powrie (1886) 13 R.777 .... 10.3, 14.1
Hay's Tr. v. Davidson (1853) 15 D.583 .... 21.15
Hayes v. Robinson, 1984 S.L.T.300 .... 2.11
Hayman & Son v. McLintock, 1907 S.C.936 .... 7.3, 21.7
Head Wrightson Aluminium Ltd. v. Aberdeen Harbour Commissioners, 1958 S.L.T.(Notes)12 .... 2.10
Healy & Young's Tr. v. Mair's Trs., 1914 S.C.893 .... 14.3
Heddle's Exrx. v. Marwick & Hourston's Tr. (1888) 15 R.698 .... 30.8
Heggie v. Heggie (1858) 21 D.31 .... 30.12
Heilbut Symons & Co. v. Buckleton [1913] A.C.30 .... 2.4
Helby v. Matthews [1895] A.C.471 .... 2.6
Henderson v. Dawson (1895) 22 R.895 .... 5.27
Henderson & Co. Ltd. v. Turnbull & Co., 1909 S.C.510 .... 1.6, 13.5
Henderson & Keay Ltd. v. A.M. Carmichael Ltd., 1956 S.L.T.(Notes)58 .... 2.2
Henderson's Tr. v. Auld and Guild (1872) 10 M.946 .... 23.4
Hendry v. Cowie & Son & Co. (1904) 12 S.L.T.31,261 .... 4.2
Henriksens A/S v. Rolimpex [1974] Q.B.233 .... 13.9
Henry v. Miller (1884) 11 R.713 .... 12.4, 12.9
—— v. Strachan & Spence (1897) 24 R.1045 .... 24.1

Table of Cases

Hepburn v. Hamilton (1661) Mor.12480 ..... 4.6
—— v. Law, 1914 S.C.918 ..... 7.3
Heriot v. Thomson (1833) 12 S.145 ..... 11.14
Heritable Reversionary Co. v. Millar (1892) 19 R.(H.L.)43 ..... 21.2, 21.15
Heritable Securities Investment Association Ltd. v. Miller's Trs. (1893) 20 R.675 ... 29.5, 29.6
—— v. Wingate & Co. (1891) 29 S.L.R.904 ..... 24.2
—— v. Wingate & Co.'s Tr. (1880) 7 R.1094 ..... 7.3
Heron v. Winfields Ltd. (1894) 22 R.182 ..... 17.4
Hertz v. Itzig (1865) 3 M.813 ..... 17.9
Hestia, The [1895] P.193 ..... 1.6
Hewats v. Robertson (1881) 9 R.175 ..... 27.1
Hibernian Bank Ltd. v. Gysin and Hanson [1939] 1 K.B.483 ..... 5.4, 6.11
High-Flex (Scotland) Ltd. v. Kentallen Mechanical Services Co., 1977 S.L.T.(Sh.Ct.)91 ..... 17.7
Highland Engineering Ltd. v. Anderson, 1979 S.L.T.122 ..... 14.5, 30.9
Highland Engineering, Liqrs. of, v. Thomson, 1972 S.C.87 ..... 13.10
Highland Leasing Ltd. v. Lyburn, 1987 S.L.T.92 ..... 1.6
Hill v. College of Glasgow (1849) 12 D.46 ..... 17.3
—— v. Hill (1872) 11 M.247 ..... 29.2
—— v. Lindsay (1847) 10 D.78 ..... 27.3, 30.12
Hill (W.H.) & Sons Ltd. v. Manning's Tr., 1951 S.L.T.(Sh.Ct.)29 ..... 17.9
Hill Samuel & Co. Ltd. v. Laing, 1989 S.L.T.760 ..... 9.15
Hill Steam Shipping Co. v. Hugo Stinnes Ltd., 1941 S.C.324 ..... 30.2
Hill's Tr. v. Macgregor (1901) 8 S.L.T.484 ..... 22.5
Hobbin v. Burns (1904) 11 S.L.T.681 ..... 16.15
Hobday v. Kirkpatrick's Trs., 1983 S.L.T.197 ..... 11.4, 14.4
Hodgmac Ltd. v. Gardiners of Prestwick Ltd., 1980 S.L.T.(Sh.Ct.)68 ..... 1.10, 2.2
Hodgson v. Hodgson's Trs., 1984 S.L.T.97 ..... 20.6
Hoey v. Butler, 1975 S.C.87 ..... 2.11
Hofford v. Gowans, 1909 1 S.L.T.153 ..... 21.3
Hogarth & Sons v. Leith Cotton Seed Oil Co., 1909 S.C.955 ..... 2.7
Hogg v. Brack (1832) 11 S.198 ..... 11.3
Holt v. City of Dundee District Council, 1990 G.W.D.8-459 ..... 14.4
—— v. National Bank of Scotland, 1927 S.L.T.484 ..... 12.2
Holt Southey Ltd. v. Catnic Components Ltd. [1978] 1 W.L.R.630 ..... 25.3
Home v. Murray (1674) Mor.863 ..... 27.4
—— v. Pringle (1706) Mor.734 ..... 17.2
Hood v. Stewart (1890) 17 R.749 ..... 5.8
Hood (George A.) & Co. v. Dumbarton District Council, 1983 S.L.T.238 ..... 14.7
Hope v. Derwent Rolling Mills Co. Ltd. (1905) 7 F.837 ..... 4.5
Hope Brothers v. Morrison, 1960 S.L.T.80 ..... 12.11
Hope Johnstone v. Cornwall (1895) 22 R.314 ..... 14.1
Hopkinson (George) Ltd. v. N.G. Napier & Son, 1953 S.C.139 ..... 2.6, 16.2, 16.8
Hopper & Co. v. Walker (1904) 20 Sh.Ct.Rep.137 ..... 17.6
Horne v. Horne's Exrs, 1963 S.L.T.(Sh.Ct.)37 ..... 1.6
Horsbrugh v. Ramsay & Co. (1885) 12 R.1171 ..... 22.7
Hostess Mobile Catering v. Archibald Scott Ltd., 1981 S.C.185 ..... 2.2, 21.7
Houston v. Aberdeen Town & County Banking Company (1849) 11 D.1490 ..... 17.8
—— v. British Road Services Ltd., 1967 S.L.T.329 ..... 11.14
—— v. Speirs (1829) 3 W.&S.392 ..... 12.5
Huber v. Banks, 1986 S.L.T.58 ..... 17.5
Hughes (C.W. & A.L.) Ltd., Re [1966] 2 All E.R.702 ..... 25.12
Hughson v. Cullen (1857) 20 D.271 ..... 19.6
Hume v. Baillie (1852) 14 D.821 ..... 17.4
Hunter v. Falconer (1835) 13 S.252 ..... 14.2
—— v. Lees (1733) Mor.736 ..... 17.4
—— v. Livingston Development Corporation, 1984 S.L.T.10 ..... 11.7
—— v. Palmer (1825) 3 S.586 ..... 16.14
—— v. Wilson (1917) 33 Sh.Ct.Rep.268 ..... 17.3
Hunter's Trs. v. Mitchell, 1930 S.C.978 ..... 12.7
Hutcheon and Partners v. Hutcheon, 1979 S.L.T.(Sh.Ct.)61 ..... 30.10

Table of Cases

Hutcheson & Co.'s Administrator v. Taylor's Exrx., 1931 S.C.484	29.6
Hutchison v. C.I.R., 1930 S.C.293	12.7
—— v. Hutchison, 1912 1 S.L.T.219	17.4
Hyslop v. Shirlaw (1905) 7 F.875	2.4
IMPERIAL MOTORS (U.K.) LTD., RE [1990] B.C.L.C.29	26.4
Importers Co. v. Westminster Bank Ltd. [1927] 2 K.B.297	6.11
Inch v. Lee (1903) 11 S.L.T.374	13.6
Independent Automatic Sales Ltd. v. Knowles & Foster [1962] 1 W.L.R.974	9.1
Inglis v. Edward (1630) Mor.2773	17.11
—— v. Inglis's Tr., 1925 S.L.T.686	4.3
—— v. Moncrieff (1851) 13 D.622	7.11
—— v. Robertson & Baxter (1898) 25 R.(H.L.)70	7.3, 17.11
Ingram Clothing Manufacturing Co. (Glasgow) Ltd. v. Lewis (1960) 76 Sh.Ct.Rep.165	30.2
Inland Revenue v. Cook, 1945 S.C.(H.L.)52	12.7
—— v. Ferguson, 1969 S.C.(H.L.)103	12.7
—— v. Goldblatt [1972] Ch.498	9.16
—— v. Highland Engineering Ltd., 1975 S.L.T.203	30.20
—— v. MacDonald, 1988 S.L.T.(Sh.Ct.)7	20.4
International Fibre Syndicate Ltd. v. Dawson (1901) 3 F.(H.L.)32	27.2
International Sponge Importers Ltd. v. Watt & Sons, 1911 S.C.(H.L.)57	12.6
International Tin Council, Re [1987] Ch.419	25.1
Interplan (Joiners and Shopfitters) Ltd. v. Reid Furniture Co. Ltd., 1984 S.L.T.(Sh.Ct.)42	11.7
Inveresk Paper Co. v. Pembry Machinery Co. Ltd., 1972 S.L.T.(Notes) 63	2.11
Inverfleet Ltd. v. Woelfell, 1976 S.L.T.(Sh.Ct.)62	4.5
Inverlochy Castle Ltd. v. Lochaber Power Co., 1987 S.L.T.466	14.8
Iona Hotels Ltd., 1991 S.L.T.11	16.13
Irvine v. King's and Lord Treasurer's Remembrancer (1949) 65 Sh.Ct.Rep.53	29.7
JACK v. Black, 1911 S.C.691	11.14
—— v. Jack (1953) 69 Sh.Ct.Rep.34	11.13
—— v. Waddell's Trs., 1918 S.C.73	16.8
Jackson v. Clyde Navigation Trust, 1961 S.L.T.(Sh.Ct.)35	11.14
—— v. Elphick (1902) 10 S.L.T.146	27.1
—— v. Fenwick's Tr. (1899) 6 S.L.T.319	22.7
—— v. MacDiarmid (1892) 19 R.528	14.1
—— v. McIver (1875) 2 R.882	10.1, 23.9
—— v. McKechnie (1875) 3 R.130	21.10
—— v. Nicoll (1870) 8 M.408	12.5
Jacob (Walter L.) & Co. Ltd. v. F.I.M.B.R.A., 1988 S.C.L.R.184	25.2
Jacobs v. Provincial Motor Cab Co. Ltd., 1910 S.C.756	11.14
Jade International v. Robert Nicholas Ltd. [1978] Q.B.917	5.9
Jaffray v. Carrick (1836) 15 S.43	7.12
Jameson v. Sharp (1887) 14 R.643	17.7, 17.8, 27.3
Jamieson v. McLeod (1880) 7 R.823	6.15
—— v. Robertson (1886) 16 R.15	29.6
Jenkins v. Horn [1979] 2 All E.R. 1141	1.2
Joachimson v. Swiss Bank Corporation [1921] 3 K.B.110	6.2, 11.1
Joel v. Gill (1859) 21 D.929	20.3, 20.,6
Johnston v. Cochran (1829) 7 S.226	29.10
—— v. Dean of Guild of Aberdeen (1676) Mor.12480	4.6
—— v. Dundas's Trs. (1837) 15 S.904	17.2
—— v. Greenock Corporation, 1951 S.L.T.(Notes)57	2.10
—— v. Johnston (1875) 2 R.986	13.4
—— v. Robertson (1861) 23 D.646	13.9
Johnstone v. Harris, 1977 S.C.365	2.11
Johnstone (C.A.) v. Duthie (1892) 19 R.624	10.3
Johnstone-Beattie v. Dalzell and Others (1868) 6 M.333	27.7
Jones & Co.'s Tr. v. Allan (1901) 4 F.374	7.3
Jones (R.E.) Ltd. v. Waring and Gillow Ltd. [1926] A.C.670	5.9

Jones' Tr. *v*. Jones (1888) 15 R.328 .... 22.6
Jopp *v*. Hay (1844) 7 D.260 .... 24.2
—— *v*. Johnston's Tr. (1904) 6 F.1028 .... 21.2, 21.3

K.H.R. FINANCINGS LTD. *v*. Jackson, 1977 S.L.T.(Sh.Ct.)6 .... 5.4
Kay *v*. Morrison's Reps., 1984 S.L.T.175 .... 29.8
Kayford Ltd., *Re* [1975] 1 W.L.R.279 .... 21.2
Keir *v*. Menzies (1739) Mor.850 .... 27.3
Keir Ltd. *v*. East of Scotland Water Board, 1976 S.L.T.(Notes)72 .... 2.9, 11.7
Keith *v*. Cairney, 1917 1 S.L.T.202 .... 19.5
—— *v*. Maxwell (1795) Mor.1163 .... 22.5
Kellas *v*. Brown (1856) 18 D.1089 .... 17.6
Kelly *v*. A. & J. Clark Ltd., 1967 S.L.T.(Notes)115 .... 2.11
Kelly & Co. *v*. Rae (1909) 25 Sh.Ct.Rep.3 .... 12.14
Kennedy *v*. Begg Kennedy & Elder Ltd., 1954 S.L.T.(Sh.Ct.)103 .... 4.1
Kerr *v*. R. & W. Ferguson, 1931 S.C.736 .... 1.10, 1.11, 17.3
—— *v*. Fife & Kinross Rlwy. Co. (1860) 22 D.564 .... 13.5
Kerr's Trs. *v*. Ker (1883) 11 R.108 .... 4.4
Ketley (A.) Ltd. *v*. Scott [1981] I.C.R.241 .... 3.2
Kettle *v*. Dunster (1928) 138 L.T.158 .... 5.14
Key *v*. Scottish Chemist Supply Co. Ltd., 1956 S.L.T.(Notes)43 .... 11.13
Kidd and Sons *v*. Bain (1913) 29 Sh.Ct.Rep.123 .... 2.9
Kilgour *v*. Kilgour (1845) 7 D.451 .... 1.12
Kilmarnock Theatre Co. *v*. Buchanan, 1911 S.C.607 .... 1.8
King *v*. British Linen Co. (1899) 1 F.928 .... 6.2
—— *v*. Johnston, 1908 S.C.684 .... 14.3
King, Sons & Paterson *v*. Ferrie (1942) 58 Sh.Ct.Rep.124 .... 4.5
Kinloch's Exrs. *v*. Kinloch (1811) Hume 178 .... 29.10
Kinmond Luke & Co. *v*. James Finlay & Co. (1904) 6 F.564 .... 23.4
Kinnear *v*. Brodie (1901) 3 F.540 .... 2.5
Kippen *v*. Hill (1822) 2 S.105 .... 19.5
Kirkcaldy District Council *v*. Household Manufacturing Ltd., 1987 S.L.T.617 ... 14.7
Kirklands Garage (Kinross) Ltd. *v*. Clark, 1967 S.L.T.(Sh.Ct.)60 .... 2.9
Kirkpatrick (G.A.) *v*. Kirkpatrick's Exrs., 1983 S.L.T.(Sh.Ct.)3 .... 13.5
Kirkwood *v*. Carroll [1903] 1 K.B.531 .... 5.27
—— *v*. Wilson (1823) 2 S.425 .... 4.6
Kirkwood & Sons *v*. Clydesdale Bank, 1908 S.C.20 .... 6.2, 6.10, 13.4
Knox *v*. Crawford (1862) 24 D.1088 .... 12.9
Kolbin & Sons *v*. Kinnear & Co., 1931 S.C.(H.L.)128 .... 11.7
Kyd *v*. Waterson (1880) 7 R.884 .... 24.2

L.A. *v*. Maritime Fruit Carriers Co. Ltd., 1983 S.L.T.357 .... 10.4
L.C.C. *v*. Agricultural Food Products Ltd. [1955] 2 Q.B.218 .... 5.13
L/F Foroya Fiskasola *v*. Charles Mauritzen Ltd., 1978 S.L.T.(Sh.Ct.)27 .... 1.5
Ladup Ltd. *v*. Shaikh [1983] Q.B.225 .... 5.20
Laidlaw (James) & Sons Ltd. *v*. Griffin, 1968 S.L.T.278 .... 30.2
Laing *v*. Cheyne (1832) 10 S.200 .... 22.1
—— *v*. Laing (1862) 24 D.1362 .... 12.14
—— *v*. Lord Advocate, 1973 S.L.T.(Notes)81 .... 13.1, 13.8
—— *v*. Taylor, 1978 S.L.T.(Sh.Ct.)59 .... 5.17
—— *v*. Westren (1858) 20 D.519 .... 2.5
Laing Brothers & Co.'s Tr. *v*. Low (1896) 23 R.1105 .... 30.13
Laing (Sir James) & Sons Ltd. *v*. Barclay Curle & Co. Ltd., 1908 S.C.82;
  S.C.(H.L.)1 .... 17.4
Laird *v*. Securities Insurance Co. Ltd. (1895) 22 R.452 .... 10.1
Lamb *v*. Thompson (1901) 4 F.88 .... 16.15
Lamberton *v*. Aiken (1899) 2 F.189 .... 5.3, 5.27
Lamonby *v*. Foulds Ltd., 1928 S.C. 89 .... 7.8
Lamond's Trs. *v*. Croom (1871) 9 M.662 .... 29.6
Lamont *v*. Hall, 1964 S.L.T.(Sh.Ct.)25 .... 16.15
Lamont & Co. *v*. Reid (1926) 42 Sh.Ct.Rep.262 .... 28.1
Lamont, Nisbett & Co. *v*. Hamilton, 1907 S.C.628 .... 30.2
Lanarkshire Health Board *v*. Banafa, 1987 S.L.T.229 .... 27.6

Lanarkshire Steel Co. Ltd. v. Caledonian Rlwy. Co. (1903) 6 F.47 . . . . 1.6
Lancashire Textiles (Jersey) Ltd. v. Thomson Shepherd & Co. Ltd., 1985 S.C.135 . 1.6
Landauer & Co. v. Alexander & Co., 1919 S.C.492 . . . . 25.3
Landcatch Ltd. v. Marine Harvest Ltd., 1985 S.L.T.478 . . . . 2.5
Landes v. Marcus (1909) 25 T.L.R.478 . . . . 5.14
Landless v. Wilson (1880) 8 R.289 . . . . 2.7
Lang v. Brown (1859) 22 D.113 . . . . 12.5
Larkin v. Morrow (1932) 48 Sh.Ct.Rep.59 . . . . 24.2
Largue v. Urquhart (1883) 10 R.1229 . . . . 7.7, 7.11
Laurie v. Denny's Tr. (1853) 15 D.404 . . . . 7.8
Lauries' Tr. v. Beveridge (1867) 6 M.85 . . . . 22.5
Lavaggi v. Pirie & Sons (1872) 10 M.312 . . . . 13.4
Law v. Humphrey (1876) 3 R.1192 . . . . 5.18, 29.6
Law Guarantee Trust and Accident Society Ltd. v. Munich Reinsurance Co. [1915]
    31 T.L.R.572 . . . . 10.1
Lawrence v. Lawrence's Trs., 1974 S.L.T.174 . . . . 22.10
Lawson v. Drysdale (1844) 7 D.153 . . . . 1.9, 13.5
Lawson's Exrs. v. Watson, 1907 S.C. 1353 . . . . 5.6
Lawsons Ltd. v. Avon Indiarubber Co. Ltd., 1915 2 S.L.T.327 . . . . 7.12
Learmonts v. Shearer (1866) 4 M.540 . . . . 19.4
Lee v. Donald, 17 May 1816, F.C. 29.7
Lees v. Dinwidie (1706) 5 Brown's Sup.35 . . . . 29.7
Legal and General Assurance Society Ltd. v. Carter, 1926 S.L.T.63 . . . . 23.1
Leggat Brothers v. Gray, 1908 S.C.67 . . . . 1.11, 11.9, 12.2, 17.2
—— v. ——, 1912 S.C.230 . . . . 17.8
Leigh (R.S.) & Co. v. Berger & Co., 1958 S.L.T.(Sh.Ct.)21 . . . . 2.2
Leith v. Garden (1703) Mor.865 . . . . 27.4
Leith Magistrates v. Lennon (1881) 18 S.L.R.313 . . . . 11.1
Lennie v. Mackie & Co. (1907) 23 Sh.Ct.Rep.85 . . . . 17.2
Lennox v. Rennie, 1951 S.L.T.(Notes)78 . . . . 2.1
Levy v. Gardiner, 1964 S.L.T.(Notes)68 . . . . 11.10
—— v. Napier, 1962 S.L.T.264 . . . . 25.3
Levy & Co. v. Thomsons (1883) 10 R.1134 . . . . 30.1
Lewis Merthyr Consolidated Collieries, Re [1929] 1 Ch.498 . . . . 9.16, 9.18
Libertas-Kommerz v. Johnson, 1977 S.C.191 . . . . 9.9, 27.1, 27.3
Libertas-Kommerz GmbH, 1978 S.L.T.222 . . . . 9.12
Liddell Brownlie & Co. v. Andrew Young & Son (1852) 14 D.647 . . . . 13.4
Lieberman v. G.W. Tait & Sons, S.S.C., 1987 S.L.T.585 . . . . 14.8
Lindsay v. Craig, 1919 S.C.139 . . . . 30.2
—— v. La Martona Rubber Estates Ltd., 1911 2 S.L.T.468 . . . . 17.3
—— v. London & North Western Rlwy. Co. (1855) 18 D.62 . . . . 11.9
Linlithgow Oil Co., Liqrs. of, v. N.B. Rlwy. Co. (1904) 12 S.L.T.421 . . . . 11.7
Little v. Burns (1881) 9 R.118 . . . . 11.14
Littlejohn v. Black (1855) 18 D.207 . . . . 8.6
—— v. Reynolds (1890) 6 Sh.Ct.Rep.321 . . . . 22.6
Liverpool Mortgage Insurance Co.'s Case [1914] 2 Ch.617 . . . . 10.1
Livesey v. Purdom & Sons (1894) 21 R.911 . . . . 30.2
Livingston v. Lindsay (1626) Mor.860 . . . . 27.4
—— v. Reid (1833) 11 S.878 . . . . 27.7
Livingstone v. Livingstone (1886) 14 R.43 . . . . 17.3
—— v. McFarlane (1842) 5 D.1 . . . . 19.3
Lloyds Bank Ltd. v. Bauld, 1976 S.L.T.(Notes)53 . . . . 2.11
—— v. Morrison & Son, 1927 S.C.571 . . . . 27.1
Lockhart v. Ferrier (1842) 4 D.1253 . . . . 30.12
Lochhead v. Graham (1883) 11 R.201 . . . . 16.1
Logan v. Stephen (1850) 13 D.262 . . . . 13.5
Logan (David) & Son Ltd. & Liquidator v. Schuldt (1903) 10 S.L.T.598 . . . . 30.2
Logan, Lady, v. Affleck (1736) Mor.5041 . . . . 12.13
Logan's Trs. v. Logan (1896) 23 R.848 . . . . 29.2
Lombard Banking Ltd. v. Central Garage and Engineering Co. Ltd. [1963] 1
    Q.B.220 . . . . 5.26
Lombard North Central Ltd. v. Lord Advocate, 1983 S.L.T.361 . . . . 7.5

Case	Reference
London & Brazilian Bank v. Lumsden's Trs., 1913 1 S.L.T.262	29.11
London & River Plate Bank Ltd. v. Bank of Liverpool [1896] 1 Q.B.7	5.21
London Joint Stock Bank Ltd. v. Macmillan [1918] A.C.777	6.12
London Scottish Transport Ltd. v. Tyres (Scotland) Ltd., 1957 S.L.T.(Sh.Ct.)48	21.7
Loudon Bros. v. Reid & Lauder's Tr. (1877) 5 R.293	22.7
Lovie v. Baird's Trs. (1895) 23 R.1	1.9
Lucarelli v. Buchanan, 1954 S.L.T.(Sh.Ct.)46	28.1
Lucas's Trs. v. Campbell & Scott (1894) 21 R.1096	17.4, 17.8
Lumsden v. Buchanan (1865) 3 M.(H.L.)89	1.8
—— v. Sym (1912) 28 Sh.Ct.Rep.168	30.13
Lupton & Co. v. Schulze & Co. (1900) 2 F.1118	2.5
Lympne Investments Ltd., Re [1972] 1 W.L.R.523	25.2
MACADAM v. Martin's Tr. (1872) 11 M.33	2.3, 21.2, 21.3
McAdam v. Scott (1912) 50 S.L.R.264	12.13
McAlister v. Swinburne & Co. (1874) 1 R.958	24.2
MacArthur v. Campbell's Tr., 1953 S.L.T.(Notes)81	22.5, 22.8
McArthur v. O'Donnell, 1969 S.L.T.(Sh.Ct.)24	2.6
—— v. Scott (1836) 15 S.270	28.1
McArthur's Exrs. v. Guild, 1908 S.C.743	29.2
McAulay v. Smith (1914) 30 Sh.Ct.Rep.162	17.7
MacBain v. MacBain, 1930 S.C.(H.L.)72	4.5
Macbride v. Clark Grierson & Co. (1865) 4 M.73	28.2
—— v. Hamilton (1875) 2 R.775	13.9
McCabe v. Andrew Middleton (Enterprises) Ltd., 1969 S.L.T.(Sh.Ct.)29	25.3
McCallum v. Wilson, 1974 S.L.T.(Sh.Ct.)72	2.9
McCallumn (Sh.Ct.) 1990 S.C.L.R.399	16.8
McCarroll v. McKinstery, 1923 S.C.94	16.15
McClelland v. Bank of Scotland (1857) 19 D.574	23.4
McConnell & Reid v. W. & G. Muir (1906) 14 S.L.T.79	13.5
McCracken v. McCracken (1928) 44 Sh.Ct.Rep.11	27.2
McCreadie's Trs. v. McCreadie (1897) 5 S.L.T.153	6.14
McCuaig v. Redpath Dorman Long Ltd., 1972 S.L.T.(Notes)42	11.7
McCutcheon v. McWilliam (1876) 3 R.565	27.2
McDonald v. Mize, 1989 S.L.T.482	11.9, 17.2
Macdonald v. North of Scotland Bank, 1942 S.C.369	1.10, 1.11, 11.1
—— v. Scott's Exrs., 1981 S.C.75	14.4
—— v. Scottish Motor Traction Co., 1948 S.C.529	11.14
—— v. Westren (1888) 15 R.988	16.2
Macdonald Fraser & Co. Ltd. v. Cairns's Exrx., 1932 S.C.699	12.5
Macdonald's Tr. v. Macdonald, 1938 S.C.536	21.9
Macdougall v. McNab (1893) 21 R.144	12.2
Macdougall's Tr. v. Lockhart (1903) 5 F.905	23.4
McDowal v. Agnew (1707) Mor.2568	1.9
—— v. Fullertoun (1714) Mor.840	27.5
McEwan's Trs. v. Macdonald, 1909 S.C.57	27.1
Macfarlane v. Glasgow Corporation (1934) 50 Sh.Ct.Rep.247	17.3
—— v. Johnston (1864) 2 M.1210	5.27
McFarlane v. Robb & Co. (1870) 9 M.370	1.10, 22.7
Macfarlane v. Sanderson (1868) 40 J.189	17.6
—— v. Watt (1828) 6 S.556	12.14
Macfie's J.F. v. Macfie, 1932 S.L.T.460	1.5
McGaan v. McGaan's Trs. (1883) 11 R.249	29.6
McGill v. Laurestoun (1558) Mor.843	27.5
McGregor v. Alley & McLellan (1887) 14 R.535	13.8
Macgregor v. City of Glasgow Bank (1865) 3 M.896	13.5
Macgregor's Tr. v. Cox (1883) 10 R.1028	13.4
McGuinness v. Anderson, 1953 S.L.T.(Notes)1	2.4
McInally v. Kildonan Homes Ltd., 1979 S.L.T.(Notes)89	11.11
MacInnes-Morrison v. Gairloch Hotel Co. Ltd., 1988 S.L.T.461	11.19
McIntosh v. Ainslie (1872) 10 M.304	14.2
Macintosh v. Nelson, 1984 S.L.T.(Sh.Ct.)82	2.9

Table of Cases

McIntosh v. Potts (1905) 7 F.765	7.12
Macintyre v. Caledonian Rlwy. Co. (1909) 25 Sh.Ct.Rep.329	17.6
McIntyre v. Macdonald (1854) 16 D.485	13.5
—— v. National Bank of Scotland, 1910 S.C.150	5.10
Macintyre Bros. v. Smith, 1913 S.C.129	2.7
Mackay v. Boswall-Preston, 1916 S.C.96	20.7
—— v. Campbell, 1967 S.C.(H.L.)53	2.11
—— v. Mackay, 1914 S.C.200	29.3
McKeand v. Laird (1861) 23 D.846	30.8
McKelvie v. Scottish Steel Scaffolding Co., 1938 S.C.278	11.17
McKenzie v. British Linen Co. (1881) 8 R.(H.L.)8	5.10, 5.21
Mackenzie v. Calder (1868) 6 M.833	22.5
McKenzie v. Campbell (1894) 21 R.904	17.12, 27.2
Mackenzie v. Cormack, 1950 S.C.183	7.10, 30.1
McKenzie v. H.D. Fraser & Sons, 1900 S.L.T.629	11.14
—— v. Jones (1926) 42 Sh.Ct.Rep.289	4.5
Mackenzie v. Macalister (1925) 41 Sh.Ct.Rep.163	1.8
—— v. Macartney (1831) 5 W.&S.504	10.1
—— v. Macleod's Exr., 1988 S.L.T.207	13.2
Mackenzie & Co. v. Finlay (1868) 7 M.27	16.1, 17.2
McKenzie's Exrx. v. Morrison's Trs., 1930 S.C.830	6.14, 12.11
Mackenzie's Trs. v. Sutherland (1895) 22 R.233	11.5, 29.6
Mackie v. McDowal (1774) Mor.2575	30.12
—— v. McMillan (1925) 41 Sh.Ct.Rep.339	24.2
—— v. Riddell (1874) 2 R.115	1.9, 13.1, 13.5
—— v. Watson (1837) 16 S.73	12.11
McKie v. Wilson, 1951 S.C.15	4.3, 4.4
McKillop v. Mutual Securities Ltd., 1945 S.C.166	2.10, 2.11
McKinlay v. McKinlay (1849) 11 D.1022	11.13
—— v. Wilson (1885) 13 R.210	12.5, 13.1
Mackinnon v. Monkhouse (1881) 9 R.393	13.10
Mackinnon's Tr. v. Bank of Scotland, 1915 S.C.411	10.1
Mackinnon's Trs. v. Dunlop, 1913 S.C.232	1.1
Mackintosh v. Macdonald (1828) 7 S.155	19.6
Mackintosh (John) & Sons Ltd. v. Baker's Bargain Stores (Seaford) Ltd. [1965] 1 W.L.R.1182	25.7
Mackintosh's Trs. v. Davidson & Gordon (1898) 25 R.554	19.3
Maclachlan v. Glasgow, 1925 S.L.T.(Sh.Ct.)77	16.15
—— v. Maxwell, 1910 S.C.87	23.4
McLaren v. Howie (1869) 8 M.106	12.12
MacLaren & Co. v. Preston (1893) 1 S.L.T.75	11.9, 17.3
McLaren's Tr. v. Argylls Ltd., 1915 2 S.L.T.241	2.6, 12.2, 21.7
—— v. National Bank (1897) 24 R.920	22.7
McLean v. Boyek (1894) 10 Sh.Ct.Rep.10	16.1
Maclean v. Campbell (1856) 18 D.609	11.7
McLean v. Clydesdale Bank (1883) 11 R.(H.L.)1	6.4, 6.8, 6.13
—— v. Galbraith Stores Ltd., 1935 S.C.165	11.14
—— v. Stuart, 1970 S.L.T.(Notes)77	30.18
McLelland v. Mackay (1908) 24 Sh.Ct.Rep.157	5.7, 5.26
Macleod v. Wilson (1837) 15 S.1043	29.7
McLetchie v. Angus Brothers (1899) 1 F.946	29.12
McMeekin v. Easton (1889) 16 R.363	5.14
McMurray v. McFarlane (1894) 31 S.L.R.531	10.1
—— v. McMurray's Trs. (1852) 14 D.1048	1.6
McNab v. Lockhart (1843) 5 D.1014	4.6
McNair v. Dunfermline Corporation, 1953 S.C.183	11.14, 28.5, 28.8
McNairn v. McNairn, 1959 S.L.T.(Notes)35	11.9
McNaught v. Milligan (1885) 13 R.366	30.10
McNaught & Co. v. Lewis (1935) 51 Sh.Ct.Rep.138	16.1
—— v. National Coal Board, 1966 S.L.T.237	11.14
McNeill & Son v. Innes, Chambers & Co., 1917 S.C.540	5.25, 19.6
McNicoll v. Kwasnica (1952) 68 Sh.Ct.Rep.295	11.2

Table of Cases

McPhail v. Cunninghame District Council, 1983 S.C.246	9.19, 14.4, 14.5
McPherson v. Cameron (1941) 57 Sh.Ct.Rep.64	29.6
Macpherson v. Macpherson's Tr. (1905) 8 F.191	16.2
Macpherson's Exrx. v. Mackay, 1932 S.C.505	6.15
Macphersons' J.F. v. Mackay, 1915 S.C.1011	27.5
Macrae v. Edinburgh Street Tramways Co. (1885) 13 R.265	11.14
—— v. Leith, 1913 S.C.901	7.10
—— v. Reed and Mallik Ltd., 1961 S.C.68	11.7
McRostie v. Halley (1850) 12 D.816	19.6
McTaggart v. Jeffrey (1828) 6 S.641	12.13
—— v. MacEachern's J.F., 1949 S.C.503	5.27
Mactavish's J.F. v. Michael's Trs., 1912 S.C.425	5.25
McVea v. Reid, 1958 S.L.T.(Sh.Ct.)60	4.4
McVey (James) Ltd. v. Budhill Social and Recreation Club, 1932 S.L.T.(Sh.Ct.)27	30.16
McWhirter v. McCulloch's Trs. (1887) 14 R.918	8.2
M.C.H. SERVICES LTD., RE [1987] B.C.L.C.535	25.14
Mace Builders (Glasgow) Ltd. v. Lunn [1987] Ch.191	9.12
Main v. Fleming's Trs. (1881) 8 R.880	22.1
Mair v. Wood, 1948 S.C.83	30.6
Malcolm v. Campbell (1889) 17 R.255	4.4
—— v. Cross (1898) 25 R.1089	2.5
Man (E.D. & F.) Ltd. v. Nigerian Sweets and Confectionery Co. Ltd. [1977] 2 Lloyd's Rep. 50	12.3
Manchester & Liverpool District Banking Co. v. Ferguson & Co. (1905) 7 F.865	5.19
Manley, Petrs., 1985 S.L.T.42	9.21
Mann v. Goldstein [1968] 1 W.L.R.1091	25.3
Manners v. Whitehead (1898) 1 F.171	2.4
Marchmont Ltd. v. Clayton, 1989 S.L.T.725	11.4
Marr's Exrx. v. Marr's Trs., 1936 S.C.64	14.8
Marren v. Ingles [1980] 1 W.L.R.983	1.1
Marshall v. Nimmo & Co. (1847) 10 D.328	1.10, 1.11, 17.3
Marshall, Earl of, v. Fraser (1682) Mor.11399	12.10
Martin's Exrx. v. McGhee, 1914 S.C.628	29.3
Martin's Tr. v. Wilson (1904) 12 S.L.T.112	23.1
Masco Cabinet Co. Ltd. v. Martin, 1912 S.C.896	13.7
Masterton v. Erskine's Trs. (1887) 14 R.712	29.11
Mather & Son v. Wilson & Co. Ltd. (1908) 15 S.L.T.946	17.3
Matthew v. Fawns (1842) 4 D.1242	17.4
—— v. Matthew's Tr. (1907) 15 S.L.T.326	1.11
Matthew Ellis Ltd., Re [1933] Ch.458	9.12
Matthew's Tr. v. Matthew (1867) 5 M.957	7.1, 22.5
Matthews v. Auld & Guild (1874) 1 R.1224	13.4
Maxwell v. McCulloch's Trs. (1738) Mor.2550	13.6
Mayfair Property Company, Re [1898] 2 Ch.28	27.1
Mechan & Sons Ltd. v. Bow McLachlan & Co. Ltd., 1910 S.C.758	2.5
Mechans Ltd. v. Highland Marine Charters Ltd., 1964 S.C.48	2.5
Medical Defence Union v. Dept of Trade [1980] Ch.82	1.11
Meier & Co. v. Küchenmeister (1881) 8 R.642	30.2
Meikle & Wilson v. Pollard (1880) 8 R.69	7.9
Mein v. McCall (1844) 6 D.1112	29.7
—— v. Towers (1829) 7 S.902	4.6
Meldrum's Trs. v. Clark (1826) 5 S.122	13.4
Mellor v. Wm. Beardmore & Co., 1927 S.C.597	2.9
Melville v. Noble's Trs. (1896) 24 R.243	11.4
—— v. Paterson (1842) 4 D.1311	21.15
Menzies v. Menzies (1893) 20 R.(H.L.)108	2.4
—— v. Murdoch (1841) 4 D.257	19.3
—— v. Poutz, 1916 S.C.143	23.12, 29.6
Mercer v. Wright (1953) 69 Sh.Ct.Rep.39	2.10
Mess v. Hay (1898) 1 F.(H.L.)22	24.2
Messenger's (J.&J.) Tr., 1990 G.W.D.26-1432	30.13

Metzenburg v. Highland Rlwy. Co. (1869) 7 M.919	17.5
Michelin Tyre Co. Ltd. v. Macfarlane (Glasgow) Ltd., 1917 2 S.L.T.205	2.3
Michie v. Young, 1962 S.L.T.(Notes)70	20.6
Microwave Systems (Scotland) Ltd. v. Electro-Physiological Instruments Ltd., 1971 S.L.T.(Notes)38	27.6
Middlemas v. Gibson, 1910 S.C.577	13.8
Middleton v. Earl of Strathmore (1743) Mor.2573	13.4
Midland Bank Ltd. v. R.V. Harris Ltd. [1963] 2 All E.R.685	6.4
—— v. Reckitt [1933] A.C.1	6.4
Milburn & Co. v. Jamaica Fruit Importing and Trading Co. of London [1900] 2 Q.B.540	1.6
Mill v. Fildes, 1982 S.L.T.147	7.3
—— v. Paul (1825) 4 S.219	13.4, 13.10
Mill's Trs. v. Mill's Trs., 1965 S.C.384	14.5
Millar v. Forage Supply Co. Ltd., 1955 S.L.T. (Sh.Ct.)18	15.5
—— v. Mitchell (1860) 22 D.833	30.2
—— v. National Bank (1891) 28 S.L.R.884	25.5
Millar & Lang v. Polak (1907) 14 S.L.T.788	11.9, 17.4
Millar & Lang v. Poole (1907) 15 S.L.T.76	11.9
Millars of Falkirk Ltd. v. Turpie, 1976 S.L.T.(Notes)66	2.5
Miller v. Baird, 1819 Hume 480	13.6
—— v. City of Glasgow District Council, 1989 S.L.T.44	14.4
—— v. Hutcheson & Dixon (1881) 8 R.489	7.10
—— v. John Finlay MacLeod & Parker, 1974 S.L.T.99	30.8
—— v. Learmonth (1870) 42 J.418	27.4
—— v. McPhun (1895) 22 R.600	11.13
—— v. Muirhead (1894) 21 R.658	27.8
—— v. Philip & Son (1883) 20 S.L.R.862	22.6
—— v. Thorburn (1861) 23 D.359	30.4, 30.8
Miller's Tr. v. Shield (1862) 24 D.821	22.8
Miln's J.F. v. Spence's Trs., 1927 S.L.T.425	7.11
Milne v. Donaldson (1852) 14 D.849	4.4
—— v. Kidd (1869) 8 M.250	10.1
Milne's Trs., 1936 S.C.706	12.7
Minha's Tr. v. Bank of Scotland, 1990 S.L.T.23	20.7
Mintons v. Hawley & Co. (1882) 20 S.L.R.126	12.2
Minty v. Donald (1824) 3 S.394	4.6
Mitchel v. Mitchel (1737) Mor.3935	29.7
Mitchell v. Berwick (1845) 7 D.382	12.11
—— v. Burn (1874) 1 R.900	17.4
—— v. Canal Basin Co. (1869) 7 M.480	30.12
—— v. Cullen (1852) 1 Macq.190	12.5
—— v. Heys & Sons (1894) 21 R.600	7.8
—— v. Mackersy (1905) 8 F.198	13.4
—— v. Motherwell (1888) 16 R.122	20.6
—— v. Moultry (1882) 10 R.378	4.6
—— v. Redpath Engineering Ltd., 1990 S.L.T.259	11.14
—— v. Scott (1881) 8 R.875	17.2, 17.9, 17.12
Mitchell & Muil Ltd. v. Ferniscliffe Products Co. Ltd., 1920 1 S.L.T.199	11.9
Mitchell & Sons v. Sirdar Rubber Co. Ltd. (1911) 27 Sh.Ct.Rep.334	2.1
Mitchell-Henry v. Norwich Union Life Insurance Society Ltd. [1918] 2 K.B.67	12.1
Modeluxe Linen Services Ltd. v. Redburn Hotel Ltd., 1985 S.L.T.(Sh.Ct.)60	11.2
Moir v. Robertson, 1924 S.L.T.435	2.8
Moncrieff v. Lord Dundas (1835) 14 S.61	11.7
Montage (G. & H.) GmbH v. Irvani [1990] 1 W.L.R.667	5.6
Monteith v. Smith (1624) Mor.12477	4.6
Montgomery (Thomas) & Sons v. Gallacher, 1982 S.L.T.138	12.5, 22.8
Montrose, Duchess of, v. Stuart (1887) 15 R.(H.L.)19	29.10
Montrose, Duke of, v. Edmonstone (1845) 7 D.759	28.1
Moore v. Gledden (1869) 7 M.1016	7.3
—— v. Young (1843) 5 D.494	4.6
Moore & Weinberg v. Ernsthausen Ltd., 1917 S.C.(H.L.)25	11.9, 17.4

Table of Cases

Moore Taggart & Co. v. Kerr (1897) 14 Sh.Ct.Rep.10 .... 30.21
Moore's Carving Machine Co. v. Austin (1896) 33 S.L.R.613 .... 7.8
Moray, Earl of, v. Mansfield (1836) 14 S.886 .... 8.6
Morel (E.J.) (1934) Ltd., Re [1962] Ch.21 .... 25.12
Morgan v. Smart (1872) 10 M.610 .... 10.3
Morison v. London County and Westminster Bank Ltd. [1914] 3 K.B.356 ..... 5.13, 6.11
Morison's Trs. v. Mitchell, 1925 S.L.T.231 .... 4.5
Moriston v. Tenants of Eastnisbet (1631) Mor.11394 .... 12.10
Morley's Tr. v. Aitken, 1982 S.C.73 .... 19.3
Morris v. Riddick (1867) 5 M.1036 .... 29.5
Morrison v. Carron Co. (1854) 16 D.1125 .... 22.5
—— v. Cornfoot (1930) 46 Sh.Ct.Rep.74 .... 29.6
—— v. Fulwell's Tr. (1901) 9 S.L.T.34 .... 7.7, 7.9
—— v. Harkness (1870) 9 M.35 .... 10.1
—— v. Harrison (1876) 3 R.406 .... 17.11, 21.13, 27.5
—— v. Hunter (1822) 2 S.68 .... 30.12
—— v. Integer Systems Control Ltd. (Sh.Ct.) 1989 S.C.L.R.495 .... 17.13
—— v. Turnbull (1832) 10 S.259 .... 1.11
Morrison & Mason v. Clarkson Bros. (1898) 25 R.427 .... 2.5
Mortgage Insurance Corporation v. C.I.R. (1888) 21 Q.B.D.352 .... 5.27
Morton (1871) 10 M.292 .... 8.6
—— v. O'Donnell, 1979 S.L.T.(Notes)26 .... 11.14
Morton's Tr. v. Fifeshire Auction Co. Ltd., 1911 1 S.L.T.405 .... 22.7
Morton's Trs. v. Robertson's J.F. (1892) 20 R.72 .... 28.7
Mosman v. Bells (1670) 2 Br.Sup.457 .... 27.3
Motherwell v. Manwell (1903) 5 F.619 .... 14.3
Mouland v. Ferguson, 1979 S.L.T.(Notes)85 .... 11.7
Mounsey (1896) 4 S.L.T.46 .... 27.4
Mowat v. Kerr, 1977 S.L.T.(Sh.Ct.)62 .... 11.10
Muir v. City of Glasgow Bank (1879) 6 R.(H.L.)21 .... 21.9
—— v. Collett (1862) 24 D.1119 .... 28.1, 30.10
—— v. Crawford (1875) 2 R.(H.L.)148 .... 10.3, 28.7
—— v. Steven (1896) 12 Sh.Ct.Rep.368 .... 4.2, 4.6
Muir's Tr. v. Braidwood, 1958 S.C.169 .... 21.10
Muirhead v. Borland, 1925 S.C.474 .... 30.14
Mullen Ltd. v. Campbell, 1923 S.L.T.497 .... 30.13
Multiservice Bookbinding Ltd. v. Marden [1979] Ch.84 .... 1.4
Munro v. Graham (1857) 20 D.72 .... 13.5
—— v. Macdonald's Exrs. (1866) 4 M.687 .... 13.5
—— v. Munro (1820) Hume 81 .... 19.6
—— v. Rothfield, 1920 S.C.118 .... 12.13, 22.5
—— v. Smith, 1968 S.L.T.(Sh.Ct.)26 .... 15.5
Murdoch v. Newman Industrial Control Ltd., 1980 S.L.T.13 .... 20.6
Murdoch & Co. Ltd. v. Greig (1889) 16 R.396 .... 21.7
Murray v. Durham (1622) Mor.855 .... 27.4
—— v. Fairlie Yacht Slip Ltd., 1975 S.L.T.(Sh.Ct.)62 .... 2.9
—— v. Laurie's Trs. (1827) 5 S.515 .... 4.6
—— v. Parlane's Tr. (1890) 18 R.287 .... 14.3
Murray (J. & C.) v. Wallace Marrs & Co., 1914 S.C.114 .... 17.2
Mushet v. Harvey (1710) Mor.14636 .... 28.1
Mycroft, Petr., 1983 S.L.T.342 .... 13.8
Myles J. Callaghan Ltd. v. City of Glasgow District Council, 1988 S.L.T.227 ... 9.18, 9.19
Mylne v. Balfour Melville (1901) 8 S.L.T.454 .... 4.1

Naismith v. Bowman (1710) Mor.2645 .... 13.7
Nakeski-Cumming v. Gordon, 1924 S.C.217 .... 20.6
Napier v. Gordon (1831) 5 W.&.S.745 .... 11.7
Napier (N.G.) Ltd. v. Crosbie, 1964 S.C.129 .... 10.3
Napier Shanks & Bell v. Halvorsen (1892) 19 R.412 .... 11.9
Nash Dredging (U.K.) Ltd. v. Kestrel Marine Ltd., 1985 S.C.96 .... 11.7
Nasmyth v. Samson (1785) 3 Pat.App.9 .... 4.1
National Bank of Australasia v. Turnbull & Co. (1891) 18 R.629 .... 5.19

Table of Cases

National Bank of Greece S.A. v. Pinios Shipping Co. (No. 1) [1990] A.C.637 ..... 11.7
National Bank of Scotland v. Campbell (1892) 19 R.885 .... 10.1
—— v. Dickie's Tr. (1895) 22 R.740 .... 13.4
—— v. Forbes (1858) 21 D.79 .... 8.1
—— v. Silke [1891] 1 Q.B.435 .... 6.11
—— v. Thomas White and Park, 1909 S.C.1308 .... 7.7, 7.11
National Bank of Scotland Glasgow Nominees Ltd. v. Adamson, 1932 S.L.T.492 .. 17.11
National Coal Board v. Thomson, 1959 S.C.353 .... 1.6, 28.6
National Commercial Bank of Scotland v. Millar's Tr., 1964 S.L.T.(Notes)57 .. 12.5, 27.2
—— v. Stuart, 1969 S.L.T.(Notes)52 .... 10.1
National Exchange Co. v. Drew (1855) 2 Macq.103 .... 13.1, 13.5
National Westminster Bank v. Halesowen Presswork [1972] A.C.785 .... 13.6
Nawab Major Sir Mohammad Akbar Khan v. Attar Singh [1936] 2 All E.R.545 ... 5.27
Neale (F.J.) (Glasgow) Ltd. v. Vickery, 1973 S.L.T.(Sh.Ct.)88 .... 30.18
Neil's Tr. v. British Linen Co. (1898) 6 S.L.T.227; (1898) 36 S.L.R.139 .... 22.5, 22.6
Neilson v. Guthrie and Gairn (1672) Mor.5878 .... 1.6, 30.21
—— v. Smiths Gowans & Roy (1821) Hume 31 .... 17.4
—— v. Stewart, 1990 G.W.D.1-4 .... 4.1
—— v. Wilson (1890) 17 R.608 .... 28.1
Neilson's Trs. v. Neilson's Trs. (1883) 11 R.119 .... 5.1, 12.11
Nelmes & Co. v. Ewing (1883) 11 R.193 .... 7.12
Nelson v. Wm. Chalmers & Co., 1913 S.C.441 .... 2.5, 21.7
—— v. Easdale Slate Quarries Co. Ltd., 1910 1 S.L.T.21 .... 5.16
—— v. Empress Assurance Corporation [1905] 2 K.B.281 .... 10.1
—— v. National Bank, 1936 S.C.570 .... 8.1
Neuchatel Asphalte Co. Ltd. v. Barnett [1957] 1 W.L.R.356 .... 11.2
New Brunswick Rlwy. Co. v. British and French Trust Corporation Ltd. [1939] A.C.1 .... 1.4
New Mining and Exploring Syndicate Ltd. v. Chalmers & Hunter, 1912 S.C.126 ... 6.13
New Timbiqui Gold Mines Ltd., Re [1961] Ch.319 .... 25.15
Newbigging v. Ritchie's Tr., 1930 S.C.273 .... 7.3, 21.7
Newlands v. McKinlay (1885) 13 R.353 .... 4.6
Newton v. Newton, 1925 S.C.715 .... 1.6
Newton & Sons' Tr. v. Finlayson & Co., 1928 S.C.637 .... 22.6
Newton's Exrx. v. Meiklejohn's J.F., 1959 S.L.T.71 .... 21.2
Nicol v. McIntyre (1882) 9 R.1097 .... 22.5, 22.6
Nicol's Tr. v. Hill (1889) 16 R.416 .... 8.6
Nicol's Trs. v. Sutherland, 1951 S.C.(H.L.)21 .... 5.7, 5.19, 5.22
Nicoll v. Reid (1878) 6 R.216 .... 12.6
Nicolson v. Johnstone & Wright 24.2
Nicolsons v. Burt (1882) 10 R.121 .... 10.3
Nimmo v. Nimmo (1873) 11 M.446 .... 4.5
Nisbet's Trs. v. Morrison's Trs. (1829) 7 S.307 .... 4.6
Niven v. Clyde Fasteners Ltd., 1986 S.L.T.344 .... 13.5
Noel v. Trust and Agency Co. of Australasia Ltd. [1937] 1 Ch.438 .... 12.7
Nordic Travel Ltd. v. Scotprint Ltd., 1980 S.C.1 .... 22.6
"Nordsoen" v. Mackie, Koth & Co., 1911 S.C.172 .... 11.10
Norman v. Baltimore and Ohio Railroad Co., 249 U.S.240 .... 1.4
Norris, Applicant, 1990 G.W.D.17-984 .... 16.9
North v. Bassett [1892] 1 Q.B.333 .... 14.2
—— v. Stewart (1890) 17 R.(H.L.) 60 .... 11.8, 11.9
North British Rlwy. Co. v. White (1881) 9 R.97 .... 11.5
North of Scotland Bank v. Inland Revenue, 1931 S.C.149 .... 5.1
North Scottish Helicopters Ltd. v. United Technologies Corporation Inc. (No. 2), 1988 S.L.T.778 .... 1.5
North-Western Bank Ltd. v. Poynter, Son and Macdonalds (1894) 22 R.(H.L.)1 .. 7.3
Northesk, Earl of, v. Gairn's Tutor (1670) Mor.2569 .... 13.4

O'Donnell v. A.M. & G. Robertson, 1965 S.L.T.155 .... 11.13
O'Driscoll v. Manchester Insurance Committee [1915] 3 K.B.499 .... 1.1
O'Hare v. Reaich, 1956 S.L.T.(Sh.Ct.)78 .... 11.9
Officers' Superannuation and Provident Fund v. Cooper, 1976 S.L.T.(Sh.Ct.)2 ... 17.3

Ogilvie & Son v. Taylor (1887) 14 R.399	24.2
Olderfleet Shipbuilding Co., *Re* [1922] 1 I.R.26	9.12
Oliphant v. Newton (1682) Mor.5035	12.13
Oncken's J.F. v. Reimers (1892) 19 R.519	1.6
Orbit Mining & Trading Co. Ltd. v. Westminster Bank Ltd. [1963] 1 Q.B. 794	5.3, 6.4, 6.13
Oriel Ltd., *Re* [1986] 1 W.L.R.180	30.20
Orleans Motor Co. Ltd., *Re* [1911] 2 Ch.41	9.12
Orr v. Jay & Co. (1911) 27 Sh.Ct.Rep.158	7.12
—— v. Metcalfe, 1973 S.C.57	11.7
Orr and Barber v. Union Bank of Scotland (1854) 1 Macq.513	6.12
Orr's Tr. v. Tullis (1870) 8 M.936	7.3
Oscar Chess Ltd. v. Williams [1957] 1 All E.R.325	2.4
Osterreichische Länderbank v. S'Elite Ltd. [1981] Q.B.565	5.9
Oswald's Trs. v. Dickson (1833) 12 S.156	30.12
Overstone Ltd. v. Shipway [1962] 1 W.L.R.117	2.6
Ovington v. McVicar (1864) 2 M.1066	1.6
PACKMAN (GEORGE) & SONS v. Dunbar's Trs., 1977 S.L.T.140	2.11
Pagan & Osborne v. Haig, 1910 S.C.341	30.16
Paisley Union Bank v. Hamilton (1831) 9 S.488	19.5
Palace Billiards Rooms Ltd. v. City Property Investment Trust Corporation Ltd., 1912 S.C.5	1.10
Palmer v. Lee (1880) 7 R.651	7.7, 14.1
—— v. S.E. Lancashire Insurance Co., 1932 S.L.T.68	17.8
Panorama Developments (Guildford) Ltd. v. Fidelis Furnishing Fabrics Ltd. [1971] 2 Q.B.711	30.18
Park, Dobson & Co. v. William Taylor & Son, 1929 S.C.571	1.11, 17.3
Parker v. Brown & Co. (1878) 5 R.979	7.8
—— v. Douglas Heron & Co. (1783) Mor.2868	16.2
—— v. Lord Advocate, 1958 S.C.426	1.11
Parkinson & Co. Ltd. v. Bowen & Sons Ltd., 1951 S.L.T.393	17.13
Parnell v. Walter (1889) 16 R.917	17.3
Paterson v. Banks, 1958 S.L.T.(Sh.Ct.)33	30.3
—— v. Cowan (1826) 4 S.477	11.10
—— v. Paterson (1897) 25 R.144	4.5
—— v. Wilson (1883) 21 S.L.R.272	6.14
Paterson's Crs. v. McAulay (1742) Mor.2646	13.7
Paterson (Robert) & Sons Ltd. v. Household Supplies Co. Ltd., 1975 S.L.T.98	13.8
Paton v. I.R.C. [1938] A.C.341	12.7
Paton's Trs. v. Finlayson, 1923 S.C.872	7.8, 21.7
Patrick v. Patrick's Trs. (1904) 6 F.836	4.5
—— v. Watt (1859) 21 D.637	12.10, 12.11
Pattison's Tr. v. Liston (1893) 20 R.806	7.3
Paul v. Boyd's Trs. (1835) 13 S.818	27.4
—— v. Craw (1956) 72 Sh.Ct.Rep.60	4.4
—— v. Henderson (1867) 5 M.1120	16.15
Paul & Frank Ltd. v. Discount Bank (Overseas) Ltd. [1967] Ch.348	9.1
Paul & Thain v. Royal Bank (1869) 7 M.361	13.5, 13.10
Pearce & Co. v. Owners of S.S. "Hans Maersk", 1935 S.C.703	11.13
Pearson v. I.R.C. [1981] A.C. 753	1.11
—— v. Scott (1878) 9 Ch.D.198	12.6
Penman v. White, 1957 S.C.338	4.4
Penman (J.) Ltd. v. Macdonald (1953) 69 Sh.Ct.Rep.284	7.9
Penney v. Aitken, 1927 S.C.673	4.6
Penson and Robertson, 6 June 1820, F.C.	7.12
Pert v. Bruce, 1937 S.L.T.475	5.18, 20.6
Pettit, *Re* [1922] 2 Ch.765	12.7
Phillips v. Italian Bank Ltd., 1934 S.L.T.78	6.5, 6.11, 6.12
Phosphate Sewage Co. v. Molleson (1874) 1 R.840	23.3
Picken v. Arundale & Co. (1872) 10 M.987	4.4
Pillans & Wilson v. Castlecary Fireclay Co. Ltd., 1931 S.L.T.532	2.9

Pirrie v. Mags. of Hawick (1901) 17 Sh.Ct.Rep.294	6.15
Pitfoddels, Lord, v. Glenkindy (1662) Mor.12454	4.6
Plotzker v. Lucas, 1907 S.C.315	30.10
Pochin & Co. v. Robinows & Marjoribanks (1869) 7 M.622	7.3
Pollich v. Heatley, 1910 S.C.469	11.7
Pollock v. Goodwin's Trs. (1898) 25 R.1051	11.2, 12.2
—— v. McCrae, 1922 S.C.(H.L.)192	2.5
Pollok (W. & J.C.) v. The Gaeta Pioneer Mining Co., 1907 S.C.182	25.3
Pommer v. Mowat (1906) 14 S.L.T.373	2.5
Poole v. Anderson (1834) 12 S.481	29.6
Porteous (George) (Arts) Ltd. v. Dollar Rae Ltd., 1979 S.L.T.(Sh.Ct.)51	14.5
Porter Spiers (Leicester) Ltd. v. Cameron [1950] C.L.Y.5329	2.5
Pow v. Pow, 1987 S.L.T.127	11.10
Prentice's Trs. v. Prentice, 1935 S.C.211	12.7
Preston v. Scot (1667) Mor.11397	12.10
Prestwick Cinema Co. v. Gardiner, 1951 S.C.98	11.7
Price & Pierce Ltd. v. Bank of Scotland, 1910 S.C.1095; 1912 S.C.(H.L.)19	7.3, 22.5
Priestley & Son v. Arthur & Co. (1882) 3 Sh.Ct.Rep.450	11.2
Primesight Bus Advertising Ltd. v. Canning and Crawford (Sh.Ct.) 1990 S.C.L.R.349	16.7
Primlaks (U.K.) Ltd., Re [1989] B.C.L.C.734	26.4
Primrose (Builders) Ltd., Re [1950] Ch.561	25.12
Primrose's Sequestration (1894) 10 Sh.Ct.Rep.238	21.7
Pringle v. Neilson (1788) Mor.1393	16.2
Pringle's Tr. v. Wright (1903) 5 F.522	22.6
Produce Marketing Consortium, Re [1989] 1 W.L.R.745	25.8
Pulsometer Engineering Co. Ltd. v. Gracie (1887) 14 R.316	7.12
Punjab National Bank v. Rome [1989] F.S.R.380	30.20
Purdie v. Hamilton (1900) 8 S.L.T.83	5.1
Purdon v. Rowat's Trs. (1856) 19 D.206	12.13
QUINN v. Bowie (No. 2), 1987 S.L.T.576	11.14, 11.19
R. v. Charles [1977] A.C.177	6.2
R. v. Lambie [1982] A.C.449	4.13
R. v. Marshall [1989] C.C.L.R.47	3.10
Rafsanjan Pistachio Producers Co-operative v. Reiss [1990] B.C.L.C.352	5.14
Railway Passengers' Assurance Co. v. Kyd (1894) 10 Sh.Ct.Rep.138	21.11
Rampgill Mill Ltd., Re [1967] Ch.1138	25.12
Ramsay v. Nairn (1708) Mor.3139	29.7
Ramsay & Son v. Brand (1898) 25 R.1212	1.6, 2.10
Ramsay's Trs. v. Souter (1864) 2 M.891	11.13
Rank Xerox Ltd. v. Lane [1981] A.C.629	5.1
Rankin v. Milne (1916) 32 Sh.Ct.Rep.109	12.13
—— v. Wither (1886) 13 R.903	1.6
Rankine v. Logie Den Land Co. (1902) 4 F.1074	28.1
Ransohoff & Wissler v. Burrell (1897) 25 R.284	30.1
Raymond Harrison & Co.'s Tr. v. North West Securities, 1989 S.L.T.718	21.4, 22.9
Reddie v. Williamson (1863) 1 M.228	11.7
Redpath Dorman Long Ltd. v. Cummins Engine Co. Ltd., 1981 S.C.370	13.9
Reed v. Young [1986] 1 W.L.R.649	30.14
Reid v. Barclay (1879) 6 R.1007	27.8
—— v. Bell (1884) 12 R.178	13.8, 13.10
—— v. Campbell, 1958 S.L.T.(Sh.Ct.)45	2.11
—— v. Chalmers (1828) 6 S.1120	30.4
—— v. Donaldson (1778) Mor.1392	16.2
—— v. Lamond (1857) 19 D.265	28.1
—— v. Morison (1893) 20 R.510	1.11, 19.4
—— v. McWalter (1878) 5 R.630	29.2
Reid & McCall v. Douglas, 11 June 1814, F.C.	30.9
Reid's Exrx. v. Reid, 1944 S.C.(H.L.)25	29.1
Renfrew Golf Club v. Ravenstone Securities Ltd., 1948 S.C.22	14.5

Rennet v. Mathieson (1903) 5 F.591	7.3
Rennie v. Ritchie (1845) 4 Bell's App.221	27.1
Renny v. Rutherford (1840) 2 D.676	7.7
Renny and Webster v. Myles & Murray (1847) 9 D.619	7.11
Renouf's Trs. v. Haining, 1919 S.C.497	29.5
Renton & Gray's Tr. v. Dickison (1880) 7 R.951	22.8
Rex v. International Trustee for the Protection of Bondholders Aktiengesellschaft [1937] A.C.500	1.4
Rhind's Tr. v. Robertson & Baxter (1891) 18 R.623	7.3, 22.5
Rhokana Corporation Ltd. v. I.R.C. [1937] 1 K.B.788	12.7
Richards & Wallington (Earthmoving) Ltd. v. Whatlings Ltd., 1982 S.L.T.66	11.10
Richmond v. Grahame (1847) 9 D.633	28.1
Richmond's Trs. v. Richmond, 1935 S.C.585	12.7
Riddell v. Galbraith (1896) 24 R.51	20.3, 20.6
Riley v. Ellis, 1910 S.C.934	1.1, 1.11, 17.3
Ritchie v. Cowan & Kinghorn (1901) 3 F.1071	12.13
—— v. McLachlan (1870) 8 M.815	11.10, 27.4
Robb v. Gow Bros. & Gemmell (1905) 8 F.90	12.1
—— v. Robb's Trs. (1884) 11 R.881	4.3, 4.5
Robbie (N.W.) & Co. Ltd. v. Witney Warehouse Co. Ltd. [1963] 1 W.L.R.1324	9.18
Roberts & Cooper Ltd. v. Salvesen & Co., 1918 S.C.794	2.1
Robertson v. Bent Colliery Co. Ltd. (1919) 35 Sh.Ct.Rep.290	12.8
—— v. British Linen Bank (1891) 18 R.1225	8.1, 27.1
—— v. Hall's Tr. (1896) 24 R.120	7.3
—— v. D.B. Marshall (Newbridge) Ltd., 1989 S.L.T.(Sh.Ct.)102	11.19
—— v. Ogilvie (1798) Mor. s.v. "Bills of Exchange" App.No.6	22.8
—— v. Ross (1887) 15 R.67	7.9
—— v. Wright (1873) 1 R.237	27.7
Robertson & Co. v. Bird & Co. (1897) 24 R.1076	1.9
Robertson Construction Co. (Denny) Ltd. v. Taylor, (O.H.) 1990 S.C.L.R.304	11.7
Robertson Durham v. Constant (1907) 15 S.L.T.131	7.5
Robertson (H.G.) v. Murray International Metals Ltd., 1988 S.L.T.747	14.5
Robertson's Tr. v. Roberts, 1982 S.L.T.22	21.15
—— v. Royal Bank (1890) 18 R.12	7.10
—— v. Riddell, 1911 S.C.14	8.1
—— v. Union Bank of Scotland, 1917 S.C.549	22.8
Rodger v. Crawfords (1867) 6 M.24	8.5
—— v. Maracas Ltd., 1990 S.L.T.45	11.11
Rodger (Builders) Ltd. v. Fawdry, 1950 S.C.483	2.11
Rodgers (H.D.) & Co. Ltd. v. The Paradise Restaurant (1955) 71 Sh.Ct.Rep.128	4.6
Rohtas Industries Ltd. v. Urquhart Lindsay and Robertson Orchar Ltd., 1950 S.L.T.(Notes)5	2.1
Rolfe Lubell & Co. v. Keith [1979] 1 All E.R.860	5.14
Rollo v. Simpson (1710) Mor.11411	12.9
Rollo (L.) v. Laird of Niddrie (1665) 1 Br.Sup.510	27.4
Rooney v. F.W. Woolworth plc, 1990 S.L.T.257	11.19
Rorie v. Stevenson, 1908 S.C.559	7.11
Rosa S., The [1989] Q.B.419	1.3
Ross v. British Railways Board, 1972 S.C.154	11.7
—— v. Cowie's Exrx. (1888) 16 R.224	14.5
—— v. Gordon's J.F., 1973 S.L.T.(Notes)91	23.1
—— v. Hutton (1830) 8 S.916	22.1
—— v. Mags. of Tayne (1711) Mor.2568	13.5
—— v. Ross (1878) 5 R.1013	11.9
—— v. —— (1895) 22 R.461	13.5, 13.10
—— v. Ross's Trs., *sub. nom.*, Rose v. Rose's Trs., 1967 S.L.T.12	29.5
—— v. Taylor, 1985 S.C.156	9.18
Ross & Co. v. Plano Manufacturing Co. (1903) 11 S.L.T.7	21.7
Ross & Duncan v. Baxter & Co. (1885) 13 R.185	7.7, 7.8
Rosslund Cycle Co. v. McCreadie, 1907 S.C.1208	30.9
Rowan's Trs. v. Rowan, 1940 S.C.30	1.6, 12.7
Rowbotham Baxter Ltd., *Re* [1990] 3 C.L.C.397	26.4

Table of Cases

Roy's Tr. v. Colville & Drysdale (1903) 5 F.769 .... 22.8
Roy's Trs. v. Stalker (1850) 12 D.722 .... 14.1
Royal Bank of Scotland v. Bain (1877) 4 R.985 .... 1.7
—— v. Brown, 1982 S.C.89 .... 10.2
—— v. Christie (1841) 2 Rob. 118 .... 12.5
—— v. Commercial Bank of Scotland (1881) 8 R.805 .... 23.6, 23.7
—— v. Dunbar, 1985 S.L.T.(Sh.Ct.)66 .... 11.7
—— v. Fairholm (1770) Mor.App. "Adjudication" No. 3 .... 17.3, 19.4
—— v. W.G.M. & C. Forbes, (O.H.) 1987 S.C.L.R.294 .... 20.3
—— v. Geddes, 1983 S.L.T.(Sh.Ct.)32 .... 11.7
—— v. McKerracher, 1968 S.L.T.(Sh.Ct.)77 .... 28.1
—— v. Millar & Co.'s Tr. (1882) 9 R.679 .... 23.4
—— v. Purdom (1877) 15 S.L.R.13 .... 23.4
—— v. Saunders & Sons' Trs. (1882) 9 R.(H.L.)67 .... 23.8, 23.9
—— v. Skinner, 1931 S.L.T.382 .... 6.2, 30.2
—— v. Watt, 1990 G.W.D.1-6 .... 6.13
—— v. Welsh, 1985 S.L.T.439 .... 10.3
Royal Trust Bank v. Buchler [1989] B.C.L.C.130 .... 26.8
Rudman v. Jay, 1908 S.C.552 .... 2.6
Russel v. Attorney-General, 1917 S.C.28 .... 1.6
—— v. Johnston (1859) 21 D.886 .... 11.5
Russell v. Dunbar (1717) Mor. 11419 .... 12.8
—— v. McNab (1824) 3 S.63 .... 30.12
—— v. Mudie (1857) 20 D.125 .... 27.8, 28.3
Rutherford (James R.) & Sons Ltd., Re [1964] 3 All E.R.137 .... 25.12
Rutherford's Exrs. v. Marshall (1861) 23 D.1276 .... 4.5
Ruthven, Lord, v. Drummond, 1908 S.C.1154 .... 11.10, 17.15
—— v. Pulford & Sons, 1909 S.C.951 .... 17.3
Ryrie v. Ryrie (1840) 2 D.1210 .... 12.11

St. Andrews Magistrates v. Forbes (1893) 31 S.L.R.225 .... 29.6
Salaman v. Rosslyn's Trs. (1900) 3 F.298 .... 7.3, 22.10, 24.2
—— v. Sinclair's Trs., 1916 S.C.698 .... 29.6
—— v. Tod, 1911 S.C.1214 .... 1.11
Salmon v. Padon & Vannan (1824) 3 S.406 .... 30.12
Sanders v. Hewat (1822) 1 S.333 .... 12.8
Sanderson v. Lockhart Mure, 1946 S.C.298 .... 1.6, 29.6
Saunders (G.L.) Ltd., Re [1986] 1 W.L.R.215 .... 9.18
Sawers v. Clark (1892) 19 R.1090 .... 4.6
Scotland v. Scotland, 1909 S.C.505 .... 4.5
Scott v. Aitken, 1950 S.L.T.(Notes)34 .... 13.2, 13.9
—— v. Hall & Bissett, June 13 1809, F.C. 30.12
—— v. J.B. Livingston & Nicol, 1990 S.L.T.305 .... 30.2
—— v. Marshall, 1949 S.L.T.(Notes)35 .... 2.2
—— v. Mills's Trs., 1923 S.C.726 .... 29.3
—— v. Price (1837) 15 S.916 .... 16.2
—— v. Scott, 1930 S.C.903 .... 1.11, 22.10, 29.5
—— v. Young, 1909 1 S.L.T.47 .... 10.1
Scott (G.M.) (Willowbank Cooperage) Ltd. v. York Trailer Co. Ltd., 1969 S.L.T.87 .... 1.6
Scott (James) & Co. (Electrical Engineers) Ltd. v. McIntosh (1960) Sh.Ct.Rep.26 .... 12.15
Scott Lithgow Ltd. v. Secretary of State for Defence, 1989 S.L.T.236 .... 14.5
Scott's Trs. v. Scott (1887) 14 R.1043 .... 13.10
Scottish and Newcastle Breweries Ltd. v. Blair, 1967 S.L.T.72 .... 5.14
—— v. Edinburgh District Council, 1979 S.L.T.(Notes)11 .... 7.12
Scottish Discount Co. Ltd. v. Blin, 1985 S.C.216 .... 2.6
Scottish Equitable Life Assurance Society v. Buist (1877) 4 R.1076; (1878) 5 R.(H.L.)64 .... 27.7
Scottish Fishermen's Organisation Ltd. v. McLean, 1980 S.L.T.(Sh.Ct.)76 .... 13.8
Scottish Heritable Security Co. v. Allan Campbell & Co. (1876) 3 R.333 .... 1.7
Scottish Heritages Co. Ltd. v. North British Property Investment Co. Ltd. (1885) 12 R.550 .... 1.7

Table of Cases

Scottish Metropolitan Co. v. Sutherlands Ltd., 1934 S.L.T.(Sh.Ct.)62	25.11
Scottish Metropolitan Property plc v. Christie, 1987 S.L.T.(Sh.Ct.)18	10.1
Scottish Milk Marketing Board v. Wood, 1936 S.C.604	20.3
Scottish Motor Traction Co. v. Murphy, 1949 S.L.T.(Notes)39	2.9
Scottish North Eastern Rlwy. Co. v. Napier (1859) 21 D.700	13.1, 13.5
Scottish Provident Institution v. Ferrier's Trs. (1871) 8 S.L.R.390	10.3
Scottish Transit Trust v. Scottish Land Cultivators Ltd., 1955 S.C.254	7.3, 21.7
Scottish Wagon Co. Ltd. v. James Hamilton's Tr. (1906) 13 S.L.T.779	23.5
Scottish Widows Fund v. Buist (1876) 3 R.1078	27.7
Seabrook Estate Co. Ltd. v. Ford [1949] 2 All E.R.94	9.17
Secretary of State for Scotland v. Coltness Industries Ltd., 1979 S.L.T.(Sh.Ct.)56	28.7
Semple v. Kyle (1902) 4 F.421	5.15
Semple's Executrices v. Semple, 1912 1 S.L.T.382	5.27
Servers of the Blind League, Re [1960] 1 W.L.R.564	25.15
Seton (1683) Mor.2566	13.5
Shankland & Co. v. McGildowny, 1912 S.C.857	11.9, 17.3
Shanks v. Central Regional Council, 1987 S.L.T.410	9.15, 14.7
Sharp v. Macdonald & Fraser (1884) 1 Sh.Ct.Rep.37	17.2
—— v. Rettie (1884) 11 R.745	13.9
Shaw v. Dow and Dobie (1869) 7 M.449	11.9
—— v. Kay (1904) 12 S.L.T.262	4.1
—— v. Wright (1877) 5 R.245	12.11
Shaw (George) Ltd. v. Duffy, 1943 S.C.350	7.1
Sheaf Steamship Co. v. Compania Transmediterranea, 1930 S.C.660	11.8
Sheldon & Ackhoff v. Milligan (1907) 14 S.L.T.703	10.1
Sherry, Re (1884) 25 Ch.D.692	12.5
Shiells v. Ferguson, Davidson & Co. (1876) 4 R.250	13.6, 27.5, 27.7
Short's Tr. v. Chung, 1990 G.W.D.28-1857	22.2
Sidlaw Industries Ltd. v. Cable Belt Ltd., 1979 S.L.T.(Notes)40	11.13
Sim v. Lundy & Blanshard (1868) 41 J.136	13.5
Simmons v. London Joint Stock Bank [1891] 1 Ch.270	5.2
Simpson v. Jack, 1948 S.L.T.(Notes)45	10.1, 14.1
Simpson & Co. v. Thomson (1877) 5 R.(H.L.)40	1.6
Simpson's Trs. v. Simpson, 1933 S.N.22	12.15
Sinclair v. Logan, 1961 S.L.T.(Sh.Ct.)10	2.9
—— v. Sinclair (1726) Mor.2793	29.7
—— v. Staples (1860) 22 D.600	17.3, 17.8
Sinclair (P.M.) v. Bamber Gray Partnership, 1987 S.L.T.674	30.2
Singer v. Gray Tool Co. (Europe) Ltd., 1984 S.L.T.149	28.6
Singh v. Cross Entertainments Ltd., 1990 S.L.T.77	1.6
Site Preparations Ltd. v. Buchan Development Co. Ltd., 1983 S.L.T.317	25.5
—— v. Secretary of State for Scotland, 1975 S.L.T.(Notes)41	2.9
Skiffington v. Dickson, 1970 S.L.T.(Sh.Ct.)24	4.5
Skinner v. Henderson (1865) 3 M.867	7.11
Skipton Building Society v. Wain, 1986 S.L.T.96	8.2
Skuce (V.L.) & Co. v. Cooper [1975] 1 W.L.R.593	3.12
Sligo v. Menzies (1840) 2 D.1478	10.4, 28.3
Sloan v. Birtwhistle (1827) 5 S.742	13.6
Smallman Construction Ltd., Re [1989] B.C.L.C.420	26.7
Smart v. Wilkinson, 1928 S.C.383	1.9, 13.9
Smart & Co. v. Stewart, 1911 S.C.668	15.1
Smeaton v. Dundee Corporation, 1941 S.C.600	11.13, 11.14
Smellie's Exrx. v. Smellie, 1933 S.C.725	11.7
Smith v. Barclay, 1962 S.C.1	11.4
—— v. Burns (1847) 9 D.1344	17.7
—— v. Cameron (1879) 6 R.1107	1.10
—— v. Chambers' Trs. (1878) 5 R.97; 5 R.(H.L.)151	17.8
—— v. Frier (1857) 19 D.384	21.15
—— v. Harding (1877) 5 R.147	28.1, 28.7
—— v. Kerr (1869) 7 M.863	12.14
—— v. Liqr. of James Birrell Ltd., 1967 S.L.T.(Notes)116	25.7
—— v. Lord Advocate, 1978 S.C.259	13.4, 25.1

Smith v. Lord Advocate, 1980 S.C.227 .... 13.8
—— v. —— (No. 2), 1981 S.L.T.19 .... 1.10, 1.11, 13.10
—— v. Macintosh (1848) 10 D.455 .... 17.15
—— v. Middleton, 1972 S.C.30 .... 11.7
—— v. North British Rlwy. (1850) 12 D.795 .... 12.6
—— v. Po and Capaldi, 1931 S.L.T.(Sh.Ct.)31 .... 7.12
—— v. Rosenbloom, 1915 2 S.L.T.18 .... 11.9
—— v. Selby (1829) 7 S.885 .... 19.6
—— v. Sim, 1954 S.C.357 .... 2.4
—— v. Smith's Trs. (1882) 19 S.L.R.552 .... 1.6
—— v. Tasker, 1955 S.L.T.347 .... 29.8
Smith & Archibald v. Ryness, Second Division, 18 July 1929; reported at 1937
    S.L.T.(News)81 .... 11.2
Smith Premier Typewriter Co. v. Cotton (1907) 14 S.L.T.764 .... 7.12
Smith's Tr. v. Smith, 1911 S.C.653 .... 4.3
Smith's Trs. v. Cranston, 1990 G.W.D. 7-381 .... 11.4
—— v. Grant (1862) 24 D.1142 .... 17.3, 29.7
Smyth v. Ninian (1826) 5 S.8 .... 17.8
Smyth & Co. v. Salem Flour Mills Co. Ltd. (1887) 14 R.441 .... 25.3
Snodgrass v. Trs. and Crs. of Bent (1744) M.1209 .... 24.2
Somervell's Tr. v. Edinburgh Life Assurance Co., 1911 S.C.1069 .... 11.7
Sommerville (1673) Mor.8325 .... 4.6
—— v. National Coal Board, 1963 S.L.T.334 .... 11.14
Souper v. Smith (1756) Mor.744 .... 17.3
Sowman v. Glasgow District Council, 1984 S.C.91 .... 8.2
Speir v. Dunlop (1827) 5 S.729 .... 22.6
Speirs (J.) & Co. v. Central Building Co. Ltd., 1911 S.C.330 .... 25.2
Spence v. Crawford, 1939 S.C.(H.L.)52 .... 2.4
—— v. Paterson's Trs. (1873) 1 R.46 .... 12.5, 12.11
Spiers v. Peterson, 1924 S.C.428 .... 2.10
Spilsbury v. Spofforth (1937) 21 T.C.247 .... 12.7
Spottiswoode v. Hopkirk (1853) 16 D.59 .... 11.4
St. George, The [1926] P.217 .... 7.5
Stafford v. McLaurin (1875) 3 R.148 .... 11.10
Stagg & Robson Ltd. v. Stirling, 1908 S.C.675 .... 5.19
Stalker v. Aiton (1759) Mor.745 .... 17.4
Stancroft Securities Ltd. (I.H.) v. McDowall, 1990 S.L.T.746 .... 11.10
Stanton (F. & E.), Re [1929] 1 Ch.180 .... 9.12
Star Motor Express Co. v. Booth Ltd. (1930) 46 Sh.Ct.Rep.239 .... 12.10
Steel v. Orbiston (1679) Mor.8467 .... 4.6
—— v. Young, 1907 S.C.360 .... 2.10
Stein's Crs. v. Forbes Hunter & Co. (1791) Mor.1142 .... 22.7
Stenhouse v. Stenhouse's Trs. (1899) 6 S.L.T.368 .... 12.10
Stenhouse London Ltd. v. Allwright, 1972 S.C.209 .... 17.3
Stephen v. Swayne (1861) 24 D.158 .... 7.8
Stephenson v. Stephenson's Trs. (1807) Mor. "Bill of Exchange" Appx. No.20 .... 5.23
Steven v. Broady Norman & Co., 1928 S.C.351 .... 28.5
Stevens v. Thomson, 1971 S.L.T.136 .... 29.8
Stevenson v. Duncan, 1805 Hume 245 .... 14.1, 14.2
—— v. Likly (1824) 3 S.291 .... 7.8
Stevenson's Tr. v. Campell & Sons (1896) 23 R.711 .... 10.1
Stewart v. Gardner (1932) 48 Sh.Ct.Rep.226 .... 16.11
—— v. Hodge (1901) 8 S.L.T.436 .... 22.10
—— v. Jarvie, 1938 S.C.309 .... 15.5
—— v. Kennedy (1890) 17 R.(H.L.)25 .... 2.4
—— v. Riddoch (1677) Mor.11406 .... 12.9
—— v. Russell, 11 July 1815, F.C. 19.6
—— v. Salmon, (Sh.Ct.) 1988 S.C.L.R.647 .... 21.16
—— v. Scott (1832) 11 S.171 .... 22.7
—— v. Shannessy (1900) 2 F.1288 .... 30.2
—— v. Steuart (1878) 6 R.145 .... 1.6
—— v. Syme, 12 Dec. 1815, F.C. 4.6

Stewart & McDonald v. Brown (1898) 25 R.1042	30.13
Stewart & Taylor v. Grimson (1904) 20 Sh.Ct.Rep.166	12.11
Stewart Roofing Co. Ltd. v. Shanlin (1958) 74 Sh.Ct.Rep.134	2.10
Stewart's Tr. v. Stewart's Exrx. (1896) 23 R.739	29.6
Stewart's Trs., 1953 S.L.T.(Notes)25	6.9
—— v. Evans (1871) 9 M.810	29.6
Stillie's Trs. v. Stillie (1898) 6 S.L.T.173	17.9, 17.11
Stiven v. Reynolds & Co. (1891) 18 R.422	17.12
Stone & Rolfe v. Kimber Coal Co., 1926 S.C.(H.L.)45	30.2
Stonehaven Magistrates v. Kincardineshire C.C., 1939 S.C.760	1.6
Strachan v. McDougle (1835) 13 S.954	17.3, 27.5
Strathdee v. Paterson, 1913 1 S.L.T.498	1.10, 20.2
"Strathlorne" S.S. Co. v. Baird & Sons Ltd., 1916 S.C.(H.L.)134	2.7
Strathmore v. Strathmore's Trs. (1825) 1 W. & S.402	29.5
Strathmore, Earl of, v. Laing (1823) 2 S.223; 2 W.&S.1	16.2
Strawbridge's Trs. v. Bank of Scotland, 1935 S.L.T.568	27.5
Strong v. Philips & Co. (1878) 5 R.770	7.10
Stroyan v. Murray (1890) 17 R.1170	29.2
Struthers v. Smith, 1913 S.C.1116	12.14
Stuart v. Lort-Phillips, 1977 S.C.244	2.11
—— v. Stuart (1705) Mor.140	17.3
—— v. —— (1869) 7 M.366	13.4, 13.5
—— v. ——, 1926 S.L.T.31	11.10
Stuart & Stuart v. Macleod (1891) 19 R.223	1.11, 20.3
Style & Mantle Ltd., Liqr. of, v. Prices Tailors Ltd., 1934 S.C.548	25.7
Summers v. Marianski (1843) 6 D.286	19.6
Sutherland decd., Re [1963] A.C.235	1.11
Sutherlands of Peterhead (Road Hauliers) Ltd. v. Allard Hewson & Co. Ltd., 1972 S.L.T.(Notes)83	11.8
Sutie v. Ross (1705) Mor.816	17.9
Sutters v. Briggs [1922] 1 A.C.1	6.13
Svenska Petroleum A.B. v. H.O.R. Ltd., 1986 S.L.T.513	11.10
Swain (J.D.), Re [1965] 1 W.L.R.909	25.14
Symington v. Campbell (1894) 21 R.434	27.6
—— v. Symington (1875) 3 R.205	11.10
Synnot v. Simpson (1854) 5 H.L.C.121	24.2
TAI HING COTTON MILL LTD. v. Liu Chong Hing Bank Ltd. [1986] A.C.80	6.12
Talbot v. Guydct (1705) Mor.5027	12.13
—— v. Von Boris [1911] 1 K.B.854	5.9
Tankexpress A/S v. Compagnie Financière Belge des Petroles S.A. [1949] A.C.79	12.1
Tawse v. Rigg (1904) 6 F.544	7.11
Tay Valley Joinery Ltd. v. C.F. Financial Services Ltd., 1987 S.L.T.207	2.3, 21.2
Taylor v. Farrie (1855) 17 D.639	22.8
—— v. Forbes (1830) 9 S.113	13.9, 29.3
—— v. Scottish and Universal Newspapers Ltd., 1981 S.C.408	9.19
—— v. Wilson's Trs., 1979 S.L.T.105	1.6
Taylor & Ferguson Ltd. v. Glass's Trs., 1912 S.C.165	29.6
Taylor's Industrial Flooring Ltd. v. M. & H. Plant Hire (Manchester) Ltd. [1990] B.C.L.C.216	25.2
Taylor's Tr. v. Paul (1888) 15 R.313	13.10
Taymech Ltd. v. Rush & Tompkins Ltd., 1990 S.L.T.681; 1990 G.W.D.21-1198	19.3, 30.19
Telford's Exr. v. Blackwood (1866) 4 M.369	11.10, 17.2
Tennant's Trs. v. Lord Advocate, 1938 S.C.224	1.1
Tennent v. Crawford (1878) 5 R.433	5.27
—— v. Glass, 1990 S.L.T.282	19.5
—— v. Martin & Dunlop (1879) 6 R.786	20.6
Thain v. Thain (1891) 18 R.1196	29.2
Thiem's Trs. v. Collie (1899) 1 F.764	6.14, 12.11
Thom v. Bridges (1857) 19 D.721	21.10
Thomas v. Thomson (1865) 3 M.1160	22.1

Thomas (M.P.) *v.* Baird (1897) 13 Sh.Ct.Rep.291 .... 20.7
Thompson *v.* J. Barke and Company (Caterers) Ltd., 1975 S.L.T.67 .... 5.9, 5.11, 6.1
Thomson *v.* Bell (1850) 12 D.1184 .... 19.6
—— *v.* —— (1894) 22 R.16 .... 5.27
—— *v.* Duncan (1855) 17 D.1081 .... 4.6
—— *v.* Fullarton (1842) 5 D.379 .... 17.11
—— *v.* Geekie (1861) 23 D.693 .... 4.1, 4.5, 11.7
—— *v.* Spence, 1961 S.L.T. 395 .... 22.1
—— *v.* Stevenson (1855) 17 D.739 .... 30.12
—— *v.* Vernon, 1983 S.L.T.(Sh.Ct.) 17 .... 2.11
Thomson & Balfour *v.* Boag & Son, 1936 S.C.2 .... 30.8
Thomson & Co. *v.* Friese-Greene's Tr., 1944 S.C.336 .... 23.1
Thomson & Gillespie *v.* Victoria Eighty Club (1905) 13 S.L.T.399 .... 30.16
Thorey *v.* Wylie & Lochhead (1890) 6 Sh.Ct.Rep.201 .... 12.1
Thow's Tr. *v.* Young, 1910 S.C.588 .... 10.1, 28.2
Tiffney *v.* Bachurzeski, 1984 S.C.108 .... 2.11
Tod's Trs. *v.* Wilson (1869) 7 M.1100 .... 21.8, 27.4, 27.5
Tompkins (H.J.), *Re* [1990] B.C.L.C.71 .... 25.14
Torbet *v.* Borthwick (1849) 11 D.694 .... 21.10
Tout and Finch Ltd. [1954] 1 All E.R.127 .... 21.2
Toynar Ltd. *v.* Whitbread & Co. plc, 1988 S.L.T. 433 .... 9.13
Trade Development Bank *v.* Warriner & Mason (Scotland) Ltd., 1980 S.C.74 .... 1.6, 8.2
Traill *v.* Actieselskabat Dalbeattie Ltd. (1904) 6 F.798 .... 27.1
—— *v.* Smith's Trs. (1876) 3 R.770 .... 6.13
Traill's Trs. *v.* Free Church of Scotland, 1915 S.C.655 .... 29.6
Train *v.* Buchanan's Tr., 1907 S.C.517; 1908 S.C.(H.L.)26 .... 1.11, 27.7
Train & McIntyre *v.* Forbes, 1925 S.L.T.286 .... 7.9
Trans Barwil Agencies (U.K.) Ltd. *v.* John S. Braid & Co. Ltd. (No. 2), 1990
  S.L.T.182 .... 11.7
Trappes *v.* Meredith (1871) 10 M.38 .... 1.11, 17.3, 27.1
Treseder-Griffin *v.* Co-operative Insurance Society [1956] 2 Q.B.127 .... 1.4
Trowsdale's Tr. *v.* Forcett Rlwy. Co. (1870) 9 M.88 .... 11.9, 16.2, 17.4
Tullis *v.* Whyte, June 18, 1817, F.C. 16.10
Turnbull *v.* McKie (1822) 1 S.353 .... 19.6
—— *v.* Scottish County Investment Co., 1939 S.C.5 .... 25.7
—— *v.* Stewart & Inglis (1751) Mor.868 .... 27.4
Turnbull & Kay *v.* Chisholm & Co. and Blair (1887) 3 Sh.Ct.Rep.379 .... 30.4
Turnbull & Sons *v.* Scott (1899) 15 Sh.Ct.Rep.268 .... 17.3
Turner *v.* Woolwich Equitable Building Society (1956) 72 Sh.Ct.Rep.300 .... 17.2
Turner's Trs. *v.* Turner, 1943 S.C.389 .... 12.7
Tweeddale, Marquis of, *v.* Hume (1848) 10 D.1053 .... 12.13
Tweeddale's Trs., Marquis of, *v.* Earl of Haddington (1880) 7 R.620 .... 11.7
Tweedie *v.* Tweedie, 1966 S.L.T.(Notes)89 .... 11.10
Tweeds Garages Ltd., *Re* [1962] Ch.406 .... 25.3
Tyler *v.* Maxwell (1892) 30 S.L.R.583 .... 5.20
Tyrie *v.* Goldie (1942) 58 Sh.Ct.Rep.24 .... 11.2

UK LIFE ASSURANCE CO. *v.* Dixon (1838) 16 S.1277 .... 27.2
Underwood (A.L.) Ltd. *v.* Bank of Liverpool [1924] 1 K.B.775 .... 6.4, 6.13
Unigate Food Ltd. *v.* Scottish Milk Marketing Board, 1972 S.L.T.137 .... 1.6
Union Bank of Scotland *v.* Calder's Tr., 1937 S.C.850 .... 23.4
—— *v.* Mills (1926) 42 Sh.Ct.Rep.141 .... 17.3
—— *v.* National Bank (1924) 40 Sh.Ct.Rep.111 .... 6.11
—— *v.* Taylor, 1925 S.C.835 .... 10.3
Union Club Ltd., Liqr. of, *v.* Edinburgh Life Assurance Co. (1906) 8 F.1143 .. 25.7, 27.1,
                                                                          27.4, 27.5
Unit 2 Windows Ltd., *Re* [1985] 1 W.L.R.1383 .... 25.12
United Collieries Ltd. *v.* Lord Advocate, 1950 S.C.458 .... 21.2
United Dominions Trust Ltd. *v.* Dickson, 1987 S.L.T.572 .... 20.2
—— *v.* Site Preparations Ltd. (No. 1), 1978 S.L.T.(Sh.Ct.)14 .... 8.2
—— *v.* —— (No. 2), 1978 S.L.T.(Sh.Ct.)21 .... 8.2
—— *v.* Taylor, 1980 S.L.T.(Sh.Ct.)28 .... 4.8

United Rentals Ltd. v. Clydesdale and North of Scotland Bank (1963) 79
    Sh.Ct.Rep.118 .... 13.4
Universal Steam Navigation Co. Ltd. v. James McKelvie & Co. [1923] A.C.492 ... 30.2
University of Glasgow v. Yuill's Tr. (1882) 9 R.643 .... 23.4
Ure v. McCubbin (1857) 19 D.758 .... 20.6
Ure & Macrae v. Davies (1917) 33 Sh.Ct.Rep.109 .... 7.7, 7.11
Urie v. Lumsden (1859) 22 D.38 .... 13.5

VALENTINE v. Grangemouth Coal Co. (1897) 5 S.L.T.47 .... 17.8
Vallance v. Forbes (1879) 6 R.1099 .... 5.27
Varney (Scotland) Ltd. v. Burgh of Lanark, 1976 S.L.T.46 .... 1.6
Veitch v. Finlay & Wilson (1894) 10 Sh.Ct.Rep.13 .... 11.10
—— v. National Bank of Scotland, 1907 S.C.554 .... 10.1, 23.7
Veitchi Co. v. Crowley Russell & Co., 1972 S.C.225 .... 21.2
Verrico (J.) & Co. Ltd. v. Australian Mutual Provident Society, 1972
    S.L.T.(Sh.Ct.)57 .... 11.9, 17.6
Vincent v. Chalmers & Co.'s Tr. (1877) 5 R.43 .... 11.10
Vitruvia S.S. Co. v. Ropner Shipping Co., 1923 S.C.574 .... 11.7

WADDEL v. Waddel (1790) 3 Pat.App.188 .... 4.5
—— v. Wadderstoun (1707) Mor.12484 .... 4.6
Waddell v. Hutton, 1911 S.C.575 .... 8.1
—— v. Waddell (1836) 15 S.151 .... 17.3
—— v. Waddell's Trs., 1932 S.L.T.201 .... 17.3
Wadham Stringer Finance Ltd. v. Meaney [1980] 3 All E.R.789 .... 4.10
Walker v. Brown (1803) Mor.App. "Solidum et pro rata" No.1 .... 28.1
—— v. Coyle (1891) 19 R.91 .... 22.5
—— v. Garlick, 1940 S.L.T.208 .... 4.4
—— v. Hunter (1933) 49 Sh.Ct.Rep.139 .... 24.2
—— v. United Creameries Ltd., 1928 S.L.T.(Sh.Ct.)21 .... 17.8
Walker & Watson v. Sturrock (1897) 35 S.L.R.26 .... 12.2
Wallace v. Davies (1853) 15 D.688 .... 27.3, 27.4
—— v. Edgar (1663) Mor.837 .... 27.5
—— v. Henderson (1875) 2 R.999 .... 11.4
—— v. Plock (1841) 3 D.1047 .... 30.9
—— v. Scot (1583) Mor.807 .... 17.9
Wallace & Brown v. Robinson Fleming & Co. (1885) 22 S.L.R.830 .... 5.18
Walls' Trs. v. Drynan (1888) 15 R.359 .... 11.8
Ward (Alexander) & Co. Ltd. v. Samyang Navigation Co. Ltd., 1975
    S.C.(H.L.)26 .... 11.8
Ward (R.V.) Ltd. v. Bignall [1967] 1 Q.B.534 .... 2.2
Wardrop v. Fairholm and Arbuthnot (1744) Mor.4860 .... 17.3
Wards v. Kelvin Tank Services Ltd., 1984 S.L.T.(Sh.Ct.)39 .... 11.10
Waterston v. City of Glasgow Bank (1874) 1 R.470 .... 6.8
Watson v. British Linen Bank, 1941 S.C.43 .... 29.6
—— v. Duncan (1879) 6 R.1247 .... 21.8
—— v. —— (1896) 4 S.L.T.75 .... 5.27
—— v. Henderson (Sh.Ct.) 1988 S.C.L.R.439 .... 20.8
—— v. Thompson (O.H.) 1990 S.C.L.R.59 .... 21.10
Watson & Sons Ltd. v. Veritys Ltd. (1907) 24 Sh.Ct.Rep.148 .... 22.5, 22.7
Watson (David) Property Management v. Woolwich Equitable Building Society
    (I.H.) 1990 S.C.L.R.517 .... 8.2
Watson's Trs. v. Brown, 1923 S.C.228 .... 29.2
Watt v. Burnett's Trs. (1839) 2 D.132 .... 12.5
Watt's Trs. v. Pinkney (1853) 16 D.279 .... 27.4
Webster & Co. Ltd. v. Hutchin (1922) 39 Sh.Ct.Rep.231 .... 6.8
Weepers v. Pearson and Jackson (1859) 21 D.305 .... 20.7
Welch's Exrs. v. Edinburgh Life Assurance Co. (1896) 23 R.772 .... 29.5
Weller v. Ker (1866) 4 M.(H.L.)8 .... 27.7
Wells v. New House Purchasers Ltd. (1963) 79 Sh.Ct.Rep.185 .... 1.7
Welsh v. Knarston, 1973 S.L.T.66 .... 30.8

Welsh v. Russell (1894) 21 R.769	2.11
Welsh & Forbes v. Johnston (1906) 8 F.453	2.7
Wemyss, Earl of, v. May (1679) Mor.782	29.4
West Lothian Oil Co. Ltd., Liqr. of, v. Mair (1892) 20 R.64	7.3
Western Bank v. Bairds (1862) 24 D.859	28.8
—— v. Douglas (1860) 22 D.447	28.1
Westminster Bank Ltd. v. Zang [1966] A.C.182	6.2, 6.4, 12.16
Westminster Corporation v. Chapman [1916] 1 Ch.161	9.10
Westraw (L.) v. Williamson & Carmichael (1626) Mor.859	27.4
Westville Shipping Co. Ltd. v. Abram Steamship Co. Ltd., 1922 S.C.571; 1923 S.C.(H.L.)68	2.4, 27.6
Whatmough's Tr. v. British Linen Bank, 1934 S.C.(H.L.)51	6.13, 22.6
White v. Briggs (1843) 5 D.1148	22.8
—— v. Stevenson, 1956 S.C.84	21.15
White & Carter (Councils) Ltd. v. McGregor, 1962 S.C.(H.L.) 1	1.6
Whitecraigs Golf Club v. Ker, 1923 S.L.T.(Sh.Ct.)23	30.16
Whitehouse & Co., Re (1878) 9 Ch.D.595	13.8
Whittall v. Christie (1894) 22 R.91	27.3
Whyte v. Neish (1622) Mor.854	27.4
—— v. Smith (1886) 2 Sh.Ct.Rep.257	4.2
Wick Harbour Trs. v. Admiralty, 1921 2 S.L.T.109	1.1
Wightman v. Wilson (1858) 20 D.779	17.5
Wilkie v. Scottish Aviation Ltd., 1956 S.C.198	2.7
Williams v. Williams, 1980 S.L.T.(Sh.Ct.)25	6.8
Williamson v. Foulds, 1927 S.N.164	10.1
—— v. McPherson, 1951 S.C.438	11.14
—— v. Rider [1963] 1 Q.B.89	5.27
—— v. Williamson's Tr., 1948 S.L.T.(Notes)72	11.7
Willison v. Ferguson (1901) 9 S.L.T.169	10.1
Wills v. Wood (1984) 128 S.J.222	3.2
Wilmot v. Wilson (1841) 3 D.815	7.7
Wilson v. Carrick (1881) 18 S.L.R.657	17.8
—— v. Drummond's Reps. (1853) 16 D.275	22.1, 22.5
—— v. Fleming (1823) 2 S.430	17.10, 29.7
—— v. Gloag (1840) 2 D.1233	17.6
—— v. Wilson (1901) 17 Sh.Ct.Rep.44	4.5
Wilson (A.) (Aberdeen) Ltd. v. Stewart & Co. Ltd. (1957) 73 Sh.Ct.Rep.217	4.6
Wilson and Corse v. Gardner, 1807 Hume 247	14.1
Winestone v. Wolifson, 1954 S.C.77	6.14
Wink v. Speirs (1868) 6 M.657	4.5
Wise v. Perpetual Trustee Co. Ltd. [1903] A.C.139	30.16
Wolifson v. Harrison, 1978 S.L.T.95	7.3
Wood v. Begbie (1850) 12 D.963	27.1
—— v. Bruce (1908) 24 Sh.Ct.Rep.24	12.4
—— v. Clydesdale Bank Ltd., 1914 S.C.397	5.2, 6.15
—— v. Gordon (1695) Mor.5035	12.13
—— v. Howden (1843) 5 D.507	4.5
—— v. Miller, 1960 S.C.86	11.14
—— v. Weir (1900) 16 Sh.Ct.Rep.356	21.8
Wood & Co. v. A. & A.Y. Mackay (1906) 8 F.625	1.6
Woodfield Finance Trust (Glasgow) Ltd. v. Morgan, 1958 S.L.T.(Sh.Ct.)14	10.3
Woodhouse Ltd. v. Nigerian Produce Ltd. [1971] 2 Q.B.23	1.5
Woodroffes (Musical Instruments) Ltd., Re [1985] 2 All E.R.908	9.16
Woods v. Royal Bank, 1913 1 S.L.T.499	17.3
Woods Parker & Co. v. Ainslie (1860) 22 D.723	24.1
Wright v. Bryson, 1935 S.C.(H.L.)49	1.11
—— v. Mitchell (1871) 9 M.516	22.5
—— v. Sheill (1676) Mor.2640	13.7
Wright (Walter) & Co. Ltd. v. Cowdray, 1973 S.L.T.(Sh.Ct.)56	2.9
Wylie & Lochhead Ltd. v. Hornsby (1889) 16 R.907	30.2
Wylie's Exrx. v. McJannet (1901) 4 F.195	7.11, 8.1
Wyper v. Carr & Co. (1877) 4 R.444	11.9

YAU v. Ogilvie & Co., 1985 S.L.T.91 .... 7.11
Yeoman Credit Ltd. v. McLean [1962] 1 W.L.R.131 .... 2.6
—— v. Waragowski [1961] 1 W.L.R.1124 .... 2.6
Yeovil Glove Co., Re [1965] Ch.148 .... 9.12, 12.5
Youle v. Cochrane (1868) 6 M.427 .... 7.8
Young v. Aktiebolaget Ofverums Bruk (1890) 18 R.163 .... 11.9, 17.4
—— v. Thomson, 1909 S.C.529 .... 12.15
Youngson, Petrs., 1911 2 S.L.T.448 .... 29.11
Yuile (Wm. S.) Ltd. v. Gibson, 1952 S.L.T.(Sh.Ct.)22 .... 16.11
Yuill's Trs. v. Maclachlan's Trs., 1939 S.C.(H.L.)40 .... 14.8

ZAHNRAD FABRIK PASSAU GMBH v. Terex Ltd., 1986 S.L.T.84 .... 2.3
Zebmoon Ltd. v. Akinbrook Investment Developments Ltd., 1988 S.L.T.146 ..... 2.11

TABLE OF STATUTES

		PARA
1592	Compensation Act (c.143) 13.1, 13.3, 13.7	
1617	Prescription Act (c.12)... 14.6	
1621	Bankruptcy Act (c.18) 22.1	
1661	c.24... 29.6	
	Bonds Act (c.32).. 29.2	
	Diligence Act (c.344) 19.4	
1672	Adjudications Act (c.45) 19.4	
1681	Bills of Exchange Act (c.86) 19.6	
1690	Confirmation Act (c.56) 29.5, 29.7	
1695	Confirmation Act (c.72) 29.6, 29.8, 29.9	
1696	Bankruptcy (Scotland) Act (8 & 9 Will. 3, c.5) 22.4	
	Inland Bills Act (c.38) 19.6	
1823	Confirmation of Executors (Scotland) Act (4 Geo. 4, c.98), s.4 .... 29.7	
1838	Debtors (Scotland) Act (7 Will. 4 & 1 Vict., c.41)—	
	s.16 .... 11.10	
	s.17 .... 11.10	
	s.18 .... 17.5	
	s.20 .... 11.10	
	s.21 .... 11.10, 17.15	
	s.22 .... 1.10, 11.10, 17.7	
	s.22(2) 17.7	
	s.22(3) 17.7, 18.6, 18.10, 18.15	
1845	Bank Notes (Scotland) Act (8 & 9 Vict., c.38)—	
	s.16 .... 5.3	
	s.20 .... 5.3	
1853	Stamp Act (16 & 17 Vict., c.59), s.19 .... 6.12	
1856	Exchequer Court (Scotland) Act (19 & 20 Vict., c.56), s.38 .... 19.5	
	Mercantile Law Amendment (Scotland) Act (19 & 20 Vict., c.60)—	
	s.6 .... 10.1	
	s.8 .... 10.1	
	s.9 .... 10.3, 28.7	
	Debts Securities (Scotland) Act (19 & 20 Vict., c.91), s.5 .... 4.1	
1857	Registration of Leases (Scotland) Act (20 & 21 Vict., c.46)................. 8.5	
1859	Confirmation and Probate Amendment Act (22 Vict., c.30), s.1 .... 29.3	
1862	Transmission of Moveable Property (Scotland) Act (25 & 26 Vict., c.44)—	
	s.2 .... 27.3	
	Sched. A 27.2	
	Sched. B 27.2	
	Sched. C 27.3	
1867	Policies of Assurance Act (30 & 31 Vict., c.144) 27.2	
	s.3 .... 27.3	
	s.6 .... 27.3	
1868	Titles to Land Consolidation (Scotland) Act (31 & 32 Vict., c.101)—	
	s.25 .... 25.7	
	s.117 .... 29.2	
	s.138 .... 19.5	
	s.155 .... 19.2	
	s.157 .... 19.3	
1874	Conveyancing (Scotland) Act (37 & 38 Vict., c.94)—	
	s.4 .... 1.8	
	s.30 .... 29.2	
	s.47 .... 1.8, 8.2, 19.5, 29.5	
1877	Writs Execution (Scotland) Act (40 & 41 Vict., c.40), s.3 .... 15.3, 19.5	
1880	Married Women's Policies of Assurance (Scotland) Act (43 & 44 Vict., c.26).. 22.2	
	s.2 .... 22.10	
	Debtors (Scotland) Act (43 & 44 Vict., c.34), s.4 .... 19.8	

1882 Bills of Exchange Act (45 & 46 Vict., c.61)—
s.2	5.4, 5.5, 5.9
s.3(1)	5.3
s.3(2)	5.3
s.3(3)	5.3
s.3(4)	5.3
s.4	5.3
s.5(1)	5.3
s.5(2)	5.3
s.6(1)	5.3
s.6(2)	5.3
s.7(1)	5.3
s.7(2)	5.3
s.7(3)	5.3, 5.21
s.8	5.4
s.8(3)	5.3
s.9	5.3
s.10(1)	5.3
s.11	5.3
s.12	5.3
s.14	5.25
s.14(1)	5.3
s.14(2)	5.3
s.15	5.3
s.17	5.3
s.21(1)	5.15
s.21(2)	5.15
s.21(3)	5.15
s.23	5.6, 5.13, 5.14
s.23(2)	5.13
s.24	5.10, 5.13, 5.21
s.25	5.13
s.26	5.14
s.26(1)	5.14
s.26(2)	5.14
s.27(1)	5.9
s.27(2)	5.9
s.27(3)	5.9
s.28(1)	5.7
s.28(2)	5.7
s.29(1)	5.9
s.29(2)	5.9
s.29(3)	5.9
s.30	6.1
s.30(1)	5.9
s.30(2)	5.9, 5.16, 5.20
s.31	5.4
s.31(2)	5.4
s.31(4)	5.8
s.31(5)	5.4
s.32	5.4
s.32(1)	6.5
s.32(4)	6.5
s.33	5.4
s.34	5.4
s.35	5.4
s.36(2)	5.9
s.36(5)	5.9
s.38(1)	5.8
s.38(2)	5.9, 5.16, 5.20
s.39	5.3
s.39(4)	5.24

1882 Bills of Exchange Act—*cont.*
- s.40 ... 5.24
- s.41(1) ... 5.24
- s.41(2) ... 5.24
- s.41(3) ... 5.24
- s.43 ... 5.5
- s.45 ... 5.25
- s.45(1) ... 5.25
- s.45(2) ... 5.25
- s.45(3) ... 5.25
- s.45(4) ... 5.25
- s.45(5) ... 5.25
- s.45(6) ... 5.25
- s.45(7) ... 5.25
- s.45(8) ... 5.25
- s.46(1) ... 5.25
- s.46(2) ... 5.25
- s.47 ... 5.5
- s.48 ... 5.5, 5.26
- s.49 ... 5.26
- s.49(12) ... 5.26
- s.49(13) ... 5.26
- s.49(14) ... 5.5, 5.26
- s.49(15) ... 5.26
- s.50(1) ... 5.26
- s.50(2) ... 5.26
- s.51 ... 5.3
- s.52 ... 5.25
- s.52(3) ... 5.26
- s.52(4) ... 5.25
- s.53(2) ... 5.5, 6.6, 6.8, 6.9, 6.10, 27.2, 27.4, 27.9
- s.54(2) ... 5.13, 5.21
- s.55 ... 5.5
- s.55(2) ... 5.13, 5.21
- s.56 ... 5.6
- s.57 ... 11.7
- s.58 ... 5.6
- s.59(1) ... 5.22
- s.59(2) ... 5.5
- s.59(2)(*a*) ... 5.22
- s.59(2)(*b*) ... 5.22
- s.59(3) ... 5.5, 5.22
- s.60 ... 6.11, 6.12
- s.62 ... 5.22
- s.63 ... 5.22
- s.64 ... 5.22
- s.65 ... 5.5
- s.66 ... 5.5
- s.67 ... 5.5
- s.68 ... 5.5
- s.69 ... 5.8
- s.70 ... 5.8
- s.71 ... 5.9
- s.72 ... 5.3
- s.73 ... 6.1
- s.74 ... 6.3
- s.75 ... 6.1, 6.8, 6.9
- s.75A ... 6.8
- s.76 ... 6.11
- s.77 ... 6.11
- s.78 ... 6.11
- s.79 ... 6.11

1882	Bills of Exchange Act—*cont.*	
	s.80	6.11, 6.12
	s.81	6.11
	s.82	6.13
	s.83(1)	5.27
	s.83(2)	5.27
	s.83(3)	5.27
	s.84	5.27
	s.85	5.27
	s.85(2)	28.1
	s.86(1)	5.27
	s.86(2)	5.27
	s.86(3)	5.27
	s.87(1)	5.27
	s.87(2)	5.27
	s.87(3)	5.27
	s.88	5.27
	s.89(1)	5.27
	s.89(2)	5.27
	s.89(3)	5.27
	s.89(4)	5.27
	s.91(1)	5.13
	s.92	5.3
	s.98	19.6
	s.100	5.19, 5.22
1889	Judicial Factors (Scotland) Act (52 & 53 Vict., c.39)—	
	s.11A	29.11
	s.11A(2)	29.11
1890	Partnership Act (53 & 54 Vict., c.49)—	
	s.1(1)	30.6
	s.3	23.10
	s.4(2)	30.9
	s.5	30.6
	s.6	30.6
	s.7	30.6
	s.8	30.6
	s.9	28.1, 30.8
	s.10	30.7
	s.11	30.7
	s.12	30.8
	s.13	30.7
	s.14(1)	30.8
	s.17	30.8
	s.17(1)	30.8
	s.18	10.3
	s.22	29.2
	s.36	30.8
	s.36(3)	30.8
1892	Sheriff Courts (Scotland) Extracts Act (55 & 56 Vict., c.17)	18.6, 18.10
	s.7(1)	15.3
	s.8	17.5
1893	Sale of Goods Act (56 & 57 Vict., c.71), s.62(1)	2.5
1899	Small Dwellings Acquisition (Scotland) Act (c.44)	8.2
1907	Limited Partnerships Act (7 Edw. 7, c.24)—	
	s.4(3)	30.14
	s.4(4)	30.14
	s.5	30.14
	s.6(1)	30.14
	s.6(3)	30.14
	s.6(5)(*b*)	27.1
	s.7	30.14

Table of Statutes

Year	Statute	Reference
1907	Sheriff Courts (Scotland) Act (7 Edw., 7, c.51)—	
	s.5(5)	16.15
	s.7	11.18
1916	Court of Session (Extracts) Act (6 & 7 Geo. 5, c.49)	19.5
1924	Carriage of Goods by Sea Act (14 & 15 Geo. 5, c.22), Sched., art. IX	1.3
	Conveyancing (Scotland) Act (15 & 16 Geo. 5, c.27)—	
	s.15	1.8, 19.5, 29.5
	s.15(1)	8.2
	s.15(2)	8.2
	s.22	29.2
	s.44(3)(*a*)	19.2
1926	Execution of Diligence (Scotland) Act (16 & 17 Geo. 5, c.16)	15.1
	s.2	15.4
	s.21	17.5
1929	Agricultural Credits (Scotland) Act (19 & 20) Geo. 5, c.13), Pt. II	7.3
1930	Third Parties (Rights against Insurers) Act (20 & 21 Geo. 5, c.24)	26.10
	s.1	21.11
	s.1(1)(*b*)	9.18, 25.7
	s.4	29.11
1938	Trade Marks Act (1 & 2 Geo. 6, c.22), s.22	8.2
1939	Currency (Defence) Act (2 & 3 Geo. 6, c.64), s.2(2)	1.2
1940	Law Reform (Miscellaneous Provisions) (Scotland) Act (3 & 4 Geo. 6, c.42)—	
	s.3(1)	28.6
	s.3(2)	1.6, 28.6
1947	Local Government (Scotland) Act (10 & 11 Geo. 6, c.43)—	
	s.247	19.7
	s.247(2)	19.7
	s.247(4)	19.7
	s.247(5)	19.7
	Crown Proceedings Act (10 & 11 Geo. 6, c.44)—	
	s.46	17.3
	s.50	13.8
1948	Companies Act (11 & 12 Geo. 6, c.38), s.327(1)(*a*)	17.14
1949	Registered Designs Act (12, 13 & 14 Geo. 6, c.88), s.19	8.2
1954	Currency and Bank Notes Act (2 & 3 Eliz. 2, c.12), s.1(2)	1.2
	Long Leases (Scotland) Act (2 & 3 Eliz. 2, c.49), s.27	8.5
1956	Administration of Justice Act (c.46)—	
	s.45	11.8
	s.46	11.8
	s.47	11.8, 11.10, 17.16
	s.48	11.8
1957	Cheques Act (5 & 6 Eliz. 2, c.36)—	
	s.1	6.4, 6.12
	s.2	6.4
	s.3	4.5
	s.4	6.4, 6.11
	s.4(1)	6.13
	s.4(2)	6.13
	s.4(3)	6.4, 6.13
1958	Interest on Damages (Scotland) Act (6 & 7 Eliz. 2, c.61)—	
	s.1	11.7
	s.1(1B)	11.7
	s.1(2)(*a*)	11.7
1961	Carriage by Air Act (9 & 10 Eliz. 2, c.27), Sched. 1, art. 22(5)	1.3
	Companies (Floating Charges and Receivers) (Scotland) Act (9 & 10 Eliz. 2, c.40), s.2(1)(*a*)	17.14
	Trusts (Scotland) Act (9 & 10 Eliz. 2, c.47), s.2	9.18
1964	Succession (Scotland) Act (c.41)—	
	s.14	29.2, 29.7
	s.14(3)	29.10
	s.18(2)	29.5
	Sched. 3	29.2, 29.6

Table of Statutes

Year	Statute	Reference
1964	Hire-Purchase Act (c.53), Pt. III	2.6
1965	Carriage of Goods by Road Act (c.37), Sched., art. 23(3)	1.3
	Hire-Purchase Act (c.66)	3.16
1966	Law Reform (Miscellaneous Provisions) (Scotland) Act (c.19), s.1	11.10
1967	Industrial and Provident Societies Act (c.48), s.3	9.9
1969	Decimal Currency Act (c.19)—	
	s.4	1.2
	s.5	1.2
	s.6	1.2
	s.7	1.2
	Sched. 1	1.2
1970	Taxes Management Act (c.9)—	
	s.63	19.7
	s.64	7.12, 15.2
	s.106(2)	12.7
	Finance Act (c.24), Sched. 7, para. 2	5.3, 12.12
	Conveyancing and Feudal Reform (Scotland) Act (c.35)—	
	s.9(3)	8.2
	s.9(4)	8.2
	s.9(6)	8.2
	s.9(7)	8.2
	s.10(1)	8.2
	s.10(3)	8.2
	s.11(1)	8.2
	s.11(2)	8.2
	s.12	8.2
	s.13	8.2
	s.14(1)	8.2
	s.14(2)	8.2
	s.15	8.2
	s.16	8.2
	s.17	8.2
	s.18(1A)	8.2
	s.19	8.2
	s.20	8.2
	s.20(1)	8.2
	s.20(2)	8.2
	s.21	8.2
	s.22	8.2
	s.23	8.2
	s.24	8.2
	s.24(1)	8.2
	s.25	8.2
	s.26	8.2
	s.26(2)	8.2
	s.27	8.2
	s.27(1)	9.18, 21.2
	s.28	8.2
	s.28(6)	8.2
	s.28(7)	8.2
	Sched. 2, Form A	8.2
	Sched. 2, Form B	8.2
	Sched. 3, standard condition 9(1)(*a*)	8.2
	Sched. 3, standard condition 9(1)(*b*)	8.2
	Sched. 3, standard condition 9(1)(*c*)	8.2
	Sched. 3, standard condition 9(2)	8.2
	Sched. 3, standard condition 10(3)	8.2
	Sched. 3, standard condition 10(4)	8.2
	Sched. 3, standard condition 10(5)	8.2
	Sched. 3, standard condition 10(6)	8.2
	Sched. 3, standard condition 12	8.2
	Sched. 4, Form A	8.2

1970	Conveyancing and Feudal Reform (Scotland) Act—*cont.*	
	Sched. 4, Form B	8.2
	Merchant Shipping Act (c.36), s.11	27.1
1971	Coinage Act (c.24)—	
	s.2	1.2
	s.13	1.2
	Interest on Damages (Scotland) Act (c.31), s.1	11.7
	Redemption of Standard Securities (Scotland) Act (c.45), s.1	8.2
	Sheriff Courts (Scotland) Act (c.58)—	
	s.35	11.16
	s.35(3)	11.15
	s.38	11.15
	Banking and Financial Dealings Act (c.80), s.3(2)	5.3
1972	Administration of Justice (Scotland) Act (c.59), s.1	7.11
1972	Companies (Floating Charges and Receivers) (Scotland) Act (c.67)	9.18
	s.1(2)	17.13
	s.15(2)(*a*)	17.13, 17.14
	s.15(4)	17.14
1973	Supply of Goods (Implied Terms) Act (c.13), ss.8–11	2.6
	Prescription and Limitation (Scotland) Act (c.52)—	
	s.1(3)	19.4
	s.6	10.2, 14.4
	s.6(1)	5.23, 5.27
	s.6(3)	5.23, 14.5
	s.7(1)	5.23, 5.27, 14.9
	s.7(2)	14.9
	s.8A	28.6
	s.9(1)	14.7
	s.9(1)(*c*)	24.2
	s.9(3)	14.7
	s.10(1)	14.8
	s.10(2)	14.8
	s.10(3)	14.8
	s.11	14.4
	s.11(4)	14.9
	s.12(1)	14.10
	s.13	14.4, 14.9
	s.14(1)(*a*)	14.6
	s.14(1)(*b*)	14.6
	s.14(1)(*c*)	14.4
	s.14(1)(*d*)	14.6
	s.14(1)(*e*)	14.6
	s.15(1)	14.4
	s.18A	14.4
	s.22A	14.4
	s.22B	14.4
	s.22C	14.4
	Sched. 1, para. 1	14.4
	Sched. 1, para. 1(*e*)	5.23, 5.27
	Sched. 1, para. 1(*g*)	10.2
	Sched. 1, para. 2	14.4
	Sched. 1, para. 2(*b*)	5.27
	Sched. 1, para. 2(*c*)	10.2
	Sched. 1, para. 3	10.2, 28.4
	Sched. 2, para. 1	14.5
	Sched. 2, para. 2	10.2, 14.5
	Sched. 2, para. 3	14.5
	Sched. 2, para. 4	14.5
	Sched. 3	14.4
	Local Government (Scotland) Act (c.65), s.31	20.7

1974 Land Tenure Reform (Scotland) Act (c.38)—	
Sched. 6, para. 1	8.5
Sched. 6, para. 5	8.5
Consumer Credit Act (c.39)—	
s.8(1)	3.3
s.8(2)	3.3
s.8(3)	3.3
s.9(1)	3.3
s.9(2)	3.3
s.9(3)	3.3, 4.10
s.9(4)	3.3
s.10	3.3
s.10(1)(b)	3.3
s.10(3)	3.3
s.11(1)	3.3
s.11(2)	3.3
s.11(3)	3.3
s.12	3.3
s.13	3.3
s.14(1)	4.13
s.14(2)	4.13
s.14(3)	4.13
s.15(1)	3.3
s.15(2)	3.3
s.16(1)	3.4
s.16(2)(a)	3.4
s.16(2)(b)	3.4
s.16(2)(c)	3.4
s.16(6A)	3.4
s.17(1)	3.5
s.17(3)	3.5
s.17(4)	3.5
s.18	3.5
s.19	3.5
s.19(3)	3.5
s.20	3.3
s.21	3.10
s.40	3.10
s.43	3.11
s.52	3.11
s.56	3.14
s.57	8.4
s.58	8.4
s.59(1)	3.12
s.60	3.12
s.61	3.12, 8.4
s.62	3.12
s.63	3.12
s.64	3.12
s.65(1)	3.12, 3.18
s.65(2)	8.4
s.67	3.13
s.68	3.13
s.69(1)	3.5
s.70	3.13
s.71	3.13
s.72	3.13
s.73	3.13
s.74(1)	3.12
s.74(4)	3.12
s.75	4.8
s.76	3.15

1974 Land Tenure Reform (Scotland) Act—*cont.*
s.77	3.15
s.78	3.15
s.79	3.15
s.81	12.5
s.82	3.15
s.82(2)	3.5
s.83	3.15
s.84	4.13
s.85	4.13
s.86	3.17
s.86(2)	3.18
s.87	3.16
s.88	3.16
s.89	3.16
s.90	4.10
s.92	4.10, 4.12
s.93	3.16
s.93A	3.18, 19.5
s.94	3.15
s.95	3.15
s.96	3.5, 3.15
s.97	3.15
s.98	3.15
s.99	4.10
s.99(3)	4.12
s.99(4)	4.10
s.99(5)	4.10
s.100	4.10
s.101	4.11
s.104	4.10, 7.12
s.105	3.21, 7.2
s.105(7)(*a*)	3.18
s.105(9)	3.21, 7.2
s.106	3.21, 7.2
s.107	3.15, 3.21, 7.2
s.108	3.15, 3.21, 7.2
s.109	3.15, 3.21, 7.2
s.110	3.21, 7.2
s.111	3.21, 7.2
s.111(2)	3.18
s.113(1)	3.21, 7.2
s.113(2)	3.21, 7.2
s.113(3)	3.21, 7.2
s.114(2)	7.4
s.115	7.4
s.116	7.4
s.117	7.4
s.118	7.4
s.119	7.4
s.120	7.4
s.121	7.4
s.122	7.4
s.123	3.20
s.123(2)	3.20
s.124	3.20
s.124(1)	3.18
s.124(2)	3.18
s.125(1)	3.20
s.125(2)	3.20
s.125(3)	3.20
s.125(4)	3.20

1974	Land Tenure Reform (Scotland) Act—*cont.*	
	s.126	8.4
	s.127	3.18
	s.127(1)	3.18
	s.127(2)	3.18
	s.127(5)	3.18
	s.128	3.18
	s.129	3.16, 3.19
	s.129(3)	3.19
	s.130(2)	4.10
	s.130(4)	4.10, 4.11
	s.131	3.19
	s.132	4.11
	s.133	4.10
	s.133(5)	4.10
	s.134	4.10
	s.135	3.19
	s.135(3)	4.11
	s.136	3.19
	s.137(1)	3.2
	s.137(2)	3.2
	s.138(1)	3.2
	s.138(2)	3.2
	s.138(3)	3.2
	s.138(4)	3.2
	s.138(5)	3.2
	s.139(1)	3.2
	s.139(2)	3.2
	s.145(2)	3.10
	s.147	3.10
	s.148	3.10
	s.149	3.10
	s.171(1)	3.3
	s.171(4)(*b*)	4.13
	s.171(6)	7.4
	s.171(7)	3.2
	s.173(3)	8.4
	s.177	8.4
	s.181(1)	3.3
	s.184	3.3
	s.187(1)	3.3
	s.187(2)	3.3
	s.187(3)	3.3
	s.187(3A)	3.3
	s.189	7.1, 8.4
	s.189(1)	3.2, 3.3, 3.5, 4.10
	s.189(2)	3.10
	Sched. 2, Ex. 9	3.3
	Sched. 2, Ex. 10	3.3
	Sched. 2, Ex. 18	3.3
	Sched. 2, Ex. 23	3.3
	Sched. 4, para. 22	2.6
	Sched. 4, para. 35	2.6
1975	Social Security Act (c.14)—	
	Pt. I	18.2
	s.87(1)	17.3, 21.9, 27.1
	District Courts (Scotland) Act (c.20), s.13A	20.7
	Oil Taxation Act (c.22)—	
	s.1	19.7
	Sched. 2	19.7
	Social Security Pensions Act (c.60)	18.2
	Sched. 3	25.12

1975	Employment Protection Act (c.71)	23.11, 25.12
1976	Damages (Scotland) Act (c.13)—	
	s.2	29.1
	s.3	27.1, 29.1
	s.4	29.1
	Police Pensions Act (c.35)	21.9
1977	Patents Act (c.37), s.31	8.2
	Unfair Contract Terms Act (c.50)—	
	s.20	2.6
	s.21	2.5
1978	Employment Protection (Consolidation) Act (c.44), s.125(2)	23.11, 25.12
1979	Customs and Excise Management Act (c.2), s.117	19.7
	Wages Council Act (c.12)	18.2
	Carriage by Air and Road Act (c.28)—	
	s.4	1.3
	s.5	1.3
	Land Registration (Scotland) Act (c.33)—	
	s.3(3)	8.5
	s.5	8.2
	s.6(1)(*c*)	19.2
	s.6(4)	8.5
	s.7	8.2
	s.9(4)	8.5
	s.12(3)(*b*)	22.5
	s.12(3)(*k*)	19.2
	s.12(3)(*o*)	8.2
	s.15(3)	8.2
	s.28	8.5, 9.9
	Banking Act (c.37)—	
	s.38	3.12
	s.47	6.13
	Sale of Goods Act (c.54)—	
	s.2(1)	2.1
	s.8(1)	2.1
	s.8(2)	2.1
	s.9	2.1
	s.11(5)	2.5, 13.9
	s.12	2.5
	s.13	2.5
	s.14	2.5
	s.15	2.5
	s.16	21.7
	s.17	21.7
	s.18	21.7
	s.19	21.7
	s.25(1)	2.3, 4.10
	s.25(2)	4.10
	s.28	2.2
	s.35	2.5
	s.36	2.5
	s.39(2)	2.2, 21.7
	s.41	2.2, 21.7
	s.42	2.2, 21.7
	s.43	2.2, 21.7
	s.44	21.7
	s.45	21.7
	s.46	21.7
	s.48(3)	2.2
	s.49(1)	2.2
	s.49(2)	2.2
	s.50	2.2
	s.51	2.5

1979	Sale of Goods Act—*cont.*	
	s.53(1)	2.5, 13.9
	s.53(1)	2.5, 12.9
	s.53(4)	2.5
	s.58	2.5
	s.61(2)	2.5
	s.62(1)	2.5
	s.62(4)	7.3, 21.7, 21.8
1980	Solicitors (Scotland) Act (c.46)—	
	s.41	23.1
	s.42	21.2
	s.42(2A)	25.7, 26.10
	s.46	29.3
	s.61	13.8
	s.62	7.3
	Tenants' Rights Etc. (Scotland) Act (c.52)—	
	s.74	4.12
	s.84	8.2
	Sched. 5	8.2
	Law Reform (Miscellaneous Provisions) (Scotland) Act (c.55), s.15	16.15
	Married Women's Policies of Assurance (Scotland) (Amendment) Act (c.56), s.3	27.1
1981	Local Government (Miscellaneous Provisions) (Scotland) Act (c.23), s.12	2.6, 16.2
	Matrimonial Homes (Family Protection) (Scotland) Act (c.59)	21.17
	Betting and Gaming Duties Act (c.63), s.29	19.7
1982	Currency Act (c.3), s.1	1.2
	Civil Jurisdiction and Judgments Act (c.27)—	
	s.20	11.8
	s.27(1)	11.10, 11.11
	Sched. 1, para. 3	11.8
	Sched. 8, para. 2(8)	11.8
	Sched. 8, rule 1	17.8
	Sched. 8, rule 2(9)	17.8
1983	Currency Act (c.9), s.1(3)	1.2
	Car Tax Act (c.53), Sched. 1, para. 3(2)	19.7
	Medical Act (c.54), s.46	2.7
	Value Added Tax Act (c.55)—	
	s.42	2.1
	Sched. 7, para. 6(5)	19.7
	Sched. 7, para. 6(6)	19.7
	Sched. 7, para. 6(7)	19.7
	Sched. 7, para. 6(8)	19.7
	Sched. 7, para. 6(9)	19.7
1984	Merchant Shipping Act (c.5)—	
	s.31	7.5
	s.32	7.5
	s.33	7.5
	s.35	7.5
	s.37	7.5
	s.38	7.5
	Law Reform (Husband and Wife) (Scotland) Act (c.15), s.6	30.21
	Inheritance Tax Act (c.51), s.237	7.3
	Rent (Scotland) Act (c.58), s.110	7.12
1985	Companies Act (c.6)	30.15
	s.24	25.9
	s.36	30.18
	s.36B	9.9, 30.18
	s.37	5.13
	s.120	27.1
	s.140	25.9
	s.182(1)	29.2
	s.349(4)	5.14

1985	Companies Act—*cont.*	
	s.395(2)	9.1
	s.395(3)	9.1, 30.19
	s.395(4)	30.19
	s.396(1)	9.1
	s.396(2)(*a*)	9.1
	s.396(2)(*b*)	9.1
	s.396(2)(*c*)	9.1
	s.396(2)(*d*)	9.1
	s.396(2)(*e*)	9.1
	s.396(2)(*f*)	9.1
	s.396(2)(*g*)	9.1
	s.396(3)	9.1
	s.397(1)	9.8
	s.397(2)	9.8
	s.397(3)	9.8
	s.397(4)	9.8
	s.397(5)	9.8
	s.398(1)	9.2
	s.398(4)	9.8
	s.398(5)	9.8
	s.399(1)	9.3
	s.400(2)	9.4
	s.400(3)(*b*)	9.4
	s.401(1)	9.5
	s.401(4)	9.8
	s.402(1)	9.5
	s.402(2)	9.5
	s.402(4)	9.5
	s.402(5)	9.5
	s.402(6)	9.5
	s.403(1)	9.6
	s.403(4)	9.8
	s.403(5)	9.6
	s.404(1)	9.3, 9.4
	s.404(2)	9.4
	s.405(1)	9.3
	s.406	9.7
	s.407(1)	9.7
	s.408	9.2
	s.408(2)	9.8
	s.411(1)	9.8
	s.411(2)	9.8
	s.411(3)	9.8
	s.412	9.8
	s.414(3)	9.2
	s.414(4)	9.2
	s.416	9.8
	s.417	9.5, 9.6
	s.419(2)	9.2
	s.419(3)	9.2
	s.462(1)	9.9, 9.18, 9.23
	s.462(2)	9.9
	s.462(5)	9.9
	s.463(1)	9.10, 9.21
	s.463(1)(*a*)	9.10, 17.13
	s.463(1)(*b*)	9.10
	s.463(1)(*c*)	9.10
	s.463(2)	9.18
	s.463(3)	9.10
	s.463(4)	9.10
	s.464(1)(*a*)	9.11

1985 Companies Act—*cont.*
  s.464(1)(*b*) 9.11
  s.464(1A) 9.11
  s.464(2) 9.10, 9.11
  s.464(3) 9.11
  s.464(4) 9.11
  s.464(5) 9.11
  s.486(1) 9.10, 9.11
  s.617(3) 9.12
  s.623(2) 25.7
  s.651 .... 25.15
  s.652 .... 25.15
  s.653 .... 25.15
  s.691 .... 30.20
  s.695 .... 30.20
  s.696 .... 30.20
  s.703D 30.20
  s.703E 30.20
  s.703L(1) 30.20
  s.703L(2) 30.20
  s.717 .... 30.14
  s.725 .... 27.3
  s.725(1) 17.6
Business Names Act (c.7)—
  s.1 .... 30.11
  s.4 .... 30.5
  s.4(3) 30.11
  s.4(6) 30.5
  s.5(1) 30.5
  s.5(2) 30.5
  s.7 .... 30.5
Companies Consolidation (Consequential Provisions) Act (c.9), s.26 .... 9.9
Reserve Forces (Safeguard of Employment) Act (c.17) 23.11, 25.12
Family Law (Scotland) Act (c.37)—
  s.13(7)(*a*) 29.5
  s.13(7)(*b*) 29.1
  s.19 .... 11.10
  s.24(1) 21.18
Bankruptcy (Scotland) Act (c.66)—
  s.3 .... 20.4
  s.4 .... 20.4, 26.12
  s.5(2)(*a*) 20.2
  s.5(2)(*c*) 20.2, 24.2
  s.5(3) 29.12
  s.5(3)(*b*) 20.2
  s.5(4) 1.11, 20.2
  s.6 .... 30.13
  s.6(1)(*c*) 30.16
  s.6(1)(*d*) 30.14
  s.6(2) 25.1
  s.6(6) 30.16
  s.7 .... 20.1, 30.13
  s.7(1) 26.12
  s.7(3)(*b*) 30.16
  s.7(4) 15.5
  s.8(1)(*a*) 20.2
  s.8(1)(*b*) 20.2
  s.8(3) 29.12
  s.8(4) 29.6
  s.9 .... 20.2
  s.9(1) 29.12
  s.9(4) 29.12

1985 Bankruptcy (Scotland) Act—*cont.*
s.9(5)	29.12
s.10	30.17
s.11(1)	20.2
s.11(5)	20.2
s.12(1)	20.2
s.12(2)	20.3
s.12(3)	20.3
s.12(4)	20.3
s.12(4)(*a*)	20.2
s.13(1)	20.3
s.14	13.8
s.14(1)	20.3
s.14(2)	20.3
s.14(4)	20.3
s.15(1)	20.3
s.15(3)	20.6
s.15(6)	20.3
s.16(1)	20.6
s.16(4)	20.6
s.17	30.17
s.17(1)	20.6
s.17(3)	20.6
s.17(4)	20.6
s.17(5)(*a*)	14.7, 20.6
s.17(5)(*b*)	20.6
s.18	20.3
s.18(2)	20.3
s.19	20.4
s.20	20.4
s.21	20.4
s.22(2)	23.2
s.22(3)	20.3, 23.1
s.23(4)	20.4
s.24	20.4
s.25	20.4
s.25(6)	20.4
s.30	20.4
s.31	21.1
s.31(1)	21.21
s.31(1)(*b*)	21.15
s.31(2)	23.5
s.31(4)	6.10, 21.6, 21.8, 25.7, 27.5
s.31(5)	21.14
s.31(6)	21.1
s.31(7)	29.12
s.31(8)	21.1, 21.21
s.31(9)	21.15
s.31(10)	21.15
s.32(1)	21.19
s.32(2)	21.19
s.32(3)	21.19
s.32(4)	21.19
s.32(5)	21.9
s.32(6)	21.20
s.32(7)	20.7, 21.20
s.32(8)	20.7
s.32(9)(*a*)	20.7
s.32(9)(*b*)	20.7
s.33(1)(*a*)	21.6
s.33(1)(*b*)	21.2
s.33(2)	7.12, 21.6

1985 Bankruptcy (Scotland) Act—*cont.*

s.33(3)	21.1
s.34(1)(*b*)(iii)	29.12
s.34(2)(*a*)	22.2
s.34(2)(*b*)(ii)	24.3
s.34(2)(*b*)(iv)	29.11
s.34(3)	22.2
s.34(4)	22.2
s.34(6)	22.2
s.34(7)	22.2
s.34(8)	22.1, 24.3, 29.11
s.35	22.11
s.35(1)(*c*)(iii)	29.11
s.35(1)(*c*)(iv)	29.11
s.35(2)	24.3
s.36(*c*)	22.4
s.36(1)	22.9
s.36(1)(*c*)(i)	29.12
s.36(1)(*c*)(ii)	29.11
s.36(2)	22.9
s.36(4)	22.9
s.36(4)(*b*)	24.3
s.36(5)	22.9
s.36(6)	24.3, 29.11
s.37	17.13, 25.7
s.37(1)	16.11, 17.12, 17.13
s.37(1)(*a*)	19.4
s.37(2)	23.5
s.37(4)	16.11, 16.12, 17.12, 18.6, 18.10
s.37(4)(*b*)	16.12, 17.13
s.37(5)	16.11, 17.13, 18.6, 18.10
s.37(5A)	18.6, 18.10
s.37(7)	29.4, 29.12
s.37(7)(*a*)	29.12
s.37(7)(*b*)	29.11
s.37(8)	19.4, 29.7, 29.12
s.37(9)	29.7
s.38	20.4
s.38(4)	7.9, 7.11
s.39	20.4
s.39(2)	20.4
s.39(4)	8.3
s.40(1)	21.16
s.40(2)	21.16
s.40(3)	21.16
s.40(4)(*a*)	21.16
s.40(4)(*b*)	21.16
s.41	21.17
s.44	20.4
s.45	20.4
s.46	20.4
s.47	20.4
s.48(1)	23.2
s.48(2)	23.2
s.48(3)	23.1
s.48(4)	23.2, 23.4
s.48(5)	23.3
s.49	25.10
s.49(3)	23.3
s.49(4)	23.3
s.49(5)	23.3
s.49(6)	23.3, 25.10

1985 Bankruptcy (Scotland) Act—*cont.*
s.51	23.10
s.51(1)(*g*)	23.2
s.51(3)(*b*)	21.18
s.51(6)	7.9
s.51(6)(*b*)	7.11
s.51(7)	23.2
s.52	23.2
s.53(1A)	20.4
s.54(1)	20.8
s.54(4)	20.8
s.54(6)	20.8
s.54(8)	20.8
s.54(9)	20.8
s.55	20.8
s.56	24.1
s.57	20.4
s.59	24.3
s.60	10.3, 25.10
s.60(1)	23.6
s.60(2)	23.6, 23.8
s.60(3)	10.1
s.61(2)	22.12
s.61(3)	22.12
s.61(4)	22.12
s.61(5)	22.12
s.61(6)	22.12
s.64	20.7, 20.8
s.67	20.7
s.67(9)	20.7
s.70	20.5, 24.2
s.73(1)	23.4
s.74	22.3, 25.8
s.74(3)	9.12
s.74(4)	22.3
Sched. 1	24.2, 25.10
Sched. 1, para. 1(1)	23.2
Sched. 1, para. 1(2)	23.2
Sched. 1, para. 1(3)	23.2
Sched. 1, para. 2	23.2
Sched. 1, para. 3	1.11
Sched. 1, para. 4	24.1
Sched. 1, para. 5	23.4
Sched. 1, para. 6	30.13
Sched. 2	20.4
Sched. 2, para. 9	20.4
Sched. 3, para. 5(2)	23.11
Sched. 3, para. 5(3)	23.11
Sched. 3, para. 6	23.11
Sched. 3, para. 6A	23.11
Sched. 4, para. 1	24.1
Sched. 4, para. 1.1	24.1
Sched. 4, para. 2	24.1
Sched. 4, para. 3	24.1
Sched. 4, para. 4	24.1
Sched. 4, para. 6	24.1
Sched. 4, para. 8	24.1
Sched. 4, para. 13	24.1
Sched. 4, para. 15	24.1
Sched. 4, para. 16	24.1
Sched. 4, para. 17	24.1
Sched. 4, para. 18	24.1

1985	Bankruptcy (Scotland) Act—*cont.*	
	Sched. 5, para. 2	24.2, 24.3
	Sched. 5, para. 3	24.2, 24.3
	Sched. 5, para. 5	24.3
	Sched. 5, para. 6	24.3
	Sched. 5, para. 7(1)(*a*)	24.3
	Sched. 5, para. 7(1)(*b*)	24.3
	Sched. 5, para. 9	24.3
	Sched. 5, para. 10	24.3
	Sched. 5, para. 11	24.3
	Sched. 7, para. 4	29.11
	Sched. 7, para. 6	29.11
	Sched. 7, para. 11	14.7, 24.2
	Sched. 7, para. 24	15.5
	Sched. 7, para. 24(3)	15.5
	Sched. 7, para. 24(5)	15.5, 17.13
	Sched. 7, para. 24(8)	15.5
	Housing Act (c.68)	3.4
	Law Reform (Miscellaneous Provisions) (Scotland) Act (c.73)	
	s.10	2.4
	s.11	6.8
1986	Drug Trafficking Offences Act (c.32)—	
	s.16	21.5
	s.17	25.4
	Gas Act (c.44)—	
	Sched. 5, para. 5(1)	2.12
	Sched. 5, para. 7(2)–(6)	2.12
	Insolvency Act (c.45)	30.15
	s.1(1)	26.1
	s.1(2)	26.1
	s.1(3)	26.1
	s.2(2)	26.1
	s.3	26.1
	s.3(2)	26.1
	s.4	26.1
	s.4(2)	26.1
	s.4(3)	26.1
	s.4(4)	26.1
	s.5(2)	26.1
	s.5(3)	26.1
	s.6	26.1
	s.7(2)	26.1
	s.7(3)	26.1
	s.8(1)	26.4
	s.8(2)	26.5
	s.8(3)	26.4
	s.8(4)	26.3
	s.9(1)	26.3
	s.9(2)	26.3
	s.9(3)	26.4
	s.9(4)	26.3
	s.10(1)	26.3
	s.10(1)(*b*)	26.8
	s.10(2)	26.3
	s.10(3)	26.3
	s.10(4)	26.3
	s.11	26.11
	s.11(1)	26.5
	s.11(2)	26.6
	s.11(3)	26.5, 26.12
	s.11(3)(*c*)	26.8
	s.11(3)(*d*)	26.10

1986	Insolvency Act—*cont.*	
	s.12	26.5
	s.14	26.6
	s.14(1)	26.6
	s.14(2)	26.6
	s.14(4)	26.6
	s.14(5)	26.6
	s.14(6)	26.6
	s.15(1)	26.9, 26.11
	s.15(2)	26.8, 26.11
	s.15(2)(*b*)	26.11
	s.15(3)	26.9, 26.11
	s.15(4)	26.9
	s.15(5)	26.8, 26.11, 26.12
	s.15(6)	26.8
	s.16(1)	26.8
	s.17(1)	26.6
	s.17(2)	26.6
	s.17(3)	26.6
	s.18	26.7
	s.19	26.7
	s.19(4)	26.9
	s.19(5)	26.9
	s.20	26.7
	s.22	26.6
	s.23	26.6
	s.24(2)	26.6
	s.24(5)	26.6
	s.25	26.7
	s.26(1)	26.6
	s.29(2)	26.3
	s.52(1)	9.13
	s.52(2)	9.13
	s.53(1)	9.14
	s.53(6)	9.14
	s.53(6)(*b*)	9.14
	s.53(7)	9.14, 9.18
	s.54(5)	9.14
	s.54(6)	9.14, 9.18
	s.55(1)	9.15, 9.23
	s.55(2)	9.15
	s.55(3)	9.15
	s.55(3)(*a*)	16.13, 17.14
	s.55(4)	9.15
	s.56(1)	9.20
	s.56(2)	9.20
	s.56(4)	9.20
	s.57(1)	9.15
	s.57(3)	9.15
	s.57(4)	9.15
	s.59	9.16
	s.59(3)	9.16
	s.60	9.17
	s.60(1)(*b*)	17.14
	s.61(1)	9.15
	s.61(3)	9.15
	s.61(4)	9.15
	s.61(5)	9.15
	s.65(1)	9.14
	s.72	17.14
	s.74	9.12
	s.74(1)	25.9

1986 Insolvency Act—*cont.*
   s.74(2)(*a*) 25.9
   s.74(2)(*b*) 25.9
   s.74(2)(*c*) 25.9
   s.74(2)(*d*) 25.9
   s.74(3) 25.9
   s.80 ..... 25.9
   s.81 ..... 29.5
   s.82(4) 23.2
   s.85 ..... 25.14
   s.86 ..... 25.14, 27.5
   s.87 ..... 25.14
   s.88 ..... 25.14
   s.89 ..... 25.14
   s.90 ..... 25.14
   s.94 ..... 25.14
   s.95 ..... 25.14
   s.96 ..... 25.14
   s.98 ..... 25.14
   s.99 ..... 25.14
   s.100 ..... 25.14
   s.100(2) 25.14
   s.101 ..... 25.14
   s.102 ..... 25.14
   s.103 ..... 25.14
   s.106 ..... 25.14
   s.107 ..... 25.14
   s.113 ..... 25.14
   s.115 ..... 25.14
   s.116 ..... 25.14
   s.120(1) 25.2
   s.120(3) 25.2
   s.122(1)(*f*) 25.2
   s.122(2) 9.10, 25.2
   s.123 ..... 26.4
   s.123(1)(*a*) 25.2
   s.123(1)(*c*) 25.2
   s.123(1)(*e*) 25.2
   s.123(2) 25.2
   s.124(1) 25.2
   s.126 ..... 25.3, 30.19
   s.127 ..... 25.5, 25.7
   s.129 ..... 25.3, 25.11, 27.5
   s.130(2) 25.3, 25.5
   s.133 ..... 25.6
   s.135 ..... 25.3
   s.135(5) 25.3
   s.138(1) 25.4
   s.138(3) 25.4
   s.142 ..... 25.4
   s.143(1) 25.4
   s.144 ..... 7.9, 7.11, 25.3, 25.4
   s.146 ..... 25.6
   s.149(3) 13.8
   s.150 ..... 25.6
   s.152 ..... 25.9
   s.161 ..... 25.6
   s.165 ..... 25.14
   s.165(5) 25.14
   s.166(2) 25.14
   s.166(3) 25.14
   s.167 ..... 25.4

1986 Insolvency Act—*cont.*
  s.169(2) 25.4
  s.172(8) 25.6
  s.175 .... 9.22, 25.11, 25.12
  s.175(2) 9.10
  s.185 .... 8.3, 25.7, 25.8
  s.185(1) 16.12, 17.13, 19.4, 23.5
  s.185(3) 16.12, 17.13, 25.3
  s.185(4) 17.13, 30.19
  s.186 .... 25.7
  s.189(4) 25.11
  s.201 .... 25.14
  s.205 .... 25.6
  s.213 .... 25.8
  s.214 .... 9.18, 25.8
  s.216 .... 25.8, 30.18
  s.217 .... 25.8, 30.18
  s.225 .... 30.20
  s.233 .... 25.4
  s.234 .... 26.6
  s.242 .... 25.8
  s.242(3) 25.8
  s.242(7) 25.8, 26.6
  s.243 .... 25.8
  s.243(1) 25.8
  s.243(6) 25.8, 26.6
  s.244 .... 25.8
  s.245 .... 9.12, 25.8, 26.4
  s.245(1) 9.12
  s.245(6) 9.12
  s.247(2) 9.10, 25.11
  s.248(*b*) 26.10, 26.12
  s.248(*b*)(ii) 26.8
  s.249 .... 9.12
  s.251 .... 9.12, 9.22, 9.23, 26.3, 26.11
  s.281 .... 30.17
  s.382(1) 30.17
  s.386 .... 25.12
  s.387(2) 26.1
  s.387(2)(*a*) 26.10
  s.387(3)(*a*) 26.10
  s.387(4)(*b*) 9.16
  s.388 .... 26.6
  s.389 .... 26.6
  s.426 .... 30.22
  s.426(1) 21.21
  s.426(2) 21.21
  s.426(3) 21.21, 30.17
  s.426(4) 21.21
  s.426(5) 21.21
  s.426(6) 21.21
  s.427 .... 20.7
  s.435 .... 9.12
  s.435(3) 9.12
  s.435(5) 9.12
  s.725 .... 30.19
  Sched. 1 .... 26.6
  Sched. 2, para. 1 .... 9.21
  Sched. 4 .... 25.4, 25.14
  Sched. 6 .... 25.12
  Sched. 8, para. 7(2) 26.10
  Sched. 13 .... 9.10

1986	Company Directors Disqualification Act (c.46)	30.15
	s.11	20.7
	Building Societies Act (c.53), Sched. 8, para. 3	6.1
	Financial Services Act (c.60), s.55(5)	21.2
1987	Debtors (Scotland) Act (c.18)—	
	s.1(1)	11.20
	s.1(3)	11.20
	s.1(4)	11.20
	s.1(5)	11.20
	s.1(6)	11.20
	s.1(8)	12.5
	s.2(1)	11.20
	s.2(2)	11.20
	s.2(3)	11.20
	s.2(4)	11.20
	s.2(5)	11.20
	s.3	11.20
	s.3(1)	11.20
	s.4(1)	11.20
	s.4(2)	11.20
	s.4(3)	11.20
	s.4(4)	11.20
	s.5(1)	15.7
	s.5(2)	15.7
	s.5(4)(b)	15.7
	s.5(4)(c)	15.7
	s.5(4)(d)	15.7
	s.5(4)(e)	15.7
	s.5(4)(f)	15.7
	s.5(5)	15.7
	s.5(7)	15.7
	s.5(8)	12.5, 15.7
	s.6(1)	15.7
	s.6(3)	15.7
	s.6(4)	15.7
	s.6(5)	15.7
	s.7	15.7
	s.9(1)	15.7
	s.9(2)	15.7
	s.9(2)(d)	15.7
	s.9(2)(e)	15.7
	s.9(3)	15.7
	s.9(4)	15.7
	s.9(5)	15.7
	s.9(8)	15.7
	s.9(10)	15.7
	s.9(11)	15.7
	s.9(12)	15.7
	s.10(1)	15.7
	s.10(4)	15.7
	s.11(1)	15.7
	s.11(2)	15.7
	s.11(3)	15.7
	s.12(1)	11.20, 15.7
	s.12(2)	11.20, 15.7
	s.13(2)	11.20, 15.7
	s.14(1)	11.20, 15.7, 16.2
	s.14(2)	11.20, 15.7
	s.14(3)	11.20, 15.7
	s.15(3)	15.7
	s.16	17.4
	s.16(1)	16.3

1987	Debtors (Scotland) Act—cont.	
	s.16(2)	16.3
	s.16(4)	16.3
	s.17	16.4
	s.17(1)	18.3, 18.7
	s.18	16.4
	s.19(1)	16.4
	s.19(3)	16.4
	s.20(2)	16.4
	s.20(4)	16.4
	s.20(5)	16.4
	s.20(6)	16.4, 16.9
	s.20(6)(*e*)	16.8
	s.20(7)	16.4
	s.21(1)	16.5
	s.21(4)	16.9
	s.21(7)	16.11
	s.21(8)	16.4
	s.21(9)	16.4
	s.22	16.6
	s.24(1)	16.9
	s.24(3)	16.9
	s.26	16.9
	s.27	16.6
	s.28(3)	16.5
	s.28(4)	16.5
	s.28(5)	16.5
	s.28(6)	16.5
	s.28(7)	16.5
	s.29(1)	16.5
	s.29(2)	16.5
	s.29(3)	16.5
	s.30	16.6
	s.30(3)	16.9
	s.31(1)	16.6
	s.31(2)	16.6
	s.32(1)	16.6, 16.7
	s.32(3)	16.7
	s.33(2)	16.9
	s.34	16.7
	s.34(1)	16.9
	s.34(2)	16.9
	s.35	16.7
	s.37(1)	16.7
	s.37(2)	16.7
	s.37(3)	16.7
	s.37(4)	16.7
	s.37(5)	16.7
	s.37(5)(*b*)	16.8
	s.37(6)	16.7
	s.37(7)	16.7
	s.37(9)	16.7
	s.38	16.7
	s.39(1)	16.7
	s.39(4)	16.7
	s.39(5)	16.7
	s.40(1)	16.8
	s.40(2)	16.8
	s.40(5)	16.8
	s.41(2)	16.8
	s.41(3)	16.8
	s.41(6)	16.8

1987 Debtors (Scotland) Act—cont.

s.41(8)	16.8
s.45	16.7
s.46	18.1
s.46(1)	17.3
s.47(1)	18.4
s.47(2)	18.6
s.48(1)	18.5
s.48(3)	18.5
s.48(4)	18.5
s.49	18.5
s.49(1)(c)	18.5
s.49(2)	18.5
s.49(3)	18.5
s.49(4)	18.5
s.49(5)	18.5
s.49(6)	18.5
s.49(8)	18.4
s.50(1)	18.6
s.50(2)	18.6
s.50(3)	18.6
s.50(4)	18.6
s.51(1)	18.8
s.51(2)	18.10
s.51(3)	18.10
s.51(4)	18.7
s.51(5)	18.7
s.51(6)	18.10
s.52	18.10
s.53(1)	18.9
s.53(2)	18.9
s.53(4)	18.8
s.53(5)	18.8
s.54(1)	18.7
s.55(1)	18.10
s.55(2)	18.10
s.55(5)	18.10
s.55(6)	18.10
s.55(8)	18.10
s.56(1)	18.10
s.56(2)	18.10
s.57(1)	18.4, 18.8
s.57(2)	18.4, 18.8
s.57(3)	18.4, 18.8
s.57(4)	18.6, 18.10
s.57(5)	18.6, 18.10
s.57(6)	18.6, 18.10
s.58	18.11
s.58(1)	18.1
s.59(1)	18.3, 18.12
s.59(2)	18.7, 18.12
s.59(3)	18.11
s.59(4)	18.11
s.59(5)	18.11
s.60	18.1
s.60(3)	18.12
s.60(4)	18.12
s.60(5)	18.14, 18.15
s.60(6)	18.12
s.60(7)	18.12
s.60(9)	18.14
s.61(1)	18.13

1987	Debtors (Scotland) Act—*cont.*	
	s.61(3)	18.13
	s.61(4)	18.13
	s.61(5)	18.13
	s.62(1)	18.3, 18.7
	s.62(5)	18.1, 18.18
	s.63(2)	18.16
	s.63(3)	18.16
	s.63(4)	18.16
	s.63(5)	18.16
	s.64	18.17
	s.65	18.15
	s.66(1)	18.15
	s.66(4)	18.15, 18.18
	s.67	18.6, 18.10, 18.15
	s.69(1)	18.4, 18.8
	s.69(2)	18.4, 18.8
	s.69(3)	18.4, 18.8
	s.69(4)	18.4, 18.8
	s.69(5)	18.6, 18.10
	s.70(1)	18.3, 18.7
	s.70(2)	18.3, 18.7
	s.70(3)	18.3, 18.7
	s.70(4)	18.3, 18.7
	s.70(5)	18.3, 18.7
	s.71	18.4, 18.8, 18.14
	s.72(2)	18.6, 18.10, 18.15
	s.72(3)	18.15
	s.72(4)	18.3, 18.6, 18.12
	s.73(1)	18.1, 18.2
	s.73(2)	18.2
	s.73(2)(*c*)	17.3
	s.73(3)	18.2
	s.73(3)(*c*)	18.2
	s.74(1)	19.7
	s.87(2)	15.3
	s.87(3)	15.3
	s.87(4)	15.3, 19.5
	s.88	15.3
	s.90(1)	15.4, 18.3
	s.90(2)	19.7
	s.90(3)	15.4
	s.90(5)	15.4
	s.90(6)	15.4
	s.91(1)	15.3
	s.91(1)(*c*)	19.5
	s.91(2)	15.3
	s.93(1)	16.7
	s.93(2)	17.8
	s.94	16.7, 17.8, 18.17
	s.94(2)	18.5
	s.95	16.7, 17.8
	s.99(1)	7.12
	s.99(2)	17.4
	Sched. 1	16.7
	Sched. 2	18.5
	Sched. 3, para. 1	18.17
	Sched. 3, para. 2	18.17
	Sched. 3, para. 3	18.17
	Sched. 4, para. 1	19.7
	Sched. 4, para. 2	19.7
	Sched. 4, para. 3	19.7

1987	Debtors (Scotland) Act—*cont.*	
	Sched. 4, para. 4	19.7
	Sched. 5	19.7
	Sched. 6, para. 3	18.10, 18.15, 18.16
	Sched. 6, para. 16	3.18, 19.5
	Sched. 6, para. 17	3.18
	Sched. 6, para. 21	19.7
	Sched. 6, para. 23	19.7
	Sched. 6, para. 26	7.12
	Sched. 6, para. 28(*a*)	15.5
	Sched. 6, para. 28(*b*)	15.5
	Banking Act (c.22), s.89	3.3
	Prescription (Scotland) Act (c.36), s.1	14.7
	Criminal Justice (Scotland) Act (c.41)—	
	s.19	15.6
	s.33	21.5
	s.35	25.4
	s.36	9.15
	s.45(5)(*b*)	20.1
	s.45(5)(*c*)	20.8
	Consumer Protection Act (c.43)	14.9
	Abolition of Domestic Rates Etc. (Scotland) Act (c.47)—	
	s.8(7)	19.8
	s.21	19.7
	Sched. 2, para. 7	19.7
	Sched. 2, para. 7(2)	19.7
	Sched. 2, para. 7(4)	19.7
	Sched. 2, para. 7(5)	19.7
	Sched. 2, para. 7(6)	19.7
1988	Income and Corporation Taxes Act (c.1)—	
	s.266(5)	12.7
	s.348	12.7
	s.349	12.7
	s.351	12.7
	s.369	12.7
	s.818	12.7
	s.819	12.7
	Merchant Shipping Act (c.12)—	
	s.21	7.5
	Sched. 1, para. 21	7.5
	Sched. 2, Pt. II	7.6
	Sched. 2, para. 3	7.6
	Sched. 2, para. 5	7.6
	Sched. 2, para. 9	7.6
	Sched. 2, para. 10	7.6
	Sched. 2, para. 11	7.6
	Sched. 3	7.5
	Criminal Justice Act (c.33)—	
	s.85	21.5
	s.86	25.4
	s.117	21.9, 27.1
	Sched. 15, para. 108	20.1
	Sched. 15, para. 109	20.8
	Court of Session Act (c.36), s.45	19.8
	Copyright, Designs and Patents Act (c.48)—	
	s.90	8.2
	s.222	8.2
	Housing (Scotland) Act (c.50)—	
	s.29	15.6
	s.118	21.15
1989	Social Security Act (c.24), Sched. 4, para. 8(2)	21.5
	Finance Act (c.26), s.155	15.2

Table of Statutes lxxi

1989	Electricity Act—*cont.*	
	Electricity Act (c.29)—	
	Sched. 6, para. 1(3)	2.12
	Sched. 6, para. 1(6)	2.12
	Sched. 6, para. 1(8)	2.12
	Sched. 7, para. 9	2.12
	Employment Act (c.38), s.19	23.11, 25.12
	Companies Act (c.40)—	
	Pt. VII	20.9, 21.5
	s.92	9.1
	s.93	9.1
	s.94	9.1
	s.95	9.1
	s.96	9.1
	s.97	9.1
	s.98	9.1
	s.99	9.1
	s.100	9.1
	s.101	9.1
	s.102	9.1
	s.103	9.1
	s.104	9.1
	s.105	9.1
	s.106	9.1
	s.107	9.1
	s.130(3)	9.9
	s.140(1)	9.10
	s.140(3)	9.11
	s.140(4)	9.11
	s.140(5)	9.11
	s.140(6)	9.11
	s.141	25.15
	s.163(4)	23.10, 25.11
	s.164(6)	23.10, 25.11
	s.165	25.8
	s.165(2)(*a*)	22.9
	s.165(2)(*b*)	22.1, 22.4
	s.175	26.3
	s.175(6)	23.10, 25.11
	s.180	15.6
	Sched. 15	30.20
	Sched. 16, para. 3(2)	26.4
	Sched. 17, para. 8	9.9
1990	Education (Student Loans) Act (c.6)—	
	Sched. 2, para. 6(*a*)	21.19
	Sched. 2, para. 6(*b*)	21.20
	Sched. 2, para. 6(*c*)(i)	20.2
	Sched. 2, para. 6(*c*)(ii)	20.8

ABBREVIATIONS

A.S.	Act of Sederunt.
A.S. (Debtors)	Act of Sederunt (Proceedings in the Sheriff Court under the Debtors (Scotland) Act 1987) 1988 (S.I. 1988/2013).
B.A.	Bankruptcy (Scotland) Act 1985.
B. Regs.	Bankruptcy (Scotland) Regulations 1985 (S.I. 1985/1925) as amended by Bankruptcy (Scotland) Amendment Regulations 1986 (S.I. 1986/1914).
C.A.	Companies Act 1985.
C.A. 1989	Companies Act 1989.
C.A.S.	Codifying Act of Sederunt.
D.A.	Debtors (Scotland) Act 1987.
I.A.	Insolvency Act 1986.
Ins. Rules	Insolvency (Scotland) Rules 1986 (S.I. 1986/1915) as amended by Insolvency (Scotland) Amendment Rules 1987 (S.I. 1987/1921).
O.C.R.	Ordinary Cause Rules–Sheriff Courts (Scotland) Act 1907, Sched. 1 as subst. by S.I. 1983/747.
R.C.	Rules of the Court of Session 1965.
Sh.Ct.Ins. Rules	Act of Sederunt (Sheriff Court Company Insolvency Rules) 1986 (S.I. 1986/2297).
Sm. Clm. R.	Act of Sederunt (Small Claim Rules) 1988 (S.I. 1988/1976).
Summ. C.R.	Act of Sederunt (Summary Cause Rules, Sheriff Court) 1976 (S.I. 1976/476).
I.L. & P.	Insolvency Law & Practice.
J.I.B.L.	Journal of International Banking Law.

PRINCIPAL WORKS CITED

Bankton	Andrew McDouall, Lord Bankton, *Institute of the Laws of Scotland in Civil Rights*, 3 vols., 1751–3.
Bell, *Comm.*	Professor G. J. Bell, *Commentaries on the Law of Scotland and the Principles of Mercantile Jurisprudence*, 7th ed., 1870.
Bell, *Prin.*	Professor G. J. Bell, *Principles of the Law of Scotland*, 10th ed., 1899.
Bell, *Lects.*	*Lectures on Conveyancing* by A. M. Bell, 3rd ed., 1882.
Byles	*Byles on Bills of Exchange*, 26th ed. by F. R. Ryder and A. Bueno, 1988.
Chalmers	*Chalmers on Bills of Exchange*, 13th ed. by David L. Smout, 1964.
Ersk	Professor John Erskine of Carnock, *An Institute of the Law of Scotland*, 8th ed., 2 vols., 1871.
Finlayson	*Law Lectures to Bankers*, by Robert Finlayson, 1939.
Gloag	*The Law of Contract*, by W. M. Gloag, 2nd ed., 1929.
Gloag & Henderson	*Introduction to the Law of Scotland*, by W. M. Gloag and R. C. Henderson, 9th ed. by A. B. Wilkinson and Others, 1987.
Gloag & Irvine	*Law of Rights in Security*, by W. M. Gloag and J. M. Irvine, 1897.
Goudy	*A Treatise on the Law of Bankruptcy in Scotland*, by Henry Goudy, 4th ed. by T. A. Fyfe, 1914.
Graham Stewart	*A Treatise on the Law of Diligence*, by J. Graham Stewart, 1898.
Gretton	*The Law of Inhibition and Adjudication*, by G. L. Gretton, 1987.
McBryde	*Bankruptcy*, by W. W. McBryde, 1989.
Macphail	*Sheriff Court Practice*, by I. D. Macphail, 1988.
Maher & Cusine	*The Law & Practice of Diligence*, by G. Maher & D. J. Cusine, 1990.
Paget	*Paget's Law of Banking*, 10th ed. by M. Hapgood, 1989.
St. Clair & Drummond Young	*The Law of Corporate Insolvency in Scotland*, by J. B. St. Clair & J. E. Drummond Young, 1988.
Thomson	*A Treatise on the Law of Bills of Exchange*, by Robert Thomson, 3rd ed., 1865.
Thorburn	*Commentary on the Bills of Exchange Act 1882*, by W. D. Thorburn, 1882.
Wallace & McNeil	Wallace and McNeil's *Banking Law*, 9th ed. by Donald B. Caskie, 1986.
Wardhaugh	*The Scottish Bankruptcy Manual*, by John B. Wardhaugh, 1955.

CHAPTER 1

THE NATURE OF DEBT

Definition

Debts are "mere rights to demand payment of money at a stipulated time."[1] They are sometimes called *nomina debitorum*. "*Nomina debitorum* are not accounted *res*; nor yet are they mere *entia rationis*: But in plain Scots, are Debts."[2]

A debt can be distinguished from an obligation to account. "In the case of a debt proper there is an obligation to pay, and an obligation to pay necessarily includes an obligation to account. But there may be an obligation to account when at the moment there is no obligation to pay."[3] A debt is a species of *jus crediti*, defined in terms of English law as "a right which the holder of it cannot make available, if it is resisted, without a suit, to compel persons to do something else in order to make the right perfect."[4] Thus, the insured under a life insurance policy has a *jus crediti*. "He was vested in the *jus crediti* or right to recover when the policy matured—a *jus crediti* which would not be enforced by him, because *ex hypothesi* he would be dead, but which would fall to, and be enforced by his personal representatives for the benefit of his estate."[5]

A "debt" may be a sum the amount of which is not ascertained.[6] But a right to the price of shares fixed by reference to the market price on the first day of dealing after a flotation of the company if a flotation should occur was held not to be a "debt"; it was merely "a contingent right . . . to receive an unascertainable amount of money at an unknown date."[7]

There may be degrees of obligation. Lord Dunedin made this classification:
(1) an ordinary debt "which you are bound to pay the moment that you are sued upon it";
(2) a debt which is good against the debtor but which cannot come into competition with his ordinary creditors;
(3) a quasi-obligation "which is truly no obligation at all, which simply says 'I promise to pay if I like to pay.' "[8]
In the case[9] cited by Lord Dunedin as an example of the second type, the words "I shall be happy to pay . . . as soon as I have it in my power" were held to justify a decree against the grantor's executor.

1.1

---

[1] Bell, *Comm.*, II, 15.
[2] *Stuart's Answers to Dirleton's Doubts, s.v. Nomina Debitorum.*
[3] *Per* L. P. Dunedin, *Riley* v. *Ellis*, 1910 S.C. 934 at 941.
[4] *Per* Lord Cranworth, *Edmond* v. *Gordon* (1858) 3 Macq. 116 at 122.
[5] *Per* L. P. Normand, *Tennant's Trs.* v. *Lord Advocate*, 1938 S.C. 224 at 231.
[6] *O'Driscoll* v. *Manchester Insurance Committee* [1915] 3 K.B. 499.
[7] *Marren* v. *Ingles* [1980] 1 W.L.R. 983.
[8] *Mackinnon's Trs.* v. *Dunlop*, 1913 S.C. 232 at 239. See, as to the use of "*ex gratia*," *Wick Harbour Trs.* v. *Admiralty*, 1921 2 S.L.T. 109.
[9] *Fair* v. *Hunter* (1861) 24 D. 1.

2   *The Nature of Debt*

Currency

1.2   The denominations of money in the currency of the United Kingdom are the pound sterling and the penny, the penny being one-hundredth part of a pound sterling.[10] Bank balances and periodical payments in so far as they were expressed in shillings and pence before February 15, 1971 are to be converted in accordance with Schedule 1 to the Decimal Currency Act 1969.[11] There are special provisions for friendly society and industrial assurance company contracts.[12]

A creditor is entitled to insist on payment in legal tender. The following are legal tender[13]:—coins of bronze, for payment of any amount not exceeding 20 pence; coins of cupro-nickel or silver of denominations of not more than 10 pence, for payment of any amount not exceeding five pounds; coins of cupro-nickel or silver of denominations of more than 10 pence, for a payment of any amount not exceeding 10 pounds; gold coins of appropriate weight, one pound and two pound nickel brass coins[14] and Bank of England notes[15] of denomination of less than five pounds for payment of any amount. It is open to the creditor and debtor to agree that gold sovereigns tendered in payment are to be treated as having a value greater than their nominal value.[16]

The pound Scots is one twelfth of the pound sterling so 100 pounds Scots is £8.33p.

International units

1.3   In legislation giving effect to international conventions, the practice, apart from the unfortunate use of "gold value" in the Carriage of Goods by Sea Act 1924,[17] was to express sums in currency units of $65\frac{1}{2}$ milligrammes of gold of millesimal fineness 900[18] (the franc Poincaré) or gold francs weighing 10/31 of a gramme and being of millesimal fineness 900[19] (the franc de germinal), the sterling equivalent being determined in each case by statutory instruments made from time to time. The legislation has now been amended to express the sums in special drawing rights as defined by the International Monetary Fund, the sterling equivalent for a particular day being determined by a certificate by the Treasury.[20]

In legislation of the European Economic Community, sums were originally fixed in units of account (u.a.), the unit being the value of

---

[10] Currency Act 1982, s.1.
[11] Decimal Currency Act 1969, ss.4, 5.
[12] ss.6, 7; Friendly Societies (Halfpenny) Regulations 1969 (S.I. 1969 No. 886); Friendly Societies (Decimal Currency) Regulations 1970 (S.I. 1970 No. 932); Industrial Assurance (Halfpenny) Regulations 1969 (S.I. 1969 No. 887); Industrial Assurance (Premium Receipt Books) (Decimal Currency) Regulations 1970 (S.I. 1970 No. 1012).
[13] Coinage Act 1971, s.2 as amended by Currency Act 1983, s.1(3).
[14] Coinage Act 1971, s.3, Proclamations of 28 April 1983 and 18 December 1985.
[15] Currency and Bank Notes Act 1954, s.1(2). Scottish bank-notes were legal tender for the war period but are not now: Currency (Defence) Act 1939, s.2(2); Order in Council dated December 20, 1945, S.R. & O. 1945 No. 1631.
[16] *Jenkins* v. *Horn* [1979] 2 All E.R. 1141.
[17] Sched., art. IX. See *The Rosa S* [1989] Q.B. 419.
[18] *e.g.* Carriage by Air Act 1961, 1st Sched., art. 22(5).
[19] *e.g.* Carriage of Goods by Road Act 1965, Sched., art. 23.3.
[20] See Carriage by Air and Road Act 1979, ss.4, 5.

·88867088 grammes of fine gold,[21] there was later a conversion to the European Currency Unit (ECU) which is based on the value of a "basket" of currencies published daily.[22]

Gold clauses
The effect of a clause requiring payment in gold or gold coin depends on a construction of the clause but where the proper law of the contract is English it will usually be construed to import an obligation to pay sterling representing the value of the gold specified and not to pay in gold itself.[23] Such a clause is known as a gold clause and is "intended to afford a definite standard or measure of value, and thus to protect against a depreciation of the currency and against the discharge of the obligation by a payment of lesser value than that prescribed."[24] A clause may, however, be construed, albeit it that it contains a reference to gold, as an obligation to pay in lawful currency.[25]

A money obligation index-linked by reference to the rate of exchange between the Swiss franc and sterling has been held in England not to be contrary to public policy.[26]

Foreign currency
A reference to a currency in an obligation may be to a "money of account" or a "money of payment." "The *money of account* is the currency in which an obligation is measured. It tells the debtor *how much* he has to pay. The *money of payment* is the currency in which the obligation is to be discharged. It tells the debtor *by what means* he is to pay."[27]

Decree can competently be granted in a foreign currency; conversion to sterling can be at the date of the extract decree but it may be that it could be later.[28] But decree in a foreign currency is not competent if the contract provides for payment in sterling.

A foreign debt falls to be converted into British currency at the rate of exchange current at the date it became payable and not that at the date of decree.

1.4

1.5

---

[21] H. Joly Dixon, "The European Unit of Account" (1977) 14 C.M.L. Rev. 191.
[22] Council Regulation 3180/1978 (O.J. L. 379, 30.12.78, p. 1) by Regulation 2626/1984 (O.J. L. 247, 15.9.84, p. 1). See Sunt, *Legal Aspects of the Ecu* (1989); J. T. Brown (1990) 18 International Business Lawyer, 203.
[23] *Feist v. Societé Intercommunale Belge D'Electricité* [1934] A.C. 161; *New Brunswick Ry. Co. v. British and French Trust Corporation Ltd.* [1939] A.C. 1.
[24] *Norman v. Baltimore and Ohio Railroad Co.*, 294 U.S. 240, quoted by Lord Maugham, *Rex v. International Trustee for the Protection of Bondholders Aktiengesellschaft* [1937] A.C. 500 at 562.
[25] *Treseder-Griffin v. Co-operative Insurance Society* [1956] 2 Q.B. 127; *Campos v. Kentucky & Indiana Terminal Railroad Co.* [1962] 2 Lloyd's Rep. 459.
[26] *Multiservice Bookbinding Ltd. v. Marden* [1979] Ch. 84.
[27] Per Lord Denning M.R., *Woodhouse Ltd. v. Nigerian Produce Ltd.* [1971] 2 Q.B. 23 at 54.
[28] *Commerzbank Aktiengesellschaft v. Large*, 1977 S.C. 375. See Marshall, 1978 S.L.T. (News) 77; *L/F Foroya Fiskasola v. Charles Mauritzen Ltd.*, 1978 S.L.T. (Sh.Ct.) 27; *Macfie's J.F. v. Macfie* 1932 S.L.T. 460; *North Scottish Helicopters Ltd. v. United Technologies Corporation Inc. (No. 2)*, 1988 S.L.T. 778; Extracts Department Regulations, reg. 5A, *Parliament House Book*, Division C.

Sources of debt

1.6 The principal sources of obligation to pay money are: (a) contracts and promises, (b) unjustified enrichment, (c) other quasi-contractual situations, (d) delict, (e) natural relationship, (f) trust, (g) succession, (h) statute.

The distinction between a debt due under the contract and a claim for damages for breach of contract may be important in that in the case of damages, firstly, the claimant must take steps to minimise his loss and, secondly, it may be argued that a claim for liquidated damages is a penalty.[29]

Many cases refer to actions of relief. "Now, relief means, of course that A is bound to relieve B of a liability which has been found against B."[30] It would seem that apart from statutory provisions for relief[31] the right of relief arises from a contractual relationship.[32] The action is limited to cases where the liability of the party from which relief is claimed is exactly commensurate with that of the party claiming the relief and the action must be founded on the same type of liability as that of the party claiming relief[33]: "where the Pursuer and the Defender were under a common obligation, which ought first to have been performed by the Defender, and which, by his neglect, was cast upon the Pursuer, so that the Pursuer, having been sued, was forced to pay damages, together with the costs of his adversary and his own costs in the suit."[34] Where B is found liable under a statute to pay compensation to C in respect of damage caused to C's property, B's action against his professional advisers whose negligence caused the damage is not an action of relief.[35]

Where one person has agreed to indemnify another, he is, on making good the indemnity subrogated to the rights of the person indemnified but he must sue in the name of the person indemnified.[36]

Obligations arising from unjustified enrichment are sometimes classified as quasi-contractual obligations. The *condictio indebiti*, or repetition, is the appropriate remedy to recover money paid under an error of fact. "The action of *condictio indebiti* implies *indebiti solutio*. It is a peculiar action well known in our law. It depends not on contract but on *quasi* contract. When a payment is made which is supposed to be due, but which is not due, the law makes a contract between the parties such as they would have made had the real truth been known."[37] The claim is not

---

[29] *Bell Brothers (H.P.) Ltd.* v. *Aitken*, 1939 S.C. 577; *Bridge* v. *Campbell Discount Co. Ltd.* [1962] A.C. 600; *White & Carter (Councils) Ltd.* v. *McGregor*, 1962 S.C. (H.L.)1; *Highland Leasing Ltd.* v. *Lyburn*, 1987 S.L.T. 92.

[30] *Per* L. P. Dunedin, *Wood & Co.* v. *A. & A. Y. Mackay* (1906) 8 F. 625 at 633.

[31] *e.g.* Law Reform (Miscellaneous Provisions) (Scotland) Act 1940, s.3(2). See *Comex Houlder Diving Ltd.* v. *Colne Fishing Co. Ltd.*, 1987 S.L.T. 442.

[32] *Buchanan & Carswell* v. *Eugene Ltd.*, 1936 S.C. 160, *per* Lord Murray at p. 181; *National Coal Board* v. *Thomson*, 1959 S.C. 353.

[33] *Caledonian Ry. Co.* v. *Colt* (1860) 3 Macq. 833, *per* Lord Chelmsford at p. 848; *Ovington* v. *McVicar* (1864) 2 M. 1066.

[34] *Caledonian Ry. Co.* v. *Colt, supra*, *per* Lord Campbell L.C. at p. 840.

[35] *British Railways Board* v. *Ross and Cromarty C.C.*, 1974 S.C. 27. See also *Lancashire Textiles (Jersey) Ltd.* v. *Thomson Shepherd & Co. Ltd.*, 1985 S.C. 135.

[36] *Simpson & Co.* v. *Thomson* (1877) 5 R. (H.L.) 40; *Esso Petroleum Co. Ltd.* v. *Hall Russell & Co. Ltd.*, 1988 S.L.T. 874.

[37] *Per* Lord Neaves, *Masters and Seamen of Dundee* v. *Cockerill* (1869) 8 M. 278 at 281.

to be sustained unless it appears that retention of the money would be inequitable.[38]

The payment must have been made in error; a payment made by a person in full knowledge of his legal rights where there was no liability to pay cannot be recovered[39]; but, to bar recovery, it must be shown that the knowledge that the sum was not due was, or should have been, present to his mind.[40] The error must be excusable,[41] as where it is due to the conduct of the other party.[42] It is not a bar to recovery that the payer had means of discovering the true facts.[43] The error must be as to fact and not law; an error as to the construction of a statute is an error of law for this purpose[44] but an error as to the construction of a private commercial contract is not, it seems.[45] It is an equitable defence that the payee had reasonable ground for believing that the money was his and acted upon his belief so as to alter his position in such a way as to make repetition unjust.[46] The doctrine has no application where there is an attempt to recover from an innocent party funds which have been improperly paid through the fraud of an intermediary.[47] There is a separate doctrine that excess charges exacted by a public body and later found unwarranted can be recovered[48]; *a fortiori*, if payment has been made under reservation.[49] It is not enough that the payment has been found to be unreasonable.[50]

The *condictio causa data causa non secuta* is appropriate where money has been paid by one of the parties to a contractual obligation and there has been a subsequent failure of consideration.[51]

The principle of recompense is that "where one has gained by the lawful act of another, done without any intention of donation, he is bound to recompense or indemnify that other to the extent of the gain."[52] The party making the demand must have been put to some expense or disadvantage which resulted in a benefit to the other party which cannot be undone.[53] The remedy is excluded when the expenditure is incurred in

---

[38] *Bell* v. *Thomson* (1867) 6 M. 64, *per* L. J.-C. Patton at p. 67; *Henderson & Co. Ltd.* v. *Turnbull & Co.*, 1909 S.C. 510; *Agnew* v. *Ferguson* (1903) 5 F. 879; *Haggarty* v. *Scottish Transport and General Workers Union*, 1955 S.C. 109; *Unigate Food* v. *Scottish Milk Marketing Board*, 1972 S.L.T. 137.

[39] *Balfour Melville* v. *Duncan* (1903) 5 F. 1079.

[40] *Dalmellington Iron Co.* v. *Glasgow and South-Western Ry. Co.* (1889) 16 R. 523.

[41] *Taylor* v. *Wilson's Trs.*, 1979 S.L.T. 105.

[42] *Duncan, Galloway & Co.* v. *Duncan, Falconer & Co.*, 1913 S.C. 265.

[43] *Balfour* v. *Smith and Logan* (1877) 4 R. 454.

[44] *Glasgow Corporation* v. *Lord Advocate*, 1959 S.C. 203; *Unigate Food Ltd.* v. *Scottish Milk Marketing Board*, 1972 S.L.T. 137; *Taylor* v. *Wilson's Trs., supra*.

[45] *Baird's Trs.* v. *Baird & Co.* (1877) 4 R. 1005; *British Hydro-Carbon Chemicals Ltd. and British Transport Commission, Petrs.*, 1961 S.L.T. 280; *cf. Rowan's Trs.* v. *Rowan*, 1940 S.C. 30.

[46] *Credit Lyonnais* v. *George Stevenson & Co. Ltd.* (1901) 9 S.L.T. 93.

[47] *G. M. Scott (Willowbank Cooperage) Ltd.* v. *York Trailer Co. Ltd.*, 1969 S.L.T. 87.

[48] *British Oxygen Co.* v. *South West Scotland Electricity Board*, 1958 S.C. 53, esp. *per* Lord Patrick at p. 79.

[49] *British Railways Board* v. *Glasgow Corporation*, 1976 S.C. 224.

[50] *Lanarkshire Steel Co. Ltd.* v. *Caledonian Ry. Co.* (1903) 6 F. 47.

[51] *Cantiere San Rocco* v. *Clyde Shipbuilding and Engineering Co.*, 1923 S.C. (H.L.) 105; *Singh* v. *Cross Entertainments Ltd.*, 1990 S.L.T. 77.

[52] Bell, *Prin.*, § 538.

[53] *Buchanan* v. *Stewart* (1874) 2 R. 78; *Stewart* v. *Steuart* (1878) 6 R. 145; *Edinburgh and District Tramways Co. Ltd.* v. *Courtenay*, 1909 S.C. 99; *Exchange Telegraph Co. Ltd.* v. *Giulianotti*, 1959 S.L.T. 293.

the expectation of benefit to the spender.[54] It is not decided whether the claim can succeed where there is no error of fact.[55] Recompense cannot be invoked if another legal remedy is available.[56] Examples of the operation of the principle are:
(a) where employers had paid a workman's fare from Kuwait to Scotland when they were under no contractual obligation to do so[57];
(b) where executors were held liable to repay with interest a bank overdraft which had been arranged by their law agent without authority[58];
(c) where a lender was allowed to recover a loan which, to his knowledge, was *ultra vires* of the borrower[59];
(d) where assignees had paid premiums on a policy which had been invalidly assigned[60];
(e) where a builder has deviated from the plans to such an extent that he cannot recover the contract price[61];
(f) where a person has expended money on melioration on a house in a bona fide belief that he was the owner[62];
(g) where a person had made payments over a period for the maintenance of a deceased person[63];
(h) where suppliers have provided clothes for a wife to the benefit of her husband.[64]

With regard to (f), it has been held that the relationship of a sub-lessee to the heritable creditor of the lessor cannot give rise to a claim of recompense.[65]

Under the heading of "other quasi-contractual situations" can be placed *negotiorum gestio*, salvage and general average.

The principle of *negotiorum gestio* is that where a person, acting without authority, undertakes the management of the affairs of another who is absent or incapacitated he has a right to be reimbursed for any expenditure incurred in the course of administration.[66] Salvage is "a reward or recompense given to those by means of whose labour, intrepidity, or perseverance, a ship, or goods . . . have been saved from shipwreck, fire or capture."[67] "Salvage in its true sense is suitable reward for services voluntarily rendered in circumstances where by the services offered on the one hand and accepted on the other there is saving of what

---

[54] *Rankin* v. *Wither* (1886) 13 R. 903.
[55] See *Rankin* v. *Wither* (1886) 13 R. 903, *per* Lord Young at p. 908; *Gray* v. *Johnston*, 1928 S.C. 659, *per* L. J.-C. Alness at p. 681.
[56] *Varney (Scotland) Ltd.* v. *Burgh of Lanark*, 1976 S.L.T. 46; *City of Glasgow D.C.* v. *Morrison McChlery & Co.*, 1985 S.C. 52.
[57] *Duncan* v. *Motherwell Bridge & Engineering Co.*, 1952 S.C. 131.
[58] *Commercial Bank of Scotland* v. *Biggar*, 1958 S.L.T. (Notes) 46.
[59] *Mags. of Stonehaven* v. *Kincardineshire County Council*, 1939 S.C. 760.
[60] *Edinburgh Life Assurance Co.* v. *Balderston*, 1909 2 S.L.T. 323.
[61] *Ramsay & Son* v. *Brand* (1898) 25 R. 1212. See para. 2.10.
[62] *Newton* v. *Newton*, 1925 S.C. 715. *Cf. Rankin* v. *Wither* (1886) 13 R. 903.
[63] *Horne* v. *Horne's Exrs.* 1963 S.L.T. (Sh.Ct.) 37; but see *Gray* v. *Johnston*, 1928 S.C. 659.
[64] *Neilson* v. *Guthrie and Gairn* (1672) Mor. 5878.
[65] *Trade Development Bank* v. *Warriner & Mason (Scotland) Ltd.*, 1980 S.C. 74.
[66] Bell, *Prin.*, § 540.
[67] Bell, *Prin.*, § 443.

otherwise was in risk of perishing or being lost."[68] The claim to salvage does not rest upon contract.[69]

The principle of general average is that "where in the danger of shipwreck or capture it is thought by those on board advisable to sacrifice any part of the cargo, or of the ship . . . for the general safety, the loss is to be adjusted by a contribution from all who have partaken of the benefit."[70] The liability does not depend on contract.[71]

Aliment has distinctive features. "A claim for aliment has many distinguishing characteristics from the ordinary claim of debt. It is in the first place rejected if the alleged debtor be unable to satisfy the demand, if he reserve enough for his own subsistence. It is in the next place rejected if the claimant have means of his own, which though contingent may be turned into money. It is also rejected if he have brains and hands enabling him to labour, accompanied by good health; and lastly, there is no claim for arrears, even although the destitute individual may have been supported by the charity of others."[72]

A decree for aliment can never be made for all time coming.[73]

Succession as a source of obligation presents some analytical difficulties. Obviously, a vitious intromitter may become liable for the debts of the deceased and an executor in respect of legacies; similarly, a person acquiring heritage is liable *quanto lucratus* under the personal obligation in a security affecting the subjects. But legal rights are described as being in the nature of debts which attach to the free succession after the claims of onerous creditors (and, in intestacy, the prior rights of the spouse) have been satisfied and they exist as debts from the date of death.[74]

Debitum fundi

A *debitum fundi* is "a real debt or lien over land, which attaches to the land itself, into whose hands soever it may come."[75] A *debitum fundi* must appear on the face of the feudal title and, except where there is a disposition of land burdened with a particular debt in favour of a third party, the creditor's right must rest upon infeftment.[76] The chief examples are feuduties, real money burdens, bonds and dispositions in security, standard securities, ground-annuals and heritably secured annuities. The *debitum fundi* affects not only the land itself but also the moveables thereon, the remedy for enforcing this right against the moveables being

1.7

---

[68] *Clan Steam Trawling Co. Ltd.* v. *Aberdeen Steam Trawling and Fishing Co. Ltd.*, 1908 S.C. 651, *per* L. J.-C. Macdonald at p. 657. See also *The Ben Gairn*, 1979 S.C. 98.
[69] *The Hestia* [1895] P. 193.
[70] Bell, *Comm.*, I, 631.
[71] *Milburn & Co.* v. *Jamaica Fruit Importing and Trading Co. of London* [1900] 2 Q.B. 540.
[72] *Smith* v. *Smith's Trs.* (1882) 19 S.L.R. 552, *per* Lord Fraser at p. 555. See also *Oncken's J. F.* v. *Reimers* (1892) 19 R. 519.
[73] *Duncan* v. *Forbes* (1878) 15 S.L.R. 371.
[74] *McMurray* v. *McMurray's Trs.* (1852) 14 D. 1048; *Russel* v. *Attorney-General*, 1917 S.C. 28; *Sanderson* v. *Lockhart-Mure*, 1946 S.C. 298.
[75] Bell's *Dictionary, s.v. Debitum Fundi.*
[76] *Scottish Heritable Security Co.* v. *Allan Campbell & Co.* (1876) 3 R. 333, *per* Lord Deas at p. 343; *Scottish Heritages Co. Ltd.* v. *North British Property Investment Co. Ltd.* (1885) 12 R. 550 *per* Lord Lee at p. 555.

a poinding of the ground.[77] The nature of a *debitum fundi* is illustrated by the form of this action. It contains no personal conclusions except for expenses and the persons called as defenders—normally the proprietor of the ground and the tenants—are called, not in respect of a conclusion directed against them, but in respect of their interest in the ground. Similarly, while an adjudication on a personal obligation covers all the debtor's heritage, an adjudication on a *debitum fundi* is restricted to the security subjects. A liability for a share of the common maintenance charges of a tenement imposed by a deed of conditions is a personal obligation.[78]

Personal liability

1.8 The question of personal liability may arise in three principal ways. Firstly, where an individual is acting in a representative capacity—as a trustee, for example—a question may arise as to whether a transaction has rendered the individual liable personally—in which case, of course, his whole property may be attached for the debt—or whether he is liable only as trustee—in which case he is liable only to the extent of the trust funds which he holds.[79] Trustees, for example, are personally liable on contracts which they make unless there is some clear stipulation that their liability is limited.[80] "Whenever a man means to bind another and not himself he should take care to say so. I think this is never to be implied. Even if a trust character is mentioned it will be held in general that this is merely descriptive of the obligant, but does not exempt him from personal liability. A trustee who does not mean to be personally bound should take care to use words which will exclude his personal liability,— for example, 'I bind not myself, but the trust-estate'; 'I bind not myself, but my constituent, or my client, for whom I act.' If he binds 'himself' it will not in general limit his responsibility that he adds, 'as agent for so and so,' or 'as trustee.' This may indicate that he claims relief, but, in general, he himself will be liable in the first place."[81] Secondly, in the case of certain debts connected in some way with land a question arises as to whether the proprietor of the land can be sued personally for the debt or whether the creditor's only remedy is to seize the land by a legal process. For example, in the case of feuduty the proprietor of the land became personally liable when the disposition in his favour was recorded;[82] he was not personally liable for the amount of a heritable security over the subjects granted by his authors unless he had signed the conveyance in his favour.[83] But the heritable creditor can, of course, operate various remedies such as an action of maills and duties or his power of sale in order to recover the amount of his bond. Debts which are recoverable from the land itself are termed "*debita fundi*." The third type of question

---

[77] *Bell* v. *Cadell* (1831) 10 S. 100; *Royal Bank* v. *Bain* (1877) 4 R. 985, *per* Lord Deas at p. 989.
[78] *Wells* v. *New House Purchasers Ltd.* (1963) 79 Sh.Ct.Rep. 185.
[79] See *Kilmarnock Theatre Co.* v. *Buchanan*, 1911 S.C. 607.
[80] *Lumsden* v. *Buchanan* (1865) 3 M. (H.L.) 89.
[81] *Brown* v. *Sutherland* (1875) 2 R. 615, *per* Lord Gifford at p. 621. See also *Mackenzie* v. *Macalister* (1925) 41 Sh.Ct.Rep. 163.
[82] Conveyancing (Scotland) Act 1874, s.4.
[83] Conveyancing (Scotland) Act 1874, s.47; Conveyancing (Scotland) Act 1924, s.15.

which arises is whether the debtor's estate is liable in respect of a debt for which the deceased was personally liable. This is dealt with elsewhere.[84]

Liquidity

The concept of a liquid debt is not altogether clear. The first characteristic of a liquid debt is that the amount should be clear: "a clear settled thing by itself."[85] "To liquidate a debt is only to make appear *quid, quale, quantum.*"[86] So a claim for damages[87] and a claim for an accounting[88] are not liquid:"The effect of a decree against a defender in an action of damages . . . is to turn a previously unliquidated claim into an ascertained and liquidated liability for a debt."[89] It has often been said that the amount must be fixed by an obligatory document or decree: "To render a claim liquid it is necessary that it should be constituted, and that its exact amount should be fixed either by an obligatory writing or by the judgment of a competent Court."[90] But there has to be some relaxation of this in some contexts because the price of goods fixed by an oral contract is regarded as liquid as is rent[91]; Lord Deas speaks of a claim for a price as "not what is called a liquid claim in the correct sense in which bonds, bills and leases constitute liquid claims," but goes on to treat it as liquid.[92] Of rent, Lord Fullerton said: "Rent is not liquid in the sense that a sum due by bond is. It is matter of contract in consideration for something to be done. It is paid for possession of the subject let . . . But the amount of the rent being mentioned in the lease does does not make it liquid in the strict sense. It is only part of a contract."[93] The second characteristic is that it must be due and not future or contingent: "A debt is deemed liquid when it is actually due and the amount ascertained, *cum certum an et quantum debeatur.*"[94] So a future or contingent debt[95] is not liquid. The third characteristic is that the debt must be proved or admitted: "Pure and Uncontroverted and Instantly Verified."[96] Erskine says liquid debts must be "ascertained either by a written obligation, the oath of the adverse party, or the sentence of a judge."[97]

1.9

Future debts

Debts are classified as pure, to a day or contingent.[98] A pure or simple debt is one which is presently due and can be exacted immediately. The

1.10

---

[84] See para. 29.5.
[85] *Per* Lord Cockburn, *Lawson* v. *Drysdale* (1884) 7 D. 153 at 155.
[86] *McDowal* v. *Agnew* (1707) Mor. 2568.
[87] *Smart* v. *Wilkinson*, 1928 S.C. 383.
[88] *Lawson* v. *Drysdale, supra.*
[89] *Comex Houlder Diving Ltd.* v. *Colne Fishing Co. Ltd.*, 1987 S.L.T. 443, *per* Lord Keith of Kinkel at p. 446.
[90] *Per* Lord Kinnear, *Robertson & Co.* v. *Bird & Co.* (1897) 24 R. 1076 at 1078.
[91] *Alexander* v. *Campbell's Trs.* (1903) 5 F. 634.
[92] *Mackie* v. *Riddell* (1874) 2 R. 115 at 117.
[93] *Graham* v. *Gordon* (1843) 5 D. 1207 at 1211; see also *Lovie* v. *Baird's Trs.* (1895) 23 R. 1, *per* Lord Kinnear at p. 4.
[94] Bell, *Comm.*, II, 122.
[95] See *infra*, paras. 10 and 11.
[96] Bankton, I, xxiv, 25.
[97] III, iv, 16.
[98] Stair, I, iii, 7; Erskine III, i, 6; Bell, *Prin.*, §§ 45-47.

obligation of a banker to his customer in respect of sums on current account is "from the first substantially operative and enforceable" and is properly classified as pure.[99] An obligation to a day, or *in diem*, or *ex die*, is one in which payment is to be made on a certain day in the future or on the occurrence of an event which must occur—*dies statim cedit, sed non venit*. The debt although it is not payable until a future time is nonetheless, in one sense of the word, "due"; it is *debitum in praesenti solvendum in futuro*. "A proper debt exists from the moment of completion of the engagement; the execution only is suspended till the arrival of the appointed day."[1] An action cannot be raised for such a debt before the date for payment.[2] Bell, in his *Commentaries*,[3] calls debts to a day "future debts" and this has been followed by later writers[4] and some judicial usage can be found to support this terminology.[5] In his *Principles*,[6] however, Bell states that debts to a day are "improperly" termed "future debts."

"Future" has been applied to the following:
(1) "a debt that is not contracted until after the date of the arrestment,"[7]
(2) the obligation of a third party liability insurer to the insured prior to decree being granted against the insured (future *and* contingent),[8]
(3) "(an obligation) the existence, and not merely the enforceability, of which depends on an event which must certainly happen, though when it will do so remains uncertain, such as an agreement to offer to sell the house to another, when the promisor's mother dies."[9]

Then there is statutory usage. The Debtors (Scotland) Act 1838, s.22, provides that arrestments upon a "future or contingent debt" will prescribe in three years "from the time when the debt shall become due and the contingency be purified." In *Jameson* v. *Sharp*[10] the arrestment of a vested interest in a trust was held to be prescribed and it does not seem to have been suggested that the 1838 Act had any application. Perhaps the "or" is exegetical and "future" is used to mean "contingent"; that would explain the "and" between "due" and "the contingency."

The existence of the category of obligations to a day gives rise to the double signification of the word "due." "'Due' is often employed as synonymous with 'payable,' but it has another meaning as referring to the creation of an obligation. A debt in this sense is often 'due' before it is 'payable.' A man is a creditor who holds a bill at three months, although he cannot enforce the obligation till the three months expire. The debt is

---

[99] *Macdonald* v. *North of Scotland Bank*, 1942 S.C. 369.

[1] Bell, *Prin.* § 46.

[2] *Crear* v. *Morrison* (1882) 9 R. 890; *Hodgmac Ltd.* v. *Gardiners of Prestwick Ltd.*, 1980 S.L.T. (Sh.Ct.) 68.

[3] I, 332.

[4] *e.g.* Graham Stewart, pp. 15, 81, 528; *Gloag*, p. 271; *cf.* Smith, *Short Commentary*, p. 617.

[5] *Smith* v. *Cameron* (1879) 6 R. 1107; *Palace Billiard Rooms Ltd.* v. *City Property Investment Trust Corporation Ltd.*, 1912 S.C. 5; *Strathdee* v. *Paterson*, 1913 1 S.L.T. 498.

[6] S.46. Graham Stewart, p. 81, n. 2, points out that Stair (III, i, 31), Bankton (III, i, 35), and Erskine (III, vi, 8), use "future" when they mean contingent.

[7] *Marshall* v. *Nimmo & Co.*, (1847) 10 D. 328 at 329 (sheriff's note).

[8] *Kerr* v. *R. & W. Ferguson*, 1931 S.C. 736 at 743. In *Smith* v. *Lord Advocate (No. 2)*, 1981 S.L.T. 19, a guarantee was held to be a contingent and not a future debt.

[9] Walker, *Contracts*, p. 306.

[10] (1887) 14 R. 643.

due from the first when it is created; the relation of debtor and creditor is constituted from the date of the contract".[11]

Contingent debts

A contingent debt is one which depends on the occurrence of an uncertain future event—an event which may or may not happen. *Dies nec credit nec venit.* Whether a debt is contingent can be important: a petition for sequestration cannot proceed on a contingent debt,[12] in a sequestration there is provision for the valuation of claims depending on a contingency[13]; a *spes successionis* is not arrestable.[14]

1.11

Graham Stewart[15] makes a distinction in discussing what debts are arrestable: "Debts and claims which are truly contingent, that is, debts and claims to which at the time of arrestment the common debtor has no vested right, which exist only *in spe*, are not arrestable. Where, however, the right has vested in the common debtor, although it is not yet prestable or is liable to be defeated by the occurrence or non-occurrence of some event before payment, arrestment will be sustained for what it may ultimately prove to be worth."

In an English Revenue appeal, Lord Reid said: " . . . conditional obligation and contingent liability have no different significance. I would, therefore, find it impossible to hold that in Scots Law a contingent liability is merely a species of existing liability. It is a liability which, by reason of something done by the person bound, will necessarily arise or come into being if one or more of certain events occur or do not occur."[16]

Consider the following:

(1) a "right" of a person to a legacy *if* someone makes a will in his favour. This is clearly not a right of any kind although it may be a liability in the Hohfeldian analysis.[17]

(2) a right to a legacy if the testator does not alter his testament; this may be called a *spes successionis*.[18]

(3) a right of a beneficiary under a discretionary trust to be considered as a potential recipient of benefit by the trustees who must exercise their discretion properly; this has been said to be more than a mere *spes*,[19] but was held not to be an "interest" for purposes of estate duty. Similar, perhaps, is the right to have a request for financial assistance fairly considered.[20] It cannot amount to a contingent debt.

(4) a right of a beneficiary to income of a trust if the trustees do not exercise a power of accumulation; this has been held not to be an "interest in possession" in the sense of a present right to present

---

[11] *Per* Lord Neaves, *McFarlane* v. *Robb & Co.* (1870) 9 M. 370 at 375.
[12] Bankruptcy (Scotland) Act 1985, s.5(4). See para. 20.2.
[13] *Ibid.* Sched. 1, para. 3.
[14] *Trappes* v. *Meredith* (1871) 10 M. 38.
[15] p. 81.
[16] *Re Sutherland decd.* [1963] A.C. 235 at 249.
[17] Paton, *Textbook of Jurisprudence* (4th ed.), p. 292.
[18] *Reid* v. *Morison* (1893) 20 R. 510, *per* Lord Rutherfurd Clark at pp. 512-514; *Wright* v. *Bryson*, 1935 S.C. (H.L.) 49, *per* Lord Alness at p. 54. See *infra* (9).
[19] *Gartside* v. *I.R.C.* [1968] A.C. 553.
[20] *Medical Defence Union* v. *Dept. of Trade* [1980] Ch. 82.

enjoyment.[21] Similarly trustees may have a discretion to reduce an interest to a liferent or to reduce revenue payments.[22] It might be said that the beneficiary has a contingent debt due to him.

(5) a right of a party who holds an award of expenses and had obtained a decree for interim execution pending an appeal to the House of Lords; this was held to be "contingent" for purposes of a sequestration petition—"Contingency may be of this nature that the debt may never become due or payable."[23] Where decree had been extracted and no appeal had been taken but appeal was still competent the debt was held not to be contingent.[24]

(6) a right of a person injured by delict to obtain payment of damages once these are assessed by a court; this has been said not to be contingent because if the claim is good it accrued from the date of the delict.[25]

(7) a right of an insured against his insurer to be indemnified against a third party claim which has not yet been the subject of an action; this has been held to be contingent for purposes of arrestment as it is both future and contingent.[26]

(8) the right of an insured against whom decree has been obtained to be indemnified by the insurers, the right being subject to arbitration; this is arrestable.[27]

(9) the right of a beneficiary to a legacy if he survives another person; this is regarded as a contingent right and is sometimes called a *spes successionis* but in the law relating to the revocation of trusts is called a *jus quaesitum* as distinct from a mere *spes*.[28] ("It is necessary to distinguish between two meanings which may attach to the term *spes successionis*. It may mean that A hopes to benefit by the will of B who is still alive, or it may mean, as here, that A has a right under the will of B, who is dead, subject to a certain contingency."[29])

(10) the right of the creditor against a cautioner before the debtor is in default or the right of the holder of a bill against the drawer before the bill is dishonoured by the acceptor; these are contingent.[30]

(11) the right of a creditor against his debtor who has given a cheque for the amount due if the cheque is not honoured; the correlative of this is described as a contingent liability which is not arrestable.[31]

---

[21] *Pearson* v. *I.R.C.* [1981] A.C. 753.
[22] *Train* v. *Buchanan's Tr.*, 1908 S.C. (H.L.) 26.
[23] *Forbes* v. *Whyte* (1890) 18 R. 182.
[24] *Mags. of Falkirk* v. *Lundie* (1892) 8 Sh.Ct.Rep. 272.
[25] *Riley* v. *Ellis*, 1910 S.C. 934, *per* Lord Johnston at p. 938.
[26] *Kerr* v. *R. & W. Ferguson*, 1931 S.C. 736.
[27] *Boland* v. *White Cross Insurance Association*, 1926 S.C. 1066.
[28] *Scott* v. *Scott*, 1930 S.C. 903, *per* L.P. Clyde at p. 916; *Parker* v. *Lord Advocate*, 1958 S.C. 426, *per* Lord Mackintosh at p. 437.
[29] *Per* Lord Mackenzie, *Salaman* v. *Tod*, 1911 S.C. 1214 at 1223. *Cf.* Stair, 1, iii, 7: "Conditional obligations are such as depend upon a condition: and so are but obligations in hope, till the condition be existent."
[30] *Morrison* v. *Turnbull* (1832) 10 S. 259; *Gordon* v. *McCubbin* (1851) 13 D. 1154; *Stuart & Stuart* v. *Macleod* (1891) 19 R. 223; *Smith* v. *Lord Advocate* (No. 2), 1981 S.L.T. 19.
[31] *Leggat Brothers* v. *Gray*, 1908 S.C. 67, *per* Lord Kinnear at p. 76.

Vesting

(12) the right of a contractor to payment if he completes the contract work; this is a conditional obligation and is arrestable.[32]
(13) a wife's claim to future aliment if the parties do not resume co-habitation; this is not even a contingent debt in a sequestration.[33]
(14) the right of the holder of a document of debt which was to be retained as a voucher for a current account until final adjustment but could not be used for suing the debtor or for diligence; this is not a contingent debt in petitioning for sequestration: "a contingent debt . . . is a debt which has no existence now but will only emerge and become due upon the occurrence of some future event."[34] Similarly, where a duty of accounting is owed to a person, his right to payment of any balance found due is not contingent and is arrestable.[35]

In cases (1) and (2) the right depends on the unrestricted volition of a party other than the possessor of the right. In (3) and (4) the right depends on the decision of persons subject to fiduciary and other duties and it is between the two cases that the line between a right which is not even a contingent right to payment and a right which is of that character is drawn. Cases (5) to (8) depend on the decision of a court or arbiter. It seems that a claim which has yet to be litigated in order to quantify it is pure and not contingent but, once it has been successfully brought to litigation, a pending appeal renders it contingent. The result in case (7) is perhaps suspect but its facts differ from the others in that there are two claims to be decided. In cases (9) to (11), the right depends on the occurrence of an event independent of the will of the parties and that makes it a contingent right. Case (12) involves only the future actings of the creditor but it is obviously contingent in some sense. It has been suggested that, to render an obligation contingent, the condition attaching to it must be casual or mixed, and not potestative.[36] Future aliment (case (13)) is obviously special as, for one thing, it involves the future actings of both creditor and debtor. The accounting situation in case (14) stands apart from the others as the existence of liability does not depend on future events or actings; it is not known whether the liability exists or not.

Vesting

Another distinction is between a right to payment of money which has vested and one which has not vested. Vesting means "a right of property in the thing vested transmissible by, or through, and in right of the person in whom it is vested."[37] "The fair meaning of vesting is nothing more than that the subject goes to a man's heirs and assignees."[38] A debt may be vested although the date of payment has not yet arrived and the essence

1.12

---

[32] *Marshall v. Nimmo & Co.* (1847) 10 D. 328; *Park, Dobson & Co. v. William Taylor & Son*, 1929 S.C. 571.
[33] *Matthew v. Matthew's Tr.* (1907) 15 S.L.T. 326.
[34] *Fleming v. Yeaman* (1884) 9 App. Cas. 966, *per* Lord Watson at p. 976.
[35] *American Mortgage Co. of Scotland Ltd. v. Sidway*, 1908 S.C. 500.
[36] *Per* Lord Jamieson, *Macdonald v. North of Scotland Bank*, 1942 S.C. 369 at 382.
[37] *Per* Lord Young, *Haldane's Trs. v. Murphy* (1881) 9 R. 269 at 295.
[38] *Per* Lord Mackenzie, *Kilgour v. Kilgour* (1845) 7 D. 451 at 456.

of vesting is that, if the person in whom the debt is vested predeceases the date of payment, the debt is transmitted in accordance with his will if he dies testate and passes to his heirs *ab intestato* if he dies intestate. A right which has not vested is sometimes said to be a mere *spes successionis*.[39]

---

[39] But see, *supra*, para, 1.11, n. 29.

CHAPTER 2

COMMON DEBTS

Sale: price

A contract of sale of goods is a contract by which the seller transfers or agrees to transfer the property in goods to the buyer for a money consideration, called the price.[1]

The price may be fixed in the contract or may be left to be fixed in a manner agreed or it may be determined by the course of dealing between the parties.[2] If the price is not determined in any of those ways the buyer must pay a reasonable price and this is a question of fact dependent on the circumstances of each particular case.[3]

If, after the contract is made, and before the goods are supplied, there is a change in the amount of value added tax charged, or a change to or from tax being charged on the transaction, unless the contract otherwise provides, there shall be added to or deducted from the price, an amount equal to the change.[4]

An order for goods which includes the words "contra account" may in some circumstances bear the meaning that the seller if he implements the order is obliged to order goods in exchange and he is not entitled to demand payment in cash.[5]

Where the contract is cancelled a question may arise as to whether a sum already paid to the seller is a forfeitable deposit or an instalment which should be returned to the buyer.[6] Where it is a deposit, and the contract is terminated by the buyer's repudiation, it cannot be recovered and the law as to penalties has no application.[7]

Failure to pay

The seller may raise an action for the price if the property has passed to the buyer and the buyer wrongfully neglects or refuses to pay according to the contract.[8] Unless otherwise agreed, the price is payable on delivery of the goods.[9] Where a period of credit has been agreed upon, the closure of the account does not affect the period of credit for past transactions.[10] The seller can also raise an action for the price if it is payable on a day certain irrespective of delivery although the property has not passed and the goods have not been appropriated to the contract.[11] A day certain is a

2.1

2.2

---

[1] Sale of Goods Act 1979, s.2(1).
[2] s.8(1).
[3] s.8(2); *Lennox* v. *Rennie*, 1951 S.L.T. (Notes) 78. See, as to prices to be fixed by a third party, s.9.
[4] Value Added Tax Act 1983, s.42.
[5] *Mitchell & Sons* v. *Sirdar Rubber Co. Ltd.* (1911) 27 Sh.Ct.Rep. 334.
[6] *Rohtas Industries Ltd.* v. *Urquhart Lindsay and Robertson Orchar Ltd.*, 1950 S.L.T. (Notes) 5.
[7] *Roberts & Cooper Ltd.* v. *Salvesen & Co.*, 1918 S.C. 794.
[8] Sale of Goods Act 1979, s.49(1).
[9] s.28.
[10] *Hodgmac Ltd.* v. *Gardiners of Prestwick Ltd.*, 1980 S.L.T. (Sh.Ct.) 68.
[11] s.49(2).

fixed day and not, for example, a day determined by the sending of an invoice.[12]

In the common case, when the question arises, the goods are in the possession of the buyer and the property has passed to him. The seller's only remedy is to sue for the price. He cannot recover the goods unless he can rescind the contract on the ground that the buyer induced him to enter into it by fraudulent misrepresentations and had no intention of making payment.[13] If the goods are in the buyer's possession but the property has not passed, the seller can bring an action for re-delivery.

If the goods are in the seller's possession and the property has passed to the buyer and the price is due, the seller can either sue for the price or claim damages for non-acceptance.[14] He may also, under his right of lien, retain possession of the goods until payment or tender of the price and he does not lose this right by reason only that he has obtained decree for the price of the goods.[15] Where the goods are of a perishable nature, or where the seller gives notice of his intention to resell and the buyer does not within a reasonable time pay or tender the price, the seller may resell the goods and recover from the buyer damages for any loss occasioned.[16] He need not account to the buyer for any profit on the resale.[17] Where the seller sues for damages for non-acceptance the conclusion in the action is normally to ordain the defender to pay the price to the pursuer in exchange for the goods with an alternative conclusion for damages for breach of contract. Such an action is not for a decree *ad factum praestandum* and an extract of the decree given cannot be used to enforce payment of the price. Its operative effect is to permit recovery of the damages for breach of contract.[18]

If the goods are in the seller's possession and the property has not yet passed to the buyer, the seller's normal remedy is to claim damages for non-acceptance[19] but he may alternatively sue for the price if it is payable on a day certain irrespective of delivery. If, while the goods are in the seller's possession, the buyer becomes insolvent or fails to pay the price when it is due, the seller can retain the goods until the price is paid or tendered.[20] Failing payment he can sell the goods after giving notice.[21]

Reservation of title

2.3   A contractual provision that the property in the goods will not pass to the buyer until the price has been paid will be given effect. On the sequestration of the buyer before payment, the goods, as they are still the seller's property, can be recovered from the trustee in the sequestration.[22]

---

[12] *Henderson & Keay Ltd.* v. *A. M. Carmichael Ltd.*, 1956 S.L.T. (Notes) 58.
[13] *Gamage* v. *Charlesworth's Tr.*, 1910 S.C. 257.
[14] s.50.
[15] ss.41–43. As to loss and revival of the right of lien, see *Hostess Mobile Catering* v. *Archibald Scott Ltd.*, 1981 S.C. 185.
[16] s.48(3).
[17] *R. V. Ward Ltd.* v. *Bignall* [1967] 1 Q.B. 534.
[18] *R. S. Leigh & Co.* v. *Berger & Co.*, 1958 S.L.T. (Sh.Ct.) 21.
[19] s.50; *Brown* v. *Carron Co.* (1898) 6 S.L.T. 231; the conclusion will be the one mentioned in the last paragraph.
[20] s.39(2).
[21] *Scott* v. *Marshall*, 1949 S.L.T. (Notes) 35.
[22] *Aluminium Industrie B.V.* v. *Romalpa Ltd.* [1976] 1 W.L.R. 676. In *Re Bond Worth Ltd.* [1980] Ch. 228, the clause was not apt to retain title in the sellers.

If the goods have been sold by the buyer the sub-purchaser gets a good title[23] and the original seller can recover the proceeds in the hands of the sub-purchaser or, if they can be identified, from the bankrupt's estate.[24] It is thought that a clause of reservation of title which purports to extend the seller's rights to a product made from, *inter alia*, the sold goods would not be given effect in Scotland as it would be an attempt to create a security over corporeal moveables *retenta possessione*.[25] It has been held by the House of Lords that a clause which reserved title until all debts due to the sellers or members of their combine had been paid is valid.[26] An enforceable part of a retention of title clause may be severable from an unenforceable part.[27]

Representations and warranties

Not infrequently the reason for the purchaser's failure to pay the price is that a statement made by or on behalf of the seller at or about the time the contract of sale was made was untrue. Whether the falsity of the statement provides a defence to an action for the price depends on whether the statement was a warranty (a term of the contract), a representation inducing the purchaser to enter the contract, or merely an expression of opinion. If the statement was a term of the contract, the purchaser's remedy is to claim damages for breach of contract and in some circumstances he may also reject the goods.[28] If the statement was an innocent misrepresentation the remedy is rescission of the contract provided that *restitutio in integrum* is possible.[29] If the misrepresentation was negligent damages may be recoverable.[30] If the misrepresentation was fraudulent the remedy is damages and the purchaser may in his

2.4

---

[23] Sale of Goods Act 1979, s.25(1), which does not, however, apply to conditional sales regulated by statute: see para. 4.10. See *Archivent Sales & Development Ltd.* v. *Strathclyde Regional Council*, 1985 S.L.T. 154. As to the seller losing ownership by industrial accession, see *Zahnrad Fabrik Passau GmbH* v. *Terex Ltd.*, 1986 S.L.T. 84.

[24] See *Macadam* v. *Martin's Tr.* (1872) 11 M. 33. If the arrangement is a "sale and return" the buyer sells as a principal and the proceeds are not recoverable by the original seller in the buyer's sequestration: *Michelin Tyre Co. Ltd.* v. *Macfarlane (Glasgow) Ltd.*, 1917 2 S.L.T. 205. Where there is an ordinary reservation of title, on the other hand, the buyer, in a question with the original seller, sells as an agent (*Aluminium B.V.* v. *Romalpa Ltd., supra*, per Roskill L.J. at p. 690) and the proceeds are recoverable by the original seller if they are identifiable: *Michelin, supra*. It is unclear whether that result can be obtained in Scotland, by the creation of a trust: *Export Credits Guarantee Department* v. *Turner*, 1981 S.L.T. 286 and *Clark Taylor & Co. Ltd.* v. *Quality Site Development (Edinburgh) Ltd.*, 1981 S.C. 111 cannot be completely reconciled with *Tay Valley Joinery Ltd.* v. *C. F. Financial Services Ltd.*, 1987 S.L.T. 207. See Reid, 1987 S.L.T. (News) 113.

[25] See *Borden (U.K.) Ltd.* v. *Scottish Timber Products Ltd.* [1981] Ch. 25.

[26] *Armour* v. *Thyssen Edelstahlwerke A.G.*, 1990 S.L.T. 891. For a criticism of the earlier decisions to the contrary see Reid and Gretton, "All Sums Retention of Title," 1989 S.L.T. (News) 185. See also Gretton, "Romalpa Clauses and the Law of Ascription," 1988 S.L.T. (News) 4.

[27] *Glen* v. *Gilbey Vintners Ltd.*, 1986 S.L.T. 553.

[28] See next paragraph.

[29] *Stewart* v. *Kennedy* (1890) 17 R. (H.L.) 25; *Menzies* v. *Menzies* (1893) 20 R. (H.L) 108; *Manners* v. *Whitehead* (1898) 1 F. 171; *Westville Shipping Co. Ltd.* v. *Abram Steamship Co. Ltd.*, 1922 S.C. 571; 1923 S.C. (H.L.) 68. The possibility of *restitutio in integrum* is a question of circumstances: *McGuiness* v. *Anderson*, 1953 S.L.T. (Notes) 1.

[30] Law Reform (Misc. Provs.) (S.) Act 1985, s.10.

option also rescind the contract.[31] Expressions of opinion honestly held and *verba jactantia* cannot be founded on by the purchaser.[32]

The principal difficulty is to distinguish a representation from a warranty. Whether a statement is a warranty depends on whether it appears on the evidence that it was intended and understood to be a warranty.[33] Generally a statement as to a collateral matter is not a warranty.[34] It seems that a verbal statement can be a warranty even although the remainder of the contract is in writing but the presumption is against this result.[35]

Breach of contract

2.5 The Sale of Goods Act 1979 establishes implied terms as to title, description, quality and fitness for purpose[36] and the extent to which it is possible to exclude these terms is restricted.[37] Breach of a condition or a warranty implied by the Sale of Goods Act 1979 constitutes a material breach of the contract.[38] In *Millars of Falkirk Ltd.* v. *Turpie*,[39] the First Division suggested, *obiter*, that breach of an implied condition, if it is minor and remediable, may not justify rescission of the contract. It is suggested, with respect, that this doubt is unfounded. The common law was that breach of a material part of the contract justified rejection of the goods. This position was preserved in 1893 by what is now s.11(5) of the 1979 Act which provides that "failure by the seller to perform any material part of a contract of sale is a breach of contract, which entitles the buyer either within a reasonable time after delivery to reject the goods and treat the contract as repudiated, or to retain the goods and treat the failure to perform such material part as a breach which may give rise to a claim for compensation or damages." The 1893 Act had, however, introduced certain implied conditions breach of which in England gave rise to a right to treat the contract as repudiated, and certain implied warranties breach of which gave rise to a claim for damages but not to a right to reject the goods and treat the contract as repudiated. To make the Scottish position clear it was provided in s.62(1) that breach of a warranty was deemed a failure to perform a material part of the contract. This is not a definition of a warranty but a direction as to the legal effect of a breach of warranty, leading the inquirer from the implied warranties in ss.12 and 14 to the remedies in s.11. There was no need for similar clarification with regard to breach of implied conditions, because the remedy provided for England was the remedy under Scots

---

[31] *Spence* v. *Crawford*, 1939 S.C. (H.L.) 52; *Smith* v. *Sim*, 1954 S.C. 357; *McGuiness* v. *Anderson*, 1953 S.L.T. (Notes) 1: as to the measure of damages see Walker, *Civil Remedies*, p. 689.
[32] *Hamilton* v. *Duke of Montrose* (1906) 8 F. 1026; *City of Edinburgh Brewery Co.* v. *Gibson's Tr.* (1869) 7 M. 886; *Flynn* v. *Scott*, 1949 S.C. 442.
[33] *Heilbut Symons & Co.* v. *Buckleton* [1913] A.C. 30; *Hyslop* v. *Shirlaw* (1905) 7 F. 875.
[34] Gloag, p. 467; McBryde, *Contract*, Chap. 3.
[35] Gloag, p. 467; *Oscar Chess Ltd.* v. *Williams* [1957] 1 All E.R. 325.
[36] Sale of Goods Act 1979, ss.12–15.
[37] Unfair Contract Terms Act 1977, ss.20–21; *Landcatch Ltd.* v. *Marine Harvest Ltd.*, 1985 S.L.T. 478.
[38] s.61(2).
[39] 1976 S.L.T. (Notes) 66.

common law. Breach of a condition is undoubtedly a breach of a material part of the contract.

If the buyer maintains that there has been a material breach of contract he can either reject the goods and claim damages for non-delivery or retain the goods and claim damages for breach of contract.[40] If he wishes to reject he must do so within a reasonable time[41] and before he does any act in relation to the goods which is inconsistent with the seller's ownership[42]; if he has intimated acceptance of them he cannot later reject them.[43] He can reject them even if the property has passed to him[44] and even if the defect has resulted in the destruction of the goods.[45]

On rejection the buyer can retain the goods in security for the repayment of the price but not in security of a claim for damages.[46] If he intimates rejection to the seller, he is not bound to return the goods but if the goods are perishable he may be bound to sell them on the seller's behalf.[47] If the seller refuses to accept the rejection the buyer should place the goods in neutral custody and obtain a warrant for sale from the sheriff.[48] Continued use of the goods after rejection is intimated may render the rejection ineffectual.[49]

A buyer who, having paid the price, later rejects the goods, can sue the seller for repetition of the price and for damages. It seems that the claim for damages may be either in respect of a material breach under s.53 or in respect of non-delivery of goods under s.51.[50] If a buyer who has rejected goods is sued for the price his course of action is to deny liability for the price as the contract has been repudiated and to counter-claim for damages.

An ineffectual rejection does not bar a subsequent claim to retain the goods and recover damages but this alternative claim must be stated in the pleadings.[51]

If the buyer, having paid the price, wishes to retain the goods and claim damages, he must raise an action for damages. If he has not paid the price, he can set off his claim for damages against the seller's claim for the price.[52] He may, however, be required, in the discretion of the court, to consign or pay into court the price or part thereof or to give reasonable security for due payment thereof.[53] It has been said that this provision

---

[40] s.11(5).
[41] s.35; what is a reasonable time is a question of fact; the Scottish case law is collected in Walker, *Civil Remedies*, pp. 668–669.
[42] s.35; *Mechan & Sons Ltd.* v. *Bow McLachlan & Co. Ltd.*, 1910 S.C. 758.
[43] s.35; *Mechans Ltd.* v. *Highland Marine Charters Ltd.*, 1964 S.C. 48.
[44] *Nelson* v. *Wm. Chalmers & Co.*, 1913 S.C. 441.
[45] *Kinnear* v. *Brodie* (1901) 3 F. 540.
[46] *Laing* v. *Westren* (1858) 20 D. 519; *Lupton & Co.* v. *Schulze & Co.* (1900) 2 F. 1118.
[47] s.36; *Pommer* v. *Mowat* (1906) 14 S.L.T. 373.
[48] *Malcolm* v. *Cross* (1898) 25 R. 1089.
[49] *Electric Construction Co.* v. *Hurry & Young* (1897) 24 R. 312.
[50] Brown, *Sale*, p. 388.
[51] *Pollock* v. *McCrae*, 1922 S.C. (H.L.) 192; *Mechans Ltd.* v. *Highland Marine Charters Ltd.*, 1964 S.C. 48.
[52] s.53(1).
[53] s.58; in *George Cohen, Sons & Co. Ltd.* v. *Jamieson & Paterson*, 1963 S.L.T. 35, it was held that s.58 had no application where the buyer was relying on s.53(1) and could be used only where the buyer relied on s.11(5). The decision is suspect but in any event it was held that there was a common law discretion to order consignation. See also *Frimokar (U.K.) Ltd.* v. *Mobile Technical Plant (International) Ltd.*, 1990 S.L.T. 180.

applies primarily to cases where a doubt has been raised as to the buyer's financial stability but its application is not restricted to such cases.[54] If the claim for damages exceeds the amount of the price the excess can be recovered by bringing the claim for damages in the form of a counter claim. Even if the buyer's claim has been set off against the price, he may raise an action for damages if further damage is sustained.[55]

It seems that where the buyer alleges a non-material breach of contract his only remedy is to retain the goods and claim damages.[56] In the case of machinery and similar goods, if there are only slight breakages or defects, the buyer should give the seller an opportunity to remedy them.[57]

If the seller fails to deliver the goods, the buyer's remedy is to claim damages for non-delivery.[58]

Hire-purchase

2.6   A contract of hire-purchase is one in which an article is let on hire and the hirer, after making a certain number of payments of hire, has an option to purchase the goods on payment of a further sum.[59] The effects of the agreement are:
(1) the article does not become the property of the hirer until the final payment has been paid; delivery of a cheque which was subsequently dishonoured is not payment for this purpose[60];
(2) during the period of hire, the article is not subject to the diligence of the hirer's creditors[61] except diligence for[62] the landlord's hypothec[63];
(3) during the period of hire, the hirer cannot give a good title to someone who purchases the article from him,[64] except in the case of a motor vehicle which can be effectually conveyed to a "private purchaser"[65];
(4) on the sequestration of the hirer during the period of hire the article does not pass to the trustee[66];
(5) Ownership may be lost if the article becomes a heritable fixture.[67]

There are implied terms as to the title to, and as to the description, quality and fitness for purpose of the article hired.[68] The extent to which it is possible to exclude these terms or restrict liability for breach of them is

---

[54] *Porter Spiers (Leicester) Ltd.* v. *Cameron* [1950] C.L.Y. 5329.
[55] s.53(4).
[56] Gloag, p. 609; the discussion in *Robey* v. *Stein* (1900) 3 F. 278 is confusing.
[57] *Morrison & Mason* v. *Clarkson Bros.* (1898) 25 R. 427.
[58] s.51.
[59] For the statutory definition see para. 4.10.
[60] *McLaren's Tr.* v. *Argylls Ltd.*, 1915 2 S.L.T. 241.
[61] *George Hopkinson Ltd.* v. *N. G. Napier & Son*, 1953 S.C. 139.
[62] Not now for rates: Local Government (Miscellaneous Provisions) (Scotland) Act 1981, s.12.
[63] *Rudman* v. *Jay*, 1908 S.C. 552.
[64] *Helby* v. *Matthews* [1895] A.C. 471.
[65] Hire Purchase Act 1964, Pt. III, now set out in Consumer Credit Act 1974, Sched. 4, para. 22.
[66] *McLaren's Tr.* v. *Argylls Ltd.*, *supra*.
[67] *Scottish Discount Co. Ltd.* v. *Blin*, 1985 S.C. 216.
[68] Supply of Goods (Implied Terms) Act 1973, ss.8–11 (as amended by Consumer Credit Act 1974, Sched. 4, para. 35). As to the common law, see *Brown* v. *Brecknell, Munro & Rogers (1928) Ltd.* (1938) 54 Sh.Ct.Rep. 254.

restricted.[69] The hirer has a title to sue for recovery of the goods from a third party.[70]

At common law, the following debts due to the owner may arise:
(1) a claim for arrears of hire payments;
(2) a claim for an amount payable in terms of the contract if the hirer exercises his option to terminate the contract; this claim cannot be treated as a penalty[71];
(3) a claim for damages; on repudiation of the contract by the hirer, the damages recoverable are the hire-purchase price under deduction of (i) instalments already paid, (ii) the value of the goods repossessed, (iii) the amount payable on exercise of the option to purchase, (iv) a discount for the earlier return to the owner of his capital outlay.[72] In England it has been held that failure to pay two instalments is not a repudiation by the hirer and the owner could only recover the arrears on retaking the goods.[73] There is no doubt that the owner can retake possession and sue for arrears.[74]

Professional services

If there is an express agreement as to the remuneration for the services, this must rule[75] even if it does not conform to the scale laid down by the professional institute.[76] If there is no express agreement, there is no presumption that the services have been rendered gratuitously.[77] If there has been a usage between the parties of payment at a certain rate this will rule.[78] If there is no such usage, the matter is regulated by the custom of the profession if this is reasonable, certain and notorious.[79] It is not necessary to prove that the employer knew of the custom if it is so well recognised that it ought to have been known.[80] A scale of charges fixed by a general consensus of the profession concerned has "very high authority"[81] but the court need not adopt such a scale if it regards the charges as unreasonable.[82] If there is no acceptable custom, the court fixes a reasonable remuneration.[83] The test is "what a man of business, having knowledge of the question, would fix as fair remuneration."[84]

2.7

A charge for medical advice or attendance or for the performance of an operation or for a medicine which the pursuer has both prescribed and

---

[69] Unfair Contract Terms Act 1977, s.20.
[70] *McArthur* v. *O'Donnell*, 1969 S.L.T. (Sh.Ct.) 24.
[71] *Bell Brothers (H.P.) Ltd.* v. *Aitken*, 1939 S.C. 577; *Granor Finance Ltd.* v. *Liqr. of Eastore Ltd.*, 1974 S.L.T. 296.
[72] *Yeoman Credit Ltd.* v. *Waragowski* [1961] 1 W.L.R. 1124; *Overstone Ltd.* v. *Shipway* [1962] 1 W.L.R. 117; *Yeoman Credit Ltd.* v. *McLean* [1962] 1 W.L.R. 131.
[73] *Financings Ltd.* v. *Baldock* [1963] 2 Q.B. 104.
[74] *Bowmaker (Commercial) Ltd.* v. *Dunnigan*, 1976 S.L.T. (Sh.Ct.) 54.
[75] *Arthur Duthie & Co. Ltd.* v. *Merson & Gerry*, 1947 S.C. 43. But, as to solicitors, see the next paragraph.
[76] *Wilkie* v. *Scottish Aviation Ltd.*, 1956 S.C. 198.
[77] *Landless* v. *Wilson* (1880) 8 R. 289; *Macintyre Bros.* v. *Smith*, 1913 S.C. 129.
[78] *Eunson* v. *Johnson & Greig*, 1940 S.C. 49.
[79] *Hogarth & Sons* v. *Leith Cotton Seed Oil Co.*, 1909 S.C. 955; *Wilkie* v. *Scottish Aviation Ltd.*, supra.
[80] *"Strathlorne" S.S. Co.* v. *Baird & Sons Ltd.*, 1916 S.C. (H.L.) 134.
[81] Per L.P. Dunedin, *Welsh & Forbes* v. *Johnston* (1906) 8 F. 453 at 456.
[82] *Wilkie* v. *Scottish Aviation Ltd.*, supra.
[83] Gloag, p. 294; *Clyde Air Extraction Ltd.* v. *Helmville Ltd.* 1964 S.L.T. (Sh.Ct.) 49.
[84] *Brownlie, Watson & Beckett* v. *Caledonian Ry. Co.*, 1907 S.C. 617.

supplied cannot be recovered unless the pursuer proves that he is a fully registered medical practitioner.[85] If a fellow of a college of physicians is prohibited by bye-law from recovering his charges, the bye-law may be pleaded in bar of proceedings.

Solicitor's account

2.8 In an action by a solicitor or his representatives for payment of an account of expenses due by a client, the court must remit the account for taxation and no decree shall be pronounced either in absence or after hearing parties, without a report having been made by the auditor.[86] Any table of fees of the Law Society of Scotland is not the full and final test by which the auditor is bound to fix the fee.[87] It seems that an agreement between solicitor and client for remuneration in excess of the authorised scale is unenforceable.[88]

Contracts for repairs, etc.

2.9 The contract may be made even although the identity of the person giving the order is not disclosed.[89] Where the owner of a damaged car has it taken to a garage and the cost of repairs is subsequently agreed by the owner's insurers before the work is done, the contract for repairs is between the insurers and the garage.[90] There is no general rule that the insurer acts as agent of the owner in instructing the repairs.[91] An "estimate" will be regarded as an offer.[92] A request for an estimate for repairs does not create a liability for work involved in putting the article in a state for inspection.[93] But there may be circumstances in which preparatory work for a contract may be the subject of a *quantum meruit* claim.[94] Additional work of an extensive and costly nature should be preceded by a further estimate and instruction by the employer.[95] If there is no estimate the account must be on a "time and materials" basis.[96] It is not enough for the contractors to prove the number of man-hours actually spent on the job; they must prove what would have been a reasonable charge for the time normally spent in carrying out the job.[97] If the evidence is sketchy the court must do its best on the material available.[98] A custom of trade can be relied upon only if it is certain, uniform, reasonable and notorious.[99] Interest is allowed on a *quantum*

---

[85] Medical Act 1983, s.46.

[86] R.C. 350(c); Macphail, *Sheriff Court Practice*, pp. 707–708; *W. & A. S. Bruce* v. *Ewans*, 1986 S.L.T. (Sh.Ct.) 20. But see Solicitors (Scotland) Act 1980, s.61A(1) and Legal Aid (Scotland) Act 1986, s.33(6).

[87] *Davidson & Syme, W.S.* v. *Booth*, 1972 S.L.T. 122.

[88] *Anstruther* v. *Wilkie* (1856) 18 D. 405; *Moir* v. *Robertson*, 1924 S.L.T. 435.

[89] *Craik* v. *Glasgow Taxicab Co. Ltd.* (1911) 27 Sh.Ct.Rep. 157.

[90] *McCallum* v. *Wilson*, 1974 S.L.T. (Sh.Ct.) 72.

[91] *Kirklands Garage (Kinross) Ltd.* v. *Clark*, 1967 S.L.T. (Sh.Ct.) 60.

[92] *Croshaw* v. *Pritchard and Renwick* (1899) 16 T.L.R. 45.

[93] *Murray* v. *Fairlie Yacht Slip Ltd.*, 1975 S.L.T. (Sh.Ct.) 62.

[94] *Pillans & Wilson* v. *Castlecary Fireclay Co. Ltd.*, 1931 S.L.T. 532. But see *Site Preparations Ltd.* v. *Secretary of State for Scotland*, 1975 S.L.T. (Notes) 41.

[95] *Walter Wright & Co. Ltd.* v. *Cowdray*, 1973 S.L.T. (Sh.Ct.) 56.

[96] *James Erskine* v. *Weibye*, 1976 S.L.T. (Sh.Ct.) 14.

[97] *Scottish Motor Traction Co.* v. *Murphy*, 1949 S.L.T. (Notes) 39.

[98] *Mellor* v. *Wm. Beardmore & Co.*, 1927 S.C. 597; *Sinclair* v. *Logan*, 1961 S.L.T. (Sh.Ct.) 10; *Robert Allan and Partners* v. *McKinstray*, 1975 S.L.T. (Sh.Ct.) 63.

[99] *Dalblair Motors Ltd.* v. *J. Forrest & Son (Ayr) Ltd.* (1954) 70 Sh.Ct.Rep. 107.

meruit claim from the date of citation.[1] A tradesman has an obligation to carry out the contract work properly unless he either makes it known to the employer before making the contract that the job requires more special skill than he commands or can show that the customer was aware of that when contracting with him.[2] Where, under the contract, work is to be done to the satisfaction of a specified person, in an action for the price there must be an averment that the person is satisfied or his judgment must be impugned in some way.[3] In the repair of machinery, the employer cannot recover the account of other repairers as damages unless he gave the original repairers an opportunity to remedy the defect.[4] Failure to pay a part of the contract price at the stipulated time may entitle the contractor to rescind the contract.[5]

Building contracts

Where there has been defective performance of a building contract, the legal position is not clear. A distinction is made between lump sum contracts and measure and value contracts. A contract which sets figures against certain branches of the work, the aggregate of which makes up the total contract price, is a lump sum contract.[6] If the contractor does not complete a lump sum contract, he cannot sue for the price. If the work has been completed but there has been an unauthorised material deviation from the terms of the contract, the contractor cannot recover the price; the employer can either call upon the contractor to remove his materials from the ground or retain them subject to the contractor's claim against him *in quantum lucratus est*.[7] If, in a lump sum contract, the deviation is not material and can be remedied, the contractor can recover the price under deduction of the cost of bringing the work into conformity with the contract.[7] If the deviation is not material but cannot be remedied, the position is doubtful; it may be that the contractor can recover the price under deduction of the damage sustained by the employer.[8] If the parties have agreed to a material alteration in a lump sum contract, it is treated on a time and material basis.[9]

2.10

In the case of a measure and value contract, the contractor can recover the appropriate sums due for items completed conform to contract even although there are other defective items.[10] It seems, however, that the

---

[1] *Keir Ltd.* v. *East of Scotland Water Board*, 1976 S.L.T. (Notes) 72.
[2] *Brett* v. *Williamson*, 1980 S.L.T. (Sh.Ct.) 56; *Macintosh* v. *Nelson*, 1984 S.L.T. (Sh.Ct.) 82.
[3] *Kidd and Sons* v. *Bain* (1913) 29 Sh.Ct.Rep. 123.
[4] *Brown* v. *Nisbet & Co. Ltd.* (1941) 57 Sh.Ct.Rep. 202.
[5] *Fixby Engineering Co. Ltd.* v. *Auchlochan Sand and Gravel Co. Ltd.*, 1974 S.L.T. (Sh.Ct.) 58.
[6] *Gray & Son Ltd.* v. *Stern*, 1953 S.L.T. (Sh.Ct.) 34.
[7] *Ramsay* v. *Brand* (1898) 25 R. 1212; *Spiers* v. *Peterson*, 1924 S.C. 428; *McKillop* v. *Mutual Securities Ltd.*, 1945 S.C. 166; *Franco-British Electrical Co.* v. *Jean Dougall Macdonald Ltd.* (1949) 65 Sh.Ct.Rep. 82; *Stewart Roofing Co. Ltd.* v. *Shanlin* (1958) 74 Sh.Ct.Rep. 134.
[8] Gloag & Henderson, p. 147; *Anderson* v. *Dow* (1907) 23 Sh.Ct.Rep. 51.
[9] *Mercer* v. *Wright* (1953) 69 Sh.Ct.Rep. 39.
[10] *Forrest* v. *Scottish County Investment Co.*, 1916 S.C. (H.L.) 28, *per* Lord Parmoor at p. 36. *Steel* v. *Young*, 1907 S.C. 360, must now be doubted—see the authorities cited in *Stewart Roofing Co. Ltd.* v. *Shanlin, supra.*

employer can deduct or set off any damage sustained by him in respect of the defective items.

In prime cost contracts, the employer should challenge any item in a monthly account at the time he receives it and once he has made payment of the monthly account, if he later challenges an item in it, the onus is on him to show why it should not stand.[11]

In a lump sum contract, if the parties agree on major modifications which are so fundamental that they result in frustration of the contract, the contractor can recover on a *quantum meruit* basis.[12]

Sale of heritage

2.11 The terms of the missives may show that a provision that the price is payable on a particular date is an essential stipulation, breach of which entitles the seller to resile from the contract. Normally, however, such a provision is not an essential stipulation; if there is unnecessary or unjustifiable delay in paying the price the seller's remedy is to intimate to the buyer a reasonable time within which payment must be made; failure to pay in the period entitles the seller to rescind.[13] His duty to mitigate his loss arises at the expiry of the period.[14] There may be circumstances in which the seller can rescind after the elapse of a reasonable time even although no limit was imposed.[15]

If the price is payable on a fixed date the seller can sue for the price provided that he is able and willing to give the buyer a good title.[16]

If the buyer has been given entry to the subjects of sale, the seller may raise an action for payment of the price with alternative conclusions for declarator that the buyer is in material breach of the contract, decree of removal and damages representing the loss on resale. It is competent to take decree for payment of the price and subsequently to obtain decree in terms of the alternative conclusions.[17] Interest is due on the price if the buyer has taken possession of the subjects.[18]

Where a contract of sale is subject to a suspensive condition, purification of which is not within the power of the parties, the contract is terminated if the condition is not fulfilled within a reasonable time, there being in this situation, of course, no breach of contract.[19] The contract may fix a date for fulfilment of the condition. A condition may be waived if it is purely in the interest of one party[20] unless it is inextricably connected with other parts of the contract and cannot be severed from them.[21] A claim to recover sums paid to account of the price of a house

---

[11] *Johnston v. Greenock Corporation*, 1951 S.L.T. (Notes) 57.

[12] *Head Wrightson Aluminium Ltd. v. Aberdeen Harbour Commissioners*, 1958 S.L.T. (Notes) 12.

[13] *Burns v. Garscadden* (1901) 8 S.L.T. 321; *Rodger (Builders) Ltd. v. Fawdry*, 1950 S.C. 483, per Lord Sorn at p. 492; *Inveresk Paper Co. v. Pembry Machinery Co. Ltd.*, 1972 S.L.T. (Notes) 63; *Lloyds Bank Ltd. v. Bauld*, 1976 S.L.T. (Notes) 53.

[14] *Johnstone v. Harris*, 1977 S.C. 365.

[15] *George Packman & Sons v. Dunbar's Trs.*, 1977 S.L.T. 140.

[16] *British Railways Board v. Birrell*, 1971 S.L.T. (Notes) 17.

[17] *Bosco Design Services Ltd. v. Plastic Sealant Services Ltd.*, 1979 S.C. 189; *Tiffney v. Bachurzewski*, 1984 S.C. 108, is a case of confused pleadings.

[18] *Thomson v. Vernon*, 1983 S.L.T. (Sh.Ct.) 17.

[19] *T. Boland & Co. Ltd. v. Dundas's Trs.*, 1975 S.L.T. (Notes) 80.

[20] See, *e.g. Gilchrist v. Paton*, 1979 S.C. 380.

[21] *Zebmoon Ltd. v. Akinbrook Investment Developments Ltd.*, 1988 S.L.T. 146.

must be founded on a probative writ.[22] A stipulation in a contract for purchase of heritage by instalments that if an instalment was unpaid when the next fell due, the buyer would lose all right to acquire the house and to recover instalments already paid, has been held not to be a penalty.[23]

The buyer may refuse to implement the contract if the seller cannot grant a disposition in compliance with the missives; he can resile from the contract and recover the price if it has been paid.[24] If the seller fails to implement the contract, the buyer may bring an action for implement of the missives together with an alternative conclusion for damages.[25]

If there is a defect in the subjects as set forth in the disposition after delivery of the disposition the buyer's only remedy is to claim damages under the warrandice clause.[26] If the disposition does not convey what is in the missives the buyer's remedy is to raise an action for reduction of the disposition and implement of the missives.[27] Where there is a breach of a collateral obligation in the missives, an obligation in respect of which the disposition does not supersede the missives, an action for damages resembling the *actio quanti minoris* is competent.[28] The buyer cannot bring such an action if he has failed to pay the price.[29]

Electricity and gas

Where gas or electricity is supplied through a meter, the register of the meter is *prima facie* evidence of the quantity supplied.[30]

2.12

A consumer of electricity must give two working days notice before he quits premises supplied with electricity. If he fails to do so he is liable to the supplier for sums in respect of supply up to the next usual meter reading or the date when the subsequent occupier requires the supplier to supply electricity to the premises or the second working day after he gives notice to the supplier, whichever shall first occur.[31] There is a similar provision for gas.[32] If the occupier of premises supplied by gas quits the premises without paying amounts due for supply, the gas supplier is not entitled to require payment from the next occupier.[33]

If a person neglects to pay a charge for electricity or any other sum due in respect of the supply of electricity, the supplier may after two working days' notice cut off the supply and recover the expenses of so doing.[34]

If a person has not, 28 days after a demand in writing, made payment of charges due by him in respect of the supply of gas, the gas supplier, after

---

[22] *Cord* v. *Gormley*, 1971 S.L.T. (Sh.Ct.) 19.
[23] *Reid* v. *Campbell*, 1958 S.L.T. (Sh.Ct.) 45. But see, now, para. 4.12.
[24] *Crofts* v. *Stewart's Trs.*, 1927 S.C. (H.L.) 65 (minerals); *Campbell* v. *McCutcheon*, 1963 S.C. 505 (minerals); *Armia Ltd.* v. *Daejan Developments Ltd.*, 1979 S.C. (H.L.) 56 (undisclosed right of access); *Stuart* v. *Lort-Phillips*, 1977 S.C. 244 (vacant possession); *Kelly* v. *A. & J. Clark Ltd.*, 1967 S.L.T. (Notes) 115 (undisclosed restrictions).
[25] *Mackay* v. *Campbell*, 1967 S.C. (H.L.) 53.
[26] *Welsh* v. *Russell* (1894) 21 R. 769.
[27] *Equitable Loan Company of Scotland Ltd.* v. *Storie*, 1972 S.L.T. (Notes) 20.
[28] *McKillop* v. *Mutual Securities Ltd.*, 1945 S.C. 166; *Bradley* v. *Scott*, 1966 S.L.T. (Sh.Ct.) 25; *Hoey* v. *Butler*, 1975 S.C. 87.
[29] *Hayes* v. *Robinson*, 1984 S.L.T. 300.
[30] Gas Act 1986, Sched. 5, para. 5(1); Electricity Act 1989, Sched. 7, para. 9.
[31] Electricity Act 1989, Sched. 6, para. 1(3).
[32] Gas Act 1986, Sched. 5, para. 7(2).
[33] para. 7(4).
[34] Electricity Act 1989, Sched. 6, para. 1(6).

seven days' notice, may cut off the supply of gas to the premises and the expense thus incurred is recoverable in like manner as charges for gas. There is no obligation to restore the supply until payment has been made of all sums due and of the expenses of reconnection.[35] These remedies cannot be used after sequestration or liquidation.[36]

---

[35] Gas Act 1986, Sched. 5, para. 7(5),(6).
[36] Electricity Act 1989, Sched. 6, para. 1(8).

CHAPTER 3

THE CONSUMER CREDIT ACT

Credit

Credit has been regarded as a species of trust: "Trust, in the vulgar acceptation, comprehends all personal obligations for paying, delivering or performing, anything where the creditor has no real right in security; for thereby he trusts more to the faithfulness of his debtors, that they did not engage to what they were not able to perform, and that they would not disappoint their performance by disposing of their means in the creditor's prejudice."[1]

3.1

A person obtains credit if he obtains an immediate benefit or advantage in consideration of an obligation to pay money at a future date. The benefit may be the use of cash, the use and possession of goods which at some time are to become his property, or services. It has been held in a matter of statutory interpretation that the receipt of money on a promise to render services or deliver goods in the future is not credit.[2]

Extortionate credit bargains

One of the most important provisions of the Consumer Credit Act 1974 is that the court is given power, if it finds a "credit bargain" to be extortionate, to reopen the credit agreement so as to do justice between the parties.[3] The operation of this power is not restricted to regulated consumer credit agreements; it is not subject to a financial limit; "exempt" agreements[4] are affected by it.

3.2

A "credit agreement" is an agreement between an individual and any other person by which that person provides credit of any amount. A "credit bargain" is the credit agreement if no other transaction is to be taken into account in computing the total charge for credit; otherwise it means the credit agreement and those other transactions taken together.[5]

A credit bargain is extortionate if it requires the debtor or a relative of his to make payments (whether unconditionally, or on certain contingencies) which are grossly exorbitant or if it otherwise grossly contravenes ordinary principles of fair dealing.[6] In considering whether the bargain is extortionate, regard is to be had to such evidence as is adduced concerning: interest rates prevailing when the bargain was made; the debtor's age, experience, business capacity and state of health; the degree to which, at the time of making the bargain, he was under financial pressure, and the nature of that pressure; the degree of risk accepted by the creditor, having regard to the value of any security provided; the creditor's relationship to the debtor; whether or not a colourable cash price was quoted for any goods or services included in the credit bargain; in relation to a linked transaction, how far the transaction was reasonably

---

[1] Stair, IV, vi, 1.
[2] *Fisher* v. *Raven* [1964] A.C. 210.
[3] s.137(1).
[4] See para. 3.4.
[5] s.137(2). As to the total charge for credit, see para. 3.6.
[6] s.138(1). See Wilkinson (1979) 8 *Anglo-American Law Review* 240.

required for the protection of the debtor or creditor or was in the interest of the debtor; any other relevant considerations.[7] There is no rule that a rate of interest not exceeding 48 per cent. cannot be exorbitant.[8] If the debtor or any "surety" alleges that the bargain is extortionate it is for the creditor to prove the contrary.[9] A "surety" is the person by whom any security is provided, or the person to whom his rights and duties in relation to the security have passed by assignation or operation of law.[10]

The credit agreement may be reopened, if the court "thinks just" on the ground that the credit bargain is extortionate: (a) on any application by the debtor or any surety to the Court of Session or sheriff court (which may be the sheriff court for the district in which the debtor or surety resides or carries on business); or (b) at the instance of the debtor or surety in any proceedings to which the debtor and creditor are parties, being proceedings to enforce the credit agreement, any security relating to it, or any linked transaction; or (c) at the instance of the debtor or surety in other proceedings in any court where the amount paid or payable under the credit agreement is relevant.[11]

In reopening the agreement the court may, to relieve the debtor or surety from payment of any sum in excess of that fairly due and reasonable, direct an accounting to be made, set aside obligations, require the creditor to make repayments, direct the return of the property to the surety or alter the terms of the credit agreement or of any security instrument.[12] These measures may be taken notwithstanding that their effect is to place a burden on the creditor in respect of an advantage unfairly enjoyed by another person who is a party to a linked transaction. The terms of the statute do not seem to allow the court to adjust a linked transaction entered into by a relative of the debtor.[13]

Consumer Credit Act: definitions

3.3   A *personal credit agreement* is "an agreement between an individual ('the debtor') and any other person ('the creditor') by which the creditor provides the debtor with credit of any amount."[14] An "individual" includes a partnership or other unincorporated body of persons not consisting entirely of bodies corporate.[15] "Credit" includes a cash loan and any other form of financial accommodation[16]; where it is provided otherwise than in sterling it is treated as provided in sterling of an equivalent amount.[17] A hire-purchase agreement is regarded as a provision of a fixed-sum credit to finance the transaction of an amount

---

[7] s.138(2)–(5). See *A. Ketley Ltd. v. Scott.* [1981] I.C.R. 241; *Davis v. Directloans Ltd.* [1986] 2 All E.R. 783; *Wills v. Wood* (1984) 128 S.J. 222.

[8] *Castle Phillips Finance Ltd. v. Williams* [1986] C.C.L.R. 13.

[9] s.171(7). See *Coldunell Ltd. v. Gallon* [1986] Q.B. 1184.

[10] s.189(1).

[11] s.139(1).

[12] s.139(2).

[13] Bennion (1977) 121 S.J. 822.

[14] s.8(1). There is a question as to whether a cheque card agreement is a personal credit agreement (notwithstanding Sched. 2, Ex. 21) as the bank does not agree to the creation of an overdraft although it must honour cheques drawn by use of the card: Dobson [1977] J.B.L. 126.

[15] s.189(1).

[16] s.9(1).

[17] s.9(2).

Definitions

equal to the total price of the goods less the aggregate of the deposit (in any) and the total charge for credit.[18] An item entering into the total charge for credit is not treated as credit even though time is allowed for its payment.[19] The amounts of the following charges are included in the total charge for credit[20]: (a) the total amount of the interest on the credit, and (b) other charges at any time payable under the transaction by or on behalf of the debtor or a relative of his whether to the creditor or any other person, notwithstanding that the whole or part of the charge may be repayable at any time or that the consideration therefor may include matters not within the transaction or subsisting at a time not within the duration of the agreement. The following are excluded from the total charge for credit:

(a) charges payable to the creditor upon failure by the debtor or his relative to do or refrain from doing anything which he is required to do or to refrain from doing;
(b) any charge relating to an agreement to finance a transaction between the debtor and the creditor, or between the debtor and a person other than the creditor, being a charge which would be payable if the transaction were for cash;
(c) any charge (other than a fee or commission charged by a credit-broker) not within (b) which relates to services or benefits incidental to the agreement and also to other services or benefits which may be supplied to the debtor and which is payable under an obligation under arrangements effected before the debtor applied to enter into the agreement, not being arrangements under which the debtor is bound to enter into any personal credit agreement;
(d) certain charges for the care, maintenance or protection of any land or goods;
(e) certain charges for money transmission services;
(f) certain insurance premiums.

A *consumer credit agreement* is a personal credit agreement by which the creditor provides the debtor with credit not exceeding £15,000.[21] (There is power to alter this amount[22]). A consumer credit agreement is a *regulated agreement* if it is not an "exempt agreement."[23] A consumer hire agreement is a regulated agreement if it is not an exempt agreement.[24] A *consumer hire agreement* is an agreement for the hiring of goods to an individual, which is not a hire-purchase agreement, which is capable of subsisting for more than three months and which does not require the hirer to make payments exceeding £15,000.[25] Value added tax is taken to be part of the payments for purposes of the limit.[26]

---

[18] s.9(3).
[19] s.9(4).
[20] s.20; Consumer Credit (Total Charge for Credit) Regulations, 1980 (S.I. 1980 No. 51) (am. by S.I.s 1985 No. 1192, 1989 No. 596) regs. 4, 5.
[21] s.8(2); Consumer Credit (Increase of Monetary Amounts) Order 1983 (S.I. 1983 No. 1878).
[22] s.181(1).
[23] s.8(3). An agreement made before April 1, 1977 is not a regulated agreement: Sched. 3, para. 1: S.I. 1977 No. 325.
[24] s.15(2).
[25] s.15(1); (S.I. 1983 No. 1878).
[26] *Apollo Leasing Ltd.* v. *Scott*, 1984 S.L.T. (Sh.Ct.) 90.

A *running-account credit* is a facility under a personal credit agreement whereby the debtor can receive cash, goods and services to a value such that, taking repayments by the debtor into account, the credit limit is not exceeded, the credit limit being in any period the maximum debit balance permissible in the period, disregarding any term of the agreement which allows the maximum to be exceeded temporarily.[27] For purposes of the £15,000 limit in the definition of a consumer credit agreement, the running-account credit is taken not to exceed £15,000 if the credit limit does not exceed £15,000; but even if there is no credit limit or a limit exceeding £15,000 the credit may be taken not to exceed £15,000 if the debtor cannot draw more than £15,000 at one time *or* if the credit charge increases or the agreement otherwise becomes more onerous when the debit balance rises above a given amount less than £15,000 *or* if "at the time the agreement is made it is probable, having regard to the terms of the agreement and any other relevant considerations, that the debit balance will not at any time rise above" £15,000.[28] If the agreement contains a term signifying that in the opinion of the parties that condition is not satisfied it shall be taken not to be satisfied unless the contrary is proved.[29] A bank overdraft is an example of a running-account credit.[30] A *fixed-sum credit* is any facility other than a running-account credit under a personal credit agreement whereby the debtor is enabled to receive credit in one amount or by instalments.[31] An ordinary loan granted in a number of instalments is a fixed-sum credit[32] and so is a hire-purchase agreement.[33]

A *restricted-use credit agreement* is a regulated consumer credit agreement:
(a) to finance a transaction between the debtor and the creditor, or
(b) to finance a transaction between the debtor and a person (the "supplier") other than the creditor, or
(c) to refinance any existing indebtedness of the debtor's whether to the creditor or another person.[34]

If the credit is supplied in such a way in fact that the debtor is free to use it as he chooses, even though certain uses would contravene the agreement or any other agreement, it is not a restricted-use agreement.[35] An *unrestricted-use credit agreement* is a regulated consumer credit agreement which is not a restricted-use agreement.[36]

A *debtor-creditor-supplier agreement*[37] is a regulated consumer credit agreement in which the creditor has a connection with the goods or services supplied. There are three kinds:

---

[27] s.10.
[28] s.10(3).
[29] s.171(1).
[30] Sched. 2, Exs. 18, 23.
[31] s.10(1)(*b*).
[32] Ex. 9.
[33] Ex. 10.
[34] s.11(1).
[35] s.11(3).
[36] s.11(2).
[37] s.12. There is a circuity in the definitions in that the debtor-creditor-supplier and debtor-creditor agreements are defined as regulated agreements. Consumer credit agreements which are not exempt agreements are regulated agreements. Some exempt agreements are defined as debtor-creditor-supplier or debtor-creditor agreements.

Exempt Agreements

(i) an agreement of type (a) *supra*, such as a hire-purchase transaction;
(ii) an agreement of type (b) *supra* made by the creditor under pre-existing arrangements,[38] or in contemplation of future arrangements, between himself and the supplier, *e.g.* a credit card agreement;
(iii) an unrestricted-use agreement made by the creditor under pre-existing arrangements between himself and a supplier in the knowledge that the credit is to be used to finance a transaction between the debtor and the supplier.

A *debtor-creditor agreement*[39] is a regulated consumer credit agreement where the creditor has no connection with the goods or services supplied. There are three kinds:
(i) an agreement of type (b) *supra*, not made by the creditor under arrangements or in contemplation of future arrangements between himself and the supplier;
(ii) an agreement of type (c) *supra*;
(iii) an unrestricted use agreement where there are no pre-existing arrangements between the creditor and a supplier.

Exempt agreements

Exempt agreements are defined partly by s.16 of the Act and partly by an order made thereunder. The first group of exemptions consists of certain agreements where the creditor is a local authority: **3.4**

(1) debtor-creditor-supplier agreements where the creditor is a local authority and the agreement finances the purchase of land or the provision of dwellings on any land and is secured on that land.[40]
(2) debtor-creditor agreements where the creditor is a local authority and the agreement is secured on land.[41]
(3) debtor-creditor-supplier agreements secured on land where the creditor is a local authority and the agreement finances a linked transaction relating to an agreement which is of the type described in (1) *supra* and relates to the security subjects or which is of the type described in (2) *supra* and finances the purchase of the security subjects or the provision of dwellings thereon.[42]

The next five exemptions are cases where the creditor is what might be termed a "reliable lender." This category includes building societies, banks and wholly owned subsidiaries of banks and then there is a list of

---

[38] An agreement is made under pre-existing arrangements if it is made in accordance with, or in furtherance of, arrangements previously made between the creditor or his associate and the supplier or his associate: s.187(1). Associates are, broadly, relatives, partners and controlled bodies corporate: s.184. An agreement is entered into in contemplation of future arrangements if it is entered into in the expectation that arrangements will subsequently be made between the creditor or his associates and a supplier or his associates for the supply of cash, goods and services to be financed by the agreement: s.187(2). Arrangements are to be disregarded if the creditor holds himself out as willing to make payments to suppliers generally: s.187(3); or if they are for the electronic transfer of funds from a current account at a bank: s.187(3A) (ins. by Banking Act 1987, s.89).
[39] s.13. See also *supra*, note 37.
[40] s.16(1), (2)(*a*).
[41] s.16(1), (2)(*b*).
[42] s.16(1), (2)(*c*).

specified bodies which consists of insurance companies, friendly societies and charities[43]:

(4) debtor-creditor-supplier agreements where the creditor is a "reliable lender" and the agreement finances the purchase of land or the provision of dwellings on any land and is secured on that land or is an agreement of the type described in (3) *supra*.[44]

(5) debtor-creditor agreements secured on land where the creditor is a "reliable lender" and the agreement is to finance the purchase of land or the provision of dwellings or business premises on any land.[45]

(6) debtor-creditor agreements secured on land where (a) the creditor is a "reliable lender," (b) the agreement is to finance the alteration, enlarging, repair or improvement of a dwelling or business premises on any land, (c) the creditor is a creditor under either (i) an agreement (whenever made) ("the related agreement") secured on that land by which the debtor was provided with credit for the purchase of that land or the provision of dwellings or business premises thereon or (ii) an agreement ("the related agreement") refinancing such an agreement, relating to and secured on that land (it should be noted that the land on which the "alteration credit agreement" is secured need not be the land on which the alterations are made).[46]

(7) a debtor-creditor agreement secured on land where the creditor is a "reliable lender," the agreement finances the alteration, enlarging, repair or improvement of a dwelling or business premises on any land and a debtor-creditor agreement ("the related agreement") to finance the alteration, enlarging, repair or improvement of a dwelling, secured on that dwelling, is made as a result of certain services provided by a housing association or another specified kind of body.[47]

(8) debtor-creditor agreements secured on land where the creditor is a "reliable lender" and the agreement refinances any existing indebtedness of the debtor's, whether to the creditor or another person, under an agreement by which the debtor was provided with credit for the purchase of land or the provision of dwellings or business premises on any land or the alteration, enlarging, repair or improvement of a dwelling or business premises on any land and there is a related agreement of the kinds described in (6) and (7).[48]

Then there are two cases where the exemption is more restricted:

(9) agreements where the creditor is not a local authority but a specified public corporation[49] and the agreement is of a description specified in relation to that body.[50]

(10) agreements where the creditor is a specified body[51] named or

---

[43] s.16(1); Consumer Credit (Exempt Agreements) Order 1989 (S.I. 1989 No. 869, am. by S.I. 1989 No. 1841 and 1989 No. 2337), Sched 1, Pt. I.
[44] S.I. 1989 No. 869, art. 2(2)(*a*).
[45] *Ibid.*, art. 2(2)(*b*).
[46] Art. 2(2)(*b*), (3)(i).
[47] Art. 2(2)(*b*), (3)(ii).
[48] Art. 2(2)(*c*).
[49] Sched. 1, Pt. II.
[50] Art. 2(4).
[51] Sched. 1, Pt. III.

referred to in the Housing Act 1985 and the agreement is of types (4) to (8) *supra* and advances money on the security of a dwelling-house.[52]

Then there are five exemptions defined by the number of payments to be made by the debtor:

(11) debtor-creditor-supplier agreements for a fixed-sum credit where the number of payments[53] to be made by the debtor does not exceed four and those payments are required to be made within a period of 12 months beginning with the date of the agreement with the exception of (a) agreements financing the purchase of land; (b) conditional sale agreements and hire-purchase agreements; and (c) agreements secured by a pledge (other than a pledge of documents of title or of bearer bonds).[54] This will cover the normal credit given by, say, a department store.

(12) debtor-creditor-supplier agreements for running-account credit providing for payments by the debtor in relation to specified periods and requiring that the number of payments[53] to be made in repayment of the whole amount of the credit provided in each such period shall not exceed one.[55] There are the same exceptions as in (11). This will cover the monthly bills for milk and newspapers and some types of credit card.

(13) debtor-creditor-supplier agreements financing the purchase of land where the number of payments[56] to be made by the debtor does not exceed four.[57]

(14) debtor-creditor-supplier agreements for fixed-sum credit to finance a premium under an insurance contract relating to land or to anything thereon where: (a) the creditor is the creditor under an agreement secured on that land which is exempt under (1)–(10) *supra* or is a personal credit agreement which would be so exempt if the credit did not exceed £15,000, (b) the credit is to be repaid within the period to which the premium relates, not being a period exceeding 12 months, (c) there is no charge for credit other than interest not exceeding the rate charged under the agreement mentioned in (a) *supra*; (d) the number of payments[56] to be made by the debtor does not exceed 12.[58]

(15) debtor-creditor-supplier agreements for fixed-sum credit where (a) the creditor is the creditor under an agreement secured on land which is exempt under (1)–(10) *supra* or is a personal credit agreement which would be so exempt if the credit did not exceed £15,000, (b) the agreement is to finance a premium under a life insurance contract which provides for payment on the death of the life insured of a sum not exceeding the amount sufficient to defray the sums which immediately after the credit under the agreement referred to in (a) *supra* has been advanced would have been payable

---

[52] Art. 2(5).
[53] "Payment" means a payment comprising an amount in respect of credit with or without any other amount.
[54] Art. 3(1)(*a*)(i).
[55] Art. 3(1)(*a*)(ii).
[56] "Payment" means a payment comprising or including an amount in respect of credit or the total charge for credit (if any).
[57] Art. 3(1)(*b*).
[58] Art. 3(1)(*c*).

to the creditor in respect of the credit and the total charge therefor, (c) there is no charge for the credit other than interest at a rate not exceeding the rate charged under the agreement referred to in (a) *supra*, and (d) the number of payments[56] to be made by the debtor does not exceed 12.[59]

Three exemptions—"the low interest exemptions"—relate to the rate charged for the credit.

(16) debtor-creditor agreements where the rate of the total charge for credit does not exceed the higher of (i) the sum of one per cent. and the highest of the base rates published by the clearing banks being the latest rates in operation on the date 28 days before the date on which the agreement is made, and (ii) 13 per cent., but excluding (a) agreements providing for an increase in, or permitting the creditor to increase, the amount or rate of any item of the total charge for credit after the agreement is in operation except by reference to the level of any index or of any other factor in accordance with any formula specified in the agreement and except when the debtor is the creditor's employee and the agreement provides for an increase on termination of the employment, and (b) any agreements under which the total amount to be repaid by the debtor to discharge his indebtedness in respect of the amount of credit provided may vary according to any formula specified in the agreement having effect by reference to movements in the level of any index or to any other factor.[60]

(17) debtor-creditor-supplier agreements satisfying conditions (a), (b) and (c) specified in (15) *supra* where the rate of the total charge for credit does not exceed the rate specified in (16) *supra* but excluding agreements specified in exception (b) to (16) *supra*.[61]

(18) debtor-creditor agreements where the only amount included in the total charge for credit is interest[62] which cannot under the agreement at any time exceed the higher of (i) the sum of one per cent. and the highest of any base rates published by the clearing banks being the latest rates in operation on the date 28 days before any such time, and (ii) 13 per cent., but excluding exception (b) in (16) *supra*.[63]

There is a last group of miscellaneous exceptions:

(19) agreements made in connection with trade in goods or services between the UK and other countries or within a country or between countries outside the UK, being agreements under which credit is provided to the debtor in the course of a business carried on by him.[64]

(20) where the creditor is listed[65] and the debtor is connected with the U.S. forces.[66]

---

[59] Art. 3(1)(*d*).
[60] Art. 4(1)(*a*), (2), (3), (4).
[61] Art. 4(1)(*b*), (4).
[62] Interest is to be determined by the formula of reg. 7 of the Consumer Credit (Total Charge for Credit) Regulations 1980 (S.I. 1980 No. 51); "period rate of charge" in the formula having the meaning given by reg. 7(2).
[63] Art. 4(1)(*c*), (4).
[64] Art. 5(*a*).
[65] Sched. 1, Pt. IV.
[66] Art. 5(*b*).

(21) consumer hire agreements for meters or metering equipment owned by electricity or water suppliers.[67]
(22) consumer credit agreements where the creditor is a housing authority and the agreement is secured on a dwelling.[68]

Further definitions

A *small agreement* is (a) a regulated consumer agreement for credit not exceeding £50 other than a hire purchase or conditional sale agreement or (b) a regulated consumer hire agreement which does not require the hirer to make payments exceeding £50, being, in either case, an agreement which is unsecured or secured only by a guarantee or indemnity.[69] There are provisions to avoid evasion by the splitting of an agreement into several small agreements.[70]

3.5

A *non-commercial agreement* is a consumer credit agreement or consumer hire agreement not made by the creditor or owner in the course of a business carried on by him.[71]

A *multiple agreement* is an agreement part of which falls within one category of agreement and part in another or an agreement which, or part of which, falls within two or more categories of agreement mentioned in the Act.[72] A part of a multiple agreement is to be treated as a separate agreement.

A transaction entered into by the debtor or his relatives other than one for the provision of a security may be a *linked transaction* in relation to an actual or prospective regulated agreement[73] (the "principal agreement").[74] There are three types. The first is where the transaction is entered into in compliance with a term of the principal agreement, *e.g.* an insurance policy over goods. The second is where the transaction is financed by a principal debtor-creditor-supplier agreement, *e.g.* a purchase made with a credit card. The third is where the other party to the transaction is a person of a specified class and the transaction is suggested by a person of a specified class. There are three sub-classes of this type. The first sub-class is where the transaction is entered into to induce the creditor to enter into the principal agreement. The second sub-class is where the transaction is for another purpose related to the principal agreement. The third sub-class is where the principal agreement is a restricted-use credit agreement and the transaction is for a purpose related to a transaction financed, or to be financed, by the principal

---

[67] Art. 6.
[68] s.16(6A).
[69] s.17(1); S.I. 1983 No. 1878.
[70] s.17(3), (4).
[71] s.189(1).
[72] s.18.
[73] Mr Bennion has pointed out that the insertion of "regulated" in s.19(1) is a drafting error because the question of whether an agreement is regulated may turn on the question of whether the charges under another agreement are to be taken into account. See [1986] J.B.L. 294, 298.
[74] s.19. Certain linked transactions are excluded from the operation of some provisions of the Act: Consumer Credit (Linked Transactions) (Exemptions) Regulations 1983 (S.I. 1983 No. 1560). See Bone and Rutherford, "Consumer Credit, Defects in the Linked Transactions Regulations" [1985] J.B.L. 209; Bennion, "Consumer Credit: the Narrowing of 'Linked Transactions' in relation to the Total Charge for credit" [1986] J.B.L. 294.

agreement. It has been suggested that a contract for the purchase of food to stock a deep-freeze acquired on credit would fall into this third subclass.[75] The specified classes of persons are the creditor, his associate, a person who knows that the principal agreement has been made or who contemplated that it might be made and a person who, in the negotiation of the transaction, is represented by a credit-broker who is also a negotiator in antecedent negotiations for the principal agreement.

A linked transaction has no effect until the regulated agreement is made.[76] Cancellation of the regulated agreement cancels the linked transaction.[77] Where, for any reason, the debtor's indebtedness under a regulated agreement is discharged before the time fixed by the agreement, he and his relatives are discharged from any liability under a linked transaction other than a debt which has already become payable.[78]

A *modifying agreement* is an agreement varying or supplementing an earlier agreement.[79] It is treated as revoking the earlier agreement and as containing provisions reproducing the combined effect of the two agreements. If the earlier agreement is a regulated one but the modifying one is not, the modifying one is to be treated as a regulated agreement unless it is for a running-account credit. The modifying agreement is treated as cancellable only in certain circumstances.

Total charges for credit: assumptions

3.6 The total charge for credit is to be calculated in accordance with regulations.[80] As the information required for the calculation will not always be available at the time the agreement is made, certain assumptions have to be made.

Unknown	Assumption
Amount of credit to be provided[81]	(a) In a running-account credit with a credit limit, the credit limit (b) In any other case, £100 (this assumption must be applied before any other)
Period for which credit is provided[82]	One year beginning with the relevant date
Level of index or factor by which rate or amount of item in total charge for credit or amount of	Level at date of making agreement

---

[75] Goode, *Consumer Credit Law* (1989), p. 662; Bennion, *Consumer Credit Control*, I, § 1880C.

[76] s.19(3).

[77] s.69(1).

[78] s.96.

[79] s.82(2).

[80] Consumer Credit (Total Charge for Credit) Regulations 1980 (S.I. 1980 No. 51, am. by S.I.s 1985 No. 1192, 1989 No. 596).

[81] Reg. 13.

[82] Reg. 14. The relevant date is the earliest specified or determinable date on which the debtor is entitled to require provision of anything under the agreement and, where there is no such date, the date of making the agreement: Reg. 1(2).

Total Charges: Assumptions

Unknown	**Assumption**
any repayment of credit is calculated[83]	
Rate or amount of item in total charge for credit which will change within one year beginning with the relevant date (where the period for which credit is to be provided cannot be ascertained)[84]	Highest rate or amount at any time obtaining under the transaction in that year
Earliest date on which credit is to be provided[85]	Date of making of agreement
Time of payment of one charge[86]	Relevant date or, where it may reasonably be expected that a debtor will not make payment on that date, the earliest date on which it may reasonably be expected that he will make payment
Times of payment of several charges of the same description[87]	The first as in the preceding entry, the last at the end of the period for which credit is provided, and the others at equal intervals between these times

The following assumptions have also to be made in the calculations[88]:
(1) the debtor will not be entitled to any income tax relief other than relief in respect of certain insurance premiums.
(2) in a transaction providing for repayment at specified times, the creditor will not exercise any right under the transaction to require repayment at other times if the debtor performs his obligations under the transaction.
(3) in a transaction without such a provision, the creditor will not exercise any right under the transaction to require repayment if the debtor performs his obligations.
(4) where the rate or amount of any item in the total charge for credit is to vary on the occurrence of any event, that that event will not occur (but this does not apply to an event which is certain to occur and of which the date of occurrence, or the earliest date of occurrence, can be ascertained at the date of making of the agreement).
(5) each provision of credit and each repayment is made at the specified time or, if there is no time specified, at the earliest time provided under the transaction.

---
[83] Reg. 15.
[84] Reg. 16.
[85] Reg. 17.
[86] Reg. 18(*a*).
[87] Reg. 18(*b*).
[88] Reg. 2.

(6) any repayment to be made before the relevant date is to be taken to be made on the relevant date.

(7) in a running-account credit or a fixed-sum credit where credit is not repayable at specified intervals or in specified amounts where, in either case, a constant period rate of charge in respect of periods of equal or nearly equal length is charged:
  (i) the amount of credit outstanding at the beginning of the period is to remain outstanding throughout the period;
  (ii) the amount of any credit provided during a period is provided immediately after the end of the period;
  (iii) any repayment made during a period is made immediately after the end of the period.

(8) any repayment of the credit or total charge for credit will, at the time when the repayment is made, be the smallest for which the agreement provides.

Time

3.7 Then there are provisions as to the way in which periods of time are to be treated.[89]

Period	Counted
Not a whole number of calendar months and not a whole number of weeks	In years and days
Whole number of calendar months but not a whole number of weeks	In calendar months
Whole number of weeks but not a whole number of calendar months	In weeks
Whole number of calendar months and a whole number of weeks where only one repayment is to be made	In calendar months
Whole number of calendar months and a whole number of weeks where more than one repayment is to be made at intervals from the relevant date of one or more weeks	In weeks
Whole number of calendar months and a whole number of weeks where more than one repayment is to be made but not at intervals of one or more weeks	In calendar months

---

[89] Reg. 11.

Period	Counted
Calendar months	Relevant number of twelfth parts of a year
Weeks	Relevant number of fifty-second parts of a year
Day	One three hundred and sixty-fifth part of a year
Every day	A working day

Computations

The "total charge for credit" is the total of the interest on the credit to be provided and all other charges at any time payable under the transaction by the debtor or his relative to the creditor or any other person.[90] Items to be included in, and items to be excluded from, the total charge have already been specified.[91]

3.8

The rate of the total charge for credit is the "annual percentage rate of charge," (A.P.R.C.) determined in accordance with the regulations to one decimal place, further decimal places being disregarded.[92]

The simplest case[93] is where a percentage rate of charge (x) comprising all charges in the total charge for credit is charged and the agreement is:
(a) an agreement under which the only charge for credit is a constant period rate of charge in respect of periods of equal length (y in a year) being either (i) an agreement for running-account credit, or (ii) an agreement for fixed-sum credit where the credit is not repayable at specified intervals or in specified amounts; or
(b) an agreement for fixed-sum credit under which (i) the only charge for credit is a constant period rate of charge in respect of periods of equal length, (ii) credit is outstanding throughout one or more such periods, and (iii) every repayment of credit and of the total charge is made at the end of such a period.

All that needs to be done here is to adjust the percentage rate if the period in respect of which it is charged is not a year; obviously, a 10 per cent. rate charged for a six month period represents an annual rate of a little over 20 per cent. The A.P.R.C. in this case is defined as:

$$100\left[(1 + \frac{x}{100})y - 1\right]$$

The second simple situation[94] is where a fixed-sum credit is provided in a lump sum (P) repayable at the end of a specified period (t in years) in a lump sum (P + C) where C is the total charge for credit. The A.P.R.C. is

$$100\left[(1 + \frac{C}{P})^{1/t} - 1\right]$$

The third definition of the A.P.R.C. is applicable to any agreement.[95]

---

[90] Reg. 4.
[91] *Supra*, para. 3.3.
[92] Reg. 6.
[93] Reg. 7.
[94] Reg. 8.
[95] Reg. 9.

It is "the rate per annum compounding annually expressed as a percentage such that: (a) the sum of the present values as at the relevant date of all repayments of credit and of the total charge for credit, and (b) the sum of the present values as at the relevant date of all credit under the agreement, would, when calculated at that rate, be equal." The relevant date is, broadly, that on which the debtor can require provision of the credit. The present value at the relevant date of a sum to be paid on or before that date, is that sum; the present value of a sum A to be paid at a later date (t years later) is:

$$\frac{A}{\left(1 + \frac{r}{100}\right)^t}$$

where r is the rate per annum expressed as a percentage. Where this method gives more than one rate, the A.P.R.C. is the positive rate nearest to zero, or, if there is none, the negative rate nearest to zero. This calculation will require the solution of an equation of the form:

$$P = \frac{a}{(1 + \frac{r}{100})^1} + \frac{b}{(1 + \frac{r}{100})^2} + \frac{c}{(1 + \frac{r}{100})^3} \ldots$$

In most cases, the value of r can be found only by trial and error, or by the use of a computer.

In the case of an agreement to which an entry in *Consumer Credit Tables* published in 1977 by HMSO exactly applies, the applicable rate in the table is to be taken to be the rate determined in accordance with the regulations.[96]

Consumer credit tables

3.9 The tables are in 15 parts. Parts 1 to 7 deal with the case where under a fixed-sum credit agreement a single advance of credit is made, the sum of the credit and the total charge for credit is to be repaid in equal instalments at equal intervals throughout the period over which the credit is to be repaid and the first instalment is payable one such interval after the credit is advanced. The user of the tables must first calculate the "charge per pound lent," which is the total charge for credit, in pounds, divided by the amount of credit to be advanced, in pounds. The user then finds the table for the appropriate interval; for example, Part 2 covers weekly intervals for 52 to 111 instalments; Part 5 covers monthly instalments for three years or over. The next step is to find in the table the column for the appropriate number of instalments and go down it until the figure for the charge per pound lent is found; reference to the end of the row then gives the annual percentage rate of charge. If there is no entry in the tables for the exact rate of charge per pound lent to the fourth decimal place, the tables cannot be used.

Parts 8 and 9 deal with the case of credit repaid with the total charge in a single sum after a specified interval. The charge per pound lent is found in the column for the appropriate length of transaction and the A.P.R.C. is again found at the end of the row.

---

[96] Reg. 10.

Part 10 covers weekly instalment (4 to 113 weeks), monthly instalment (3 to 32 months) and single repayment (4 to 53 weeks and 1 to 10 months) cases where the A.P.R.C. is 100 or over.

Parts 11 to 13 cover transactions of the same types as are covered by Parts 1 to 7. Here the calculation begins with the computation of the "annual flat rate" which is:

$$\frac{C \times 100 \times 52}{P \times t}$$

where C is the total charge for credit in pounds, P is the amount of credit in pounds and t is the period, in weeks, over which the credit is to be repaid. The next step differs from the method used in the earlier parts. The columns are for numbers of instalments as before but the rows are annual flat rates at intervals of a quarter of a per cent. The row for the appropriate annual flat rate is found and then the user moves along it to the column for the number of instalments and the figure at that point is the A.P.R.C. If the intervals are monthly the formula for the annual flat rate is

$$\frac{C \times 100 \times 12}{P \times t}$$

where t is the repayment period in months; if the intervals are quarterly, half yearly or yearly the formula is

$$\frac{C \times 100}{P \times t}$$

where t is the repayment period in years. Parts 11 to 13 are thus to some extent an alternative to Parts 1 to 7 but the range of transactions covered is slightly different.

Part 14 deals with single repayment transactions where an annual flat rate can be calculated by the formula:

$$\frac{C \times 100}{P \times t}$$

where t is the length of the transaction in years. Again the columns are lengths of transaction and the rows are annual flat rates; the A.P.R.C. is the figure in the appropriate row and column.

Part 15 applies where there is a "constant period rate of charge" (*i.e.* a percentage rate of charge for a period comprising all the charges included in the total charge for credit) and the agreement is a running-account credit agreement *or* a fixed-sum credit agreement where the credit is not repayable at specified intervals or in specified amounts *or* a fixed-sum credit agreement where the credit is repayable at the end of a specified period in a single lump sum comprising the credit and the total charge for credit. The page for the period for which the period rate of charge is charged is found and there each period rate has the appropriate A.P.R.C. opposite it.

Licensing[97]

3.10 A person who carries on a business consisting of the provision of credit under regulated consumer credit agreements or the hiring of goods under regulated consumer hire agreements is required to have a licence.[98] A person is not treated as carrying on a particular type of business merely because occasionally he enters into transactions belonging to a business of that type.[99] If a regulated agreement, other than a non-commercial agreement, is made when the creditor or owner is unlicensed, it is enforceable against the debtor or hirer only where the Director of Fair Trading has made an order that the agreement is to be treated as if the trader had been licensed.[1]

A person carrying on an ancillary credit business (*i.e.* credit brokerage, debt-adjusting, debt counselling, debt-collecting or a credit reference agency) also requires a licence.[2] An agreement for the services of such a person made when he is unlicensed is enforceable against the customer only where the Director has made an appropriate order[3] and a regulated agreement made by a debtor who was introduced to the creditor by an unlicensed credit-broker is in the same position.[4] Credit brokerage is the effecting of introductions of individuals desiring credit or goods on hire to persons carrying on the appropriate business or to other credit-brokers.[5]

Advertising and quotations

3.11 There is regulation of the contents of advertisements and quotations issued by a person carrying on a consumer credit business, a consumer hire business, a business in the course of which individuals are provided with credit secured on land, or certain other types of business.[6] The regulations allow for some relaxation of the rules applying to the calculation of the rate of the total charge for credit.

General requirements

3.12 The following general requirements apply to the making of regulated agreements[7]:

---

[97] See Borrie, "Licensing Practice under the Consumer Credit Act" [1982] J.B.L. 91.

[98] s.21. The Consumer Credit Act 1974 (Commencement No. 2) Order 1977 (S.I. 1977 No. 325) exempted from the licensing requirement a business carried on by an individual in the course of which the only agreements made were for fixed-sum credit not exceeding £30 or for running-account credit where the credit limit did not exceed £30: but this exemption has now been removed (Consumer Credit Act 1974 (Commencement No. 10) Order 1989 (S.I. 1989 No. 1128)).

[99] s.189(2); *R. v. Marshall* [1989] C.C.L.R. 47.

[1] s.40.

[2] s.147. Certain exceptions are made in the Consumer Credit Act 1974 (Commencement No. 4) Order 1977 (S.I. 1977 No. 2163).

[3] s.148.

[4] s.149.

[5] s.145(2).

[6] ss.43, 52; Consumer Credit (Advertisements) Regulations 1989 (S.I. 1989 No. 1125); Consumer Credit (Quotations) Regulations 1989 (S.I. 1989 No. 1126) (and reg. 2 of S.I.s 1983 No. 110, 1983 No. 1721, 1984 No. 1055, 1985 No. 619).

[7] They do not apply to non-commercial agreements nor to a debtor-creditor agreement enabling the debtor to overdraw on a current account: s.74(1). Requirements (2)–(5) do not apply to a small debtor-creditor-supplier agreement for restricted-use credit unless a term is expressed in writing in which case requirement (1) applies: s.74(4) amended by Banking Act 1979, s.38.

Agency

(1) the agreement must have the specified content and be in the specified form[8];
(2) a document embodying all the terms of the agreement other than implied terms, the terms being readily legible, must be signed by the debtor or hirer and by or on behalf of the creditor or owner[9];
(3) the debtor or hirer must be given a copy or copies of the agreement[10];
(4) the debtor or hirer must be given notice of his right (if any) to cancel the agreement.[11]

If these requirements are not satisfied the agreement is not properly executed and it is enforceable against the debtor or hirer on an order of the court only.[12]

With some exceptions,[13] an agreement is void if, and to the extent that, it purports to bind a person to enter as debtor into a prospective regulated agreement.[14]

Cancellation

A regulated agreement may be cancelled if the antecedent negotiations included oral representations made in the debtor's presence by the negotiator unless (a) the agreement is secured on land, or is a restricted use agreement to finance the purchase of land or an agreement for a bridging loan in connection with the purchase of land, or (b) the unexecuted agreement is signed by the debtor at the business premises of the creditor, owner or negotiator or of a party to a linked transaction (other than the debtor or his relative).[15] The cancellation may normally be made before the end of the fifth day following the completion of the documentation.[16] The general effect of cancellation is that sums paid by the debtor are repayable, any credit extended is repayable and goods must be returned.[17] An unscrupulous consumer may take unfair advantage of these provisions where a car has been taken in part-exchange at a "written-up" value; a borrower may obtain a month's interest-free credit.[18]

3.13

Agency

"Antecedent negotiations" are negotiations with the debtor conducted by the creditor in relation to the making of an agreement, *or* by a credit-broker in relation to goods to be sold to the creditor who will then enter

3.14

---

[8] s.60; Consumer Credit (Agreements) Regulations 1983 (S.I. 1983 No. 1553), am. by S.I.s 1984 No. 1600, 1985 No. 666, 1988 No. 2047.

[9] s.61.

[10] ss.62–63; Consumer Credit (Cancellation Notices and Copies of Documents) Regulations 1983 (S.I. 1983 No. 1557) am. by S.I.s 1984 No. 1108, 1985 No. 666, 1988 No. 2047). As to "sent," see *V. L. Skuce & Co.* v. *Cooper* [1975] 1 W.L.R. 593.

[11] s.64; S.I. 1983 No. 1557; Consumer Credit (Notice of Cancellation Rights) (Exemptions) Regulations 1983 (S.I. 1983 No. 1558).

[12] s.65(1).

[13] Consumer Credit (Agreements to Enter Prospective Agreements) (Exemptions) Regulations 1983 (S.I. 1983 No. 1552).

[14] s.59(1).

[15] s.67.

[16] s.68.

[17] ss.70–73; Consumer Credit (Repayment of Credit on Cancellation) Regulations (S.I. 1983 No. 1559).

[18] Dobson (1978) 128 N.L.J. 56.

an agreement with the debtor relating to the goods *or* by the supplier in relation to a transaction to be financed by a debtor-creditor-supplier agreement. The person conducting the negotiations on behalf of the credit-broker or supplier is deemed to be conducting them as agent of the creditor as well as in his actual capacity.[19]

Currency of agreement

3.15 During the currency of the regulated agreement, the creditor must give the debtor and the surety information as to the state of the transaction if requested to do so.[20] The creditor cannot during the specified term of duration of the agreement, without giving seven days' notice in the prescribed form, enforce a term of the agreement (other than one arising from the debtor's breach of the agreement) by demanding earlier payment of any sum, recovering possession of any goods or land, or treating any right conferred on the debtor as terminated, restricted or deferred[21]; this does not prevent the creditor treating a right to draw on credit as restricted or deferred.

If the creditor varies the agreement under a power therein, the variation does not take effect until notice is given in the prescribed manner.[22]

The debtor under a regulated consumer credit agreement is not liable for any loss arising from the use of the credit facility by someone not acting, or to be treated as acting, as his agent but this does not apply to a non-commercial agreement nor to a loss arising from misuse of a cheque or banker's draft.[23]

The debtor under a regulated consumer credit agreement is entitled to receive on request a statement by the creditor of the amount required to discharge the debt,[24] and he is entitled to make payment to discharge his indebtedness under the agreement at any time.[25] A rebate must be allowed.[26] This discharge of indebtedness has the effect of discharging him from liability under a linked transaction other than a debt which has already become payable.[27]

The creditor cannot terminate an agreement during its specified period of duration under a power in the agreement unless he gives the debtor seven days' notice in the prescribed manner.[28]

---

[19] s.56.

[20] ss.77–79, 107–109; Consumer Credit (Prescribed Periods for Giving Information) Regulations 1983 (S.I. 1983 No. 1569); Consumer Credit (Running-Account Credit Information) Regulations 1983 (S.I. 1983 No. 1570).

[21] s.76; Consumer Credit (Enforcement, Default and Termination Notices) Regulations 1983 (S.I. 1983 No. 1561) reg. 2(1).

[22] s.82; Consumer Credit (Notice of Variation of Agreements) Regulations 1977 (S.I. 1977 No. 328).

[23] s.83.

[24] s.97; Consumer Credit (Settlement Information) Regulations 1983 (S.I. 1983 No. 1564).

[25] s.94.

[26] s.95; Consumer Credit (Rebate on early settlement) Regulations [1983] (S.I. 1983 No. 1562) (am. by S.I. 1989 No. 596).

[27] s.96.

[28] s.98; Consumer Credit (Enforcement, Default and Termination) Regulations 1983 (S.I. 1983 No. 1561), reg. 2(3).

Default

On breach of a regulated agreement by the debtor, the creditor must serve a default notice before he is entitled: **3.16**
(a) to terminate the agreement;
(b) to demand earlier payment of any sum;
(c) to recover possession of goods or land;
(d) to treat any of the debtor's rights as terminated, restricted or deferred;
(e) to enforce any security (an act by which a floating charge becomes fixed is not enforcement).[29]

The default notice must be in the prescribed form and must specify the breach and the action required to remedy it before a specified date not earlier than seven days after service of the notice, or, if the breach is not capable of remedy, the sum required to be paid as compensation before a specified date. If the action is taken or the sum paid before the specified date the breach is treated as not having occurred.[30]

On service of the notice the debtor may apply to the court for a time order.[31]

The debtor in a regulated consumer credit agreement cannot be obliged to pay interest on sums unpaid in breach of the agreement at a rate exceeding any rate of interest included in the total charge for credit or, if no interest is so included, what would be the rate of the total charge for credit if amounts payable under linked transactions were not included in the total charge.[32]

It would seem that the rebate on early settlement provisions[33] should be given effect when decree is granted in an action for earlier payment of the sum due. The rebate should be calculated at the date of decree and interest can then run on.[34]

Debtor's death

The creditor is not entitled to do the acts (a) to (e) specified in the preceding paragraph by reason of the death of the debtor if at the death the agreement is fully secured. If it is unsecured or partly secured, the creditor can do these acts on an order of the court only.[35] The creditor is not prevented from treating the right to draw on any credit as restricted or deferred. Nor is there anything to prevent the payment of sums due under the agreement out of the proceeds of a policy of assurance on the debtor's life. The restraint on terminating the agreement applies only where there is specified in the agreement a period of duration which has not ended when the creditor purports to terminate the agreement. **3.17**

---

[29] s.87.
[30] ss.88, 89; Consumer Credit (Enforcement, Default and Termination Notice) Regulations 1983 (S.I. 1983 No. 1561), reg. 2(2). See *Eshun* v. *Moorgate Mercantile Co. Ltd.* [1971] 1 W.L.R. 722 (Hire-Purchase Act 1965).
[31] s.129. See *infra*, para. 3.19.
[32] s.93.
[33] See para. 3.15.
[34] *Cf. Forward Trust Ltd.* v. *Whymark* [1989] 3 All E.R. 915. County court judgments do not bear interest.
[35] s.86.

Enforcement orders

3.18 The Act frequently provides that in certain circumstances an agreement is enforceable against the debtor on an order of the court only.[36] The court cannot make an enforcement order if there was failure to comply with certain provisions as to notice of the right to cancel, as to the giving of a copy agreement to the debtor, or as to the signing of the agreement.[37] Where the debtor has died an order can be made only if the creditor proves that he has been unable to satisfy himself that the present and future obligations of the debtor are likely to be discharged.[38] The court may dismiss the application if it considers it just to do so having regard to the prejudice caused to any person by the contravention in question and the degree of culpability for it and having regard also to the court's powers to make conditional or suspended orders or to vary the terms of the agreement.[39] In an enforcement order the court may reduce or discharge any sum payable by the debtor or by a surety to compensate him for any loss suffered as a result of the contravention.[40] Where the agreement is not in the correct form but the debtor did sign a document containing all the prescribed terms, the order may direct that the agreement is to have effect as if it did not include a term omitted from that document.[41]

Time orders

3.19 A "time order" may be made (a) when the creditor applies for an enforcement order, (b) on an application by the debtor, after service of a default notice, a notice of termination of the agreement or a notice of intention to demand early payment, or repossess goods or land or treat a right as terminated, restricted or deferred, and (c) when the creditor brings an action to enforce the agreement, or a security, or recover possession of any goods or land. A time order cannot be made if there has already been made a time to pay direction[42] or a time to pay order[43] in relation to the debt.[44]

A "time order" provides for payment by instalments or for the remedying of any breach by the debtor within a specified time.[45] In any order made in relation to an agreement the court may make the operation of a term conditional on the doing of certain acts by any party or suspend the operation of any term.[46] The court may also include in the order such provision as it considers just for amending the agreement or security in consequence of a term of the order.[47] On the application of the creditor or

---

[36] ss.65(1), 86(2), 105(7)(*a*), (*b*), 111(2), 124(1), (2). Summary diligence cannot be used to enforce payment of a debt due under a regulated agreement or under any security related thereto: s.93A (inserted by D.A. Sched. 6, para. 16).
[37] s.127.
[38] s.128.
[39] s.127(1).
[40] s.127(2).
[41] s.127(5).
[42] See para. 11.20.
[43] See para. 15.7.
[44] s.129(3) (inserted by D.A. Sched. 6, para. 17); A.S. (Debtors) 7.
[45] s.129.
[46] s.135.
[47] s.136.

owner, the court may make such order as it thinks just for the protection of his property or property subject to a security pending the determination of the proceedings.[48]

Negotiable instruments

Except in the case of a non-commercial agreement, a negotiable instrument cannot be taken as a security for discharge of a sum due under a regulated agreement and a negotiable instrument other than a banknote or cheque cannot be taken from a debtor or surety in discharge of a sum payable.[49] The person taking the negotiable instrument is not a holder in due course and is not entitled to enforce it.[50] A cheque taken in discharge cannot be negotiated except to a banker[51] and negotiation to a non-banker is a defect in the negotiator's title.[52] Contravention of these provisions makes the agreement or security enforceable on order of the court only.[53] The rights of a holder in due course of a negotiable instrument are not affected but where the debtor or surety becomes liable to a holder in due course as a result of a contravention of these provisions the creditor must indemnify him.[54]

3.20

Securities

Documents embodying regulated agreements have to embody any security provided in relation to the agreement by the debtor.[55] If the person by whom a security is provided (the "surety") is not the debtor, the security must be expressed in writing in the prescribed form, the document containing all the terms of the security other than implied terms must be signed by or on behalf of the surety and a copy of the document and the principal agreement given to him.[56] If these requirements are not satisfied, the security is enforceable against the surety only on an order of the court and if an application for such an order is dismissed (except on technical grounds) the security is treated as never having effect, property lodged with the creditor for purposes of the security must be returned, any entry relating to the security in any register must be cancelled and any amount received by the creditor on realisation of the security must be repaid to the surety[57]; there is a partial exemption for heritable securities. The creditor is obliged to give the surety on request a copy of the principal agreement and of the security instrument and information about the present state of the debtor's indebtedness.[58]

3.21

---

[48] s.131.
[49] s.123. There is an exception for consumer hire agreements connected with a country outside the U.K.: Consumer Credit (Negotiable Instruments) (Exemption) Order 1984 (S.I. 1984 No. 435).
[50] s.125(1).
[51] s.123(2).
[52] s.125(2).
[53] s.124.
[54] s.125(3), (4).
[55] s.105(9).
[56] s.105. The power to prescribe form and content has been exercised only with respect to guarantees and indemnities—Consumer Credit (Guarantees and Indemnities) Regulations 1983 (S.I. 1983 No. 1556)—see para. 10.1.
[57] s.106.
[58] ss.107–110.

A copy of any default notice served on the debtor must be served on the surety.[59] A security cannot be enforced so as to benefit the creditor to an extent greater than would be the case if there were no security and the obligations of the debtor were carried out to the extent (if any) to which they would be enforced under the Act.[60] Accordingly, if a regulated agreement is enforceable only on a court order or on an order of the Director the security is enforceable only where an order has been made[61] and, generally, if the agreement is cancelled or becomes unenforceable, the security becomes ineffective.[62]

---

[59] s.111.
[60] s.113(1).
[61] s.113(2).
[62] s.113(3).

CHAPTER 4

CREDIT TRANSACTIONS

Loan of money

Mutuum is defined by Bell as "a real contract, by which one gives and transfers a fungible to another without hire, for use by consumption, on an engagement to restore as much of the same thing at the stipulated time."[1] Although interest is usually payable on a loan of money, such a loan can be treated as a species of *mutuum*. The borrower's obligation is to restore the sum lent. The lender has only a personal right to repayment.

4.1

It is possible for advances of money to be made on the footing that they will be repaid only if the receiver is able to do so.[2] Where a loan between mercantile men was "to be repaid by instalments as found most convenient to" the borrower, it was held that this referred to mercantile convenience—a time when the borrower had money sufficient in amount and free from the ordinary purposes of his business—and that the onus of proof as to this was on the lender.[3]

If a loan is made, the creditor is entitled to demand repayment at any time unless this is precluded by some conventional provision.[4]

If there is a stipulation that the loan will not be called up so long as interest is paid "punctually" on a specified day, a payment on a later date is not made "punctually."[5]

A penalty for failure in punctual payment is not enforceable.[6] There may be a provision that the rate of interest will be lower if the interest is paid punctually.[7]

A loan falls under the quinquennial prescription.[8] If the contract stipulates the date for repayment, that date is the *terminus a quo*; if there is no stipulation as to the date of repayment, the prescriptive period runs from the date when a written demand for repayment is made by or on behalf of the creditor to the debtor.[9]

Proof of loan

As a general rule, a loan of money exceeding 100 pounds Scots (£8·33) can be proved only by writ or oath of the borrower.[10] The defender must state a plea to this effect and if he fails to do so and a proof *prout de jure* is allowed, the case will be decided on the whole evidence led.[11]

4.2

---

[1] *Prin.*, § 200.

[2] *Forbes* v. *Forbes* (1869) 8 M. 85; *Mylne* v. *Balfour Melville* (1901) 8 S.L.T. 454.

[3] *Shaw* v. *Kay* (1904) 12 S.L.T. 6, 262.

[4] *Thomson* v. *Geekie* (1861) 23 D. 693, per L.J.-C. Inglis at p. 701; *Neilson* v. *Stewart*, 1990 G.W.D. 1–4.

[5] *Gatty* v. *Maclaine*, 1921 S.C. (H.L.) 1; *Kennedy* v. *Begg Kennedy & Elder Ltd.*, 1954 S.L.T. (Sh.Ct.) 103.

[6] *Nasmyth* v. *Samson* (1785) 3 Pat.App. 9; Debts Securities (Scotland) Act 1856, s.5.

[7] *Gatty* v. *Maclaine, supra*.

[8] Prescription and Limitation (Scotland) Act 1973, Sched. 1, para. 1.

[9] Sched. 2, para. 2(2).

[10] Erskine, IV, ii, 20; Bell, *Prin.*, § 2257. But see para. 11.15 as to evidence in small claims.

[11] *Dick's Exrx.* v. *Dick*, 1964 S.L.T. (Sh.Ct.) 41; *Cuthbertson* v. *Paterson*, 1968 S.L.T. (Sh.Ct.) 21.

The rule does not apply to an advance which was to form the pursuer's contribution to the capital of a partnership, if it was formed.[12] It has also been held that the rule does not apply where the borrower stands in a special fiduciary relationship to the lender—for example, the relationship between director and company.[13]

A loan not exceeding 100 pounds Scots can be proved *prout de jure*,[14] but, where a loan of over that amount is averred, parole proof is not admitted by restricting the sum sued for to £8·33.[15] An advance of £16 to pay wages of three servants, each wage being less than £8·33, was held to be one loan.[16] Parole evidence is not allowed to prove a payment made on behalf of the debtor if the debtor holds a receipt for the payment.[16]

Series of transactions

4.3 It seems that the general rule as to proof suffers an exception where there is alleged, not an isolated loan transaction, but a series of transactions. The limits of this exception are not at all clear. In one case it was held that indorsed cheques were sufficient to vouch advances constituting items in a current account between agent and client, there being other advances shown in the account and vouched by bills, IOUs or receipts.[17] In another case, where the defender admitted that heritage held in his name was truly the property of his father but claimed that it was so held by him in security of advances made by him to his father over a period, it was held that in "a going series of transactions" proof was not necessarily restricted to writ or oath, the series must be taken as a whole and the question was "what would be the natural way of preserving evidence of what was done among ordinary business men."[18] The basis of the decision was, however, that the question was not whether a loan was constituted but upon what terms was property to be reconveyed. This distinction has been emphasised subsequently in a case in which it was said that, in any event, the exception could not extend to a loan made in instalments.[19] Where a father made a series of advances to a forisfamiliated son and took no document of debt therefor but made entries in his books, it was held that these facts did not amount to "natural proof" of loan.[20] Three separate loans made at intervals of several months are not sufficient to form a series of transactions for purposes of the exception.[21]

Pleading

4.4 Any admission made by the defender in his pleadings must be taken with any qualification adjected to it. The distinction between intrinsic and

---

[12] *Hendry* v. *Cowie & Son & Co.* (1904) 12 S.L.T. 31, 261.
[13] *John S. Boyle Ltd.* v. *Boyle's Trs.*, 1949 S.L.T. (Notes) 45.
[14] *Annand's Trs.* v. *Annand* (1869) 7 M. 526. See also *Muir* v. *Steven* (1896) 12 Sh.Ct.Rep. 368.
[15] *Whyte* v. *Smith* (1886) 2 Sh.Ct.Rep. 257.
[16] *Annand's Trs.* v. *Annand*, supra.
[17] *Robb* v. *Robb's Trs.* (1884) 11 R. 881.
[18] *Smith's Tr.* v. *Smith*, 1911 S.C. 653. See *Grant's Exrx.* v. *Grant*, 1922 S.L.T. 156; *Boyd* v. *Millar*, 1934 S.N. 7. See also *Inglis* v. *Inglis's Tr.*, 1925 S.L.T. 686.
[19] *McKie* v. *Wilson*, 1951 S.C. 15.
[20] *Grant's Exrx.* v. *Grant*, supra.
[21] *Ainslie* v. *McGowan*, 1974 S.L.T. (Sh.Ct.) 19.

extrinsic qualifications has no application to judicial admissions.[22] So if it is admitted that there was a loan which has been repaid or abandoned, the pursuer must still rebut the qualification by writ or oath.[23] Similarly, if the receipt of money is admitted but it is averred that the sum was paid for services rendered, the loan must still be established by writ or oath.[24] On the other hand, when the defender avers that the money was received as a gift, it seems that the onus is on him to prove this unless the alleged donor was under a natural obligation to provide for the recipient.[25]

Writ

The writ need not be holograph or tested.[26] It need not be granted contemporaneously with the making of the loan but an acknowledgment granted by the borrower after his sequestration cannot be used.[27] A writ of the borrower's agent may be constructively the borrower's writ.[28] Parole evidence is admissible to prove the borrower's handwriting and signature, the borrower's instructions to his agent and the fact of delivery.[29] Parole evidence may also be admitted to prove that a document was signed by the grantor as a partner and authorised agent of a firm,[30] or by the grantors as directors and agents of a company.[31]

It would appear that the writ must be a *chirographum*—a document which was given by the recipient to the payer of the money as a record of the transaction and which is retained in the possession of the payer.[32] It is therefore doubtful whether an entry in the debtor's books *per se* can establish loan although it has been said that "no better proof can be found" of *payment* of money.[33] It may be that it is a question of the regularity and authenticity of the books.[34] Entries made in a pass-book by the creditor on the debtor's instructions, the pass-book being retained by the debtor, are sufficient.[35] Where an unqualified acknowledgment of the receipt of money is produced, there is a presumption of loan which the defender may rebut.[36] If, however, the acknowledgment is qualified by an explanation that the money was received on some footing other than that

4.5

---

[22] *Gray* v. *Munro* (1829) 8 S. 221; *Milne* v. *Donaldson* (1852) 14 D. 849; *Picken* v. *Arundale & Co.* (1872) 10 M. 987.
[23] *Walker* v. *Garlick*, 1940 S.L.T. 208; *Kerr's Trs.* v. *Ker* (1883) 11 R. 108.
[24] *Gow's Exrs.* v. *Sim* (1866) 4 M. 578; *McKie* v. *Wilson*, 1951 S.C. 15.
[25] *Malcolm* v. *Campbell* (1889) 17 R. 255; *Penman* v. *White*, 1957 S.C. 338; *McVea* v. *Reid*, 1958 S.L.T. (Sh.Ct.) 60; Walker & Walker, *Evidence*, p. 66, n. 2. Cf. *Paul* v. *Craw* (1956) 72 Sh.Ct.Rep. 60.
[26] *Paterson* v. *Paterson* (1897) 25 R. 144.
[27] *Carmichael's Tr.* v. *Carmichael*, 1929 S.C. 265.
[28] *Bryan* v. *Butters Bros. & Co.* (1892) 19 R. 490; *Clark's Exrs.* v. *Brown*, 1935 S.C. 110 (banker); *Dryburgh* v. *Macpherson*, 1944 S.L.T. 116.
[29] Per L. P. Inglis, *Haldane* v. *Speirs* (1872) 10 M. 537 at 541; per Lord Kinnear, *Dunn's Tr.* v. *Hardy* (1896) 23 R. 621 at 633.
[30] *King, Sons & Paterson* v. *Ferrie* (1942) 58 Sh.Ct.Rep. 124 (creditor's averment); *McKenzie* v. *Jones* (1926) 42 Sh.Ct.Rep. 289 (debtor's averment).
[31] *Field* v. *R. H. Thomson & Co.* (1902) 10 S.L.T. 261.
[32] Per L. P. Inglis, *Haldane* v. *Speirs, supra*, at p. 541; per Lord Neaves, *Duncan's Trs.* v. *Shand* (1873) 11 M. 254 at 259.
[33] Per Lord Neaves, *ibid*.
[34] *Wink* v. *Speirs* (1868) 6 M. 657; *Waddel* v. *Waddel* (1790) 3 Pat.App. 188; *Hope* v. *Derwent Rolling Mills Co. Ltd.* (1905) 7 F. 837.
[35] *Bruce* v. *Calder* (1904) 20 Sh.Ct.Rep. 288.
[36] *Thomson* v. *Geekie* (1861) 23 D. 693; *Christie's Trs.* v. *Muirhead* (1870) 8 M. 461.

of loan, the debt is not established.[37] Similarly where the qualification is that the debt was repaid, this must be taken with the admission and resting-owing must be proved by the defender's writ or oath.[38] The acknowledgment must be so expressed as to imply existing indebtedness.[39] A cheque in favour of the defender and indorsed by him establishes payment of money but not loan.[40] A post-dated cheque may, however, establish a loan.[41] Similarly, a deposit-receipt in the pursuer's name and indorsed by the defender on the back does not prove loan.[42] But if payment of money is proved by a cheque, other writs may be used to show *quo animo* the money passed[43]; and if the cheque has a receipt by the defender on its face, that is sufficient.[44] Letters which do not specify the nature or amount of the loan are not sufficient.[45] Non-repudiation does not amount to an admission.[46] If there is a clear admission of liability, a creditor's letter may be looked at to identify the debt.[46]

An income tax return has been held to be sufficient acknowledgment.[47]

Where the creditor holds a receipt in which a third party acknowledges a payment by the debtor, the creditor may prove *prout de jure* that the creditor made the payment from his own funds on the debtor's behalf[48]; *a fortiori* such proof is competent where the receipt bore that the payment was "per" the creditor.[49] Receipts for interest granted by the creditor have been held to be constructively the writ of the debtor.[50]

Reference to oath

4.6   If the pursuer wishes to resort to proof by the oath of the defender, he must lodge a minute of reference.[51] It is important that the minute should make clear what is referred. The effect of an oath does not, as a rule, depend on credibility. The only question for the court is *quid juratum est*.[52] The principal difficulty arises where an admission in the oath is in some way qualified. The effect of the qualification depends upon whether

---

[37] *Duncan's Trs.* v. *Shand, supra*; *Morison's Trs.* v. *Mitchell*, 1925 S.L.T. 231.
[38] *Burns* v. *Burns*, 1964 S.L.T. (Sh.Ct.) 21.
[39] *Patrick* v. *Patrick's Trs.* (1904) 6 F. 836.
[40] *Haldane* v. *Speirs* (1872) 10 M. 537; *Dunn's Tr.* v. *Hardy* (1896) 23 R. 621; *Scotland* v. *Scotland*, 1909 S.C. 505; *Skiffington* v. *Dickson*, 1970 S.L.T. (Sh.Ct.) 24. An unindorsed cheque which appears to have been paid by the banker on whom it is drawn is evidence of the receipt by the payee of the sum payable by the cheque: Cheques Act 1957, s.3. Payments in a current account may be vouched by indorsed cheques: *Robb* v. *Robb's Trs.* (1884) 11 R. 881.
[41] *A.* v. *B.C. & Co.* (1956) 72 Sh.Ct.Rep. 29.
[42] *Nimmo* v. *Nimmo* (1873) 11 M. 446.
[43] *Hope* v. *Derwent Rolling Mills Co. Ltd.* (1905) 7 F. 837.
[44] *Gill* v. *Gill*, 1907 S.C. 532.
[45] *Rutherford's Exrs.* v. *Marshall* (1861) 23 D. 1276; *Morison's Trs.* v. *Mitchell*, 1925 S.L.T. 231; *Inverfleet Ltd.* v. *Woelfell*, 1976 S.L.T. (Sh.Ct.) 62.
[46] *MacBain* v. *MacBain*, 1930 S.C. (H.L.) 72 (a prescription case).
[47] *Clarkson* v. *Johnston* (1934) 50 Sh.Ct.Rep. 318.
[48] *Fairbairn* v. *Fairbairn* (1868) 6 M. 640.
[49] *Brand* v. *Allan* (1913) 29 Sh.Ct.Rep. 76.
[50] *Wood* v. *Howden* (1843) 5 D. 507; *Wilson* v. *Wilson* (1901) 17 Sh.Ct.Rep. 44.
[51] See Walker & Walker, *Evidence*, pp. 339–341; *Muir* v. *Steven* (1896) 12 Sh.Ct.Rep. 368.
[52] *Per* Lord Deas, *Cowbrough* v. *Robertson* (1879) 6 R. 1301 at 1306; see, however, Walker & Walker, *op. cit.*, at p. 346.

it is intrinsic or extrinsic. If it is intrinsic it is given effect; if it is extrinsic it is ignored. So the oath is negative if the defender admits the receipt of a sum of money from the pursuer but says that it was received as a gift,[53] or in payment of services previously rendered,[54] or in payment of a debt due for lodgings,[55] or in payment of a debt due to the defender by a third party.[56] If the defender admits the constitution of the loan but says that it was subsequently repaid or extinguished by some other method agreed upon by the parties at the time the loan was made, the oath is negative because these are treated as intrinsic qualifications.[57] On the other hand, if the constitution of the loan is admitted but the defender says that the debt was subsequently extinguished by compensation this is an extrinsic qualification and the oath is affirmative unless, it seems, the compensation was effected by an express agreement. A qualification that the debt was subsequently remitted by the creditor is intrinsic.[58]

In certain circumstances reference may be made to the oath of someone other than the alleged debtor:

(a) *Agents*—As a general rule reference cannot be made to the oath of the debtor's agent. This has been held with regard to the debtor's solicitor[59] and to a son contracting as his father's agent.[60] But it has been suggested that where the debtor has entrusted the whole conduct of his business to a general manager, reference can be made to the manager's oath.[61] Reference can be made to the wife's oath to prove the constitution of a debt in respect of household supplies and to the husband's oath to establish resting-owing.[62]

(b) *Incapaces*—Where the debt is allegedly due by a pupil reference may be made to the oath of the tutor or factor *loco tutoris*[63] but not in relation to transactions prior to his appointment[64] or after he is *functus*.[65] But a debt allegedly due by a minor cannot be referred to the curator's oath.[66]

(c) *Executors and Trustees*—A debt incurred by the deceased cannot be proved by the oaths of his executors or trustees unless they are also the beneficiaries.[67] Debts incurred in the administration of a testamentary or public trust can, however, be referred to the oaths of the trustees.[68]

(d) *Bankrupt*—It is not competent to refer a debt to the oath of a

---

[53] *Penney* v. *Aitken*, 1927 S.C. 673.
[54] *Gow's Exrs.* v. *Sim* (1866) 4 M. 578.
[55] *Thomson* v. *Duncan* (1855) 17 D. 1081.
[56] *Minty* v. *Donald* (1824) 3 S. 394.
[57] *Newlands* v. *McKinlay* (1885) 13 R. 353; *Adam's Trs.* v. *Burns* (1939) 55 Sh.Ct.Rep. 196.
[58] *Galbraith* v. *Cuthbertson* (1866) 4 M. 295; *Cowbrough* v. *Robertson* (1879) 6 R. 1301.
[59] *Sawers* v. *Clark* (1892) 19 R. 1090.
[60] *Kirkwood* v. *Wilson* (1823) 2 S. 425.
[61] *Encyclopaedia of the Laws of Scotland*, Vol. X., p. 400.
[62] *Mitchell* v. *Moultry* (1882) 10 R. 378, *per* Lord Young at p. 381.
[63] Erskine, IV, ii, 10; *Hepburn* v. *Hamilton* (1661) Mor. 12480.
[64] *Stewart* v. *Syme*, 12 Dec. 1815, F.C.
[65] *Waddel* v. *Wadderstoun* (1707) Mor. 12484.
[66] *Forbes* v. *Pitsligo* (1628) Mor. 12479.
[67] *Monteith* v. *Smith* (1624) Mor. 12477; Erskine, IV, ii, 10.
[68] *Murray* v. *Laurie's Trs.* (1827) 5 S. 515; *Moore* v. *Young* (1843) 5 D. 494.

54   *Credit Transactions*

bankrupt who is undischarged or discharged on payment of a composition.[69]

(e) *Firms and Corporate Bodies*—A debt due by a firm can be referred to the oath of a managing partner[70] but where all the partners are acting,[71] or where the firm has been dissolved,[72] the debt cannot be referred to the oath of one. It seems that reference is competent to the oath of the managing director, manager or officer of a limited company who "in some real sense represents the corporation."[73] Reference was made to the oath of the magistrates of a burgh.[74]

(f) *Co-obligants*—The oath of one co-obligant[75] or co-owner[76] binds himself alone.

(g) *Assignations*—The oath of the cedent binds the assignee before intimation but not thereafter[77] unless the debt was litigious before intimation[78] or the assignation was gratuitous.[79]

Consumer Credit Act

4.7   If payment of the amount of the loan is made to the borrower and the agreement is not made by the creditor under pre-existing arrangements between himself and a supplier in the knowledge that the loan is to be used to finance a transaction between the debtor and the supplier, the agreement is a debtor-creditor agreement.[80]

The rate of the total charge for credit may be such that it is an exempt agreement falling under category (16) or (18).[81]

Connected lender liability

4.8   In a debtor-creditor-supplier agreement in which there are "arrangements" between the creditor and the supplier (*e.g.* a credit card) if the debtor has, in relation to a transaction financed by the agreement, any claim against the supplier in respect of a misrepresentation or breach of contract, he has a like claim against the creditor who is jointly and severally liable with the supplier but has a right to be indemnified by the supplier.[82] The liability is not affected by the fact that the debtor exceeded the credit limit or otherwise contravened a term of the agreement. The provision does not apply to a non-commercial agreement nor where the claim relates to any single item to which the supplier has attached a cash

---

[69] *Mein* v. *Towers* (1829) 7 S. 902; *Dyce* v. *Paterson* (1846) 9 D. 310.
[70] *Gow* v. *McDonald* (1827) 5 S. 472.
[71] *McNab* v. *Lockhart* (1843) 5 D. 1014.
[72] *Nisbet's Trs.* v. *Morrison's Trs.* (1829) 7 S. 307.
[73] *H. D. Rodgers & Co. Ltd.* v. *The Paradise Restaurant* (1955) 71 Sh.Ct.Rep. 128; *A. Wilson (Aberdeen) Ltd.* v. *Stewart & Co. Ltd.* (1957) 73 Sh.Ct.Rep. 217.
[74] *Johnston* v. *Dean of Guild of Aberdeen* (1676) Mor. 12480.
[75] *Allan* v. *Ormiston* (1817) Hume 477.
[76] *Dickson* v. *Blair* (1871) 10 M. 41.
[77] *Lord Pitfoddels* v. *Glenkindy* (1662) Mor. 12454; *Boyd* v. *Storie* (1674) Mor. 12456.
[78] *Sommerville* (1673) Mor. 8325.
[79] *Steel* v. *Orbiston* (1679) Mor. 8467.
[80] See para. 3.3.
[81] See para. 3.4.
[82] Consumer Credit Act 1974, s. 75. It is possible for the section to apply to buildings: see Adams (1975) 39 *Conveyancer* 94.

price not exceeding £100 or more than £30,000. In the case cited[83] rescission of the supply contract was treated as a "claim" which affected the credit agreement; the better view is that the rescission of the supply contract gives rise to a claim for repetition and damages which can be set off against the debt due under the credit agreement. What is not clear is whether the debtor having rescinded the supply contract is entitled to terminate the credit agreement without payment of interest and other charges.[84]

The creditor may, of course, be liable to the debtor in respect of misrepresentations made by the supplier as his deemed agent.[85]

Credit-sale agreement

4.9 A credit-sale agreement is an agreement for the sale of goods under which the price or part of it is payable by instalments but which is not a conditional sale agreement.[86] If the purchaser is not a body corporate, and the amount payable by instalments does not exceed £15,000, the agreement is a debtor-creditor-supplier agreement.[87] It may be an exempt agreement if the number of payments to be made by the debtor does not exceed four.[88]

Hire-purchase and conditional sale

4.10 A hire-purchase agreement is an agreement, other than a conditional sale agreement, under which (a) goods are hired in return for periodical payments by the person to whom they are hired, and (b) the property in the goods will pass to that person if the terms of the agreement are complied with and one of the following occurs: (i) the exercise of an option to purchase by that person, (ii) the doing of any other specified act by any party to the agreement, (iii) the happening of any other specified event.[89]

The agreement is treated as providing fixed-sum credit to finance the transaction of an amount equal to the total price of the goods less the aggregate of the deposit (if any) and the total charge for credit.[90] A hire-purchase agreement is a debtor-creditor-supplier agreement.[91] It does not qualify as an exempt agreement.

A conditional sale agreement is a sale agreement under which the price or part of it is payable by instalments and the property in the goods is to remain in the seller (notwithstanding that the buyer is to be in possession of them) until such conditions as to the payment of instalments or otherwise as may be specified in the agreement are fulfilled.[92] If the purchaser is not a body corporate and the amount payable by instalments

---

[83] *United Dominions Trust* v. *Taylor*, 1980 S.L.T. (Sh.Ct.) 28. See Gane [1980] J.B.L. 277; Davidson (1980) 86 L.Q.R. 343.
[84] Dobson [1981] J.B.L. 179.
[85] See para. 3.14; Fairest & Rudkin (1978) 128 N.L.J. 243.
[86] See next paragraph.
[87] See para. 3.3.
[88] See para. 3.4 (Category 11).
[89] Consumer Credit Act 1974, s.189(1).
[90] s.9(3).
[91] See para. 3.3.
[92] s.189(1).

does not exceed £15,000, the agreement is a debtor-creditor-supplier agreement.[93] It does not qualify as an exempt agreement.

The buyer under a conditional sale agreement which is a consumer credit agreement is not to be taken as a person who has bought or agreed to buy goods for purposes of s.25(1) of the Sale of Goods Act 1979, and he thus cannot give a good title to a sub-purchaser.[94] In consequence, the differences between a hire-purchase and conditional sale under the 1974 Act are slight and most of the special regulatory provisions apply to both transactions. The "total price" under a hire-purchase or conditional sale agreement is the total sum payable thereunder, including any sum payable on the exercise of an option to purchase but excluding any sum payable as a penalty or as compensation or damages for a breach of the agreement.

The following provisions apply to both hire-purchase and conditional sale agreements:

(1) if the debtor is in breach of the agreement after he has paid one-third or more of the total price of the goods and while the goods are still the creditor's property, the creditor cannot recover possession of the goods (which in this context are "protected goods") except on an order of the court[95]; if he does take the goods without a court order, the agreement terminates, the debtor is released from all liability thereunder and is entitled to recover all sums already paid from the creditor. Where there is an installation charge specified in the agreement the one-third figure is the sum of the installation charge and one third of the remainder of the total price. The protection does not apply if the debtor has terminated the agreement. On the debtor's death the protection continues until confirmation is expede. In certain circumstances there may be protection although one-third of the price has not been paid if there had been such payment under a prior agreement relating to the same goods or some of them.

(2) If, without a court order, the creditor enters premises to take possession of the goods, the entry is actionable as a breach of statutory duty.[96]

(3) At any time before the final payment, the debtor is entitled to terminate the agreement by giving notice.[97] On termination, the debtor is liable, unless the agreement provides for a smaller payment or for no payment, to pay to the creditor the amount by which one-half of the total price exceeds the aggregate of the sums paid and the sums due in respect of the total price immediately before termination.[98] The liability may be reduced by the court to an amount representing the loss sustained by the creditor in consequence of the termination. The debtor is also liable to recompense the creditor if he has failed to take reasonable care of the goods. If the debtor wrongfully retains possession of the goods, the court may order delivery of the goods to the creditor without giving the debtor an

---

[93] See para. 3.3.
[94] Sale of Goods Act 1979, s.25(2).
[95] Consumer Credit Act 1974, s.90.
[96] s.92.
[97] s.99. See *Wadham Stringer Finance Ltd.* v. *Meaney* [1980] 3 All E.R. 789.
[98] s.100.

option to pay the value of the goods. If, under a conditional sale agreement, the property in the goods has passed to the debtor and has then been transferred to a third party who did not become the debtor under the agreement, the debtor cannot terminate the agreement.[99] If the property has passed to the debtor but there has been no further transfer to a third party the debtor can terminate the agreement and the property will vest in the person who owned the goods before they became the property of the debtor.[1]

(4) The goods, if they have not become the debtor's property, are not subject to the landlord's hypothec in the period between service of a default notice and the date of its expiry or compliance with it; nor are they so subject in the period between the commencement and the termination of an action by the creditor to enforce an agreement which is enforceable on the order of a court only.[2]

(5) A time order[3] providing for instalment payments may deal with sums which, although not payable at the time of the order, would if the agreement continued become payable subsequently.[4]

(6) After the making of a time order the debtor is treated as custodier of the goods notwithstanding that the agreement has terminated.[5]

(7) In an action for an enforcement order or for a time order or for recovery of the goods, the court may make a "return order" or a "transfer order."[6] A return order is for return of the goods to the creditor. A transfer order is for the transfer to the debtor of the creditor's title to such part of the goods as seems just and the return of the remainder of the goods to the creditor. Such an order can be made only when the "paid-up sum" exceeds the part of the total price referable to the transferred goods by an amount equal to at least one-third of the unpaid balance of the total price. The "paid-up sum" is the part of the total price which has been paid with any adjustments made by the court in its discretion. Where a return order or transfer order has been made, the debtor has the option to pay the balance of the total price and on fulfilment of any other necessary conditions retain all the goods. If the debtor fails to return the goods as ordered, the court may revoke the order and order the debtor to pay the unpaid portion of so much of the total price as is referable to those goods.

(8) If, under a time, return or transfer order, the total price is paid and any other necessary conditions are fulfilled, the creditor's title to the goods vests in the debtor.[7] There is a curious provision about "adverse detention"[8] which seems to have no relevance in Scotland.

---

[99] s.99(4).
[1] s.99(5).
[2] s.104.
[3] See para. 3.19.
[4] s.130(2).
[5] s.130(4).
[6] s.133.
[7] s.133(5).
[8] s.134.

Consumer hire agreements

4.11 It should be noted that the provisions which make the dealer the supplier's agent in antecedent negotiations do not apply to consumer hire agreements.[9] The hirer can terminate the agreement by giving notice but the notice cannot expire earlier than 18 months after the making of the agreement.[10] A minimum period of notice is prescribed. There is no statutory right to terminate if (a) the total annual payments exceed £900, or, (b) the goods are hired for purposes of a business carried on by the hirer or the hirer holds himself out as requiring the goods for those purposes and the goods are selected by the hirer and acquired by the owner at the hirer's request from any person other than the owner's associate, or (c) the hirer requires, or holds himself out as requiring, the goods for the purpose of hiring them to other persons in the course of his business. The Director may give a dispensation from this termination provision to a person carrying on a consumer hire business.

The debtor is treated as custodier of the goods if he is in possession of them notwithstanding that the agreement has been terminated following the making of a time order.[11]

If the owner recovers possession of the goods otherwise than by action, the hirer may ask the court to order that any sums paid by the hirer in respect of the goods shall be repaid and the obligation to pay the whole or part of any sum owed by the hirer to the owner shall cease. A like provision may be made in an order for delivery of the goods.[12]

In making a suspension order, the court shall not use its powers so as to extend the period for which, under the agreement, the hirer is entitled to possession of the goods.[13]

Conditional sale of land

4.12 On breach of a regulated conditional sale agreement relating to land, the creditor can recover possession of the land on an order of the court only.[14] Such an agreement cannot be terminated by the debtor after the title has passed to him.[15]

Credit-tokens

4.13 A credit-token agreement is a regulated agreement for the provision of credit in connection with the use of a credit-token.[16] A credit-token is a card, check, voucher, coupon, stamp, form, booklet or other document or thing given to an individual by a person carrying on a consumer credit business, who undertakes: (a) that on production of it (whether or not some other action is also required) he will supply cash, goods and services (or any of them) on credit, or (b) that, where, on the production of it to a third party (whether or not any other action is also required) the third

---

[9] Dobson [1983] J.B.L. 312, 316.
[10] s.101.
[11] s.130(4).
[12] s.132.
[13] s.135(3).
[14] s.92. As to the court's discretion when the agreement is for purchase of a dwelling-house by three or more instalments, see Tenant's Rights (Scotland) Act 1980, s.74.
[15] s.99(3).
[16] s.14(2).

party supplies cash, goods and services (or any of them) he will pay the third party for these (whether or not deducting any discount or commission), in return for payment to him by the individual.[17] The credit is provided when the third party supplies the cash, goods or services.[18]

The debtor is liable for loss to the creditor from the use of the token by a person who possessed it with the debtor's consent.[19] The debtor is also liable to a maximum of £50 for loss to the creditor from the use of the token by persons not authorised by the debtor. Neither liability can arise from use of the token after notice of the loss or theft of the token has been given orally (in which case written confirmation may be required), or in writing, to the creditor at an address stated in the agreement.[20] If the debtor avers that any use was unauthorised the onus is on the creditor to prove that the use was authorised or that the use occurred before notice had been given to the creditor.[21] Except in the case of a small agreement, on the renewal of a token, the creditor must give the debtor a copy of the executed agreement and of any document referred to in it; the agreement cannot be enforced during default.[22]

---

[17] s.14(1); *Elliott* v. *Director General of Fair Trading* [1980] 1 W.L.R. 977; *R.* v. *Lambie* [1982] A.C. 449.
[18] s.14(3).
[19] s.84.
[20] Consumer Credit (Credit-Token Agreements) Regulations 1983 (S.I. 1983 No. 1555).
[21] s.171(4)(*b*).
[22] s.85.

CHAPTER 5

BONDS AND BILLS

Bond

5.1 "A bond in Scots law, is—broadly—neither more nor less than a written obligation to pay or perform."[1] The essential part of a bond for money is "an engagement, absolutely or conditionally, at a day certain or in a specified event, to pay a definite sum of money."[2] A clause of registration for execution is not a requisite.[3] The document must be attested or holograph.[4]

The most important characteristic of a bond is that the holder "need not concern himself with the debt for which it was granted, so long as the instrument retains its virtue—for he sues on it, and not on the debt, while the holder of a mere acknowledgment of debt must sue on the debt with the acknowledgment as evidence, which may be sufficient or not, according to circumstances, whether *per se* or aided by other evidence."[5]

Negotiable instruments

5.2 The characteristics of a negotiable instrument are (a) "when transferred it passes in its own *corpus* the thing it represents without intimation,"[6] (b) a good title is acquired by a party who takes it bona fide for value, notwithstanding any defect of title in the party from whom it is so taken.[7] It can be contrasted with other documents of debt in that assignation followed by intimation is not required to transfer it and the maxim *assignatus utitur jure auctoris* does not apply. A document may be transferable by indorsation and yet not negotiable[6]—a deposit receipt, for example.[8] A bill of lading can be transferred by delivery but it does not always give the transferee a better title than that of the transferor.[9] Debenture bonds payable to bearer are negotiable instruments.[10]

A document acquires the privilege of negotiability only by statute or by mercantile usage and the parties themselves cannot make a document negotiable.[11]

Definition of a bill

5.3 Bills of exchange, "the simplest of all obligations in form, and the least trammelled with solemnities, are, in respect of performance, the most

---

[1] *North of Scotland Bank* v. *Inland Revenue*, 1931 S.C. 149, *per* L. P. Clyde at p. 154.
[2] Bell, *Comm.*, I, 352.
[3] *Purdie* v. *Hamilton* (1900) 8 S.L.T. 83.
[4] Bell, *Comm.*, I, 352. But a unilateral binding obligation to pay money need not be probative: *Rank Xerox Ltd.* v. *Lane* [1981] A.C. 629, *per* Lord Keith of Kinkel at p. 648.
[5] *Neilson's Trs.* v. *Neilson's Trs.* (1883) 11 R. 119, *per* Lord Young at p. 123.
[6] *Per* Lord Neaves, *Connal & Co.* v. *Loder* (1868) 6 M. 1095 at 1102.
[7] *Crouch* v. *Credit Foncier of England Ltd.* (1873) 8 Q.B.D. 374.
[8] *Wood* v. *Clydesdale Bank Ltd.*, 1914 S.C. 397.
[9] *Simmons* v. *London Joint Stock Bank* [1891] 1 Ch. 270.
[10] *Bechuanaland Exploration Co.* v. *London Trading Bank Ltd.* [1898] 2 Q.B. 658; *Edelstein* v. *Schuler & Co.* [1902] 2 K.B. 144.
[11] *Dixon* v. *Bovill* (1856) 3 Macq. 1.

Definition of a Bill

strict, and in execution the most rapid, of all the obligations known in law."[12] A bill of exchange[13] is an unconditional order in writing, addressed by one person to another, signed by the person giving it,[14] requiring the person to whom it is addressed to pay on demand, or at a fixed or determinable future time, a sum certain in money to or to the order of a specified person, or to bearer. A bill is payable to bearer which is expressed to be so payable or on which the only or last indorsement is an indorsement in blank.[15] No stamp is required now.[16] The person who gives the order is the *drawer*; the person to whom the order is addressed is the *drawee*; and the specified person to whom the money is to be paid is the *payee*.

Polite expressions such as "please" do not mean that the document is not an order.[17] A document which orders an act to be done in addition to the payment of money is not a bill.[18] An order to pay out of a particular fund is not unconditional but an unqualified order to pay, coupled with (a) an indication of a particular fund out of which the drawee is to reimburse himself, or a particular account to be debited with the amount, or (b) a statement of the transaction which gives rise to the bill, is unconditional.[19]

The drawee must be named or indicated with reasonable certainty.[20] There may be two or more drawees but not in the alternative nor in succession.[21] If the drawer and the drawee are the same person or the drawee is fictitious or is *incapax*, the holder may treat the instrument, at his option, as a bill or as a promissory note.[22]

If the bill is not payable to bearer, the payee must be named or indicated with reasonable certainty.[23] There may be joint payees or the bill may be payable in the alternative to one of two, or one or some of several payees. A bill may be payable to the holder of an office for the time being.[24] If the payee is a fictitious or non-existing person the bill may be treated as payable to bearer.[25] An order "Pay Cash or Order" is not a bill.[26]

A sum "together with any interest that may accrue thereon" is not certain.[27] A sum is certain although it is to be paid with interest or by instalments, by instalments with a provision that on default the whole will become due, or at an indicated rate of exchange or rate to be ascertained

---

[12] Bell, *Comm.*, I, 411.
[13] Bills of Exchange Act 1882, s.3(1).
[14] A mark attested by witnesses is sufficient but not effectual for summary diligence: *Adair* v. *Cunningham* (1887) 4 Sh.Ct.Rep. 51.
[15] s.8(3). As to foreign bills, see. ss.4, 51, 72.
[16] Finance Act 1970, Sched. 7, para. 2.
[17] *Provost of Airdrie* v. *French* (1915) 31 Sh.Ct.Rep. 189.
[18] s.3(2).
[19] s.3(3).
[20] s.6(1).
[21] s.6(2). As to a referee in case of need, see s.15.
[22] s.5(2).
[23] s.7(1). The bill may be payable to, or to the order of, the drawer or drawee: s.5(1).
[24] s.7(2).
[25] s.7(3), See Byles, pp. 27–31.
[26] *Orbit Mining & Trading Co. Ltd.* v. *Westminster Bank Ltd.* [1963] 1 Q.B. 794.
[27] *Lamberton* v. *Aiken* (1899) 2 F. 189. But see Chalmers, p. 29; *cf.* Byles, p. 21.

as directed. Where there is a discrepancy between words and figures, the sum denoted by words is the amount payable.[28]

A bill is payable on demand if it is expressed to be payable on demand, or at sight or on presentation or in which no time of payment is expressed.[29] A bill is payable at a determinable future time if it is expressed to be payable at a fixed period after date or sight or on or at a fixed period after the occurrence of a specified event which is certain to happen, though the time of happening may be uncertain.[30] An instrument expressed to be payable on a contingency is not a bill.

The bill is due and payable in all cases on the last day of the time of payment as fixed by the bill or, if that is a non-business day, on the succeeding business day. There are now no days of grace.[31] Non-business days are Saturday, Sunday, Good Friday, Christmas Day, a bank holiday and a day appointed as a public fast or thanksgiving day.[32]

A bill is not invalid by reason that it is not dated, that it does not specify the value given or that any value has been given therefor or that it does not specify the place where it is payable.[33] The usual procedure is that the drawer delivers the bill to the payee who may present it to the drawee for acceptance. The drawee, if he is prepared to obey the order, normally accepts the bill by writing "accepted" across its face and signing his name beneath; but a mere signature is sufficient.[34] The drawee, who becomes by his acceptance the *acceptor*, returns the bill to the payee. On the day the bill falls due the payee presents the bill to the acceptor for payment and receives the sum due.

If the bill is payable at sight or on demand, presentment for acceptance is obviously unnecessary; if the bill is payable at a fixed period after sight, or if the bill expressly stipulates that it shall be presented for acceptance, or if it is payable elsewhere than at the residence or place of business of the drawee, presentment for acceptance is necessary[35]; in other cases, presentment for acceptance is optional but it is advantageous in that it obtains the drawee's liability on the bill.

Negotiation

5.4   The payee may *negotiate* the bill if (a) it is expressed to be payable to order, (b) it is payable to a particular person and does not contain words prohibiting transfer or indicating an intention that it should not be transferable, (c) it is expressed to be payable to bearer.[36] In cases (a) and (b) the bill is negotiated by the payee's indorsing it, *i.e.* placing his

---

[28] s.9. Bills and notes (other than cheques) for sums less than £1 are prohibited in Scotland: Bank Notes (Scotland) Act 1845, ss.16, 20.
[29] s.10(1).
[30] s.11. The fixed period is calculated by excluding the day from which it runs and including the day of payment: s.14(2).
[31] s.14(1) as substituted by Banking and Financial Dealings Act 1971, s.3(2).
[32] s.92.
[33] s.3(4). The holder may insert a date: s.12.
[34] s.17.
[35] s.39.
[36] s.8. An intention that the bill should not be transferable is evinced by the words "Pay X only" or, in the case of a bill other than a cheque, "Not Negotiable": *Hibernian Bank Ltd.* v. *Gysin and Hanson* [1939] 1 K.B. 483, but see Byles, p. 85, as to that decision.

Liability

signature on the bill and delivering it to the *indorsee*.[37] The indorsement may be *special*, *i.e.* it may specify the person to whom or to whose order the bill is to be payable; or it may be *in blank*, *i.e.* specify no indorsee, in which case it becomes payable to bearer.[38] A bill expressed to be payable to bearer is negotiated by delivery.[39] The payee or indorsee of a bill who is in possession of it or the person in possession of a bill which is payable to bearer is a holder.[40] The holder is in right of the bill and can present it for acceptance, if that has not been done already, and present it for payment; he can also, of course, negotiate the bill further.

Dishonour

If the bill is dishonoured by non-acceptance, *i.e.* if the drawee refuses to accept it, an immediate right of recourse against the drawer and indorsers accrues to the holder and he need not present the bill for payment.[41] A similar right accrues to the holder where a bill is dishonoured by non-payment, *i.e.* when payment is refused or cannot be obtained[42]; here, of course, the holder may have a right against the acceptor as well. In all cases of dishonour by non-acceptance or non-payment, the holder, to preserve his right of recourse, must give notice of dishonour to the drawer and to each indorser; a drawer or indorser to whom notice is not given is discharged.[43] Further, if the bill is to be enforced by summary diligence against any of the parties liable thereon it must be protested for non-acceptance or non-payment, as the case may be.[44] An indorser who has been compelled to pay the bill may in his turn seek payment from the drawer or any prior indorsers, provided that he has given notice of dishonour to them.[45] A drawer who has been compelled to pay the bill can enforce payment of it against the acceptor.[46]

5.5

Liability

It will therefore be seen that no one is liable on a bill unless his signature appears thereon as acceptor, drawer or indorser.[47] A *transferor by delivery*, *i.e.* a holder of a bill payable to bearer who has negotiated it by delivery without indorsing it, is not liable on the bill.[48] The acceptor is the party primarily liable and the drawer and indorsers have a secondary liability in the event of dishonour.

5.6

A document in the form of a bill which bears the signature of the

---

[37] ss.31, 32. See, as to indorsement on the back of the document, *K. H. R. Financings Ltd.* v. *Jackson*, 1977 S.L.T. (Sh.Ct.) 6. As to restrictive and conditional indorsements, see ss.31(5), 33 and 35.
[38] s.34.
[39] s.31(2).
[40] s.2.
[41] s.43. The drawee may be liable to the holder by virtue of the assignation effected under s.53(2)—see para. 6.6.
[42] s.47. As to acceptance and payment for honour, see ss.65–68.
[43] s.48.
[44] See para. 19.6.
[45] s.55. See also s.49(14).
[46] s.59(2) (unless it is an accommodation bill: s.59(3)).
[47] s.23; a person who signs a bill otherwise than as drawer or acceptor thereby incurs the liabilities of an indorser to a holder in due course (s.56); such a signature is called an "aval"—see *G. & H. Montage Gmbh* v. *Irvani* [1990] 1 W.L.R. 667.
[48] s.58.

acceptor, but not that of the drawer, is not a valid bill but it is evidence of the acceptor's indebtedness to the person to whom he had delivered it.[49]

Accommodation bills

5.7 For the purpose of lending his name to some other person, a person may sign a bill as drawer, acceptor, or indorser without receiving value therefor. For example, the drawee may accept a bill although he in fact does not owe money to the drawer. Such a person is known as an "accommodation party."[50] An accommodation party is liable on the bill to a holder for value even if the holder for value, when he took the bill, knew that he was an accommodation party.[51] The accommodation party is not, however, liable in a question with the accommodated party and the true relationship of the parties *inter se* can be proved by parole evidence.[52]

Enforcement by action; lost bills

5.8 The holder,[53] or a transferee for value,[54] can sue on the bill in his own name. Where a bill has been lost before it is overdue, the person who was the holder of it may apply to the drawer to give him another bill of the same tenor, giving security to the drawer if required to indemnify him against all persons whatever in case the bill alleged to have been lost shall be found again.[55] If the drawer on request refuses to give such a duplicate bill, he may be compelled to do so. In any action or proceeding upon a bill, the court may order that the loss of the instrument shall not be set up, provided an indemnity be given to the satisfaction of the court against the claims of any other person upon the instrument in question.[56]

Holder in due course

5.9 A holder in due course is a holder who has taken a bill, complete and regular on the face of it,[57] under the following conditions:
(a) that he became the holder of it before it was overdue, and without notice that it had been previously dishonoured, if such was the fact;
(b) that he took the bill in good faith and for value, and that at the time the bill was negotiated to him he had no notice of any defect in the title of the person who negotiated it.[58] The title of the person who negotiated the bill is defective if he obtained the bill, or the acceptance thereof, by fraud, duress, or force and fear, or other unlawful means, or for an illegal consideration or if he negotiated it in breach of faith or under such circumstances as amount to a fraud.[59]

---

[49] *Lawson's Exrs.* v. *Watson*, 1907 S.C. 1353.
[50] s.28(1); *McLelland* v. *Mackay* (1908) 24 Sh.Ct.Rep. 157.
[51] s.28(2); he is also liable to a transferee for value: *Hood* v. *Stewart* (1890) 17 R. 749; the accommodation is not a defect: *Downie* v. *Saunders' Trs.* (1898) 6 S.L.T. 134.
[52] *Nicol's Trs.* v. *Sutherland*, 1951 S.C. (H.L.) 21, *per* Lord Simonds at p. 27.
[53] s.38(1).
[54] s.31(4); *Hood* v. *Stewart* (1890) 17 R. 749.
[55] s.69.
[56] s.70; see *Enever* v. *Craig*, 1913 2 S.L.T. 30.
[57] "Looking at the bill, front and back, without the aid of outside evidence, it must be complete and regular in itself," *per* Denning L.J., *Arab Bank Ltd.* v. *Ross* [1952] 2 Q.B. 216 at 226.
[58] s.29(1). As to a bill drawn in a set, see s.71.
[59] s.29(2); the list of defects is perhaps not exhaustive: Chalmers, p. 98.

Value may be constituted by "any consideration sufficient to support a simple contract," or by an antecedent debt or liability.[60] If the holder has a lien on the bill, by contract or implication of law, he is deemed to be a holder for value to the extent of the sum for which he has a lien.[61] Once value has been given for a bill the holder is deemed to be a holder for value as regards the acceptor and all parties to the bill who became parties prior to such time.[62] Every party whose signature appears on a bill is prima facie deemed to have become a party thereto for value.[63]

A holder in due course holds the bill free from any defect of title of prior parties as well as from mere personal defences available to prior parties among themselves, and may enforce payment against all parties liable on the bill.[64]

Every holder of a bill is prima facie deemed to be a holder in due course, but if in an action on the bill it is admitted or proved that the acceptance, issue, or subsequent negotiation of the bill is affected with fraud, duress, or force and fear, or illegality, the burden of proof is shifted, unless and until the holder proves that, subsequent to the alleged fraud or illegality, value has in good faith been given for the bill.[65] Except where an indorsement bears a date after the maturity of the bill, every negotiation is prima facie deemed to have been effected before the bill was overdue.[66]

A holder (whether for value or not) who derives his title through a holder in due course, and who is not himself a party to any fraud or illegality affecting it, has all the rights of that holder in due course as regards the acceptor, and all parties to the bill prior to that holder.[67] So, if the bill is negotiated by a holder in due course back to the drawer, the latter has the rights of a holder in due course.[68] The same would apply to a payee, to whom the bill had been negotiated by a holder in due course.

The payee as such, although he is a holder,[69] is not a holder in due course because the bill has not been "negotiated" to him as required by s.29(1)[70] and he is not affected by the provisions of s.30(2) of the Act.[71] As regards the drawer, the payee is merely in the position of the holder of a writ *in re mercatoria* which bears the grantor's signature and which *ex facie* records an obligation of the grantor to the holder.[72]

A person to whom an overdue bill is negotiated acquires it subject to any defect of title affecting it at its maturity and cannot acquire or give a better title than that which the person from whom he took it has.[73] A

---

[60] s.27(1).
[61] s.27(3).
[62] s.27(2).
[63] s.30(1).
[64] s.38(2).
[65] s.30(2). A fraudulent preference in bankruptcy was not *per se* fraud: *Osterreichische Länderbank* v. *S'Elite Ltd.* [1981] Q.B. 565.
[66] s.36(4).
[67] s.29(3).
[68] *Jade International* v. *Robert Nicholas Ltd.* [1978] Q.B. 917.
[69] s.2.
[70] *R. E. Jones Ltd.* v. *Waring and Gillow Ltd.* [1926] A.C. 670.
[71] *Talbot* v. *Von Boris* [1911] 1 K.B. 854.
[72] *Thompson* v. *J. Barke and Company (Caterers) Ltd.*, 1975 S.L.T. 67.
[73] s.36(2).

demand bill is overdue for this purpose when it appears on the face of it to have been in circulation for an unreasonable length of time.

Where a bill which is not overdue has been dishonoured, any person who takes it with notice of dishonour takes it subject to any defect of title attaching to it at the time of dishonour.[74]

Forgery

5.10 The person against whom the bill is being enforced may deny that he signed it. The onus of proving that a signature is genuine is on the person founding on the bill.[75] However, a person may bar himself by his conduct from relying on the forgery, as where he has said that the signature was his or has failed to notify interested parties once the forgery has come to his knowledge.[76]

Ultra vires

5.11 A cheque drawn on the account of a company by two directors in order to repay a personal debt of one of them was held to be not enforceable by the payee against the company because the circumstances of its issue were such as to put him on his inquiry.[77]

Unauthorised signature

5.12 Even if the defender did not himself write his name on the bill, he may have to meet an allegation that the name was written by his agent acting within the scope of his authority.

Agency

5.13 Liability on a bill may be incurred through an agent. The principal's name must be written on the bill before he can be liable and, although it is provided that no one can be liable on a bill unless he has signed it,[78] there is a further provision that the signature may be written by another person by authority of the first.[79] Accordingly, the agent may write his principal's name on the bill and, if this is within his actual or ostensible authority, the principal will be liable. Alternatively, there may be a *per procurationem* signature, *i.e.* the agent signs "pp. Jones & Co., James Smith" or uses expressions such as "on behalf of" or "for."[80] Such a signature operates as notice that the agent has but a limited authority to sign and the principal is only bound if the agent was acting within the actual limits of his authority.[81] If the agent merely signs his own name followed by words indicating that he is an agent but not disclosing the principal's name, the

---

[74] s.36(5).

[75] *McIntyre* v. *National Bank of Scotland*, 1910 S.C. 150.

[76] s.24; *Brook* v. *Hook* (1871) L.R. 6 Ex. 89; *Greenwood* v. *Martins' Bank Ltd.* [1933] A.C. 51; see also *McKenzie* v. *British Linen Co.* (1881) 8 R. (H.L.) 8; *British Linen Co.* v. *Cowan* (1906) 8 F. 704.

[77] *Thompson* v. *J. Barke and Company (Caterers) Ltd.*, *supra*.

[78] s.23; but a person who signs a trade or assumed name is liable as if he had signed his own name.

[79] s.91(1).

[80] Byles, pp. 68–70.

[81] s.25; as to *per procurationem* signatures generally, see *L.C.C.* v. *Agricultural Food Products Ltd.* [1955] 2 Q.B. 218; *Morison* v. *London County and Westminster Bank Ltd.* [1914] 3 K.B. 356.

principal is not liable even if the party transacting with the agent knew his identity.[82]

There is one exceptional situation in which the principal may be liable even although his name is not written on the bill. Where the bill is drawn on the principal, and the agent, acting within his authority, accepts it in his own name, with representative words added, it seems that the principal is liable.[83]

The agent's authority can be proved by parole evidence.[84] If the signature is unauthorised it is wholly inoperative and no right to retain the bill or to give a discharge therefor or to enforce payment thereof against any party thereto can be acquired through or under the signature,[85] but (a) the signature may be ratified if it does not amount to a forgery, (b) the party against whom it is sought to retain or enforce payment may be precluded from setting up the lack of authority, (c) the acceptor cannot deny to a holder in due course the drawer's authority to draw,[86] (d) an indorser cannot deny to a holder in due course the regularity in all respects of the drawer's signature and of all previous indorsements.[87]

The signature of a firm name is equivalent to the signatures of all the persons liable as partners.[88] A bill or promissory note is deemed to have been signed on behalf of a company if it is signed in the name of, or by or on behalf or on account of, the company by a person acting under its authority.[89] If the company's articles provide that one director may be authorised by the board to sign bills on behalf of the company, a party transacting with the company is not bound to inquire whether the power was in fact granted.[90] The secretary of a company may be presumed to have authority to sign bills on its behalf.[91]

Personal liability of agent

In certain circumstances a person who has intended to sign a bill as an agent is personally liable thereon. He is not liable if his name is not written on the bill. As a general rule, he is not liable if he has added words to his signature indicating that he signs for and on behalf of a principal, or in a representative character.[92] But the mere addition to the signature of words describing him as an agent, or as filling a representative character—"a description for the purpose merely of showing who he is and how he came to sign"[93]—does not exempt him from personal liability. So the addition of "director" followed by the company name is not sufficient to elide liability[94]; it is necessary to use an expression such as

5.14

---

[82] Chalmers, p. 68.
[83] Bowstead, *Agency* (15th ed., 1985), p. 329.
[84] Thorburn, p. 27.
[85] s.24.
[86] s.54(2).
[87] s.55(2).
[88] s.23(2).
[89] Companies Act 1985, s.37.
[90] *Dresdner Bank* v. *Wolfson & Sons Ltd.* (1928) 44 Sh.Ct.Rep. 262.
[91] *Commercial Bank* v. *Fraser Ross & Co. Ltd.* (1906) 22 Sh.Ct.Rep. 169.
[92] 1882 Act, s.26(1).
[93] *per* Scrutton L.J., *Elliott* v. *Bax-Ironside* [1925] 2 K.B. 301 at 307.
[94] *Brebner* v. *Henderson*, 1925 S.C. 643; see also *Brown* v. *Sutherland* (1875) 2 R. 615; *McMeekin* v. *Easton* (1889) 16 R. 363; *Landes* v. *Marcus* (1909) 25 T.L.R. 478; *Kettle* v. *Dunster* (1928) 138 L.T. 158.

"on behalf of"[95] or "for and on behalf of Jones as agent."[96] The construction most favourable to the validity of the instrument is adopted.[97]

There is a doubt about the effect of words which clearly indicate that the signature is as an agent but which do not disclose the principal's name.[98]

Where the bill is drawn on the agent and the agent accepts it by writing the principal's name thereon, it seems that neither is liable because only the drawee can accept[99]; if such a bill is accepted by the agent's signing his own name, the principal is obviously not liable and the agent obviously is[1]; if such a bill is accepted by the agent's signing his own name followed by words indicating that the acceptance is on behalf of the principal, it seems that the principal is not liable and the question of the agent's liability is in doubt.[2]

Where the bill is drawn on the principal and the agent accepts by signing his own name without qualification, it seems that the agent is not liable.[3]

An agent who signs as agent a bill outwith his authority is not personally liable on the bill.[4]

If an officer of a company or any person on its behalf signs or authorises to be signed on behalf of the company any bill, promissory note, endorsement or cheque wherein the company's name is not correctly stated in legible characters, he is personally liable to the holder of the bill, note or cheque for the amount thereof unless it is duly paid by the company[5]; liability may be elided if the incorrect wording was written by the person enforcing the bill.[6]

Delivery

5.15   If the bill is in the hands of a holder in due course a valid delivery of the bill by all parties prior to him so as to make them liable to him is conclusively presumed.[7]

If the bill is in the hands of an immediate party or a remote party who is not a holder in due course, it is a defence that delivery was not made by or under the authority of the party drawing, accepting, or indorsing as the

---

[95] *per* Lord Sands, *Brebner* v. *Henderson, supra*, at p. 648. See also *Rolfe Lubell & Co.* v. *Keith* [1979] 1 All E.R. 860.

[96] *per* Scrutton L.J., *Elliott* v. *Bax-Ironside, supra*, at p. 307; *cf. Bondina Ltd.* v. *Rollaway Shower Blinds Ltd.* [1986] 1 W.L.R. 517.

[97] s.26(2).

[98] Powell, *Law of Agency* (2nd ed., 1961), p. 25.

[99] Bowstead, *op. cit.*, p. 454, Chalmers, *op. cit.*, p. 42.

[1] ss.23, 26.

[2] Powell, *op. cit.*, p. 251; *cf. Encyclopaedia of the Laws of Scotland*, Vol. II., p. 245.

[3] Bowstead, *op. cit.*, p. 454.

[4] Bowstead, *op. cit.*, p. 454.

[5] Companies Act 1985, s.349(4); *Scottish and Newcastle Breweries Ltd.* v. *Blair*, 1967 S.L.T. 72; *British Airways* v. *Parish* [1979] 2 Lloyd's Rep. 361; *Blum* v. *OCP Repartition SA* [1988] B.C.L.C. 170; *Rafsanjan Pistachio Producers Co-operative* v. *Reiss* [1990] B.C.L.C. 352.

[6] *Durham Fancy Goods Ltd.* v. *Michael Jackson (Fancy Goods) Ltd.* [1968] 2 Q.B. 839. The use of the abbreviations "Ltd." and "Co." does not make the name incorrect: *Banque de l'Indochine et de Suez S.A.* v. *Euroseas Group Finance Co. Ltd.* [1981] 3 All E.R. 198.

[7] 1882 Act, s.21(2); but see *Encyclopaedia of the Laws of Scotland*, Vol. II, p. 212.

case may be.[8] Where, however, the bill is no longer in the possession of a party who has signed it as drawer, acceptor or indorser, a valid and unconditional delivery by him is presumed until the contrary is proved.[9] It is also a defence to show that the delivery was conditional or for a special purpose only and not for the purpose of transferring the property in the bill.[10] Such a condition can be proved by parole evidence.[11]

Although the general rule is that every contract on a bill—the drawer's, the acceptor's, or an indorser's—is incomplete and revocable until delivery to give effect thereto, if an acceptance is written on a bill and the drawee gives notice to or according to the directions of the person entitled to the bill that he has accepted it, the acceptance then becomes complete and irrevocable.[12]

Fraud or force and fear
These are not defences against a holder in due course,[13] but if it is proved that the acceptance, issue or subsequent negotiation of a bill was affected with fraud, or force and fear, the burden of proof is shifted unless and until the holder proves that, subsequently, value was in good faith given for the bill.[14]

They are defences against an immediate party or a remote party who is not a holder in due course.[15]

5.16

Incapacity
Intoxication is not a defence unless it amounts to loss of reason.[16]

5.17

Absence of consideration
Non-onerosity is not *per se* a defence.[17] A bill granted as a gift is valid.[18] Failure of the consideration may constitute a defence in a question with an immediate party but not against a holder in due course. So, where a bill had been accepted for the price of goods, and the goods were subsequently rejected, the seller's agent could not enforce payment.[19] Where a bill had been granted in terms of an agreement to form a partnership, and the contract was subsequently resiled from, it was held that the consideration could be impeached by parole evidence.[20]

5.18

Agreements qualifying obligation
Agreements qualifying the obligation on the bill are ineffectual unless

5.19

---

[8] s.21(2).
[9] s.21(3).
[10] s.21(2).
[11] *Semple* v. *Kyle* (1902) 4 F. 421; s.100.
[12] s.21(1).
[13] s.38(2); by the former law of Scotland force and fear was a defence even in a question with a holder in due course and the extent of the change made by the Act has been questioned: Thorburn, p. 83; *Encyclopaedia of the Laws of Scotland*, Vol. II, p. 210; as to fraud, see *Clydesdale & North of Scotland Bank Ltd.* v. *Diamond* (1963) 79 Sh.Ct.Rep. 145.
[14] s.30(2); *Nelson* v. *Easdale Slate Quarries Co. Ltd.*, 1910 1 S.L.T. 21.
[15] *Ayres* v. *Moore* [1940] 1 K.B. 278 (fraud).
[16] *Laing* v. *Taylor*, 1978 S.L.T. (Sh.Ct.) 59.
[17] *Law* v. *Humphrey* (1876) 3 R. 1192.
[18] Thorburn, p. 76.
[19] *Wallace & Brown* v. *Robinson Fleming & Co.* (1885) 22 S.L.R. 830.
[20] *Pert* v. *Bruce*, 1937 S.L.T. 475.

they can be proved by writ or oath. This rule is not affected by the terms of s.100 which provides that any fact relating to a bill which is relevant to any question of liability thereon may be proved by parole evidence. So where the holder sued the drawer it was held incompetent for the defender to prove by parole evidence an arrangement that the acceptor alone would be liable on the bill[21]; where bills had been granted for the price of goods in terms of a written agreement it was held incompetent to prove parole a verbal agreement that the bills were to be renewed at maturity if the goods had not been delivered by then[22]; and, in an action by the holder against the acceptor, the averment of an agreement that the bill was not to be demandable until the indorser had raised "sufficient working capital" was held to be irrelevant.[23] It seems that a customer can prove by parole evidence that a bill was indorsed to his bank only for purposes of collection and not with the intention of transferring the property in the bill.[24]

Illegality

5.20 In a question with an immediate party or a remote party other than a holder in due course it is a valid defence that the bill was granted for an illegal consideration. It is not a defence against a holder in due course,[25] but if it is admitted or proved that the acceptance, issue or negotiation of the bill is affected with illegality, the burden of proof is shifted unless and until the holder proves that, subsequently, value was in good faith given for the bill.[26]

Forgery of another party's signature

5.21 The person against whom the bill is being enforced may claim that the signature of some other party is not genuine. For example, the acceptor may claim that an indorsement has been forged. If a signature is forged, it is wholly inoperative and no right to retain the bill or to give a discharge therefor or to enforce payment against any party thereto can be acquired through or under that signature.[27] If payment has been made, it can be recovered.[28] It is doubtful if a forged signature can be ratified.[29] There are, however, certain circumstances in which a person against whom the bill is being enforced may be precluded from setting up a forgery; (a) the acceptor cannot deny the genuineness of the drawer's signature to a holder in due course; but if the bill is payable to the drawer's order, he can

---

[21] *National Bank of Australasia* v. *Turnbull & Co.* (1891) 18 R. 629. Acceptors cannot prove that they are merely cautioners: *Exchange Loan Co.* v. *McAweeny* (1907) 24 Sh.Ct. Rep. 217.
[22] *Stagg & Robson Ltd.* v. *Stirling*, 1908 S.C. 675; see also *Gibson's Trs.* v. *Galloway* (1896) 23 R. 414. *Drybrough & Co. Ltd.* v. *Roy* (1903) 5 F. 665, was disapproved in *Nicol's Trs.* v. *Sutherland*, 1951 S.C. (H.L.) 21.
[23] *Manchester & Liverpool District Banking Co.* v. *Ferguson & Co.* (1905) 7 F. 865.
[24] *Clydesdale Bank* v. *Liqrs. of James Allan Senior & Son*, 1926 S.C. 235.
[25] s.38(2); Gloag, p. 589; *Ladup Ltd.* v. *Shaikh* [1983] Q.B. 225.
[26] s.30(2); for a case where the burden of proof was not discharged, see *Tyler* v. *Maxwell* (1892) 30 S.L.R. 583.
[27] s.24.
[28] *London & River Plate Bank Ltd.* v. *Bank of Liverpool* [1896] 1 Q.B. 7. See also *Alexander Beith Ltd.* v. *Allen*, 1961 S.L.T. (Notes) 80.
[29] Chalmers, p. 74; *cf. McKenzie* v. *British Linen Co.* (1881) 8 R. (H.L.) 8.

dispute the genuineness of the drawer's indorsement; and if the bill is payable to the order of a third party he can dispute the genuineness of the indorsement[30]; (b) an indorser cannot deny to a holder in due course the genuineness of the drawer's signature and of all previous indorsements[31]; (c) if the person has barred himself by his conduct from relying on the forgery as where he has failed to notify interested parties once the forgery has come to his knowledge.[32] A further possible exception to the general rule arises where the payee is a fictitious or non-existing person. The bill may then be treated as payable to bearer and the authenticity of the indorsement is consequently of no account.[33]

Payment
The bill is discharged if the drawee or acceptor, or someone on his behalf, makes payment in due course, *i.e.* payment at or after the maturity of the bill to the holder thereof in good faith and without notice that his title to the bill is defective.[34] So if a bank pays a cheque drawn on it when the grantor has no funds at credit, it cannot sue the grantor on the cheque as a document of debt.[35] Payment by a drawer or indorser, however, does not discharge the bill. If a bill payable to, or to the order of, a third party is paid by the drawer, he may enforce the bill against the acceptor but cannot re-issue the bill.[36] If a bill is paid by the indorser, or if a bill payable to the drawer's order is paid by the drawer, the party paying it is remitted to his former rights as regards the acceptor or antecedent parties and he may, if he thinks fit, strike out his own and subsequent indorsements and again negotiate the bill.[37] Where an accommodation bill is paid in due course by the party accommodated the bill is discharged.[38]

5.22

Notwithstanding the terms of s.100,[39] it is not competent to prove payment by parole evidence; proof *scripto vel juramento* is required.[40] The debtor's possession of the bill raises a presumption of payment.[41]

Prescription
A bill of exchange is subject to the quinquennial and vicennial prescriptions but in neither case is the running of the prescriptive period subject to interruption by an acknowledgment of the subsistence of the obligation.[42] The *terminus a quo* is the date when the obligation became enforceable. Under the prior law the *terminus a quo* was the date when

5.23

---

[30] s.54(2).
[31] s.55(2).
[32] s.24; *Brook* v. *Hook* (1871) L.R. 6 Ex. 89; *Greenwood* v. *Martins' Bank Ltd.* [1933] A.C. 51; see also *McKenzie* v. *British Linen Co.* (1881) 8 R. (H.L.) 8; *British Linen Co.* v. *Cowan* (1906) 8 F. 704.
[33] s.7(3). See Byles, pp. 27–31.
[34] s.59(1). As to discharge by waiver, cancellation and material alteration, see ss.62–64.
[35] *Coats* v. *Union Bank of Scotland*, 1929 S.C. (H.L.) 114.
[36] s.59(2)(*a*).
[37] s.59(2)(*b*).
[38] s.59(3).
[39] The section allows "any fact relating to a bill of exchange . . . which is relevant to any question of liability thereon" to be proved by parole evidence.
[40] *Nicol's Trs.* v. *Sutherland*, 1951 S.C. (H.L.) 21.
[41] Ersk., III, iv, 5.
[42] Prescription and Limitation (Scotland) Act 1973, ss.6(1), 7(1). Sched. 1, para. 1(*e*).

the bill was "exigible" and it would seem that the former rules still apply; if the bill is payable on demand the *terminus* is the date of the bill, if the bill is payable at a specified period after sight, it is the date of demand for payment; if the bill is payable at a fixed future date, it is the date when the bill is due; if acceptance is refused it runs from the date of refusal.[43]

Not presented for acceptance

5.24 If a bill payable after sight is negotiated, the holder must either present it for acceptance or negotiate it within a reasonable time. If he does not do so, the drawer and all indorsers prior to that holder are discharged.[44] The presentment must be made by or on behalf of the holder to the drawee or to some person authorised to accept or refuse acceptance on his behalf at a reasonable hour on a business day and before the bill is overdue. If there are two or more drawees, who are not partners, presentment must be made to them all, unless one has authority to accept for all, in which case presentment may be made to him only. If the drawee is dead, presentment may be made to his personal representative; where the drawee is bankrupt, presentment may be made to him or to his trustee. A presentment through the post office is sufficient where authorised by agreement or usage.[45]

Where the holder of a bill, drawn payable elsewhere than at the place of business or residence of the drawee, has not time, with the exercise of reasonable diligence, to present the bill for acceptance before presenting it for payment on the day that it falls due, the delay caused by presenting the bill for acceptance before presenting it for payment is excused and does not discharge the drawer and indorsers.[46] Presentment is excused where (a) the drawee is dead or bankrupt or is a fictitious person or a person not having capacity to contract by bill, (b) after the exercise of reasonable diligence presentment cannot be effected, (c) although the presentment has been irregular, acceptance has been refused on some other ground.[47] The fact that the holder has reason to believe that the bill, on presentment, will be dishonoured does not excuse presentment.[48]

Not presented for payment

5.25 If a bill is not duly presented for payment the drawer and indorsers are discharged.[49] Presentment must be made on the day the bill falls due; if the bill is payable on demand presentment must be made a reasonable time after its issue to render the drawer liable and within a reasonable time after its indorsement to render the indorser liable.[50] Presentment must be made by the holder or some person authorised on his behalf at a reasonable hour on a business day at the proper place either to the person designated by the bill as payer or to some person authorised to pay or

---

[43] *Ibid.*, s.6(3); *Broddelius* v. *Grischotti* (1887) 14 R. 536; *Stephenson* v. *Stephenson's Trs.* (1807) Mor. "Bill of Exchange" App. No. 20; *Ferguson* v. *Douglas* (1796) 3 Pat.App. 503; Thomson, p. 462.
[44] 1882 Act, s.40.
[45] s.41(1).
[46] s.39(4).
[47] s.41(2).
[48] s.41(3).
[49] s.45.
[50] s.45(1), (2); see as to the due date s.14 and, as to a reasonable time, s.45(2).

refuse payment on his behalf if with the exercise of reasonable diligence such person can there be found.[51] If the bill is drawn upon or accepted by two or more persons who are not partners and no place of payment is specified, presentment must be made to them all.[52] If the drawee or acceptor is dead and no place of payment is specified presentment must be made to a personal representative, if such there be, and with the exercise of reasonable diligence he can be found.[53] Presentment through the post office is sufficient where authorised by agreement or usage.[54]

Where a bill is presented at the proper place, and after the exercise of reasonable diligence no person authorised to pay or refuse payment can be found there, no further presentment to the drawee or acceptor is required.[55] Delay in presentment is excused if it is caused by circumstances beyond the holder's control and not imputable to his default, misconduct or negligence; presentment must be made with reasonable diligence when the cause of delay ceases to operate.[56] Presentment is dispensed with where (a) it cannot be effected after the exercise of reasonable diligence (the fact that the holder has reason to believe that the bill will, on presentment, be dishonoured does not dispense with the necessity for presentment); (b) the drawee is a fictitious person, (c) as regards the drawer, where the drawee or acceptor is not bound as between himself and the drawer to accept or pay the bill and the drawer has no reason to believe that the bill would be paid if presented[57]; (d) as regards an indorser, where the bill was accepted or made for the accommodation of that indorser, and he has no reason to expect that the bill would be paid if presented; (e) by waiver of presentment, express or implied.[58]

If the bill is accepted generally, presentment for payment is not necessary to render the acceptor liable.[59] If a qualified acceptance requires presentment, the acceptor is not discharged by failure to present for payment at maturity unless there is an express stipulation to that effect. Summary diligence may proceed against the acceptor although the bill was not presented for payment on the day it fell due but within six months thereafter.[60]

No notice of dishonour

Notice of dishonour is not necessary to render the acceptor liable.[61]   **5.26**

Any drawer or indorser to whom notice of dishonour by non-acceptance or non-payment is not given is discharged, but (a) if a bill is dishonoured by non-acceptance and notice of dishonour is not given, the

---

[51] s.45(3); as to the proper place, see s.45(4); the bill must be exhibited to the person from whom payment is demanded: s.52(4).
[52] s.45(6).
[53] s.45(7).
[54] s.45(8).
[55] s.45(5).
[56] s.46(1).
[57] See *Bank of Scotland* v. *Lamont & Co.* (1889) 16 R. 769.
[58] s.46(2); see, as to waiver made in error, *Mactavish's J. F.* v. *Michael's Trs.*, 1912 S.C. 425.
[59] s.52.
[60] *McNeill & Son* v. *Innes, Chambers & Co.*, 1917 S.C. 540.
[61] s.52(3).

rights of a holder in due course subsequent to the omission are not prejudiced by the omission, (b) if a bill is dishonoured by non-acceptance and due notice of dishonour is given, it shall not be necessary to give notice of a subsequent dishonour by non-payment unless the bill has in the meantime been accepted.[62]

Notice must be given by or on behalf of the holder or an indorser who, at the time of giving it, is himself liable on the bill; it may be given by an agent in his own name or in the name of any party entitled to give notice, whether that party be his principal or not.[63] A notice given by or on behalf of a holder enures for the benefit of all subsequent holders and all prior indorsers who have a right of recourse against the party to whom it is given; a notice given by or on behalf of an indorser entitled to give notice enures for the benefit of the holder and all indorsers subsequent to the party to whom notice is given.

The notice may be in writing or by personal communication and may be given in any terms which sufficiently identify the bill and intimate that the bill has been dishonoured. The return of the bill is sufficient. A written notice need not be signed and, if insufficient, may be supplemented and validated by verbal communication. A misdescription of the bill does not vitiate the notice unless the party to whom the notice is given is in fact misled thereby.

The notice may be given to the party or his agent. If the drawer or indorser is dead, notice must be given to a personal representative if such there be, and with the exercise of reasonable diligence he can be found. If the drawer or indorser is bankrupt, notice is given to the party himself or to the trustee. Where there are two or more drawers or indorsers who are not partners, notice must be given to each of them, unless one of them has authority to receive such notice for the others.

A notice of dishonour can be posted before the due date for payment of the bill but it is bad if it is received before the bill itself was dishonoured; where on the evidence it is not clear whether the receipt of the notice preceded dishonour of the bill, the maxim *ut res magis valeat quam pereat* applies.[64]

Notice must be given within a reasonable time of dishonour which means that, in the absence of special circumstances, where the two parties reside in the same place, notice must be given in time to reach the recipient on the day after dishonour; and where the parties reside in different places, notice must be sent off on the day after dishonour if there is a post at a convenient hour, and if there be no such post, then by the next post thereafter.[65] If the bill is dishonoured in the hands of an agent he may give notice to the party liable or to his principal in which event he must do so within the same time as if he were the holder, and the principal upon receipt of such notice has himself the same time for giving notice as if the agent had been an independent holder.[66] Where a party receives due notice of dishonour, he has the same time after receipt for

---

[62] s.48.
[63] s.49.
[64] *Eaglehill Ltd.* v. *J. Needham Ltd.* [1973] A.C. 992.
[65] s.49(12); *Lombard Banking Ltd.* v. *Central Garage and Engineering Co. Ltd.* [1963] 1 Q.B. 220.
[66] s.49(13).

giving notice to antecedent parties that the holder has after dishonour.[67]

Where a notice of dishonour is duly addressed and posted, the sender is deemed to have given due notice of dishonour, notwithstanding any miscarriage by the post office.[68]

Delay in giving notice is excused if it is caused by circumstances beyond the control of the giver and not imputable to his default, misconduct, or negligence; where the cause of delay ceases to operate the notice must be given with reasonable diligence.[69]

Notice of dishonour is dispensed with: (a) when after the exercise of reasonable diligence, notice cannot be given to or does not reach the drawer or indorser concerned, (b) by waiver, express or implied, occurring before or after the omission,[70] (c) as regards the drawer, (i) where drawer and drawee are the same person, (ii) where the drawee is a fictitious person, or a person not having capacity to contract, (iii) where the drawer is the person to whom the bill is presented for payment, (iv) where the drawee or acceptor is as between himself and the drawer under no obligation to accept or pay the bill, (v) where the drawer has countermanded payment, (d) as regards the indorser, (i) where the drawee is a fictitious person or a person not having capacity to contract and the indorser was aware of the fact at the time he indorsed the bill, (ii) where the indorser is the person to whom the bill is presented for payment, (iii) where the bill was accepted or made for his accommodation.[71]

Promissory notes

A promissory note is an unconditional promise in writing made by one person to another signed by the maker, engaging to pay, on demand or at a fixed or determinable future time, a sum certain in money, to, or to the order of, a specified person or to bearer.[72] A note payable to the maker's order is not a promissory note until it has been indorsed by the maker.[73] A note may contain a pledge of collateral security with authority to sell or dispose thereof,[74] but apart from that it must be a promise to pay money and nothing more.[75] The consideration may be stated and provisions relating to the "giving of time" are acceptable.[76]

For purposes of stamp duty a promissory note was defined as including any document or writing (except a banknote) containing a promise to pay any sum of money. This definition included a document which was a

5.27

---

[67] s.49(14).
[68] s.49(15).
[69] s.50(1).
[70] *Aberdeen Town and County Bank* v. *Davidson* (1885) 1 Sh.Ct.Rep. 212; *McLelland* v. *Mackay* (1908) 24 Sh.Ct.Rep. 157.
[71] s.50(2); *McLelland* v. *Mackay, supra.*
[72] s.83(1); a promise to repay "on or before" a specified date is not a promissory note because the time is not determinable: *Williamson* v. *Rider* [1963] 1 Q.B. 89; *Claydon* v. *Bradley* [1987] 1 W.L.R. 521. *Cf. Creative Press* v. *Harman* [1973] I.R. 313.
[73] s.83(2).
[74] s.83(3).
[75] *Nawab Major Sir Mohammad Akbar Khan* v. *Attar Singh* [1936] 2 All E.R. 545; *Mortgage Insurance Corporation* v. *C.I.R.* (1888) 21 Q.B.D. 352; *Dickie* v. *Singh*, 1974 S.L.T. 129.
[76] *Kirkwood* v. *Carroll* [1903] 1 K.B. 531.

promissory note within the meaning of s.83 of the 1882 Act[77] but its terms were obviously much wider. The definition was, however, restricted by judicial interpretation. The sum of money had to be definite.[78] There had to be in substance a promise to pay although the use of the word "promise" was not necessary.[79] To be a promissory note the document had to be unilateral in the sense that it became effectual on delivery and required nothing done on the other side to make it operative.[80] It was not necessary that the time of payment or the payee should have been stated.[81] A record of an obligation constituted against the grantor with no direct expression of a promise to pay was not a promissory note.[82]

A promissory note may be made by two or more makers who are liable thereon jointly, or jointly and severally, according to its tenor. A note which runs "I promise to pay" and is signed by two or more persons is deemed to be their joint and several note.[83]

A note is inchoate and incomplete until it is delivered to the payee or bearer.[84] The maker engages that he will pay the note according to its tenor and is precluded from denying to a holder in due course the existence of the payee and his then capacity to indorse.[85]

Presentment for payment is not necessary to make the maker liable unless the note is in the body of it made payable at a particular place.[86]

Presentment on the date of payment is not necessary to render the maker liable.[87] To make the indorser liable, however, presentment for payment is necessary and where the note is in the body of it made payable at a particular place, presentment at that place is necessary; where the place is indicated by way of memorandum only, presentment to the maker elsewhere will suffice.[88]

If a note payable on demand has been indorsed and has not been presented for payment within a reasonable time of the indorsement, the indorser is discharged.[89] What is a reasonable time depends on the nature of the instrument, the usage of trade and the facts of the case.[90] Where a note payable on demand is negotiated, it is not deemed to be overdue, for the purpose of affecting the holder with defects of title of which he had no notice, by reason that it appears that a reasonable time for presenting it for payment has elapsed since its issue.[91]

---

[77] Alpe, *Law of Stamp Duties* (23rd ed.), p. 93; *McTaggart* v. *MacEachern's J.F.*, 1949 S.C. 503. No stamp is required now.

[78] *Tennent* v. *Crawford* (1878) 5 R. 433; *Henderson* v. *Dawson* (1895) 22 R. 895, *per* Lord McLaren at p. 901; *Lamberton* v. *Aiken* (1899) 2 F. 189.

[79] *Macfarlane* v. *Johnston* (1864) 2 M. 1210; *Vallance* v. *Forbes* (1879) 6 R. 1099; *Watson* v. *Duncan* (1896) 4 S.L.T. 75; *Bell* v. *Bell* (1897) 4 S.L.T. 214; *Thomson* v. *Bell* (1894) 22 R. 16; *Cairney* v. *Macgregor's Trs.*, 1916 1 S.L.T. 357.

[80] *Thomson* v. *Bell*, *supra*, *per* Lord McLaren at p. 18.

[81] *McTaggart* v. *MacEachern's J.F.*, *supra*.

[82] *Semple's Executrices* v. *Semple*, 1912 1 S.L.T. 382; see also *Dick* v. *Dick*, 1950 S.L.T. (Notes) 44.

[83] s.85.

[84] s.84.

[85] s.88.

[86] s.87(1).

[87] *Gordon* v. *Kerr* (1898) 25 R. 570.

[88] s.87(2), (3).

[89] s.86(1).

[90] s.86(2).

[91] s.86(3).

In general the provisions of the 1882 Act relating to bills apply to promissory notes, the maker being deemed to correspond with the acceptor of a bill and the first indorser of the note being deemed to correspond with the drawer of an accepted bill payable to drawer's order.[92] The provisions of the Act relating to acceptance, presentment for acceptance, acceptance *supra* protest and bills in a set do not apply to notes.[93] Protest of a dishonoured foreign note is unnecessary.[94]

A promissory note is subject to the quinquennial and vicennial prescriptions but in neither case is the running of the prescriptive period interrupted by an acknowledgment of the subsistence of the obligation.[95]

---

[92] s.89(1), (2).
[93] s.89(3).
[94] s.89(4).
[95] Prescription and Limitation (Scotland) Act 1973, Sched. 1, para. 1(*e*); ss.6(1), 7(1). A banknote is exempt from the quinquennial prescription: Sched. 1, para. 2(*b*).

CHAPTER 6

CHEQUES

Cheque

6.1 A cheque is a bill of exchange drawn on a banker payable on demand.[1] A building society which provides banking services is treated as a bank.[2] The banker on whom the cheque is drawn is known as "the *paying banker.*" The banker who collects the amount of the cheque on behalf of the payee or indorsee is "the *collecting banker.*"[3] Broadly, the law as to bills of exchange applies to cheques but the following special features must be noticed:
(a) it is at least doubtful whether a cheque can be accepted[4]; certification of a cheque is not acceptance;
(b) special duties arise from the relationship of banker and customer;
(c) the duty and authority of the bank to pay a cheque drawn by a customer are determined by countermand of payment and also by notice of the customer's death[5];
(d) summary diligence on a cheque is incompetent[6];
(e) there are relaxations of the rules relating to indorsement;
(f) certain precautions can be taken against theft and forgery of cheques;
(g) special protection is given to the paying banker and to the collecting banker.

Before the 1882 Act value was not presumed in the case of a cheque. Now, it is clear that value is presumed in a question between remote parties.[7] So far as a cheque held by the payee is concerned it is sometimes said that value is not presumed[8] but it is doubtful whether this view gives sufficient weight to the fact that the 1882 Act makes a cheque a species of bill.[9]

Banker and customer

6.2 A banker who opens an account-current with a customer undertakes to honour his cheques as presented to the extent to which there are funds at the credit of the customer in the account; if he fails to do so he is liable in damages for the injury to the customer's credit arising out of his breach of contract.[10] The principle does not apply to a deposit account.[11] If the banker has been in the habit of honouring cheques to the extent of the

---

[1] Bills of Exchange Act 1882, s.73.
[2] Building Societies Act 1986, Sched. 8, para. 3.
[3] See *Barclays Bank plc* v. *Bank of England* [1985] 1 All E.R. 385.
[4] See *Bank of Baroda* v. *Punjab National Bank* [1944] A.C. 176. As to the Scottish practice of "marking" cheques, see Marshall, *Scots Mercantile Law*, p. 391.
[5] Bills of Exchange Act 1882, s.75.
[6] *Glickman* v. *Linda*, 1950 S.C. 18.
[7] s.30.
[8] *Thompson* v. *J. Barke & Co. (Caterers) Ltd.*, 1975 S.L.T. 67, *per* Lord Dunpark at p. 69.
[9] Thorburn, p. 174.
[10] *King* v. *British Linen Co.* (1899) 1 F. 928; see also *Joachimson* v. *Swiss Bank Corporation* [1921] 3 K.B. 110; *Royal Bank* v. *Skinner*, 1931 S.L.T. 382.
[11] *Gibb* v. *Lombank Scotland Ltd.*, 1962 S.L.T. 288.

customer's credit upon an account-current, he is not entitled without notice at any moment to refuse to honour a cheque on the ground that if the account-current was massed together with the customer's loan and cash accounts, there would be a debit balance.[12] The fact that the banker holds a security against a debit balance does not mean that there are funds available for payment of cheques,[12] but if the customer has been allowed to overdraw against a security the banker cannot, without giving notice, refuse to honour further cheques.[13] Where money has been paid in for credit of the customer's account, it cannot be drawn upon until a reasonable time for the necessary book-keeping operations has elapsed.[14] Where cheques have been lodged for credit of the customer, they are not available until they have been cleared unless the bank has expressly or implicitly agreed to allow the customer to draw against uncleared effects.[15] The banker can, of course, at any time terminate his relationship with his customer by intimating that he will refuse to honour cheques in future but, if he does this, he must nevertheless honour any cheques drawn prior to the date of intimation.[16] Two sentences printed on the cover of a new cheque-book may not be sufficient notice of a proposed alteration in the contractual relationship.[17]

The bank has no authority to pay a post-dated cheque before the date which it bears and, if it does pay, it takes the risk of a countermand arriving before business hours of the date on which the cheque bears to be drawn.[18]

Where a cheque card has been given to the customer, the bank undertakes to pay cheques of the amount stipulated on presentation, if the conditions of issue of the card have been complied with.[19]

Stale cheques

Where a cheque is not presented for payment within a reasonable time of its issue, and the drawer or the person on whose account it is drawn had the right at the time of such presentment as between him and the banker to have the cheque paid and suffers actual damage through the delay, he is discharged to the extent of such damage, that is to say, to the extent to which such drawer or person is a creditor of such banker to a larger amount than he would have been had such cheque been paid. If the drawer or person is discharged in this way, the holder of the cheque becomes a creditor, in lieu of the drawer or person, of the banker to the extent of the discharge and is entitled to recover the amount from him.[20]

What is a reasonable time depends on the nature of the instrument, the usage of trade and of bankers, and the facts of the particular case. In practice cheques presented more than six months after date are not paid before confirmation has been obtained from the drawer.

6.3

---

[12] *Kirkwood & Sons* v. *Clydesdale Bank*, 1908 S.C. 20.
[13] Wallace & McNeil, p. 12.
[14] Paget, p. 201.
[15] See *Westminster Bank Ltd.* v. *Zang* [1966] A.C. 182.
[16] *King* v. *British Linen Co.*, *supra*.
[17] *Burnett* v. *Westminster Bank* [1966] 1 Q.B. 742.
[18] *Commercial Bank* v. *Henderson* (1897) 13 Sh.Ct.Rep. 136.
[19] Byles, p. 8; Wallace & McNeil, p. 71. See *Regina* v. *Charles* [1977] A.C. 177; Dobson [1977] J.B.L. 126.
[20] s.74.

Cheques

The necessity of indorsement

6.4 Prior to 1957, the rules as to the indorsement of cheques did not differ from those applicable to the indorsement of other bills of exchange. The payee or indorsee of the cheque had to indorse it when he paid it into his bank (the collecting bank) for credit of his account. Moreover, the paying banker required the payee's indorsement even where the payee presented the cheque personally. In 1957 the Mocatta Committee[21] recommended that, in order to achieve "a substantial saving of unproductive work," indorsement should not be necessary on a cheque being collected by a bank on behalf of a customer who was the payee. Following upon this report, the Cheques Act 1957 provided that: (1) where the paying banker in good faith and in the ordinary course of business pays a cheque drawn on him, which is not indorsed or is irregularly indorsed, he does not, in doing so, incur any liability by reason only of the absence of, or irregularity in, indorsement, and he is deemed to have paid it in due course,[22] (2) that the collecting banker is not to be treated for purposes of s.4 of the 1957 Act as having been negligent by reason only of his failure to concern himself with absence of, or irregularity in, indorsement of an instrument.[23]

Now, it would seem that these provisions apply, not only to cheques being collected by a bank on behalf of a customer who is the payee, but also to cheques collected by a bank on behalf of a customer who is not the payee but an indorsee. The banks, however, have not interpreted the Act so widely and in their view: "The intention of the Act is to relieve customers from the task of endorsing instruments which are to be collected for the payees' Accounts . . . "[24] In practice, therefore, the banks still require indorsement in the following cases: (i) cheques paid in for the credit of someone other than the ostensible payee, (ii) where the payee's name is mis-spelt or the payee is incorrectly designated and the surrounding circumstances are suspicious, (iii) cheques payable to joint payees which are tendered for credit of an account to which all are not parties, (iv) combined cheque and receipt forms marked "R" on the face, (v) bills of exchange other than cheques, (vi) promissory notes, (vii) drafts and other instruments drawn on the General Post Office or payable at a post office, (viii) Inland Revenue warrants, (ix) drafts drawn on H.M. Paymaster General or the Queen's and Lord Treasurer's Remembrancer, (x) drafts drawn on the Crown Agents, High Commissioners for Pakistan or India, and other paying agents, (xi) travellers'

---

[21] Cmnd. 3 (1956).

[22] s.1; the section applies to some documents other than cheques, *viz.* a document issued by the banker's customer which, though not a bill of exchange, is intended to enable a person to obtain payment from him of the sum mentioned in the document (*e.g.* an instrument in which the order is "Pay cash or order"—*Orbit Mining and Trading Co. Ltd.* v. *Westminster Bank Ltd.* [1963] 1 Q.B. 794); and a draft payable on demand drawn by him upon himself, whether payable at the head office or some other office of his bank; in these cases, payment in good faith and in the ordinary course of business discharges the instrument.

[23] s.4(3); see also para. 6.13, *infra.*

[24] Circular dated 23 September 1957 issued by the Committee of London Clearing Bankers; see also J. Milnes Holden, *The Bankers' Magazine* (1957) Vol. CLXXXIV, page 101; F. R. Ryder, *The Bankers' Magazine* (1962) Vol. CXCIII, p. 266; Antonio, *The Scottish Bankers' Magazine* (1957) Vol. XLIX, p. 139.

cheques, (xii) instruments payable by banks abroad. The paying banker requires the payee's signature on cheques cashed at the counter.

The result probably is that these requirements now form part of the "ordinary course of business" for purposes of s.1 of the 1957 Act.[25]

Indorsement is, of course, still necessary when the payee negotiates the cheque to a third party.

Another important section of the 1957 Act is designed to put a collecting banker who has given value for a cheque in the position of a holder even although it is not indorsed. It is provided that a banker who gives value for, or has a lien on, a cheque payable to order which the holder delivers to him for collection without indorsing it, has such (if any) rights as he would have had if, on delivery, the holder had indorsed it in blank.[26] The section applies where the holder delivers the cheque to the bank for collection for the credit of an account other than his own.[27] Where the managing director and controlling shareholder of a company delivered to the bank an unindorsed cheque in favour of himself for collection for credit of the company's account, it was held that he did so as a "holder."[27] The bank gives value for the cheque (i) if it cashes it, (ii) if it in fact allows the customer to draw against the uncleared cheque,[28] (iii) if there is an express or implied agreement that the customer is to be entitled to draw against uncleared effects,[29] (iv) if the bank has a lien on the cheque,[30] (v) if the bank accepts the cheque as a conditional payment in reduction of an overdraft.[31]

Method of indorsement

The indorsement is written on the cheque and is signed by the indorser. A simple signature without additional words is sufficient.[32] If the payee or indorsee is wrongly designated or if his name is mis-spelt, he should indorse as he is described and add his correct signature.[33] The payee's initials or Christian names are an essential part of the indorsement but titles are not. If the cheque is payable to "Mrs. A.B." the indorsement should be the payee's normal signature followed by "wife of A.B." If there are two or more payees, all must indorse unless either the one indorsing has the authority to indorse for the others or the payees are partners in which case one partner may sign the firm name or sign in his own name expressly on behalf of the firm. In the case of joint stock companies the indorsement should be by a duly authorised officer, normally a director, secretary or manager.[34] If there are only two trustees or executors, both must indorse, but if there are more than two a majority

6.5

---

[25] Paget, p. 398; Ellinger, *Modern Banking Law*, p. 309.
[26] s.2; see *Midland Bank Ltd. v. R. V. Harris Ltd.* [1963] 2 All E.R. 685.
[27] *Westminster Bank v. Zang* [1966] A.C. 182.
[28] *Westminster Bank v. Zang*, supra.
[29] *A. L. Underwood Ltd. v. Bank of Liverpool* [1924] 1 K.B. 775.
[30] *Barclays Bank v. Astley Industrial Trust Ltd.* [1970] 2 Q.B. 527.
[31] *McLean v. Clydesdale Bank* (1883) 11 R.(H.L.) 1; *Midland Bank v. Reckitt* [1933] A.C. 1; *Barclays Bank Ltd. v. Astley Industrial Trust Ltd.*, supra.
[32] 1882 Act, s.32(1).
[33] s.32(4); Chalmers, p. 115.
[34] *Phillips v. Italian Bank Ltd.*, 1934 S.L.T. 78.

will suffice. Where the cheque is payable to the holder of an office, the official's signature with his designation appended is necessary.[35]

Transfer

6.6 Obviously, when the paying banker honours a cheque a transfer of funds is effected. It is, however, important to notice that by s.53(2) *presentation* of a bill operates as an assignation of the sum for which it is drawn in favour of the holder if the bank has in its hands funds available for payment thereof.[36] Any doubt as to whether this subsection applies to cheques as fully as it does to other bills is, it is submitted, unfounded; the reservations expressed by Lord President Inglis in *British Linen Co. Bank* v. *Carruthers and Fergusson*[37] were the product of a state of the law prior to the 1882 Act in which it was not clear that a cheque was a species of bill. It seems that the subsection applies even if the cheque is post-dated or not properly indorsed.[38]

Insufficient funds

6.7 If the funds at credit of the customer are less than the amount of the cheque, the cheque is returned marked "insufficient funds" and the amount at credit is transferred to a separate account bearing reference to the cheque as the presentation of the cheque has operated as an assignation.[39] Payment of the sum in that account can be made to the holder of the cheque if he delivers up the cheque.

Countermand

6.8 The banker's duty and authority to pay a cheque are determined if there is a countermand of payment by the customer.[40] The notice of countermand must be given to the branch on which the cheque is drawn.[41] To be effectual, the countermand must, of course, be communicated to the bank before payment has been made.[42]

Where countermand is made before presentation of the cheque for payment or after presentation but before payment has been made, the banker cannot in safety make payment.[43] Section 53(2) does not now operate to effect an assignation when payment is countermanded because s.75A[44] provides that on countermand of payment of a cheque the banker is treated as having no funds available for payment of the cheque. The result is that payment of the cheque is refused and the drawer continues to have at his disposal the funds at credit of his account.

---

[35] For a fuller treatment of this subject see Wallace & McNeil, pp. 113–115.

[36] The assignation is in favour of a *holder* as defined in the 1882 Act: *Dickson* v. *Clydesdale Bank Ltd.*, 1937 S.L.T. 585.

[37] (1883) 10 R. 923. See Mr D. J. Cusine's illuminating article at 1977 J.R. 98.

[38] Finlayson, pp. 55–56.

[39] *British Linen Co. Bank* v. *Carruthers and Fergusson* (1883) 10 R. 923; Wallace & McNeil, p. 12.

[40] s.75. The terms of the agreement between bank and customer on the issue of a cheque card will provide that the customer cannot countermand cheques accepted on production of the card.

[41] Wallace & McNeil, p. 134.

[42] Holden, *Banker and Customer*, p. 227.

[43] See *Waterston* v. *City of Glasgow Bank* (1874) 1 R. 470 (pre-Act).

[44] Added by Law Reform (Miscellaneous Provisions) (Scotland) Act 1985, s.11. See Gretton (1983) 28 J.L.S. 333, 389.

Where the countermand is effectual in this way, the holder can sue the drawer and any indorsers on the cheque.[45] The onus is on the drawer to justify the countermand.[46] He will not usually succeed if the holder is a holder in due course.

Customer's death

6.9 Notice of his customer's death determines the duty and authority of the banker to pay cheques drawn on him by the customer.[47] However, presentment of the cheque after notice of death has been received still operates as an assignation of any funds available for payment of the amount of the cheque.[48] Whether there are funds available for payment must be determined on a true state of all the accounts between the customer and the bank and not merely on the state of the current account.[49]

Customer's insolvency

6.10 If the customer is sequestrated, the sum at credit of the account (or the balance where there are several accounts[50]) vests in the trustee as at the date of sequestration.[51] If, however, a cheque has been presented before the date of sequestration, and payment has been refused because of insufficient funds, the credit balance is nevertheless transferred to the holder of the cheque,[52] at least to the extent that the cheque was in payment of a debt which was due by the bankrupt at the date of presentation.[53] The position in liquidation is the same.[54] The attachment of a floating charge freezes the bank account[55] (if it is subject to the charge), and transfers it to the receiver. An administration order does not affect the bank's duty to pay cheques.[56]

Precautions against theft and forgery

6.11 A cheque is crossed generally by putting on its face two parallel transverse lines with or without the words "and company" or any abbreviation thereof between the lines; a cheque is crossed specially to a banker by putting across its face the name of the banker.[57] A cheque may be crossed by the drawer or holder and a holder may cross specially a cheque crossed generally. The banker to whom a cheque is crossed specially may cross it specially to another banker for collection. A

---

[45] *McLean* v. *Clydesdale Bank* (1883) 11 R.(H L.) 1. He can arrest the bank account on the dependence of the action.
[46] *Webster & Co. Ltd.* v. *Hutchin* (1922) 39 Sh.Ct.Rep. 231; *cf. Williams* v. *Williams*, 1980 S.L.T.(Sh.Ct.) 25. The onus probably depends on what is admitted as to the circumstances in which the cheque was delivered.
[47] s.75; an undated cheque cannot be given testamentary effect: *Stewart's Trs.*, 1953 S.L.T.(Notes) 25.
[48] s.53(2); *Bank of Scotland* v. *Reid* (1886) 2 Sh.Ct.Rep. 376.
[49] *Kirkwood & Sons* v. *Clydesdale Bank*, 1908 S.C. 20.
[50] *Kirkwood & Sons* v. *Clydesdale Bank*, 1908 S.C. 20.
[51] Bankruptcy (Scotland) Act 1985, s.31(4).
[52] s.53(2): *British Linen Co. Bank* v. *Carruthers and Fergusson* (1883) 10 R. 923.
[53] *Commercial Bank* v. *Lyon* (1909) 25 Sh.Ct.Rep. 312
[54] See para. 25.7.
[55] See para. 9.18.
[56] See Wallace & McNeil, p. 38, for a contrary view.
[57] 1882 Act, s.76.

84   *Cheques*

collecting banker may cross specially to himself an uncrossed cheque or a cheque crossed generally.[58] The crossing is a material part of the cheque and it is unlawful to obliterate it or, except as authorised by the Act, to add to or alter it.[59]

The crossing is a direction to the paying banker that, if it is crossed generally, he must pay only to a banker, or, if it is crossed specially, he must pay only to the banker to whom it is crossed or his agent for collection being a banker. If the paying banker disregards this direction he is liable to the true owner of the cheque for any loss he may sustain owing to the cheque having been paid otherwise than as directed.[60] If, however, the crossing has been obliterated or altered so that at payment it does not appear to be crossed or to have had a crossing obliterated or altered, and the paying banker pays it in good faith and without negligence to someone other than a banker, he does not incur liability. The paying banker is protected by s.80 if he pays in accordance with the crossing.[61]

Crossing is only a partial safeguard because, of course, the person who has misappropriated the cheque may manage to obtain payment through a banker or he may transfer the cheque to someone else who obtains payment in good faith through a banker. If the indorsement of the payee has been forged the person taking the cheque from the thief cannot be a holder in due course; but if the cheque has been validly indorsed in blank before the theft the person to whom the cheque is negotiated by the thief can be a holder in due course. To avoid this result, it is possible to write on the face of a crossed cheque the words "not negotiable."[62] The effect of this is that the cheque can still be transferred but a person taking such a cheque does not have and cannot give a better title to the cheque than that which the person from whom he took it had.[63] In other words, no one can be a holder in due course of such a cheque.

The addition of the words "Account Payee" to a cheque has no statutory basis but it is not an unlawful addition to the crossing.[64] It does not affect the negotiability of the cheque.[65] It is a direction to the collecting banker that payment of the proceeds should be made for credit of the payee's account.[66] If the collecting banker accepts such a cheque for credit of another account without a satisfactory explanation he is probably negligent and loses the protection of s.4 of the Cheques Act 1957.[67] A question has been raised as to whether the paying banker might lose the protection of ss.60 and 80 of the 1882 Act if he acts upon such a

---

[58] s.77.
[59] s.78.
[60] s.79; see *Phillips* v. *Italian Bank*, 1934 S.L.T. 78.
[61] See para. 12, *infra*.
[62] s.76; the cheque must be crossed: Paget, p. 375; Byles, p. 288; *Union Bank* v. *National Bank* (1924) 40 Sh.Ct.Rep. 111; the section does not apply to bills of exchange other than cheques: *Hibernian Bank Ltd.* v. *Gysin and Hanson* [1939] 1 K.B. 483.
[63] s.81; *Great Western Railway Co.* v. *London & County Banking Co. Ltd.* [1901] A.C. 414.
[64] *Akrokerri (Atlantic) Mines Ltd.* v. *Economic Bank* [1904] 2 K.B. 465.
[65] *National Bank* v. *Silke* [1891] 1 Q.B. 435. *Cf.* Ellinger, *Modern Banking Law*, p. 257.
[66] *Morison* v. *London County and Westminster Bank Ltd.* [1914] 3 K.B. 356, *per* Lord Reading C.J. at p. 373.
[67] *Importers Company* v. *Westminster Bank Ltd.* [1927] 2 K.B. 297.

cheque which bears indorsements subsequent to that of the payee and which, therefore, is presumably being collected for someone else.[68] It is thought that "Account Payee Only" has the same significance as "Account Payee."[69]

The paying banker

The paying banker is not protected if he honours as a cheque a document on which the signature of his customer, the drawer, has been forged.[70] He cannot debit his customer with the amount paid unless the customer is in some way barred from relying on the forgery.[71] Nor can he debit his customer if the amount on the cheque has been fraudulently increased unless the customer has negligently drawn the cheque in such a way as to facilitate fraud or forgery.[72] The customer's duties are to draw cheques so as not to facilitate fraud or forgery and to notify the bank immediately if he becomes aware of the existence of unauthorised cheques; he has no wider duty to take precautions in the management of his business to prevent forged cheques being presented to the bank or to check bank statements to discover payments on forged cheques.[73]

6.12

The paying banker is, however, protected where an indorsement has been forged or made without authority. If he pays a cheque in good faith and in the ordinary course of business he is deemed to have paid it in due course even although the indorsement was forged or made without authority[74] and he can debit his customer. Payment across the counter of a cheque indorsed in blank can be protected but there may be circumstances in which such payment is not in the ordinary course of business.[75]

Secondly, where a banker pays a crossed cheque in accordance with the crossing, and in good faith and without negligence, he is entitled to the same rights and is placed in the same position as if payment had been made to the true owner of the cheque even although he has in fact paid to a banker collecting for a thief or finder.[76] This section, of course, does not give protection where the drawer's signature is forged.

The third protection of the paying banker is that, under s.1 of the Cheques Act 1957, where he pays in good faith and in the ordinary course of business a cheque[77] which is not indorsed or is irregularly indorsed, he does not, in doing so, incur any liability by reason only of the absence of, or irregularity in, indorsement, and he is deemed to have paid in due course.

---

[68] Paget, p. 401.
[69] Paget, p. 378.
[70] *Orr and Barber* v. *Union Bank of Scotland* (1854) 1 Macq. 513.
[71] See para. 5.10.
[72] *London Joint Stock Bank Ltd.* v. *Macmillan* [1918] A.C. 777.
[73] *Tai Hing Cotton Mill Ltd.* v. *Liu Chong Hing Bank Ltd.* [1986] A.C. 80.
[74] s.60.
[75] *Bank of England* v. *Vagliano Brothers* [1891] A.C. 107, *per* Lord Halsbury L.C. at p. 117; *Auchteroni & Co.* v. *Midland Bank Ltd.* [1928] 2 K.B. 294; *Phillips* v. *Italian Bank Ltd.*, 1934 S.L.T. 78.
[76] s.80.
[77] s.1(2) gives similar protection in respect of drafts (which are also affected by Stamp Act 1853, s.19) and certain other documents.

Liability of collecting banker

6.13 In collecting a cheque, a bank may be acting merely as an agent for its customer or it may be collecting for itself. Where the bank acts as an agent: "The customer says to his banker—'Act as my agent and collect this bill.' The bill is delivered for a special and limited purpose. There is no transfer of the property. The only right the banker has to the bill is to carry out the instructions of his customer regarding it."[78] On the other hand, the bank may have given value to its customer for the cheque and be collecting the proceeds for itself. The determination of the capacity in which the bank is acting is a question of fact.[79] The mere fact that the bank in its books enters the value of the cheque on the credit side of the account does not without more constitute the bank a holder for value.[80] It seems that even if the bank is acting as an agent for collection it may be a "holder" or "holder for value" of the cheque.[81]

If the bank was acting merely as an agent and was in good faith it is not liable if it has collected a cheque on which the signatures of the drawer and the indorser were forged.[82] If the bank has constituted itself a holder in due course of a cheque it does not, of course, incur any liability in respect of the proceeds. When, however, the bank has collected for itself a cheque to which it had no title because the customer from whom the cheque was acquired had a defective title, the bank may be liable to pay the proceeds to the true owner of the cheque even if, because it had given value for the cheque, it has not been enriched by the transaction.[83] There is also a general principle that a person cannot retain a benefit obtained by the fraud of another, even though himself innocent of fraud, unless a valuable consideration has been given.[84] It seems that all these forms of liability are based on repetition or other principles of unjust enrichment.

Section 4(1) of the Cheques Act 1957[85] is primarily intended to give protection against the English tort of conversion but it may serve to protect Scottish banks against some of the foregoing liabilities:

"Where a banker in good faith and without negligence (*a*) receives payment for a customer of [a cheque]; or, (*b*) having credited a customer's account with the amount of [a cheque], receives payment thereof for himself; and the customer has no title, or a defective title, to [the cheque] the banker does not incur any liability to the true owner of [the cheque] by reason only of having received payment thereof." A defence of contributory negligence is available where the banker has

---

[78] *Clydesdale Bank* v. *Liqrs. of James Allan Senior & Son*, 1926 S.C. 235, *per* L.J.-C. Alness at p. 241.
[79] *McLean* v. *Clydesdale Bank* (1883) 11 R.(H.L.) 1.
[80] *Whatmough's Tr.* v. *British Linen Bank*, 1934 S.C.(H.L.) 51, *per* Lord Thankerton at p. 60. This was supported by reference to the opinion of Atkin L.J. in *A. L. Underwood Ltd.* v. *Barclays Bank* [1924] 1 K.B. 775, which is criticised by Paget (p. 433) as ignoring *Sutters* v. *Briggs* [1922] 1 A.C.1. *Whatmough's Tr.* is not cited in Paget or Byles.
[81] *Sutters* v. *Briggs, supra*; *Barclays Bank* v. *Astley Industrial Trust* [1970] 2 Q.B. 527.
[82] *Clydesdale Bank* v. *Royal Bank* (1876) 3 R. 586.
[83] *Alexander Beith Ltd.* v. *Allan*, 1961 S.L.T.(Notes) 80.
[84] *Clydesdale Bank* v. *Paul* (1877) 4 R. 626. See also *Traill* v. *Smith's Trs.* (1876) 3 R. 770; *New Mining and Exploring Syndicate Ltd.* v. *Chalmers & Hunter*, 1912 S.C. 126; *Royal Bank of Scotland plc* v. *Watt*, 1990 G.W.D. 1–6.
[85] This section replaces section 82 of the 1882 Act which, however, applied only to crossed cheques; s.4 of the 1957 Act applies to all cheques, crossed and uncrossed, and also to the other instruments defined in subs.(2). See Cusine, 1978 J.R. 233.

been negligent in some degree.[86] A banker is not to be treated as having been negligent by reason only of his failure to concern himself with the absence of, or irregularity in, indorsement of the cheque.[87]

The wording of paragraph (*b*) of s.4(1) is rather odd in that it seems to be based on the view that crediting the customer's account does put the bank in the position of receiving payment for itself.[88]

IOU

An IOU is a document consisting of the expression "I owe you" or "IOU" and indicating a sum of money. It must be holograph of the granter and signed by him.[89] It need not be dated or addressed to a creditor.[90] It does not require a stamp.[91]

6.14

An IOU is an acknowledgment of debt due by the granter to the grantee and it implies an obligation to repay on demand.[92] "If nothing more is known about an IOU except what can be gathered from the terms of the document, it is thus *per se* a good warrant for a claim on the part of the creditor named in the document to whom it has been delivered to sue for repayment."[93] This would indicate that the IOU is a document of debt and not merely an adminicle of evidence[94] and the pursuer is under no obligation to explain to the court how the indebtedness arose.[95] The genuineness of the handwriting has, of course, to be proved.[96] In the absence of express stipulation, interest does not begin to run on the principal sum *ex lege* until repayment is demanded.[97]

Payment can be proved only by the writ or oath of the creditor.[98] It is not a relevant defence to prove that no money passed at the granting of the document[99]; or that there was no antecedent debt[98]; or that the document is a sham.[1] The following defences can be proved parole: (a) a collateral agreement as to the date at which payment is to be made[2]; (b) that "facts and circumstances have arisen which really show that the party putting forward the IOU has no proper right to have the document of

---

[86] Banking Act 1979, s.47.
[87] s.4(3); as to negligence see *Orbit Mining & Trading Co. Ltd.* v. *Westminster Bank Ltd.* [1963] 1 Q.B. 794, and the cases cited therein.
[88] See Paget, p. 471; Byles, pp. 314, 317–319; Ellinger, p. 440.
[89] *per* Lord Deas, *Bowe and Christie* v. *Hutchison* (1868) 6 M. 642 at 646; *per* L. P. Inglis, *Haldane* v. *Speirs* (1872) 10 M. 537 at 541.
[90] *Brunton* v. *Bone* (1858) 1 S.L.J. 58; *Ferenze Spinning Co.* v. *Wallace* (1858) 1 S.L.J. 93.
[91] *per* Lord Trayner, *Thiem's Trs.* v. *Collie* (1899) 1 F. 764 at 777.
[92] *per* L. P. Normand, *Black* v. *Gibb*, 1940 S.C. 24 at 26.
[93] *per* Lord Moncrieff, *Black* v. *Gibb*, *supra*, at p. 28.
[94] It has been suggested that this is a distinction without a difference (*per* Lord Johnston, *Bishop* v. *Bryce*, 1910 S.C. 426 at 435; see also *Thiem's Trs.* v. *Collie*, *supra*, *per* Lord Trayner at p. 774), but it does affect the form of the action—see *Encyclopaedia of Scottish Legal Styles*, Vol. VI, p. 19; Dobie, *Sheriff Court Styles*, p. 257, n. 7.
[95] But see *Bertram* v. *McIntyre* (1934) 50 Sh.Ct.Rep. 194.
[96] *per* L. P. Inglis, *Haldane* v. *Speirs*, *supra*, at p. 541.
[97] *Winestone* v. *Wolifson*, 1954 S.C. 77.
[98] *Thiem's Trs.* v. *Collie* (1899) 1 F. 764.
[99] *Black* v. *Gibb*, *supra*. Cf. *Paterson* v. *Wilson* (1883) 21 S.L.R. 272.
[1] *McCreadie's Trs.* v. *McCreadie* (1897) 5 S.L.T. 153; *Gray* v. *Bain* (1954) 70 Sh.Ct.Rep. 65.
[2] *Black* v. *Gibb*, *supra*.

debt with him"[3]; (c) that there exists a state of facts which is inconsistent with the continued subsistence of the debt[4] (d) where the granting of the IOU is admitted, that it was destroyed by the instructions of the creditor who intended that the money advanced should be a gift to the defender.[5] Moreover, if both parties agree that the IOU is not a true record of the transaction between them and that in fact no debt was outstanding which the debtor *ex facie* of the document undertook to repay, the document is ignored and the pursuer must prove his debt by other means.[6] As to prescription, see Chapter 14, paras. 4 *et seq.*

An IOU is not a negotiable instrument and can be transferred only by intimated assignation.[7]

Deposit receipt

6.15   A deposit receipt is a contract whereby a bank promises to pay upon a certain order but it does not give any indication as to the person to whom the money belongs after it has been paid.[8] There are two distinct questions: (a) what is the obligation to pay which the bank has undertaken? and (b) who is the true owner of the fund which is the subject of the deposit?[9] The terms of the receipt are not conclusive evidence as to the ownership of the fund and *per se* do not instruct an *inter vivos* donation,[10] a *mortis causa* donation,[11] or a testamentary bequest[12]; with other evidence, however, some of these effects may be established.[13] In general, the ownership of the fund has to be determined on the evidence.[14]

Questions of retention[15] and the effect of arrestment[16] in the hands of the bank are treated elsewhere.

The deposit receipt is not a negotiable document and right to the fund is not transferred by indorsation; it can be assigned.[17] If the receipt is lost, the bank may refuse payment unless caution is given or there is a judicial order for payment.[18]

---

[3] *per* L. P. Dunedin, *Bishop* v. *Bryce*, 1910 S.C. 426 at 430; Gloag, p. 716, interprets this decision thus: "that the document of debt was granted for a particular purpose, that this purpose has been carried into effect, and that the document ought to have been given up."
[4] *McKenzie's Exrx.* v. *Morrison's Trs.*, 1930 S.C. 830.
[5] *Anderson's Trs.* v. *Webster* (1883) 11 R. 35.
[6] *Black* v. *Gibb, supra.*
[7] Gloag & Irvine, p. 575.
[8] *Dickson* v. *National Bank*, 1917 S.C.(H.L.) 50, *per* Lord Dunedin at p. 53.
[9] *Anderson* v. *North of Scotland Bank* (1901) 4 F. 49, *per* Lord McLaren at p. 54.
[10] *Barstow* v. *Inglis* (1857) 20 D. 230; *Lord Advocate* v. *Galloway* (1884) 11 R. 541.
[11] *Jamieson* v. *McLeod* (1880) 7 R. 1131.
[12] *Crosbie's Trs.* v. *Wright* (1880) 7 R. 823.
[13] *Grant's Trs.* v. *McDonald*, 1939 S.C. 448 (*inter vivos* donation); *Macpherson's Exrx.* v. *Mackay*, 1932 S.C. 505; *Graham's Trs.* v. *Gillies*, 1956 S.C. 437 (donation *mortis causa*).
[14] *Bank of Scotland* v. *Robertson* (1870) 8 M. 391.
[15] See para. 13.4.
[16] See para. 17.3.
[17] See *Wood* v. *Clydesdale Bank Ltd.*, 1914 S.C. 397.
[18] *Pirrie* v. *Mags. of Hawick* (1901) 17 Sh.Ct.Rep. 294.

CHAPTER 7

SECURITIES: CORPOREAL MOVEABLES

Securities

A right in security is "any right which a creditor may hold for ensuring   7.1
the payment or satisfaction of his debt, distinct from, and in addition to, his right of action and execution against the debtor under the latter's personal obligation."[1] The right may be a *jus in personam*, a right against persons other than the debtor, or a *jus in re*, a right over specific property. It has been held that the granting of a voucher for an existing debt—an IOU or a promissory note, for example—is not the constitution of a security unless its effect is to give the creditor a preference as regards diligence.[2] However, the word "security" is used in more than one way: "The word 'security' has two meanings. It may refer to some property deposited or made over or some obligation entered into by or on behalf of a person in order to secure his fulfilment of an obligation he has undertaken. Or it may refer to a document held by a creditor as evidence or a guarantee of his right to repayment."[3] A promissory note was held to be a "security" for purposes of the Moneylenders Acts[4] and bonds, bills and notes are within the definition of "security" in the Consumer Credit Act 1974.[5]

In the Consumer Credit Act 1974, a "security" means a "mortgage" (including a heritable security), charge, pledge, bond, debenture, indemnity, guarantee, bill, note or other right provided by the debtor or at his request to secure the carrying out of his obligations.[6]

A mere pecuniary obligation is not a security even if it designates a fund of the debtor out of which it is to be paid.[7]

Consumer Credit Act 1974

Documents embodying regulated agreements have to embody any   7.2
security provided in relation to the agreement by the debtor.[8] If the person by whom a security is provided (the "surety") is not the debtor, the security must be expressed in writing, the document containing all the terms of the security other than implied terms must be signed by or on behalf of the surety and a copy of the document and the principal agreement given to him.[9] If these requirements are not satisfied, the security is enforceable against the surety only on an order of the court and if an application for such an order is dismissed (except on technical

---

[1] Gloag & Irvine, p. 1.
[2] *Matthew's Tr.* v. *Matthew* (1867) 5 M. 957.
[3] *per* Lord Migdale, *Cleveleys Investment Trust Co.* v. *Inland Revenue*, 1971 S.C. 233 at 243.
[4] *George Shaw Ltd.* v. *Duffy*, 1943 S.C. 350.
[5] s.189.
[6] Consumer Credit Act 1974, s.189.
[7] *Graham & Co.* v. *Raeburn & Verel* (1895) 23 R. 84.
[8] s.105(9); Consumer Credit (Agreements) Regulations, 1983 (S.I. 1983 No. 1553), reg. 2(8).
[9] s.105.

grounds) the security is treated as never having effect, property lodged with the creditor for purposes of the security must be returned, any entry relating to the security in any register must be cancelled and any amount received by the creditor on realisation of the security must be repaid to the surety[10]; there is a partial exemption for heritable securities. The creditor is obliged to give the surety on request a copy of the principal agreement and of the security instrument and information about the present state of the debtor's indebtedness.[11]

A copy of any default notice served on the debtor must be served on the surety.[12] A security cannot be enforced so as to benefit the creditor to an extent greater than would be the case if there were no security and the obligations of the debtor were carried out to the extent (if any) to which they would be enforced under the Act.[13] Accordingly, if a regulated agreement is enforceable only on a court order or an order of the Director the security is enforceable only where an order has been made[14] and, generally, if the agreement is cancelled or becomes unenforceable, the security becomes ineffective.[15]

Corporeal moveables

7.3   The general principle is that a security cannot be created over corporeal moveables unless they are delivered to the creditor.[16] There may be some relaxation of the rule where delivery is impossible[17] and there are the following exceptions:

(i)   floating charges,[18]
(ii) agricultural charges in favour of banks[19];
(iii) Inland Revenue charges for unpaid inheritance tax[20];
(iv) maritime liens[21];
(v)   mortgages of ships and aircraft.[22]

A solicitor's "charge" for expenses on property recovered or preserved in an action may prevail in a sequestration or liquidation although it yields to a bona fide purchaser or lender.[23]

There have been attempts to evade the principle. It is not possible to constitute a security over corporeal moveables *retenta possessione* by means of a fictitious sale. The provisions of the Sale of Goods Act 1979 do not apply to a transaction in the form of a contract of sale which is intended to operate by way of mortgage, pledge, charge or other

---

[10] s.106.
[11] ss.107-110.
[12] s.111.
[13] s.113(1).
[14] s.113(2).
[15] s.113(3).
[16] Bell, *Comm.*, II, 21; *Clark* v. *West Calder Oil Co.* (1882) 9 R. 1017; *cf. Rhind's Tr.* v. *Robertson & Baxter* (1891) 18 R. 623; *Pattison's Tr.* v. *Liston* (1893) 20 R. 806.
[17] *Darling* v. *Wilson's Tr.* (1887) 15 R. 180.
[18] See para. 9.9.
[19] Agricultural Credits (Scotland) Act 1929, Pt. II.
[20] Inheritance Tax Act 1984, s.237.
[21] See, as to the enforcement of a maritime lien, *Mill* v. *Fildes*, 1982 S.L.T. 147.
[22] See *infra*, paras. 5 and 6.
[23] Solicitors (Scotland) Act 1980, s.62.

security.[24] In particular, a sale followed by a letting or hire-purchase back to the seller will not be effectual if there has been no delivery.[25] A genuine *pactum de retrovendendo* is not struck at.[26]

It has been suggested that the recent affirmation[27] that an individual can declare a trust of his own property with himself as sole trustee opens a further way of evasion but the difficulty may be that a trust for creditors is superseded by sequestration.[28]

Pledge is the form of security appropriate to corporeal moveables. It is defined as "a real contract, by which one places in the hands of his creditor a moveable subject, to remain with him in security of a debt or engagement, to be re-delivered on payment or satisfaction; and with an implied mandate, on failure to fulfil the engagement at the stipulated time or on demand, to have the pledge sold by judicial authority."[29] Actual delivery may be effected either by physical transfer or by placing the goods in a separate part of the debtor's premises, the key of which is given to the creditor.[30] Mere labelling or setting apart of the goods is not sufficient.[31]

The creditor, being owner of the premises on which the goods are situated, may have possession of them although the debtor, as contractor or lessee, has the use of them.[32] In the case of a bill of lading there may be symbolic delivery, the bill being regarded as equivalent to the goods it represents.[33] Possession is not lost if the bill is returned to the debtor so that he may, as the creditor's agent, sell the goods.[34] When the goods are in the hands of an independent third party[35] such as a storekeeper, there may be constructive delivery.[36] This is effected by an intimation to the custodier in the form of a delivery order that the goods are to be held for the transferee. The goods must be specific in the sense that they are either a total undivided quantity stored in a particular place or a specified quantity forming part of an identified whole.[37]

---

[24] 1979 Act, s.62(4). See *Robertson* v. *Hall's Tr.* (1896) 24 R. 120; *Jones & Co.'s Tr.* v. *Allan* (1901) 4 F. 374; *Hepburn* v. *Law*, 1914 S.C. 918. Evasion by use of a lease and the landlord's hypothec is ineffectual: *Heritable Securities Investment Association Ltd.* v. *Wingate & Co.'s Tr.* (1880) 7 R. 1094.

[25] *Rennet* v. *Mathieson* (1903) 5 F. 591; *Newbigging* v. *Ritchie's Tr.*, 1930 S.C. 273; *Scottish Transit Trust* v. *Scottish Land Cultivators Ltd.*, 1955 S.C. 254; *G. & C. Finance Corporation Ltd.* v. *Brown*, 1961 S.L.T. 408.

[26] *Gavin's Tr.* v. *Fraser*, 1920 S.C. 674; but see Gloag's view of this decision— *Encyclopaedia of the Laws of Scotland*, Vol. XIII, p. 311.

[27] *Allan's Trs.* v. *Lord Advocate*, 1971 S.C. (H.L.) 45.

[28] *Salaman* v. *Rosslyn's Trs.* (1900) 3 F. 298.

[29] Bell, *Prin.*, § 203.

[30] *Liqr. of West Lothian Oil Co. Ltd.* v. *Mair* (1892) 20 R. 64.

[31] *Gibson* v. *Forbes* (1833) 11 S.916; *Boak* v. *Megget* (1844) 6 D. 662; *Orr's Tr.* v. *Tullis* (1870) 8 M. 936.

[32] *Moore* v. *Gledden* (1869) 7 M. 1016; *Orr's Tr.* v. *Tullis* (1870) 8 M. 936.

[33] Bell, *Prin.*, § 417; *Hayman & Son* v. *McLintock*, 1907 S.C. 936.

[34] *North-Western Bank Ltd.* v. *Poynter, Son and Macdonalds* (1894) 22 R. (H.L.) 1. See Gretton, 1990 J.R. 23.

[35] *Anderson* v. *McCall* (1866) 4 M. 765; *Dobell, Beckett & Co.* v. *Neilson* (1904) 7 F. 281.

[36] *Pochin & Co.* v. *Robinows & Marjoribanks* (1869) 7 M. 622, *per* L. P. Inglis at p. 628; *Inglis* v. *Robertson & Baxter* (1898) 25 R. (H.L.) 70; *Hayman & Co.* v. *McLintock*, *supra*; *Price & Pierce Ltd.* v. *Bank of Scotland*, 1910 S.C. 1095; 1912 S.C. (H.L.) 19. See, as to the technical nature of the transaction, Rodger, 1971 J.R. 193.

[37] *Pochin & Co.* v. *Robinows & Marjoribanks*, *supra*, *per* L. P. Inglis at p. 629.

On the debtor's default, the creditor can sell the subject of pledge if he is expressly authorised by the contract to do so. Otherwise, he must apply to the sheriff for a warrant for sale.[38] It seems that the subject cannot be retained for payment of debts other than the one for which it was pledged.[39] The security may be destroyed if the creditor by donation loses legal possession of the article.[40]

Where the security is in the form of an *ex facie* absolute transfer of the property in the subjects, the creditor can sell on default at his own hand and can retain the security against any debt due to him by the debtor.[39]

Pledges: Consumer Credit Act

7.4   The provisions of the Consumer Credit Act as to pledges do not apply to pledges of documents of title or bearer bonds or to non-commercial agreements. It is an offence to take an article in pawn from a minor.[41] It is also an offence for the "pawnee" to fail to give the "pawner" a copy of the agreement, notice of his cancellation rights and a pawn-receipt with a specified form and content.[42] The period during which the pawn is redeemable (the "redemption period") is six months after it was taken or the period fixed for the duration of the credit, if longer, or such longer period as the parties may agree; the pawn remains redeemable after the expiry of the redemption period until it is realised or the property in it passes to the pawnee.[43] No special charges or higher charges for safe keeping of the pawn can be made on redemption after the expiry of the redemption period.

The pawnee must deliver the pawn on surrender of the receipt and payment of the amount owing unless he knows or suspects that the bearer of the receipt is not the owner of the pawn.[44] If the owner claiming the pawn does not have the receipt he may make a statutory declaration (or, where the loan is not over £25, a written statement in prescribed form) which is treated as the receipt.[45] It is an offence to fail without reasonable cause to allow redemption of a pawn.[46] Where a pawn is an article which has been stolen or obtained by fraud the court which has convicted a person of the offence may order delivery of the pawn to the owner subject to such conditions as to payment of the debt as it thinks fit.[47]

If the credit does not exceed £25, and the pawn has not been redeemed at the end of the redemption period of six months, the property in the pawn passes to the pawnee.[48] In other cases, the pawn becomes realisable if it has not been redeemed at the end of the redemption period. The pawner must be given 14 days' notice of the pawnee's intention to sell

---

[38] Bell, *Prin.*, § 207.

[39] *Hamilton* v. *Western Bank of Scotland* (1856) 19 D. 152.

[40] *Wolifson* v. *Harrison*, 1978 S.L.T. 95.

[41] Consumer Credit Act 1974, s.114(2).

[42] s.115; Consumer Credit (Pawn-Receipts) Regulations 1983 (S.I. 1983 No. 1566). Where the receipt is not separate from the document embodying the regulated agreement, Consumer Credit (Agreements) Regulations 1983 (S.I. 1983 No. 1553), reg. 4, applies.

[43] s.116.

[44] s.117.

[45] s.118; Consumer Credit (Loss of Pawn-Receipt) Regulations 1983 (S.I. 1983 No. 1567).

[46] s.119; s.171(6).

[47] s.122.

[48] s.120.

unless the credit does not exceed £50 and, within 21 working days after the sale, information as to the sale, its proceeds and expenses. If the net proceeds are not less than the debt, the debt is discharged and any surplus is payable to the pawner; otherwise the debt is reduced *pro tanto*. On challenge, it is for the pawnee to prove that he used reasonable care to ensure that the true market value was obtained and that the expenses of sale were reasonable.[49]

Ships

A mortgage over a registered ship or a share therein may be registered by the registrar of the ship's port of registry.[50] The mortgagee has power to sell the ship but not without the concurrence of any prior mortgagee unless a court order is obtained.[51] He may also enter into possession of the ship. There are provisions as to the discharge and transfer of mortgages.[52] Mortgages rank according to the date of registration.[53] They are postponed to bottomry bonds,[54] and maritime liens[55] but a mortgagee in possession is preferred to an arrester.[56] A mortgage may be reduced where the grantee was in bad faith.[57]

There are similar provisions as to the registration of mortgages of registered fishing vessels.[58]

7.5

Aircraft

A security can be created over an aircraft together with its spare parts[59] by executing a mortgage[60] which is entered in the Register of Aircraft Mortgages kept by the Civil Aviation Authority. Delivery of the aircraft to the mortgagee is not necessary.[61] A priority notice, that is, a notice of intention to make an application to enter a contemplated mortgage in the register, may be entered in the register.[62] On the mortgagor's default the mortgagee can either apply to the Court of Session for warrant to take possession of the aircraft[63] or sell the aircraft by a prescribed procedure;[64] the proceeds of the sale are held by the mortgagee in trust for payment in the following priority[65]: (i) the expenses of sale; (ii) amounts due under prior mortgages; (iii) amounts due under his mortgage and any mortgage

7.6

---

[49] s.121; Consumer Credit (Realisation of Pawn) Regulations 1983 (S.I. 1983 No. 1568).
[50] Merchant Shipping Act 1894, s.31 (as substituted by Merchant Shipping Act 1988, Sched. 1, para. 21).
[51] s.35. See *Robertson Durham* v. *Constant* (1907) 15 S.L.T. 131; *Banque Indo Suez* v. *Maritime Co. Overseas Inc.*, 1984 S.C. 120.
[52] ss.32, 37, 38.
[53] s.33.
[54] *The St. George* [1926] P. 217.
[55] *The Athena* (1921) 8 Ll.L.R. 482.
[56] *Clydesdale Bank* v. *Walker & Bain*, 1926 S.C. 72.
[57] *Lombard North Central Ltd.* v. *Lord Advocate*, 1983 S.L.T. 361.
[58] Merchant Shipping Act 1988, s.21, Sched. 3.
[59] Mortgaging of Aircraft Order 1972 (S.I. 1972 No. 1268), arts. 3, 4; Mortgaging of Aircraft (Amendment) Order 1981 (S.I. 1981 No. 611); Insolvency (Amendment of Subordinate Legislation) Order 1986 (S.I. 1986 No. 2001).
[60] Sched. 2, Pt. II.
[61] Sched. 2, para. 3.
[62] Art. 5.
[63] Sched. 2, para. 11.
[64] Sched. 2, para. 9.
[65] Sched. 2, para. 10.

ranking *pari passu*; (iv) amounts due under postponed mortgages; (v) amounts due under unregistered mortgages. Any residue is paid to the owner.

A registered mortgage has priority over an unregistered one.[66] Registered mortgages rank according to the time of entry in the register except that where a priority notice has been entered and the contemplated mortgage has been entered within 14 days thereafter that mortgage has priority from the time of registration of the priority notice.[67] A registered mortgage is postponed to any possessory lien in respect of work done on the aircraft and to any right to detain the aircraft under any Act of Parliament.[68]

Liens in general

7.7   A lien is a right to retain possession of goods or documents belonging to another until a debt has been paid.[69] The owner of the property must have been in a position to give a good title of possession.[70] Possession must have been obtained with the owner's consent, not by mistake.[71] The articles must have come into the creditor's possession in the course of the legal relationship which gives rise to the lien.[72] The lien must be consistent with the terms of the contract under which possession is given so if articles are appropriated to a particular purpose there cannot be a lien over them.[73] Whether the creditor has possession is a question of fact.[74] The possession must be that of someone more than a mere servant of the debtor.[75] Civil possession may be retained by the creditor if the articles are given to a broker or borrower.[76] The lien falls with loss of possession and does not revive upon subsequent recovery of possession.[77] Relinquishing possession of part of the goods or documents does not affect the lien over the remainder for the full amount of the debt.[78] A lien held in one relationship cannot be used in respect of a debt arising from another relationship.[79] Taking a bill for the debt may be a resignation of the lien.[80] Where possession of goods is relinquished on the granting of a bond the terms of the bond must be carefully considered.[81]

---

[66] Art. 14(1).
[67] Art. 14(2).
[68] Art. 14(5). See *Channel Airways* v. *Manchester Corporation* [1974] 1 Lloyd's Rep. 456.
[69] Bell, *Prin.*, § 1410.
[70] *National Bank of Scotland* v. *Thomas White and Park*, 1909 S.C. 1308.
[71] *Louson* v. *Craik* (1842) 4 D. 1452.
[72] *National Bank of Scotland* v. *Thomas White and Park*, 1909 S.C. 1308.
[73] *Borthwick* v. *Bremner* (1833) 12 S. 121.
[74] *Barr & Shearer* v. *Cooper* (1875) 2 R. (H.L.) 14; *Ross & Duncan* v. *Baxter & Co.* (1885) 13 R. 185.
[75] *Dickson* v. *Nicholson* (1885) 17 D. 1011; *Callum* v. *Ferrier* (1825) 1 W. & S. 399; *Gladstone* v. *McCallum* (1896) 23 R. 783; *Barnton Hotel Co.* v. *Cook* (1899) 1 F. 1190.
[76] *Renny* v. *Rutherford* (1840) 2 D. 676; *Wilmot* v. *Wilson* (1841) 3 D. 815; *Gairdner* v. *Milne and Co.* (1858) 20 D. 565; *Ure & Macrae* v. *Davies* (1917) 33 Sh.Ct.Rep. 109.
[77] *Morrison* v. *Fulwell's Tr.* (1901) 9 S.L.T. 34.
[78] *Gray* v. *Graham* (1855) 2 Macq. 435.
[79] *Largue* v. *Urquhart* (1883) 10 R. 1229.
[80] *Palmer* v. *Lee* (1880) 7 R. 651.
[81] *Georgia Pacific Corporation* v. *Evalend Shipping Co. S.A.*, 1988 S.L.T. 683.

Special liens

A right of retention or special lien arises wherever property comes into the possession of someone other than the proprietor under a contract which creates rights *hinc inde*. The right "is part of the law of mutual contract, entitling one to withhold performance, or retain possession of that which forms the subject of the contract, till the counter obligation be performed."[82]

So a person who has carried out work on goods under contract is entitled to retain the goods in his possession until he is paid for the work done on the goods[83] or until he is paid damages for breach of contract.[84] This right arises from an implied condition of the contract. It has been recognised in Scotland in the cases of an engine-builder,[85] a storekeeper,[86] and a carrier.[87]

In the case of a bleacher, the implied right is over each parcel of goods for his whole account for work done within the year.[88]

It has been held in the sheriff court that repairers exercising a lien over a car are not entitled to recover garage dues covering the period of the lien but it is not clear that this is justified by the authority cited.[89]

There is Scottish authority to the effect that a repairer cannot acquire a lien over an article on hire-purchase if the hire-purchase contract excludes the hirer's right to create a lien. The decision seems wrong.[90]

The owner is entitled to delivery of the goods on payment of the unpaid account and is not bound to find security for the expenses of the action for delivery.[91] The creditor's ultimate remedy is to petition the court to have the goods sold.[92]

7.8

Lien over papers

The principle of lien has been extended to give an accountant the right to retain books and papers until he has been paid for the work done with them[93]; and a factor is in the same position.[94] The lien falls with loss of possession and does not revive upon recovery of possession.[95] On the sequestration or liquidation of the debtor, the books and papers must be delivered up to the trustee or liquidator under reservation of the lien[96];

7.9

---

[82] Bell, *Prin.*, § 1419; *Moore's Carving Machine Co.* v. *Austin* (1896) 33 S.L.R. 613; *Paton's Trs.* v. *Finlayson*, 1923 S.C. 872.
[83] Bell, *Comm.*, II, 87.
[84] *Moore's Carving Machine Co.* v. *Austin*, supra.
[85] *Ross & Duncan* v. *Baxter & Co.* (1885) 13 R. 185.
[86] *Laurie* v. *Denny's Tr.* (1853) 15 D. 404.
[87] *Stevenson* v. *Likly* (1824) 3 S. 291; *Youle* v. *Cochrane* (1868) 6 M. 427.
[88] *Anderson's Tr.* v. *Fleming* (1871) 9 M. 718.
[89] *Carntyne Motors* v. *Curran*, 1958 S.L.T. (Sh.Ct.) 6; *Stephen* v. *Swayne* (1861) 24 D. 158.
[90] *Lamonby* v. *Foulds Ltd.*, 1928 S.C. 89; *Mitchell* v. *Heys & Sons* (1894) 21 R. 600. See Gow, *Law of Hire-Purchase* (2nd ed.), p. 164.
[91] *Garscadden* v. *Ardrossan Dry Dock Co. Ltd.*, 1910 S.C. 178.
[92] *Gibson and Stewart* v. *Brown & Co.* (1876) 3 R. 328; *Parker* v. *Brown & Co.* (1878) 5 R. 979.
[93] *Meikle & Wilson* v. *Pollard* (1880) 8 R. 69; *Findlay* v. *Waddell*, 1910 S.C. 670; *J. Penman Ltd.* v. *Macdonald* (1953) 69 Sh.Ct.Rep. 284.
[94] *Robertson* v. *Ross* (1887) 15 R. 67.
[95] *Morrison* v. *Fulwell's Tr.* (1901) 9 S.L.T. 34.
[96] B.A., ss.38(4), 51(6); I.A., s.144; Ins. Rule 4.22(4); *Train & McIntyre* v. *Forbes*, 1925 S.L.T. 286.

the effect of the reservation is that if eventually a valid lien is found to have existed, the person who held the documents is entitled to a preference in the liquidation, presumably similar to that obtained by a solicitor's lien but is, of course, in the case of an accountant limited to the amount of the account for the work done on the papers held.

General lien

7.10   A general lien is a right of retention until payment of any balance due on trade operations. If the relationship between the debtor and creditor is not one of those giving rise to a general lien, goods cannot be retained for all debts which may be due.[97] A general lien rests on express or implied contract[98] or usage of trade[99] or, in the case of a factor, on the nature of the contract.[1] The following have a general lien: a banker,[2] a stockbroker,[1] a solicitor,[3] an auctioneer,[4] and a hotel proprietor.[5] The innkeeper's lien extends to all the guest's possessions on the premises, including those belonging to third parties.[6]

A factor has a general lien if he is required to make payment or undertake liabilities for his principal and goods of his principal come into his possession in the ordinary course of his employment[1]; it is suggested that this lien is confined to cases of mercantile agency.[7]

A bank has a general lien over negotiable instruments belonging to a customer and in its possession.[8] The lien does not apply to securities deposited for safe custody.[9] The lien does not apply when the documents have been delivered for a special purpose.[8]

Solicitor's lien

7.11   A solicitor has a general lien over his client's titles, securities, documents of debt and other papers for payment of his professional account and ordinary disbursements.[10] It does not cover advances to the client.[11]

It does not cover accounts incurred on behalf of the client which the solicitor has not in fact paid and for which he is not personally liable.[12] It does not, in the case of a country solicitor, cover his Edinburgh agent's account.[13] There cannot be a lien over a company register.[14] The client

---

[97] *Harper* v. *Faulds* (1791) Mor. 2666.
[98] *Miller* v. *Hutcheson & Dixon* (1881) 8 R. 489.
[99] *Strong* v. *Philips & Co.* (1878) 5 R. 770.
[1] *Glendinning* v. *Hope & Co.*, 1911 S.C. (H.L.) 73.
[2] Bell, *Comm.*, II, 113.
[3] See *infra*, para. 11.
[4] *Crockart's Tr.* v. *Hay & Co. Ltd.*, 1913 S.C. 509; *Mackenzie* v. *Cormack*, 1950 S.C. 183. Only one judge in *Miller* v. *Hutcheson & Dixon*, supra, which is cited in these decisions, opined that an auctioneer has a general lien but an auctioneer is in any event a factor or mercantile agent.
[5] Bell, *Prin.*, § 1428; Hotel Proprietors Act 1956, ss. 1, 2.
[6] *Bermans & Nathans Ltd.* v. *Weibye*, 1983 S.C. 67.
[7] *Macrae* v. *Leith*, 1913 S.C. 901.
[8] *Robertson's Tr.* v. *Royal Bank* (1890) 18 R. 12.
[9] *Brandao* v. *Barnett* (1846) 12 Cl. & F. 787.
[10] Bell, *Prin.*, § 1438.
[11] *Wylie's Exrx.* v. *McJannet* (1901) 4 F. 195.
[12] *Liqr. of Grand Empire Theatres* v. *Snodgrass*, 1932 S.C. (H.L.) 73.
[13] *Largue* v. *Urquhart* (1883) 10 R. 1229.
[14] *Liqr. of the Garpel Haematite Co.* v. *Andrew* (1866) 4 M. 617.

must have been in a position to give a good title of possession.[15] The lien terminates with loss of possession.[16] There is no lien over titles which did not come into the solicitor's possession until after the relationship of solicitor and client had terminated.[17] If the solicitor has acted for lender and borrower he cannot exercise his lien against the borrower to the prejudice of the lender.[18] The solicitor for a proprietor or postponed heritable creditor cannot acquire a lien over writs against a heritable creditor after the date of recording of that creditor's security.[19] The solicitor for the heritable creditor cannot retain titles against the proprietor for payment of amounts due by his client.[20] Relinquishing possession of some papers does not prevent the exercise of the lien over the rest for the full account.[21] The papers cannot be sold for payment of the debt.[22] Production can be withheld until the account is paid or secured even where the client is petitioning for recovery of the papers under s.1 of the Administration of Justice (Scotland) Act 1972.[23]

On sequestration or liquidation of the client, the solicitor must deliver up the documents to the trustee or liquidator under reservation of his lien; he will retain his preference if he can show that if there had been no order for delivery he would have had an effectual lien.[24]

The effect of the lien is to give the solicitor a preferential right to payment of the sums due to him from the general assets of the estate[25]; he is not restricted to the assets to which the papers relate. But if the trustee or liquidator does not demand the titles and abandons the property to which they relate, there is no preference.[26] The preference is postponed to the expenses of administration of the sequestration or liquidation.[27] It it not clear how it ranks in relation to other preferential debts but there is some authority for the view that it ranks before other preferential debts.[28] The court has an equitable power to control the solicitor's lien.[29] The trustee in the solicitor's sequestration can have no higher right in respect of the lien than the solicitor himself.[30]

Hypothec

The landlord has a right of security over the *invecta et illata* on the subjects let for the current year's rent and the arrears of the past year's rent if sequestration for rent proceeds within three months of the term of

7.12

---

[15] *National Bank* v. *Thomas White and Park*, 1909 S.C. 1308.
[16] *Tawse* v. *Rigg* (1904) 6 F. 544.
[17] *Renny and Webster* v. *Myles & Murray* (1847) 9 D. 619.
[18] *Drummond* v. *Muirhead & Guthrie Smith* (1900) 2 F. 585.
[19] Conveyancing (Scotland) Act 1924, s.27.
[20] *Boyd* v. *Turnbull & Findlay*, 1911 S.C. 1006.
[21] *Gray* v. *Graham* (1855) 2 Macq. 435.
[22] *Ferguson and Stuart* v. *Grant* (1856) 18 D. 536.
[23] *Yau* v. *Ogilvie & Co.*, 1985 S.L.T. 91.
[24] B.A., ss.38(4), 51(6)(b); I.A., s.144; Ins. Rule 4.22(4); *Renny and Webster* v. *Myles & Murray, supra*; *Rorie* v. *Stevenson*, 1908 S.C. 559; *Garden Haig Scott & Wallace* v. *Stevenson's Tr.*, 1962 S.C. 51.
[25] *Skinner* v. *Henderson* (1865) 3 M. 867.
[26] *Ure & Macrae* v. *Davies* (1917) 33 Sh.Ct.Rep. 109.
[27] *Miln's J.F.* v. *Spence's Trs.*, 1927 S.L.T. 425.
[28] Bell, *Comm.*, II, 108; Gloag & Henderson, p. 270.
[29] *Ferguson and Stuart* v. *Grant, supra*.
[30] *Inglis* v. *Moncreiff* (1851) 13 D. 622.

payment.[31] Broadly, the hypothec now exists only in urban subjects and agricultural subjects where the land does not exceed two acres in extent.[32]

The hypothec does not apply to the articles exempted from poinding.[33]

The hypothec does apply to goods or a single article on hire or hire-purchase,[34] to goods on sale or return,[35] to goods in the gratuitous possession of the tenant after expiry of the hiring agreement,[36] and containers temporarily on the premises,[37] but it does not apply to a single article belonging to a third party, and hired to someone living with the tenant where the remainder of the furniture does not fall under the hypothec and the rent is payable in advance[38]; a hired article which is the only article on the premises not belonging to the landlord,[39] possibly, articles on hire for a very short period[40]; possibly, a hired article where the hiring arrangement excludes the hypothec and this has been intimated to the landlord[41]; articles already sold under diligence but remaining on the premises[42]; articles which the tenant is wrongfully withholding from the true owner[43]; articles under a hire-purchase or conditional sale agreement subject to the Consumer Credit Act 1974 in the period between the service of a default notice and the date on which the notice expires or is complied with, or, if the agreement is enforceable on the order of the court only, during the period between the commencement and the termination of the creditor's action to enforce the agreement,[44] articles stored in the premises in respect of which the tenant is receiving a rent[45]; articles sent to the tenant as samples.[46] The hypothec is not affected by the sequestration of the debtor[47] but the landlord's right is postponed to the superior's hypothec for feuduty, all privileged debts, and certain taxes.[48]

The superior has a hypothec over the crop and stock or *invecta et illata* for the last or current feuduty, similar but preferable to the landlord's hypothec.[49]

The hypothec is enforced by a sequestration for rent; in some cases the sheriff has a discretion to sist or adjourn the proceedings.[50]

---

[31] Bell, *Prin.*, § 1277.
[32] Hypothec Abolition (Scotland) Act 1880, s.1.
[33] D.A., s.99(1); see para. 16.3.
[34] *Penson and Robertson*, 6 June 1820, F.C.; *Nelmes & Co. v. Ewing* (1883) 11 R. 193; *Dundee Corporation v. Marr*, 1971 S.C. 96; *Smith v. Po and Capaldi*, 1931 S.L.T. (Sh.Ct.) 31. See also *McIntosh v. Potts* (1905) 7 F. 765.
[35] *Lawsons Ltd. v. Avon Indiarubber Co. Ltd.*, 1915 2 S.L.T. 327.
[36] *Smith Premier Typewriter Co. v. Cotton* (1907) 14 S.L.T. 764.
[37] *Scottish & Newcastle Breweries Ltd. v. Edinburgh District Council*, 1979 S.L.T. (Notes) 11.
[38] *Bell v. Andrews* (1885) 12 R. 961.
[39] *Edinburgh Albert Buildings Co. v. General Guarantee Corporation*, 1917 S.C. 239.
[40] *Adam v. Sutherland* (1863) 2 M. 6, *per* Lord Deas at p. 8.
[41] *Jaffray v. Carrick* (1836) 15 S. 43; *Orr v. Jay & Co.* (1911) 27 Sh.Ct.Rep. 158.
[42] *Adam v. Sutherland, supra.*
[43] *Jaffray v. Carrick, supra.*
[44] Consumer Credit Act 1974, s.104.
[45] Bell, *Comm.*, II, 31.
[46] *Pulsometer Engineering Co. Ltd. v. Gracie* (1887) 14 R. 316.
[47] Bankruptcy (Scotland) Act 1985, s.33(2).
[48] Bell, *Prin.*, § 1241; Taxes Management Act 1970, s.64; Graham Stewart, p. 489.
[49] Bell, *Prin.*, § 698.
[50] Rent (Scotland) Act 1984, s.110 (substituted by D.A., Sched. 6, para. 26).

CHAPTER 8

SECURITIES: OTHER PROPERTY

Incorporeal moveables

A security over incorporeal moveables is effected by assignation followed by intimation.[1] Mere delivery of the document of title has no effect, nor has a mere contractual obligation to create a security.[2] If the assignation is *ex facie* absolute, it is a security for any debt due by the debtor to the creditor notwithstanding that a back letter mentions a specific debt; if the assignation specifies the debt for which it is to constitute a security, the creditor must grant a retrocession on payment of that debt.[3]

8.1

In the case of shares in a company the only fully satisfactory method of creating a security is to obtain and register a duly executed transfer. A deposit of the share certificates has no effect.[4] The identical shares should be retransferred on repayment of the loan.[5] The creditor may be liable to the debtor if he fails to subscribe for a "rights issue"[6] or if he sells more shares than are required to pay the debt.[7]

A security can be granted over intellectual property.[8]

Heritage

A security cannot be created over heritage by mere deposit of the titles.[9] In general, the only method by which a security can be created over heritage is by the granting of a standard security.[10] Where a deed which is not in the form of a standard security, for the purpose of securing a debt, contains a disposition or assignation of an interest in land, it is to that extent void and unenforceable and the creditor may be required to grant a deed to clear the register.[11] The granter of a standard security need not have a recorded or registered title and can deduce his title.[12] The

8.2

---

[1] See Chap. 27.

[2] *Christie* v. *Ruxton* (1862) 24 D. 1182; *Robertson* v.*British Linen Bank* (1891) 18 R. 1225; *Wylie's Exrx.* v. *McJannet* (1901) 4 F. 195; *Bank of Scotland* v. *Liqrs. of Hutchison Main & Co. Ltd.*, 1914 S.C. (H.L.) 1.

[3] *National Bank* v. *Forbes* (1858) 21 D. 79; *Robertson's Tr.* v. *Riddell*, 1911 S.C. 14. It may be different if the back letter specifically limits the future advances to be secured: *Anderson's Tr.* v. *Somerville & Co.* (1899) 36 S.L.R. 833.

[4] *Gourlay* v. *Mackie* (1887) 14 R. 403.

[5] *Crerar* v. *Bank of Scotland*, 1921 S.C. 736; 1922 S.C. (H.L.) 137.

[6] *Waddell* v. *Hutton*, 1911 S.C. 575.

[7] *Nelson* v. *National Bank*, 1936 S.C. 570.

[8] See McLean, "Security over Intellectual Property: A Scottish Perspective" [1988] 3 J.I.B.L. 135; Trade Marks Act 1938, s.22; Registered Designs Act 1949, s.19; Patents Act 1977, s.31; Copyright, Designs and Patents Act 1988, ss.90, 222.

[9] *Christie* v. *Ruxton* (1862) 24 D. 1182.

[10] Conveyancing and Feudal Reform (Scotland) Act 1970, s.9(3). A security could be created by bond and disposition in security under the Small Dwellings Acquisition (Scotland) Acts 1899–1923: 1970 Act s.9(7); but s.9(7) was repealed by Tenants Rights, Etc. (Scotland) Act 1980, s.84, Sched. 5. Securities over entailed estates can be created by bond and disposition in security. For an example of a special statutory security, see *Sowman* v. *Glasgow D.C.*, 1984 S.C. 91.

[11] 1970 Act, s.9(4).

[12] s.12. Under registration of title, a deduction of title is not necessary if the midcouples or links are produced to the Keeper: Land Registration (Scotland) Act 1979, s.15(3).

security is in a specified form.[13] Unless specially qualified the import of the clause imposing a personal obligation is[14]:

(a) where the security is for a fixed amount advanced or payable at, or prior to, the delivery of the deed, the clause undertaking to make payment to the creditor imports an acknowledgment of receipt by the debtor of the principal sum advanced or an acknowledgment by the debtor of liability to pay that sum and a personal obligation undertaken by the debtor to repay or pay to the creditor on demand in writing at any time after the date of delivery of the standard security the said sum, with interest at the rate stated payable on the dates specified, together with all expenses for which the debtor is liable;

(b) where the security is for a fluctuating amount, whether subject to a maximum amount or not and whether advanced or due partly before and partly after delivery of the deed or whether to be advanced or to become due wholly after such delivery, the clause undertaking to make payment to the creditor imports a personal obligation by the debtor to repay or pay to the creditor on demand in writing the amount, not being greater than the maximum amount, if any, specified in the deed, advanced or due and outstanding at the time of demand, with interest on each advance from the date when it was made until repayment thereof, or on each sum payable from the date on which it became due until payment thereof, and at the rate stated payable on the dates specified, together with all expenses for which the debtor is liable.

The sum secured need not be specified.[15] The clause of consent to registration in the specified form imports a consent to registration in the Books of Council and Session, or in the books of the appropriate sheriff court, for execution.[16] The security is regulated by the "standard conditions" set out in Schedule 3 to the Act unless these have been varied.[17] A third party has no notice of a variation of the conditions which has not entered the Sasine Register but a reference in the standard security to the possibility of variation by a document not on the register is sufficient to put the third party on inquiry.[18] When the security is recorded or registered it vests the interest over which it is granted in the grantee as a security for the performance of the contract to which the security relates.[19]

Ranking of a standard security, in the absence of express provision, is

---

[13] Sched. 2, Forms A or B.

[14] s.10(1). Under standard condition 12, the debtor is personally liable for the expenses of creating, varying, restricting, discharging, calling-up the security and of realising the security subjects.

[15] s.9(6). Under registration of title there is no indemnity by the Keeper of the Registers in respect of a claim relating to the amount due under a heritable security: Land Registration (Scotland) Act 1979, s.12(3)(*o*).

[16] s.10(3).

[17] s.11(2).

[18] *Trade Development Bank* v. *Warriner & Mason (Scotland) Ltd.*, 1980 S.C. 74.

[19] s.11(1). Under registration of title, a security is registered by amending the title sheet of the relevant interest in land. The creditor will be given a charge certificate containing details of his security and disclosing any prior or *pari passu* security: Land Registration (Scotland) Act 1979, s.5.

by date of recording in the Sasine Register. Under registration of title, registered interests rank according to date of registration. A registered interest and an interest recorded in the Sasine Register rank according to the respective dates of registration and recording.[20]

The ranking of the security may be regulated by the agreement of the debtor and the creditors concerned but, apart from that, where the creditor receives notice of the creation of a subsequent recorded or registered [21] security over the same subjects or of a subsequent recorded or registered[21] conveyance of the subjects themselves, his preference is restricted to security for his advances up to that time and any future advances which he may be required to make under the contract to which the security relates and interest present or future thereon (including any such interest which has accrued or may accrue) and for any expenses or outlays (including interest thereon) which may be, or may have been, reasonably incurred in the exercise of any power conferred on any creditor by the deed expressing the existing security.[22] The recording of a deed is not, but a conveyance of the security subjects by operation of law is, sufficient notice to the creditor. It is thought that the effect of the section is to restrict the preference of the first creditor in a question with the notifying creditors; the first creditor still has a security for any post-notification advances but it is postponed to the security of the notifying creditor[23]

The security may be transferred in whole or in part by assignation in the statutory form,[24] recording or registration of which vests the security in the assignee as if it had been granted in his favour. The assignation also has the effect of vesting in the assignee the full benefit of all corroborative or substitutional obligations for the debt, or any part thereof, whether these obligations are contained in any deed or arise by operation of law or otherwise.[25]

There is provision for restriction, variation and discharge of the security.[26] The debtor has a right to redeem the security on giving two months' notice but this is subject to any agreement to the contrary.[27]

If the creditor intends to require discharge of the debt secured, he must serve a calling-up notice on the proprietor and on any other person against whom he wishes to preserve any right of recourse in respect of the debt. The debtor is in default if he does not comply with the notice and the creditor can proceed to sell the security subjects and exercise his other remedies under the Act.[28] The debtor is also in default if he has failed to comply with any other requirements arising out of the security; the creditor may serve a "notice of default" requiring fulfilment of the obligation; if that is not complied with, the creditor can exercise his

---

[20] Land Registration (Scotland) Act 1979, s.7.
[21] Halliday, *Conveyancing Law and Practice in Scotland*, Vol. III, p. 325.
[22] 1970 Act, s.13.
[23] Halliday, *op. cit.*, p. 326; but see Gretton (1980) 25 J.L.S. 275.
[24] s.14(1); Sched. 4, Forms A or B.
[25] s.14(2).
[26] ss.15–17.
[27] s.18(1A) added by Redemption of Standard Securities (Scotland) Act 1971, s.1.
[28] ss.19, 20(1), (2); Sched. 3, standard condition 9(1)(*a*). Remedies other than those provided by the 1970 Act (*i.e.*(1), (2), (6) and (7) *infra*) can be exercised without complying with the statutory conditions.

remedies under the Act other than entering into possession.[29] Alternatively he can, instead of serving a notice, apply to the court for warrant to exercise any of his remedies under the Act. The third type of default arises where the debtor is insolvent[30]; the creditor can apply to the court for warrant to exercise his remedies.[31]

The creditor's remedies[32] are:
(1) to raise an action on the personal obligation. The obligation transmits against a person taking by succession, gift or bequest, *quanto lucratus*, but it transmits against a person taking by onerous conveyance only where there is an agreement to that effect *in gremio* of the conveyance and the conveyance is signed by him.[33]
(2) to execute summary diligence under the personal obligation. This can, of course, be done only where the deed contained a clause of consent. Where the personal obligation is created by succession, gift or bequest, summary diligence is competent thereon only if the obligant has executed an agreement to the transmission of the obligation.[34]
(3) to enter into possession of the security subjects and receive the rents.[35]
(4) to sell the security subjects in accordance with the statutory procedure.[36] The money received is held by the creditor in trust for payment in the following priority:[37] (i) his expenses of sale, (ii) the whole amount due under any prior security to which the sale is not made subject, (iii) the whole amount due under his security and any security ranking *pari passu* with his, (iv) the amounts due under any postponed securities. The residue is payable to the person entitled to the security subjects at the time of sale or any person authorised to give receipts for the proceeds of sale. The recording or registration of the disposition to the purchaser, bearing to be in implement of the sale, disburdens the subjects of the security and of *pari passu* and postponed securities.[38]
(5) to apply to the court for decree of foreclosure after a failure to sell the subjects at a price not exceeding the amount due under the security and any *pari passu* or prior securities.[39] The court may order another sale at a price fixed by the court at which the creditor can bid and purchase or it may grant a decree of foreclosure declaring the creditor's right to the subjects at the price at which they were last exposed. The result of decree of foreclosure on its being recorded or

---

[29] Sched. 3, standard condition 9(1)(*b*); ss.21, 23(2).
[30] Sched. 3, standard conditions 9(1)(*c*), 9(2). See *United Dominions Trust Ltd.* v. *Site Preparations Ltd.* (No. 1), 1978 S.L.T. (Sh.Ct) 14. *Cf. United Dominions Trust Ltd.* v. *Site Preparations Ltd.* (No. 2), 1978 S.L.T. (Sh.Ct.) 21.
[31] s.24(1).
[32] He has the choice of remedy: *McWhirter* v. *McCulloch's Trs.* (1887) 14 R. 918.
[33] Conveyancing (Scotland) Act 1874,. s.47; Conveyancing (Scotland) Act 1924, s.15(1).
[34] 1924 Act, s.15(2).
[35] 1970 Act, Sched. 3, standard condition 10(3)–(6); *David Watson Property Management* v. *Woolwich Equitable Building Society*, 1990 S.C.L.R. 517 (I.H.); *Skipton Building Society* v. *Wain*, 1986 S.L.T. 96.
[36] 1970 Act, ss.20–25.
[37] s.27.
[38] s.26. A prior security is not affected but the selling creditor can redeem it: s.26(2).
[39] s.28.

registered is to extinguish any right of redemption, to vest the subjects in the creditor as if he had received an irredeemable disposition thereof duly recorded from the proprietor, to disburden the subjects of the security and all postponed securities and diligences and to give the creditor the same right as the debtor to redeem prior or *pari passu* securities.[40] The debtor's personal obligation remains in force so far as not extinguished by the price at which the subjects have been acquired.[41]

(6) to attach the moveables belonging to the proprietor or the subjects by a poinding of the ground.[42] The procedure is by raising an action in the sheriff court or Court of Session. Service creates a nexus over the moveables on the subjects at that time. A warrant to poind is granted and when the moveables have been inventoried a warrant for sale can be obtained.

(7) to raise an action of adjudication.[42] Adjudications on *debita fundi* are preferable to adjudications on personal debts and rank *inter se* according to priority of infeftment.

Heritable securities: insolvency

The trustee in the sequestration can sell heritable estate over which there is a heritable security only with the concurrence of the creditor unless he can obtain a sufficiently high price to discharge the security. The creditor cannot take steps to enforce his security after the trustee has intimated to him that he intends to sell it and the trustee cannot commence the procedure for sale after the creditor has intimated that he intends to proceed to a sale; if, however the party who has given intimation unduly delays in proceeding with the sale, the other may obtain authorisation from the court to proceed with the sale.[43] There is a similar provision for liquidations.[44]

8.3

Heritable securities: Consumer Credit Act

In the language of the Act, a "land mortgage" is any security "charged" on land, "land" being defined to include heritable subjects of whatever description.[45] Documents embodying a regulated consumer credit agreement must "embody" any security given by the debtor, but this may be done by reference to another document.[46]

8.4

The general provisions as to the cancellation of regulated agreements[47] do not apply to agreements secured on land but before sending to the debtor for signature an unexecuted agreement where the prospective

---

[40] s.28(6).
[41] s.28(7).
[42] This remedy is not mentioned in the 1970 Act but it is thought to be available: Halliday, *The Conveyancing and Feudal Reform (Scotland) Act 1970* (2nd ed.), p. 205.
[43] B.A., s.39(4).
[44] I.A., s.185; Ins. Rules 4.22(5).
[45] Consumer Credit Act 1974, s.189. Many heritable securities will relate to exempt agreements: see para. 3.4. For the requirements of the Act which apply to all securities, see para. 3.21.
[46] Consumer Credit (Agreements) Regulation 1983 (S.I. 1983 No. 1553), reg. 2(8). See Wood, "The Consumer Credit Act 1974" (1985) 30 J.L.S. 130, 181; Foley, "Loan Agreements and Standard Securities" (1985) 30 J.L.S. 222.
[47] para. 3.13.

regulated agreement is to be secured on land, the creditor must give the debtor a copy of the unexecuted agreement containing a notice indicating the debtor's right to withdraw from the prospective agreement and how and when the right is exercisable.[48] This does not apply to a restricted-use agreement to finance the purchase of the land or to an agreement for a bridging loan in connection with the purchase of the security subjects or other land. The regulated agreement is not properly executed unless (a) the copy agreement and notice of the withdrawal right is sent to the debtor, (b) the unexecuted agreement is sent by post to the debtor for his signature not less than seven days after the copy was given to him, (c) in the period between the giving of that copy and the expiry of seven days after the sending of the unexecuted agreement for his signature (or its return signed if earlier) the creditor refrained from approaching the debtor, in person, by telephone or letter or otherwise except in response to a specific request made by the debtor, (d) no notice of withdrawal by the debtor was received by the creditor before the sending of the unexecuted agreement.[49]

A "land mortgage" securing a regulated agreement is enforceable (so far as provided in relation to the agreement) on an order of the court only; retaking of the land is an enforcement.[50] There would appear to be no sanction for breach of this provision. The debtor could no doubt obtain an interdict. The provision does not prevent enforcement with the consent of the debtor given at that time.[51]

There is a general saving provision that nothing in the Act is to affect the rights of a heritable creditor, other than one carrying on the business of debt-collecting, who became the creditor for value and without notice of any defect in title arising by virtue of the other provisions of the Act or who derived title from such a creditor.[52]

Leases

8.5   A security can be granted over a lease which is not registrable by assignation followed by possession; if the lease is registrable, a standard security must be used.

A lease is registrable if it is probative, it is for a period exceeding 20 years and it contains a description of the subjects.[53] An assignee who has taken possession before recording of the standard security prevails.[54]

Under registration of title, however, a lessee under a long lease (*i.e.* a probative lease for a period which exceeds, or at the option of the grantee, could exceed, 20 years) obtains a real right only by registration and registration is the only means of making rights or obligations relating to the lease real rights or obligations or of affecting such real rights or

---

[48] s.58; Consumer Credit (Cancellation and Copies of Documents) Regulations 1983 (S.I. 1983 No. 1557), reg. 4.
[49] s.61. As to the enforcement of improperly executed agreements, see, para. 3.18. As to the effects of withdrawal, see s.57.
[50] ss.126, 65(2).
[51] s.173(3).
[52] s.177.
[53] Registration of Leases (Scotland) Act 1857 as amended by Long Leases (Scotland) Act 1954, s.27, and Land Tenure Reform (Scotland) Act 1974, Sched. 6, paras. 1, 5.
[54] *Rodger* v. *Crawfords* (1867) 6 M. 24, *per* Lord Neaves at p. 31.

obligations.[55] But two kinds of interest under leases are "overriding interests" which can prevail over registered interests. The first is the interest of a lessee under a lease which is not a long lease; the second is the interest of a lessee under a long lease who, prior to the commencement of the Land Registration (Scotland) Act 1979, has acquired a real right to the subjects of the lease by possession.[56] The second of these, but not the first, may be noted in the Land Register.[57]

Catholic and secondary securities
A catholic creditor is one whose security extends over two or more subjects; a secondary creditor is one whose security is over one of these subjects and is postponed to that of the catholic creditor. Where there is one secondary creditor, the catholic creditor is not entitled to proceed so as to injure the secondary creditor while not obtaining any benefit for himself. So if his security extends over subjects B and C, and the postponed security of the secondary creditor is over B, the catholic creditor must either take payment so far as possible from C or if he takes payment from B, assign his security right to the secondary creditor.[58] This equitable right of the secondary creditor can however be defeated by the sale of C, by the debtor creating a postponed security over C, or by the creditor renouncing his security over C.[59] The principle does not apply where the catholic creditor has a postponed security over C for a separate debt.[60] Where there is a secondary security over each subject the catholic creditor must not unfairly benefit one secondary creditor to the prejudice of the other. The debt must be paid proportionally out of the two subjects.[61]

The foregoing principles apply whether the property is heritable or moveable and whether the question arises on operation of the security or in a sequestration.[62] They do not apply to a receiver choosing which property to which a floating charge has attached should be ingathered and realised.[63] It is thought that they apply where the sale of the security subjects has been initiated by the secondary creditor.

8.6

---

[55] Land Registration (Scotland) Act 1979, s.3(3).
[56] 1979 Act, s.28.
[57] 1979 Act, ss.6(4), 9(4).
[58] *Littlejohn* v. *Black* (1855) 18 D.207; *Nicol's Tr.* v. *Hill* (1889)16 R. 416
[59] *Morton* (1871) 10 M. 292.
[60] Gloag & Irvine, p. 63.
[61] *Littlejohn* v. *Black, supra, per* L.P. McNeill at p. 213; *Earl of Moray* v. *Mansfield* (1836) 14 S. 886.
[62] *Littlejohn* v. *Black, supra.*
[63] *Forth & Clyde Construction Co. Ltd.* v. *Trinity Timber & Plywood Co. Ltd.*, 1984 S. C. 1.

CHAPTER 9

SECURITIES GRANTED BY A COMPANY

Registration of Securities[1]

9.1 Certain "charges" created by a company are void if they are not registered in the Companies Register.

A "charge" is defined as "any form of security interest (fixed or floating) over property, other than an interest arising by operation of law."[2] The charges which have to be registered are[3]:

(a) a charge on land or any interest in land, other than (i) in England and Wales, a charge for rent or any other periodical sum issuing out of the land, (ii) in Scotland, a charge for any rent, ground annual or other periodical sum payable in respect of the land;

(b) a charge on goods or any interest in goods, other than a charge under which the chargee is entitled to possession of the goods or of a document of title to them; goods are any corporeal moveable property other than money[4]; a charge is not excluded from this requirement because the chargee is entitled to take possession in case of default or on the occurrence of some other event[5];

(c) a charge on goodwill;

(d) a charge on intellectual property, *i.e.* any patent, trade mark, service mark, registered design, copyright or design right or any licence under or in respect of any such right[6];

(e) a charge on book debts (whether book debts of the company or assigned to the company); a debenture which is part of an issue or series is not a book debt[7]; the deposit by way of security of a negotiable instrument given to secure the payment of a book debt is not to be treated as a charge on book debts[8]; nor is a shipowner's lien on subfreights[9]; a book debt is a debt arising in the course of a business which would or could in the ordinary course of business be entered in well-kept books relating to that business whether it is in fact entered in the books of the business or not[10]; sums due under hire-purchase agreements were held to be book debts but rights under an Export Credits Guarantee policy were held not to be[11]; evidence of accountancy practice is relevant;

(f) a charge on uncalled share capital of the company or on calls made but not paid;

---

[1] The provisions of the Companies Act 1985 dealing with registration of securities were inserted by the Companies Act 1989, ss.92–107. They are not yet in force.
[2] C.A., s.395(2).
[3] s.396(1).
[4] s.396(2)(*b*).
[5] s.396(2)(*c*).
[6] s.396(2)(*d*).
[7] s.396(2)(*e*).
[8] s.396(2)(*f*).
[9] s.396(2)(*g*).
[10] *Independent Automatic Sales Ltd.* v. *Knowles & Foster* [1962] 1 W.L.R. 974. A bank account is not a book debt: *Re Brightlife* [1987] Ch. 200.
[11] *Paul & Frank Ltd.* v. *Discount Bank (Overseas) Ltd.* [1967] Ch. 348.

(g) a charge for securing an issue of debentures;
(h) a floating charge on the whole or part of the company's property; a shipowner's lien on subfreights is not a floating charge for this purpose.[9]

A charge on a debenture forming part of an issue or series does not fall within (a) or (b) *supra* by reason of the fact that the debenture is secured by a charge on land or goods or on an interest in land or goods.[12]

It is immaterial where the property subject to the charge is situated.[13] Whether a charge is one which requires to be registered is determined at the date the charge is created or the date at which the company acquires the property subject to the charge.[14]

Registration

Although the charge can be registered by any person having an interest in it, the duty to register is placed on the company which created the charge or which acquired property subject to a charge.[15] The variation of a charge which is not registrable so as to include property by virtue of which it becomes registrable is treated as the creation of a charge.[16] The prescribed particulars of the charge in the prescribed form[17] must be delivered to the registrar within 21 days after the date of the charge's creation or the date of acquisition.[18] A floating charge is taken to be created when the instrument creating it is executed by the company; other charges are taken to be created when the security right is constituted as a real right.[19] Where a charge is created inside the United Kingdom but affects property outside the United Kingdom, any further proceedings necessary to make the charge valid or effectual under the law of the country where the property is situated are disregarded in ascertaining the date of creation.[20] The date of acquisition of property is taken to be the date on which the transaction was settled.[21] Where a charge securing an issue of debentures has been registered, the company has a duty to deliver to the registrar particulars of the date on which the debentures were taken up and of the amount taken up; this has to be done within 21 days after the date on which the debentures were taken up.[22]

9.2

Failure to register

If the prescribed particulars are not delivered for registration within the 21-day period or at any time a charge created by the company is void against an administrator or liquidator of the company who is subsequently appointed.[23] It is also void against a person who has subsequently acquired for value an interest in or right over the property

9.3

---

[12] s.396(2)(*a*).
[13] s.395(3).
[14] s.396(3).
[15] s.398(1).
[16] s.419(2).
[17] Regulations not yet made.
[18] s.398(1).
[19] s.414(3).
[20] s.414(4).
[21] s.419(3).
[22] s.408.
[23] s.399(1).

subject to the charge except where the acquisition was expressly subject to the charge.[24] However, it is void against a subsequent charge only if some or all of the particulars of the subsequent charge relating to rights inconsistent with the earlier charge, are delivered within 21 days of creation of the later charge or at a later time.[25] If the particulars of the subsequent charge are incomplete or inaccurate, the earlier charge is void against that charge only to the extent that rights are disclosed by registered particulars of the subsequent charge.

Late registration

9.4 Where the particulars are delivered after the end of the 21-day period, the charge is void against an administrator or liquidator subsequently appointed only if the company was at the date of delivery of the particulars unable to pay its debts or subsequently became unable to pay its debts in consequence of the transaction under which the charge was created, and a petition for an administration order or for winding up of the company was presented or a voluntary winding-up resolution was passed within a specified period from the date of delivery of the particulars.[26] The specified period is two years in the case of a floating charge in favour of a person connected with the company, one year in the case of a floating charge in favour of a person not connected with the company and six months in any other case.[27] The charge is not void against a subsequent charge if the latter has not been registered before the late registration of the earlier charge.[28] If the particulars of the subsequent charge are incomplete or inaccurate, the earlier charge is void against that charge only to the extent that rights are disclosed by particulars of the subsequent charge registered before the corresponding particulars of the earlier charge.[29]

Defective registration

9.5 Where the registered particulars are not complete and accurate the validity of the charge may be affected to the extent that rights are not disclosed by the particulars which would be disclosed if they were complete and accurate.[30] The charge is void to that extent as against an administrator or liquidator of the company if the petition for the administration order or for winding up was presented or the winding-up resolution was passed at a time when the particulars were incomplete or inaccurate in a relevant respect[31]; however, the court, on the application of the chargee, may order that the charge is to be effective as against the administrator or liquidator if it is satisfied that the omission or error is not likely to have misled materially to his prejudice any unsecured creditor of the company, or that no person became an unsecured creditor of the company at a time when the particulars were incomplete or inaccurate in

---

[24] s.405(1).
[25] s.404(1).
[26] s.400(2).
[27] s.400(3)(*b*).
[28] s.404(1).
[29] s.404(2).
[30] s.402(1).
[31] s.402(2).

a relevant respect.[32] As against a person who for value acquires an interest in or right over the property subject to the charge at a time when the particulars were incomplete or inaccurate the charge is void to the extent that rights are not disclosed by the registered particulars which would be disclosed if they were complete and accurate[33]; however, the court, on the application of the chargee, may order that the charge is effective as against the acquirer if it is satisfied that he did not rely, in connection with the acquisition, on registered particulars which were incomplete or inaccurate in a relevant respect.[34] An omission or inaccuracy with respect to the name of the chargee is not regarded as a failure to disclose the rights of the chargee.[35]

Further particulars may be registered at any time.[36] If it is not possible to obtain a signature of the chargee or the company the court may authorise delivery of the particulars without the signature.[37]

Termination

9.6 Where a registered charge ceases to affect the company's property a memorandum signed by the company and the chargee may be delivered to the registrar[38]; however, if such a memorandum is delivered where the charge in fact continues to affect the company's property, the charge is void as against an administrator or liquidator if the date of presentation of the petition for the administration order or for the winding up or the winding-up resolution was after the delivery of the memorandum; it is void as against an acquirer if the acquisition is after the delivery of the memorandum.[39]

Void charges

9.7 Where a charge becomes void to any extent under these registration requirements the whole of the sum secured by the charge, including any interest payable, is payable forthwith on demand even if the sum secured by the charge is also the subject of another security.[40]

There is a curious provision as to a chargee exercising a power of sale[41]: "A chargee exercising a power of sale may dispose of property to a purchaser freed from any interest or right arising from the charge having become void to any extent by virtue of this Part—(a) against an administrator or liquidator of the company, or (b) against a person acquiring a security interest over property subject to the charge, and a purchaser is not concerned to see or inquire whether the charge has become so void." A "purchaser" means "a person who in good faith and for valuable consideration acquires an interest in the property." The effect of this seems to be that the chargee can effectually exercise the power of sale even although the charge is void and give a good title to a

---

[32] s.402(4).
[33] s.402(2).
[34] s.402(5).
[35] s.402(6).
[36] s.401(1).
[37] s.417.
[38] s.403(1). As to signature of the memorandum see s.417.
[39] s.403(5).
[40] s.407(1).
[41] s.406.

bona fide purchaser. However, the proceeds of sale are to be held by the chargee in trust and applied in a certain order which is subject to any other statutory provision or rule of law applicable in any case. The order is (i) discharge of any sum secured by prior incumbrances to which the sale is not made subject, including any incumbrance to the extent that the charge is void as against it; (ii) in payment of all costs, charges and expenses of the sale and any previous attempted sale; (iii) in discharge of any sum effectively secured by the charge and incumbrances ranking *pari passu* with the charge but no sum is effectively secured by the charge to the extent that it is void as against the administrator or liquidator; (iv) in discharge of any sum effectively secured by incumbrances ranking after the charge; any residue is payable to the company or to a person authorised to give a receipt for the proceeds of sale.

The registers

9.8   In the Companies Register there is kept a register of charges on the property of the company consisting of a file containing with respect to each charge the particulars and other information which have been delivered to the registrar.[42] When particulars or further particulars are delivered to the registrar he must send a copy of the material delivered and a note of the date of delivery to the company, to the person appearing to be the chargee and to the person delivering the material.[43] Similarly when a memorandum of a charge ceasing to affect a company's property has been delivered for registration a copy of it and a note of the date of delivery must be sent to these persons.[44] Any person may require the registrar to give him a certificate stating the date on which any specified particulars of, or other information relating to, a charge were delivered to him; such a certificate is conclusive evidence that the particulars or other information were delivered to the registrar no later than the date stated in the certificate and it is presumed unless the contrary is proved that they were not delivered earlier than that date.[45] A person taking a charge over the company's property is taken to have notice of any matter requiring registration and disclosed on the register at the time the charge was created. Otherwise a person is not to be taken to have notice of any matter by reason of its having been disclosed on the register or by reason of his failing to search the register in the course of making such inquiries as ought reasonably to be made.[46]

A company must keep at its registered office a copy of every instrument creating or evidencing a charge over the company's property.[47] It must also keep there a register of all such charges, containing entries for each charge giving a short description of the property charged, the amount of the charge and, except in the case of securities to bearer, the names of the persons entitled to it.[48] These two requirements apply to any charge,

---

[42] s.397(1), (2).
[43] s.398(4), (5), s.401(4), s.408(2).
[44] s.403(4).
[45] s.397(3)–(5).
[46] s.416.
[47] s.411(1).
[48] s.411(2).

whether or not it is one which has to be registered.[49] The copy instruments and the register are open to inspection by a creditor or member of the company without fee and any person can obtain copies on payment of a fee.[50]

FLOATING CHARGES

SECURITIES GRANTED BY A COMPANY

Floating charge: creation

A company may create a floating charge over all or any part of the property (including uncalled capital) which may from time to time be comprised in its property and undertaking.[51] The charge may secure any debt or other obligation (including a cautionary obligation) incurred or to be incurred by, or binding upon, the company or any other person. The floating charge is created by a written instrument subscribed by the company.[52]

9.9

Prescribed particulars of the charge must be delivered to the registrar of companies within 21 days after the date on which the instrument creating the charge was executed by the company.[53] If it is not so registered it may be void as against an administrator or liquidator of the company subsequently appointed. It affects heritage even if it is not recorded in the Sasine Register.[54] It is an "overriding interest" under registration of title to land.[55]

Operation

The floating charge now attaches when the company "goes into liquidation,"[56] which is when a resolution for voluntary winding up is passed or the winding up order is made when there has been no such resolution.[57] Previously the charge attached "on the commencement of winding up" which could, of course, be earlier than the date of the order.[58]

9.10

The creditor may apply to the court for winding up of the company if his security is in jeopardy, that is, that events have occurred or are about to occur which render it unreasonable in the interests of the creditor that the company should retain power to dispose of the property which is subject to the floating charge.[59] When the company goes into liquidation

---

[49] s.411(3).
[50] s.412.
[51] C.A., 462(1). A floating charge can be granted by a European Economic Interest Grouping (see para. 30.15) and a co-operative society (Industrial and Provident Societies Act 1967, s.3, subst. by Companies Consolidation (Consequential Provisions) Act 1985, s.26).
[52] C.A., 462(2) (C.A. 1989, Sched. 17, para. 8). As to subscription see C.A., s.36B (Law Reform (Misc. Provs.) (Scotland) Act 1990, s.72). A charge is assignable: *Libertas-Kommerz* v. *Johnston*, 1977 S.C. 191.
[53] See paras. 9.1–9.7.
[54] C.A., s.462(5).
[55] Land Registration (Scotland) Act 1979, s.28.
[56] C.A., s.463(1) (as amended by C.A. 1989, s.140(1)).
[57] I.A., s.247(2).
[58] See para. 25.3.
[59] I.A., s.122(2).

the floating charge attaches to the property then comprised in the company's property and undertaking (or part thereof) and has effect as if the charge were a fixed security over the property to which it has attached in respect of the principal of the debt or obligation to which it relates and any interest due or to become due thereon.[60] Interest accrues until payment of the sum due under the charge.[61] A fixed security is a security, other than a floating charge or a charge having the nature of a floating charge, which on winding up in Scotland would be treated as an effective security; a heritable security is a fixed security.[62]

The attaching of the charge is, however, subject to:
(1) the rights of any person who has "effectually executed diligence" on the property or any part of it.[63]
(2) the rights of the holder of a fixed security arising by operation of law,[64] *e.g.* a lien, the landlord's hypothec.
(3) the rights of the holder of a fixed security or another floating charge over the property ranking in priority to the floating charge.[65]
(4) payment of the preferential debts specified in para. 25.12 in so far as the assets of the company available for payment of general creditors are insufficient to meet them.[66]

The liquidator acting in the name of the company is the appropriate pursuer to recover a contribution from the floating charge assets to the preferential debts once the assets available for payment of general creditors have been exhausted.[67]

Ranking

9.11　Where property is subject both to a floating charge and to a fixed security arising by operation of law, the fixed security has priority over the floating charge.[68] The instrument creating the floating charge or a document relating to the charge executed by the debtor or creditor before the registration of the charge or an instrument of alteration[69] may contain provisions prohibiting or restricting the creation of any fixed security or any other floating charge having priority over, or ranking *pari passu* with, the floating charge[70]; such a provision is effective to confer priority on the floating charge over any fixed security or floating charge created after the date of the instrument.[71] An instrument creating the floating charge or an ancillary document, may, with the consent of the holder of any subsisting floating charge or fixed security which would be adversely affected, contain provisions regulating the order in which the floating charge is to

---

[60] C.A., s.463(1). As to attachment, see para. 9.18.
[61] C.A., s.463(4).
[62] C.A., s.486(1).
[63] C.A., s.463(1)(*a*); see paras.
[64] C.A., s.464(2).
[65] C.A., s.463(1)(*b*), (*c*); see para. 9.11.
[66] I.A., s.175(2); C.A., s.463(3) (I.A., Sched. 13).
[67] *Westminster Corporation* v. *Chapman* [1916] 1 Ch. 161.
[68] C.A., s.464(2). The landlord's hypothec is a fixed security. *Cumbernauld Development Corporation* v. *Mustone Ltd.*, 1983 S.L.T. (Sh.Ct) 55 is wrong.
[69] Referred to hereafter as an "ancillary document" (C.A. s.486(1)).
[70] C.A., s.464(1)(*a*).
[71] C.A., s.464(1A) (added by C.A. 1989, s.140(4)).

rank with any other subsisting or future floating charges or fixed securities.[72]

If there are no such provisions,[73] a fixed security has priority over a floating charge if it has been constituted as a real right before the floating charge attached to the property; floating charges rank with one another according to the time of registration; floating charges received by the registrar for registration by the same postal delivery rank with one another equally.[74]

Where the holder of a floating charge receives intimation in writing of the subsequent registration of another floating charge over the same property or part thereof, his preference is restricted to security for: (a) his present advances, (b) future advances which he may be required to make under the instrument creating the floating charge or under an ancillary document,[75] (c) interest due or to become due on all such advances, (d) any expenses or outlays reasonably incurred by him, and (e) in the case of a floating charge to secure a contingent liability other than a liability arising under any further advances made from time to time, the maximum sum to which that contingent liability is capable of amounting whether or not it is contractually limited.[76] It is thought that although the preference of the first charge holder over the second is restricted, he retains a security for any subsequent advances postponed to that of the second charge holder.[77] The rules as to catholic and secondary securities do not apply to a floating charge.[78]

Avoidance of the floating charge

A liquidator or an administrator can impugn the validity of a floating charge in three situations[79]:

(1) Where within two years of the date of commencement of the winding up or the making of the administration order the floating charge was created in favour of a person who is connected with the company. A person is connected with the company if he is a director or a shadow director of the company or an associate of a director or shadow director or an associate of the company.[80] A shadow director is a person in accordance with whose directions or instructions the directors of the company are accustomed to act.[81] The definition of "associate" in the Insolvency Act 1986[82] differs slightly from that of the Bankruptcy Act[83] in that there is the additional provision that a

9.12

---

[72] C.A., s.464(1)(*b*) (amended by C.A. 1989, s.140(3)).
[73] C.A., s.464(3) (subst. by CA 1989, s.140(5)).
[74] C.A., s.464(4).
[75] See n. 69, *supra*.
[76] C.A., s.464(5) (amended by C.A. 1989, s.140(6)).
[77] Halliday, *Conveyancing Law and Practice in Scotland*, Vol. III, p. 496. The same ambiguity arises with regard to standard securities: see para. 8.2.
[78] *Forth & Clyde Construction Co. Ltd.* v. *Trinity Timber & Plywood Co. Ltd.*, 1984 S.C. 1.
[79] I.A., s.245.
[80] I.A., s.249.
[81] I.A., s.251.
[82] I.A., s.435.
[83] I.A., s.74. See para. 22.3

trustee is an associate of a beneficiary and of an associate of a beneficiary.[84]

(2) Where within the 12 months ending with the date of commencement of winding up or the making of the administration order the floating charge was created in favour of any other person and the company was at that time unable to pay its debts or it became unable to pay its debts in consequence of the transaction under which the charge was created.

(3) Where the floating charge was created between the presentation of a petition for the making of an administration order in relation to the company and the making of an order on the petition.

If any of these conditions is satisfied the charge is invalid except to the extent of the aggregate of

"(a) the value of so much of the consideration for the creation of the charge as consists of money paid, or goods or services supplied, to the company at the same time as, or after, the creation of the charge, (b) the value of so much of that consideration as consists of the discharge or reduction, at the same time as, or after, the creation of the charge, of any debt of the company, and (c) the amount of such interest (if any) as is payable on the amount falling within paragraph (a) or (b) in pursuance of any agreement under which the money was so paid, the goods or services were so supplied or the debt was so discharged or reduced."[85]

It will be appreciated that these are *novum debitum* provisions[86] or, at least, are intended to be so. Before the 1986 Act the wording of the corresponding provision was "at the time" rather than "at the same time" and it was held in England[87] that payments made slightly before the creation of the charge could qualify, but it may be that that "*unico contextu*" approach is not possible under the changed wording. Again, the earlier wording was "in consideration for" rather than "so much of that consideration as consists," and it was held that it was sufficient if advances were made in reliance on the existence of the charge and it was not necessary that they should be in implement of a binding obligation made at the time the charge was created[88]; that reading is perhaps more difficult now.

The value of goods or services supplied is to be taken as market value.[89] Paragraph (b) is new and is apparently intended to cover the case in which the lender makes payment directly to other creditors of the company. It is not clear whether it is intended to cover the case where the lender repays a prior debt due to himself and enjoys a security for his new advance, thus in effect obtaining a security for a prior debt. There is also the possibility of collusion between a creditor and his assignee.

An arrangement that the cash paid to the company will be applied in

---

[84] I.A., s.435(5). There is a slight difference between B.A., s.74(3) and I.A., s.435(3).
[85] I.A., s.245(1).
[86] See para. 22.8.
[87] *Re Columbian Fireproofing Co. Ltd.* [1910] 2 Ch. 120; *Re Olderfleet Shipbuilding Co.* [1922] 1 I.R. 26.
[88] *Re F. & E. Stanton* [1929] 1 Ch. 180.
[89] I.A., s.245(6).

payment of specified debts does invalidate the charge[90] but if the object and effect of the transaction under which the cash was paid was to benefit certain creditors and not to benefit the company the charge is invalid.[91] Where the company had an overdrawn account at the granting of the charge to the bank, it was held that each advance after the creation of the charge was cash paid to the company in consideration of the charge and that the bank was entitled under the rule in *Clayton's* case to apply subsequent payment in by the company to the pre-charge indebtedness.[92]

If a receiver appointed by the floating charge holder realises assets and applies the proceeds in repayment of the debts secured by the charge, the repayment cannot be invalidated on the subsequent liquidation of the company on the ground that the floating charge was invalid under s.245.[93]

It seems that a floating charge can be reduced as an unfair or fraudulent preference or as a gratuitous alienation.[94]

Receivers

The alternative remedy of the holder of the floating charge is to have a receiver appointed. 9.13

The holder may appoint a receiver himself on the occurrence of an event specified in the instrument creating the charge as entitling him so to do and, unless the instrument otherwise provides, on the occurrence of:
(a) the expiry of 21 days after a demand for payment of the whole or part of the principal sum secured, without payment having been made;
(b) the expiry of two months during the whole of which interest due and payable under the charge has been in arrears;
(c) the making of an order or the passing of a resolution to wind up the company;
(d) the appointment of a receiver by virtue of another floating charge created by the company.[95]

A receiver may be appointed by the court in any of these circumstances (including the events specified in the instrument) except (d) and also where the court, on the application of the holder of the charge, pronounces itself satisfied that the position of the holder is likely to be prejudiced if no appointment is made.[96]

Receiver: appointment

The holder appoints the receiver by an instrument of appointment, a certified copy of which, along with a notice,[97] must be sent to the Registrar of Companies within seven days so that the particulars can be entered in the register of charges.[98] The appointment is of no effect unless 9.14

---

[90] *Re Matthew Ellis Ltd.* [1933] Ch. 458.
[91] *Re Destone Fabrics Ltd.* [1941] Ch. 319; *Re Orleans Motor Co. Ltd.* [1911] 2 Ch. 41. See also *Re Ambassadors (Bournemouth)* (1961) 105 S.J. 969; *Libertas-Kommerz GmbH*, 1978 S.L.T. 222.
[92] *Re Yeovil Glove Co.* [1965] Ch. 148.
[93] *Mace Builders (Glasgow) Ltd.* v. *Lunn* [1987] Ch. 191 (decided on the Scottish legislation). But see *Palmer's Company Law*, p. 1621, n. 78.
[94] *Cf.* C.A. 1985, s.617(3), which has not been re-enacted.
[95] I.A., s.52(1).
[96] I.A., s.52(2).
[97] Receivers (Scotland) Regulations 1986, Sched., Fm. 1.
[98] I.A., s.53(1).

it is accepted before the end of the business day next following that on which the instrument was received by the appointee.[99] The acceptance need not be in writing but it must be intimated to the floating charge holder or his agent.[1] The appointee must endorse on the instrument of appointment a docquet evidencing the day and the time of receipt and a further docquet indicating acceptance.[2] As soon as possible thereafter he must deliver a copy of the endorsed instrument to the floating charge holder or his agent.[3] Subject to the requirement as to the time of acceptance, the appointment is deemed to have been made on the day on and at the time at which the instrument of appointment was received as evidenced by the docquet.[4] The appointment of joint receivers is made when the last of them receives the instrument of appointment and he has the duty of sending a copy of the endorsed instrument to the floating charge holder.[5] At the date of the appointment the charge attaches to the property subject to it as if it were a fixed security.[6]

Where the appointment is made by the court, a certified copy of the interlocutor along with a notice[7] must be sent to the registrar[8]; the charge attaches at the date of appointment by the court.[9]

When a receiver is appointed, he must forthwith send to the company and publish a notice of his appointment and he must within 28 days send such a notice to all the creditors of the company in so far as he is aware of their addresses.[10]

Receiver: powers

9.15   A receiver is given a wide range of powers in relation to the company's property attached by the charge but they are subject to the rights of creditors who have effectually executed diligence and the rights of those creditors who hold securities ranking prior to or *pari passu* with the floating charge by virtue of which he was appointed.[11] First, he has the powers given to him by the instrument creating the charge[12] and power to do all other things incidental to the exercise of these powers.[13] Secondly, in so far as they are not inconsistent with the provisions of the instrument creating the charge, he has the wide powers contained in Schedule 2 of the Insolvency Act 1986.[14] These include power to take possession of the company's property, to sell or otherwise dispose of that property, to bring and defend actions on behalf of the company and to carry on the

---

[99] I.A., s.53(6).
[1] Ins. Rules, 31(1).
[2] I.A., s.53(6)(*b*); Ins. Rules 3.1(1), (2).
[3] Ins. Rules, 3.1(3).
[4] I.A., s.53(6)(*b*).
[5] Receivers (Scotland) Regulations, reg. 5.
[6] I.A., s.53(7).
[7] Receivers (Scotland) Regulations 1986, Sched., Fm. 2.
[8] I.A., s.54(5), (6).
[9] I.A., s.54(5), (6).
[10] I.A., s.65(1); Receivers (Scotland) Regulations, Sched., Fm. 4.
[11] I.A., s.55(3).
[12] I.A., s.55(1).
[13] I.A., Sched. 2, para. 23.
[14] I.A., s.55(2). As to the directors' power to raise an action, see *Shanks* v. *Central Regional Council*, 1987 S.L.T. 410. The receiver's powers may be restricted by the drugs legislation: Criminal Justice (Scotland) Act 1987, s.36.

business of the company or any part of it. A person dealing with the receiver in good faith and for value is not concerned to inquire whether the receiver is acting within his powers.[15] The receiver is deemed to be the agent of the company in relation to the property subject to the charge.[16]

The receiver is personally liable on any contract entered into by him in the performance of his functions except in so far as the contract otherwise provides.[17] Where he is so personally liable he is entitled to be indemnified out of the property subject to the charge.[18] Prior contracts entered into by the company continue in force notwithstanding the receiver's appointment, subject to their terms, but the receiver does not by virtue only of his appointment incur any personal liability on such contracts.[19]

Where property subject to the floating charge is subject to a security (prior, *par passu* or postponed) or is affected or attached by effectual diligence, and the receiver cannot obtain the consent of the creditor to a sale, he can apply to the court to authorise the sale of the property free of the security or diligence on such terms and conditions as the court thinks fit.[20] Authorisation will not be given where a fixed security ranking prior to the floating charge has not been met or provided for in full unless it is satisfied that the sale would be likely to provide a more advantageous realisation of the company's assets than would otherwise be effected.[21] It must be a condition of such an authorisation that the net proceeds of such a disposal shall be applied towards discharging the sums secured by the fixed security, and that a further sum will also be so applied to make good any difference between the proceeds and the net amount which would be realised on the sale of the property or interest in the open market by a willing seller.[22] Where such a condition relates to two or more fixed securities, the condition shall require the sums to be applied towards discharging the sums secured by the securities in the order of their priorities.[23] These provisions can be used where the receiver wishes to sell heritage which is subject to an inhibition, even, apparently, where the inhibition cannot be regarded as "effectual diligence."[24] The disencumbering of the property has effect from the date of delivery of the document of transfer or conveyance of the property, or from the date of recording, intimation or registration thereof where one of these is required.

Receiver: preferential debts

A very important qualification of the rights of the floating charge holder is that they are postponed to the claims of the preferential creditors. The receiver must pay out of the assets coming into his hands in

9.16

---

[15] I.A., s.55(4).
[16] I.A., s.57(1). But see *Gomba Holdings Ltd.* v. *Minories Finance Ltd.* [1987] B.C.L.C. 115, *per* Fox L.J. at p. 117
[17] I.A., s.57(1); *Hill Samuel & Co. Ltd.* v. *Laing*, 1989 S.L.T. 760.
[18] I.A., s.57(3).
[19] I.A., s.57(4).
[20] I.A., s.61(1).
[21] I.A., s.61(3).
[22] I.A., s.61(4).
[23] I.A., s.61(5).
[24] *Armour and Mycroft, Petrs.*, 1983 S.L.T. 453.

priority to any claim for principal or interest by the holder of the floating charge the preferential debts specified in para. 25.12, in so far as these have become known to him within six months after advertisement by him for claims.[25] The periods of time for computing these debts are reckoned from the date of the receiver's appointment.[26] He will be liable to the preferential creditors if he disposes of the assets without paying them.[27] He may recoup the payments he makes as far as may be out of the assets of the company available for payment of ordinary creditors.[28] Where the same creditor holds a floating charge and a fixed security over the same assets, the fixed security prevails and has priority over the preferential debts.[29] Where there is a fixed security postponed to the floating charge there is a circularity problem in that the floating charge prevails over the fixed security which prevails over the preferential debts which prevail over the floating charge; in England, the floating charge holder is subrogated to the rights of the fixed security holder and prevails to that extent over the preferential creditors[30]; this would seem to be applicable in Scotland.

Distribution of funds

9.17 Moneys received by the receiver are paid to the holder of the floating charge in or towards satisfaction of the debt secured but subject to the rights of holders of prior or *pari passu* fixed securities, persons who have effectually executed diligence, creditors in respect of debts incurred by the receiver, the receiver in respect of his liabilities, expenses and remuneration and indemnities and preferential creditors.[31] Any balance is paid in accordance with their respective rights and interests, as the case may require, to (a) any other receiver, (b) the holder of a fixed security over property subject to the floating charge, (c) the company or its liquidator.

It has been held in England that the receiver is not a debtor to the company for the balance which may ultimately be due to it and there is therefore, during the course of the receivership and before the final accounting, no debt which can be attached by a creditor.[32]

Attachment

9.18 On liquidation the floating charge attaches to the property subject to the charge and the provisions of the Insolvency Act relating to winding up have effect "as if the charge were a fixed security over the property to which it has attached."[33] On the appointment of a receiver the floating charge attaches to the property subject to it and the attachment has effect "as if the charge was a fixed security over the property to which it has

---

[25] I.A., s.59.
[26] I.A., s.387(4)(*b*).
[27] *I.R.C.* v. *Goldblatt* [1972] Ch. 498.
[28] I.A., s.59(3).
[29] *Re Lewis Merthyr Consolidated Collieries* [1929] 1 Ch. 498.
[30] *Re Woodroffes (Musical Instruments) Ltd.* [1985] 2 All E.R. 908 (*ex concessione*); Goode, *Principles of Corporate Insolvency Law* (1990), p. 76.
[31] I.A., s.60.
[32] *Seabrook Estate Co. Ltd.* v. *Ford* [1949] 2 All E.R. 94.
[33] C.A., 463(2).

attached."[34] The operation of this statutory hypothesis has given rise to difficulties. The corresponding provisions of the Companies (Floating Charges and Receivers) (Scotland) Act 1972 were considered in *Forth & Clyde Construction Co. Ltd.* v. *Trinity Timber & Plywood Co. Ltd.*[35] The First Division rejected an argument that "the effect of the floating charge is to create a new species of security in a general form, the effect of which is not determined by the kind of security appropriate to each type of property under the general law." Lord President Emslie said[36]:

"By the language of section 13(7) [now Insolvency Act 1986, s.53(7)] one is, in my opinion, drawn to ask, in defining the effect of the attachment of particular property, what kind of security over that property, other than by way of diligence, would be treated by the law of Scotland on the winding up of the company in this jurisdiction as an 'effective security.'"

He went on to hold that in the case of a book debt the appropriate security must be an intimated assignation in security.

Corporeal moveables subject to the floating charge are treated as if they were the subject of a pledge even although they are not in the possession of a creditor. Goods which have been sold but were still in the company's ownership and possession at the date of attachment are subject to the security of the holder of the floating charge even if the price has been paid.

Goods which are on conditional sale or hire-purchase and which were still in the company's property but which are in the possession of the acquirer are not, it is thought, affected by the attachment of the charge. The floating charge creditor should not be in this respect in a better position than a liquidator; the acquirer has a right of retention over the goods which, being a security arising by operation of law, prevails over the floating charge.

On the sale in the ordinary course of business of corporeal moveables which were the property of the company at attachment, the resultant debt is clearly still subject to the charge—the sale is by a pledgee.[37]

Incorporeal moveable property will be subject to the attached security which will prevail over assignees who have not intimated or registered their transfer at the date of attachment. There would seem to be no ground for importing here the rule of the "race to register" which obtains in sequestration.[38] In recovering a debt which was owing to the company, however, the receiver cannot sue in his own name; he must raise the action in the name of the company and give some indication that he as receiver is associated with the claim.[39]

The appointment of a receiver is one of the events on which the company's rights under a third party liability insurance policy are transferred to the third party.[40]

---

[34] I.A., s.53(7). See also s.54(6)—"as if the charge *were* a fixed security."
[35] 1984 S.C. 1.
[36] at p. 10.
[37] *N. W. Robbie & Co. Ltd.* v. *Witney Warehouse Co. Ltd.* [1963] 1 W.L.R. 1324.
[38] See para. 21.13.
[39] *Forth & Clyde Construction Co. Ltd.* v. *Trinity Timber & Plywood Co. Ltd., supra*; *Myles J. Callaghan Ltd.* v. *City of Glasgow D.C.*, 1988 S.L.T. 227.
[40] Third Parties (Rights against Insurers) Act 1930, s.1(1)(*b*).

The floating charge affects heritage in the form of a hypothetical standard security. It will be a burden on the right of a purchaser who had not recorded or registered his title at the date of attachment.

It is thought that English dicta[41] which may suggest that the surplus of proceeds of the realisation of a fixed security after payment of the debt secured are not subject to a postponed floating charge could not be applied in Scotland because of the different wording of, for example, s.27(1) of the Conveyancing and Feudal Reform (Scotland) Act 1970.

It has been cogently argued[42] that property held by the company in trust is subject to the floating charge because of (a) the principle established by *Redfearn* v. *Sommervails*,[43] that a *bona fide* onerous transferee is not affected by latent trusts, and (b) the effect of the Trusts (Scotland) Act 1961, s.2, which provides that where "trustees under any trust enter into a transaction with any person" ("the second party"), the transaction being one of a class which includes the borrowing of money on security, "the validity of the transaction and of any title acquired by the second party under the transaction shall not be challengeable by the second party or any other person on the ground that the act in question is at variance with the terms or purposes of the trust." It is not easy to counter these arguments, but it is felt that the conclusion cannot be right. As to (a), the position of one who has taken a real right over a specific subject and is held to take it free of a latent trust is not quite the same as the position of one who has taken a floating charge over the whole assets of a company; the floating charge creditor can only ascertain the subjects of his security by examining the company accounts from time to time. As to (b), the statutory provision can operate only when the trust was in existence at the time of creation of the floating charge and, in any event, it is not clear that a provision designed to remove doubts as to the powers of trustees should be used to interpret the terms of a conveyance by the trustee. A company has power to create a floating charge over "all or any part of the property . . . which may from time to time be comprised in its property and undertaking"[44]; it might be argued that although trust assets are in a sense the property of the company they are not comprised in its property and undertaking. It is of course always possible to deal with the matter expressly in the instrument creating the charge. A sum recovered as a fraudulent preference after the receiver's appointment is attached by the floating charge; that follows either from the fact that the terms of the charge extend to future property of the company or from a further attachment of the charge which, at least in the view of the First Division, occurs on liquidation.[45] Sums recovered in misfeasance proceedings and, probably, contributions ordered in respect of wrongful trading under the Insolvency Act, s.214, go to the floating charge creditor.[46]

---

[41] *Re Lewis Merthyr Consolidated Collieries, supra; Re G. L. Saunders Ltd.* [1986] 1 W.L.R. 215.

[42] Reid, "Trusts and Floating Charges," 1987 S.L.T. (News) 113.

[43] (1813) 1 Dow 50.

[44] C.A., s.462(1).

[45] *Ross* v. *Taylor*, 1985 S.C. 156.

[46] *Re Anglo-Austrian Printing and Publishing Union* [1895] 2 Ch. 891. As to wrongful trading contributions (para. 25.8) see Prentice [1990] *Oxford Journal of Legal Studies*, at pp. 271–273.

Set off

Considerable problems have arisen in relation to set off when the receiver is attempting to recover a debt due to the company. As has already been stated it is clear from *Forth & Clyde*[47] that the appointment of the receiver has effect in relation to a book debt of the company as if there had been an intimated assignation of the debt in security to the floating charge holder. *In limine*, however, it is necessary to say that there is a major qualification of this in that it is well established that the receiver cannot sue for the debt in his own name; he must sue in the name of the company and should give some indication that he as receiver is associated with the claim; this is perhaps a practical device although it is not completely logical. That qualification made, however, the rigour of the doctrine of assignation applies. After the appointment of the receiver, a creditor of the company cannot arrest the debt because it is no longer due to the company. Again, the maxim *assignatus utitur jure auctoris* applies and the debtor can take against the receiver any defence which he could have taken against the company before the receiver was appointed. It seems clear that the debtor cannot set off against the receiver's claim a debt due by the company which the debtor acquired after the receiver's appointment; the decision of Lord Ross to the contrary in *Taylor*[48] cannot stand with *Forth & Clyde*. The debtor can obviously set off a debt which was due to him and payable before the date of the receiver's appointment or an illiquid claim which had arisen before that date out of the same contract as the receiver is suing on.[49] It seems probable that an illiquid claim can be set off even if it arises out of another contract; receivership can be treated as an insolvency situation.[50]

9.19

Several charges

Where two or more equally ranking floating charges affect the same property and a receiver has been appointed under each, the receivers act jointly.[51] The two charges may not be in precisely the same position if the dates of appointment of the receivers are different and a fixed security has been constituted as a real right between these dates.

9.20

Where the two or more floating charges do not rank equally the receiver appointed under the one having priority exercises the powers of a receiver to the exclusion of any other receiver.[52] In consequence, a receiver may be superseded by a receiver appointed under a prior charge; his powers are suspended but revive when the prior charge ceases to attach to the property then subject to the charge.[53]

If the company is not in liquidation before the appointment of any of the receivers, and the receivers are not appointed at the same time, the charges will have different dates of attachment.

---

[47] 1984 S.C. 1.
[48] *Taylor* v. *Scottish and Universal Newspapers Ltd.*, 1981 S.C. 408.
[49] *Myles J. Callaghan Ltd.* v. *City of Glasgow D.C.*, 1988 S.L.T. 227.
[50] *McPhail* v. *Cunninghame D.C.*, 1983 S.C. 246.
[51] I.A., s.56(2).
[52] I.A., s.56(1).
[53] I.A., s.56(4).

Appointment after liquidation

9.21 Where the company is in liquidation prior to the receiver's appointment, he recovers the property subject to the floating charge from the liquidator. The charge has attached to the property at the commencement of winding up.[54] The receiver has power "to take possession of, collect and get in the property from the company on a liquidation thereof."[55] It would appear that the receiver is primarily responsible for payment of the secured and preferential debts.[56]

Supervening liquidation

9.22 The company may be put into liquidation before the receivership is completed. This of course does not affect the receiver's control of the assets which were subject to the floating charge, but it seems that new preferential debts arising at the date of liquidation have to be paid by the receiver in priority to the claims of the floating charge holder. This seems to follow from s.175 of the Insolvency Act which requires such debts to be paid "out of any property comprised in or subject to that charge" and the definition of "floating charge" as "a charge which, as created, was a floating charge"[57]; assets to which the floating charge attached on the receiver's appointment and which have not been realised at the date of liquidation are therefore to be applied in payment of the preferential debts.

Partial charge

9.23 A floating charge may be created over only a part of the company's property.[58] A receiver appointed under such a charge may not be an "administrative receiver"[59] and the floating charge creditor will not be in a position to prevent the making of an administration order.[60] The receiver's powers are only in relation to such part of the company's property as is attached by the charge.[61] There will be other assets of the company available to meet the preferential debts unless, of course, all such assets are subject to fixed securities. If the company is not subsequently put into liquidation it is not clear what mechanism exists to enable the payments of preferential debts to be recouped from the assets available for payment of ordinary creditors.

---

[54] C.A., s.463(1).
[55] I.A., Sched. 2, para. 1.
[56] *Manley Petr.*, 1985 S.L.T. 42.
[57] I.A., s.251.
[58] C.A., s.462(1).
[59] I.A., s.251.
[60] See para. 24.4.
[61] I.A., s.55(1).

CHAPTER 10

CAUTIONARY OBLIGATIONS

Cautionary obligations

A cautionary obligation is "an accessory obligation or engagement, as surety for another, that the principal obligant shall pay the debt or perform the act for which he has engaged, otherwise the cautioner shall pay the debt or fulfil the obligation."[1] It has to be distinguished from an independent obligation,[2] delegation,[3] a representation as to credit,[4] an indemnity[5] and insurance.[6] An indemnity is an obligation to relieve the other contracting party of any loss incurred by him by entering into a certain transaction; it is bilateral while cautionry is trilateral. Insurance is an obligation to pay a sum on the occurrence of an event. If C pays only a dividend on his liability to D, he can recover the full amount of the liability from B under a contract of insurance but if it is a contract of indemnity he can only recover from B what he has paid.[7] 10.1

A cautionary obligation must be in writing[8]; it is not clear whether the writing must be either attested or holograph but in many cases the question has been avoided by invoking either the doctrine of *rei interventus* or the privilege of documents *in re mercatoria*.[9] Guarantees and indemnities provided in relation to regulated agreements under the Consumer Credit Act must comply with requirements as to content and form.[10] There must be a prominent heading to the security instrument which must contain the names and addresses of the creditors, debtor and surety and a description of the subject-matter to which the security relates. There must also be a statement of the surety's rights and a "signature box" in specified forms. The lettering must be easily legible and of a colour readily distinguishable from the colour of the paper.

Cautionry is proper when the fact that the parties are principal debtor and cautioner appears on the face of the deed; it is improper where they are bound as co-obligants although in fact they are principal and cautioner.[11] The significance of the distinction is that in proper caution the creditor has certain duties to the cautioner; in improper caution he can treat the cautioner as a co-obligant although the rules of cautionry apply between the cautioner and the principal debtor. Even if the debtor

---

[1] Bell, *Prin.*, § 245.

[2] *Morrison* v. *Harkness* (1870) 9 M. 35; *Stevenson's Tr.* v. *Campbell & Sons* (1896) 23 R. 711; *Aitken & Co.* v. *Pyper* (1900) 38 S.L.R. 74.

[3] See para. 14.2.

[4] *Fortune* v. *Young*, 1918 S.C. 1.

[5] *Milne* v. *Kidd* (1869) 8 M. 250; *Simpson* v. *Jack*, 1948 S.L.T. (Notes) 45.

[6] *Laird* v. *Securities Insurance Co. Ltd.* (1895) 22 R. 452.

[7] *Nelson* v. *Empress Assurance Corporation* [1905] 2 K.B. 281; *Liverpool Mortgage Insurance Co.'s Case* [1914] 2 Ch. 617; *Law Guarantee Trust and Accident Society Ltd.* v. *Munich Reinsurance Co.* [1915] 31 T.L.R. 572.

[8] Mercantile Law Amendment Act (Scotland) 1856, s.6.

[9] *National Bank* v. *Campbell* (1892) 19 R. 885; *B.O.C.M. Silcock Ltd.* v. *Hunter*, 1976 S.L.T. 217; Walker & Walker, *Evidence*, p. 109.

[10] Consumer Credit (Guarantees and Indemnities) Regulations 1983 (S.I. 1983 No. 1556). See also para. 7.2.

[11] Bell, *Prin.*, § 247.

and cautioner are co-obligants *ex facie* of the deed, if the creditor knows at the time of entry to the obligation that they are in fact principal and cautioner he must treat them as such.[12]

Cautionry is an accessory obligation and the cautioner's liability cannot exceed that of the principal debtor.[13] Where the obligation is partial, the extent of the cautioner's liability and his right to rank on the estate of the principal debtor depend on the construction of the deed.[14] There may also be a question of construction as to whether the obligation covers interest as well as the sum stated.[15]

Unless there is a stipulation to the contrary, the creditor need not proceed against the debtor before proceeding against the cautioner.[16] It is, however, necessary that the debtor should be in default and whether there is a default is a question of fact.[17] The creditor need not await the result of a sequestration or liquidation to ascertain the amount of his loss.[18] He is not required to constitute the debt by an action against the debtor; he can constitute it in an action against the cautioner.[19] In general, the creditor is not obliged to give intimation to the cautioner that the debtor is in default.[20] It should be noticed that if the creditor does commence diligence against the debtor he cannot cease to prosecute it without good reason because this in effect is to give up a security.[21]

On payment of the debt, the cautioner is entitled to relief from the principal debtor unless, possibly, there was an agreement that the debtor would repay only when his circumstances allowed.[22] On full payment (not merely a dividend) he is entitled to an assignation from the creditor of the debt, any securities held and any diligence done.[23] He has no right to securities granted by third parties.[24]

In proper caution, where there is more than one cautioner for the same debt, unless they are bound jointly and severally, they have the *beneficium divisionis* and each is liable only for his *pro rata* share unless the others are insolvent.[25] A cautioner who has paid more than his share has a right of relief against his co-cautioners.[26] He cannot obtain a joint and several decree against them because each solvent cautioner is only liable for his *pro rata* share.[27] The right of relief does not emerge until the amount of the whole debt has been ascertained.[28] A cautioner in the

---

[12] *Mackenzie* v. *Macartney* (1831) 5 W. & S. 504; Gloag & Irvine, p. 674.
[13] *Jackson* v. *McIver* (1875) 2 R. 882.
[14] *Harvie's Trs.* v. *Bank of Scotland* (1885) 12 R. 1141; *Veitch* v. *National Bank*, 1907 S.C. 554; *Mackinnon's Tr.* v. *Bank of Scotland*, 1915 S.C. 411.
[15] *National Commercial Bank* v. *Stuart*, 1969 S.L.T. (Notes) 52.
[16] Mercantile Law Amendment Act (Scotland) 1856, s.8; *Scottish Metropolitan Property plc* v. *Christie*, 1987 S.L.T. (Sh.Ct.) 18.
[17] Gloag & Irvine, p. 789.
[18] *Willison* v. *Ferguson* (1901) 9 S.L.T. 169.
[19] *Morrison* v. *Harkness* (1870) 9 M. 35; *Sheldon & Ackhoff* v. *Milligan* (1907) 14 S.L.T. 703. See also *Clydesdale Bank* v. *D. & H. Cohen*, 1943 S.C. 244.
[20] *Britannia Steamship Insurance Association Ltd.* v. *Duff*, 1909 S.C. 1261.
[21] Gloag & Irvine, p. 789.
[22] *McMurray* v. *McFarlane* (1894) 31 S.L.R. 531; *Williamson* v. *Foulds*, 1927 S.N. 164.
[23] *Ewart* v. *Latta* (1865) 3 M.(H.L.) 36; Bankruptcy (Scotland) Act 1985, s.60(3).
[24] *Thow's Trustee* v. *Young*, 1910 S.C. 588.
[25] Bell, *Prin.*, § 267.
[26] *Op. cit.*, § 270.
[27] *Buchanan* v. *Main* (1900) 3 F. 215; *Anderson* v. *Dayton* (1884) 21 S.L.R. 787.
[28] *Beaton* v. *Wilkie* (1927) 43 Sh.Ct. Rep. 193.

absence of agreement to the contrary,[29] is entitled to share the benefit of any security held by his co-cautioners[30] unless it was given by a third party and not the debtor.[31]

Cautionry: prescription

A proper cautionary obligation is subject to the quinquennial prescription even although it is constituted or evidenced by a probative writ.[32] An improper cautionary obligation created by probative writ is also subject to the quinquennial prescription unless the original creditor was not aware at the time when the writ was delivered to him that the obligant was not truly a principal debtor.[33]

There was some doubt as to the *terminus a quo* of the prescriptive period. For most types of obligation, the *terminus* is the date when the obligation becomes enforceable. It was suggested that a cautionary obligation fell under para. 2 of Sched. 2 to the Prescription and Limitation (Scotland) Act 1973 as being an "obligation to repay the whole, or any part of, a sum of money lent to . . . the debtor under a contract of loan . . . " and that the *terminus a quo* was accordingly the date stipulated for repayment or, if there was no stipulation, the date when a written demand for repayment was made.[34] This view, however, has been held to be wrong.[35] The *terminus a quo* in the case of a cautionary obligation is the date when the obligation became enforceable which is the date of a demand for payment from the cautioner if it is payable "on demand"; if there is no such provision, the obligation is enforceable at least from the date of the creditor's claim in the liquidation of the principal debtor. A "performance bond" which was held to be a cautionary obligation was enforceable on the default of the contractor.[36]

A cautionary obligation is, of course, also subject to the vicennial prescription.

Discharge

The cautionary obligation is discharged by:
(1) direct discharge of the cautioner.
(2) extinction of the principal obligation. This may be by discharge,[37] but not by the creditor's assent to the debtor's discharge in his sequestration or any composition.[38] If the creditor merely agrees not to sue the principal debtor but reserves his rights against the cautioner, the cautioner is not discharged.[39]

10.2

10.3

---

[29] *Hamilton & Co.* v. *Freeth* (1889) 16 R. 1022.
[30] Bell, *Prin.*, § 270.
[31] *Scott* v. *Young*, 1909 1 S.L.T. 47.
[32] Prescription and Limitation (Scotland) Act 1973, s.6, Sched. 1, paras. 1(*g*), 2(*c*).
[33] Sched. 1, para. 3.
[34] See Antonio, 1977 S.L.T. (News) 41; Halliday, *The Conveyancing and Feudal Reform (Scotland) Act 1970* (2nd ed.), p. 128.
[35] *The Royal Bank of Scotland* v. *Brown*, 1982 S.C. 89
[36] *City of Glasgow D.C.* v. *Excess Insurance Co. Ltd.*, 1986 S.L.T. 585. Cf. *City of Glasgow D.C.* v. *Excess Insurance Co. Ltd. (No. 2)*, 1990 S.L.T. 225, where the effect of a special clause of the contract was considered.
[37] *Aitken's Trs.* v. *Bank of Scotland*, 1944 S.C. 270.
[38] Bankruptcy (Scotland) Act 1985, s.60.
[39] *Muir* v. *Crawford* (1875) 2 R.(H.L.) 148.

(3) giving time. "In the language of the law, to give time does not consist in refraining from suing, but in the creditor putting himself under a disability to sue by agreeing to postpone payment of his debt."[40] The cautioner is discharged because he is deprived of his chance of considering whether he will have recourse to his remedy against the principal debtor or not and because it is then out of his power to operate the same remedy against him as he would have had under the original contract.[41] Postponing the date of repayment of a loan is giving time.[42] The taking of bills at a currency is giving time[41] unless the period of credit given is not unreasonable in the trade.[43] Prejudice resulting to the cautioner need not be shown.[41] The cautioner is not discharged if the creditor in giving time to the debtor reserved his rights against the cautioner,[44] nor if the cautionary agreement allows the creditor to give time.[45]

(4) alteration of the contract. If the creditor and debtor make a material alteration in the principal obligation the cautioner is discharged.[46]

(5) discharge of a co-cautioner without the consent of the other cautioners discharges all the cautioners.[47] It has been held that this applies only where the cautioners are bound jointly and severally.[48] If there are two separate debts the rule does not apply.[48] If the cautioners are bound in respect of the same debt, but not jointly and severally, it has been suggested that the discharge of one does not discharge the others because the others retain their right of relief against the one.[49]

The following terminate the obligation in the sense that it does not apply to future advances:

(1) recall by the cautioner in terms of the agreement.[50] If the creditor bank then closes the account the cautioner has no right to require future lodgements by the debtor to be applied to redeem the indebtedness.[51]

(2) the death of the principal debtor.[52]

---

[40] *per* Lord Rutherfurd Clark, *Hay & Kyd* v. *Powrie* (1886) 13 R. 777, at 782. See *Hamilton's Exr.* v. *Bank of Scotland*, 1913 S.C. 743.

[41] *C. & A. Johnstone* v. *Duthie* (1892) 19 R. 624.

[42] *Scottish Provident Institution* v. *Ferrier's Trs.* (1871) 8 S.L.R. 390.

[43] *Calder & Co.* v. *Cruikshank's Tr.* (1889) 17 R. 74. A bill at sight is different: *Nicolsons* v. *Burt* (1882) 10 R. 121.

[44] *Muir* v. *Crawford* (1875) 2 R.(H.L.) 148.

[45] *Hamilton's Exr.* v. *Bank of Scotland*, 1913 S.C. 743.

[46] Bell, *Prin.*, § 259; *Allan Buckley Allan & Milne* v. *Pattison* (1893) 21 R.195; *N. G. Napier Ltd.* v. *Crosbie*, 1964 S.C. 129.

[47] Mercantile Law Amendment Act (Scotland) 1856, s.9. In the proviso to the section that "nothing herein contained shall be deemed to extend to the case of a cautioner consenting to the discharge of a co-cautioner who may have become bankrupt," "cautioner" should be "creditor," probably: Bell, *Prin.*, § 261A. n.(a); *Royal Bank* v. *Welsh*, 1985 S.L.T. 439.

[48] *Morgan* v. *Smart* (1872) 10 M. 610. But see Bell, *Prin.* (10th ed.), § 261A.

[49] *Union Bank of Scotland* v. *Taylor*, 1925 S.C. 835, *per* L.P. Clyde at p. 841.

[50] *Doig* v. *Lawrie* (1903) 5 F. 295.

[51] *Buchanan* v. *Main* (1900) 3 F. 215.

[52] *Woodfield Finance Trust (Glasgow) Ltd.* v. *Morgan*, 1958 S.L.T. (Sh.Ct.) 14. The cautioner's death does not terminate the obligation: *British Linen Co.* v. *Monteith* (1858) 20 D. 557.

(3) a change in the constitution of a firm which is the creditor or principal debtor in the absence of agreement to the contrary.[53]

The equities and privileges of the cautioner can of course be renounced in the contract.[54]

Pro tanto discharge

The giving up of a security by the creditor,[55] or the creditor's failure to make a security effectual,[56] liberates the cautioner to the extent of the security. **10.4**

---

[53] Partnership Act 1890, s.18.
[54] *Bank of Scotland* v. *MacLeod*, 1986 S.L.T. 504.
[55] *Sligo* v. *Menzies* (1840) 2 D. 1478.
[56] *Fleming* v. *Thomson* (1826) 2 W. & S. 277; *L.A.* v. *Maritime Fruit Carriers Co. Ltd.*, 1983 S.L.T. 357.

CHAPTER 11

RECOVERY OF DEBTS

Demand for payment

11.1 Whatever the position may be in England,[1] there is no requirement in Scotland that the creditor must preface his action by a demand for payment. "The worst that can happen to any Scottish pursuer who raises a petitory action without prefacing it by a demand is that he may be found liable in the expenses of an *ex hypothesi* premature and unnecessary action."[2] "I am clearly of the opinion that when a debt of money is demanded, and the defender is not first told how much is asked of him, and when it is to be paid, but a summons is raised at once, and the pursuers then ask expenses, the defender is entitled to expenses, and not the pursuer."[3] On the same principle, where the pursuer in an action of reparation had failed without reasonable cause to intimate a claim before service of the summons and had accepted a tender lodged with the defences, the defenders were awarded expenses.[4] The debtor cannot avoid liability for expenses by consigning the amount of the debt in the hands of the court before the creditor has raised an action.[5]

Partial payment

11.2 When a debtor sends his creditor a cheque for a sum less than the amount claimed and states that it is sent "in full and final settlement," a question arises as to whether the creditor, if he cashes the cheque, can thereafter sue for the balance. Two cases have been distinguished.[6] Where the cheque is sent for the purpose of compromising a dispute, it is a question of fact to be ascertained from the circumstances whether the creditor has accepted the compromise. Thus, when the creditor replied to the debtor that he was not accepting the cheque in full settlement and, on receiving no answer, cashed the cheque, it was held that the creditor could recover the balance.[7] The onus of proving acceptance of the compromise rests on the debtor. In the second type of case the sending of the cheque in purported settlement of a larger amount admittedly due is merely an attempt to escape from a contractual obligation. Here, it seems, the retention and cashing of the cheque have no effect on the

---

[1] *Joachimson* v. *Swiss Bank Corporation* [1921] 3 K.B. 110.
[2] per L.J.-C. Cooper, *Macdonald* v. *North of Scotland Bank*, 1942 S.C. 369.
[3] per Lord Shand, *Magistrates of Leith* v. *Lennon* (1881) 18 S.L.R. 313 at 315.
[4] *Crombie* v. *British Transport Commission*, 1961 S.L.T. 115.
[5] *Alexander* v. *Campbell's Trustees* (1903) 5 F. 634; *A.B. & Co.* v. *C.D.* (1909) 25 Sh.Ct. Rep. 106.
[6] *McNicoll* v. *Kwasnica* (1952) 68 Sh.Ct.Rep. 295.
[7] *Smith & Archibald* v. *Ryness*, Second Division, 18 July 1929, reported at 1937 S.L.T. (News) 81; *Day* v. *McLea* (1889) 22 Q.B.D. 610; *Neuchatel Asphalte Co. Ltd.* v. *Barnett* [1957] 1 W.L.R. 356; *Gilbey Vintners Scotland Ltd.* v. *Perry*, 1978 S.L.T. (Sh.Ct.) 48; *Modeluxe Linen Services Ltd.* v. *Redburn Hotel Ltd.*, 1985 S.L.T. (Sh.Ct.) 60. Most of the extensive prior case law on this topic is set forth in *Lord Doune* v. *John Dye & Son Ltd.*, 1972 S.L.T. (Sh.Ct.) 30 in which Sheriff Kydd pointed out that a dictum of Lord McLaren in *Pollock* v. *Goodwin's Trs.* (1898) 25 R. 1051, which has been frequently cited in prior cases on this subject, relates to an entirely different situation. See also *Duthie & Co.* v. *Merson & Gerry*, 1947 S.C. 43.

creditor's claim for the full sum due[8]; if the debtor had been sued, his admission would have resulted in interim decree for the lower amount being granted.[9] In either case, it is important that the creditor, on retaining the cheque, should immediately inform the debtor that he is still demanding the balance.

Action of payment

A debt is normally recovered by an action for payment which is a type of petitory action, *i.e.* an action in which "some demand is made upon the defender, in consequence either of a right of property or credit in the pursuer."[10] The terms of the conclusion or crave are for payment to the pursuer by the defender of a certain sum, with interest thereon to a certain date, and of the expenses of the action.

11.3

Accounting

An action of accounting, more properly called an action of count, reckoning and payment, is appropriate "wherever there is a right to demand and liability to render an account."[11] It may be brought, for example, by a beneficiary against a trustee, by a principal against his agent, and by a ward against his guardian. It is not a suitable form of action for the determination of conflicting claims on a trust estate which involves questions of vesting.[12] Nor should it be a vehicle for general criticisms of trust administration but the question of the liability of trustees for a higher rate of interest than was in fact realised can be entertained.[13] An employer cannot bring such an action against his manager or other employee because the latter is not an independent person keeping his own books.[14] The action is competent even although accounts have admittedly been lodged.[15]

11.4

The conclusion of the summons is for a count and reckoning and payment of the balance due or, alternatively, for payment of a specified sum. Decree may be granted for any sum found due although it exceeds the sum specified in the alternative.[16] The date to which the accounting is sought should be specified if it is later than the date of citation.[17]

If there is no appearance, decree in absence is given for the specified sum. If the action is defended, the first question to be determined is the existence of the liability to account.[18] If there is such a liability, the defender is ordered to lodge accounts. The pursuer may then frame objections to items of the account. Any dispute arising from the accounts can be pursued in an objection.[19] The purpose of the objections is to show

---

[8] *McNicoll* v. *Kwasnica, supra*; *Tyrie* v. *Goldie* (1942) 58 Sh.Ct.Rep. 24.

[9] *Priestley & Son* v. *Arthur & Co.* (1882) 3 Sh.Ct.Rep. 450.

[10] Ersk., IV, i, 47.

[11] Mackay, *Manual of Practice in the Court of Session*, p. 372. See Maxwell, *Practice of the Court of Session*, p. 357; Macphail, pp. 684–688.

[12] *Davidson* v. *Davidson's Trs.*, 1952 S.L.T. (Notes) 3.

[13] *Melville* v. *Noble's Trs.*, (1896) 24 R. 243.

[14] *Govan Old Victualling Society Ltd.* v. *Wagstaff* (1907) 44 S.L.R. 295; *Marchmont Ltd.* v. *Clayton*, 1989 S.L.T. 725.

[15] *Cunningham-Jardine* v. *Cunningham-Jardine's Trs.*, 1979 S.L.T. 298.

[16] *Spottiswoode* v. *Hopkirk* (1853) 16 D. 59.

[17] *Wallace* v. *Henderson* (1875) 2 R. 999.

[18] See "Procedure in Actions of Accounting" (1950) 66 S.L.R. 276. See also *Smith* v. *Barclay*, 1962 S.C. 1; *Smith's Trs.* v. *Cranston*, 1990 G.W.D. 7–381.

[19] *Hobday* v. *Kirkpatrick's Trs.*, 1983 S.L.T. 197.

that the balance brought out should be larger either because the defender has credited an item which he is not entitled to credit or because he has failed to debit an item he should have debited. Each objection should deal with a particular item and must be supported by relevant averments.[20] The defender answers the objections, a record is made up and the action proceeds to debate or proof. There may be a remit to an accountant for a report.

Multiplepoinding

11.5 Multiplepoinding is the form of action most appropriate where two or more parties have competing claims to the same fund or property. It may be raised by the holder of the fund, who in this event is the pursuer and real raiser, or by a claimant, in which event the holder is the pursuer and nominal raiser and the claimant is the defender and real raiser. It is difficult to delimit the circumstances in which this form of action is competent. There must be double distress—a "double claim to one fund or property on separate and hostile grounds."[21] In the strict sense double distress is competition created by rival diligence but practice has extended the meaning of the term.

Circumstances in which a multiplepoinding has been held competent are:
(a) where property is claimed by an arrester and another party[22];
(b) where the proceeds of an insurance policy are claimed by the policy holder and by an arrester[23];
(c) where a share of an executry estate was claimed by a beneficiary and by the assignees of the beneficiary[24];
(d) where trustees are unable to obtain a discharge from the beneficiaries.[25]

In outline, the procedure is[26]:
(1) The summons calls all known claimants as defenders. If the action is raised by the holder a condescendence of the fund *in medio* is annexed to the summons. If the action is not raised by the holder he must lodge a condescendence of the fund.
(2) A claimant need only enter appearance at this stage if he wishes to challenge the competency of the action. This objection is then disposed of.
(3) If no defences are lodged, claimants can then object to the condescendence of the fund *in medio* and these objections are then disposed of.
(4) When the fund is settled, an order is made for claims to be lodged. Claims are then lodged, a record is made up and the action proceeds in the ordinary way.

The creditor of a claimant whose debt is liquid and constituted can

---

[20] *Guthrie v. McKimmie's Tr.*, 1952 S.L.T. (Sh.Ct.) 49.
[21] *Russel v. Johnston* (1859) 21 D. 886, *per* Lord Kinloch at p. 887. See Maxwell, *Practice of the Court of Session*, p. 369; Macphail, pp. 701–707; *Adam Cochran & Co. v. Conn*, 1989 S.L.T. (Sh.Ct.) 27.
[22] *North British Ry. Co. v. White* (1881) 9 R. 97.
[23] *Colonial Mutual Life Assurance Society Ltd. v. Brown*, 1911 1 S.L.T. 158.
[24] *Fraser's Exrx. v. Wallace's Trs.* (1893) 20 R. 374.
[25] *Mackenzie's Trs. v. Sutherland* (1895) 22 R. 233.
[26] R.C. 175–185; O.R.C. 113–127; Summ. C.R. 57–63.

lodge a riding claim in the multiplepoinding and may be ranked on any portion of the fund *in medio* to which the debtor is found entitled *primo loco*.

A multiplepoinding does not stop diligence by creditors who are not claimants but the holder of the fund can use the dependence of the multiplepoinding as a ground for suspension of diligence used against him.[27]

Partial claim

The general law is that if a pursuer sues and obtains decree for only a part of a debt due to him, he is held to have abandoned all claim to the balance. He can, however, expressly reserve any further claim arising out of the same grounds of action and he is not then precluded from recovering the balance in another action.[28]

11.6

Interest

The general rule[29] is that in the absence of an express or implied contractual provision interest does not run on a debt until there has been either a judicial demand for payment[30] or intimation by the creditor that if payment is not made by a specified date interest will begin to run.[31] Rendering of an account is not sufficient to make interest run.[32] So it has been held that interest *ex lege* does not run on a solicitor's fees,[33] arrears of feuduty,[34] or rent,[35] demurrage,[36] or sums due under an obligation of relief from public burdens.[37] But it is competent to stipulate that interest will run after a specified period of credit.[38] This may be done by a statement on an invoice, for example.[39] Again, interest may be due by virtue of a custom of trade.[40] Then there is "a very limited class of debts"[41] on which interest does run *ex lege*, *viz*. (a) loans[42]: an obligation to pay interest is implied in the contract of loan although there may be circumstances which show that this was not the lender's intention[43]; a law

11.7

---

[27] *Ferguson* v. *Bothwell* (1882) 9 R. 687.
[28] *Findlay's Trs.* v. *Shanks*, 1930 S.L.T. (Sh.Ct.) 32.
[29] *Carmichael* v. *Caledonian Ry. Co.* (1870) 8 M.(H.L.) 119, *per* Lord Westbury at p. 131; *Blair's Trs.* v. *Payne* (1884) 12 R. 104.
[30] See *supra*, para. 11.3.
[31] *Liqrs. of Linlithgow Oil Co.* v. *N.B. Ry. Co.* (1904) 12 S.L.T. 421.
[32] *Cardno & Darling* v. *Steuart* (1869) 7 M. 1026; *Blair's Trs.* v. *Payne, supra*; *Hunter* v. *Livingston Development Corporation*, 1984 S.L.T. 10.
[33] *Blair's Trs.* v. *Payne*; *supra Bunten* v. *Hart* (1902) 9 S.L.T. 476; *Somervell's Tr.* v. *Edinburgh Life Assurance Co.*, 1911 S.C. 1069; but as to advances by a law agent see *infra*.
[34] *Marquis of Tweeddale's Trs.* v. *Earl of Haddington* (1880) 7 R. 620.
[35] *Moncreiff* v. *Lord Dundas* (1835) 14 S. 61.
[36] *per* L.P. Dunedin, *Pollich* v. *Heatley*, 1910 S.C. 469 at 478.
[37] *Durie's Trs.* v. *Ayton* (1894) 22 R. 34.
[38] *Per* Lord Westbury, *Carmichael* v. *Caledonian Ry. Co.* (1870) 8 M. (H.L.) 119 at 131; *Liqrs. of Linlithgow Oil Co.* v. *N.B. Ry. Co.*, *supra*.
[39] *per* Lord Fraser, *Blair's Trs.* v. *Payne, supra*, at p. 112.
[40] *Findlay Bannatyne & Co.'s Assignee* v. *Donaldson* (1864) 2 M. (H.L.) 86.
[41] *Per* Lord Dunedin, *Pollich* v. *Heatley, supra*, at p. 478.
[42] *Thomson* v. *Geekie* (1861) 23 D. 693, L.J.-C. Inglis at p. 701; *Cuninghame* v. *Boswell* (1868) 6 M. 890.
[43] *Forbes* v. *Forbes* (1869) 8 M. 85; *Christie* v. *Matheson* (1871) 10 M. 9; *Smellie's Exrx.* v. *Smellie*, 1933 S.C. 725; *Williamson* v. *Williamson's Tr.*, 1948 S.L.T. (Notes) 72.

agent, therefore, can recover interest on advances to a client[44]; (b) where money has been paid under protest on the footing that it will be repaid in a certain event[45]; (c) where the purchaser of heritage obtains entry to the subjects interest runs on the unpaid price until settlement or consignation[46]; (d) interest is due on bills of exchange and promissory notes[47]; (e) interest is due on the accounts of mercantile agents[48]; (f) where a cautioner has paid on behalf of the principal debtor, interest runs[49]; (g) partners are entitled to interest at 5 per cent. on advances made to the firm.[50] There seems to be a class of case in which interest can be awarded from the date at which payment was wrongfully withheld.[51]

In the foregoing cases, the summons should conclude for interest from the appropriate date. In actions for an ascertained sum, such as the price of goods, the pursuer is entitled to interest from the date of citation.[52] This applies also to a *quantum meruit* claim.[53] When a claim only entered the record after the action was raised interest cannot be awarded on the claim from a date earlier than that of amendment of the record.[54] Interest may be awarded from the date of a judicial demand first made in the English courts.[55] The court is not restricted to the legal rate and may fix a rate appropriate in the circumstances.[56]

The court has no common law power to award interest on statutory compensation from a date prior to the date on which the amounts are agreed or determined.[57]

Compound interest with annual rests is allowed only "in the case of a fixed usage in commercial dealings, or where there has been an abuse in a party trusted with funds, and violating his trust."[58] However, when arrears of interest are the subject-matter of the action interest without rests may be allowed thereon.[59]

In actions of damages, the common law rule was that unless there was

---

[44] *Blair's Trs.* v. *Payne, supra.*

[45] *Glasgow Gas Light Co.* v. *Barony Parish of Glasgow* (1868) 6 M. 406; *Haddon's Exrx.* v. *Scottish Milk Marketing Board*, 1938 S.C. 168.

[46] *Grandison's Trs.* v. *Jardine* (1895) 22 R. 925; *Greenock Harbour Trs.* v. *Glasgow & South Western Ry. Co.*, 1909 S.C. (H.L.) 49; *Prestwick Cinema Co.* v. *Gardiner*, 1951 S.C. 98.

[47] Bills of Exchange Act 1882, s.57.

[48] *Findlay Bannatyne & Co.'s Assignee* v. *Donaldson, supra.*

[49] Ersk., III, iii, 78; Bell, *Prin.*, § 32.

[50] Partnership Act 1890, s.24, r. 3.

[51] *Carmichael* v. *Caledonian Ry. Co.* (1870) 8 M. (H.L.) 119, per Lord Westbury at p. 131; *Farrans (Construction) Ltd.* v. *Dunfermline D.C.*, 1988 S.L.T. 466; *Robertson Construction Co. (Denny) Ltd.* v. *Taylor*, (O.H.) 1990 S.C.L.R. 304.

[52] *F.W. Green & Co. Ltd.* v. *Brown & Gracie Ltd.*, 1960 S.L.T. (Notes) 43; *Dean Warwick Ltd.* v. *Borthwick*, 1983 S.L.T. 533.

[53] *Keir Ltd.* v. *East of Scotland Water Board*, 1976 S.L.T. (Notes) 72.

[54] *H.M.V. Fields Properties Ltd.* v. *Skirt 'n' Slack Centre of London Ltd.*, 1987 S.L.T. 2.

[55] *Trans Barwil Agencies (U.K.) Ltd.* v. *John S. Braid & Co. Ltd. (No. 2)*, 1990 S.L.T. 182.

[56] *Interplan (Joiners and Shopfitters) Ltd.* v. *Reid Furniture Co. Ltd.*, 1984 S.L.T. (Sh.Ct.) 42.

[57] *British Railways Board* v. *Ross and Cromarty C.C.*, 1974 S.C. 27.

[58] *Douglas* v. *Douglas's Trs.* (1867) 5 M. 827, per L.J.-C. Patton at p. 836. See also *Reddie* v. *Williamson* (1863) 1 M. 228; *National Bank of Greece S.A.* v. *Pinios Shipping Co. (No. 1)* [1990] A.C. 637.

[59] *Napier* v. *Gordon* (1831) 5 W. & S. 745; *Maclean* v. *Campbell* (1856) 18 D. 609; *Nash Dredging (U.K.) Ltd.* v. *Kestrel Marine Ltd.*, 1985 S.C. 96.

unreasonable delay, interest ran only from the date of the final decree because it is only then that the illiquid claim is quantified and made liquid.[60] There are some cases in which interest was awarded because the pursuer had been deprived of an interest-bearing security or a profit-producing chattel.[61]

However, by statute,[62] the interlocutor awarding damages may include interest at a specified rate on the whole or part of the sum awarded for the whole or any part of the period between the date when the right of action arose and the date of the interlocutor. Where the sum includes damages or solatium in respect of personal injuries, the court must award interest on such part of each of the damages and solatium as it considers appropriate unless it is satisfied "that there are reasons special to the case why no interest should be given."[63] Interest can be awarded on parts only where the award of damages has identifiable elements.[63] Pre-decree interest should not be awarded on damages representing future loss.[64] The rate of pre-decree interest should be the average of the rates obtaining for post-decree interest during the period in question.[65] Although s.1(2)(a) provides that nothing in the Act authorises the granting of interest on interest, the pre-decree interest should be included in the sum on which interest is awarded from the date of decree.[66] A tender is to be taken to be in full satisfaction of any claim to interest.[67]

In cases other than those of personal injury, it has been said that interest should be awarded only where there is some special circumstance such as undue delay and that the fact that the damages are substantial is not such a circumstance.[68] It has also been said that interest from a date prior to decree should be awarded only on quantified loss.[69]

In actions of damages for breach of contract it seems that, apart from the 1958 Act, interest can be awarded from the date of citation only if the sum can be quantified at that date.[70] It has been suggested that interest can be awarded under the statute more readily in breach of contract cases.[71]

---

[60] *Flensburg Steam Shipping Co.* v. *Seligmann* (1871) 9 M. 1011; *Clancey* v. *Dixon's Ironworks Ltd.*, 1955 S.L.T. 36.
[61] *Kolbin & Sons* v. *Kinnear & Co.*, 1931 S.C. (H.L.) 128, *per* Lord Atkin at p. 137; *Dunn & Co.* v. *Anderston Foundry Co. Ltd.* (1894) 21 R. 880; *Vitruvia S.S. Co.* v. *Ropner Shipping Co.*, 1923 S.C. 574.
[62] Interest on Damages (Scotland) Act 1958, s.1, as substituted by Interest on Damages (Scotland) Act 1971, s.1.
[63] *Ross* v. *British Railways Board*, 1972 S.C. 154; *Orr* v. *Metcalfe*, 1973 S.C. 57.
[64] *Macrae* v. *Reed and Mallik Ltd.*, 1961 S.C. 68; *McCuaig* v. *Redpath Dorman Long Ltd.*, 1972 S.L.T. (Notes) 42.
[65] *Smith* v. *Middleton*, 1972 S.C. 30.
[66] *Smith* v. *Middleton, supra*; *Mouland* v. *Ferguson*, 1979 S.L.T. (Notes) 85.
[67] s.1(1B).
[68] *R. & J. Dempster Ltd.* v. *Motherwell Bridge and Engineering Co. Ltd.*, 1964 S.L.T. 353; *Buchanan* v. *Cameron*, 1973 S.C. 285.
[69] *Fraser* v. *J. Morton Wilson Ltd.*, 1965 S.L.T. (Notes) 85; *Bell's Sports Centre (Perth) Ltd.* v. *William Briggs & Sons Ltd.*, 1971 S.L.T. (Notes) 48.
[70] *F.W. Green & Co. Ltd.* v. *Brown & Gracie Ltd., supra.*
[71] *Macrae* v. *Reed & Mallik Ltd., supra, per* Lord Mackintosh at p. 81.

Post-decree interest can be awarded at the rate agreed in the contract.[72] The rate may be related to a fluctuating base rate.[73]

Where a decree includes interest, it is deemed to be at 15 per cent. per annum, unless otherwise stated.[74] Interest should be asked for before the decree for damages is given.[75]

Arrestment ad fundandam jurisdictionem

11.8 A person who is not otherwise subject to the jurisdiction of the Scottish courts and who is not domiciled in the United Kingdom or in another member state of the European Community may be rendered subject to the jurisdiction if funds or property held for him in Scotland are arrested to found jurisdiction.[76] A ship can be arrested.[77] The procedure is by inserting a warrant for arrestment to found jurisdiction in the summons or initial writ.[78] The arrestment should be executed before or at the same time as the service of the summons.[79] Arrestment to found jurisdiction does not place a nexus on the subjects of arrestment and a separate arrestment on the dependence is necessary to obtain this result.[80] The schedule of arrestment must bear that the arrestment is to found jurisdiction.[81] In the summary cause procedure, an arrestment executed before service of the summons must be reported forthwith to the sheriff clerk and the summons must be served within 42 days of the execution of the arrestment.[82] Warrant to arrest to found jurisdiction can be included in an order granting leave to serve a third party notice.[83]

Subjects arrestable

11.9 The subjects which can be arrested to found jurisdiction are the same as those which can be arrested in execution.[84] Corporeal moveables, to be arrestable, must have a commercial value[85] but the value may be quite small[86] as long as it is not elusory.[87] The arrestee must be under an

---

[72] *Bank of Scotland* v. *Davis*, 1982 S.L.T. 20.
[73] *Royal Bank* v. *Dunbar*, 1985 S.L.T. (Sh.Ct.) 66; *Bank of Scotland* v. *Logie*, 1986 S.L.T. (Sh.Ct.) 47. *Cf. Royal Bank* v. *Geddes*, 1983 S.L.T. (Sh.Ct.) 32.
[74] R.C. 66; A.S. (Interest in Sheriff Court Decrees or Extracts) 1985 (S.I. 1985 No. 1179).
[75] *Handren* v. *Scottish Construction Co. Ltd.*, 1967 S.L.T. (Notes) 21.
[76] Civil Jurisdiction and Judgments Act 1982, s.20, Sched. 1, Art. 3, Sched. 8, para. 2(8).
[77] *Sheaf Steamship Co.* v. *Compania Transmediterranean*, 1930 S.C. 660, but see Administration of Justice Act 1956, ss.45–48.
[78] R.C. 74; O.C.R. 6.
[79] *Walls' Trs.* v. *Drynan* (1888) 15 R. 359; *North* v. *Stewart* (1890) 17 R. (H.L.) 60.
[80] *Fraser-Johnston Engineering Co.* v. *Jeffs*, 1920 S.C. 222; *Alexander Ward & Co. Ltd.* v. *Samyang Navigation Co. Ltd.*, 1975 S.C. (H.L.) 26.
[81] *Sutherlands of Peterhead (Road Hauliers) Ltd.* v. *Allard Hewson & Co. Ltd.*, 1972 S.L.T. (Notes) 83.
[82] Summ. C.R. 47.
[83] R.C. 85(1)(*b*); O.C.R. 50(7).
[84] *Trowsdale's Tr.* v. *Forcett Ry. Co.* (1870) 9 M. 88; *Leggat Bros.* v. *Gray*, 1908 S.C. 67; see paras. 17.3, 4.
[85] *Trowsdale's Tr.* v. *Forcett Ry. Co., supra.*
[86] *Shaw* v. *Dow and Dobie* (1869) 7 M. 449 (£1 : 8 : 6d); *Ross* v. *Ross* (1878) 5 R. 1013 (9/3d.); *Dalrymple's Trs.* v. *Lancashire Trust Corporation* (1894) 2 S.L.T. 79 (brass door plate).
[87] *Lindsay* v. *London & North Western Ry. Co.* (1855) 18 D. 62, aff. (1858) 3 Macq. 99; *Millar & Lang* v. *Polak* (1907) 14 S.L.T. 788; *Millar & Lang* v. *Poole* (1907) 15 S.L.T. 76; *Shankland & Co.* v. *McGildowny*, 1912 S.C. 857.

obligation to the common debtor at the date of arrestment,[88] but jurisdiction can be established even if the obligation is contingent[89] or defeasible.[90] The obligation need not rest on an express contract.[91] An obligation to account is sufficient even if in the event nothing is due to the common debtor.[92] If it appears that *prima facie* an obligation to account exists, the court will not generally allow an investigation of the accounts between the arrestee and the common debtor.[93] If, however, the court in its discretion does allow a preliminary proof which establishes that nothing is due by the arrestee, the arrestment is ineffectual to found jurisdiction.[94] If the arrestee denies the existence of any obligation to account, there is no jurisdiction.[95] It has been held that where the defender deposited funds with a building society at its London office jurisdiction can be established in Scotland by arresting in the hands of the building society at its Scottish branch[96] but if under the terms of an insurance policy payments can only be made at the insurer's London office, the debt is localised in London and there is nothing to arrest in Scotland.[97] It is not possible to create jurisdiction in Scotland against a foreign debtor by assigning the debt to a third party who then arrests in the hands of the cedent a smaller counter claim due to the debtor.[98] A creditor cannot arrest in his own hands.[99]

Arrestment on the dependence
The object of this type of arrestment, which is a matter of right to anyone who raises an action, is to keep fixed some asset of the defender so that the asset may be made good to satisfy the decree which the pursuer assumes he is going to obtain. Arrestment on the dependence is competent wherever there is a conclusion or crave for a pecuniary claim other than expenses.[1] The claim may be alternative or subsidiary. It is not warranted to arrest on the dependence of an action to enforce a future debt unless the defender is *vergens ad inopiam* or *in meditatione fugae*.[2]

11.10

---

[88] *Young* v. *Aktiebolaget Ofverums Bruk* (1890) 18 R. 163; *North* v. *Stewart* (1890) 17 R. (H.L.) 60; *McDonald* v. *Mize*, 1989 S.L.T. 482.
[89] *MacLaren & Co.* v. *Preston* (1893) 1 S.L.T. 75.
[90] *North* v. *Stewart, supra*; *Baird* v. *Baird*, 1910 1 S.L.T. 95; similarly it did not matter that the arrestee might have been able to plead the triennial prescription: *Shaw* v. *Dow and Dobie, supra*.
[91] *Moore & Weinberg* v. *Ernsthausen Ltd.*, 1917 S.C. (H.L.) 25.
[92] *Baines and Tait* v. *Compagnie Generale des Mines d'Asphalte* (1879) 6 R. 846; *MacLaren & Co.* v. *Preston* (1893) 1 S.L.T. 75.
[93] *Douglas* v. *Jones* (1831) 9 S. 856.
[94] *Wyper* v. *Carr & Co.* (1877) 4 R. 444; *Napier Shanks & Bell* v. *Halvorsen* (1892) 19 R. 412; *Mitchell & Muil Ltd.* v. *Ferniscliffe Products Co. Ltd.*, 1920 1 S.L.T. 199.
[95] *Smith* v. *Rosenbloom*, 1915 2 S.L.T. 18.
[96] *McNairn* v. *McNairn*, 1959 S.L.T. (Notes) 35.
[97] *J. Verrico & Co. Ltd.* v. *Australian Mutual Provident Society*, 1972 S.L.T. (Sh.Ct.) 57.
[98] *O'Hare* v. *Reaich*, 1956 S.L.T. (Sh.Ct.) 78.
[99] *Grant Melrose & Tennent Ltd.* v. *W. & G. DuCros Ltd.* (1927) 43 Sh.Ct. Rep. 347.
[1] Debtors (Scotland) Act, 1838, s.16; *Stafford* v. *McLaurin* (1875) 3 R. 148. The Court of Session may grant warrant for arrestment where proceedings have commenced elsewhere in the UK or EEC: Civil Jurisdiction and Judgments Act 1982, s.27(1); *Stancroft Securities Ltd.* v. *McDowall*, 1990 S.L.T. 746; *Clipper Shipping Co. Ltd.* v. *San Vincente Partners*, 1989 S.L.T. 204.
[2] *Symington* v. *Symington* (1875) 3 R. 205; *Burns* v. *Burns* (1879) 7 R. 355; *Brash* v. *Brash*, 1966 S.L.T. 157; *Pow* v. *Pow*, 1987 S.L.T. 127.

There is a special provision for actions for aliment and claims for orders for financial provision on divorce.[3] There may be arrestment on the dependence of a counter claim.[4]

A warrant for arrestment can be inserted in a Court of Session summons and can be craved for in a sheriff court initial writ.[5] If this is not done, a warrant can be obtained by motion in the Court of Session action and in the sheriff court a precept of arrestment can be obtained from the sheriff clerk on production of a writ containing pecuniary conclusions upon which a warrant of citation has been granted or of a liquid document of debt.[6] Warrant to arrest on the dependence can be included in an order for service of a third party notice.[7] A caveat cannot extend to warrants for arrestment on the dependence.[8]

The arrestment can be executed before service of the action on the defender but in the Court of Session the action must be served within 20 days and the summons called within 20 days of the diet of compearance. In the ordinary sheriff court the arrestment must be forthwith reported to the sheriff clerk and the action must be served within 20 days of the execution and tabled within 20 days of the first court day after the expiry of the *induciae*; if it is undefended decree in absence must be taken within 20 days of the expiry of the *induciae*.[9] In the summary cause procedure, the arrestment must be reported forthwith to the sheriff clerk and the arrestment falls unless the summons is served within 42 days from the execution of the arrestment.[10] Arrestment on the dependence is competent at any time up to the issue of the extract of the final decree.

The subjects which can be arrested on the dependence are broadly those which can be arrested in execution.[11] It is not competent to arrest on the dependence any wages or salary (including fees, bonuses, commission, overtime pay or other emoluments) or pension (including any annuity in respect of past services, any periodical payments in compensation for loss of employment, and any disability pension).[12] There are some restrictions on the arrestment of ships.[13]

The arrestee must be subject to the jurisdiction of the Scottish courts. The effect of the arrestment is to interpel the arrestee from paying over the arrested funds. If the schedule of arrestment states a sum followed by the words "more or less" the sum attached by the arrestment is not necessarily restricted to the sum stated.[14] As a matter of practice, the Scottish banks refuse to disclose whether anything has in fact been

---

[3] Family Law (Scotland) Act 1985, s.19.
[4] R.C. 84(*c*); O.C.R. 53.
[5] R.C. 74; O.C.R. 5; Summ. C.R. 3(2).
[6] R.C. 74(*d*); O.C.R. 42.
[7] R.C. 85(1)(*b*); O.C.R. 50(7).
[8] *Wards* v. *Kelvin Tank Services Ltd.*, 1984 S.L.T. (Sh.Ct.) 39.
[9] Debtors (Scotland) Act 1838, s.17; O.C.R. 112.
[10] Summ. C.R. 47.
[11] See paras. 17.3–4.
[12] Law Reform (Miscellaneous Provisions) (Scotland) Act 1966, s.1.
[13] Administration of Justice Act 1956, s.47; *Gatoil International Inc.* v. *Arkwright-Boston Manufacturers Mutual Insurance Co.*, 1985 S.L.T. 68; *William Batey (Exports) Ltd.* v. *Kent*, 1987 S.L.T. 557; *The "Aifanourios,"* 1980 S.C. 346. But see, as to the effect of the Civil Jurisdiction and Judgments Act 1982, *Clipper Shipping Co. Ltd.* v. *San Vincente Partners*, 1989 S.L.T. 204.
[14] *Ritchie* v. *McLachlan* (1870) 8 M. 815.

attached by an arrestment on the dependence.[15] The effect of the arrestment continues even after a final decree of *absolvitor* if the pursuer appeals.[16] The three-year period for the prescription of arrestment runs, in the case of an arrestment on the dependence, from the date of the final decree in the cause.[17]

Once the pursuer has obtained decree he may raise an action of furthcoming on the arrestment on the dependence, a further arrestment in execution not being necessary.[18] The arrestment covers the principal debt, the interest thereon and the expenses of the action constituting it but not the expenses of the arrestment itself.[19] In the sheriff court summary cause the expenses of the furthcoming are covered.[20] If in the end of the day the arrestment is released the common debtor cannot recover interest on the sum arrested from the arrestee.[21]

Interdict may be obtained against the threatened use of arrestment on the dependence if malice and oppression can be instantly verified[22] or if caution is found.[23] Once an arrestment has been used, the defender can apply to have it loosed on finding caution or to have it recalled, or restricted.[24] The grounds of recall may be that the debt is future or contingent or that the arrestment is nimious or oppressive, *e.g.* that the pursuer's claim is for a random figure,[25] that the pursuer has delayed in proceeding with the action,[26] or that there was a procedural irregularity.[27]

As a rule, the validity of the arrestment must be determined in the furthcoming and not in a petition for recall[28] but in special circumstances the question of whether a fund is arrestable can be decided in the petition for recall.[29]

The application may be made either to the Court of Session or to the sheriff from whose books the warrant of arrestment has been issued. In the Court of Session the application is generally made by way of motion before the Lord Ordinary before whom the action depends or, if the arrestment is used before the calling of the action, by letter to the Deputy Principal Clerk.[30] In the sheriff court, the procedure is by summary application before call and by motion after call.[31]

Unless there are exceptional circumstances[32] the arrestee cannot

---

[15] *Veitch* v. *Finlay & Wilson* (1894) 10 Sh.Ct.Rep. 13.
[16] *Countess of Haddington* v. *Richardson* (1822) 1 S. 362.
[17] Debtors (Scotland) Act 1838, s.22; *Paterson* v. *Cowan* (1826) 4 S. 477; Graham Stewart, p. 223.
[18] Graham Stewart, p. 231.
[19] *Ibid.*, p. 133.
[20] Summ. C.R. 64.
[21] *Glen Music Co. Ltd.* v. *City of Glasgow D.C.*, 1983 S.L.T. (Sh.Ct.) 26.
[22] *Beattie & Son* v. *Pratt* (1880) 7 R. 1171.
[23] *Duff* v. *Wood* (1858) 20 D. 1231.
[24] *Tweedie* v. *Tweedie*, 1966 S.L.T. (Notes) 89.
[25] *Cullen* v. *Buchanan* (1862) 24 D. 1280; *Levy* v. *Gardiner*, 1964 S.L.T. (Notes) 68. *Cf. Svenska Petroleum A.B.* v. *H.O.R. Ltd.*, 1986 S.L.T. 513.
[26] *Telford's Exr.* v. *Blackwood* (1866) 4 M. 369; *Mowat* v. *Kerr*, 1977 S.L.T. (Sh.Ct.) 62.
[27] *Richards & Wallington (Earthmoving) Ltd.* v. *Whatlings Ltd.*, 1982 S.L.T. 66.
[28] *Vincent* v. *Chalmers & Co.'s Tr.* (1877) 5 R. 43.
[29] *Lord Ruthven* v. *Drummond*, 1908 S.C. 1154.
[30] Debtors (Scotland) Act 1838, s.20; R.C. 74(*g*), (*h*); *Stuart* v. *Stuart*, 1926 S.L.T. 31.
[31] Debtors (Scotland) Act 1838, s.21; *Mowat* v. *Kerr*, 1977 S.L.T. (Sh.Ct.) 62; Summ.C.R. 48.
[32] *Svenska Petroleum A.B.* v. *H.O.R. Ltd.*, 1983 S.L.T. 493.

petition for recall if the subject of the arrestment is a debt or a corporeal moveable which is admittedly the property of the common debtor but he can seek recall if the subject arrested is a corporeal moveable which, in his contention, is not the property of the common debtor. In such a case the arrestment will be recalled unless the arrester can establish a *prima facie* case that the subject arrested is the property of the common debtor.[33] A person who is neither the arrestee nor the common debtor cannot petition for recall on the ground that the subjects arrested truly belong to him.[34]

Inhibition on the dependence

11.11 It is possible to inhibit on the dependence of an action for payment of money other than expenses. If the action is for a future debt, inhibition on the dependence is appropriate only if the debtor is *vergens ad inopiam* or *in meditatione fugae*. In a Court of Session action a warrant for inhibition on the dependence can be inserted in the will of the summons and, when the summons has been signeted, the messenger can serve an inhibition.[35] Alternatively a warrant can be obtained at any later stage by motion to the Lord Ordinary.[36] In a sheriff court action, it is necessary to present the initial writ and warrant, or a certified copy thereof, together with a Bill for Letters of Inhibition to the Petition Department of the Court of Session. A *fiat* is obtained and the Letters of Inhibition can then be signeted. Partial recall of an inhibition on the dependence is competent.[37] There may be a recall if the diligence is nimious and oppressive.[38] Applications may be made before[39] or after[40] calling of the action. An inhibition on the dependence of a sheriff court action has to be recalled by a Court of Session petition.[41]

Diligence in security

11.12 Where the debt is liquid but future or contingent—a bond or bill which is not yet due, for example—it is possible to arrest and inhibit in security on the document of debt without the necessity of a summons if the debtor is *vergens ad inopiam* or *in meditatione fugae*.[42] In the Court of Session the procedure is by bill. In the sheriff court, a precept of arrestment can be obtained.[43]

Partial admissions

11.13 There are three cases here:
(a) where it is conceded that a distinct part of the sum sued for, definite

---

[33] *Barclay Curle & Co. Ltd.* v. *Sir James Laing & Sons Ltd.*, 1908 S.C. 82. Cf. *William Batey (Exports) Ltd.* v. *Kent*, 1987 S.L.T. 557.
[34] *Brand* v. *Kent* (1892) 20 R. 29; *"Nordsoen"* v. *Mackie, Koth & Co.*, 1911 S.C. 172.
[35] R.C. 74. Where proceedings have commenced elsewhere in the UK or EEC the court can grant a warrant of inhibition: Civil Jurisdiction and Judgments Act 1982, s.27(1).
[36] R.C. 74(*d*), See also R.C. 84(*c*) (counterclaim) and R.C. 85 (1)(*b*) (third party notice).
[37] *McInally* v. *Kildonan Homes Ltd.*, 1979 S.L.T. (Notes) 89.
[38] *Rodger* v. *Maracas Ltd.*, 1990 S.L.T. 45.
[39] R.C. 74(*g*).
[40] R.C. 74(*h*).
[41] R.C. 189(*a*)(xv).
[42] Graham Stewart, pp. 15, 528.
[43] O.C.R. 42.

in amount, is due to the pursuer, *e.g.* where the action is for the sum of the prices of two articles and it is admitted that the price of one of them is due, or where the only defence is compensation and there is a balance of the sum sued for after deduction of the amount set off;
(b) where it is conceded that something is due to the pursuer in respect of his whole claim but the parties are not agreed as to the *quantum* of the claim, *e.g.* in an action of reparation for personal injuries where liability is admitted;
(c) where the defender disputes that any amount is due but is willing to make some payment to the pursuer "for the sake of peace."[44]

In (a) the defender should make the appropriate admission in the defences. The pursuer can then move for *interim* decree; the court may in its discretion grant such a decree prior to the closing of the record.[45] The decree is extractable in the ordinary way.

In (b) and (c) the appropriate course is to make, by formal minute, a judicial tender including an offer of expenses down to its date. Such a tender should not be referred to on record, and should not be mentioned in evidence or in any other way brought to the notice of the judge or jury.[46] If the pursuer has not intimated a claim to the defender prior to the raising of the action, a tender lodged with the defences need not include an offer of expenses and, even if the tender is accepted immediately, the defender may be awarded expenses against the pursuer.[47] If an extrajudicial offer has been made by the defender prior to the raising of the action, it may be repeated on record but should not be brought to the notice of the jury or referred to in evidence or debate.[48] If such a tender has been so repeated and the pursuer accepts it, the defender may be entitled to full expenses against the pursuer; it is a question of circumstances.[49] If an extrajudicial offer is not repeated on record and the pursuer after the raising of the action accepts the amount offered, no expenses are due to or by either party.[50] If he is awarded less than the offer the whole expenses may be awarded to the defender.[51] An extrajudicial tender during the course of the action may be taken into consideration.[52]

A tender by the defender is appropriate where a liquid claim is met by an illiquid counterclaim.[53]

---

[44] *per* L.J.-C. Inglis, *Ramsay's Trs.* v. *Souter* (1864) 2 M. 891, at p. 892.

[45] *McKinlay* v. *McKinlay* (1849) 11 D. 1022; *Conacher* v. *Conacher* (1857) 20 D. 252; Maclaren, *Court of Session Practice*, p. 1090; *George Hotel (Glasgow) Ltd.* v. *Prestwick Hotels Ltd.*, 1961 S.L.T. (Sh.Ct.) 61.

[46] *Smeaton* v. *Dundee Corporation*, 1941 S.C. 600; *Avery* v. *Cantilever Shoe Co. Ltd.*, 1942 S.C. 469; *Key* v. *Scottish Chemist Supply Co. Ltd.*, 1956 S.L.T. (Notes) 43; in the sheriff court where a tender has been lodged the sheriff should be asked to reserve consideration of expenses until the merits have been dealt with—*Jack* v. *Jack* (1953) 69 Sh.Ct.Rep. 34; *Associated Portland Cement Manufacturers Ltd.* v. *McInally*, 1970 S.L.T. (Sh.Ct.) 9.

[47] *Crombie* v. *British Transport Commission*, 1961 S.L.T. 115.

[48] *Avery* v. *Cantilever Shoe Co. Ltd., supra.*

[49] *Gunn* v. *Hunter* (1886) 13 R. 573.

[50] *Ramsay's Trs.* v. *Souter, supra; Critchley* v. *Campbell* (1884) 11 R. 475; but see the doubts expressed in *Miller* v. *McPhun* (1895) 22 R. 600.

[51] *O'Donnell* v. *A.M. & G. Robertson*, 1965 S.L.T. 155.

[52] *Pearce & Co.* v. *Owners of S.S. "Hans Maersk,"* 1935 S.C. 703.

[53] *Sidlaw Industries Ltd.* v. *Cable Belt Ltd.*, 1979 S.L.T. (Notes) 40.

Tenders

11.14 A tender is an offer by the defender to pay part of the sum sued for. It must, as a rule, include the expenses of process to its date.[54] The offer of expenses should be free from limitation.[55] An offer of "the expenses of process" does not necessarily mean expenses on the Court of Session scale; it means the appropriate expenses as determined by the court.[56] The tender must be unconditional although it is competent and usual to state that liability is not admitted and to reserve all rights and pleas. If there is more than one pursuer a lump sum cannot be offered to them without apportionment.[57]

A tender has an important effect on expenses. If the pursuer eventually recovers more than the amount tendered, he is awarded full expenses[58] unless there was in substance divided success in the action as a whole.[59] If he is awarded the amount tendered or less, he is entitled to his expenses down to the date of the tender and the defender is entitled to his expenses incurred in the natural progress of the cause against the pursuer from that date.[60] If the tender is accepted within a reasonable time, the pursuer is entitled to expenses down to the date of acceptance. If the tender is accepted more than a reasonable time after its date the pursuer is entitled to expenses down to the date at which it was reasonable to expect the tender to be accepted or refused and the defender is entitled to his expenses against the pursuer from that date.[61] The determination of the date should normally be left to the Auditor.[62]

A tender, until it is withdrawn, can be accepted at any time unless there has been an important change of circumstances, *e.g.* the death of the original pursuer,[63] the pronouncement of judgment by the Lord Ordinary,[64] the lodging of a report by a judicial referee.[65]

The acceptance of a tender made by one defender does not preclude the pursuer from continuing to proceed against another defender.[66] Where one defender tenders "expenses to date" this may include the expenses for which the pursuer is liable to another defender who is to be assoilzied.[67] Where each of two defenders who were sued jointly and severally lodged a tender, and the award to the pursuer against both jointly and severally was more than either tender but less than the total

---

[54] *Little* v. *Burns* (1881) 9 R. 118; *Graham* v. *Graham*, 1955 S.L.T. (Notes) 15.
[55] *Banks* v. *D.R.G. plc.*, 1988 S.L.T. 825.
[56] *McKenzie* v. *H.D. Fraser & Sons*, 1990 S.L.T. 629.
[57] *Flanagan* v. *Dempster Moore & Co.*, 1928 S.C. 308; *McNeil* v. *National Coal Board*, 1966 S.L.T. 237.
[58] *Heriot* v. *Thomson* (1833) 12 S. 145. See *Quinn* v. *Bowie (No. 2)*, 1987 S.L.T. 576.
[59] *Alvis* v. *Harrison*, 1989 S.L.T. 746.
[60] *Jacobs* v. *Provincial Motor Cab Co. Ltd.*, 1910 S.C. 756; *McLean* v. *Galbraith Stores Ltd.*, 1935 S.C. 165.
[61] *Jack* v. *Black*, 1911 S.C. 691.
[62] *Smeaton* v. *Dundee Corporation*, 1941 S.C. 600; *Wood* v. *Miller*, 1960 S.C. 86.
[63] *Sommerville* v. *N.C.B.*, 1963 S.L.T. 334.
[64] *Bright* v. *Low*, 1940 S.C. 280.
[65] *Macrae* v. *Edinburgh Street Tramways Co.* (1885) 13 R. 265.
[66] *McNair* v. *Dunfermline Corporation*, 1953 S.C. 183. See para. 28.5.
[67] *Macdonald* v. *Scottish Motor Traction Co.*, 1948 S.C. 529. *Cf. Mitchell* v. *Redpath Engineering Ltd.*, 1990 S.L.T. 259.

sum of the two tenders, the defenders were awarded expenses against the pursuer from the date of the second tender.[68]

Where, in an action for damages against two defenders, the first defender lodged a "tender" whereby, subject to the concurrence of the second defender, he offered to admit liability jointly and severally with the second defender on the basis that the defenders would be liable *inter se* to contribute to damages and expenses in the proportion of three-quarters to the first defender and one-quarter to the second defender, and the jury awarded two-thirds of the damages against the first defender and one-third against the second defender, it was held that all the pursuer's expenses to the date of the tender and his subsequent expenses so far as applicable to the quantification of damages should be paid in the proportion of two-thirds by the first defender and one-third by the second defender, each defender bearing his own expenses; and that the expenses of the pursuer and first defender incurred subsequent to the date of the tender and attributable to the determination and apportionment of liability should be paid by the second defender.[69]

Sheriff court small claims

Small claims in the sheriff court are (a) actions for payment of money not exceeding £750, exclusive of interest and expenses, other than actions for aliment and interim aliment and actions of defamation; (b) actions *ad factum praestandum* and actions for the recovery of moveable property where there is an alternative claim for payment of a sum not exceeding £750, exclusive of interest and expenses.[70] A small claim is commenced by a summons which should give fair notice of the claim and which should state the basis of the claim including relevant dates, and, where the claim arises from the supply of goods or services, details of the nature of the goods or services and the date or dates on or between which they were ordered and supplied; there should be a reference to any agreement giving jurisdiction in the claim to another court and to any proceedings pending in another court about the same claim.[71] The period of notice of the summons to be given to the defender is 21 days if he is resident or has a place of business within Europe and otherwise 42 days.[72] If the defender does not lodge a response to the summons by the "return date" the pursuer can obtain a decree without a court appearance.[73] The defender, not later than 14 days after the execution of a charge or the execution of an arrestment, whichever first occurs, following on the decree, can apply for recall of the decree.[74]

11.15

Enactments or rules of law relating to the admissibility or corrobora-

---

[68] *Jackson* v. *Clyde Navigation Trust*, 1961 S.L.T. (Sh.Ct.) 35—the court has a discretion because one defender might be a man of straw.

[69] *Williamson* v. *McPherson*, 1951 S.C. 438. As to delay in accepting such a tender, see *Morton* v. *O'Donnell*, 1979 S.L.T. (Notes) 26. As to the effect of acceptance of such a tender after refusal of a previous tender, see *Houston* v. *British Road Services Ltd.*, 1967 S.L.T. 329.

[70] Small Claims (Scotland) Order 1988 (S.I. 1988 No. 1999), Art. 2. Actions for count, reckoning and payment are not actions *ad factum praestandum*.

[71] Sm.Clm.R. 3.

[72] r. 4.

[73] r. 10.

[74] r. 27(2).

tion of evidence do not apply in a small claim.[75] Any hearing is conducted in an informal manner.[76] There is an appeal to the sheriff principal on a point of law.[77] In a small claim there is no award of expenses unless the value of the claim exceeds £200, in which case expenses not exceeding £75 may be awarded.[78] An extract may be issued 14 days after the granting of decree.[79]

Summary cause

11.16　The sheriff court summary cause includes actions for payment of money not exceeding £1,500 in amount, exclusive of interest and expenses, and actions of multiplepoinding, furthcoming and sequestration for rent where the sum involved does not exceed £1,500.[80] It is commenced by a summons in the statutory form, the *induciae* being 21 days if the defender's residence or place of business is within Europe and 42 days if it is outwith Europe.[81] If the defender lodges neither a notice of intention to appear nor an application for a time to pay direction on or before the "return day" specified in the summons (which must be after the expiry of the *induciae*) the pursuer can, by entering a minute in the Book of Summary Causes, obtain decree in absence on the day specified in the summons as the "first calling day" (which is seven days after the "return day").[82] The defender may within 14 days after execution of a charge or an arrestment, whichever first occurs, following on the decree, apply for recall of the decree.[83]

There is an appeal to the sheriff principal on a question of law and from the sheriff principal to the Court of Session if the sheriff principal certifies the cause as suitable for such appeal.[84] An extract may be issued 14 days after the granting of the decree.[85]

Ordinary court action

11.17　An ordinary action in the sheriff court is appropriate if the sum sued for exceeds £1,500. It is commenced by an initial writ, the *induciae* being the same as in a summary cause.[86] Decree in absence may be granted at any time after the expiry of the *induciae*.[87] An extract may be issued after the expiry of 14 days from the date of the decree.[88] The defender may be reponed at any time before implement of the decree.[89] The decree is entitled to the privilege of a decree *in foro* after 20 years or in six months

---

[75] Sheriff Courts (Scotland) Act 1971, s.35(3).
[76] r. 19.
[77] 1971 Act, s.38(*a*); r. 29.
[78] Small Claims (Scotland) Order 1988, Art. 4.
[79] Summ. C.R. 89 applied by Sm.Clm.R. 2.
[80] Sheriff Courts (Scotland) Act 1971, s.35; A.S. (Summary Cause Rules, Sheriff Court) 1976 (S.I. 1976 No. 476); S.I. 1988 No. 1993.
[81] Summ. C.R. 4.
[82] Summ. C.R. 55.
[83] Summ. C.R. 19.
[84] 1971 Act, s.38.
[85] Summ. C.R. 89.
[86] O.C.R. 7—see para. 16 *supra*.
[87] O.C.R. 21.
[88] O.C.R. 25.
[89] O.C.R. 28–32; see *McKelvie* v. *Scottish Steel Scaffolding Co.*, 1938 S.C. 278.

from its date or the date of a charge on it if the service of the writ or charge was personal.[90]

On decree being granted in a defended action, extract may be issued when it is no longer possible to mark an appeal.[91] An appeal may be taken within 14 days of the decree if it has not sooner been extracted.[92] The appeal may be to the Court of Session or the sheriff principal.

Court of Session action

An action for debt in the Court of Session must be for a sum exceeding £1,500 in amount exclusive of interest and expenses.[93] The action is commenced by a summons, the *induciae* being in the case of citation within Europe 21 days after execution of service, and, outside Europe, 21 days if there was personal citation and 42 days if there was not; where execution is by registered or recorded delivery letter, the *induciae* is reckoned from 24 hours after the date of posting.[94]

The summons cannot be called before the day on which the *induciae* expires.[95] If the defender wishes to defend he must enter appearance within three days of the calling.[96] If he fails to do so, the pursuer can enrol a motion for decree in absence and the cause appears on the Roll of Undefended Causes on the first available day.[97] The defender may have the decree in absence recalled within 10 days.[98] Extract is obtainable after 11 days on a decree in absence; after eight days in other causes.

A reclaiming motion may be taken within 21 days of the date of the interlocutor,[99] but a reclaiming motion may not be brought to recall a decree in absence.[1]

11.18

Expenses

A pursuer who has had to raise an action to recover his debt is entitled to his expenses. If the debtor has paid before service of the summons upon him but after the pursuer has obtained a warrant for citation, the pursuer is entitled to the expenses of obtaining the warrant.[2] Expenses may be modified as the court deems fit and this power may be exercised where the principal sum awarded could have been recovered in a lower court.[3]

11.19

---

[90] O.C.R. 26.
[91] O.C.R. 90.
[92] O.C.R. 91.
[93] 1907 Act, s.7; Sheriff Courts (Scotland) Act 1971 (Privative Jurisdiction and Summary Cause) Order 1988 (S.I. 1988 No. 1993).
[94] R.C. 72.
[95] R.C. 78.
[96] R.C. 81.
[97] R.C. 89. The special provisions of this rule as to defenders furth of Scotland should be noted.
[98] R.C. 89(*f*).
[99] R.C. 264.
[1] R.C. 89(*ab*).
[2] *Cadzow Finance Co. Ltd.* v. *Fleming*, 1985 S.L.T. (Sh.Ct.) 37; *Clark & Rose Ltd.* v. *Mentiplay*, 1989 S.L.T. (Sh.Ct.) 66.
[3] R.C. 347(*c*); A.S. (Fees of Solicitors in the Sheriff Court) 1989, Sched., para. 5; *Quinn* v. *Bowie (No. 2)*, 1987 S.L.T. 576; *MacInnes-Morrison* v. *Gairloch Hotel Co. Ltd.*, 1988 S.L.T. 461; *Banks* v. *D.R.G. plc*, 1988 S.L.T. 825; *Carr* v. *L.A.*, 1990 S.L.T. 225; *Rooney* v. *F.W. Woolworth plc*, 1990 S.L.T. 257; *Robertson* v. *D. B. Marshall (Newbridge) Ltd.*, 1989 S.L.T. (Sh.Ct.) 102.

Time to pay directions

11.20 On granting decree for payment of any principal sum of money, the court may make a time-to-pay direction—a direction that any sum decerned for in the decree shall be paid either by instalments at specified intervals or in a lump sum at the end of a specified period; the payment by instalments commences at a specified time after, and the period for payment of the lump sum begins to run from, the date of intimation by the creditor to the debtor of an extract of the decree containing the direction.[4] The direction can also apply to expenses in relation to which the decree contains a finding as to liability or it can apply to such expenses alone. Where a finding as to expenses is made and a direction is made in respect of these expenses but the court does not decern for payment of the expenses or decerns for payment of them as taxed by the auditor but does not specify the amount of them, the relevant times begin to run from the date of intimation of an extract of the decree specifying the amount of the expenses.[5] On making the direction, the court may recall or restrict any arrestment on the dependence of the action or arrestment in security which is in effect,[6] but the recall or arrestment may be made subject to the fulfilment by the debtor of such conditions within such period as the court thinks fit and the granting of decree is then postponed until the conditions are fulfilled or the end of the period, whichever is the earlier.[7] The recall of the arrestment does not prevent the creditor from being ranked *pari passu* on the proceeds of any other arrestment or poinding under the Bankruptcy Act.[8]

(a) *Where direction competent.* A direction can be made only where the debtor is an individual and only if and to the extent that he is liable personally for the debt or liable as a tutor, *factor loco tutoris*, *factor loco absentis* or *curator bonis*.[9] A direction cannot be made in the following cases: where the sum decerned for, exclusive of interest and expenses, exceeds £10,000; where the decree contains an award of a capital sum on divorce or the granting of a nullity; in connection with a maintenance order; in an action by the Inland Revenue for payment of tax; in an action for rates or community charge; in an action for payment of betting duty, car tax or value added tax.[10] A direction cannot be made if there has already been a time order under the Consumer Credit Act.[11] If the court makes a finding as to liability for expenses and does not at the same time make a direction, it is not competent for the court subsequently to make a direction in respect of these expenses.[12]

(b) *The effect of a direction.* The effect of the direction is that it is not competent to serve a charge for payment of the debt or to commence or execute to recover the debt an arrestment, furthcoming, poinding and

[4] D.A., s.1(1).
[5] s.1(4).
[6] s.2(3).
[7] s.2(4).
[8] s.13(2). See para. 15.5.
[9] s.14(1).
[10] s.1(5).
[11] s.14(3). See para. 3.19.
[12] s.1(3).

sale, earnings arrestment or adjudication for debt.[13] If there is in effect an arrestment on the dependence or in security it is not competent to commence an action of furthcoming or sale, but the arrestment remains in effect unless it is recalled or restricted.[14] If there is interest payable under the decree, other than interest awarded as a specific sum in the decree, the creditor can recover it only by serving a notice on the debtor stating that he is claiming interest and specifying the amount; that must be done not later than 14 days before the date on which the last instalment is due to be paid or the date on which the lump sum is to be paid. Any sum paid by the debtor under the direction is not ascribed to interest until the debt other than interest has been discharged.[15] While the direction is in effect, the creditor cannot found on the debt in presenting, or concurring in the presentation of, a petition for sequestration of the debtor's estate.[16]

(c) *Cessation*. When the direction is recalled or ceases to have effect otherwise than on the debtor's sequestration or by reason of the debt being paid or otherwise extinguished, the debt in so far as it remains outstanding and interest thereon, whether or not awarded as a specific sum in the decree, becomes again enforceable by diligence.[17]

The direction ceases to have effect if
(i) on the day on which an instalment payable under the direction becomes due, there remains unpaid a sum, due under previous instalments, of not less than the aggregate of two instalments[18];
(ii) at the end of the period of three weeks immediately following the day on which the last instalment payable under the direction becomes due, any part of the debt remains outstanding[19];
(iii) any sum payable in a lump sum at the end of a period under the direction remains unpaid 24 hours after the end of the specified period[20];
(iv) the debtor dies or the obligation to pay the debt transmits to another person during the debtor's life[21];
(v) an award of sequestration of the debtor's estate is granted[22];
(vi) the debtor grants a voluntary trust deed for his creditors[22];
(vii) the debtor enters into a composition contract with his creditors.[22]

If there is a direction made in relation to both a principal sum and expenses and decree for payment of the expenses is granted after the decree for the principal sum and if the direction ceases to have effect under (i), (ii) or (iii) above in relation to the sum due under one of the decrees the direction also ceases to have effect in relation to the sum due under the other decree.[23]

(d) *Procedure*. The defender has to be given notice with the summons

---

[13] s.2(1).
[14] s.2(2).
[15] s.1(6), (7), (8); R.C. 88H; A.S. (Debtors) 3.
[16] s.12(1).
[17] s.2(5).
[18] s.4(1).
[19] s.4(2).
[20] s.4(3).
[21] s.14(2).
[22] s.12(2).
[23] s.4(4).

that he can apply for a direction[24] and there are provisions to allow him to apply for a direction at various stages in the action.[25] The court, on the application of the debtor or the creditor, may vary or recall a direction if it seems reasonable to do so and it may also recall or restrict an arrestment with or without conditions.[26] A variation comes into effect when it is intimated to the debtor and creditor by the sheriff clerk.[27]

---

[24] R.C. 88B; O.C.R. 5(5); Summ.C.R. 17A; Smll.C.R. 3(2).
[25] R.C. 88C–F; O.C.R. 21B–C; Summ.C.R. 17A; Smll.C.R. 24.
[26] s.3; R.C. 88F; A.S. (Debtors) 4, fm. 1.
[27] s.3(3).

CHAPTER 12

PAYMENT

Mode of payment
A creditor is entitled to require payment in legal tender.[1] The validity of methods of payment depends on the instructions of the creditor and the normal way of doing business. Unless there is a request to remit a cheque by post, the cheque is sent at the risk of the sender.[2] It is not normal business practice to send large sums of notes by post and the loss falls on the sender.[3] If the creditor has accepted payment in one form he cannot require payment in another form in strict compliance with the contract without giving fair notice to the debtor.[4] If the ordinary way of paying is by post an account will be held to have been paid by a remittance duly posted although the remittance does not reach the creditor.[5]

12.1

Payment by cheque
Payment by cheque is equivalent to payment in cash. It was held that an amount had been "paid and received" on the day on which the cheque was received although it could not be presented until the following day[6]; and when a cheque sent in payment of a debt has been received by the creditor there is no debt in existence which can be arrested in the hands of the sender of the cheque.[7] On the other hand, a creditor is not bound to accept payment by cheque or otherwise than by legal tender.[8] He is entitled to reject the cheque by returning it to the debtor although it has been doubted whether in the absence of some reasonable doubt as to the debtor's solvency, he is entitled to proceed with diligence forthwith.[9] If he retains the cheque, however, he must countermand any diligence which has been commenced,[10] although it would seem that he can still take decree in absence against the debtor.[11] Again, once the cheque has been accepted and paid into the creditor's bank, he cannot reject it[12]; and if he has rejected the cheque on some other ground which is later shown to be invalid, he cannot then rely on the point that the cheque was not legal tender.[13] If, of course, the cheque is dishonoured there is no payment and the debt revives.[14]

12.2

---

[1] *Glasgow Pavilion Ltd.* v. *Motherwell* (1903) 6 F. 116, *per* Lord Young at p. 119. See para. 1.2.
[2] *Baker* v. *Lipton* (1899) 15 T.L.R. 435; *Robb* v. *Gow Bros. & Gemmell* (1905) 8 F. 90; *Coats* v. *Glasgow Corporation* (1912) 28 Sh.Ct.Rep. 38.
[3] *Mitchell-Henry* v. *Norwich Union Life Insurance Society Ltd.* [1918] 2 K.B. 67.
[4] *Tankexpress A/S* v. *Compagnie Financière Belge des Petroles S.A.* [1949] A.C. 76.
[5] *Thorey* v. *Wylie & Lochhead* (1890) 6 Sh.Ct.Rep. 201.
[6] *Glasgow Pavilion Ltd.* v. *Motherwell* (1903) 6 F. 116.
[7] *Leggat Brothers* v. *Gray*, 1908 S.C. 67.
[8] *per* Lord Young, *Glasgow Pavilion Ltd.* v. *Motherwell, supra*, at p. 119.
[9] Gloag, p. 709.
[10] *Macdougall* v. *McNab* (1893) 21 R. 144.
[11] *Pollock* v. *Goodwin's Trs.* (1898) 25 R. 1051.
[12] *Mintons* v. *Hawley & Co.* (1882) 20 S.L.R. 126.
[13] *Holt* v. *National Bank of Scotland*, 1927 S.L.T. 484.
[14] *Walker & Watson* v. *Sturrock* (1897) 35 S.L.R. 26; *Leggat Brothers* v. *Gray*, 1908 S.C. 67; *McLaren's Tr.* v. *Argylls Ltd.*, 1915 2 S.L.T. 241.

Other modes of payment

12.3 Payment by credit card is not conditional; if the credit card company fails to pay the supplier he has no recourse against the purchaser.[15] On the other hand, payment by letter of credit is conditional.[16]

Place of payment

12.4 In general, the debtor should tender payment at the creditor's residence or place of business.[17] It has been held that payment by the debtor in good faith into the creditor's bank account, with intimation to the creditor, but without his authority, is ineffectual discharge of the debt but it is doubtful if this is correct.[18]

Ascription of payments

12.5 Where the same person is debtor in more than one debt to the same creditor a question may arise as to the debt to which a payment by the debtor is to be ascribed. The rule is that the debtor may appropriate the payment to a particular debt.[19] He may not, however, appropriate a payment to principal rather than interest.[20] If the debtor does not appropriate, the creditor may do so, either in his receipt or at a later point. It has been said that he can appropriate "up to the last moment"[21] but not after issue has been joined.[22] The creditor's ascription cannot preclude challenge of the validity of the debt.[23] If the creditor does not appropriate expressly, his implied or presumed intention governs.[24] The intention may be inferred from the form and statement of the account but the entry in the creditor's own books is not conclusive.[25] In the case of an account-current, there is a presumption by virtue of the rule in *Devaynes* v. *Noble*[26] that the earliest credit is applied to extinguish the earliest debit. The presumption is redargued however if the course of dealing between the parties shows a different intention[27] or if the form and statement of the account or other evidence shows that the creditor's intention was

---

[15] *Re Charge Card Services Ltd.* [1987] Ch. 150; [1989] Ch. 497; *Customs and Excise Commr.* v. *Diners Club Ltd.* [1989] 1 W.L.R. 1196.

[16] *W. J. Alan & Co. Ltd.* v. *El Nasr Export and Import Co.* [1972] 2 Q.B. 189; *E. D. & F. Man Ltd.* v. *Nigerian Sweets and Confectionery Co. Ltd.* [1977] 2 Lloyd's Rep. 50.

[17] *Haughhead Coal Co.* v. *Gallocher* (1903) 11 S.L.T. 156; *Bank of Scotland* v. *Seitz*, 1989 S.L.T. 641; 1990 S.L.T. 584.

[18] *Wood* v. *Bruce* (1908) 24 Sh.Ct.Rep. 24.

[19] *Allan* v. *Allan & Co.* (1831) 9 S.519; *Mitchell* v. *Cullen* (1852) 1 Macq. 190.

[20] *Gourlay* v. *Clydesdale Bank Ltd.* (1900) 7 S.L.T. 473. When, however, there is a time to pay direction or order see D.A., ss.1(8), 5(8)

[21] *Cory Brothers & Co. Ltd.* v. *Owners of "Mecca,"* L.R. [1897] A.C. 286, *per* Lord Macnaghten at p. 294.

[22] *Jackson* v. *Nicoll* (1870) 8 M. 408—"before action and while the debtor is solvent": Gloag & Irvine, p. 852.

[23] *Dougall* v. *Lornie* (1899) 1 F. 1187.

[24] *Cory Brothers & Co. Ltd.* v. *Owners of "Mecca," supra*.

[25] *Cory Brothers & Co. Ltd.* v. *Owners of "Mecca," supra*; *Jackson* v. *Nicoll, supra*; but see *National Commercial Bank of Scotland* v. *Millar's Tr.*, 1964 S.L.T. (Notes) 57.

[26] (1816) 1 Mer. 572 (known in England as *Clayton's Case*). This was accepted as the law of Scotland in *Houston* v. *Speirs* (1829) 3 W. & S. 392, and *Royal Bank* v. *Christie* (1841) 2 Rob. 118.

[27] *Hay* v. *Torbet*, 1908 S.C. 781; *Macdonald Fraser & Co. Ltd.* v. *Cairns's Exrx.*, 1932 S.C. 699. See also *Deeley* v. *Lloyds Bank Ltd.* [1912] A.C. 756; *Thomas Montgomery & Sons* v. *Gallacher*, 1982 S.L.T. 138.

different.[28] Between banker and customer the presumption is rebutted by the existence of two accounts or the closing of one account and the opening of another.[29] An account-current is normally between banker and customer[30] but it may be between agent and client,[31] mercantile houses,[32] or dealers.[33] The rule does not apply to a tradesman's account; there, payments go against general indebtedness.[34] Where the debtor owes both principal and interest a payment will be first appropriated to interest even although the interest is not payable at fixed terms.[35]

Where a debtor is liable to make to the same person payments in respect of two or more regulated agreements under the Consumer Credit Act 1974 he may appropriate any sum paid by him towards the sum due under any one of the agreements or towards the sum due under two or more agreements in such proportions as he thinks fit. If he fails to make an appropriation where one of the agreements is a hire-purchase agreement, a conditional sale agreement, a consumer hire agreement or an agreement in relation to which any security is provided the payment is appropriated towards the satisfaction of the sums due under the several agreements respectively in the proportions which these sums bear to one another.[36]

A payment by a debtor to his creditor is presumed to be on account of the debt.[37]

Payment to third parties

Payment of the amount of a debt to the creditor's agent who has, or appears to have, authority to receive it, is valid.[38] Notice on the invoice that payment is to be made direct to the principal is sufficient to negative the agent's authority.[39] The onus is on the debtor to prove the actual or ostensible authority.[40] A solicitor has ostensible authority to receive a sum sued for[41] and to receive the price of shares which have been sold through him.[42] An agent who has acted for both parties in a loan transaction has no implied authority to receive repayment.[43] Payment by a litigant to his country agent may not be payment to his Edinburgh agent.[44] A factor authorised to uplift interest has no power to give a

12.6

---

[28] *Cory Brothers & Co. Ltd.* v. *Owners of "Mecca," supra.*
[29] *Re Sherry* (1884) 25 Ch.D. 692; *Buchanan* v. *Main* (1900) 3 F. 215; *Bradford Old Bank Ltd.* v. *Sutcliffe* [1918] 2 K.B. 833; *Commercial Bank* v. *Turner* (1944) 60 Sh.Ct.Rep. 95.
[30] As in *Cuthill* v. *Strachan* (1894) 21 R. 549. The rule can apply to bank accounts other than current accounts—*Re Yeovil Glove Co. Ltd.* [1963] Ch. 528.
[31] *Lang* v. *Brown* (1859) 22 D. 113.
[32] *Houston* v. *Speirs, supra.*
[33] *McKinlay* v. *Wilson* (1885) 13 R. 210.
[34] *Dougall* v. *Lornie* (1899) 1 F. 1187; *Hay* v. *Torbet, supra.*
[35] *Watt* v. *Burnett's Trs.* (1839) 2 D. 132.
[36] Consumer Credit Act 1974, s.81.
[37] *Spence* v. *Paterson's Trs.* (1873) 1 R. 46, *per* Lord Deas at p. 60.
[38] *International Sponge Importers Ltd.* v. *Watt & Sons*, 1911 S.C. (H.L.) 57; *Gemmell* v. *Annandale & Son Ltd.* (1899) 36 S.L.R. 658.
[39] *Ell Bros.* v. *Sneddon* (1929) 45 Sh.Ct.Rep. 351.
[40] *Encyclopaedia of the Laws of Scotland*, Vol. XI., p. 168; *British Bata Shoe Co. Ltd.* v. *Double M. Shah Ltd.*, 1980 S.C. 311.
[41] *Smith* v. *North British Ry.* (1850) 12 D. 795.
[42] *Pearson* v. *Scott* (1878) 9 Ch.D. 198.
[43] *Falconer* v. *Dalrymple* (1870) 9 M. 212.
[44] *Clark & Macdonald* v. *Schulze* (1902) 4 F. 448.

discharge for the principal sum even although the document of debt is in his possession.[45] The partner of a firm who made a contract is entitled to discharge payments under it.[46] Payment to the *curator bonis* of a minor who had not extracted or found caution was not valid.[47]

Deduction of tax

12.7 Tax at the basic rate may be deducted from the following when payable wholly out of profits or gains brought into charge for income tax[48]:
(1) annuities and other annual payments except interest[49];
(2) a royalty or other sum in respect of the user of a patent;
(3) rents and royalties in respect of mines, quarries and similar concerns.

The accumulation or capitalisation of interest does not constitute a "payment" so as to entitle the debtor to recover the tax.[50] "Payment" does, however, include payment by cheque or bill, by transfer of marketable securities, by making of credit entries in books of account, by the discharge of an obligation expressed in foreign currency or, in general, by any method which is in a commercial sense a payment.[51] The deduction is at the basic rate for the year in which the payment becomes due. The payee must allow the deduction on receipt of the residue, and the payer is acquitted and discharged of the sum represented by the deduction.[52] Where the amount paid is to be set off against a debt due by the payee to the payer, only the net amount can be set off.[53] The question of whether tax is deductible from a payment can be determined in an action to which the Revenue is not a party.[54] The payer, if requested by the payee, must furnish a certificate of deduction of tax. It has been said that in the case of royalties, at least, a payer who has failed to deduct may recover the tax from the payee by a *condictio indebiti*.[55] In the case cited,[56] it was held that a debtor who, for a long number of years, failed to deduct bond interest at the time of payment could not claim the deduction in a subsequent settlement with the creditor. Trustees who have misconstrued the trust deed cannot recover from the beneficiary the tax which they failed to deduct.[57]

A person making a termly payment is entitled to deduct only in respect of a sum that he is currently paying, and not in respect of the full termly payment, the balance of which alone is currently being paid.[58]

---

[45] *Duncan* v. *River Clyde Trs.* (1851) 13 D. 518; aff. (1853) 25 Sc.Jur. 331.
[46] *Nicoll* v. *Reid* (1878) 6 R. 216.
[47] *Donaldson* v. *Kennedy* (1833) 11 S. 740.
[48] Income and Corporation Taxes Act 1988, s.348. The effect of the section (and of s.349) is restricted by s.347A (ins. by Finance Act 1988, s.36). As to life insurance premiums, see 1988 Act, s.266(5).
[49] 1988 Act, s.351.
[50] *Paton* v. *I.R.C.* [1938] A.C. 341.
[51] *Rhokana Corporation Ltd.* v. *I.R.C.* [1937] 1 K.B. 788.
[52] Income and Corporation Taxes Act 1988, s.348(1)(*b*).
[53] *Butler* v. *Butler* [1961] P. 33.
[54] *David Allen & Sons Billposting Ltd.* v. *Bruce*, 1933 S.C. 253.
[55] *Agnew* v. *Ferguson* (1903) 5 F. 879.
[56] *Galashiels Provident Building Society* v. *Newlands* (1893) 20 R. 821.
[57] *Rowan's Trs.* v. *Rowan*, 1940 S.C. 30.
[58] *Fletcher* v. *Young*, 1936 S.L.T. 572.

Deduction must be made from certain payments not made wholly out of profits or gains already taxed.[59] The relevant payments are (1), (2) and (3) mentioned at the beginning of this section, and: yearly interest paid (a) by a company or local authority, otherwise than in a fiduciary or representative capacity, (b) by a partnership of which a company is a member, (c) by any person to another person whose usual place of abode is outside the UK but there is an exception of bank interest and some other types of payment. Deduction is made at the basic rate in force at the time of the payment. A certificate of deduction of tax must be provided on request. It is implied that the payee must allow the deduction and treat the payer as acquitted of liability in respect of the amount deducted.[60] The payer must account for the tax to the Revenue.

Mortgage interest is paid under deduction of tax.[61]

Any provision, written or oral, for the payment of interest "less tax" or using words to that effect, is to be construed, in relation to interest payable without deduction of tax, as if the words were not included.[62]

It is a question of construction whether a deed directs payment of a sum without deduction of tax. A reference to "all deductions" may not suffice.[63] It is also a question of construction whether the direction covers higher rates of income tax.[64]

If the clause is effectual, and the payment is one from which the payer is obliged by law to deduct tax, the result is to increase the sum payable and the amount of tax deducted.

Every agreement for payment of interest, rent or other annual payment in full without allowing for the authorised deduction is void.[65] A promissory note is an "agreement"[66] but the provision clearly does not apply to payments made under a will or an order of court.[67] The provision does not avoid an agreement to pay a sum "free of tax"; such an agreement is construed as an obligation to pay, in addition to the stated sum, any tax becoming due by reason of the payments being made.[68] It does not affect an agreement between a trust beneficiary and another party whereby the trustees are directed to pay to the other party a fraction of the income due to the beneficiary after deduction of tax coupled with a stipulation that the sum paid shall not fall below a certain amount.[69] An obligation to make such an annual payment that, after deduction of tax, a certain sum of money will be available is not void.[70] An obligation by A to pay B's tax on the whole or a portion of his income is not struck at.[71]

Special statutory provisions alter the effect of wills taking effect, and

---

[59] Income and Corporation Taxes Act 1988, s.349. But see n. 48, *supra*.
[60] *Allchin* v. *South Shields Corporation* [1943] 25 T.C. 445, *per* Viscount Simon at p. 461.
[61] Income and Corporation Taxes Act 1988, s.369.
[62] 1988 Act, s.818.
[63] *Belk* v. *Best* [1942] 1 Ch. 77.
[64] See, *e.g. Prentice's Trs.* v. *Prentice*, 1935 S.C. 211.
[65] Taxes Management Act 1970, s.106(2).
[66] *C.I.R.* v. *Hartley* (1956) 36 T.C. 348.
[67] *Spilsbury* v. *Spofforth* (1937) 21 T.C. 247.
[68] *Inland Revenue* v. *Ferguson*, 1969 S.C. (H.L.) 103.
[69] *Brooke* v. *Price* [1917] A.C. 115.
[70] *Booth* v. *Booth* [1922] 1 K.B. 66; *Noel* v. *Trust and Agency Co. of Australasia Ltd.* [1937] 1 Ch. 438.
[71] *Hutchison* v. *C.I.R.*, 1930 S.C. 293.

instruments made on or after September 3, 1939 which provided for payments free of income tax.[72] Payment of a stated amount free of income tax other than surtax is taken to be payment of a stated amount free of income tax other than such as exceeds the amount to which the payee would be liable if all income tax were charged at the basic rate to the exclusion of any higher rate. Payment of an amount which after deduction of income tax at the standard rate is equal to a stated amount is taken to be payment of an amount which after deduction of tax at the basic rate is equal to the stated amount.

Where there is an effectual clause in the normal form the payer is entitled to deduct the gross amount from his total income. The payee has the gross amount added to his total income and may have to pay higher rate tax thereon. On the other hand if he is entitled to reliefs he may be able to recover tax which he can retain. However, in some cases the language of the cause may be susceptible of the interpretation that the sum of £X has to be arrived at not merely by taking into account the basic rate of income tax but also any reliefs which the payee may be able to claim. Under the rule in *Re Pettit*,[73] the payee must claim the relief due from the Revenue and repay it to the payer. It seems that this rule applies in Scotland.[74]

Onus of proof

12.8 As a general rule, once the creditor has proved the constitution of the debt, the onus of proving payment is on the debtor.[75] There are, however, certain circumstances in which there is a presumption of payment.

First of all, certain types of debt are presumed to have been paid. There is a conclusive presumption that counsel's fees have been paid except where there is some special promise or contract.[76] Tavern and hotel bills are presumed to have been paid if the guest has left as this is "a presumption of practical life." The creditor may rebut the presumption *prout de jure*.[77] There was, at one time, a presumption that physician's fees had been paid but this is now of doubtful validity.[78]

Where wages were distributed in envelopes the onus of proving correct payment is on the employer.[79]

Possession of voucher

12.9 *Chirographum apud debitorem repertum praesumitur solutum.* If the written voucher which constitutes the obligation is found in the hands of the debtor (or cautioner[80]), it is presumed that the debt has been paid.[81]

---

[72] Income and Corporation Taxes Act 1988, s.819.
[73] [1922] 2 Ch. 765.
[74] *Hunter's Trs.* v. *Mitchell*, 1930 S.C. 978; *Milne's Trs.*, 1936 S.C. 706. *Cf. Richmond's Trs.* v. *Richmond*, 1935 S.C. 585; *Rowan's Trs.* v. *Rowan*, 1940 S.C. 30. In *Turner's Trs.* v. *Turner*, 1943 S.C. 389, the point was conceded. See also *Inland Revenue* v. *Cook*, 1945 S.C. (H.L.) 52.
[75] Gloag, p. 744.
[76] Bell, *Prin.*, § 568.
[77] *Barnett* v. *Colvill* (1840) 2 D. 337.
[78] *Russell* v. *Dunbar* (1717) Mor. 11419; *Sanders* v. *Hewat* (1822) 1 S. 333; Gloag, p. 718.
[79] *Robertson* v. *Bent Colliery Co. Ltd.* (1919) 35 Sh.Ct.Rep. 290.
[80] *Gordon* v. *Johnston's Heirs* (1703) Mor. 11408.
[81] Ersk., III, iv, 5.

Mode of Proof

This applies to heritable bonds[82] as well as other obligations but not to bilateral deeds.[83] The creditor can prove *prout de jure* that the voucher reached the debtor's possession otherwise than by payment, *e.g.* by force or fraud or without the creditor's consent.[84] An averment that the document was returned to the debtor for a special purpose without abandonment of the creditor's right must be proved by writ or oath.[85]

Apocha trium annorum

If three consecutive discharges of periodical payments—rent, interest, feuduties or salaries, for example—are produced, payment of all preceding is presumed.[86] The presumption can be rebutted by parole evidence.[87] The presumption does not apply where there have been three consecutive payments but no discharge in writing[88]; nor where one discharge has been granted for three consecutive payments[89]; nor where arrears have been constituted by bill or bond even although there are three consecutive discharges for subsequent terms[90]; nor where two discharges have been granted unknown to the heir, by an ancestor and a third by the heir[91]; nor where the receipts are for hire and the claim is for overtime charges.[92] The position where the discharges have been granted by a factor is doubtful.[93]

12.10

Mode of proof

Parole proof of payment is competent in a ready-money transaction— "where payment of the price is the counterpart and the immediate counterpart of the delivery at the same time of the subject sold."[94] A short time may elapse between delivery and payment but they must be *unico contextu*. But even where the transaction on credit is verbal, and even where the sum involved is under £100 Scots, a payment made under an antecedent obligation is in general provable only by the writ or oath of the creditor.[95]

There are, however, certain exceptional cases where payment under an antecedent obligation can be proved by parole evidence. There must be "a state of facts, capable of being proved by parole evidence, which is

12.11

---

[82] *Rollo* v. *Simpson* (1710) Mor. 11411.
[83] *Stewart* v. *Riddoch* (1677) Mor. 11406.
[84] *Edward* v. *Fyfe* (1823) 2 S. 431; *Knox* v. *Crawford* (1862) 24 D. 1088; *per* L. P. Inglis, *Henry* v. *Miller* (1884) 11 R. 713 at 717.
[85] Dickson, *Evidence*, § 933.
[86] Stair, I, xviii, 2; Ersk., III, iv, 10.
[87] *per* Lord Kincairney (Ordinary), *Cameron* v. *Panton's Trs.* (1891) 18 R. 728 at 729; *Stenhouse* v. *Stenhouse's Trs.* (1899) 6 S.L.T. 368.
[88] *Moriston* v. *Tenants of Eastnisbet* (1631) Mor. 11394.
[89] Ersk., III, iv, 10; Dickson, *Evidence*, § 177.
[90] *Patrick* v. *Watt* (1859) 21 D. 637.
[91] *Gray* v. *Reid* (1699) Mor. 11399.
[92] *Star Motor Express Co.* v. *Booth Ltd.* (1930) 46 Sh.Ct.Rep. 239.
[93] Dickson, *Evidence*, § 180; *Preston* v. *Scot* (1667) Mor. 11397; *Earl of Marshall* v. *Fraser* (1682) Mor. 11399; *Grant* v. *Maclean* (1757) Mor. 11402.
[94] *Shaw* v. *Wright* (1877) 5 R. 245, *per* Lord Gifford at p. 247.
[95] *Burt* v. *Laing*, 1925 S.C. 181; *Hope Brothers* v. *Morrison*, 1960 S.L.T. 80. As to reference to a manager's oath, see *Craig & Rose Ltd.* v. *Lamarra*, 1975 S.C. 316.

inconsistent with the continued subsistence of the debt."[96] It has also been said that there must be proof of "some transaction or settlement between the creditor and the debtor subsequent to the contraction of the debt which necessarily leads to the conclusion that the debt was discharged,"[97] but in a later case[98] it was held that a transaction was not indispensable. Mere lapse of time,[99] or the absence of correspondence about the debt,[1] is not *per se* sufficient.

Part payment can be inferred from an account rendered by the creditor to the debtor.[2]

Receipts—execution

12.12   A debt constituted by a probative document requires a probative receipt to discharge it.[3] Otherwise, the general rule is that a receipt need not be probative.[4] In particular, a receipt for rent,[5] a receipt *in re mercatoria*,[5] a receipt for a legacy,[6] and a discharge of a claim for damages[7] need not be probative. The onus of proof of authenticity is, of course, in such cases on the person founding on the document.[7]

A receipt does not now require a stamp.[8]

Construction of discharge

12.13   Where the discharge bears to be in respect of specified debts it will not cover by implication other debts due to the grantor which are not specified.[9] Where a bond and disposition in security had been granted in favour of a building society and was subsequently discharged, the discharge did not affect a liability under the society's rules to pay interest on arrears of interest due under the bond.[10] Where specified debts are followed by a general discharge the latter covers only debts of the same kind as those specified.[11] A general discharge covers all debts due at its date even although the term of payment has not arrived[12] but it does not cover debts of an uncommon kind which were not in the contemplation of the parties,[13] *e.g.* a cautioner's right of relief against the principal debtor where no payment has been made by the cautioner at the date of the

---

[96] *per* Lord McLaren, *Chrystal* v. *Chrystal* (1900) 2 F. 373 at 379; see also *Mackie* v. *Watson* (1837) 16 S. 73; *Ryrie* v. *Ryrie* (1840) 2 D. 1210; *Mitchell* v. *Berwick* (1845) 7 D. 382; *Spence* v. *Paterson's Trs.* (1873) 1 R. 46; *Neilson's Trs.* v. *Neilson's Trs.* (1883) 11 R. 119; *British Bata Shoe Co. Ltd.* v. *Double M. Shah Ltd.*, 1981 S.L.T. (Notes) 5.
[97] *per* Lord Moncreiff, *Thiem's Trs.* v. *Collie* (1899) 1 F. 764 at 780.
[98] *McKenzie's Exrx.* v. *Morrison's Trs.*, 1930 S.C. 830.
[99] *Thiem's Trs.* v. *Collie, supra.*
[1] *Patrick* v. *Watt* (1859) 21 D. 637.
[2] *Stewart & Taylor* v. *Grimson* (1904) 20 Sh.Ct.Rep. 166.
[3] *per* L.J.-C. Aitchison, *Davies* v. *Hunter*, 1934 S.C. 10 at 15.
[4] Bell, *Prin.*, § 565; *Encyclopaedia of the Laws of Scotland*, Vol. V., p. 587.
[5] Bell, *Prin.*, § 565.
[6] *McLaren* v. *Howie* (1869) 8 M. 106.
[7] *Davies* v. *Hunter, supra.*
[8] Finance Act 1970, Sched. 7, para. 2.
[9] *Marquis of Tweeddale* v. *Hume* (1848) 10 D. 1053.
[10] *Galashiels Provident Building Society* v. *Newlands* (1893) 20 R. 821.
[11] Stair, IV, xl, 34; Ersk., III, iv, 9; Bell, *Prin.*, § 583; *Talbot* v. *Guydet* (1705) Mor. 5027.
[12] *Adam* v. *Macdougall* (1831) 9 S. 570; *British Linen Co.* v. *Esplin* (1849) 11 D. 1104.
[13] Stair, I, xviii, 2; Ersk., III, iv, 9; Bell, *Prin.*, § 584; *Wood* v. *Gordon* (1695) Mor. 5035.

discharge.[14] Similarly, if the grantor of the discharge was unaware of the existence of a debt it is not affected.[15] A general discharge does not include a debt which has been assigned by the grantor before the date of the discharge but has not yet been intimated to the debtor.[16]

Although it has been said that in construing a discharge the court must look only at the instrument and not at extrinsic evidence,[17] it seems that parole evidence is admissible to show what was in the contemplation of the parties at the time the instrument was granted.[18]

A compromise made by the creditor as a result of an *error calculi* when he had the means of knowing the true facts cannot be rectified.[19]

A discharge on composition with an expressed understanding that the debtor would pay the balance when he was able to do so has been held to discharge the debt completely, the qualification being merely an obligation of honour.[20]

An agreement between an insolvent debtor and some of his creditors by which they bind themselves not to sue for their debts if they receive payment by instalments may be reducible at the instance of another creditor as a fraudulent preference but it is not a *pactum illicitum* and is binding on the creditors who are parties to it.[21]

Eliding receipt

If a receipt is in possession of the debtor, proof that the debt was not in fact paid is competent only by the debtor's writ or oath.[22] It is, however, competent to prove by parole evidence that the receipt got into the debtor's hands by fraud, error, or accident or was given to the debtor for some special purpose.[23] A bank may prove parole that an entry in a customer's pass-book was made in error.[24]

12.14

Where an account was discharged with the words "paid by cheque" with a date, the creditor could prove only by writ or oath that the cheque was for less than the amount of the account and that there was a balance resting owing; it was suggested that the object of the words was to prevent the discharge being founded on as conclusive if the cheque should be dishonoured.[25]

Between banker and customer, a pay-in slip[26] is *prima facie* evidence of

---

[14] *Campbell* v. *Napier* (1678) Mor. 5035; *Oliphant* v. *Newton* (1682) Mor. 5035; *McTaggart* v. *Jeffrey* (1828) 6 S. 641; revd. (1830) 4 W. & S. 361; see also *Dickson's Trs.* v. *Dickson's Trs.*, 1930 S.L.T. 226—discharge by legatee did not cover later claim arising as heir *in mobilibus*.

[15] *Greenock Banking Co.* v. *Smith* (1844) 6 D. 1340; *Dickson* v. *Halbert* (1854) 16 D. 586; *Purdon* v. *Rowat's Trs.* (1856) 19 D. 206.

[16] *Lady Logan* v. *Affleck* (1736) Mor. 5041.

[17] *per* Lord Wynford, *McTaggart* v. *Jeffrey*, *supra*, at p. 367.

[18] *McAdam* v. *Scott* (1912) 50 S.L.R. 264 (here the discharge was ambiguous).

[19] *Belhaven Engineering & Motors Ltd.* v. *Reid* (1910) 26 Sh.Ct.Rep. 234.

[20] *Ritchie* v. *Cowan & Kinghorn* (1901) 3 F. 1071; *Rankin* v. *Milne* (1916) 32 Sh.Ct.Rep. 109.

[21] *Munro* v. *Rothfield*, 1920 S.C. 118.

[22] *Macfarlane* v. *Watt* (1828) 6 S. 556; *Gordon* v. *Trotter* (1833) 11 S. 696; *Anderson* v. *Forth Marine Insurance Co.* (1845) 7 D. 268; *cf. Crawford* v. *Bennet* (1827) 2 W. & S. 608.

[23] *Smith* v. *Kerr* (1869) 7 M. 863; *Henry* v. *Miller* (1884) 11 R. 713.

[24] *Commercial Bank of Scotland* v. *Rhind* (1860) 3 Macq. 643.

[25] *Kelly & Co.* v. *Rae* (1909) 25 Sh.Ct.Rep. 3.

[26] *Docherty* v. *Royal Bank*, 1962 S.L.T. (Notes) 102.

156 Payment

payment and, similarly, a bank passbook[27] which passes between banker and customer is *prima facie* evidence against the banker. On the other hand, if the customer has in writing acknowledged that the balance at credit of his account is correct he is barred from subsequently impugning it because the account has become a fitted or settled account which is probative.[28]

It may be, however, that the rigour of that rule is confined to the banker-customer relationship and whether the admission results in more than a shift in the onus of proof depends on the degree of formality with which approval is given.

Generally where parties have agreed by signing or docqueting an account as to the position between them the account is known as a fitted or settled account to be distinguished from an open account.[29] Such an account raises a presumption that there has been a final settlement between the parties; it is still possible to dispute the accuracy of the account but there is a heavy onus on the challenger.[30]

Lost receipt

12.15 It seems possible to prove payment by parole evidence to the effect that the receipt has been lost. This was allowed where a passbook vouching receipt had been lost by the creditor[31]; where a receipt had been lost by the debtor[32]; and where a letter acknowledging repayment of a loan had been lost.[33]

Cheques

12.16 Prior to 1957, it was established that a cheque indorsed by the payee was evidence of receipt by him of the amount of the cheque.[34] Section 1 of the Cheques Act 1957 rendered indorsement by the payee unnecessary and, in consequence, section 3 of the Act provided that: "An unindorsed cheque which appears to have been paid by the banker on whom it is drawn is evidence of the receipt by the payee of the sum payable by the cheque." This section sets up only a *prima facie* presumption and it has been said that the unindorsed cheque does not appear to be as cogent evidence as a cheque indorsed by the payee.[35]

---

[27] *Commercial Bank* v. *Rhind* (1860) 3 Macq. 643; *Couper's Trs.* v. *National Bank* (1889) 16 R. 412.

[28] *Connochie* v. *British Linen Bank* (1943) 59 Sh.Ct.Rep. 44, in which the opinion of Lord Carmont in *Dickson* v. *Clydesdale Bank*, Dec. 18, 1936, unreported, is quoted and followed. See also *British Linen Co.* v. *Thomson* (1853) 15 D. 314.

[29] *Commercial Bank* v. *Rhind* (1860) 3 Macq. 643, *per* Lord Campbell L.C. at p. 650.

[30] *Laing* v. *Laing* (1862) 24 D. 1362; *Struthers* v. *Smith*, 1913 S.C. 1116.

[31] *Young* v. *Thomson*, 1909 S.C. 529.

[32] *James Scott & Co. (Electrical Engineers) Ltd.* v. *McIntosh* (1960) 76 Sh.Ct.Rep. 26 (this goes further than *Young* in that there was no course of dealing between the parties).

[33] *Simpson's Trs.* v. *Simpson*, 1933 S.N. 22.

[34] *Haldane* v. *Speirs* (1872) 10 M. 537.

[35] *Westminster Bank Ltd.* v. *Zang* [1966] A.C. 182.

CHAPTER 13

COMPENSATION AND RETENTION

"Set-off"[1]

The question now to be considered is, in general terms, whether a debt due by the pursuer to the defender can be set off against the pursuer's claim for a debt due to him by the defender. The preliminary question is whether there are in fact two separate debts or whether there are merely two items in a running account in which case the question of set-off disappears and the balance on the account is the only debt due. A running account or account-current is one in which the intention of the parties was that the transactions should be set down on different sides of the account against each other and a balance struck at the end with periodical settlements.[2]

13.1

If there are two separate debts there arise two distinct questions which are often confused. The first is: in an action for debt is it a relevant defence to plead that a debt is due by the pursuer to the defender? The second is: in an action for debt, what types of debt can form the basis of a counterclaim by the defender? The answers to these questions are not necessarily the same because a debt due by the pursuer to the defender may be the basis of a counterclaim even although it is not a relevant defence; the pursuer will be granted decree for the full amount of his claim but the counterclaim may be allowed to continue as a substantive action.

The answer to the first question is that the debt is a relevant defence only in circumstances where the doctrines of compensation, balancing of accounts in bankruptcy or retention operate.

Compensation under the Act 1592, c. 143 operates where both debts are liquid and certain other conditions are fulfilled; retention operates where both debts, liquid or illiquid, arise out of the same contract; balancing of accounts in bankruptcy operates where the creditor or debtor in the liquid claim is bankrupt. If one of these doctrines is applicable the pursuer's claim is extinguished or reduced *pro tanto*. If none of these doctrines is applicable the existence of the defender's claim is no defence and is no bar to the pursuer's obtaining decree for his claim because it is clearly established that in general an illiquid claim is not an answer to a liquid claim.[3] As has already been indicated, however, this does not necessarily mean that the debt due to the defender cannot form the basis of a counterclaim.

Competent counterclaims

It is hardly necessary to say that a counterclaim will lie only where an

13.2

---

[1] "Set-off" is used as a convenient neutral term. It is not a term of art in Scots law: *Laing* v. *Lord Advocate*, 1973 S.L.T. (Notes) 81.
[2] *McKinlay* v. *Wilson* (1885) 13 R. 210.
[3] *per* Lord Cranworth L.C., *National Exchange Co.* v. *Drew* (1855) 2 Macq. 103 at p. 122; *Scottish N.E. Ry. Co.* v. *Napier* (1859) 21 D. 700; *Burt* v. *Bell* (1861) 24 D. 13; *Mackie* v. *Riddell* (1874) 2 R. 115; *Armour & Melvin* v. *Mitchell*, 1934 S.C. 94.

independent action could be brought—"a counterclaim is a sword, whereas compensation is only a shield, and the right to defend one's self with the latter does not imply the right to wield the former."[4]

In the Court of Session, in terms of rule 84, the defender may counterclaim in respect of "any matter forming part of, or arising out of the grounds of, the pursuer's action, or the decision of which is necessary for the determination of the question in controversy between the parties, or which, if the pursuer had been a person not otherwise subject to the jurisdiction of the court, might competently have formed the subject of an action against such pursuer in which jurisdiction would have arisen *ex reconventione*; provided that, in any case, the counterclaim is such as might have formed matter of a separate action, and that, if such separate action had been raised, it would not have been necessary to call as defender thereto any person other than the pursuer." It has been held that the connection between the principal claim and the counterclaim can be of a tenuous nature; if both are liquid, or both illiquid, they can be heard together.[5] Where the counterclaim is for damages and arises out of the same course of dealing as the pursuer's claim, but not out of the same contract, and thus cannot be set off against the pursuer's claim, the pursuer can be granted interim decree *de plano* for the amount of his claim and the defenders can then be allowed to proceed with the counterclaim as if it was an independent claim.[6]

In the sheriff court,[7] a defender may lodge a counterclaim and the sheriff may deal with it as if it had been stated in a substantive cause and may grant decree for it in whole or in part, or for the difference between it and the sum claimed. A restrictive view was taken of an earlier form of this rule and it was thought that only items which could be set off against the pursuer's claim could found a counterclaim.[8] It was eventually established that a claim which could not be set off could form a counterclaim.[9] It is thought that the position is the same under the current form of the rule.[10] If the pursuer's claim is admitted, the pursuer is given interim decree for its amount together with expenses[11] and the counterclaim may proceed as an independent substantive action. The court, however, probably has a discretionary power to prevent a counterclaim quite unconnected with the pursuer's claim proceeding.[12]

If the pursuer's claim has to go to proof, the counterclaim falls to be dismissed.[12] If the pursuer's action is abandoned or dismissed as irrelevant the counterclaim can proceed.[13] It has been suggested that in

---

[4] *J. E. Binstock Miller & Co.* v. *E. Coia & Co. Ltd.* (1957) 73 Sh.Ct.Rep. 178.

[5] *Mackenzie* v. *Macleod's Exr.*, 1988 S.L.T. 207.

[6] *Scott* v. *Aitken*, 1950 S.L.T. (Notes) 34; *Fulton Clyde Ltd.* v. *J. F. McCallum & Co. Ltd.*, 1960 S.C. 78.

[7] O.C.R. 51, 54; Summ. C.R. 21.

[8] *Christie* v. *Birrells*, 1910 S.C. 986; *Fingland & Mitchell* v. *Howie*, 1926 S.C. 319.

[9] *Armour & Melvin* v. *Mitchell*, 1934 S.C. 94.

[10] *Bank of Scotland* v. *Baird* (Sh.Ct.), 1987 S.C.L.R. 18; Macphail, *Sheriff Court Practice*, pp. 402–406.

[11] *Grant* v. *McAlister* (1948) 64 Sh.Ct.Rep. 261.

[12] *Croall & Croall* v. *Sharp* (1954) 70 Sh.Ct.Rep. 129; *James Allan & Sons (Contractors) Ltd.* v. *Gourlay*, 1956 S.L.T. (Sh.Ct.) 77.

[13] *Feld British Agencies Ltd.* v. *Jas. Pringle Ltd.*, 1961 S.L.T. 123.

some circumstances the defender could obtain decree before judgment is issued on the pursuer's claim.[14]

In the summary cause procedure, it is probably competent to counterclaim for a sum in excess of the summary cause limit.[15]

Compensation

The Compensation Act 1592, provides: "that any debt *de liquido in liquidum*, instantly verified by writ, or oath of party, before the giving of decree, be admitted by all judges within this realm by way of exception, but not after the giving thereof in the suspension, or in reduction of the same decree." The conditions for the operation of compensation are: (1) the debts must be of the same kind, (2) the debts must both be due and liquid, (3) there must be *concursus debiti et crediti*, (4) it must be pleaded before decree.[16]

Concursus debiti et crediti

Each party must be debtor and creditor in the same capacity. A sum due to the defender as an executor cannot be compensated against a sum due by him personally,[17] unless, perhaps, where he is also the sole beneficiary of the executry estate.[18] Although a tutor who is sued on a bond granted by himself *qua* tutor can set off a debt due to the pupil,[19] he cannot set off a debt due to the pupil against a debt due by him personally.[20]

Where A, acting as agent for C, contracts with B, the agency being disclosed, then A cannot set off a sum due under the contract by B to C against a debt due by him as an individual to B.[21] Similarly B cannot set off a debt due to him by A against the amount due to C under the contract.[22] It seems, however, that B can set off a sum due to him and collected by A as agent for C against his debt to C.[23] C can obviously set off an amount due by B to A as agent against a debt due by him to B and this holds even in *del credere* agency.[24]

Where the existence of the agency is revealed but the principal's name is undisclosed, B nevertheless cannot set off sums due to him by A against sums due by him to C under the contract.[25] Where the agency is not disclosed, however, B is entitled to set off A's debt to him against the amount due to C.[26]

An executor is *eadem persona cum defuncto* and a creditor of the deceased may plead compensation against a debt due by him to the estate

13.3

13.4

---

[14] *per* Lord Skerrington, *British Motor Body Co. Ltd.* v. *Thomas Shaw (Dundee) Ltd.*, 1914 S.C. 922 at 930.
[15] Macphail, *op. cit.*, p. 832.
[16] Bell, *Prin.*, § 575.
[17] *Stuart* v. *Stuart* (1869) 7 M. 366.
[18] *per* L. P. Inglis, *Stuart* v. *Stuart*, *supra*, at 367; Bell, *Comm.*, II, 125.
[19] *Earl of Northesk* v. *Gairn's Tutor* (1670) Mor. 2569.
[20] *Elliot* v. *Elliots* (1711) Mor. 2658.
[21] *Ferguson* v. *Muir* (1711) Mor. 2659.
[22] *Liddell Brownlie & Co.* v. *Andrew Young & Son* (1852) 14 D. 647.
[23] *Macgregor's Tr.* v. *Cox* (1883) 10 R. 1028.
[24] *Ferrier* v. *British Linen Co.*, Nov. 20, 1807, F.C.
[25] *Lavaggi* v. *Pirie & Sons* (1872) 10 M. 312; *Matthews* v. *Auld & Guild* (1874) 1 R. 1224; *National Bank of Scotland* v. *Dickie's Tr.* (1895) 22 R. 740.
[26] *Gall* v. *Murdoch* (1821) 1 S. 77.

which resulted from a transaction with the executor after the death.[27] An heir who was sued for his ancestor's debt could plead compensation on a debt due by the creditor to the deceased even although the debt was moveable and would fall to the executor.[28] A beneficiary cannot set off a debt due to the trustees against a debt due by her personally.[29]

In bankruptcy, the *concursus* must have existed prior to the date of sequestration. A debtor of the bankrupt cannot plead compensation against the trustee on a debt due by the bankrupt which was acquired by assignation after the date of sequestration.[30] A creditor of the bankrupt cannot plead compensation against a debt due to the trustee which arose after sequestration.[31] A person who is both creditor of, and debtor to, the bankrupt prior to sequestration can interdict the trustee from endorsing to a third party the bill due by him.[32] The same principles apply where a trust deed for creditors has been executed and also in liquidations.[33] It is not permissible to set off a claim in respect of breach of contract by the company against a sum payable in respect of a contract carried out by the liquidator.[34] However, when the liquidator has re-engaged employees of the company, any redundancy payments subsequently due to them in respect of periods of employment prior to liquidation can be set off by the Secretary of State against sums due by him to the liquidator.[35]

A sum due to one of several co-obligants by the creditor can be set off against the debt for which the co-obligants are liable.[36] But it is not possible to compensate a debt due by one of several co-creditors against the debt due to the co-creditors jointly and severally.[37] Where a deposit receipt was payable to either A or B or the survivor, it was held that the bank could not set off a debt due to it by A against a demand for payment by B.[38]

A bank can set off one account against another of the same customer but not if one is a fiduciary account.[39]

Liquidity

13.5 The debt used to compensate must be liquid in the sense that it is certain in amount, presently payable and not disputed. A claim cannot be used as a ground of compensation if it is future or contingent[40]; if it is an

---

[27] *Mitchell* v. *Mackersy* (1905) 8 F. 198 (overruling *Gray's Trs.* v. *Royal Bank of Scotland* (1895) 23 R. 199).
[28] *Hay* v. *Crawford* (1712) Mor. 2571; *Middleton* v. *Earl of Strathmore* (1743) Mor. 2573.
[29] *Johnston* v. *Johnston* (1875) 2 R. 986.
[30] *Cauvin* v. *Robertson* (1783) Mor. 2581.
[31] *Mill* v. *Paul* (1825) 4 S. 219.
[32] *Harvey Brand & Co.* v. *Buchanan Hamilton & Co.'s Tr.* (1886) 4 M. 1128.
[33] *Meldrum's Trs.* v. *Clark* (1826) 5 S.122; *Mill* v. *Paul, supra*.
[34] *Asphaltic Limestone Co.* v. *Corporation of Glasgow*, 1907 S.C. 463. But see para. 13.10.
[35] *Smith* v. *Lord Advocate*, 1978 S.C. 259.
[36] *Dobson* v. *Christie* (1835) 13 S. 582. As to compensation in partnership, see para. 30.12.
[37] *Burrell* v. *Burrell's Trs.*, 1916 S.C. 729.
[38] *Anderson* v. *North of Scotland Bank Ltd.* (1901) 4 F. 49.
[39] *Kirkwood & Sons* v. *Clydesdale Bank Ltd.*, 1908 S.C. 20; *United Rentals Ltd.* v. *Clydesdale and North of Scotland Bank* (1963) 79 Sh.Ct.Rep. 118.
[40] *Paul & Thain* v. *Royal Bank* (1869) 7 M. 361.

unquantified claim for damages[41]; if it requires investigation and proof[42], or if it requires something in the nature of an accounting to expiscate it.[43] But the rule *de liquido in liquidum* is to be understood *cum aliquo temperamento* and, in accordance with the brocard *quod statim liquidari potest, pro jam liquido habetur*,[44] the court has a discretion to allow an illiquid counterclaim to be admitted if it can be ascertained almost immediately,[45] or is in the fair course of being made liquid,[46] or if it can be instantly verified by reference to the pursuer's oath,[47] or if it is equitable to admit it in the circumstances.[48] It seems that an illiquid claim is also admitted where the pursuer is *vergens ad inopiam*.[49]

Operation

Compensation does not operate *ipso facto*; it must be pleaded and sustained.[50] The mere fact that the two debts existed at the same time does not extinguish them. Nor is the statement of the plea sufficient; it must be sustained.[51] Compensation is "the operation of the judge rather than of the law."[52] So, a debt which has been extinguished by prescription cannot be pleaded to compensate a debt which has not prescribed even although an action for its recovery during the prescriptive period would have been met by a plea of compensation founded on the other debt.[53] The same result followed in the case of the triennial[54] and quinquennial[55] prescriptions but there it was possible to refer the prescribed debt instantly to the debtor's oath.[56] Other consequences of the general principle are that the party pleading compensation may abandon the plea before decree, substitute another defence and use his claim for some other purpose[57]; where the defender is creditor in several debts he may

13.6

---

[41] *National Exchange Co. v. Drew* (1855) 2 Macq. 103; *Scottish North Eastern Ry. Co. v. Napier* (1859) 21 D. 700; *Mackie v. Riddell* (1874) 2 R. 115.

[42] *Logan v. Stephen* (1850) 13 D. 262; *Drew v. Drew* (1855) 17 D. 559; *Urie v. Lumsden* (1859) 22 D. 38; *Kerr v. Fife & Kinross Ry. Co.* (1860) 22 D. 564; *Munro v. Graham* (1857) 20 D. 72; *Macgregor v. City of Glasgow Bank* (1865) 3 M. 896.

[43] *Lawson v. Drysdale* (1844) 7 D. 153; *McIntyre v. Macdonald* (1854) 16 D. 485; *Blair Iron Co. v. Alison* (1855) 18 D. (H.L.) 49; 6 W. & S. 56.

[44] Ersk., III, iv, 16; *Seton* (1683) Mor. 2566; *Brown v. Elies* (1686) Mor. 2566.

[45] *Logan v. Stephen* (1850) 13 D. 262, per Lord Cuninghame at p. 267; *Henderson & Co. Ltd. v. Turnbull & Co.*, 1909 S.C. 510. *Cf. Niven v. Clyde Fasteners Ltd.*, 1986 S.L.T. 344.

[46] *Munro v. Macdonald's Exrs.* (1866) 4 M. 687.

[47] *Stuart v. Stuart* (1869) 7 M. 366; *Ross v. Magistrates of Tayne* (1711) Mor. 2568.

[48] *Ross v. Ross* (1895) 22 R. 461; *G. & A. Kirkpatrick v. Kirkpatrick's Exrs.*, 1983 S.L.T. (Sh.Ct.) 3. *Cf. McConnell & Reid v. W. & G. Muir* (1906) 14 S.L.T. 79.

[49] *Sim v. Lundy & Blanshard* (1868) 41 J. 136; *Paul & Thain v. Royal Bank* (1869) 7 M. 361.

[50] Ersk., III, iv, 12; Bell, *Comm.*, II, 124; Bell, *Prin.*, § 575; *National Westminster Bank v. Halesowen Presswork* [1972] A.C. 785, per Lord Kilbrandon at p. 822.

[51] *Cowan v. Gowans* (1878) 5 R. 581 (this case is relevant to the principle of balancing accounts in bankruptcy rather than compensation; it creates an exception to that principle because of the special position of a shareholder in relation to calls).

[52] Ersk., III, iv, 12.

[53] *Carmichael v. Carmichael* (1719) Mor. 2677.

[54] *Galloway v. Galloway* (1799) Mor. 11122.

[55] *Baillie v. McIntosh* (1753) Mor. 2680.

[56] *Miller v. Baird*, 1819 Hume 480; Bell, *Comm.*, II, 123; Bell, *Prin.*, § 574.

[57] *Lord Balmerino v. Dick's Crs.* (1664) Mor. 2681.

choose which he pleases as a ground for compensation[58]; and prescription on the debt founded on is not interrupted till the plea is sustained.[59]

What might appear to be an exception to the rule arises where a debt has been assigned. If *concursus* existed before intimation, the debtor can plead against the assignee compensation on a debt due to him by the cedent.[60]

It is, of course possible for debts to be extinguished by an express agreement to compensate. There must be a specific agreement and probably writing is required.[61]

Where the plea of compensation has been sustained, however, it operates *retro* so that the debts are extinguished from the start of the *concursus* and interest on them is also extinguished from that time.[62] Liquifaction is also drawn back to the date of *concursus* so that if one debt was illiquid at the time of concourse but was liquified before the action was raised both debts are extinguished from the date of concourse.[63]

Pleaded before decree

13.7　In terms of the Compensation Act 1592, compensation must be pleaded before decree; it cannot be used in a suspension.[64] So a debt due by the pursuer which is acquired by the defender after decree cannot be used as a ground of compensation.[65] The rule applies even where the decree is given in absence[66] but exceptions are allowed where the creditor is bankrupt,[67] where there were several debtors,[68] and where the decree is null.[69] An award of expenses is outwith the general rule because the plea cannot be taken against it prior to decree.[70] The principle does not apply where the plea has been proponed and wrongfully repelled.[71]

Exceptions

13.8　Compensation cannot be pleaded against certain debts:
(a) where the money was a deposit.[72]
(b) where money has been paid to someone to be used for a specific purpose and that purpose fails, compensation cannot be pleaded against a claim for repayment.[73]

---

[58] *Maxwell* v. *McCulloch's Trs.* (1738) Mor. 2550.

[59] *Sloan* v. *Birtwhistle* (1827) 5 S. 742.

[60] *Shiells* v. *Ferguson, Davidson & Co.* (1876) 4 R. 250; see the argument in *Carmichael* v. *Carmichael, supra*, and Hume, *Lectures*, III, pp. 43–44.

[61] *Cowan* v. *Shaw* (1878) 5 R. 680.

[62] *Cleland* v. *Stevenson* (1669) Mor. 2682.

[63] *Inch* v. *Lee* (1903) 11 S.L.T. 374.

[64] Erskine, III, iv, 19; *Paterson's Crs.* v. *McAulay* (1742) Mor. 2646; *Naismith* v. *Bowman* (1710) Mor. 2645.

[65] *Anderson* v. *Schaw* (1739) Mor. 2646.

[66] *Cuninghame Stevenson & Co.* v. *Wilson*, Jan. 17, 1809, F.C.

[67] *Barclay* v. *Clerk* (1683) Mor. 2641.

[68] *Corbet* v. *Hamilton* (1707) Mor. 2642; *A.* v. *B.* (1747) Mor. 2648.

[69] *Wright* v. *Sheill* (1676) Mor. 2640.

[70] *Fowler* v. *Brown*, 1916 S.C. 597. See also *Masco Cabinet Co. Ltd.* v. *Martin*, 1912 S.C. 896; *Galloway* v. *MacKinnon* (1936) 52 Sh.Ct.Rep. 135.

[71] Erskine, III, iv, 19.

[72] Stair, I, xiii, 8; Ersk., III, iv, 17; Bell, *Prin.*, § 574; *McGregor* v. *Alley & McLellan* (1887) 14 R. 535; *Mycroft, Petr.*, 1983 S.L.T. 342.

[73] *Middlemas* v. *Gibson*, 1910 S.C. 577; *Mycroft, Petr., supra*.

(c) compensation is not pleadable against a demand for alimentary payments but arrears of an alimentary fund are not protected.[74]

(d) it is not competent to take a set-off or counterclaim in any proceedings by the Crown without leave of the court if the subject-matter of the counterclaim does not relate to the Government department on whose behalf the proceedings are brought. Similarly, the Crown in any proceedings against a Government department cannot without leave of the court take a set-off or counterclaim if the subject-matter thereof does not relate to that department. A set-off or counterclaim cannot be taken in any proceedings by the Crown for recovery of taxes, duties or penalties and a subject cannot found a set-off or counterclaim on a claim for repayment of such sums.[75]

(e) in a liquidation, a contributory cannot set-off amounts due by the company to him against calls unless all the creditors have been paid in full.[76]

(f) a bank or building society at which a solicitor keeps a special account for client's money cannot, in respect of any liability of the solicitor to the bank or building society (not being a liability in connection with that account) have or obtain any recourse or right, "whether by way of set-off, counterclaim, charge or, otherwise, against money standing to the credit of that account."[77]

(g) where the debt is due under a contract the terms of which exclude set-off against the debt.[78]

Retention

The principle of retention is that "in cases of mutual contract a party in defence is entitled to plead and maintain claims in reduction or extinction of a sum due under his obligation where such claims arise from the failure of the pursuer to fulfil his part of the contract."[79] This is an aspect of the wider principle that "one party to a mutual contract, in which there are mutual stipulations, cannot insist on having his claim under the contract satisfied, unless he is prepared to satisfy the corresponding and contemporaneous claims of the other party to the contract."[80] Thus, a claim for freight can be met with a claim for damages for defective carriage[81]; and the rule has been applied to contracts of sale,[82] storage,[83] and service[84] and

13.9

---

[74] *Reid* v. *Bell* (1884) 12 R. 178; *Drew* v. *Drew* (1870) 9 M. 163.

[75] Crown Proceedings Act 1947, s.50; as to the granting of leave see *Atlantic Engine Co. (1920) Ltd.* v. *Lord Advocate*, 1955 S.L.T. 17; *Smith* v. *L.A.*, 1980 S.C. 227. The rules apply to balancing of accounts in bankruptcy: *Laing* v. *L.A.*, 1973 S.L.T. (Notes) 81.

[76] *Re Whitehouse & Co.* (1878) 9 Ch.D. 595; I.A., s.149(3). S.14 of the 1985 Act does not prevent set-off if the company is not in liquidation: *Scottish Fishermen's Organisation Ltd.* v. *McLean*, 1980 S.L.T. (Sh.Ct.) 76.

[77] Solicitors (Scotland) Act 1980, s.61.

[78] *Robert Paterson & Sons Ltd.* v. *Household Supplies Co. Ltd.*, 1975 S.L.T. 98.

[79] per Lord Shand, *Macbride* v. *Hamilton* (1875) 2 R. 775 at 779n., approved by L. P. Strathclyde in *British Motor Body Co. Ltd.* v. *Thomas Shaw (Dundee) Ltd.*, 1914 S.C. 922 at 928.

[80] per Lord Benholme, *Johnston* v. *Robertson* (1861) 23 D. 646 at 652.

[81] *Taylor* v. *Forbes* (1830) 9 S.113; cf. *Henriksens A/S* v. *Rolimpex* [1974] Q.B. 233.

[82] *British Motor Body Co. Ltd.* v. *Thomas Shaw (Dundee) Ltd.*, *supra*; here, of course, there are also sections 11(5) and 53(1) of the Sale of Goods Act 1979.

[83] *Gibson and Stewart* v. *Brown & Co.* (1876) 3 R. 328.

[84] *Sharp* v. *Rettie* (1884) 11 R. 745.

to building contracts.[85] The contract may be implied as where a storekeeper enforces his lien.[86] The principle has some application between landlord and tenant but there are complexities which cannot be treated here.[87]

It is not altogether clear whether the rule applies to a building contract where the price is payable by instalments.[88] In a contract where the price is payable by instalments, the employer cannot set a claim for damages against a claim for the earlier instalments due if the damages claim does not exceed the amount of the last instalment.[89]

The right to retain is, it seems, subject to the equitable control of the court and the defender may be prevented from taking advantage of a plea of retention for the purpose of delay or to try to establish a claim which probably could not be established in a cross action by the court refusing to give effect to the plea or by ordering consignation.[90]

A contract may expressly or by necessary implication exclude the right of retention.[91]

It should be noted that a claim for damages in respect of fraudulent misrepresentations which induced the defender to enter the contract arises *ex delicto* and not from the contract, so such a claim cannot be pleaded against a sum due under the contract.[92] To allow retention, it is not enough that both claims arise from the same course of dealing between the parties; they must both arise from a contract which is one and indivisible; a person cannot transform a series of contracts into one by delaying payment of the accounts until several have been accumulated and re-rendered as one account.[93]

Balancing accounts in bankruptcy

13.10 Where one party is bankrupt or in liquidation, an illiquid claim can be set-off against a liquid claim.[94] So a future or contingent debt due by the bankrupt can be used to set-off a debt presently due to him.[95] Unquantified claims can similarly be utilised. It has been said that the debt used must be one which is capable of being ranked for.[96] It has been doubted, however, whether an illiquid claim for damages—one in respect of defamation, for example—can be set-off against a liquid claim.[97] This

---

[85] *Johnston* v. *Robertson, supra.*
[86] *Gibson and Stewart* v. *Brown & Co., supra.*
[87] See Gloag, pp. 628–630.
[88] *Field & Allan* v. *Gordon* (1872) 11 M. 132.
[89] *Dick & Stevenson* v. *Woodside Steel & Iron Co.* (1888) 16 R. 242.
[90] *per* Lord Ardwall, *Garscadden* v. *Ardrossan Dry Dock Co. Ltd.*, 1910 S.C. 178 at 180; *per* Lord Skerrington, *British Motor Body Co. Ltd.* v. *Thomas Shaw (Dundee) Ltd., supra*, at p. 929.
[91] *Redpath Dorman Long Ltd.* v. *Cummins Engine Co. Ltd.*, 1981 S.C. 370.
[92] *Smart* v. *Wilkinson*, 1928 S.C. 383.
[93] *Grewar* v. *Cross* (1904) 12 S.L.T. 84; *Scott* v. *Aitken*, 1950 S.L.T. (Notes) 34; *Fulton Clyde Ltd.* v. *J. F. McCallum & Co. Ltd.*, 1960 S.L.T. 253; *J. W. Chafer (Scotland) Ltd.* v. *Hope*, 1963 S.L.T. (Notes) 11.
[94] *Mill* v. *Paul* (1825) 4 S. 219, *per* Lord Glenlee at p. 220; *Scott's Trs.* v. *Scott* (1887) 14 R. 1043, *per* L. P. Inglis at p. 1051; *Ross* v. *Ross* (1895) 22 R. 461; *per* Lord McLaren at p. 465.
[95] *Hannay & Sons' Tr.* v. *Armstrong & Co.* (1875) 2 R. 399; (1877) 4 R. (H.L.) 43; *Smith* v. *Lord Advocate (No. 2)*, 1981 S.L.T. 19.
[96] Goudy, p. 553.
[97] Gloag, p. 626; Gloag & Irvine, p. 315.

principle of balancing accounts in bankruptcy resembles compensation in that there must have been a *concursus debiti et crediti* prior to sequestration.[98] In other words, a debt contracted after notice of bankruptcy cannot be set-off against a debt due to the bankrupt estate which arose before bankruptcy; but this does not prevent a debt arising after sequestration or liquidation being set-off against one which also arose after that time.[99] There is one case which seems suspect.[1] A company had entered into two contracts with a corporation. On the liquidation of the company the liquidator adopted one contract and repudiated the other. When he had completed the first contract he claimed payment of the contract price but the corporation contended that they should be allowed to set-off their claim for damages in respect of the failure to complete the other contract. This contention was rejected. Lord McLaren, after referring to the principle of balancing accounts in bankruptcy, said[2]:

"But this principle of bankruptcy law presupposes reciprocal obligations which are both existing at the time of the declaration of insolvency, although only one of them is, it may be, immediately exigible. It has no application to the case of a new obligation arising after bankruptcy or declaration of insolvency when the rights of the parties are irrevocably fixed."

There is no doubt that the decision would have been right if the liquidator's claim had arisen from a completely new contract negotiated with the corporation after the liquidation but that is not what happened. The difficulty is that the obligation was not new; it had existed prior to the liquidation in a contingent form; the corporation was bound by the contract before the liquidation and remained bound by the liquidator's adoption of it. It is doubtful whether a claim acquired within six months of bankruptcy can be used.[3] As in compensation some types of debt cannot be used to set-off.[4] In the case of a company it is sufficient for the application of the principle that the company is in liquidation and need not be insolvent.[5] It seems that sequestration or liquidation is not necessary to bring the principle into operation; it is sufficient that the party is *vergens ad inopiam* or that his pecuniary responsibility and circumstances have materially altered to the worst.[6]

There is one major exception to the operation of the principle. Suppose A and B are jointly and severally liable to C but B is the primary debtor. A and B are both sequestrated and C ranks for the debt on both estates. A owes a debt of some other kind to B and B's trustee claims this in A's sequestration. A's trustee contends that he can set-off a claim for relief against B's estate in respect of the dividend paid to C. This cannot be done, however, because C has ranked for the same debt on B's estate

---

[98] *Mill* v. *Paul, supra*; *Cauvin* v. *Robertson* (1783) Mor. 2581; *Taylor's Tr.* v. *Paul* (1888) 15 R. 313.
[99] *Liqrs. of Highland Engineering* v. *Thomson*, 1972 S.C. 87.
[1] *Asphaltic Limestone Co.* v. *Corporation of Glasgow*, 1907 S.C. 463.
[2] at p. 474.
[3] Bell, *Comm.*, II, 124.
[4] *Campbell* v. *Little* (1823) 2 S. 484; *Reid* v. *Bell* (1884) 12 R. 178.
[5] *G. & A. (Hotels) Ltd.* v. *T.H.B. Marketing Services Ltd.*, 1983 S.L.T. 497.
[6] *per* Lord Ormidale, *Paul & Thain* v. *Royal Bank of Scotland* (1869) 7 M. 361 at p. 364; *Busby Spinning Co. Ltd.* v. *BMK Ltd.*, 1988 S.L.T. 246.

and if A's trustee is allowed to set-off there would be a double ranking.[7] This applies only in sequestration and it does not extend to the case where C has got a composition from B.[8]

There is further exception to the principle in the case of calls. After liquidation, a shareholder cannot set-off a debt due to him by the company against a call made before liquidation.[9]

Normally the bankrupt is creditor in the liquid claim and debtor in the illiquid claim but there is one case[10] in which an insurance company had a liquid claim against the bankrupt in respect of advances and was debtor to the bankrupt in respect of a future and contingent obligation under a policy. The company was relieved of its obligation under the policy on deducting the surrender value from its liquid claim.

---

[7] *Anderson* v. *Mackinnon* (1876) 3 R. 608; *cf. Christie* v. *Keith* (1838) 16 S. 1224.

[8] *Gibb* v. *Brock*, May 12, 1838, F.C.; *Mackinnon* v. *Monkhouse* (1881) 9 R. 393.

[9] *Cowan* v. *Gowans* (1878) 5 R. 581; see *supra*, para. 8.

[10] *Borthwick* v. *Scottish Widows' Fund* (1864) 2 M. 595. *Cf. Campbell* v. *Carphin*, 1925 S.L.T. (Sh.Ct.) 30.

CHAPTER 14

OTHER DEFENCES

Novation

Novation is "the substitution of a new engagement or obligation by the same debtor to the same creditor, to the effect of extinguishing the original debt."[1] There is a presumption against novation.[2] So the taking of a bill or other document of debt for the amount of an account does not extinguish the original debt,[3] and the creditor does not lose any lien he may have in respect of the original debt unless the period for which the bill is granted is so long as to make it unreasonable to suppose that the parties intended the lien to remain in force.[4] The taking of a renewal bill does not extinguish the liability on the original bill if the latter is retained by the creditor[5]; and where a party liable on a bill granted a heritable bond in favour of the creditor it was held that in the absence of evidence of an intention that the bond was to be substituted for the bill, the liability on the bill remained.[6] It has been said that before the defence of novation can be sustained either the original document of debt must have been given up or there must be a letter or other evidence to show that it was departed from.[7] So the giving up of a bill when a new bill is taken forms novation[8]; and an express declaration by the creditor that the prior obligations are discharged[9] or a statement to that effect in the narrative of a new bond[10] precludes the creditor from relying on the original debt.

14.1

The effect of novation is to extinguish the debt with its accessories.[11]

Delegation

Delegation is "the substitution of a new debtor for the old, with consent of the creditor."[12] It is sometimes treated as a species of novation.[13] Delegation is not to be presumed[14]; there must be clear evidence of the intention of the three parties concerned to effect delegation but such intention may be inferred from facts and circumstances.[15] It may rest upon a usage of trade.[16] As in the case of novation, the surrender of the original document of debt supports the inference of

14.2

---

[1] Bell, *Prin.*, § 576.
[2] Stair, I, xviii, 8.
[3] *Wilson and Corse* v. *Gardner*, 1807 Hume 247.
[4] *Gairdner* v. *Milne & Co.* (1858) 20 D. 565; *Palmer* v. *Lee* (1880) 7 R. 651.
[5] *Hay & Kyd* v. *Powrie* (1886) 13 R. 777.
[6] *Roy's Trs.* v. *Stalker* (1850) 12 D. 722.
[7] per L.J.-C. Hope, *Roy's Trs.* v. *Stalker, supra*, at p. 723.
[8] *Stevenson* v. *Duncan*, 1805 Hume 245; *Simpson* v. *Jack*, 1948 S.L.T. (Notes) 45. *Hope Johnstone* v. *Cornwall* (1895) 22 R. 314, is a special case.
[9] *Cox* v. *Tait* (1843) 5 D. 1283.
[10] *Jackson* v. *MacDiarmid* (1892) 19 R. 528.
[11] Bell, *Prin.*, § 579.
[12] Bell, *Prin.*, § 577.
[13] Ersk., III, iv, 22.
[14] *McIntosh* v. *Ainslie* (1872) 10 M. 304.
[15] *Dudgeon* v. *Reid* (1829) 7 S. 729; *Hunter* v. *Falconer* (1835) 13 S. 252; *Fox* v. *Anderson* (1849) 11 D. 1194.
[16] *North* v. *Bassett* [1892] 1 Q.B. 333.

delegation.[17] Where one limited company has amalgamated with another, strict proof is required before it can be held that a creditor of the first company has agreed to accept the amalgamated company as his debtor in place of the first.[18] Questions of delegation in relation to partnership are dealt with elsewhere.[19]

Confusio[20]

14.3 Where the same person in the same capacity becomes both creditor and debtor in the same obligation, the debt is extinguished *confusione*.[21] *Confusio* takes place only when the full and absolute right of the creditor and the full and absolute right of the debtor merge in one and the same person.[22] The principle operates *ipso jure* and independently of intention.[23] It does not operate where the person has an interest to maintain the debt in existence.[24] Where the cautioner acquires the creditor's right, the cautionary obligation is extinguished but the principal obligation is not.[25] Where a bondholder purchases the security subjects and pays the proprietor only the balance of the price after deduction of the bond, the debt is extinguished, even although the bond is not discharged.[26] The result is the same where the debtor pays off the bond and obtains an assignation thereof.[27] An *ex facie* absolute disposition to the bondholder in further security does not extinguish the bond.[28] Ground annuals cannot be extinguished *confusione*.[29] Feuduties are extinguished *confusione* when the superior and vassal are one.[30]

Quinquennial prescription

14.4 An obligation to which the prescription applies is extinguished if it has subsisted for a continuous period of five years without any relevant claim having been made in relation to it and without its subsistence having been relevantly acknowledged.[31] It is not possible to contract out of the prescription,[32] but this does not prevent the parties from agreeing to postpone the enforceability of an obligation.[33]

The prescription applies[34]:
    (a) to any obligation to pay a sum of money due in respect of a particular period by way of interest; an instalment of an

---

[17] *Stevenson* v. *Duncan*, 1805 Hume 245.
[18] *Re Family Endowment Society* (1870) L.R. 5 Ch. 118.
[19] See para. 30.8.
[20] The English term is merger.
[21] Bell, *Prin.*, § 580; *Motherwell* v. *Manwell* (1903) 5 F. 619, *per* Lord Kinnear at p. 631.
[22] *per* Lord Ardwall, *King* v. *Johnston*, 1908 S.C. 684 at 689.
[23] *Healy & Young's Tr.* v. *Mair's Trs.*, 1914 S.C. 893.
[24] *Fleming* v. *Imrie* (1868) 6 M. 363.
[25] Ersk., III, iv, 24.
[26] *Hogg* v. *Brack* (1832) 11 S. 198.
[27] *Murray* v. *Parlane's Tr.* (1890) 18 R. 287.
[28] *King* v. *Johnston, supra.*
[29] *Healy & Young's Tr.* v. *Mair's Trs., supra.*
[30] *Motherwell* v. *Manwell, supra per* Lord Adam at p. 627.
[31] Prescription and Limitation (Scotland) Act 1973, s.6. The qualification as to acknowledgment does not apply to bills of exchange or promissory notes.
[32] s.13.
[33] *McPhail* v. *Cunninghame D.C.*, 1983 S.C. 246.
[34] Sched. 1, para. 1.

annuity; feuduty or other periodical payment under a feu grant; ground annual or other periodical payment under a contract of ground annual; rent or other periodical payment under a lease; a periodical payment in respect of the occupancy or use of land; a periodical payment under a land obligation;
- (b) to any obligation based on redress of unjustified enrichment, including without prejudice to that generality any obligation of restitution, repetition or recompense;
- (c) to any obligation arising from *negotiorum gestio*;
- (d) to any obligation arising from liability (whether arising from any enactment or from any rule of law) to make reparation[35];
- (e) to any obligation under a bill of exchange or a promissory note;
- (f) to any obligation of accounting, other than accounting for trust funds; this does not cover a liability to pay tax[36];
- (g) to any obligation arising from, or by reason of any breach of, a contract or promise.

The prescription does not apply[37]:
- (i) to any obligation to recognise or obtemper a decree of court, an arbitration award or an order of a tribunal or authority exercising jurisdiction under any enactment;
- (ii) to any obligation arising from the issue of a banknote;
- (iii) to any obligation constituted or evidenced by a probative writ, not being a cautionary obligation nor being an obligation to make a periodical payment specified in (a), *supra*;
- (iv) to any obligation under a contract of partnership or of agency, not being an obligation remaining, or becoming prestable on or after the termination of the relationship between the parties under the contract;
- (v) to any obligation relating to land (including an obligation to recognise a servitude) except obligations to make periodical payments;
- (vi) to any obligation to satisfy any claim to terce, courtesy, *legitim*, *jus relicti* or *jus relictae*, or to any prior right of a surviving spouse under s.8 or 9 of the Succession (Scotland) Act 1964;
- (vii) to any obligation to make reparation in respect of personal injuries or in respect of the death of any person as a result of such injuries[38];
- (viii) to any obligation to make reparation or otherwise make good in respect of defamation[39];
- (ix) to any obligation arising under the Consumer Protection Act 1987 to make reparation for damage caused wholly or partly by a defect in a product[40];

---

[35] A trustee's obligation to account is not a liability to make reparation: *Hobday* v. *Kirkpatrick's Trs.*, 1985 S.L.T. 197. See also *Miller* v. *City of Glasgow D.C.*, 1989 S.L.T. 44; *Holt* v. *City of Dundee D.C.*, 1990 G.W.D. 8–459 (planning compensation).

[36] *Lord Advocate* v. *Hepburn*, 1990 G.W.D. 3–143.

[37] Sched. 1, para. 2.

[38] Reparation claims are subject to a three-year limitation under ss.17 and 18 of the 1973 Act.

[39] Defamation claims are subject to a three-year limitation under s.18A of the 1973 Act.

[40] Product liability claims are subject to a 10-year prescription (s.22A, 1973 Act) and a three-year limitation (ss.22B, 22C, 1973 Act).

170   *Other Defences*

(x) to any imprescriptible obligation.

Imprescriptible obligations are[41]:
- (a) any real right of ownership in land;
- (b) the right in land of the lessee under a recorded lease;
- (c) any right exercisable as a *res merae facultatis*;
- (d) any right to recover property *extra commercium*;
- (e) any obligation of a trustee:
  - (i) to produce accounts of the trustee's intromissions with any property of the trust;
  - (ii) to make reparation or restitution in respect of any fraudulent breach of trust to which the trustee was a party or was privy;
  - (iii) to make furthcoming to any person entitled thereto any trust property, or the proceeds of any such property, in the possession of the trustee, or to make good the value of any such property previously received by the trustee and appropriated to his own use;
- (f) any obligation of a third party to make furthcoming to any person entitled thereto any trust property received by the third party otherwise than in good faith and in his possession;
- (g) any right to recover stolen property from the person by whom it was stolen or from any person privy to the stealing thereof;
- (h) any right to be served as heir to an ancestor or to take any steps necessary for making up or completing title to any interest in land.

Terminus a quo

14.5   As a general rule, the prescription runs from the date when the obligation became enforceable.[42] A claim to recompense becomes enforceable when the defenders are *lucrati*.[43] There are special provisions for loans, deposits, obligations arising from partnership or agency, obligations to pay money or execute work by instalments and series of transactions for the supply of goods or services.

Where the obligation is to repay the whole, or any part, of a sum of money lent to, or deposited with, the debtor under a contract of loan or deposit, if the contract contains a stipulation which makes provision with respect to the date on or before which repayment of the sum or the part thereof is to be made, the appropriate date is the date on or before which, in terms of that stipulation, the sum or part thereof is to be repaid; if the contract contains no such stipulation, but a written demand for repayment of the sum, or the part thereof, is made by or on behalf of the creditor to the debtor the appropriate date is the date when such demand is made or first made.[44]

In the case of an obligation under a contract of partnership or of agency, being an obligation remaining, or becoming, prestable on or after the termination of the relationship between the parties under the contract, if the contract contains a stipulation which makes provision with

---
[41] Sched. 3. A trustee includes anyone holding property in a fiduciary capacity for another: s.15(1). See, as to (h), *Macdonald* v. *Scott's Exrs.*, 1981 S.C. 75.
[42] s.6(3). See *Scott Lithgow Ltd.* v. *S. of S. for Defence*, 1989 S.L.T. 236.
[43] *N. V. Devos Gebroeder* v. *Sunderland Sportswear Ltd.*, 1989 S.L.T. 382.
[44] Sched. 2, para. 2. As to a cautionary obligation, see para. 10.2.

respect to the date on or before which performance of the obligation is to due, the appropriate date is the date on or before which, in terms of that stipulation, the obligation is to be performed; in any other case the appropriate date is the date when the relationship terminated.[45]

Where the obligation is to pay an instalment of a sum of money payable by instalments, or to execute any instalment of work due to be executed by instalments, the appropriate date is the date on which the last of the instalments is due to be paid or, as the case may be, to be executed.[46]

Where the obligation, not being part of a banking transaction, is to pay money in respect of:
(a) goods supplied on sale or hire (including credit sale, conditional sale and hire-purchase),
(b) services rendered (not including the keeping of the account)
in a series of transactions between the same parties (whether under a single contract or under several contracts) and charged on continuing account,[47] the appropriate date is the date on which payment for the goods last supplied, or, as the case may be, the services last rendered, became due.[48] A continuing account arises where there are repeated transactions which are recorded by the creditor, but a specific invoice is not rendered on the occasion of each transaction.[49]

Where there is a series of transactions between a partnership and another party, the series is regarded as terminated (without prejudice to any other mode of termination) if the partnership or any partner therein becomes bankrupt; but, subject to that, if the partnership is dissolved and is replaced by a single new partnership having among its partners any person who was a partner in the old partnership, then, the new partnership is regarded as if it were identical with the old partnership.

The liability of a partner for a partnership debt is enforceable from the date of constitution of the debt against the firm.[50] A claim to legal rights becomes enforceable at the date of death or at the date estate first falls into intestacy.[51] Where, under a building contract, payments have to be certified by the architect, the obligation is enforceable only on issue of a certificate.[52]

An obligation to make reparation for loss, injury or damage (whether arising from any enactment or rule of law or from, or by reason of any breach of, a contract or promise) becomes enforceable when the loss, injury or damage occurs.[53] The *terminus a quo* is the date when *injuria* concurs with *damnum* even although some items of loss arise after that date.[54] If the loss, injury or damage results from a continuing neglect, act or default, it is deemed to have occurred when the act, neglect or default

---

[45] Sched. 2, para. 3.
[46] Sched. 2, para. 4.
[47] See *Ross* v. *Cowie's Exrx.* (1888) 16 R. 224; *Christison* v. *Knowles* (1901) 3 F. 480.
[48] Sched. 2, para. 1.
[49] *H. G. Robertson* v. *Murray International Metals Ltd.*, 1988 S.L.T. 747.
[50] *Highland Engineering Ltd.* v. *Anderson*, 1979 S.L.T. 122.
[51] *Campbell's Trs.* v. *Campbell's Trs.*, 1950 S.C. 48; *Mill's Trs.* v. *Mill's Trs.*, 1965 S.C. 384.
[52] *McPhail* v. *Cunninghame D.C.*, 1983 S.C. 246.
[53] s.11.
[54] *Dunlop* v. *McGowans*, 1980 S.C. (H.L.) 73. See also *George Porteous (Arts) Ltd.* v. *Dollar Rae Ltd.*, 1979 S.L.T. (Sh.Ct.) 51; *Renfrew Golf Club* v. *Ravenstone Securities Ltd.*, 1984 S.C. 22.

ceased. If, at the time of occurrence of the loss, injury or damage, the creditor was not aware, and could not with reasonable diligence have been aware, that loss, injury or damage had occurred giving rise to an obligation to make reparation,[55] the *terminus a quo* is the date when the creditor first became, or could with reasonable diligence have become, so aware.

If the commencement of the period falls at a time other than the beginning of a day, the period is deemed to commence at the beginning of the next following day.[56]

The period

14.6 Except where the Act provides otherwise regard is to be had to the prior law applicable to the computation of periods of prescription for the purpose of the Prescription Act 1617.[57] The running of the period is interrupted (but not terminated) by any period during which the original creditor, while he was the creditor, was under legal disability by reason of nonage or unsoundness of mind.[58] Nonage comprises both minority and pupillarity.[59] Other forms of disability do not interrupt.[60] It is also interrupted by any period in which the creditor is induced to refrain from making a claim in relation to the obligation because of the fraud of the debtor or his agent or error induced by words or conduct of the debtor or his agent but this does not include any time occurring after the creditor could with reasonable diligence have discovered the fraud or error.[58] If the last day of the period is a Saturday, Sunday or bank holiday, the period is extended to include the next day which is not one of these.[61] Time before the commencement of the relevant part of the Act (July 25, 1976) is reckonable towards the period but such time cannot exceed the prescriptive period so at least one day must be after the commencement date.[62]

Relevant claim

14.7 A relevant claim[63] is a claim for implement or part-implement of the obligation made against the debtor[64]:

(a) in a court of competent jurisdiction in Scotland or elsewhere except proceedings in the Court of Session initiated by a summons which is not subsequently called; a summons served within the prescriptive period constitutes a relevant claim unless it is not called within a year and a day after service or within a lesser period fixed by protestation[65];

---

[55] *Dunfermline D.C.* v. *Blyth & Blyth Associates*, 1985 S.L.T. 345.
[56] s.14(1)(*c*).
[57] s.14(1)(*e*).
[58] s.6(4).
[59] *Fyfe* v. *Crondace Ltd.*, 1986 S.L.T. 528; *Forbes* v. *House of Clydesdale Ltd.*, 1988 S.L.T. 594.
[60] s.14(1)(*b*).
[61] s.14(1)(*d*).
[62] s.14(1)(*a*); *Dunlop* v. *McGowans, supra*.
[63] s.9(1) as amended by Prescription (Scotland) Act 1987. See as to the content of the summons or writ, *Bank of Scotland* v. *W. & G. Fergusson* (1898) 1 F. 96; *British Railways Board* v. *Strathclyde Regional Council*, 1980 S.L.T. 63.
[64] *Kirkcaldy D.C.* v. *Household Manufacturing Ltd.*, 1987 S.L.T. 617.
[65] *Barclay* v. *Chief Constable, Northern Constabulary*, 1986 S.L.T. 562.

(b) in an arbitration in Scotland;
(c) in an arbitration elsewhere the award in which would be enforceable in Scotland;
(d) by presenting or concurring in a petition for sequestration[66] or liquidation[67] of the debtor or by lodging a claim in the sequestration[66] or liquidation[67];
(e) by a creditor to the trustee acting under a trust deed[68];
(f) by the execution of any form of diligence directed to the enforcement of the obligation.

Where the nature of the claim has been stated in the notice served by one party to an arbitration on the other requiring him to agree to an arbiter or to submit the dispute to a named or designated arbiter, the date of service of the notice is taken to be the date of making of the claim.[69] It has been suggested that the raising of an action which is fundamentally null cannot be a relevant claim,[70] but a summons containing defects which can be cured by amendment may be a relevant claim.[71] The raising of an action based on breach of contract does not interrupt the prescriptive period in a claim of recompense.[72] Once an action has been raised, a fresh prescriptive period does not begin to run until the action has been abandoned.[73]

Acknowledgment

The subsistence of the obligation is acknowledged if, and only if, either there has been such performance by or on behalf of the debtor towards implement of the obligation as clearly indicates that the obligation still subsists[74] or there has been made by or on behalf of the debtor to the creditor or his agent an unequivocal written admission clearly acknowledging that the obligation still subsists.[75] Payment of interest on a bond and disposition in security does not prevent prescription of a bond of corroboration.[76]

Where there are joint debtors so that each is liable for the whole debt, acknowledgment by part performance has effect as respects the liability of each debtor but acknowledgment by admission has effect only as respects the liability of the person who makes it.[77] Acknowledgment by one of several trustees has effect as respects the liability of the trust estate and any liability of each of the trustees.[78]

14.8

---

[66] The recall of the award of sequestration does not affect the interruption of prescription: B.A., s.17(5)(a).
[67] Inserted by Prescription (Scotland) Act 1987, s.1.
[68] Inserted by B.A., Sched. 7, para. 11.
[69] s.9(3). As to prescription of claims subject to arbitration, see *Douglas Milne Ltd.* v. *Borders R.C.*, 1990 G.W.D. 8–445.
[70] *Shanks* v. *Central R.C.*, 1987 S.L.T. 410.
[71] *British Railways Board* v. *Strathclyde R.C.*, 1981 S.C. 90.
[72] *N.V. Devos Gebroeder* v. *Sunderland Sportswear Ltd.*, 1990 S.L.T. 473.
[73] *George A. Hood & Co.* v. *Dumbarton D.C.*, 1983 S.L.T. 238.
[74] See *Inverlochy Castle Ltd.* v. *Lochaber Power Co.*, 1987 S.L.T. 466; *Gibson* v. *Carson*, 1980 S.C. 356.
[75] s.10(1); see *Marr's Exrx.* v. *Marr's Trs.*, 1936 S.C. 64; *Lieberman* v. *G. W. Tait & Sons*, S.S.C., 1987 S.L.T. 585; *Greater Glasgow Health Board* v. *Baxter Clark & Paul*, 1990 G.W.D. 12–625.
[76] *Yuill's Trs.* v. *Maclachlan's Trs.*, 1939 S.C. (H.L.) 40.
[77] s.10(2).
[78] s.10(3).

Vicennial prescription

14.9 An obligation to which the prescription applies is extinguished if it has subsisted for a continuous period of 20 years without any relevant claim having been made in relation to it and without its subsistence having been relevantly acknowledged.[79] It is not possible to contract out of the prescription.[80] The prescription applies to obligations of any kind (including the obligations to which the quinquennial prescription applies), other than imprescriptible obligations, obligations to make reparation in respect of personal injury or death and obligations to make reparation under the Consumer Protection Act 1987.[81] The *terminus a quo* is the date when the obligation became enforceable except in the case of obligations to make reparation where the provisions for the five-year prescription for such obligations, with the exception of the rule as to the creditor's knowledge, apply.[82] There is no interruption of the period by disability, fraud or error. The rules as to the relevant claim, the relevant acknowledgment and the first and the last days of the period are as for the quinquennial prescription.

Transitional provisions

14.10 Where by virtue of an enactment made before July 25, 1973 a claim to establish a right or enforce implement of an obligation may be made only within a specified period of limitation, and if by the operation of the quinquennial or vicennial prescription the right or obligation would be extinguished before the expiration of the period of limitation, the prescriptive period is extended so that it expires on the date when the limitation period expires or, if on that date any such claim made within the period has not finally been disposed of, on the date when the claim is so disposed of.[83]

---

[79] s.7(1). The last requirement does not apply to bills of exchange or promissory notes.
[80] s.13.
[81] s.7(2).
[82] s.11(4). See *Beard v. Beveridge, Herd and Sandilands, W.S.*, 1990 S.L.T. 609.
[83] s.12(1).

CHAPTER 15

DILIGENCE

General features of diligence

15.1 Diligence is the legal process by which a debtor's person, lands or effects are attached for recovery of the debt. The principal forms of diligence are arrestment and poinding in relation to moveable property and inhibition and adjudication in relation to heritable property. Some of the special forms of diligence appropriate to particular types of debt, such as poinding of the ground and actions of mails and duties, are not dealt with in this work.

In general, diligence on a Court of Session decree must be executed by a messenger-at-arms and diligence on an ordinary sheriff court decree by a messenger or sheriff officer but in the islands and in a sheriff court district where there is no resident messenger a sheriff officer has the powers of a messenger.[1] For simplicity, reference is made hereafter only to sheriff officers. A creditor is not entitled to seize the debtor's goods at his own hand to satisfy the debt. If he does so he can be made to restore the goods or their value or, if the value is unknown, to pay the debts of other creditors.[2]

Prior claims

15.2 There are two types of claim which have a priority as regards diligence:
(a) If at any time at which any moveable goods and effects belonging to any person are liable to be taken by virtue of any poinding, sequestration for rent, or other diligence, the person is in arrears in respect of certain amounts due to the Inland Revenue, the goods and effects may not be so taken unless on demand made by the collector of taxes the person proceeding to take the said goods and effects pays such sums as have fallen due at or before the date of the diligence. The relevant sums are amounts due for deduction of PAYE and deductions from payments made to the sub-contractors in the building industry (these are debts which are preferred debts due to the Inland Revenue in sequestration and liquidation). If the sums are not paid within 10 days of the date of the demand the sums are, notwithstanding any proceedings for the purpose of taking the said moveable goods and effects, recoverable by poinding and selling the said moveable goods and effects under a summary warrant.[3]
(b) the landlord's hypothec[4] is preferred to the diligence of ordinary creditors. If poinding takes place before the term of payment of the rent, the landlord can interdict the procedure until security for the rent is given.[5] After the term of payment, a poinding creditor can proceed with diligence only if he leaves sufficient goods to pay the rent.

---

[1] Execution of Diligence (Scotland) Act 1926, s.1.
[2] *Crawford* v. *Black* (1829) 8 S.158; *Smart & Co.* v. *Stewart*, 1911 S.C. 668.
[3] Taxes Management Act 1970, s.64 (amended by Finance Act 1989, s.155).
[4] See para. 7.12.
[5] Graham Stewart, pp. 483–484.

Warrants for diligence

15.3 The warrants on which diligence commonly proceeds are:
(a) that contained in a Court of Session decree for payment of money[6];
(b) that contained in a sheriff court decree for payment of money;
(c) that inserted in an extract of a document registered in the Books of Council and Session or in sheriff court books which contains an obligation to pay a sum of money.[7]

Any of these warrants authorises the following diligence[8]:
(i) in relation to an ordinary debt (*i.e.* a debt other than maintenance), the charging of the debtor to pay within the period specified in the charge the sum specified in the extract and any interest accrued thereon and in the event of failure to pay, the execution of an earnings arrestment and the poinding of articles belonging to the debtor and, if necessary for the purpose of executing the poinding, the opening of shut and lockfast places;
(ii) in relation to an ordinary debt, an arrestment other than arrestment of the debtor's earnings in the hands of his employer;
(iii) in relation to a debt for maintenance, a current maintenance arrestment.

The warrants may be executed anywhere in Scotland.[9] A warrant may be executed by a sheriff officer of the court which granted it or the sheriff court district in which it is to be executed.[10]

Where a person has acquired a warrant for diligence by assignation, confirmation as executor or otherwise, he may obtain a warrant authorising execution of diligence at his instance by submitting to the appropriate clerk of court the decree or other document containing the original warrant together with the assignation (along with evidence of its intimation to the debtor), the confirmation or other document establishing his right and the warrant applied for will be granted if the clerk is satisfied that the applicant's right has been established.[11] Where a charge has been served in pursuance of the original warrant and the applicant submits with the other documents the certificate of execution of the charge the warrant granted to the applicant will authorise diligence in pursuance of that charge.

The charge

15.4 The execution of a poinding or an earnings arrestment (other than one under a summary warrant) is not competent unless it has been preceded by the service on the debtor of a formal warning to pay, known as a "charge,"[12] in the prescribed form.[13] The period for payment of the debt

---

[6] R.C. 64.
[7] See, as to summary diligence, para. 19.5.
[8] D.A., s.87(2); Sheriff Courts (Scotland) Extracts Act 1892, s.7(1) (subst. by D.A., s.87(3); Writs Execution (Scotland) Act 1877, s.3 (subst. by D.A., s.87(4)).
[9] D.A., s.91(1).
[10] D.A., s.91(2).
[11] D.A., s.88.
[12] D.A., s.90(1). If the defender's address is unknown service is made on the sheriff clerk (S.I. 1990 No. 661).
[13] A.S. (Form of Charge for Payment) 1988; Act of Adjournal (Consolidation) 1988, Rules 83A, 126A, inserted by S.I. 1989 No. 1020. A charge upon a summary cause decree may in some circumstances be executed by registered post: Execution of Diligence (Scotland) Act 1926, s.2.

specified in the charge is 14 days if the debtor is in the United Kingdom and 28 days if he is outside the United Kingdom or his whereabouts are unknown.[14] The poinding or earnings arrestment cannot be executed more than two years after the date of service of the charge but another charge can be served to reconstitute the creditor's right.[15]

Equalisation of diligence

Apparent insolvency has the effect of equalising certain diligence. All arrestments and poindings executed within 60 days prior to the constitution of apparent insolvency of the debtor, or within four months thereafter, are ranked *pari passu* as if they had all been executed on the same date.[16] The result is that arrestments and poindings of different subjects are equalised. The rule applies to arrestments of ships[17] but not to an earnings arrestment, a current maintenance arrestment or a conjoined arrestment order.[18] Although a company cannot be sequestrated, its apparent insolvency can be constituted[19] and that has the effect of equalising diligence.[20]

15.5

To benefit from the equalisation it is not necessary that a creditor should have executed his diligence. Any creditor judicially producing in a process relative to the subject of an arrestment or poinding liquid grounds of debt or decree of payment within the 60-day or four-month period is entitled to rank as if he had executed an arrestment or a poinding.[21] If the first or any subsequent arrester obtains in the meantime a decree or furthcoming or recovers payment, or a poinding creditor carries through a sale, or gets payment in respect of a poinded article on its redemption, he is accountable to those who are eventually found to have a right to rank *pari passu* thereon and must pay to them proportionately after allowing the expense of recovery out of the fund; it seems that he is not entitled to an allowance for the expenses in a question with creditors who have executed a poinding or arrestment.

The rule has a surprisingly wide effect where there is a sequestration because a sequestration has the effect in relation to diligence of an arrestment and a completed poinding in favour of creditors according to their respective entitlements and accordingly, if sequestration occurs within four months of apparent insolvency, any poinding or arrestment within the prescribed period is cut down.[22] Under the former law it was held[23] that where an arrestment was executed within 60 days of notour bankruptcy and sequestration followed within four months of notour bankruptcy but the arrested funds were paid to the arrester under mandate before the sequestration, the trustee could not recover from the arrester because the arrestment had not been "used"; the new wording

---

[14] D.A., s.90(3).
[15] D.A., s.90(5), (6).
[16] B.A., Sched. 7, para. 24.
[17] *Harvey* v. *McAdie* (1888) 4 Sh.Ct.Rep. 254; *Munro* v. *Smith*, 1968 S.L.T. (Sh.Ct) 26.
[18] B.A., Sched. 7, para. 24(8) added by D.A., Sched. 6, para. 28(*b*).
[19] B.A., s.7(4).
[20] Sched. 7, para. 24(5).
[21] para. 24(3) (amended by D.A., Sched. 6, para. 28(*a*)).
[22] *Stewart* v. *Jarvie*, 1938 S.C. 309; *Galbraith* v. *Campbell's Trs.* (1885) 22 S.L.R. 602.
[23] *Millar* v. *Forage Supply Co. Ltd.*, 1955 S.L.T. (Sh.Ct.) 18.

has "executed" instead of "used" so the result would now, it is thought, be different.

Extremely complicated questions can arise where there are multiple apparent insolvencies. Suppose one arrestment is executed within 60 days before apparent insolvency, a second arrestment within four months after apparent insolvency and sequestration follows more than four months after that apparent insolvency but within 60 days of the second arrestment; it seems that the arrestments are equalised but the second arrester's share goes to the trustee.[24]

The equalisation of diligence can operate where there is no sequestration. Indeed, for ordinary creditors there is a certain advantage in proceeding in this way rather than by sequestration as arrestments can be equalised without satisfying the claims of preferential creditors.[25]

Special restrictions on diligence

15.6 Sundry statutes place restrictions on the use of diligence, *e.g.* diligence cannot be done for the rent of any house let under an assured tenancy except with the leave of the sheriff.[26] Diligence cannot be carried out against property other than land which is held by a recognised investment exchange or clearing house as margin or which is subject to a "market charge" except with the consent of the exchange or clearing house or the person in whose favour the charge was granted.[27]

Time to pay order

15.7 A time to pay order is a means of suspending the operation of diligence which has been begun. It can be granted where a charge has been served or an arrestment executed or an action of adjudication for debt has been commenced[28] in relation to a debt due under a "decree or other document" which is defined as a court decree, an extract registered in court books, an order enforceable as if it were an extract registered decree arbitral, or an enforceable foreign judgment but not a maintenance order or a summary warrant.[29] The debtor must be an individual liable personally for the debt or liable as a tutor, factor *loco tutoris* or *loco absentis* or *curator bonis*.[30] The order cannot be made if there has already at some time been a time to pay direction or a time order to pay order or a time under the Consumer Credit Act in relation to the debt.[31] It cannot be made if a summary warrant has been granted.[32] If certain types of diligence have reached a certain stage an order cannot be made until the diligence has been completed or has otherwise ceased to have effect; that applies where a warrant of sale has been granted in a poinding but has not been executed, where after an arrestment a furthcoming decree has been granted but not enforced or warrant of sale granted but not executed and

---

[24] See Gretton, (1983) 28 J.L.S. 18.
[25] Goudy, p. 243; Wardhaugh, p. 9; *Campbell* v. *McKellar*, 1926 S.L.T. (Sh.Ct.) 82.
[26] Housing (Scotland) Act 1988, s.29. There are also restrictions where an administrator has been appointed under the drugs legislation: Criminal Justice (Scotland) Act 1987, s.19.
[27] C.A., 1989, s.180.
[28] D.A., s.5(1).
[29] s.15(3).
[30] s.14(1).
[31] ss.5(4)(*b*), 14(3); A.S. (Debtors) 7.
[32] s.5(4)(*c*).

where a decree in an action for adjudication for debt has been granted and the creditor has with the debtor's consent entered into possession of the property or obtained a decree of maills and duties or a decree of removing or ejection.[33] An order cannot be made where the outstanding debt exclusive of interest exceeds £10,000 or where the debt includes tax due to the Inland Revenue, rates, community charge, betting duty, car tax or value added tax or is maintenance, a capital sum awarded on divorce or nullity or a fine or order of a criminal court.[34]

(a) *Procedure.* The debtor must submit an application for the order stating the amount of the outstanding debt and including an offer to pay it by instalments or in a lump sum after a period.[35] On receipt of the application the sheriff may make an interim order sisting diligence[36]; while that order is in effect it is not competent to grant a warrant of sale in a poinding, execute an earnings arrestment, commence an action of furthcoming or sale or grant decree in such an action, or commence an action of adjudication or, if such an action has commenced, take any but certain specified steps in such an action.[37] The interim order comes into effect on intimation to the creditor and remains in effect until intimation to the parties of the sheriff's decision on the application for the order.[38] The sheriff may require the creditor to furnish details of the decree or document on which the debt is founded and if the creditor fails to comply any existing diligence may be recalled or extinguished and he may be interdicted from executing further diligence.[39] The application is disposed of after a hearing.[40]

The order is that the debt will be paid by instalments or in a lump sum after a specified period.[41] While the order is in effect it is not competent to serve a charge or to commence or execute an arrestment and action of furthcoming or sale, a poinding and sale, an earnings arrestment or an adjudication for debt to enforce payment of the debt.[42]

The making of the order may be subject to the fulfilment of conditions by the debtor.[43] On the making of the orders any existing earnings arrestment is recalled, the debt is excluded from any existing conjoined arrestment order, and there is a prohibition of taking any steps in an adjudication which has been commenced other than those which are specifically allowed.[44] An order may be made recalling a poinding and it may be subject to conditions.[45] An order may be made recalling or restricting an arrestment other than an earnings arrestment and this again

---

[33] s. 5(5).
[34] ss.5(4)(*d*)–(*f*), 15(3).
[35] s.6(1); A.S. (Debtors) 5, fm. 2.
[36] s.6(3).
[37] s.8(1).
[38] s.8(2).
[39] s.6(4), (5); A.S. (Debtors) 5 (2).
[40] s.7.
[41] s.5(2).
[42] s.9(1).
[43] s.9(3).
[44] s.9(2).
[45] s.9(2)(*d*).

may be subject to conditions.[46] If a poinding or arrestment is not recalled, the creditor must be ordered to take no further steps in the diligence other than, in the case of a poinding, applying for an order to protect the goods or reporting the execution of the poinding.[47] While that order is in force it is not competent to grant a warrant of sale (other than for perishable goods) or a decree of furthcoming or sale.[48] All these orders must specify the diligence affected[49] and a diligence not specified remains in effect.[50] If a charge has been served before the making of the time to pay order it lapses if the period for payment has not expired at the making of the order; if the period has expired the charge can still operate to constitute apparent insolvency.[51] While the order is in effect the creditor cannot found on the debt to obtain the debtor's sequestration[52] but he can by virtue of an arrestment or poinding which has been recalled on the making of the time to pay order be ranked *pari passu* on the proceeds of another arrestment or poinding under the Bankruptcy Act.[53]

(b) *Cessation*. The order ceases to have effect:
 (a) if the debtor dies;
 (b) if the obligation is transmitted to another person in the debtor's lifetime[54];
 (c) if the debtor is sequestrated, grants a trust deed for creditors or enters into a composition contract[55];
 (d) if on the day on which an instalment is due there remains unpaid a sum, due under previous instalments, of not less than the aggregate of two instalments[56];
 (e) if at the end of the period of three weeks immediately following the day on which the last instalment becomes due, any part of the debt remains outstanding[57];
 (f) if 24 hours after the end of the period for payment of the lump sum, any part of it remains unpaid.[58]

If the time to pay order is recalled or ceases to have effect for any reason other than the debtor's sequestration or the payment or extinction of the debt, the debt again becomes enforceable by diligence including, where there was a poinding in progress at making of the order, another poinding in these premises.[59]

(c) *Variation*. While the time to pay order is in force it may be varied by the sheriff and any poinding or arrestment in effect can be recalled with or

---

[46] s.9(2)(e).
[47] s.9(4).
[48] s.9(8).
[49] s.9(5).
[50] s.9(11).
[51] s.9(10).
[52] s.12(1).
[53] s.13(2); see para. 15.5.
[54] s.14(2).
[55] s.12(2).
[56] s.11(1).
[57] s.11(2).
[58] s.11(3).
[59] s.9(12).

without conditions.[60] If it comes to the knowledge of the sheriff that the debt is being enforced by diligence which has not been stopped by the various orders, he can, after a hearing, recall the time to pay order or make any of the orders he could have made at the time the time to pay order was made.[61]

If the creditor wishes to recover interest on the debt which is not awarded as a specific sum in the decree he must give notice of this to the debtor[62]; any sum paid by the debtor under the time to pay order is not ascribed to such interest until the remainder of the debt has been discharged.[63]

---

[60] s.10(1); A.S. (Debtors) 6, fm. 3.
[61] s.10(4).
[62] s.5(7); A.S. (Debtors) 3.
[63] s.5(8).

CHAPTER 16

POINDING

Its use

16.1 Poinding is the form of diligence appropriate to attach corporeal moveables belonging to the debtor which are in the custody or control of the debtor himself. It can also be used where corporeal moveables belonging to the debtor are in the possession of the creditor.[1] At one time it was used where the debtor's moveables were in the possession of a third party but in modern practice arrestment is used in this situation.[2] A poinding must be preceded by the expiry of a charge.[3]

Subjects of poinding

16.2 The subjects of poinding are corporeal moveables—"things corporeally valuable and capable of being sold by the Sheriff's warrant."[4] "The essence of poinding is that the goods poinded may be taken to the market-cross and sold."[5] So books, papers and evidents cannot be poinded.[6] Growing crops can be poinded if they are of sufficient maturity to be capable of valuation.[7] The following cannot, however, be poinded: the debtor's wearing apparel[8]; his working tools,[9] ships and goods on board them[10] (the appropriate diligence is arrestment,[11]); goods within the Palace of Holyroodhouse;[12] subjects which have become *ex contractu* not moveable.[13] There is some doubt as to whether banknotes can be poinded.[14]

The goods poinded must be the property of the debtor so the following cannot be poinded: the property of a partnership for a debt due by a partner,[15] goods liferented by the debtor,[16] goods held on trust by the debtor even if the trust is latent[17] (but goods held in security of a debt due to the debtor can be poinded *tantum et tale*); goods on sale or return[18];

---

[1] *Lochhead* v. *Graham* (1883) 11 R. 201.
[2] *Mackenzie & Co.* v. *Finlay* (1868) 7 M. 27. But see *McLean* v. *Boyek* (1894) 10 Sh.Ct.Rep. 10; *McNaught & Co.* v. *Lewis* (1935) 51 Sh.Ct. Rep. 138.
[3] See para. 15.4; as to the warrant for poinding, see para. 15.3.
[4] Bell, *Prin.*, § 2289.
[5] *per* Lord Neaves, *Trowsdale's Tr.* v. *Forcett Ry. Co.* (1870) 9 M. 88 at 95.
[6] *Trowsdale's Tr.* v. *Forcett Ry. Co., supra.*.
[7] Ersk., III, vi, 22; *Parker* v. *Douglas Heron & Co.* (1783) Mor. 2868; *Elders* v. *Allen* (1833) 11 S. 902.
[8] *Pringle* v. *Neilson* (1788) Mor. 1393.
[9] Ersk., IV, iii, 27, n.; *Reid* v. *Donaldson* (1778) Mor. 1392; for what is included see Graham Stewart, p. 346; *Macpherson* v. *Macpherson's Tr.* (1905) 8 F. 191.
[10] For a discussion of this anomaly see Dirleton's *Doubts*, 385; Bell, *Comm.*, II, 60.
[11] See para. 17.16.
[12] *Earl of Strathmore* v. *Laing* (1823) 2 S. 223, revd. 2 W. & S. 1.
[13] *Elders* v. *Allen* (1833) 11 S. 902.
[14] See *Alexander* v. *McLay* (1826) 4 S. 439; *Encyclopaedia of the Laws of Scotland*, Vol. XI, p. 356.
[15] *Dawson* v. *Cullen* (1825) 4 S. 39.
[16] *Scott* v. *Price* (1837) 15 S. 916.
[17] Graham Stewart, pp. 67–68.
[18] *Macdonald* v. *Westren* (1888) 15 R.988 *per* Lord Young at p. 990; *Bell, Rannie & Co.* v. *Smith* (1885) 22 S.L.R. 597.

goods on hire-purchase;[19] goods which have been poinded and bought back by, or given to, the debtor.[20] Goods owned in common by the debtor and a third party can be poinded.[21]

Exempt articles

The following articles belonging to the debtor are exempt from the poinding[22]:

16.3

(a) clothing reasonably required by the debtor or any member of his household;
(b) implements, tools of trade, books or other equipment reasonably required for the use of the debtor or any member of his household in the practice of the debtor's or that member's profession, trade or business, not exceeding in aggregate value £500;
(c) medical aids or medical equipment reasonably required for the use of the debtor or any member of his household;
(d) books or other articles reasonably required for the education or training of the debtor or any member of his household not exceeding in aggregate value £500;
(e) toys for the use of any child who is a member of the debtor's household;
(f) articles reasonably required for the care and upbringing of a child who is a member of the debtor's household;
(g) specified articles of furniture and household equipment if they are at the time of the poinding in a dwelling-house and are reasonably required for the use in the dwelling-house of the person residing there or a member of his household.[23]

The debtor, a person owning the article in common with the debtor or a person in possession of a poinded article can apply within 14 days of the execution of the poinding to the sheriff for an order releasing the article from the poinding on the ground that it is exempt.[24]

Procedure

The officer, accompanied by one witness, proceeds to the premises between 8 a.m. and 8 p.m. on a day which is not a public holiday or a Sunday.[25] Unless he has given four days notice he cannot enter a dwelling-house if there is no adult present.[26] He exhibits the warrant to poind and the certificate of execution of the charge and demands payment of the sum due from the debtor. He should make inquiry from any person present as to the ownership of the articles proposed to be poinded and in particular whether they are in common ownership.[27] He then proceeds with the poinding. He can poind only to the extent

16.4

---

[19] *George Hopkinson Ltd.* v. *N. G. Napier & Son*, 1953 S.C. 139. This is so even if the creditor is a local authority for rates: Local Government (Miscellaneous Provisions) (Scotland) Act 1981, s.12.
[20] *Anderson* v. *Buchanan* (1848) 11 D. 270.
[21] D.A., s.41(1). See para. 16.8.
[22] D.A., s.16(1).
[23] D.A., s.16(2).
[24] D.A., s.16(4); A.S. (Debtors) 8, fm. 4.
[25] D.A., s.17.
[26] s.18; A.S. (Debtors) 10.
[27] s.20(2).

necessary to ensure that the amount due would be realised if the articles were sold at the values fixed.[28] He can assume that articles in the possession of the debtor are owned by him and he is not precluded from relying on that assumption by the fact that an assertion has been made that the article does not belong to the debtor or by the fact that the article is of a type commonly held on hire-purchase or a similar arrangement.[29] The officer values the articles according to the prices they would be likely to fetch if sold on the open market unless he considers that a valuation by a professional valuer is advisable.[30] He prepares a poinding schedule which sets forth the names of the creditor and the debtor, the articles poinded and their values, the sum recoverable and the place where the poinding was executed.[31] He and the witness sign the schedule and deliver it to the person in possession of the articles; if that is not the debtor a copy is sent by post to the debtor. The date of delivery is the date of execution of the poinding. The debtor must be informed of his rights to redeem the articles and to have articles released from the poinding. A person who owns a poinded article in common with the debtor must also be informed of his rights.[32] The articles are left at the place where they were poinded, but if that place is not a dwelling-house or other premises and there is not time in which to obtain an order from the court, he may remove them for security to the nearest convenient premises of the debtor or the person in possession of the articles or, if no such premises are available, to the nearest suitable secure premises.[33] He may conjoin another creditor in the poinding if the creditor has a warrant to poind other than a summary warrant.[34]

Effect of poinding

16.5   The poinding places a nexus on the articles. If the articles are removed by the debtor or any person who knows of the poinding without the consent of the creditor or the authorisation of the court it is a breach of the poinding and a contempt of court.[35] Restoration may be ordered and warrant to search for them granted.[36] The removal of the articles to another location does not release them from the poinding,[37] but if they have been acquired for value by someone who did not know about the poinding the sheriff will order their release.[38] A third party who knew of the poinding and had removed the articles so that they were acquired by another party from or through him may be ordered to consign a compensating sum in court.[39] If the debtor was at fault in the circumstances of the removal, the sheriff may authorise the poinding of other articles belonging to the debtor.[40] Wilful damage or destruction of the

---

[28] s.19(1).
[29] s.19(3).
[30] s.20(4).
[31] s.20(5); A.S. (Debtors) 11, fm. 5.
[32] s.20(6).
[33] s.20(7).
[34] s.21(8), (9).
[35] s.28(3).
[36] s.28(4).
[37] s.28(7).
[38] s.28(5)
[39] s.29(3).
[40] s.28(6).

articles is also a breach of the poinding and a contempt of court.[41] If the debtor was responsible a further poinding may be ordered.[42] The sheriff may make an order for the security of the poinded articles or for the immediate disposal of perishable articles.[43]

Warrant of sale

Within 14 days of the execution of the poinding, the officer of court must make to the sheriff a report of the poinding, signed by him and the witness and noting any assertion that any poinded article did not belong to the debtor.[44] The creditor may then apply to the sheriff for a warrant of sale, a copy of the application and a note of his rights being served on the debtor.[45] The application must be made within one year of the execution of the poinding unless an extension has been given.[46] The warrant of sale must provide that the sale will be by public auction at a specified location,[47] which must not be in a dwelling-house except with the consent in the prescribed written form of the occupier and, if he is not the occupier, the debtor.[48] The warrant appoints an officer of court to arrange the sale, specifies a period in which the sale must be held and empowers the officer to open shut and lockfast places for the purpose of executing the warrant.[49]

16.6

The sale

If articles are poinded in a dwelling-house they must be taken to an auction room for the sale unless the occupier and the debtor consent to the sale being held in the house; if the removal to the auction room would be too expensive the sale may be held in premises offered by the creditor.[50] A sale cannot be held in premises, other than a house or auction room, occupied by a person other than the debtor or creditor, except with consent of the occupier.[51]

The sale must be intimated to the debtor and advertised.[52] The arrangements for the sale may be varied on application to the sheriff.[53]

If he is not appointed as auctioneer, the officer must attend the sale and keep a record of the proceedings.[54] If he is acting as auctioneer he must be accompanied by one witness.[55] Unless the creditor chooses there is no reserve price, but if there is one it must not be more than the fixed value.[56]

16.7

---

[41] s.29(1).
[42] s.29(2).
[43] s.21(1); A.S. (Debtors) 12, 13, fms. 6, 7.
[44] s.22; A.S. (Debtors) 15, fm. 9.
[45] s.30; A.S. (Debtors) 26, fm. 20.
[46] s.27.
[47] s.31(1).
[48] s.32(1).
[49] s.31(2).
[50] s.32(3).
[51] s.32(4); A.S. (Debtors) 27, fm. 22.
[52] s.34; A.S. (Debtors) 29.
[53] s.35; A.S. (Debtors) 30, fm. 24 but see *Primesight Bus Advertising Ltd.* v. *Canning and Crawford* (Sh.Ct.), 1990 S.C.L.R. 349.
[54] s.37(1).
[55] s.37(2).
[56] s.37(3).

The fixed value and the reserve price need not be disclosed to bidders.[57] Any creditor and any person owning an article in common with the debtor can purchase at the sale.[58] Ownership of an article which remains unsold after exposure for sale passes to the creditor but if the sale is in the debtor's premises he must uplift it within a specified time.[59] Where an article is unsold or is sold below the fixed value the debtor is credited with the amount of the fixed value.[60]

After the sale the officer pays to the creditor the proceeds so far as necessary to meet the sum recoverable or, if the sheriff so directs, he consigns them in court.[61] The officer must also make a report of the sale to the sheriff.[62] The report is remitted to the auditor of court and after he has reported to the sheriff the sheriff makes an order declaring the balance due by or to the debtor.[63]

The sum recoverable is the amount outstanding of the sum due under the decree or document with interest and expenses decerned for and the expenses incurred in serving the charges and in the process of poinding and sale.[64] The expenses chargeable against the debtor are specified[65] and are recoverable by the poinding but not by any other legal process; any expenses not recovered by the time the diligence is completed cease to be chargeable against the debtor.[66] Sums recovered are ascribed first to expenses of diligence then to the interest due under the decree and then to the principal sum (including expenses) due under the decree.[67] The poinding ceases to have effect when the full amount recoverable is paid to the creditor or sheriff officer.[68]

Third party rights

16.8   A third party who owns an article which has been poinded can recover it if he satisfies the sheriff officer that it belongs to him and the debtor or the possessor of the article does not deny that it belongs to him.[69] Alternatively, at any time between the execution of the poinding and the warrant sale, the third party can apply to the sheriff for an order releasing the article from the poinding.[70] Such an application does not prejudice the taking of other proceedings and the third party can interdict the sale[71] or even recover the article from a purchaser[72] or the creditor.[73]

A person who owns an article in common with the debtor can obtain release of the article from the poinding by paying to the sheriff officer a

---

[57] s.37(4).
[58] s.37(5).
[59] s.37(6), (7).
[60] s.37(9).
[61] s.38.
[62] s.39(1); A.S. (Debtors) 31, fm. 26.
[63] s.39(4), (5).
[64] s.45.
[65] Sched. 1.
[66] s.93(1).
[67] s.94.
[68] s.95.
[69] D.A., s.40(1).
[70] D.A., s.40(2); A.S. (Debtors) 34, fm. 27.
[71] *Jack v. Waddell's Trs.*, 1918 S.C. 73.
[72] *Carlton v. Miller*, 1978 S.L.T. (Sh.Ct.) 36.
[73] *George Hopkinson v. Napier & Sons*, 1953 S.C. 139.

sum equal to the value of the debtor's interest in the article before the warrant sale unless the debtor or the possessor of the article denies the claim.[74] Alternatively, he can apply to the sheriff who may order release of the article on payment of the value of the debtor's interest or on the ground that the continued poinding would be unduly harsh to the third party.[75] The third party can purchase at the sale.[76] If the third party does not seek release of the article from the poinding, the creditor must pay him an appropriate fraction of the proceeds of sale.[77]

A third party common owner must be given notice of his rights at the time when the poinding is executed.[78] When an article has been released from the poinding because of third party ownership or on the ground of harshness, the sheriff officer can poind other articles belonging to the debtor in the same premises.[79]

The debtor's rights

The debtor has a right to be told of his right to redeem the poinded articles at the time of the poinding and of his rights to apply for orders releasing articles from the poinding.[80] A copy of the application for a warrant of sale must be served on him and he can object to the application.[81] He must be given intimation of the date arranged for the sale[82] and, if the sale is not to be held in the premises where the poinded articles are situated, of the place and date of removal.[83] He can redeem any article at the fixed value within 14 days of the execution of the poinding[84] and again within the period of seven days after the service on him of the application for the warrant of sale.[85] He can apply to the sheriff for an order that the poinding is invalid or has ceased to have effect[86] or for an order recalling the poinding on the ground that it would be unduly harsh for the warrant of sale to be granted, or that the aggregate of values fixed is substantially below what the articles would have been likely to fetch on the open market or that the likely proceeds of sale would probably not exceed the expenses of the remaining procedure.[87] The debtor or another person residing in a caravan, houseboat or other moveable structure which has been poinded can apply for an order sisting the proceedings.[88]

16.9

Competitions[89]

Where two poindings have not been conjoined, preference depends

16.10

---

[74] s.41(2).
[75] s.41(3); A.S. (Debtors) 35, fm. 28. *McCallum* (Sh.Ct.), 1990 S.C.L.R. 399 treats partnership property as common property!
[76] s.37(5)(*b*).
[77] s.41(8).
[78] s.20(6)(*e*).
[79] ss.40(5), 41(6).
[80] s.20(6); *Norris, Applicant*, 1990 G.W.D. 17–984.
[81] s.30(3); A.S. (Debtors) 26(8).
[82] s.34(1).
[83] s.34(2).
[84] s.21(4).
[85] s.33(2).
[86] s.24(1); A.S. (Debtors), 17(1)(*a*), fm.11.
[87] s.24(3); A.S. (Debtors), 17 (1)(*b*), fm.11.
[88] s.26; A.S. (Debtors), 18, fm. 12.
[89] As to the landlord's hypothec, see para. 15.2.

188 *Poinding*

upon priority of execution. In the case of a sale of goods, if the property has passed before the execution, the purchaser is obviously preferred; if the sale and delivery of the goods take place after execution of the poinding the purchaser is preferred but on notice that he must retain the price for the benefit of the poinder; if the price is paid but the goods have not been delivered it seems that the poinder is preferred.[90]

Poinding is, of course, preferred to a pledge, if the execution was prior to completion of the security by delivery.

A personal poinding is defeated by a poinding of the ground if the heritable creditor serves his action before the sale in the personal poinding is complete, unless the infeftment of the poinder of the ground was after the execution of the personal poinding in which event preference depends upon priority of execution.[91]

It is, apparently, competent for the *poinder's* creditor to arrest in the hands of the owner of the poinded goods.[92]

In a competition with an arrestment the poinding is preferred if the sale is completed before the date of the decree in the furthcoming.[93]

Effect of sequestration

16.11 A poinding executed on or after the 60th day prior to sequestration is ineffectual and the goods poinded or the proceeds thereof must be handed over to the trustee.[94] The poinder thus deprived of his diligence has a preference out of the goods or proceeds for the expense incurred by him in procuring the warrant for and executing such diligence.[95] This clearly applies where the execution of the poinding has taken place within the 60-day period and no sale has taken place under the former law. Where the poinding was executed before the 60 days but no sale had taken place at the date of sequestration, it seems that the diligence was struck down, even where there had been no unreasonable delay in carrying out the sale.[96] Now, however, the section refers to when the poinding was "executed" and the poinding is executed when the schedule is delivered,[97] so a poinding carried out before the 60 days is not affected by the section.[98]

Sequestration may affect a poinding executed before the 60-day period by virtue of the equalisation of diligence provisions.[99] Sequestration is equivalent to an arrestment and a completed poinding[1] and where sequestration is within four months of apparent insolvency, a poinding within 60 days before or four months after the apparent insolvency will, in effect, be cut down.

---

[90] Graham Stewart, pp. 365–366.
[91] *Tullis* v. *Whyte*, June 18, 1817, F.C.; Graham Stewart, p. 366.
[92] *Ferguson* v. *Bothwell* (1882) 9 R. 687.
[93] Graham Stewart, p. 159.
[94] B.A., s.37(4).
[95] s.37(5).
[96] *Wm. S. Yuile Ltd.* v. *Gibson*, 1952 S.L.T. (Sh.Ct.) 22; *cf.* Graham Stewart, p. 364; *Bendy Brothers Ltd.* v. *McAlister* (1910) 26 Sh.Ct.Rep. 152.
[97] D.A., s.21(7).
[98] See, however, McBryde, p. 178.
[99] See para. 15.5.
[1] B.A., s.37(1).

No poinding on or after the date of sequestration can give a preference over the bankrupt estate.[2]

If poinded property is sold, not under the poinding but by agreement between the creditor and debtor, the transaction may be reducible as a fraudulent preference.[3]

Liquidation

A poinding of the company's estate executed within the period of 60 days before the day on which the winding up order was made in a compulsory liquidation, or the date of the resolution, in the case of a voluntary liquidation, and whether or not subsisting at that date, is not effectual to create a preference for the poinder.[4] The estate poinded or the proceeds of sale thereof, must be handed over to the liquidator. The poinder is entitled to the expenses of the diligence out of the proceeds. Moreover, the liquidation is equivalent to a completed poinding in favour of the creditors according to their respective entitlements; accordingly, as in the case of sequestration, a poinding more than 60 days before liquidation may be cut down through the equalisation of diligence provisions.[5] A poinding on or after the date of liquidation is ineffectual.[6] 16.12

Appointment of receiver

If a receiver is appointed by virtue of a floating charge his powers over property are subject to the rights of any person who has effectually executed diligence thereon.[7] A poinding which has not been followed by a warrant of sale is not effectual diligence.[8] However, as a poinding, like an arrestment, renders the subject litigious[9] it would seem that a poinding executed before the creation of the floating charge gives a preference over the receiver.[10] 16.13

English bankruptcy

It seems that a receiving order in England has no effect on prior diligence executed on assets in Scotland.[11] 16.14

Suspension of poindings

Diligence may be stayed by an action of suspension which is competent, unless excluded by statute, where a decree or document exists on which a charge may follow.[12] If a charge has not yet been given, or if a charge has been given and the days of charge have not expired, or if the expired charge has not been followed out by poinding, the 16.15

---

[2] s.37(4).
[3] *Stewart* v. *Gardner* (1932) 48 Sh.Ct. Rep. 226.
[4] I.A., s.185(1), (3) applying B.A., s.37 (4).
[5] See para. 15.5.
[6] I.A., s.185(1) applying B.A., s.37(4)(*b*).
[7] I.A., s.55(3)(*a*).
[8] *Lord Advocate* v. *Royal Bank of Scotland*, 1977 S.C. 155.
[9] Graham Stewart, p. 362.
[10] *Iona Hotels Ltd.*, 1991 S.L.T. 11.
[11] *Hunter* v. *Palmer* (1825) 3 S. 586; Graham Stewart, p. 187; *cf.* Anton, *Private International Law*, p. 442.
[12] Mackay, *Manual of Practice in the Court of Session*, p. 421. In many cases the usual remedy will be an application for an order under D.A., s.24—see para. 16.9.

appropriate procedure is by a simple suspension.[13] If a poinding has followed on an expired charge but an order for sale has not been obtained, the procedure is a suspension and interdict. If an order for sale has been obtained the correct remedy is a suspension and suspension and interdict.[14] A simple suspension is the appropriate process to stay diligence for recovery of imperial taxes[15] but a suspension and interdict was required in the case of diligence proceeding on a warrant for collection of rates.[16]

Where the objection is to the diligence itself or is founded on a defect in the extract decree the sheriff court of the domicile of the person charged has jurisdiction in suspensions of charges or threatened charges on decrees granted by the sheriff.[17] The same sheriff court also has jurisdiction where the objection is to a decree of registration proceeding upon bonds, bills or other documents registered in any sheriff court books or the Books of Council and Session where, for example, it is alleged that the decree proceeded upon a promissory note the signature to which had been obtained by fraud.[18] The sheriff court cannot suspend its own decrees *in foro* apart from these cases.[19] The Court of Session can review the merits of decrees of lower courts but it cannot suspend its own decrees *in foro* unless the extract is defective or the decree is one of registration.[20] An objection to a decree *in foro* must be pursued in an action of reduction.[21]

The grounds for suspension of diligence are, broadly, defects in the extract decree or the diligence procedure,[22] a charge for an excessive amount,[23] and partial or total extinction of the debt subsequent to decree.[24]

In the Court of Session the first interlocutor orders intimation and answers and includes an interim sist of execution which may or may not require caution or consignation.[25] This prevents poinding and imprisonment but not arrestment, inhibition or adjudication. In the sheriff court, on sufficient caution being found for the sum charged for interest and expenses and for the expenses of the suspension, the sheriff may sist diligence, order intimation and answers, and proceed to dispose of the cause in a summary manner.[26] This, when intimated, prevents poinding and imprisonment but not arrestment or inhibition.[27]

---

[13] *Paul v. Henderson* (1867) 5 M. 1120.
[14] *Hobbin v. Burns* (1904) 11 S.L.T. 681.
[15] *Encyclopaedia of the Laws of Scotland*, Vol. XIV, p. 332.
[16] *Op. cit.*, Vol. VIII, p. 342.
[17] Sheriff Courts (Scotland) Act 1907, s.5(5), O.C.R. 108.
[18] 1907 Act, s.5(5) amended by Law Reform (Miscellaneous Provisions) (Scotland) Act 1980, s.15); *Maclachlan v. Glasgow*, 1925 S.L.T. (Sh.Ct) 77.
[19] *Lamont v. Hall*, 1964 S.L.T. (Sh.Ct.) 25.
[20] *Lamb v. Thompson* (1901) 4 F. 88.
[21] *McCarroll v. McKinstery*, 1923 S.C. 94; *Greenwood v. Mundle*, 1957 S.L.T. (Notes) 15.
[22] *Encyclopaedia of the Laws of Scotland*, Vol. VIII, p. 343.
[23] *Haughhead Coal Co. v. Gallocher* (1903) 11 S.L.T. 156—the charge is suspended *quoad* the excess.
[24] *Fowler v. Brown*, 1916 S.C. 597. See also *McCarroll v. McKinstery*, 1923 S.C. 94.
[25] Maclaren, *Bill Chamber Practice*, pp. 63–64.
[26] O.C.R. 109.
[27] Graham Stewart, p. 755.

CHAPTER 17

ARRESTMENT

Its use

17.1 Arrestment is the diligence appropriate to attach obligations to account to the debtor by a third party and corporeal moveables belonging to the debtor which are in the hands of a third party. In relation to the arrestment, the arresting creditor is known as "the arrester," the third party as "the arrestee" and the debtor as "the common debtor."[1] Arrestment to enforce payment of a decree is known as arrestment in execution; arrestment to found jurisdiction and arrestment on the dependence are treated elsewhere.[2]

The arrestee

17.2 The arrestee must be subject to the jurisdiction of the Scottish courts.[3] The arrestment must be made in the hands of a third party who is indebted to, or is under an obligation to account to, or holds goods which are the property of, the common debtor. It cannot be made in the hands of the arrester himself.[4] It cannot be made in the hands of a debtor of the common debtor's debtor.[5] It cannot be made in the hands of the common debtor himself or of "persons who are in law identified with him"[6] such as his wife,[7] his servants,[8] his factor,[9] or steward.[10] It can be made in the hands of someone who is under an obligation to account to the common debtor such as a trustee,[11] a commissioner,[12] a factor *loco absentis*,[13] an agent,[14] his law agent who holds the proceeds of a bond due to him,[15] the purchaser of heritage from him,[16] and an auctioneer.[17] A creditor of the exposer cannot arrest in the hands of a purchaser at an auction if the purchaser's obligation is to the auctioneer alone.[18]

A question arises where the arrestee has given the common debtor a cheque or bill for the amount due prior to the date of arrestment and it

---

[1] See as to the ambiguity of this nomenclature, Bell, *Comm.*, II, 63, n. 6.
[2] para. 11.8; para. 11.10.
[3] *Brash* v. *Brash*, 1966 S.C. 56; as to the locality of the debt, see para. 11.9.
[4] *Anderson* v. *Scottish N.E. Ry. Co.* (1867) 3 S.L.R. 270. But see *E. & A. Denholm Young & Co.* v. *MacElwee* (1918) 34 Sh.Ct.Rep. 193.
[5] Bell, *Prin.*, § 2276; *J. & C. Murray* v. *Wallace Marrs & Co.*, 1914 S.C. 114; (a bank instructed by the common debtor's bank); *McDonald* v. *Mize*, 1989 S.L.T. 482.
[6] Bell, *Comm.*, II, 70.
[7] More's *Notes to Stair*, p. 287.
[8] *Cuningham* v. *Home* (1760) Mor. 747.
[9] *Dunlop* v. *Weir* (1823) 2 S. 167.
[10] Bell, *Comm.*, II, 70.
[11] *Johnston* v. *Dundas's Trs.* (1837) 15 S. 904.
[12] *Brown* v. *Duff's Tr.* (1850) 13 D. 149.
[13] *Mitchell* v. *Scott* (1881) 8 R. 875.
[14] *Home* v. *Pringle* (1706) Mor. 734.
[15] *Telford's Exr.* v. *Blackwood* (1866) 4 M. 369; for a case where the agent acted both for the vendor and the building society in a sale of heritage, see *Turner* v. *Woolwich Equitable Building Society* (1956) 72 Sh.Ct.Rep. 300.
[16] *Benjedward's Crs.* (1753) Mor. 743.
[17] *Adam* v. *Anderson* (1837) 15 S. 1225; *Mackenzie & Co.* v. *Finlay* (1868) 7 M. 27.
[18] *Sharp* v. *Macdonald & Fraser* (1884) 1 Sh.Ct.Rep. 37.

has not been presented for payment prior to that date. If the cheque is not post-dated there is nothing to arrest.[19] If a post-dated cheque or a bill payable at a currency is given there is still a debt which can be attached prior to the date for payment of the instrument, at least where there has been no transfer to a bona fide indorsee for value.[20] In that situation the arrestee cannot require delivery of the bill as a condition of payment to the arrester.[21]

The fact that the common debtor has refused to accept the sum owed to him by the arrestee and has unsuccessfully sued for a larger sum is of no significance.[22]

Subjects arrestable—debts

17.3 Apart from corporeal moveables, it is not only debts which are arrestable: "It is the obligation to account which is the proper subject of attachment."[23] The following debts and obligations are arrestable:

(a) *Contract Payments.* Payments under a contract of *locatio operis* are arrestable even although the payment is not yet due and even although the obligation to pay is conditional upon completion of the work to the employer's satisfaction.[24] If payment is to be by instalments, only the next instalment is caught by the arrestment.[25]

(b) *Rents* are arrestable (but see para. 17.7 *infra*).

(c) *Insurance Policies.* The proceeds of a life insurance policy can be arrested during the life of the insured.[26] In the furthcoming the policy may be sold or surrendered.[27] It is thought that the arrestment is not affected by payment of subsequent premiums.[28] In the case of indemnity insurance, the insurer is under no liability to the insured until judgment is given against the insured and nothing can be arrested in the hands of the insurer till then.[29]

(d) *Cash on Deposit Receipt.* Where a deposit receipt acknowledges that money received from A and B is "payable to either or the survivor," and the fund is arrested by a creditor of B, the bank is entitled to refuse to make payment to A.[30] A deposit receipt in the name of the common debtor "in trust" is arrestable.[31]

(e) *Bonds.* Personal bonds and heritable bonds upon which infeftment has not followed can be arrested as to principal and interest.[32] Heritable bonds on which infeftment has followed can be arrested

---

[19] *Leggat Bros.* v. *Gray*, 1908 S.C. 67.
[20] *Elmslie* v. *Hunter* (1936) 52 Sh.Ct.Rep. 181.
[21] *Evans* v. *Pinchere* (1907) 23 Sh.Ct.Rep. 111.
[22] *Lennie* v. *Mackie & Co.* (1907) 23 Sh.Ct.Rep. 85.
[23] Bell, *Comm.*, II, 71.
[24] *Marshall* v. *Nimmo & Co.* (1847) 10 D. 328; *Park Dobson & Co. Ltd.* v. *Wm. Taylor & Son*, 1929 S.C. 571; *MacLaren & Co.* v. *Preston* (1893) 1 S.L.T. 75.
[25] *Park Dobson & Co. Ltd.* v. *Wm. Taylor & Son, supra.*
[26] *Strachan* v. *McDougle* (1835) 13 S. 954.
[27] *Clark* v. *Scottish Amicable Insurance Co.* (1922) 38 Sh.Ct. Rep. 170.
[28] *Bankhardt's Trs.* v. *Scottish Amicable Life Assurance Society* (1871) 9 M. 443.
[29] *Kerr* v. *R. & W. Ferguson*, 1931 S.C. 736; *Boland* v. *White Cross Insurance Association*, 1926 S.C. 1066.
[30] *Allan's Exr.* v. *Union Bank of Scotland Ltd.*, 1909 S.C. 206.
[31] *Union Bank* v. *Mills* (1926) 42 Sh.Ct.Rep. 141.
[32] Arrestments Act 1661.

only as to interest due and current, the appropriate diligence to attach the principal being adjudication.[33]

(f) *Partnership Interest.* A share in a partnership is arrestable.[34] A debt due to an English partnership is not due to one of the partners.[35]

(g) *Shares* in a limited company registered in Scotland are arrestable.[36] A subsidiary company can arrest shares of its holding company in the hands of the latter although a subsidiary company cannot acquire the shares of its holding company.[37] In the case of other corporate bodies the position may be regulated by special statutory provisions.[38]

(h) *Calls* on shares may be arrested in the hands of the shareholders.[39] The amount unpaid on shares cannot be arrested before a call is made, however.[40]

(i) *Liability to Account.* In general a liability to account is arrestable. Where a bank held shares in security of a customer's overdraft, it was held that an arrestment in the hands of the bank attached any balance due to the customer after realisation of the shares and extinction of the overdraft.[41]

(j) *Expenses.* An award of expenses is arrestable even if it has not been quantified.[42]

(k) *Legitim.* A right to legitim is arrestable from the date of the ancestor's death even if the descendant has to elect between legitim and a non-vested conventional provision.[43]

(l) *Trust Interest.* A vested right in a trust estate is arrestable if the beneficiary's interest is moveable in character.[44] This depends on the terms of the trust deed and not on the nature of the estate. The interest is moveable "so long as it is not a claim several or *pro indiviso* to heritage, but merely a right to payment out of the general estate."[45] It seems that an interest which has vested subject to defeasance is arrestable.[46]

The following debts are not arrestable:
(a) Earnings as defined[47] are not subject to arrestment.[48]
(b) Alimentary payments are not arrestable[49] except (i) as to arrears,[50]

---

[33] *Stuart* v. *Stuart* (1705) Mor. 140.
[34] Bell, *Comm.*, II, 536; *Cassells* v. *Stewart* (1879) 6 R. 936, *per* Lord Gifford at p. 956.
[35] *Parnell* v. *Walter* (1889) 16 R. 917.
[36] *Sinclair* v. *Staples* (1860) 22 D. 600; *American Mortgage Co. of Scotland Ltd.* v. *Sidway*, 1908 S.C. 500.
[37] *Stenhouse London Ltd.* v. *Allwright*, 1972 S.C. 209.
[38] *Royal Bank* v. *Fairholm* (1770) Mor. App., "Adjudication," No. 3.
[39] *Hill* v. *College of Glasgow* (1849) 12 D. 46.
[40] Graham Stewart, p. 46; *Lindsay* v. *La Martona Rubber Estates Ltd.*, 1911 2 S.L.T. 468.
[41] *Commercial Bank of Scotland Ltd.* v. *Eagle Star Insurance Co. Ltd.*, 1950 S L.T. (Notes) 30.
[42] *Agnew* v. *Norwest Construction Co.*, 1935 S.C. 771.
[43] *Waddell* v. *Waddell's Trs.*, 1932 S.L.T. 201.
[44] *Smith's Trs.* v. *Grant* (1862) 24 D. 1142.
[45] Graham Stewart, p. 62.
[46] *Chambers' Trs.* v. *Smith* (1878) 5 R.(H.L.) 151.
[47] See para. 18.2.
[48] D.A., s.46(1).
[49] Bell, *Comm.*, I, 125. See *Douglas Gardiner & Mill* v. *Mackintosh's Trs.*, 1916 S.C. 125.
[50] *Drew* v. *Drew* (1870) 9 M. 163.

(ii) *quoad excessum*[51] (iii) for alimentary debts.[52] A person declared to be alimentary is subject to diligence against earnings.[53] Alimentary debts are "all articles of annual expenditure required for the comfort, or suitable to the situation of the party; and in regard to articles in which ready-money dealing is unusual and inconvenient, and in which an absolute disability to contract debt would operate to his advantage, that disability has been departed from."[54] What is alimentary depends on the party's station in life.[55] The price of liquor may be an alimentary debt.[56] The expenses of an alimentary decree are alimentary.[57] Law accounts are not alimentary unless they are incurred for the defence of the alimentary fund.[58] A creditor who has made an advance for alimentary purposes is an alimentary creditor.[59] Arrears of contractual aliment do not constitute an alimentary debt.[60]

(c) Sums appropriated for a special purpose.[61]

(d) Any money payable by the Crown the assignation, charging or taking in execution of which is prohibited or restricted by statute.[62]

(e) A *spes successionis*.[63]

(f) The position of a right to damages in respect of delict or breach of contract is not clear. Where the wrong is of a personal nature—seduction, slander or personal injury, for example—nothing is arrestable until an action is raised or possibly, until a claim is intimated.[64] There may be exceptions. Even if an action has been raised the arrestment may be nugatory if the arrestee's insurers make an extra-judicial settlement.[65]

A contractual provision that a debt will not be arrestable has no effect.[66] Where a debt which is not arrestable is paid into the common debtor's bank account the sum may still be protected if it can be identified.[67]

---

[51] *Livingstone* v. *Livingstone* (1886) 14 R. 43.
[52] *Lord Ruthven* v. *Pulford & Sons*, 1909 S.C. 951.
[53] D.A., s.73(2)(c).
[54] *Per* Lord Fullerton, *Greig* v. *Christie* (1837) 16 S. 242 at 244.
[55] *Earl of Buchan* v. *His Creditors* (1835) 13 S. 1112.
[56] *Turnbull & Sons* v. *Scott* (1899) 15 Sh.Ct.Rep. 268.
[57] *Hunter* v. *Wilson* (1917) 33 Sh.Ct.Rep. 209.
[58] *Greig* v. *Christie, supra*.
[59] *Waddell* v. *Waddell* (1836) 15 S. 151.
[60] *Officers' Superannuation and Provident Fund* v. *Cooper*, 1960 S.L.T. (Sh.Ct.) 2.
[61] *Souper* v. *Smith* (1756) Mor. 744. Few of the cases usually cited on this matter are satisfactory. In *Baillie* v. *Wilson* (1840) 2 D. 495 the sum was due under an agreement made directly between the arrestee and the person to whom the appropriation was made. In *British Linen Co.* v. *Kansas Investment Co. Ltd.* (1895) 3 S.L.T. 138 and 202 the fund was provided by a third party, not the debtor. As to sums consigned in court, see *Shankland & Co.* v. *McGildowny*, 1912 S.C. 857.
[62] Crown Proceedings Act 1947, s.46; *e.g.* Social Security Act 1975, s.87(1). See *Macfarlane* v. *Glasgow Corporation* (1934) 50 Sh.Ct.Rep. 247.
[63] *Trappes* v. *Meredith* (1871) 10 M. 38.
[64] Lord Dunedin's dissenting opinion in *Riley* v. *Ellis*, 1910 S.C. 934, was approved by the House of Lords in *Caldwell* v. *Hamilton*, 1919 S.C. (H.L.)100; *Wardrop* v. *Fairholm and Arbuthnot* (1744) Mor. 4860 establishes that the claim is arrestable once the action has been raised.
[65] *Mather & Son* v. *Wilson & Co. Ltd.* (1908) 15 S.L.T. 946.
[66] *Fritz's Agency Ltd.* v. *Moss' Empires Ltd.* (1922) 38 Sh.Ct.Rep. 124.
[67] *Woods* v. *Royal Bank*, 1913 1 S.L.T. 499.

Subjects arrestable: corporeal moveables

17.4 The corporeal moveables arrested must be the property of the common debtor and the arrestee must be under an obligation to the common debtor with regard to the moveables although the obligation need not rest upon an express contract.[68] It is not sufficient that the moveables belong to the common debtor if the arrestee is under an obligation to someone else in respect of them.[69] Similarly, it is not sufficient that the arrestee is under an obligation to the common debtor in respect of them if the moveables are not the property of the common debtor.[70] Property owned jointly by the common debtor and another party cannot be arrested.[71]

Goods can, therefore, be arrested in the hands of a depositary,[72] a carrier,[73] a consignee,[74] and ship-owners[75] (unless the ship is on a time charter at the disposal of the owner of the goods.)[76] It is not competent to arrest the furniture of a landlord in the hands of his tenant.[77] Possession sufficient to create a lien is not necessarily sufficient to permit arrestment, so a guest's baggage cannot be arrested in the hands of a host or innkeeper[78] and a horse being shod cannot be arrested in the hands of a blacksmith.[79]

The following are not arrestable:

(a) articles which are exempted from poinding under Debtors (Scotland) Act 1987, s.16.[80]

(b) books, documents and evidents;[81]

(c) stolen property in the hands of the procurator fiscal or police;[82]

(d) the corpus of bills.[83] If the common debtor is payee, the debt can be arrested in the hands of the acceptor. The arrestment can, however, be defeated if the payee indorses the bill to a bona fide holder for value who does not have notice of the arrestment.

Service of arrestment

17.5 The warrant for arrestment in execution is normally an extract of a Court of Session decree, of a sheriff court decree or of a decree proceeding on a deed or protest registered in the Books of Council and

---

[68] *Sir James Laing & Sons Ltd.* v. *Barclay Curle & Co. Ltd.*, 1908 S.C. 82; S.C.(H.L.) 1; *Moore & Weinberg* v. *Ernsthausen Ltd.*, 1917 S.C.(H.L.) 25.

[69] *Young* v. *Aktiebolaget Ofverums Bruk* (1890) 18 R. 163; *Heron* v. *Winfields Ltd.* (1894) 22 R. 182.

[70] *Millar & Lang* v. *Polak* (1907) 14 S.L.T. 788.

[71] *Byng* v. *Campbell* (1893) 1 S L.T. 371; *Lucas's Trs.* v. *Campbell & Scott* (1894) 21 R. 1096.

[72] *Bridges* v. *Ewing* (1836) 15 S. 8.

[73] *Matthew* v. *Fawns* (1842) 4 D. 1242; *Frederic Braby & Co. Ltd.* v. *Edwin Danks & Co. (Oldbury) Ltd.* (1907) 15 S.L.T. 161 (goods despatched by arresters).

[74] *Stalker* v. *Aiton* (1759) Mor 745.

[75] *Mitchell* v. *Burn* (1874) 1 R. 900.

[76] Graham Stewart, p. 108.

[77] *Hunter* v. *Lees* (1733) Mor. 736; *Davidson* v. *Murray* (1784) Mor. 761 (poinding is competent).

[78] *Hume* v. *Baillie* (1852) 14 D. 821; *Hutchison* v. *Hutchison*, 1912 1 S.L.T. 219.

[79] *Neilson* v. *Smiths Gowans & Roy* (1821) Hume 31.

[80] D.A., s.99(2). See para. 16.3.

[81] *Trowsdale's Tr.* v. *Forcett Ry Co.* (1870) 9 M. 88.

[82] *Guthrie* v. *Morren* (1939) 55 Sh.Ct.Rep. 172.

[83] Ersk., III, 6, 7; Bell, *Comm.*, II, 68; Graham Stewart, p. 78.

Session or sheriff court books.[84] The warrant must be regular. It can, of course, be used for any number of arrestments.[85]

If the arrestee is furth of Scotland an arrestment proceeding on an extract of a Court of Session decree can be served on him edictally[86] but the arrestment is not held to have interpelled such person from paying the common debtor unless it is proved that the arrestee or those having authority to act for him were previously in the knowledge of such arrestment having been so served.[87] An arrestment proceeding on an extract sheriff court decree cannot be served edictally. The common debtor need not be subject to the jurisdiction when the arrestment is used.[88]

No charge is necessary before service of an arrestment. Service must be made by a sheriff officer.[89] The officer must deliver the schedule to the arrestee personally or leave it at his dwelling-house. If it is not personally served, to make it effectual a copy must also be sent by registered post or recorded delivery to the arrestee's last known place of abode, or, if that is unknown, or if the arrestee is a firm or corporation, to the arrestee's principal place of business, if known, or, if that is not known, to any known place of business.[90]

There is no statutory form of schedule.[91] The funds or property to be arrested need not be specified.[92] The capacity in which the funds are held need not be stated.[93]

Types of arrestee

17.6 Where the arrestee is a pupil or *incapax* the arrestment is made in the hands of the tutor, judicial factor or *curator bonis*[94] but in the case of a minor service should be on the minor, not his curator.[95] In the case of trustees the arrestment should be served on all the accepting trustees, or at least a quorum.[96] Service is made on a corporation[97] or partnership by putting the notice in the hands of one of their servants at their principal office or branch office.[98] In the case of a limited company the notice may be served by leaving it at, or sending it by post to, the registered office or

---

[84] For the procedure where a person has acquired right to an extract, see para. 15.3.
[85] Graham Stewart, p. 26.
[86] 1838 Act, s.18.
[87] Debts Securities (Scotland) Act 1856, s.1.
[88] *Wightman* v. *Wilson* (1858) 20 D. 779.
[89] 1892 Act, s.8. In a summary cause an arrestment can be executed by registered letter: Execution of Diligence (Scotland) Act 1926, s.21.
[90] O.C.R. 111; S.C.R. 3(2); Smll. C.R. 2(1).
[91] Graham Stewart, p. 34; see also as to defects in the schedule and execution, *ibid.* pp. 35, 36.
[92] As to this see *Metzenburg* v. *Highland Ry. Co.* (1869) 7 M. 919.
[93] *Huber* v. *Banks*, 1986 S.L.T. 58. But see, as to arrestments served on the Lord Advocate, 1980 S.L.T. (News) 146.
[94] Ersk., III, 6, 4: Bell, *Prin.*, § 2121.
[95] *Binning* v. *Macdoual* (1738) Mor. 736.
[96] *Black* v. *Scott* (1830) 8 S. 367; *Gracie* v. *Gracie*, 1910 S.C. 899.
[97] *Campbell* v. *Watson's Tr.* (1898) 25 R. 690; *Macintyre* v.*Caledonian Ry. Co.* (1909) 25 Sh.Ct. Rep. 329; *Abbey National Building Society* v. *Strang*, 1981 S.L.T. (Sh.Ct.) 4.
[98] See O.C.R. 111.

branch office.[99] It seems that where the company is in liquidation, service should be on the company itself and the liquidator as such.[1] While it has been stated that service at a branch of a bank affects only funds held at that branch[2] it is not clear that this is in accordance with principle;[3] the usual practice is to serve on both the head office and the branch at which there is an account.

Where goods are on a ship, instead of service on the owners, the arrestment may be made in the hands of the master[4] and, possibly, if the ship is in harbour, the shipbrokers.[5]

Effect of arrestment

The effect of the arrestment is to interpel the arrestee from paying over the sum attached to the common debtor. If he does so he is liable to the arrester for the loss caused thereby. Similarly, the arrestee cannot pay over the funds to the arrester without either the authority of the court or the consent of the common debtor.[6] **17.7**

An arrestment of a periodical payment attaches only the payment in respect of the current term which may be only a day.[7] If under the contract, the payment is made in advance, the arrestment cannot attach anything except payments in arrears.[8]

The practice of the Scottish banks is to disclose what sum has been attached by an arrestment in execution.

If they are not pursued or insisted on, arrestments in execution prescribe in three years from the date of service except where the debt is future or contingent when the three years run from the date the debt becomes due and the contingency is purified.[9] A period in which the debt which the arrestment secures was subject to a time to pay direction or a time to pay order, or in which the arrestment was subject to an interim order pending disposal of an application for a time to pay order is disregarded.[10] In an arrestment on the dependence, prescription runs from the date of decree in the action. These provisions do not apply to an earnings arrestment, a current maintenance arrestment or a conjoined arrestment order.[11]

---

[99] Companies Act 1985, s.725(1); *Hopper & Co.* v. *Walker* (1904) 20 Sh.Ct.Rep. 137.
[1] *Burns* v. *Gillies, supra.*
[2] Graham Stewart, p. 33.
[3] See *J. Verrico & Co. Ltd.* v. *Australian Mutual Provident Society*, 1972 S.L.T. (Sh.Ct.) 57.
[4] *Kellas* v. *Brown* (1856) 18 D. 1089.
[5] *Carron Co.* v. *Currie & Co.* (1896) 33 S.L.R. 578.
[6] *High-Flex (Scotland) Ltd.* v. *Kentallen Mechanical Services Co.*, 1977 S.L.T. (Sh.Ct.) 91.
[7] *McAulay* v. *Smith* (1914) 30 Sh.Ct.Rep. 162.
[8] *Smith* v. *Burns* (1847) 9 D. 1344 (annuity).
[9] Debtors (Scotland) Act 1838, s.22. From *Jameson* v. *Sharp* (1887) 14 R. 643, it would appear that the exemption applies only to what are properly called contingent debts; when the debt is due at a future date but is not yet payable the period runs from the date of service of the arrestment. See para. 1.10.
[10] *Ibid.*, s.22(2) added by D.A. Sched. 6, para. 3.
[11] Debtors (Scotland) Act 1838, s.22(3) added by D.A., Sched. 6, para.3.

Furthcoming

17.8 The arresting creditor completes his diligence by bringing an action of furthcoming against the arrestee and the common debtor in order to obtain "a decree effectually transferring from the common debtor to the arresting creditor the obligation which was originally prestable to the former by the arrestee."[12] The purposes of the action are to ascertain the existence and extent of the arrestee's obligation to the common debtor and to determine whether the arrester is now in right of that obligation. The action is brought in the Court of Session or in the sheriff court where the fund is situated or to whose jurisdiction the arrestee is subject.[13] The common debtor does not need to be subject to the court's jurisdiction but he must receive fair notice of the action.[14] The usual conclusion or crave is to ordain payment of the sum arrested by the arrestee to the arrester but where the subject arrested is not a pecuniary obligation the summons must be framed so as to be applicable to the subject attached.[15] In the case of corporeal moveables the court will grant a warrant for sale on a conclusion for payment[16] but if the subjects arrested are shares[17] or an insurance policy[18] or an interest in a partnership,[19] a special conclusion is necessary. Any expenses chargeable against the debtor incurred in the service of the schedule or in the furthcoming are recoverable out of the arrested property and decree will be given in the furthcoming for any balance not so recovered.[20] The common debtor may defend the action on the ground that the arrestment was invalid or that he is not indebted to the arrester; the latter course is not open to him if his liability to the arrester has been established in a prior action.[21] The arrestee has no interest to plead that nothing is due by the common debtor to the arrester[22] but he can defend on the grounds that the common debtor has not been duly called[23] or that the arrestment was invalid, or that nothing was arrested. He may take against the arrester any defence which he could have maintained against the common debtor because the arrester acquires the common debtor's right *tantum et tale*.[24] If the arrestee's liability to the common debtor is contingent upon the result of an arbitration, the furthcoming will be sisted to await the result of the arbitration proceedings.[25] The fact that the common debtor would have

---

[12] Per Lord Kinnear, *Lucas's Trs.* v. *Campbell & Scott* (1894) 21 R. 1096 at 1103.
[13] Civil Jurisdiction and Judgments Act 1982, Sched. 8, rules 1,2(9).
[14] *Burns* v. *Monro* (1844) 6 D. 1352; *Leggat Bros.* v. *Gray*, 1912 S.C. 230.
[15] *Lucas's Trs* v. *Campbell & Scott, supra.*
[16] *Ibid.*
[17] *Sinclair* v. *Staples* (1860) 22 D. 600; *Valentine* v. *Grangemouth Coal Co.* (1897) 5 S.L.T. 47.
[18] *Clark* v. *Scottish Amicable Life Assurance Society*, 1922 S.L.T. (Sh.Ct.) 88.
[19] *Green* v. *Miller's Debt Recovery Services*, 1954 S.L.T. (Sh.Ct.) 26.
[20] D.A., s.93(2).
[21] *Donaldson* v. *Ord* (1855) 17 D. 1053.
[22] *Houston* v. *Aberdeen Town & County Banking Company* (1849) 11 D. 1490.
[23] *Smyth* v. *Ninian* (1826) 5 S. 8.
[24] *Houston* v. *Aberdeen Town & County Banking Company, supra*; *Wilson* v. *Carrick* (1881) 18 S.L.R. 657 (compensation); *Smith* v. *Chambers' Trs.* (1878) 5 R. 97; 5 R.(H.L.) 151 (defeasible claim).
[25] *Boland* v. *White Cross Insurance Association*, 1926 S.C. 1066; *Palmer* v. *S.E. Lancashire Insurance Co.*, 1932 S.L.T. 68; *Cant* v. *Eagle Star Insurance Co.*, 1937 S.L.T. 444.

been entitled to deduct tax in paying the arrester does not mean that the arrestee is entitled to do so.[26] Any party having an interest in the arrested funds or property can appear in the action. If a prior arrester on the dependence who has not yet obtained decree in his principal action appears, the action of furthcoming will be sisted.[27] If the action is defended it proceeds as an ordinary action. The action is not affected by the death of the arrestee; it proceeds against his representatives.[28] The furthcoming may be raised before the arrested fund is payable and it may be necessary to do this to interrupt the prescription of the arrestment.[29]

Sums recovered are ascribed first to the expenses of diligence, then to interest and then to the principal sum including expenses.[30] The arrestment ceases to have effect when the full amount recoverable is paid to the creditor or sheriff officer.[31]

Competition: arrestments inter se

Arrestments rank *inter se* according to priority of service[32] and the arrestment which is executed first is preferred even although the arrester is not the first to obtain a decree of furthcoming[33] or, in the case of arrestment on the dependence, decree of constitution.[34] Priority is determined by the hour shown in the execution.[35] If neither execution mentions the hour, arrestments served on the same day are ranked *pari passu*.[36] If one execution mentions the hour and the other is silent, the former is preferred[37] unless the hour mentioned is late in the day in which case they are ranked *pari passu*.[38] It is probably not competent to prove the hour of service by parole evidence.[39] If there is undue delay in following up the arrestment first served, a subsequent arrester who has obtained and extracted decree in a furthcoming will be preferred.[40] Where an arrestment on the dependence is subsequent to an arrestment to found jurisdiction, the arrester on the dependence cannot enforce a furthcoming until a citation has followed upon the arrestment to found jurisdiction, but once citation has followed he is preferred to the arrestment to found jurisdiction.[41]

A second or subsequent arrestment has effect subject to the prior arrestment and results in a preference over any balance remaining after satisfaction of the claim of the prior arrester.[42]

17.9

---

[26] *Fletcher* v. *Young*, 1936 S.L.T. 572.
[27] Graham Stewart, p. 232; *Walker* v. *United Creameries Ltd.*, 1928 S.L.T. (Sh.Ct.) 21.
[28] Graham Stewart, p. 228.
[29] *Jameson* v. *Sharp* (1887) 14 R. 643.
[30] D.A., s.94.
[31] D.A., s.95.
[32] Stair, III, i, 46; Ersk., III, vi, 18.
[33] *Wallace* v. *Scot* (1583) Mor. 807.
[34] *Baynes* v. *Graham* (1796) Mor. 2904; *Mitchell* v. *Scott* (1881) 8 R. 875.
[35] Ersk., III, vi, 18.
[36] Bankton, III, i, 41; *Sutie* v. *Ross* (1705) Mor. 816.
[37] Bankton, III, i, 41; *Hertz* v. *Itzig* (1865) 3 M. 813.
[38] *Douglas* v. *Palmer* (1777) 5 Brown's Supp. 381.
[39] Bankton, III, i, 41; *Sutie* v. *Ross, supra*; *Hertz* v. *Itzig, supra*.
[40] Bankton, III, i, 41; Graham Stewart, p. 141.
[41] *Stillie's Trs.* v. *Stillie* (1898) 6 S.L.T. 173.
[42] *W.H. Hill & Sons Ltd.* v. *Manning's Tr.*, 1951 S.L.T. (Sh.Ct.) 29.

17.10 Competition: other diligence[43]

In competition with confirmation by an executor-creditor, the arrestment is preferred only if a decree of furthcoming has been obtained before the executor has confirmed to the arrested fund.[44] It seems that in competition with an adjudication, the criterion of preference is whether decree of furthcoming was obtained before the date of adjudication.[45] Such a competition could arise only in the limited field where both diligences are competent, *e.g.* heritable bonds not followed by infeftment.

Competition: assignations

17.11 In competition with a voluntary assignation an arrestment is preferred if it is executed before the date of intimation of the assignation even if the date of the assignation itself was prior to the arrestment.[46] If the arrestment and intimation are on the same day, priority is determined by the hour.[47] If the hours are not specified, the arrestment and the assignation rank *pari passu*.[48] If either the execution of arrestment or the intimation specified an hour and the other document does not, the former is preferred.[49] Intimation of a transfer of shares in a limited company has the effect of giving the transfer priority over a subsequent arrestment even if the transfer is not registered before the execution of the arrestment.[50]

Effect of insolvency

17.12 An arrestment executed within the period of sixty days before the date of the common debtor's sequestration, and whether or not subsisting at that date, is ineffectual to create a preference for the arrestor.[51] It does place a nexus on the fund which prevents the arrestee paying it away to the prejudice of the trustee.[52] The day of sequestration itself is excluded in computing the period so an arrestment on April 20 is affected by a sequestration on June 19.[53] An arrestment executed outwith the 60 days is not cut down even although decree in the furthcoming was obtained within the period.[54] An arrestment which was executed before the 60 days but which has not been followed up by a furthcoming prior to sequestration is effectual if there has been no undue delay in bringing the

---

[43] For competition with a poinding of the ground and a heritable creditor collecting rents, see Graham Stewart, p. 163.

[44] Bell, *Comm.*, II, 69; *Wilson* v. *Fleming* (1823) 2 S. 430.

[45] Bell, *Comm.*, II, 69; Graham Stewart, p. 161.

[46] Stair, III, i, 43, 44; Erskine, III, 6, 19; *Inglis* v. *Robertson & Baxter* (1898) 25 R.(H.L.) 70. Where the arrestment is on the dependence, it does not matter that decree of constitution has not been obtained at the time intimation is made—*A* v. *B* (1618) Mor. 2771.

[47] *Davidson* v. *Balcanqual* (1629) Mor. 2773; presumably this arises only where the intimation is formal.

[48] *Inglis* v. *Edward* (1630) Mor. 2773.

[49] Stair, III, i, 43.

[50] *Thomson* v. *Fullarton* (1842) 5 D. 379; *Stillie's Trs.* v. *Stillie* (1898) 6 S.L.T. 173; *Harvey's Yoker Distillery* v. *Singleton* (1901) 8 S.L.T. 369; *National Bank of Scotland Glasgow Nominees Ltd.* v. *Adamson*, 1932 S.L.T. 492. It is arguable that this result is consistent with *Morrison* v. *Harrison* (1876) 3 R. 406—see Graham Stewart, p. 143.

[51] B.A., s.37(4); *Dow & Co.* v. *Union Bank* (1875) 2 R. 459.

[52] *McKenzie* v. *Campbell* (1894) 21 R. 904.

[53] *Stiven* v. *Reynolds & Co.* (1891) 18 R. 422, *arguendo*.

[54] Graham Stewart, p. 186.

furthcoming;[55] this is so even where the arrestment is on the dependence of an action in which decree on the merits has not yet been obtained before sequestration; in such cases, however, where there has been not furthcoming prior to sequestration, the arrestee does not pay over the funds to the arrester and must make them available to the trustee who then gives a preference to the arrester in the sequestration in respect of the funds recovered.[56] Where the arrestment is executed within the 60 days and decree in a furthcoming has not been obtained before the sequestration, the arrestment is cut down; the arrestee must make the funds available to the trustee and he cannot pay them away to the trustee's prejudice;[57] the arrester is, however, entitled to payment out of the arrested estate or out of the proceeds of sale thereof of the expenses incurred in obtaining the extract or other document on which the arrestment proceeded, in executing the arrestment and in taking any further action in respect of the arrestment.

Where the arrestment is executed within the 60 days and the funds have been paid over to the arrester prior to sequestration, he must pay them to the trustee under deduction of these expenses.

As has been indicated above, sequestration has a still wider effect on arrestments by virtue of the equalisation of diligence provisions.[58] Sequestration at its date is equivalent to an arrestment in execution and decree of furthcoming and an arrestment in execution and warrant of sale in favour of the creditors according to their respective entitlements.[59] Therefore, when sequestration takes place within four months of apparent insolvency it ranks equally with any arrestment executed within 60 days before, or four months after, apparent insolvency and the arrestment is, in effect, cut down.

No arrestment on or after the date of sequestration can give a preference over the bankrupt estate.[60]

Liquidation

An arrestment of the company's estate executed within the period of 60 days before the day on which the winding up order was made in a compulsory liquidation,[61] or the date of the resolution, in the case of a voluntary liquidation, and whether or not subsisting at that date, is not effectual to create a preference for the arrester.[62] (An arrestment prior to the 60 days is effectual and, even if there has been no furthcoming prior to liquidation, the arrested fund does not fall to the liquidator.[63]) The estate arrested, or the proceeds of sale thereof, must be handed over to the

17.13

---

[55] It is thought that this is not affected by what was said about the nature of an arrestment in *Lord Advocate* v. *Royal Bank of Scotland Ltd.*, 1977 S.C. 155, but see, for the position in a liquidation, para. 17.13.

[56] *Mitchell* v. *Scott* (1881) 8 R. 875; *Benhar Coal Co.* v. *Turnbull* (1883) 10 R. 558 (liquidation); *James Gilmour (Crossford) Ltd.* v. *John Williams (Wishaw) Ltd.*, 1970 S.L.T. (Sh.Ct.) 6.

[57] *McKenzie* v. *Campbell* (1894) 21 R. 904.

[58] See para. 15.5.

[59] B.A., s.37(1).

[60] s.37(4).

[61] I.A., s.185(3); *Morrison* v. *Integer Systems Control Ltd.* (Sh.Ct.) 1989 S.C.L.R. 495.

[62] I.A., s.185(1) applying B.A., s.37.

[63] *Commercial Aluminium Windows Ltd.* v. *Cumbernauld Development Corporation*, 1987 S.L.T. (Sh.Ct.) 91.

liquidator. The arrester is entitled to the expenses of the diligence out of the proceeds.[64] Moreover, the liquidation is equivalent to an arrestment in execution and a decree of furthcoming, and an arrestment in execution and warrant of sale;[65] accordingly, as in the case of sequestration, an arrestment more than 60 days before liquidation may be cut down through the equalisation of diligence provisions.[66] An arrestment on or after the date of liquidation is ineffectual.[67]

The First Division has held[68] that an arrestment which has not been followed up by a furthcoming was not "effectually executed diligence" in terms of the Companies (Floating Charges and Receivers) (Scotland) Act 1972, s.15(2)(a)[69] and accordingly did not prevail against a receiver subsequently appointed under a floating charge. The expression "effectually executed diligence" also occurs in s.463(1)(a) of the Companies Act 1985[70] in relation to the attachment of a floating charge on the liquidation of the company. If effect is given to the presumption that the same meaning is to be given to the same words in Acts *in pari materia* this means that an arrestment executed more than 60 days before liquidation and not followed by a furthcoming does not prevail against the rights of the holder of a floating charge over the arrested property but would prevail against the general creditors if there were no floating charge. Where a liquidator was appointed on the common debtor company between the raising of the furthcoming and the granting of decree therein, and the liquidator intimated that he claimed the arrested funds, the court granted a sist of execution to prevent the arrester proceeding to do diligence against the arrestees on the furthcoming decree.[71] The equalisation of diligence provisions[72] apply to companies.[73]

The foregoing provision as to the effect of liquidation applies to the estate in Scotland of a company registered in England.[74]

Appointment of receiver

17.14 When a receiver is appointed by virtue of a floating charge, the rights of the floating charge holder are postponed to the rights of all persons who have "effectually executed diligence" on any part of the company's property which is subject to the charge prior to the appointment of the receiver.[75] In *Lord Advocate* v. *Royal Bank of Scotland Ltd.*[76] the First Division held that an arrestment which has not been followed by a furthcoming was not "effectually executed diligence" and that the receiver was entitled to the sum arrested. It was suggested that a case in which an arrester would have a preference over property of the company

---

[64] B.A., s.37(5).
[65] B.A., s.37(1).
[66] See para. 15.5.
[67] B.A. s.37(4)(b).
[68] *Lord Advocate* v. *Royal Bank of Scotland Ltd.* 1977 S.C. 155. See para. 17.14.
[69] Now I.A. s.55(3)(a).
[70] Formerly, s.1(2) of the 1972 Act.
[71] *Parkinson & Co. Ltd.* v. *Bowen & Sons Ltd.* 1951 S.L.T. 393.
[72] See para. 15.5.
[73] B.A., Sched. 7, para. 24(5). The reference should be to s.7(4), not s.7(5).
[74] I.A., s.185(4).
[75] I.A., ss.55(3)(a), 60(1)(b).
[76] 1977 S.C. 155. See, however, the effect of consignation; *Hawking* v. *Hafton House Ltd.*, 1990 G.W.D. 6–333.

would be where a decree of furthcoming has proceeded on an arrestment of corporeal moveables. It is submitted that this decision is clearly wrong; it makes arrestment on the dependence of an action against a company almost useless; it leads to a circuitous situation if an arrestment has been followed by intimation of an assignation of the fund which in turn has been followed by the receiver's appointment; it is suggested that when "effectually executed diligence" was first used in the Companies (Floating Charges) (Scotland) Act 1961, s.2(1)(*a*), and later in the Companies (Floating Charges and Receivers) (Scotland) Act 1972, s.15(2)(*a*), the intended meaning was diligence which had not been rendered ineffectual under the Companies Act 1948, s.327(1)(*a*), by reason of liquidation commencing within 60 days thereafter.

The effect of *Lord Advocate* v. *Royal Bank* has been modified by the later decision of the First Division in *Iona Hotels Ltd., Petrs.*,[77] where it was held that the receiver did not prevail over an arrestment on the dependence which was executed before the registration of the floating charge. The ground of the decision is that arrestment renders the subject litigious so that the common debtor cannot defeat the arrestment by any posterior voluntary deed such as the instrument creating the floating charge.

It is clear that the appointment of a receiver under a floating charge created by a company registered in England renders ineffectual any subsequent arrestment of assets in Scotland.[78] The validity of prior diligence would seem to be the same as in the case of a Scottish receiver as the English receiver may exercise his powers "so far as their exercise is not inconsistent with the law applicable" in Scotland.[79]

Preventing arrestment

It is possible to prevent, by interdict, a threatened use of arrestment in execution if caution is offered or if malice and oppression can be instantly verified.[80] When arrestments have been used, it is possible to have an arrestment in execution recalled by the statutory procedure available in the case of arrestment on the dependence.[81] The sheriff may recall or restrict arrestments proceeding on a warrant issued from his books with or without caution as appears just, his judgment being subject to review in the Court of Session.[82] A contention that the subjects are not arrestable can be raised in a petition for recall if there is a delay in bringing the furthcoming.[83] The suspension of a charge on the decree on which the arrestment has been used is a ground for recall of the arrestment on caution.[84]

17.15

---

[77] 1991 S.L.T. 11.
[78] *Gordon Anderson (Plant) Ltd.* v. *Campsie Construction Ltd.*, 1977 S.L.T. 7 (decided under s.15(4) of the 1972 Act).
[79] I.A., s.72.
[80] *Beattie & Son* v. *Pratt* (1880) 7 R. 1171.
[81] *Gillies* v. *Bow*, 1877, Guthrie's Select Cases I, 196. See para. 11.10.
[82] Debtors (Scotland) Act 1838, s.21.
[83] *Lord Ruthven* v. *Drummond*, 1908 S.C. 1154.
[84] *Smith* v. *Macintosh* (1848) 10 D. 455.

Arrestment of Ships

17.16 Arrestment is the appropriate diligence to attach a ship.[85] This differs from other forms of arrestment in that it is not used in the hands of a third party but is used as a real diligence against the ship itself.[86] The ship must be in harbour or lying in a roadstead before it is subject to arrestment.[87] The schedule is attached to the mast and the Royal initials are chalked above it. Special authority to dismantle the ship may be obtained. The diligence is completed by an action of sale. Arrestment *in rem* is permissible only in certain circumstances.[88]

---

[85] See generally Graham Stewart, pp. 23–24, 41–42, 242–245; Dobie, *Sheriff Court Practice*, pp. 272, 275.
[86] See *Clan Line Steamers Ltd.* v. *Earl of Douglas Steamship Co. Ltd.*, 1913 S.C. 967.
[87] *The "Grey Dolphin,"* 1982 S.C. 5.
[88] Administration of Justice Act 1956, s.47.

CHAPTER 18

DILIGENCES AGAINST EARNINGS

The general scheme

The general scheme of diligence against earnings introduced by the Debtors (Scotland) Act 1987 is that "earnings," as defined, can no longer be attached by the normal form of arrestment and furthcoming and can be attached only by the three new forms of diligence: the earnings arrestment, the current maintenance arrestment and the conjoined arrestment order.[1] **18.1**

For the purposes of these diligences, debts are divided into two categories: ordinary debts and current maintenance. An ordinary debt is any debt other than current maintenance. Current maintenance is maintenance currently payable under a "maintenance order" which is defined to include orders for payment of aliment or periodical allowance on divorce and analogous orders. Ordinary debts include a fine or any sum due under an order of a court in criminal proceedings in respect of which a warrant for civil diligence has been issued, arrears of maintenance and the expenses of current maintenance arrestments.[2]

A creditor seeking to enforce payment of an ordinary debt uses an earnings arrestment to attach earnings in the hands of the debtor's employer; a creditor seeking to enforce payment of current maintenance uses a current maintenance arrestment in the hands of the employer. The effect of these diligences is that the employer has to make certain deductions from the debtor's earnings and pay them to the creditor. However, at one time, there can be in force against the same earnings of the same debtor from the same employer only one earnings arrestment and one current maintenance arrestment.[3] A creditor who finds that he cannot use one of these diligences because of that restriction can apply to the sheriff for a conjoined arrestment order the effect of which is to recall any earnings arrestment and any current maintenance arrestment in force and to require the employer to make certain deductions from the earnings and pay them to the sheriff clerk who then disburses the sums to the various creditors.[4] A creditor who finds that there is already a conjoined arrestment order in force can apply to the sheriff to vary the order so that his debt is included amongst those being enforced by the order.[5]

Earnings

The following are earnings[6]: wages; salary; fees, bonuses, commission or other emoluments payable under a contract of service or apprenticeship; pensions including pensions declared to be alimentary, an annuity in respect of past services (whether or not the services were rendered to **18.2**

---

[1] D.A., s.46.
[2] s.73(1).
[3] s.58(1).
[4] s.60.
[5] s.62(5).
[6] s.73(2).

the person paying the annuity) and any periodical payments of compensation for loss, abolition, relinquishment, or diminution in earnings of any office or employment; statutory sick pay. But the following are not treated as earnings[7]: pay of the armed services; a disablement or disability pension or allowance; an occupational pension payable under an enactment which precludes the assignation of the pension or exempts it from diligence; a social security pension, allowance or benefit; a guaranteed minimum pension within the meaning of the Social Security Pensions Act 1975; a redundancy payment. The wages of a seaman (other than a member of the crew of a fishing boat) are not to be treated as earnings in relation to the enforcement by an earnings arrestment of a debt other than maintenance.[8]

"Net earnings" are the earnings which remain payable to the debtor after the employer has deducted income tax, primary class 1 contributions under Part I of the Social Security Act 1975 and amounts deductible under any enactment, or in pursuance of a request in writing by the debtor, for the purposes of a superannuation scheme under the Wages Council Act 1979.[9]

Earnings Arrestments

Procedure

18.3 An earnings arrestment is not competent if another earnings arrestment or a conjoined arrestment order is already in effect against the same earnings.[10] Before an earnings arrestment can be executed a charge for payment must have been served on the debtor not more than two years previously and the period for payment specified in the charge must have expired without payment having been made[11]; there is an exception where the arrestment is executed in pursuance of a summary warrant. The arrestment cannot be executed after the date of the debtor's sequestration to enforce a debt which the creditor is entitled to claim in the sequestration.[12] The arrestment is executed by an officer of the court serving an earnings arrestment schedule[13] on the employer by registered or recorded delivery letter or, if such a letter cannot be delivered, by any other competent mode of service.[14] If it is reasonably practicable to do so, he must intimate a copy of the schedule to the debtor[15] but failure to do so does not of itself make the arrestment invalid.[16] The certificate of execution of the arrestment is signed by the officer of court who effected the service.[17] Except where the service is by post it cannot be executed on a Sunday, Christmas Day, New Year's Day or Good Friday.[18]

---

[7] s.73(3).
[8] s.73(3)(c).
[9] s.73(1).
[10] ss.59(1), 62(1).
[11] s.90(1).
[12] s.72(4).
[13] A.S. (Debtors) 38, form 30.
[14] s.70(3). As to the notice on the envelope, see A.S. (Debtors) 66.
[15] s.70(1).
[16] s.70(2).
[17] s.70(4); A.S. (Debtors) 67, form 60.
[18] ss.17(1), 70(5).

Effect

18.4 The arrestment requires the employer, while the arrestment is in effect, to make a deduction from the debtor's net earnings on every pay-day and, as soon as reasonably practicable, to pay the sum deducted to the creditor.[19] On making each payment the employer can charge the debtor a fee of 50p which is deductible from the net earnings after the deduction for the creditor.[20] Payment to the creditor may be by cheque unless a cheque has been dishonoured or for any other reason the method of payment has been ineffectual in which case the creditor can insist that the payment and future payments shall be tendered in cash.[21] If the employer fails to comply with the arrestment he is liable to pay the creditor the sum he would have paid if he had complied and he is not entitled to recover any sum he has paid to the debtor in contravention of the arrestment.[22] Where a pay-day occurs within seven days of service of the schedule the employer is entitled but not required to operate the arrestment on that pay-day[23]; where he does not operate the arrestment on such a pay-day he cannot make a deduction in respect of the earnings on that pay-day on a subsequent pay-day.[24] Where regulations have been made altering the provisions as to the amount of the deduction, they do not apply to an existing arrestment until the debtor or creditor intimates them to the employer[25]; the employer, however, is entitled to apply them before intimation[26]; he cannot be required to apply them at a pay-day within seven days of intimation to him.[27]

Deduction

18.5 The amount of the deduction is determined by tables in Schedule 2 to the Debtors (Scotland) Act 1987 which show in one column bands of net earnings and in another column the appropriate deduction; Table A is for weekly earnings and Table B for monthly earnings.[28] There are special provisions for the cases where the earnings are payable at regular intervals of a whole number of weeks or months,[29] where payment is at other regular intervals,[30] where payments are at irregular intervals,[31] where earnings payable at regular intervals and earnings payable at irregular intervals are paid on the same day[32] or on different pay-days,[33] and where earnings are paid by two or more series of payments at regular intervals.[34]

---

[19] s.47(1).
[20] s.71.
[21] s.57(2), (3).
[22] s.57(1). The creditor's claim must be made within a year; s.69(4).
[23] s.69(2).
[24] s.69(3).
[25] s.49(8).
[26] s.69(1).
[27] s.69(2).
[28] s.49.
[29] s.49(1)(c).
[30] s.49(2).
[31] s.49(3).
[32] s.49(4).
[33] s.49(5).
[34] s.49(6).

The debt recoverable by the arrestment consists of the following sums so far as still outstanding:

(a) any debt other than current maintenance and any expenses due under the decree or other document on which the earnings arrestment proceeds;

(b) any interest on these sums which has accrued at the date of execution of the arrestment; and

(c) the expenses incurred in executing the arrestment and the charge which preceded it.[35] Sums are recoverable only if they have been specified in the arrestment schedule.[36] Interest after the date of execution of the arrestment is therefore not recoverable by the arrestment. If the expenses of service of the schedule of arrestment are not recovered by the diligence they cannot be recovered in any other way.[37] Two or more debts due to the same creditor can be recovered by the same arrestment executed in pursuance of the the same warrant or different warrants.[38] Sums recovered are applied first towards expenses of diligence then to interest and then to the principal sum including expenses.[39]

Duration

18.6   The arrestment remains in effect until the debt has been paid or otherwise extinguished, the debtor has ceased to be employed by the employer or the arrestment has been recalled or abandoned by the creditor.[40] The employer is not liable to the debtor in respect of any deduction unless he has received intimation of one of these events.[41] The creditor has a duty to intimate to the employer if the debt is paid or extinguished or ceases to be enforceable by diligence[42]; if he fails to do so, any excess payment is recoverable by the debtor from the creditor with interest at the rate specified in the decree, order or extract or the rate specified under the Sheriff Courts (Scotland) Extracts Act 1892[43] and the sheriff, on the debtor's application, may order the creditor to pay to the debtor, in addition, an amount not exceeding twice the amount recoverable by the debtor.[44] Equalisation of diligence[45] does not apply to an earnings arrestment.[46] The arrestment ceases to have effect at the date of the debtor's sequestration[47] and it is not competent to execute after the date of sequestration an earnings arrestment to enforce a debt which can be claimed in the sequestration.[48] The statutory prescription of arrestments does not apply to an earnings arrestment.[49]

On the application of the debtor or the person on whom the earnings

---

[35] s.48(1).
[36] s.48(3).
[37] s.93(1).
[38] s.48(4).
[39] s.94(2).
[40] ss.47(2), 95.
[41] s.69(5).
[42] s.57(4); A.S. (Debtors) 50.
[43] s.57(5).
[44] s.57(6); A.S. (Debtors) 51, form 41.
[45] See para. 15.5.
[46] s.67.
[47] s.72(2).
[48] s.72(4). B.A., s.37(4), (5) do not apply: B.A., s.37(5A).
[49] Debtors (Scotland) Act 1838, s.22(3), ins. by D.A., Sched. 6, para. 3.

arrestment schedule was served, the sheriff may make an order declaring that an arrestment was invalid or has ceased to have effect.[50] The order is intimated to the debtor, the creditor and the person on whom the schedule was served. There is no appeal.[51] The sheriff may also make an order as to the operation of an earnings arrestment[52] and order the reimbursement of payments which ought not to have been made and the payment with interest of sums which ought to have been paid.[53]

CURRENT MAINTENANCE ARRESTMENTS

Procedure

A current maintenance arrestment is not competent if another current maintenance arrestment or a conjoined arrestment order is already in effect against the same earnings.[54] Before the arrestment can be executed the creditor must have intimated to the debtor the making or registration in Scotland of the maintenance order, four weeks must have elapsed and a sum not less than the aggregate of three instalments of maintenance must remain unpaid.[55] The arrestment is executed by an officer of the court serving a current maintenance arrestment schedule on the employer.[56] The schedule must specify the maintenance payable as a daily rate arrived at by multiplying a monthly rate by 12 and dividing it by 365 or by multiplying a quarterly rate by 4 and dividing it by 365.[57] The schedule is served by registered or recorded delivery letter or, if such a letter cannot be delivered, by any other competent mode of service.[58] If it is reasonably practicable to do so, the officer must intimate a copy of the schedule to the debtor[59] but failure to do so does not of itself make the arrestment invalid.[60] The certificate of execution of the arrestment is signed by the officer of court who effected the service.[61] Except where the service is by post it cannot be executed on a Sunday, Christmas Day, New Year's Day or Good Friday.[62]

Effect

The arrestment requires the employer, while the arrestment is in effect, to make a deduction from the debtor's net earnings on every payday and, as soon as reasonably practicable, to pay the sum deducted to the creditor.[63] On making each payment the employer can charge the debtor a fee of 50p which is deductible from the net earnings after the

18.7

18.8

---

[50] s.50(1); A.S. (Debtors) 40, form 32.
[51] s.50(2).
[52] s.50(3); A.S. (Debtors) 41, form 33.
[53] s.50(4).
[54] ss.59(2), 62(1).
[55] s.54(1); A.S. (Debtors) 45, form 37 (except where an order is varied or superseded by another order).
[56] s.70(1).
[57] s.51(4), (5).
[58] s.70(3).
[59] s.70(1).
[60] s.70(2).
[61] s.70(4).
[62] ss.17(1), 70(5).
[63] s.51(1).

deduction for the creditor.[64] Payment to the creditor may be by cheque unless a cheque has been dishonoured or for any other reason the method of payment has been ineffectual in which case the creditor can insist that the payment and future payments shall be tendered in cash.[65] If the employer fails to comply with the arrestment he is liable to pay the creditor the sum he would have paid if he had complied and he is not entitled to recover any sum he has paid to the debtor in contravention of the arrestment.[66] Where a pay-day occurs within seven days of service of the schedule the employer is entitled but not required to operate the arrestment on that pay-day[67]; where he does not operate the arrestment on such a pay-day he cannot make a deduction in respect of the earnings on that pay-day on a subsequent pay-day.[68] Where regulations have been made altering the provisions as to the amount of the deduction, or the tax rules as to small income limits have been altered, the changes do not apply to an existing arrestment until the debtor or creditor intimates them to the employer[69]; the employer, however, is entitled to apply them before intimation[70]; he cannot be required to apply them at a pay-day within seven days of intimation to him.[71]

Deduction

18.9   The employer must deduct the debtor's net earnings whichever is the lesser of the two following amounts, less any sum which the debtor is entitled to deduct in respect of income tax[72]:

(a) the sum arrived at by multiplying the daily rate of maintenance specified in the current maintenance arrestment schedule by the number of days since the last pay-day when a deduction was made in respect of the arrestment or, if there was no such pay-day, since the date of execution of the arrestment; or

(b) any net earnings in so far as they exceed the sum of £5 per day for that number of days.[73]

Duration

18.10   The current maintenance arrestment remains in effect until the debtor has ceased to be employed by the employer, the arrestment has been recalled or abandoned by the creditor, an order or decree varying, superseding or recalling the maintenance order has come into effect, or the obligation to pay maintenance has ceased to be enforceable in Scotland.[74] The employer is not liable to the debtor in respect of any deduction unless he has received intimation of one of these events.[75] The creditor has a duty to intimate to the employer if the maintenance order

---

[64] s.71.
[65] s.57(2), (3).
[66] s.57(1). The creditor's claim must be made within a year: s.69(4).
[67] s.69(2).
[68] s.69(3).
[69] ss.53(4), 69(2).
[70] ss.53(5), 69(1).
[71] s.69(2).
[72] s.53(1).
[73] s.53(2).
[74] ss.51(2), 55(8).
[75] s.69(5).

ceases to have effect[76]; if he fails to do so, any excess payment is recoverable by the debtor from the creditor with interest at the rate specified in the decree, order or extract or the rate specified under the Sheriff Courts (Scotland) Extracts Act 1892[77] and the sheriff, on the debtor.[78] Equalisation of diligence[79] does not apply to a current addition, an amount not exceeding twice the amount recoverable by the debtor.[78] Equalisation of diligence[79] does not apply to an current maintenance arrestment.[80] The arrestment ceases to have effect at the date of the debtor's sequestration.[81] The statutory prescription of arrestments does not apply to a current maintenance arrestment.[82]

On the application of the debtor or the person on whom the current maintenance arrestment schedule was served, the sheriff may make an order declaring that an arrestment was invalid or has ceased to have effect.[83] The sheriff may make an order determining any dispute as to the operation of the arrestment and order the reimbursement of sums which ought not to have been paid and the payment with interest of sums which ought to have been paid.[84] The sheriff may, on the debtor's application, recall the arrestment if he is satisfied that the debtor is unlikely to default again in paying maintenance.[85]

The expenses of executing a current maintenance arrestment are recoverable from the debtor as an ordinary debt and are recoverable by any diligence other than the current maintenance arrestment in pursuance of the warrant which authorised that arrestment.[86] No interest accrues on arrears of the maintenance while the arrestment is in effect.[87] Where one or more maintenance orders provide for payment to one person of maintenance in respect of more than one individual, the obligations may be enforced by a single arrestment against the same earnings and the schedule specifies one daily rate being the aggregate of the daily rates in respect of the individuals.[88] Where a maintenance order is varied or superseded by another order or decree, the later order may provide that it will not come into effect until the earlier of the expiry of the period needed to give notice to the employer of the new order or the service of a new schedule in pursuance of the later order[89]; this does not apply where the earlier order is for aliment and the later order is for periodical allowance on divorce or nullity.[90]

Priority

Where an earnings arrestment and a current maintenance arrestment **18.11**

---

[76] s.57(4).
[77] s.57(5).
[78] s.57(6).
[79] See para. 15.5.
[80] s.67.
[81] s.72(2). B.A., s.37(4), (5), do not apply: B.A., s.37(5A).
[82] Debtors (Scotland) Act 1838, s.22(3) ins. by D.A., Sched. 6, para. 3.
[83] s.55(1).
[84] s.55(5), (6).
[85] s.55(2).
[86] s.51(3).
[87] s.51(6).
[88] s.52.
[89] s.56(1).
[90] s.56(2).

are in effect simultaneously and the net earnings are insufficient to satisfy the requirements of both, the employer must first operate the earnings arrestment and then operate the current maintenance arrestment against the balance.[91] If an employer receives on the same day two or more earnings arrestments or two or more current maintenance arrestments against the earnings of the same debtor, he must give effect to the first one received if he knows when they were received; if they came at the same time or he does not know when they were received he can choose which shall have effect.[92] Where an arrestment is in effect and another arrestment of the same kind is served, the employer must give the second creditor details of the prior diligence and he can be ordered to do so by the sheriff.[93]

Conjoined Arrestment Orders

Procedure

18.12   There can be only one earnings arrestment and one current maintenance arrestment in force against the same earnings.[94] A creditor who, but for that rule, would be able to execute one of these diligences must apply to the sheriff for the making of a conjoined arrestment order. An order cannot be made where all the debts concerned are maintenance payable to the same person for his own or another's benefit; where there are only two debts, one being maintenance and one an ordinary debt; or where the same person is creditor in all the debts.[95] An order cannot be made after the date of sequestration to enforce a debt which the creditor is entitled to claim in the sequestration.[96] The order recalls the arrestments which are in force and requires the employer to make deductions from the debtor's net earnings and pay the sum as soon as is reasonably practicable to the sheriff clerk.[97] The order specifies the amount of any ordinary debts recoverable and the daily rate of maintenance if current maintenance is being enforced.[98] The sheriff clerk serves the order on the employer, the debtor and the creditors whose arrestments have been recalled.[99]

The debt

18.13   In the case of an ordinary debt, there is recoverable any sum, including expenses due under the decree or document, interest accrued to the date of execution of the arrestment (or if there was no arrestment, to the date of the making of the conjoined arrestment order), and the expenses of executing any earnings arrestment and the charge preceding it.[1] The creditor who applied for the order can get his expenses connected with

---

[91] s.58.
[92] s.59(3).
[93] s.59(4), (5).
[94] s.59(1), (2).
[95] s.60(4); A.S. (Debtors) 53, form 43.
[96] s.72(4).
[97] s.60(3).
[98] s.60(6); A.S. (Debtors) 54, form 45.
[99] s.60(7).
[1] s.61(1).

the application but not the expenses of any arrestment schedule served after the date of the application.[2] No interest accrues on arrears of maintenance while the order is in effect.[3]

Effect

The order comes into effect seven days after a copy of it has been served on the employer[4]; it will be noted that this is later than is the case with the other earnings diligences. If the employer fails to comply with the order, he is liable to pay to the sheriff clerk any sum he should have deducted, he cannot recover from the debtor any sum he paid him in contravention of the order, and the sheriff clerk may obtain a warrant for diligence against the employer for recovery of the sums.[5] The employer may make a further deduction of 50p from the net earnings on making each payment to the sheriff clerk.[6]

18.14

Duration

The order remains in effect until an order recalling it is served on the employer, the debtor ceases to be employed by the employer, or the date of the debtor's sequestration.[7] Sums paid to the sheriff clerk prior to the date of sequestration can be disbursed by him after that date.[8] The equalisation of diligence provisions[9] do not apply to a conjoined arrestment order.[10] The statutory prescription of arrestments does not apply to a conjoined arrestment order.[11] The sheriff may make orders recalling the conjoined arrestment order,[12] or determining any dispute as to its operation,[13] or varying the amount recoverable.[14]

18.15

Deduction

Where all the debts are ordinary debts, the employer deducts and pays to the sheriff clerk the sum which he would have had to pay to the creditor if the debts were one debt being enforced by an earnings arrestment.[15] Where all the debts are current maintenance, the sum is the lesser of two specified amounts less any sum which the debtor is entitled to deduct in respect of income tax.[16] The specified amounts are[17]:

(a) the aggregate of the sums arrived at by multiplying each of the daily rates of maintenance specified in the conjoined arrestment order by the number of days since the last pay-day when a deduction was made in respect of the maintenance obligation or, if there is no such pay-day, since the date when the order was made or varied:

18.16

---

[2] s.61(4), (5).
[3] s.61(3).
[4] s.60(5).
[5] s.60(9).
[6] s.71.
[7] ss.60(5), 72(2).
[8] s.72(3).
[9] See para. 15.5.
[10] s.67.
[11] Debtors (Scotland) Act 1838, s.22(3), ins. by D.A. Sched 6, para. 3.
[12] s.66(1).
[13] s.65.
[14] s.66(4).
[15] s.63(2).
[16] s.63(3).
[17] s.63(4).

(b) any net earnings in excess of £5 per day for that number of days.

Where the debts comprise ordinary debts and current maintenance the sum deducted is the aggregate of:
(a) the sum which would be deductible if the ordinary debts were treated as one debt and it was being enforced by an earnings arrestment;
(b) the sum which would be deductible under the order if all the debts were current maintenance and so much of the debtor's net earnings as were left after deduction of the sum specified in (a) were his whole net earnings.[18]

Disbursements

18.17   If all the debts are ordinary debts, the sheriff clerk pays each creditor the same proportion of the amount of his debt.[19] If all the debts are current maintenance, and if the sum for disbursement is sufficient to satisfy every creditor in respect of the amount of maintenance to be deducted in respect of his debt on that pay-day, each creditor is paid that amount; if it is insufficient to make these payments, each creditor is paid the same proportion of the amount to be deducted in respect of his debt on that pay-day.[20] Where the debts comprise both ordinary debts and current maintenance:
(a) if only one of the debts is an ordinary debt, the creditor gets the sum which would be payable to him if the debt were being enforced by an earnings arrestment;
(b) if more than one debt is an ordinary debt, each creditor in one of those debts is paid the same proportion of the amount of his debt out of the sum which would be payable to a creditor if the debt were a single debt being enforced by an earnings arrestment;
(c) if only one of the debts is current maintenance, the creditor is paid the sum which would be payable to him if the debt were being enforced by a current maintenance arrestment;
(d) if more than one of the debts is current maintenance each creditor will be paid the same proportion of the amount of maintenance to be deducted in respect of his debt on that pay-day[21];
(e) priority is given in the disbursement to ordinary debts.[22] So far as each ordinary debt is concerned, sums are applied first to expenses of diligence, then to interest and then to the principal sum including expenses.[23]

Variation

18.18   Where another creditor appears who would be in a position to do diligence against the earnings but for the order, he can apply to the sheriff to vary the order to include his debt.[24] Where a debt which is being enforced under the order has been paid or otherwise extinguished, the debtor, a creditor, the employer or the sheriff clerk can apply to the sheriff to vary the order appropriately.[25]

---

[18] s.63(5).
[19] s.64; Sched. 3, para. 1.
[20] Sched. 3, para. 2.
[21] para. 3.
[22] para. 4.
[23] s.94.
[24] s.62(5).
[25] s.66(4).

CHAPTER 19

OTHER DILIGENCE

Inhibition

An inhibition is "a writ passing under the signet, prohibiting the debtor from alienating any part of his estate, and from contracting debt by means of which it may be carried off, to the prejudice of the creditor inhibitor; and interdicting third parties from taking conveyances of the heritage."[1] It affects only the heritable estate of the debtor. It is not a complete diligence and its effect is merely prohibitory and preventive.

19.1

Inhibition may proceed on a decree of the Court of Session or the ordinary sheriff court.[2] It may also proceed on a liquid document of debt such as a bond or bill and it is not necessary that the document should be capable of registration for execution.[3]

Procedure

Even in the case of a sheriff court decree, an inhibition must be effected through the Petition Department of the Court of Session. A Bill for Letters of Inhibition is presented with the decree or document of debt in the Petition Department. A *fiat* is obtained and Letters of Inhibition can then be signeted. The Letters authorise a messenger-at-arms to serve a copy of them on the debtor. Before service, it is competent to register in the Register of Inhibitions and Adjudications a Notice of Inhibition. After service, the execution, together with the Letters, is registered and, if this is done not later than 21 days from the date of registration of the notice, the inhibition takes effect from the date of registration of the notice; otherwise, the effective date is the date of registration of the Letters.[4] An inhibition prescribes on the lapse of five years from its effective date.[5]

19.2

Effect of inhibition

The inhibition affects all heritage owned by the debtor whether or not he is infeft therein[6]; it also affects heritable securities if notarial intimation is made to the debtor in the security[7]; it does not affect *acquirenda* except in certain special circumstances.[8] The effect of the inhibition is to prohibit the debtor from granting future voluntary deeds to the inhibitor's prejudice. This does not affect the recording of a deed

19.3

---

[1] Bell, *Prin.*, § 2306.
[2] Graham Stewart, p. 527.
[3] Graham Stewart, *loc. cit.*
[4] Titles to Land Consolidation (Scotland) Act 1868, s.155. Under registration of title, on registration of an interest, any subsisting entry in the Register of Inhibitions and Adjudications adverse to the interest is entered in the title sheet; the mode of entry of subsequent inhibitions is not yet clear: Land Registration (Scotland) Act 1979, s.6(1)(*c*) (as to indemnity by the Keeper, see s.12(3)(*k*)).
[5] Conveyancing (Scotland) Act 1924, s.44(3)(*a*).
[6] *Dryburgh* v. *Gordon* (1896) 24 R. 1, *per* Lord Kincairney at p. 3.
[7] Graham Stewart, p. 549; but see *Mackintosh's Trs.* v. *Davidson & Gordon* (1898) 25 R. 554.
[8] Titles to Land Consolidation (Scotland) Act 1868, s.157.

already granted[9]; nor does it affect the granting of a disposition in implement of missives completed prior to the inhibition because this is not a voluntary act.[10] It did not affect further advances made on a bond of cash credit.[11] Acts of ordinary administration, *e.g.* the granting of a lease of ordinary duration, are not struck at.[12] A deed which is affected by the inhibition may be reduced *ex capite inhibitionis* by the inhibitor; the right transmits to his representatives and assignees.[13] The inhibition operates only against the debtor; his successors are not constrained by it.[14] Where the debtor has granted a heritable security and another creditor has then inhibited, on the sale of the security subjects, the heritable creditor is entitled to be paid in full from the proceeds and the inhibiting creditor, who has adjudged before the sale, or arrested the balance in the hands of the heritable creditor, is entitled to the balance in preference to creditors whose debts were contracted after the date of the inhibition but not, in preference to other creditors whose debts were contracted before the date of the inhibition.[15] An inhibition also has an effect on the ranking on the heritable estate in the debtor's sequestration.[16] An English trustee in bankruptcy is affected by an inhibition relating to Scottish heritage.[17]

Adjudication

19.4 Adjudication is the appropriate diligence to attach the heritable property of the debtor.[18] The subjects of the diligence are: land and heritable rights generally including liferents, annuities and rights having a *tractum futuri temporis*; heritable securities; a heritable interest in a trust[19]; bank stock where the charter excludes arrestment.[20] Where a security over heritage has been constituted by *ex facie* absolute disposition, the disponer's reversionary right is adjudgeable.[21] A *spes successionis* cannot be adjudged.[22] An action of adjudication to enforce a debt payable under a liquid document of debt is not competent unless there is a decree or the debt is a *debitum fundi* or there is a document of debt which has been registered for execution.[23] The procedure is by an action which can be raised only in the Court of Session. Service of the summons together with registration of a notice in the Register of Inhibitions and Adjudications makes the subjects litigious and prevents voluntary conveyances by the debtor to the prejudice of the creditor. Decree in the action when recorded in the Sasine Register vests the

---

[9] Graham Stewart, p. 563.
[10] *Livingstone* v. *McFarlane* (1842) 5 D. 1.
[11] *Campbell's Tr.* v. *De Lisle's Exrs.* (1870) 9 M. 252.
[12] Bell, *Comm.*, II, 142.
[13] Bankt., I, vii, 140; Graham Stewart, p. 552.
[14] Ersk., II, xi, 2; *Menzies* v. *Murdoch* (1841) 4 D. 257.
[15] Gretton, pp. 104–111; *Halifax Building Society* v. *Smith*, 1985 S.L.T. (Sh.Ct.) 25.
[16] See para. 23.5.
[17] *Morley's Tr.* v. *Aitken*, 1982 S.C. 73. As to an English receiver see *Taymech Ltd.* v. *Rush & Tompkins Ltd.*, 1990 S.L.T. 681.
[18] As adjudication is not a satisfactory form of diligence in the general case, it is dealt with here in a summary fashion.
[19] *Learmonts* v. *Shearer* (1866) 4 M. 540.
[20] *Royal Bank* v. *Fairholm* (1770) Mor.App. "Adjudication" No. 3.
[21] Graham Stewart, p. 606.
[22] *Reid* v. *Morison* (1893) 20 R. 510.
[23] D.A., s.101.

property in the adjudger subject to the debtor's right of redemption. Redemption may be effected at any time until *either* a period of 10 years (the "legal") has expired and the adjudger has obtained decree in an action of declarator of expiry of the legal *or* possession for the period of 10 years of positive prescription has followed the expiry of the legal.[24] Adjudications of the same subjects within a year and a day of the first effectual adjudication are equalised.[25] The adjudication is cut down by sequestration or liquidation within a year and a day.[26]

It is incompetent to raise or insist in an adjudication against the debtor's estate after the date of sequestration.[27]

Summary diligence

If a document of debt incorporates a clause of consent to registration for execution, the creditor may do diligence against the debtor without first resorting to a court action. The document is registered in the court books and an extract therefrom is a warrant for diligence. In other words, the clause is "a consent given *ab ante* that the Court of Session may issue a decree which is to have the same effect as if the parties had entered into a suit before the Court, and decree had been pronounced in that action."[28] The extract is "a constructive decree." Summary diligence is not competent to enforce payment of a debt due in respect of a regulated agreement under the Consumer Credit Act or any security related thereto.[29]

19.5

The document of debt must be probative.[30] It must contain the clause "I consent to registration for execution"[31] although this is not necessary in a bond in favour of the Crown.[32] The sum due must be definitely ascertainable on the face of the document or the document must state the mode in which the sum due is to be ascertained. For example, the sum may be ascertained by a separate certified account which need not be registered.[33]

If the debtor resides anywhere in Scotland, registration may be made in the Books of Council and Session. Registration may be made in the books of a sheriff court if the debtor is designed in the document as residing within the appropriate sheriff court district. Anyone may lodge the document for registration. An extract is then issued with a warrant for diligence inserted in it. The warrant authorises diligence by poinding or earnings arrestment after a charge, by arrestment and, where the document is a maintenance order, by a current maintenance arrestment.[34] In the case of a sheriff court extract, if the debtor has changed his

---

[24] Prescription and Limitation (Scotland) Act 1973, s.1(3). See Gretton, 1983 J.R. 177.
[25] Diligence Act 1661; Adjudications Act 1672.
[26] B.A., s.37(1)(*a*); I.A., s.185(1).
[27] B.A., s.37(8).
[28] Wood, *Lectures*, p. 160.
[29] Consumer Credit Act 1974, s.93A (inserted by D.A. Sched. 6, para. 16).
[30] *Carnoway* v. *Ewing* (1611) Mor. 14988.
[31] *Erskine* (1710) Mor. 14997; Titles to Land Consolidation (Scotland) Act 1868, s.138.
[32] Exchequer Court (Scotland) Act 1856, s.38.
[33] *Fisher* v. *Stewart* (1828) 7 S. 97; *Paisley Union Bank* v. *Hamilton* (1831) 9 S. 488; *Keith* v. *Cairney*, 1917 1 S.L.T. 202; *Tennent* v. *Glass*, 1990 S.L.T. 282.
[34] Titles to Land Consolidation (Scotland) Act 1868, s.138; Writs Execution (Scotland) Act 1877, s.3 (subst. by D.A. 1987, s.87(4)); Court of Session (Extracts) Act 1916.

residence to another jurisdiction, the warrant can be executed anywhere in Scotland by a sheriff officer of the court which granted it or of the district in which it is to be executed.[35]

If the original debtor has died, summary diligence is incompetent and the debt must be constituted against his representatives by an action[36] except where, in the case of a heritable security, a person taking the security subjects by conveyance, succession, gift or bequest has executed an agreement to the transmission of the personal obligation.[37]

On bills of exchange

19.6 Summary diligence may also be done on a bill of exchange or a promissory note[38] but not on a cheque.[39] On non-acceptance or non-payment the protest is registered in the books of a court having jurisdiction over the party against whom diligence is to be executed.[40] In the case of non-acceptance the registration must be within six months from the date of the bill; in the case of non-payment within six months from the date it fell due.[41] If the bill is payable on demand, the six months runs from the date of presentation for payment.

A bill may be a valid document of debt and yet not be a valid ground of summary diligence, "the whole grounds and warrants of the diligence must be entire, and must be apparently and manifestly entire".[42] The bill must itself prove liability and require no extrinsic evidence to support it or to identify the parties.[43] The debt must be exigible without any qualification or condition whatsoever.[44] The bill must be *ex facie* complete and regular. Summary diligence cannot follow upon a bill which is signed with initials[45] or a mark,[46] or which is undated[47] or unstamped[48] or which has been torn up and pasted together.[49] It is vitiated if the date[50] or date of payment[51] is written upon an erasure. A procuration signature is not objectionable if the procuration is notorious.[52]

Summary warrant procedure

19.7 There is a special summary procedure for the collection of rates and

---

[35] D.A., s.91(1)(c).
[36] *Kippen* v. *Hill* (1822) 2 S. 105.
[37] Conveyancing (Scotland) Act 1874, s.47; Conveyancing (Scotland) Act 1924, s.15.
[38] Bills of Exchange Act 1681; Inland Bills Act 1696; 12 Geo. III, c. 72, s.42; Bills of Exchange Act 1882, s.98. As to the warrant for diligence, see para. 15.3.
[39] *Glickman* v. *Linda*, 1950 S.C. 18.
[40] The diligence may proceed on a householder's certificate in place of a protest: Bills of Exchange Act 1882, s.94; *McRobert* v. *Lindsay* (1898) 14 Sh.Ct.Rep. 89.
[41] *McNeill* v. *Innes Chambers & Co.*, 1917 S.C. 540.
[42] *per* Lord Gillies, *Smith* v. *Selby* (1829) 7 S. 885 at 886.
[43] *Summers* v. *Marianski* (1843) 6 D. 286; *Fraser* v. *Bannerman* (1853) 15 D. 756.
[44] Bell, *Prin.*, § 316; *Hughson* v. *Cullen* (1857) 20 D. 271.
[45] *Munro* v. *Munro* (1820) Hume 81.
[46] *Stewart* v. *Russell*, 11 July 1815, F.C.; *Mackintosh* v. *Macdonald* (1828) 7 S. 155.
[47] Bell, *Prin.*, § 343.
[48] Bell, *Comm.*, I, 415.
[49] *Thomson* v. *Bell* (1850) 12 D. 1184.
[50] *Armstrong* v. *Wilson* (1842) 4 D. 1347; *McRostie* v. *Halley* (1850) 12 D. 816.
[51] *Hamilton* v. *Kinnear & Sons* (1825) 4 S. 102.
[52] *Turnbull* v. *McKie* (1822) 1 S. 353.

certain taxes. It applies to rates,[53] community charge,[54] income tax,[55] car tax[56] and value added tax.[57] The appropriate authority presents an application to the sheriff certifying that the amount remains unpaid after a demand for payment was made. The sheriff then grants a summary warrant authorising the recovery of the amount due by a poinding and sale in accordance with Schedule 5 of the Debtors (Scotland) Act 1987, an earnings arrestment, or an arrestment and action of furthcoming or sale.[58] In the case of rates and community charge a surcharge of 10 per cent. is added to the amount due.[59] A warrant cannot be granted in respect of a liability for community charge arising under s.8(7) of the Abolition of Domestic Rates Etc. (Scotland) Act 1987 which imposes a joint and several liability on spouses and cohabitees.[60] In the case of rates and community charge a warrant cannot be granted if an action for recovery of the amount has already been raised; an action cannot be raised if any of the diligences has been executed; if an action is raised any existing summary warrant ceases to have effect.[61] It should be noted that the poinding is under a separate code contained in Schedule 5 of the Debtors (Scotland) Act 1987; the provisions of the schedule follow the general law fairly closely but no charge is necessary,[62] there is no report of the poinding or the sale to the sheriff and there is no need to apply to the sheriff for a warrant of sale. There are separate poinding procedures for betting and gaming duties[63] and customs and excise.[64]

Civil imprisonment

Imprisonment in respect of non-payment of debt is competent only in the following cases:

19.8

(a) fines imposed for contempt of court or under the Court of Session Act 1988, s.45;
(b) wilful failure to pay aliment, the maximum period being six weeks.[65] The failure is presumed to be wilful until the contrary is proved but the warrant will not be granted if it is proved that the debtor has not since the commencement of the action possessed or been able to earn the means of paying the sums due or such instalments thereof as are considered reasonable. The warrant may be granted of new at

---

[53] Local Government (Scotland) Act 1947, s.247 (subst. by D.A., s.74(1), Sched. 4, para. 1).

[54] Abolition of Domestic Rates Etc. (Scotland) Act 1987, s.21, Sched. 2, para. 7.

[55] Taxes Management Act 1970, s.63 (subst. by D.A., s.74(1), Sched. 4, para. 2) (applied to petroleum revenue tax by Oil Taxation Act 1975, s.1, Sched. 2).

[56] Car Tax Act 1983, Sched. 1, para. 3(2) (subst. by D.A., s.74(1), Sched. 4, para. 3).

[57] Value Added Tax Act 1983, Sched. 7, para. 6(5)–(9) (subst. by D.A., s.74(1), Sched. 4, para. 4).

[58] A.S. (Proceedings in the Sheriff Court under the Debtors (Scotland) Act 1987) 1988, Forms 61–63.

[59] Local Government (Scotland) Act 1947, s.247(2); Abolition of Domestic Rates Etc. (Scotland) Act 1987, Sched. 2, para. 7(2).

[60] 1987 Act, Sched. 2, para. 7(4).

[61] 1947 Act, s.247(4), (5); 1987 Act, Sched. 2, para. 7(5), (6).

[62] D.A., s.90(2).

[63] Betting and Gaming Duties Act 1981, s.29, as amended by D.A., Sched. 6, para. 23.

[64] Customs and Excise Management Act 1979, s.117 (as amended by D.A., Sched. 6, para. 21).

[65] Debtors (Scotland) Act 1880, s.4.

intervals of not less than six months in respect of failure to pay the same sums or sums afterwards accruing. Imprisonment does not extinguish the debt or interfere with other remedies. The creditor is not liable for the debtor's aliment.

CHAPTER 20

SEQUESTRATION

Apparent insolvency

"The principle of sequestration is that it is a process by which the whole property of a bankrupt person is ingathered by a trustee for the purpose of division *pari passu* among the creditors."[1]   20.1

To be sequestrated, the debtor must be in a condition known as "Apparent Insolvency." Apparent insolvency is constituted whenever[2]:
(a) the debtor's estate is sequestrated or he is adjudged bankrupt in England or Wales or Northern Ireland; or
(b) he gives written notice to his creditors that he has ceased to pay his debts in the ordinary course of business; or
(c) any of the following circumstances occurs:
  (i) he grants a trust deed;
  (ii) following the service on him of a charge for payment of a debt, the days of charge expire without payment;
  (iii) following a poinding or seizure of any of his moveable property under a summary warrant for the recovery of rates or taxes, 14 days elapse without payment;
  (iv) a decree of adjudication of any part of his estate is granted, either for payment or in security;
  (v) his effects are sold under a sequestration for rent due by him; or
  (vi) a receiving order is made against him in England or Wales, unless it is shown that at the time when any such circumstance occurred, the debtor was able and willing to pay his debts as they became due; or
(d) a creditor of the debtor, in respect of a liquid debt which amounts (or liquid debts which in aggregate amount) to not less than £750, has served on the debtor by personal service by an officer of the court a demand in the prescribed form[3] requiring him either to pay the debt or debts or to find security for its or their payment and within three weeks after the date of service of the demand the debtor has not
  (i) complied with the demand, or
  (ii) intimated to the creditor, by recorded delivery, that he denies that there is a debt or that the sum claimed by the creditor as the debt is immediately payable.

The petition

The petition may be at the instance of creditors but it can also be brought by the trustee under a trust deed for creditors granted by the debtor.[4] The debtor himself may petition with the concurrence of   20.2

---

[1] *per* Lord Dunedin, *Caldwell* v. *Hamilton*, 1919 S.C. (H.L.) 100 at 107. The sequestration of the estate of a deceased debtor is dealt with elsewhere—see para. 29.12.

[2] B.A., s.7. The provisions are qualified where the debtor is affected by drug legislation: Criminal Justice (Scotland) Act 1987, s.45(5)(*b*); Criminal Justice Act 1988, Sched. 15, para. 108.

[3] B. Regs. Form 1.

[4] B.A., s.5(2)(*c*). As to trust deeds, see para. 24.2.

qualified creditors; he need not be apparently insolvent and sequestration will be awarded forthwith.[5] A petition by creditors must be at the instance or with the concurrence of one or more creditors whose debt or debts together amount to not less than £750. The debts may be secured or unsecured, liquid or illiquid, provided they are not future, contingent or payable under a drugs confiscation order.[6] A contingent debt is "a debt which has no existence now but will only emerge and become due upon the occurrence of some future event."[7] It means "only some element in the debt itself, and which covers only some 'contingency' arising, *ex facie*, upon the documents of debt, or which can be instantly verified." The making of an appeal after the expiry of a charge does not make the debt contingent.[8] Liability for future rent is not contingent.[9] While a time to pay direction[10] or order[11] is in effect, the creditor is not entitled to found on the debt concerned in presenting or in concurring in the presentation of, a petition for the sequestration of the debtor's estate.[12]

The petition is presented in the Court of Session or in the sheriff court of any sheriffdom within which the debtor had an established place of business or was habitually resident at any time in the year immediately preceding the date of presentation of the petition.[13] The petition must be lodged with the court office within four months of the constitution of apparent insolvency.[14] The four month period does not run while a charge is suspended.[15]

Every petitioning and concurring creditor must produce an oath as to the existence of his debt, specifying its amount, the dates when it was incurred and payable and whether any security is held for it.[16] There must also be produced an extract decree, account or voucher which constitutes prima facie evidence of the debt. A document of debt should be produced for a loan. If the debt is an open trading account, an account in the form of an extract from the creditor's books is sufficient provided the items are specified. The petitioning creditor must in addition produce such evidence as is available to him to show the apparent insolvency of the debtor.[17]

Procedure

20.3   On presentation of the petition, the court grants warrant to cite the debtor to appear before it on a specified date not less than six nor more than 14 days after the date of citation to show cause why sequestration

---

[5] B.A., ss.5(2)(*a*), 8(1)(*a*), 12(1). The date of sequestration is the date when sequestration is awarded: B.A. s.12(4)(*a*).
[6] B.A., s.5(3)(*b*), (4). A student loan is not a debt for this purpose: Education (Student Loans) Act 1990, Sched. 2, para. 6(*c*)(i).
[7] *per* Lord Watson, *Fleming* v. *Yeaman* (1884) 9 A.C. 966 at 976.
[8] *British General Insurance Co.* v. *Borthwick* (1924) 40 Sh.Ct.Rep. 198.
[9] *Strathdee* v. *Paterson*, 1913 1 S.L.T. 498.
[10] See para. 11.20.
[11] See para. 15.7.
[12] D.A., s.12(1).
[13] B.A., s.9.
[14] B.A., s.8(1)(*b*).
[15] *United Dominions Trust Ltd.* v. *Dickson*, 1987 S.L.T. 572 (but see McBryde, p. 21).
[16] s.11(1); B. Regs. Fm. 2.
[17] s.11(5).

should not be awarded.[18] The date on which the warrant is granted is the date of the sequestration.[19] On cause shown, an interim trustee may be appointed at this stage. The clerk of court sends a certified copy of the court order to the keeper of the register of inhibitions and adjudications for recording in that register.[20] The recording has the effect as from the date of sequestration of an inhibition and of a citation in an adjudication of the debtor's heritable estate at the instance of the creditors who subsequently have claims accepted in the sequestration[21]; that effect expires after three years unless it is renewed by the recording by the permanent trustee of a memorandum before the expiry of the three years; it also expires, of course, on the recording of a certified copy of an order refusing or recalling sequestration.[22] At the next diet, if the court is satisfied that proper citation has been made of the debtor (if he has not appeared), that the petition has been presented in accordance with the provisions of the Bankruptcy Act, and that the requirements as to apparent insolvency have been fulfilled, sequestration is awarded forthwith unless cause is shown why sequestration cannot competently be awarded or the debtor forthwith pays or satisfies or produces written evidence of payment or satisfaction of, or gives sufficient security for the payment of the debt in respect of which he became apparently insolvent and any other debt due by him to the petitioner and any creditor concurring in the petition.[23] There is a doubt as to whether a pre-existing security is sufficient.[24]

The debtor may show cause why sequestration cannot competently be awarded. If the statutory conditions are satisfied, however, the court has no discretion and is bound to award sequestration.[25] Consequently the valid grounds of objection are restricted to questions of jurisdiction and defects in the documents produced with the petition.[26] It is not an answer for the debtor to offer to prove his general solvency.[27] It is the practice to dispose of objections without proof and on *ex parte* statements.[28] But sometimes further inquiry may be necessary.[29]

An interim trustee is appointed by the court on sequestration being awarded or as soon as may be thereafter.[30] He publishes a notice in the Edinburgh and London Gazettes stating that sequestration has been awarded and inviting creditors to submit claims to him.[31]

---

[18] s.12(2).
[19] s.12(4).
[20] s.14(1).
[21] s.14(2).
[22] s.14(4). R.C. 201A(2), Fm. 34B. A.S.; (Bankruptcy) 1986, para. 4(2), Fm. 2.
[23] s.12(3). As to concurrent proceedings see para. 30.17.
[24] *The Royal Bank of Scotland* v. *Forbes*, 1987 (O.H.) S.C.L.R. 294. *Cf. Drybrough & Co. Ltd., Petrs.*, (Sh.Ct.) 1989 S.C.L.R. 279; *Bank of Scotland* v. *Mackay*, 1991 S.L.T. 163.
[25] *Joel* v. *Gill* (1859) 21 D. 929; *Stuart & Stuart* v. *Macleod* (1891) 19 R. 223.
[26] *Riddell* v. *Galbraith* (1896) 24 R. 51.
[27] *Scottish Milk Marketing Board* v. *Wood*, 1936 S.C. 604.
[28] *Scottish Milk Marketing Board* v. *Wood, supra*, per L. P. Normand at p. 611.
[29] *Royal Bank of Scotland* v. *Forbes, supra*; see also *James Finlay Corporation Ltd.* v. *McCormack*, 1986 S.L.T. 106.
[30] s.13(1). For his powers, see s.18(2).
[31] s.15(6); B. Regs. Fm. 3. He must write to a foreign creditor: s.22(3).

Where sequestration has been awarded by the Court of Session it is remitted to such sheriff court as is considered appropriate.[32]

Conspectus of further procedure

20.4 The interim trustee takes measures to safeguard the estate,[33] investigates the debtor's affairs[34] and reports thereon to the Accountant in Bankruptcy.[35] Within 28 days after the date of award of sequestration, he calls a meeting of the creditors[36] at which the permanent trustee (there cannot be more than one)[37] is elected[38]; his functions are to recover, manage and realise the estate, ascertain the state of the debtor's liabilities and assets, ascertain the reasons for the debtor's insolvency and the circumstances surrounding it and distribute the estate among the creditors. Between one and five commissioners may also be elected to advise the trustee and supervise his intromissions with the estate.[39] The proceedings are reported to the sheriff who confirms the election of the trustee and the Act and Warrant, the trustee's title, is then issued.[40] The trustee gives notice of his confirmation in the Edinburgh Gazette[41] and proceeds to recover, manage and realise the estate.[42] He ascertains the reasons for the insolvency and he can examine the debtor, his wife, and other persons as to the debtor's assets, dealings and conduct.[43] He can carry on the debtor's business, bring proceedings, create a security over the estate and sell the estate by public roup or private bargain.[44] In due course the creditors submit claims, the trustee adjudicates thereon and he then proceeds to distribute the estate. Eventually the debtor[45] and the trustee[46] are discharged.

If the interim trustee reports to the creditors' meeting that the debtor's assets are unlikely to be sufficient to pay any dividend, the sheriff appoints the interim trustee as the permanent trustee,[47] a modified procedure is applied to the sequestration[48] and the trustee's outlays and remuneration are if necessary met from public funds.[49]

Supplies by utilities

20.5 A special provision prevents the suppliers of gas, water, electricity and telecommunication services from refusing to supply the trustee until he pays the amount due by the debtor. If, after a petition for sequestration has been presented and a warrant for citation of the debtor granted, the

---

[32] s.15(1).
[33] s.18.
[34] s.19.
[35] s.20.
[36] s.21.
[37] *Inland Revenue Commissioners* v. *MacDonald*, 1988 S.L.T. (Sh.Ct.) 7.
[38] ss.3, 24.
[39] ss.4, 30.
[40] s.25; A.S. (Bankruptcy) 1986, Fm. 3.
[41] s.25(6); B. Regs., Fm. 6.
[42] ss.38, 39.
[43] ss.44–47.
[44] s.39(2).
[45] See para. 20.8.
[46] s.57.
[47] s.23(4).
[48] Sched. 2.
[49] s.53(1A) ins. by Sched. 2, para. 9.

trustee makes a request for supplies for the purposes of any business which is or has been carried on by the debtor, the supplier can make it a condition of giving the supply that the trustee personally guarantees the payment of any charges in respect of the supplies to be made but he cannot make a condition, or do anything which has the effect of making it a condition, that any outstanding charges in respect of supplies given to the debtor are paid.[50]

Recall of sequestration

While the creditor can appeal against an order refusing to award sequestration,[51] there is no appeal against an order awarding sequestration but the debtor can petition for recall. The Court of Session can recall an award of sequestration if it is satisfied that in all the circumstances of the case (including those arising after the award of the sequestration) it is appropriate to do so and in particular, if it is satisfied that the debtor has paid his debts in full or has given sufficient security for their payment or if a majority in value of the creditors reside in a country other than Scotland and it is more appropriate that the estate be administered there or if other awards of sequestration or an analogous remedy have been granted.[52] The petition for recall may be presented by the debtor, any creditor, any other person having an interest, the interim or permanent trustee or the Accountant in Bankruptcy.[53] The petition must be presented within 10 weeks after the date of sequestration unless it is on one of the three particular grounds specified above, in which case it can be presented at any time.[54] On recalling the award, the court may direct that the outlays and remuneration of the interim and the permanent trustee and the expenses of the petitioning creditor shall be paid out of the debtor's estate and the court may make such further order as it considers necessary or reasonable in the circumstances of the case.[55] The effect of recall is, so far as practicable, to restore the debtor and any other person affected by the sequestration to the position he would have been in if the sequestration had not been awarded[56] but the recall does not affect the interruption of prescription constituted by the presentation of the petition or the submission of a creditor's claim[57]; nor does it invalidate any transaction entered into before the recall by the interim or permanent trustee with a person acting in good faith.[58]

20.6

The most important grounds of recall are:

(a) Defects in the proceedings. If the defect appears *ex facie* of the proceedings—for example, if the account produced by a concurring creditor was not sufficiently specific in its terms[59]—the court must recall the sequestration. If the defect is latent—for example, if the petitioning creditor's affidavit was invalid because the granter had

---

[50] B.A., s.70.
[51] B.A., s.15(3).
[52] B.A., s.17(1).
[53] B.A., s.16(1).
[54] B.A., s.16(4).
[55] B.A., s.17(3).
[56] B.A., s.17(4).
[57] B.A., s.17(5)(*a*).
[58] B.A., s.17(5)(*b*).
[59] *Riddell* v. *Galbraith* (1896) 24 R. 51.

not been put on oath[60]—the granting of the petition for recall is in the discretion of the court.[61] The matters to be considered in the exercise of this discretion are whether the defect was substantial, whether the irregularity was due to the fraud of the petitioning creditor, whether creditors not responsible for the irregularity would be prejudiced by recall and whether the debtor suffered prejudice because of the irregularity.[62] Where the defect is latent a creditor who has taken part in the sequestration proceedings may be barred by acquiescence if he petitions for recall.[63]

(b) Solvency: The court has a discretion to recall the sequestration if the debtor shows that he was at the time of the award in a position to meet his current obligations,[64] but the court can take into account the debtor's situation at the date of the hearing for recall.[65]

(c) That the debt founded on by the petitioning creditor was not due. The court's power is again discretionary,[66] but will not normally be exercised if no steps have been taken to reduce the decree for the debt.[65]

(d) That the award of sequestration was obtained by fraud or an unfair use of process.[67]

Considerations of equity and expediency are not grounds for recall.[68]

The debtor

20.7 Any dealing of or with the debtor relating to his estate vested in the permanent trustee is of no effect in a question with the trustee[69] unless the trustee has abandoned the property to the debtor or has expressly or impliedly authorised the dealing or is otherwise personally barred from challenging the dealing.[70] The following dealings may also have effect if the person dealing with the debtor was, at the time of the dealing, unaware of the sequestration and had no reason to believe that the debtor's estate had been sequestrated or was the subject of sequestration proceedings:

(a) the performance of an obligation undertaken before the sequestration by a person obliged to the debtor in the obligation;

(b) the purchase from the debtor of goods for which the purchaser has given value to the debtor or is willing to give value to the trustee;

(c) a banking transaction in the ordinary course of business between the debtor and the banker.[71] The debtor must notify the trustee of any assets acquired by him after the date of sequestration.[72] The debtor

---

[60] *Blair v. North British and Mercantile Insurance Co.* (1889) 16 R. 325.
[61] *Ballantyne v. Barr* (1867) 5 M. 330; *Mitchell v. Motherwell* (1888) 16 R. 122.
[62] *Nakeski-Cumming v. Gordon*, 1924 S.C. 217; *Hodgson v. Hodgson's Trs.*, 1984 S.L.T. 97.
[63] *Ure v. McCubbin* (1857) 19 D. 758; *Tennent v. Martin & Dunlop* (1879) 6 R. 786.
[64] *Aitken v. Kyd* (1890) 28 S.L.R. 115; *Michie v. Young*, 1962 S.L.T. (Notes) 70.
[65] *Murdoch v. Newman Industrial Control Ltd.*, 1980 S.L.T. 13.
[66] *Pert v. Bruce*, 1937 S.L.T. 475.
[67] *Joel v. Gill* (1859) 22 D. 6; *Gardner v. Woodside* (1862) 24 D. 1133.
[68] *Joel v. Gill, supra.*
[69] B.A., s.32(8).
[70] B.A., s.32(9)(*a*).
[71] B.A., s.32(9)(*b*). The relevant knowledge is that of the bank and not that of the individual teller: *Minhas's Tr. v. Bank of Scotland*, 1990 S.L.T. 23.
[72] B.A., s.32(7).

has a duty to cooperate with the trustee in the performance of his functions.[73] The debtor commits an offence if he, either alone or jointly with another person, obtains credit to the extent of £250 without giving the person from whom he obtained it the information that he has been sequestrated and has not obtained his discharge.[74] Certain criminal offences may arise out of the debtor's conduct before and during the sequestration.[75]

The debtor may carry on a business after sequestration but the profits of the business will be available to the trustee. The assets of the business are available for the diligence of the creditors of the business[76] The trustee cannot, after a long interval, claim them as *acquirenda*.[77] The debtor cannot insist in any action raised by him which the trustee wishes to take up unless it is of a personal character.[78] An action may be brought against the debtor but it is not *res judicata* in a question with the trustee.[79] A debtor who raises an action may be required to find caution for expenses.[80] A bankrupt defender is not normally required to find caution.[81] An undischarged bankrupt is disqualified from holding certain public offices[82] and cannot be a company director without the leave of the court.[83]

Discharge

The debtor is automatically discharged on the expiry of three years from the date of the sequestration[84] and can obtain a certificate of discharge from the Accountant in Bankruptcy[85] unless the trustee or a creditor, not later than two years and nine months after the date of sequestration, applies to the sheriff for a deferment of the discharge and the sheriff makes an order deferring the discharge for a period not exceeding two years.[86] On the application being made the sheriff orders the debtor to lodge in court a declaration that he has made a full and fair surrender of his estate and a full disclosure of all claims which he was entitled to make against other persons and that he has delivered to the trustee every document under his control relating to his estate or his business or financial affairs; if the declaration is not lodged within 14 days, the discharge is deferred without a hearing. If the declaration is lodged, the sheriff, after considering a report by the trustee on the debtor's assets and liabilities, his financial and business affairs and his conduct in relation thereto and upon the sequestration and his conduct in

20.8

---

[73] B.A., s.64.
[74] B.A., s.67(9); B. Reg. 13.
[75] B.A., s.67.
[76] *Abel* v. *Watt* (1883) 11 R. 149.
[77] *M.P. Thomas* v. *Baird* (1897) 13 Sh.Ct.Rep. 291.
[78] Goudy, p. 364.
[79] Goudy, p. 372.
[80] *Weepers* v. *Pearson and Jackson* (1859) 21 D. 305; *Maltman* v. *Tarmac Civil Engineering Ltd.*, 1967 S.L.T. (Notes) 102.
[81] *Mackay* v. *Boswall-Preston*, 1916 S.C. 96.
[82] I.A., s.427; District Courts (Scotland) Act 1975, s.13A; Local Government (Scotland) Act 1973, s.31.
[83] Company Directors Disqualification Act 1986, s.11.
[84] B.A., s.54(1).
[85] B. Regs. Fm. 8.
[86] s.54(4).

the course of it, and after hearing representations by the applicant, the debtor and any creditor, may defer the discharge or dismiss the application.[87] Where the discharge is deferred, the debtor may petition for discharge during the period of deferment[88]; the trustee or a creditor can apply, not later than three months before the expiry of the period of deferment, for a further deferment.[89] The effect of the discharge is that the debtor is discharged within the United Kingdom of all debts and obligations contracted by him, or for which he was liable, at the date of the sequestration[90] but there are the following exceptions:

(a) any liability to pay a fine due under a confiscation order or other penalty due to the Crown;
(b) any liability to forfeiture of a sum of money deposited in court under the Bail etc. (Scotland) Act 1980;
(c) any liability incurred by reason of fraud or breach of trust;
(d) any obligation to pay aliment or any sum of an alimentary nature under any enactment or rule of law or any periodical allowance payable on divorce under a court order or under an obligation, not being a sum which could have been claimed in the sequestration;
(e) the debtor's statutory duty to cooperate with the trustee.[91] The debtor is not discharged from his post-sequestration debts. The sequestration itself can continue after the debtor's discharge.

The financial markets régime

20.9 The Companies Act 1989 established a special régime for the treatment of certain transactions connected with financial markets.[92] The broad effect is to take these transactions out of the general insolvency law which is made subject to the provisions of the 1989 Act. Contracts connected with a recognised investment exchange or clearing house and securities related thereto are not affected by insolvency proceedings if a party is unable to meet his obligations under the contracts. The contractual liabilities are worked out under the default rules of the exchange or clearing house and the net sum payable by or to the party is taken into account in the insolvency proceedings.

---

[87] s.54(6). See *Watson* v. *Henderson* (Sh.Ct.) 1988 S.C.L.R. 439; *Crittal Warmlife Ltd.* v. *Flaherty*, 1988 G.W.D. 22–930.

[88] s.54(8).

[89] s.54(9).

[90] s.55. (amended by Criminal Justice (S.) Act 1987, s.45(5)(*c*); Criminal Justice Act 1988, Sched. 15, para. 109.) A student loan is not discharged: Education (Student Loans) Act 1990, Sched. 2, para. 6(*c*)(ii).

[91] s.64.

[92] C.A. 1989, Part VII. See Rajani & Hickmott, "*Financial Markets and Insolvency*" (1989) 6 I.L. & P. 167.

CHAPTER 21

SEQUESTRATION: THE ESTATE

Vesting in trustee

By virtue of the Act and Warrant the whole estate of the debtor, wherever situated, vests as at the date of sequestration and from the beginning of that day[1] in the permanent trustee for the benefit of the creditors.[2] The estate includes any income or estate vesting in the debtor on the date of sequestration and the capacity to exercise and to take proceedings for exercising all such powers in, over or in respect of any property as might have been exercised by the debtor for his own benefit as at or on the date of sequestration or might be exercised between the date of sequestration and the date of the debtor's discharge.[3] "A bankrupt may have had property scattered in his own name all over the world. But the sequestration vests it all in the trustee."[4] The vesting in the trustee is, of course, without prejudice to the right of any secured creditor which is preferable to the trustee's right.[5] Any person claiming a right to any estate claimed by the trustee can apply to the court for the estate to be excluded from that vesting in the trustee.[6]

21.1

Trust property

Property held by the debtor on trust for any other person does not vest in the trustee.[7] This is so even where heritage is held on an unqualified feudal title subject to a latent trust.[8] A trust obligation must, however, be distinguished from a mere liability created by personal contract.[9] Trust property cannot be recovered if it has been so mixed with the debtor's own funds as to be indistinguishable.[10] The fact that shares have been pledged with other securities under a general letter of hypothecation does not make them unidentifiable.[11]

21.2

The terms of a building contract may be such that payments made by the employer to the principal contractor in respect of work done by a sub-contractor are held in trust by the principal contractor.[12] Money representing the price of goods sent in with an order may be treated by the recipient in such a way as to create a trust of it, *e.g.* by putting it into a

---

[1] *Cook's Tr., Petr.*, 1985 S.L.T. 33.
[2] B.A., s.31.
[3] B.A., s.31(8).
[4] *Per* Lord Cockburn, *Adam* v. *McRobbie* (1845) 7 D. 276 at 282.
[5] B.A., s.33(3).
[6] B.A., s.31(6).
[7] B.A., s.33(1)(*b*).
[8] *Heritable Reversionary Co.* v. *Millar* (1892) 19 R. (H.L.) 43.
[9] *Bank of Scotland* v. *Liquidators of Hutchison Main & Co. Ltd.*, 1914 S.C. (H.L.) 1. See also *Export Credits Guarantee Department* v. *Turner*, 1979 S.C. 286; *Clark Taylor and Co. Ltd.* v. *Quality Site Development (Edinburgh) Ltd.*, 1981 S.C. 111; *Tay Valley Joinery Ltd.* v. *C. F. Financial Services Ltd.*, 1987 S.L.T. 207. Consignation "for behoof of" another person creates a trust: *United Collieries Ltd.* v. *Lord Advocate*, 1950 S.C. 458.
[10] Goudy, p. 289.
[11] *Newton's Exrx.* v. *Meiklejohn's J.F.*, 1959 S.L.T. 71.
[12] *Tout and Finch Ltd.* [1954] 1 All E.R. 127; *Veitchi Co.* v. *Crowley Russell & Co.*, 1972 S.C. 225; *Dunbarton C.C.* v. *George W. Sellars & Sons Ltd.*, 1973 S.L.T. (Sh.Ct.) 67.

bank account denominated as a trust account.[13] Funds held by the debtor as an agent do not pass to the trustee if they can be identified.[14] Scottish legislative draftsmen seem to prefer the device of agency to trust.[15] There are now numerous situations in which a statutory trust or agency is created.[16]

Special appropriation

21.3 Property which has been lodged with the debtor for a specific purpose does not pass to the trustee if it can be identified in the debtor's hands.[17] If the debtor has mixed the deposited funds with his own in a bank account and has later made a withdrawal, he is presumed to have withdrawn his own funds.[18]

Acquisitions by fraud

21.4 The trustee cannot take advantage of the debtor's fraud and property acquired by fraud can be recovered if it can be identified.[19]

Statutory exceptions

21.5 Where the debtor holds property which is affected by an order under drugs legislation the property is excluded from the debtor's estate for purposes of the Bankruptcy Act.[20] The powers of the trustee may also be restricted by the special provisions relating to financial markets.[21] Where the debtor is receiving compensation in respect of accident, injury or disease the sum to be deducted in respect of social security benefits which is payable to the Department of Social Security does not form part of the debtor's estate.[22]

Corporeal moveables

21.6 Corporeal moveables vest in the trustee as if at the date of sequestration the trustee had taken delivery or possession of the property.[23] Property exempted from poinding for the purpose of protecting the debtor and his family does not, however, vest in the trustee.[24] The landlord's hypothec is not affected by the sequestration.[25]

---

[13] *Re Kayford Ltd.* [1975] 1 W.L.R. 279.
[14] Bell, *Comm.*, I, 287; Goudie, p. 290; *Macadam* v. *Martin's Tr.* (1872) 11 M. 33; *Jopp* v. *Johnston's Tr.* (1904) 6 F. 1028.
[15] See Financial Services Act 1986, s.55(5).
[16] See Conveyancing and Feudal Reform (S.) Act 1970, s.27(1); Solicitors (S.) Act 1980, s.42 (solicitor's client bank account); Financial Services (Clients' Money) Regulations 1987, reg. 2.2(1)(*b*).
[17] *Macadam* v. *Martin's Tr.* (1872) 11 M. 33.
[18] *Jopp* v. *Johnston's Tr.* (1904) 6 F. 1028; but see *Hofford* v. *Gowans*, 1909 1 S.L.T. 153.
[19] *Colquhouns' Tr.* v. *Campbell's Trs.* (1902) 4 F. 739. Cf. *Raymond Harrison & Co.'s Tr.* v. *North West Securities*, 1989 S.L.T. 718.
[20] Drug Trafficking Offences Act 1986, s.16; Criminal Justice (Scotland) Act 1987, s.33; Criminal Justice Act 1988, s.85.
[21] C.A., 1989, Part VII; see para. 20.9.
[22] Social Security Act 1989, Sched. 4, para. 8(2).
[23] B.A., s.31(4).
[24] B.A., s.33(1)(*a*). See para. 16.3.
[25] s.33(2).

Sale of goods

Where the debtor has in his possession goods which he has bought but not paid for, the disposal of the goods depends largely on whether the property has passed.[26] If the property had not passed to the debtor, the seller can recover them.[27] If there is an appropriate clause in the contract the seller may be able to recover the proceeds of a sub-sale of the goods if they can be identified.[28] If the property has passed he cannot recover the goods,[29] except, possibly, where the buyer induced the contract of sale by fraudulent representations as to his solvency and the seller has raised an action of rescission prior to the sequestration[30]; or where the buyer fraudulently took delivery on the eve of sequestration or after the presentation of the sequestration petition; but mere knowledge of insolvency does not constitute fraud.[31] If the buyer before sequestration rejected the goods the seller can recover them.[32] If the goods are not in the debtor's possession at the sequestration the seller can exercise his rights of lien[33] or stoppage in transit[34] if the property has passed or his co-extensive right of withholding delivery if the property has not passed.[35]

21.7

Where the debtor has sold goods and received payment of the price the buyer can recover the goods if the property has passed to him[36] unless the transaction was in substance a security in the form of a sale.[37]

In the case of goods on hire-purchase the goods do not pass to the hirer's trustee.[38] If the goods were originally owned by the debtor and the hire-purchase transaction was preceded by a purported sale, the transaction may be struck at by s.62(4) of the Sale of Goods Act 1979.[39]

If goods have been let on hire-purchase by the debtor, the trustee acquires the property in the goods and the right to receive payments under the contract. It is thought that the trustee cannot prevent the hirer completing the contract and obtaining property in the goods.[40]

Incorporeal moveables

Incorporeal moveable property vests in the trustee as if intimation of its assignation to the trustee had been made at the date of sequestration.[41] So where a life insurance policy was assigned for value but the assignation

21.8

---

[26] For the rules as to passing of property, see Sale of Goods Act 1979, ss.16–19.
[27] *Ross & Co.* v. *Piano Manufacturing Co.* (1903) 11 S.L.T. 7 (sale or return).
[28] See para. 2.3.
[29] *London Scottish Transport Ltd.* v. *Tyres (Scotland) Ltd.*, 1957 S.L.T. (Sh.Ct.) 48 (approved in *Hostess Mobile Catering* v. *Archibald Scott Ltd.*, 1981 S.C. 185).
[30] *A. W. Gamage Ltd.* v. *Charlesworth's Tr.*, 1910 S.C. 257. The many reservations in the opinions should be noted.
[31] Goudy, p. 281; *Allan* v. *Murray* (1894) 10 Sh.Ct.Rep. 103; *Primrose's Seqn.* (1894) 10 Sh.Ct.Rep. 238.
[32] Goudy, p. 281; and see *Nelson* v. *Chalmers & Co. Ltd.*, 1913 S.C. 441.
[33] ss.41–43; *Paton's Trs.* v. *Finlayson*, 1923 S.C. 872.
[34] ss.44–46.
[35] s.39(2).
[36] *Hayman & Son* v. *McLintock*, 1907 S.C. 936.
[37] See para. 7.3.
[38] *Murdoch & Co. Ltd.* v. *Greig* (1889) 16 R. 396; *McLaren's Tr.* v. *Argylls Ltd.*, 1915 2 S.L.T. 241.
[39] *Newbigging* v. *Ritchie's Tr.*, 1930 S.C. 273; *Scottish Transit Trust* v. *Scottish Land Cultivators*, 1955 S.C. 254; *G. & C. Finance Corporation Ltd.* v. *Brown*, 1961 S.L.T. 408.
[40] Gow, *Law of Hire-Purchase* (2nd ed.), p. 223.
[41] B.A., s.31(4).

not intimated to the insurance company before the cedent's sequestration, the trustee had a right to the policy preferable to that of the assignee[42]; the result was the same where the unintimated assignation was of a trust fund.[43] A bank draft in favour of a creditor which is still in the bankrupt's possession falls to the trustee.[44]

State pensions

21.9 Certain state pensions, by statute, do not vest in the trustee, *e.g.* pensions under the Police Pensions Act 1976, and social security benefits.[45] They may, however, be treated as alimentary provisions so that any excess is recoverable by the trustee.[46]

Rights of action

21.10 The trustee has a title to sue for patrimonial loss suffered by the debtor's estate but he cannot raise an action to recover *solatium* for personal injuries suffered by the debtor because the claim, being personal in character, does not transmit to him.[47] Where the debtor has raised an action, however, the trustee can have himself sisted as pursuer and acquire for the creditors any sum recovered.[48] But if he is unsuccessful he will be personally liable for the expenses before, as well as after, the sist.[49] Once decree has been granted in an action by the debtor for *solatium* in respect of an injury sustained after the sequestration, the debtor must account to the trustee for the proceeds.[50] Where a claim for solatium and patrimonial loss arises after sequestration the debtor and the trustee should sue in one action.[51] If the trustee has abandoned a claim, the debtor is entitled to pursue it.[52]

Rights against insurers

21.11 Where the debtor is insured against liabilities to third parties which he may incur and such a liability is incurred before or after sequestration, his rights against the insurer are transferred to the third party.[53]

The proceeds of a claim under a personal accident policy are *acquirenda* but the debtor has a right to be indemnified co-extensive with the amount of the proceeds.[54]

Building contracts

21.12 Where a building contract provided that the principal contractor could

---

[42] *Wood* v. *Weir* (1900) 16 Sh.Ct.Rep. 356.
[43] *Tod's Trs.* v. *Wilson* (1869) 7 M. 1100 (but see *Watson* v. *Duncan* (1879) 6 R. 1247, *per* Lord Deas at p. 1252).
[44] *Brown* v. *Hunter-Arundell's Trs.* (1899) 15 Sh.Ct.Rep. 281.
[45] Social Security Act 1975, s.87(1). An award under the statutory Criminal Injuries Compensation Scheme (when it is in force) will not pass to the trustee: Criminal Justice Act 1988, s.117.
[46] *Macdonald's Tr.* v. *Macdonald*, 1938 S.C. 536.
[47] *Muir's Tr.* v. *Braidwood*, 1958 S.C. 169.
[48] *Thom* v. *Bridges* (1857) 19 D. 721; *Watson* v. *Thompson* (O.H.), 1990 S.C.L.R. 59.
[49] *Torbet* v. *Borthwick* (1849) 11 D. 694.
[50] *Jackson* v. *McKechnie* (1875) 3 R. 130.
[51] *Grindall* v. *John Mitchell (Grangemouth) Ltd.*, 1987 S.L.T. 137.
[52] *Dickson* v. *United Dominions Trust Ltd.*, 1988 S.L.T. 19.
[53] Third Parties (Rights against Insurers) Act 1930, s.1.
[54] *Railway Passengers' Assurance Co.* v. *Kyd* (1894) 10 Sh.Ct.Rep. 138.

not obtain an architect's certificate for payment until he had paid the sums due to sub-contractors under previous certificates, it was held that on the liquidation of the principal contractor the provision was still operative.[55]

Registered titles

Where property is held on a registered title (*e.g.* shares in a limited company), the Act and Warrant does not confer a real right on the trustee as at the date of sequestration and his title is not complete until he is placed on the register. An assignee whose transfer was granted before and registered after the date of sequestration but before registration of the trustee's title is preferred.[56] The rule applies not only to shares, but also to ships, patents and trade-marks.[57] This is the "race to the register."

21.13

Spes successionis

A non-vested contingent right of succession in favour of the debtor vests in the trustee as if an assignation by the debtor had been intimated at the date of sequestration.[58]

21.14

Heritage

The Act and Warrant has, in respect of the heritable estate in Scotland, the same effect as if a decree of adjudication in implement of sale, as well as a decree of adjudication for payment and in security of debt, subject to no legal reversion, had been pronounced in favour of the permanent trustee.[59] However, the trustee's title is not complete until he has recorded his title. The trustee will be preferred to the holder of an unrecorded security if he completes his title first.[60] The position is probably the same where there is an unrecorded disposition granted by the debtor prior to sequestration.[61] Where the debtor has concluded missives, received payment of the price and given possession to the purchaser but no disposition has been granted prior to sequestration, the subjects pass to the trustee, the purchaser having only a *jus crediti* and not a real right.[62] Property of the debtor on a disposition *ex facie* absolute but truly in security does not vest in the trustee.[63] Where the debtor had a one-half *pro indiviso* share in a lease subject to a survivorship destination and the debtor died after the date of sequestration it was held that the

21.15

---

[55] *Veitchi Co.* v. *Crowley Russell & Co.*, 1972 S.C. 225.
[56] *Morrison* v. *Harrison* (1876) 3 R. 406.
[57] Goudy, p. 254. There is more than one principle underlying this rule. In the case of shares, the rationale is that the bilateral character of membership of a company which involves both rights and liabilities requires entry on the register to complete the transfer (see the opinions in *Morrison*); in the case of heritage the reason is to give heritable creditors a reasonable time in which to complete their securities (see Bell, *Comm.*, II, 33).
[58] B.A., s.31(5).
[59] B.A., s.31(1)(*b*).
[60] Bell, *Comm.*, II, 338; *Cormack* v. *Anderson* (1829) 7 S. 868; *Melville* v. *Paterson* (1842) 4 D. 1311, *per* Lord Ivory at p. 1315; *Smith* v. *Frier* (1857) 19 D. 384; Bell, *Lectures on Conveyancing* (3rd ed.), p. 812; Craigie, *Scottish Law of Conveyancing: Heritable Rights* (3rd ed.), p. 514; Wallace, *Bankruptcy* (2nd ed.), p. 238; Burns, *Conveyancing Practice* (4th ed.), p. 409.
[61] Reid (1985) 30 J.L.S. 110. *Cf.* McDonald (1985) 30 J.L.S. 20.
[62] *Gibson and Hunter Home Designs Ltd.*, 1976 S.C. 23.
[63] *Heritable Reversionary Co.* v. *Millar* (1892) 19 R. (H.L.) 43.

trustee had no right to the subjects but it is not clear that this decision is correct.[64]

The trustee can have the debtor ejected from the heritable property.[65] When the debtor has constituted a security over the subjects by *ex facie* absolute disposition the trustee acquires the right to redeem the property, and is entitled to an accounting.[66]

The interest of the debtor as a tenant under an assured, protected or secure tenancy is not treated as part of the debtor's estate and does not vest in the trustee until the trustee serves notice on the debtor to that effect.[67]

The family home

21.16   The "family home" is any property in which, on the day immediately preceding the date of sequestration, the debtor had, alone or in common with another person, a right or interest, and which was occupied as a residence at that time by the debtor's spouse or former spouse, with or without a child of the family, or by the debtor with a child of the family.[68] The trustee cannot dispose of any right or interest in the debtor's family home unless either he obtains the consent of the occupying spouse or former spouse, or, where the debtor is residing there with a child, the consent of the debtor.[69] If he is unable to obtain consent, the trustee has to apply to the court for authority; the court will have regard to all the circumstances, including the needs and financial resources of the spouse or former spouse and of any child of the family, the interests of creditors, and the length of the period during which, before or after the date of sequestration, the home was used as a residence by the spouse, former spouse or child; the court may refuse to grant the application, or postpone the granting of it for such period not exceeding 12 months as it may consider reasonable in the circumstances, or grant the application subject to such conditions as it may prescribe.[70] The court may exercise the same powers if the trustee brings an action for division and sale of the family home or an action to obtain vacant possession of the family home.[71]

The matrimonial home

21.17   Where the sequestrated estate includes a matrimonial home within the meaning of the Matrimonial Homes (Family Protection) (Scotland) Act 1981, of which the debtor, immediately before the issue of the Act and Warrant was an entitled spouse and the other spouse was a non-entitled spouse and the court is satisfied that the purpose of the petition for sequestration was wholly or mainly to defeat the occupancy rights of the non-entitled spouse the court may recall the sequestration or make such

---

[64] *Robertson's Tr. v. Roberts*, 1982 S.L.T. 22.
[65] *White v. Stevenson*, 1956 S.C. 84.
[66] *Hay's Tr. v. Davidson* (1853) 15 D. 583.
[67] B.A., ss.31(9) and (10), inserted by Housing Act 1988, s.118.
[68] s.40(4)(*a*). A "child of the family" includes any child of the debtor, his spouse or his former spouse, and any person brought up or accepted by these persons as if he were his or her child whatever the age of the child, grandchild or person may be (s.40(4)(*b*)).
[69] B.A., s.40(1).
[70] B.A., s.40(2).
[71] B.A., s.40(3); *Stewart v. Salmon* (Sh.Ct.) 1988 S.C.L.R. 647.

order as it thinks appropriate to protect the occupancy rights of the non-entitled spouse.[72] The trustee must inform the non-entitled spouse of the award of sequestration within 14 days after the issue of the Act and Warrant and the non-entitled spouse can petition the Court of Session within 40 days of the issue of the Act and Warrant or within 10 weeks from the date of sequestration.

Property of the debtor's spouse

21.18 The property of the debtor's spouse is not liable for his debts.[73] However, a loan by the debtor's spouse to the debtor is a postponed debt in the sequestration.[74]

The debtor's income

21.19 Any income of whatever nature received by the debtor between his sequestration and discharge, other than income arising from estate which is vested in the trustee, vests in the debtor.[75] It is not competent to execute diligence against such income vesting in the debtor in respect of a debt of which the debtor would be discharged in the course of the sequestration.[76] The trustee may apply to the sheriff to determine a suitable amount to allow for the aliment of the debtor and the debtor's obligations to pay aliment or to pay a periodical allowance to a former spouse; the amount allowed need not be sufficient for compliance with a subsisting order or agreement relating to the aliment or periodical allowance.[77] If the debtor's total income is in excess of the total amount allowed the sheriff fixes the amount of the excess and orders that it shall be paid to the trustee.[78] The order may be varied or recalled on a change in the debtor's circumstances.[79] The provisions as to income are wide enough to cover alimentary income and it would appear that such income is not now treated differently from other income in sequestration.

Acquirenda

21.20 Any estate, wherever situated, acquired by the debtor between his sequestration and his discharge, which would have vested in the trustee if it had been part of the debtor's estate at the date of sequestration, vests in the trustee for the benefit of the creditors as at the date of acquisition.[80] The holder of any such estate must convey or deliver it to the trustee on production to him of a certified copy Act and Warrant. A person who has in good faith and without knowledge of the sequestration conveyed the estate to the debtor or to anyone on the debtor's instructions incurs no liability to the trustee except to account to the trustee for any proceeds of the conveyance which are in his hands. Rights and interests acquired in

---

[72] B.A., s.41.
[73] Family Law (S.) Act 1985, s.24(1).
[74] B.A., s.51(3)(b).
[75] s.32(1).
[76] s.32(5).
[77] s.32(3).
[78] s.32(2). A student loan is not to be treated as income: Education (Student Loans) Act 1990, Sched. 2, para. 6(a).
[79] s.32(4).
[80] s.32(6). Sums paid as a student loan do not go to the trustee: Education (Student Loans) Act 1990; Sched. 2, para. 6(b).

the estate in good faith and for value are not prejudiced. It is a criminal offence if the debtor fails to notify the trustee of any assets acquired by him.[81]

Property furth of Scotland

21.21 The Act and Warrant vests in the trustee the whole estate of the debtor wherever situated[82] but the Bankruptcy Act provides remarkably little machinery to enable the trustee to exercise his powers in relation to property outwith Scotland.[83] However, some provision of a rather unsatisfactory character is made by s.426 of the Insolvency Act 1986. First, it is enacted that an order of a court exercising insolvency jurisdiction in one part of the United Kingdom will be enforced in any other part as if it were made by a court having jurisdiction in that other part.[84] That is then immediately qualified to the effect that it does not require a court in one part of the United Kingdom to enforce, in relation to property situated in that part, any order made by a court in any other part.[85] That provision is, however, to be without prejudice to the following provisions of the section, of which four are material. First, there is power to make by order provision which would give a Scottish trustee the same powers in relation to property in England as an English trustee or assignee would have[86]; this order has not yet been made. Then it is provided that the courts in one part of the UK shall assist the courts having the corresponding insolvency jurisdiction in any other part of the UK[87]; a request by the one court to the other is authority for the court to whom the request is made to apply in the matter "the insolvency law which is applicable by either court in relation to comparable matters falling within its jurisdiction" having regard to the rules of private international law.[88] Lastly, where a trustee under the insolvency law of one part of the UK claims property in another part, the submission of that claim to a court in that other part is treated as a request made by a court under the preceding provision.[89]

Outwith the UK the trustee's powers will depend on the law of the state in which property is situated; in some cases there will be special reciprocal arrangements.

---

[81] s.32(7).
[82] B.A., 31(1), (8).
[83] See Lewis (1988) 4 I.L. & P. 155.
[84] I.A., s.426(1).
[85] s.426(2).
[86] s.426(3).
[87] s.426(4). This and the next two subsections are extended to Guernsey: Insolvency Act 1986 (Guernsey) Order 1989 (S.I. 1989 No. 2409).
[88] s.426(5).
[89] s.426(6).

CHAPTER 22

ANTECEDENT TRANSACTIONS

Certain antecedent transactions can be impugned by the trustee to the effect of recovering assets for the benefit of the creditors. The principal transactions affected are (a) gratuitous alienations, (b) fraudulent and unfair preferences, (c) *inter vivos* trusts, (d) divorce orders, and (e) extortionate credit transactions.

Gratuitous alienations—common law

At common law, the trustee, or any onerous creditor, can challenge a gratuitous alienation made by the debtor when he was insolvent. This right is preserved by the Bankruptcy (Scotland) Act 1985.[1] The onus is on the challenger to show that the alienation was gratuitous, that the debtor was insolvent at the date of the alienation, that the debtor is still insolvent, and that the alienation was made to the prejudice of creditors. The difficulty of proving these matters is such that in practice resort was usually made to the Bankruptcy Act 1621, which struck at gratuitous alienations to conjunct and confident persons. That Act has now been repealed but it is thought that some of the case law decided under it may be relevant to the common law position.

22.1

The Act applied to "all alienations, dispositions, assignations, and translations, whatsoever made by the debtor of any of his lands, teinds, reversions, actions, debts, or goods whatsoever." The subjects of the alienation had to be attachable by the diligence of creditors.[2] The following were held to be alienations: the assignation of a life interest or life insurance policy; a lease[3]; the granting of a bill[4] or promissory note[5]; the discharge of a claim[6]; the abandonment of an action[7]; a decree allowed to pass in absence.[8] The conveyance might be direct or indirect.[9] So, a conveyance from the seller to the conjunct or confident person, the price being paid by the insolvent, was an alienation.[10] In the insolvency of a partnership where one partner exercised a power of appointment under an ante-nuptial marriage contract so as to divert a *spes successionis* from her partner to her grandchild, it was held that there had been an alienation because the creditors of the appointer were prejudiced.[11] Cash

---

[1] B.A., s.34(8). There may not be a challenge where the financial markets régime applies: C.A. 1989, s.165(2)(*b*). See para. 20.9.

[2] Bell, *Comm.*, II, 178–179.

[3] *Gorrie's Tr.* v. *Gorrie* (1890) 17 R. 1051.

[4] Bell, *Comm.*, II, 177.

[5] *Thomas* v. *Thomson* (1865) 3 M. 1160; but a mere voucher was not an alienation. The point seems to be that a voucher neither attaches a fund nor gives a right to do diligence.

[6] *Laing* v. *Cheyne* (1832) 10 S. 200.

[7] *Wilson* v. *Drummond's Reps.* (1853) 16 D. 275.

[8] Mackenzie, *Works*, II, p. 8.

[9] Bell, *Comm.*, II, 174.

[10] *Ross* v. *Hutton* (1830) 8 S. 916; *Bolden* v. *Ferguson* (1863) 1 M. 522.

[11] *Thomson* v. *Spence*, 1961 S.L.T. 395.

payments were not alienations under the Act[12] but they are under the common law.[13]

Gratuitous alienations—1985 Act

22.2 A gratuitous alienation by the debtor may be challenged by the trustee or by a creditor under s.34 of the Act.[14] The alienation may be one by which any of the debtor's property was transferred or any claim or right of the debtor was discharged or renounced.[15] The alienation must have become completely effectual not earlier than two years before the date of sequestration, or, if it was in favour of an associate[16] of the debtor, not earlier than five years before the sequestration.[17]

If a challenge is brought, the court will grant decree of reduction[18] or for such restoration of property to the debtor's estate or other redress as may be appropriate but not if it is established that:
(a) immediately, or at any other time, after the alienation the debtor's assets were greater than his liabilities, or
(b) the alienation was made for adequate consideration, or
(c) the alienation was a birthday, Christmas or other conventional gift which, having regard to all the circumstances, it was reasonable for the debtor to make or a reasonable gift to a person who is not an associate of the debtor for a charitable, benevolent or philanthropic purpose whether or not it was charitable within the meaning of any rule of law.[19] An alienation in implement of a prior obligation is deemed to be one for which there was no consideration or no adequate consideration to the extent that the prior obligation was undertaken for no consideration or no adequate consideration.[20] Rights or interests acquired in good faith and for value from or through the transferee in the alienation are not affected by the challenge.[21] A policy under the Married Women's Policies of Assurance (Scotland) Act 1880 is not affected.[22]

Associates

22.3 An associate is the modern form of the "conjunct and confident person"—someone who is so close to the debtor by blood, marriage or business connection that he may be favoured by the debtor or trusted by the debtor to secrete his assets for him. First, it is necessary to define "relative." A relative of an individual is that individual's brother, sister, uncle, aunt, nephew, niece, lineal ancestor or lineal descendant. The half blood is treated as the whole blood and stepchildren, adopted children and illegitimate children are treated as children. A spouse includes a

---

[12] *Gilmour Shaw & Co.'s Tr.* v. *Learmonth*, 1972 S.C. 137.
[13] *Dobie* v. *Mitchell* (1854) 17 D. 97; *Main* v. *Fleming's Trs.* (1881) 8 R. 880.
[14] But not where the financial markets régime applies: C.A. 1989, s.165(2)(*a*). See para. 20.9.
[15] B.A., s.34(2)(*a*).
[16] See next paragraph.
[17] s.34(3).
[18] An action of reduction must be brought in the Court of Session.
[19] s.34(4); *Short's Tr.* v. *Chung* (1990) G.W.D. 28–1857.
[20] s.34(6).
[21] s.34(4).
[22] s.34(7).

former and a reputed spouse.[23] Then, an associate of an individual is that individual's husband or wife; relative; relative's spouse; spouse's relative; spouse's relative's spouse; partner; partner's associate; firm of which he is a partner; employee; employer; company of which he has control or of which he and his associates have control. A person is taken to have control of a company if the directors of it or of another company which controls it are accustomed to act in accordance with his directions or instructions or if he can exercise, or control the exercise of, one third or more of the voting power at any general meeting of the company or of another company which controls it; if two or more persons together satisfy either of these conditions they are taken to control the company. Directors and officers of the company are treated as employees of the company.

A company is an associate of another company if (i) the same person controls both, or (ii) a person controls it and his associates or he and his associates control the other, or (iii) a group of persons controls each company and the groups consist of the same persons or could be regarded as so consisting by treating members of one group as replaced by persons of whom they are associates.[24]

Fraudulent preferences

A fraudulent preference arises where a debtor "after his funds have become inadequate to the payment of all his debts, intentionally, and in contemplation of his failing, confers on favourite creditors a preference over the rest."[25] Such fraudulent preferences are challengeable at common law if they are made by the debtor (i) voluntarily (ii) during insolvency, and (iii) while conscious of his insolvency. It seems that the challenge can be at the instance of any creditor who is prejudiced by the transaction. The right is preserved by the Bankruptcy Act 1985.[26] Formerly, most challenges were under the Bankruptcy Act 1696, now repealed, but some of the case law decided on that Act is relevant to the common law and may be of relevance to the construction of the new provisions.

22.4

Transactions affected

The Act was applied to: a disposition of heritage[27]; the transfer of moveables[28]; the return of moveables bought but not paid for under an arrangement made in view of the buyer's insolvency[29]; the granting of a delivery order for moveables[30]; an assignation[31]; a mandate for pay-

22.5

---

[23] s.74(4).
[24] s.74 as amended by B. Regs. 11.
[25] Bell, *Comm.*, II, 226.
[26] s.36(6). There may not be the possibility of challenge where the financial markets régime applies: C.A. 1989, s.165(2)(*b*). See para. 20.9.
[27] *Hill's Tr.* v. *Macgregor* (1901) 8 S.L.T. 484. Under registration of title, there is no indemnity in respect of the reduced title: Land Registration (Scotland) Act 1979, s.12(3)(*b*).
[28] *Rhind's Tr.* v. *Robertson & Baxter* (1891) 18 R. 623; *Walker* v. *Coyle* (1891) 19 R. 91.
[29] *Watson & Sons Ltd.* v. *Veritys Ltd.* (1908) 24 Sh.Ct.Rep. 148.
[30] *Wright* v. *Mitchell* (1871) 9 M. 516; *Price & Pierce Ltd.* v. *Bank of Scotland*, 1910 S.C. 1095; 1912 S.C. (H.L.) 19.
[31] Bell, *Comm.*, II, 196.

ment[32]; the indorsation of a bill or cheque[33]; a bond and disposition in security[34]; a security constituted by an *ex facie* absolute disposition of heritage[35]; a mortgage of a ship[36]; a trust deed for creditors[37]; the discharge of a right[38]; the renunciation of a lease[39]; the abandonment of a competent defence[40]; the allowance of decree by default[41]; possibly, an agreement to pay several creditors by instalments provided they did not sue for recovery of their debts.[42] The principle applies even where the creditor is given an advantage by means of a circuitous device. It appears that the granting of a mere acknowledgment of a subsisting debt is not affected at least where effectual diligence has not followed upon it.[43]

There are, however, certain transactions which are not affected, *viz.* cash payments, transactions in the ordinary course of business and *nova debita*.

Cash payments

22.6 A cash payment in ordinary course of business made to extinguish a debt already due is not challengeable unless it is collusive.[44] An insolvent debtor can prefer which creditors he pleases by paying their due debts in cash until the eve of sequestration, although he cannot give them securities for their debts.[45] Cash payments for this purpose include not only currency but also cheques drawn by the debtor,[46] bank drafts,[46] bills drawn by the debtor on his banker[47] and orders for payment signed by the debtor and addressed to persons who are obliged, or have agreed, to honour the debtor's drafts.[48] Consignation may be a cash payment.[49] On the other hand, a bill of exchange drawn on an ordinary debtor,[50] and a bill[51] or cheque[52] *indorsed* to a creditor (whether by the debtor or his agent[53]) are assignations, not cash payments, and are struck at. Where, however, the debtor has indorsed a bill to his banker[54] or has indorsed a cheque to his bank as an agent for collection,[55] the transaction is regarded

---

[32] *Dods* v. *Welsh* (1904) 12 S.L.T. 110.
[33] *Nicol* v. *McIntyre* (1882) 9 R. 1097; *Carter* v. *Johnstone* (1886) 13 R. 698.
[34] *Neil's Tr.* v. *British Linen Co.* (1898) 6 S.L.T. 227.
[35] *MacArthur* v. *Campbell's Tr.*, 1953 S.L.T. (Notes) 81.
[36] *Anderson* v. *Western Bank* (1859) 21 D. 230.
[37] *Douglas* v. *Gibson-Craig* (1832) 10 S. 647; *Mackenzie* v. *Calder* (1868) 6 M. 833.
[38] *Keith* v. *Maxwell* (1795) Mor. 1163.
[39] *Morrison* v. *Carron Co.* (1854) 16 D. 1125.
[40] *Wilson* v. *Drummond's Reps.* (1853) 16 D. 275.
[41] *Lauries' Tr.* v. *Beveridge* (1867) 6 M. 85.
[42] *Munro* v. *Rothfield*, 1920 S.C. 118.
[43] *Matthew's Tr.* v. *Matthew* (1867) 5 M. 957.
[44] *Forbes* v. *Brebner* (1751) Mor. 1128; per L. P. McNeill, *Guild* v. *Orr Ewing & Co.* (1858) 20 D. 392 at 397.
[45] per Lord Young, *Coutts' Tr. and Doe* v. *Webster* (1886) 13 R. 1112 at 1116.
[46] per Lord Shand, *Carter* v. *Johnstone* (1886) 13 R. 698 at 707.
[47] *Dixon* v. *Cowan* (1828) 7 S.132.
[48] *Miller* v. *Philip & Son* (1883) 20 S.L.R. 862; *Craig* v. *Hunter & Son* (1905) 13 S.L.T. 525.
[49] *Gordon* v. *Brock* (1838) 1 D. 1; *Littlejohn* v. *Reynolds* (1890) 6 Sh.Ct.Rep. 321.
[50] *Carter* v. *Johnstone, supra*.
[51] *Nicol* v. *McIntyre* (1882) 9 R. 1097.
[52] *Carter* v. *Johnstone, supra*.
[53] *Anderson's Tr.* v. *John Somerville & Co. Ltd.* (1899) 36 S.L.R. 833.
[54] *Blincow's Tr.* v. *Allan & Co.* (1828) 7 S. 124; (1833) 7 W. & S. 26.
[55] *Whatmough's Tr.* v. *British Linen Bank*, 1934 S.C. (H.L.) 51.

as a cash payment. As a rule the debt must be due at the time of payment and anticipatory payments are not protected,[56] but there may be circumstances where this does not hold.[57]

A cash payment is not protected if the transaction is simulate or collusive.[58] It is not collusive by reason only of the fact that both debtor and creditor knew of the debtor's insolvency.[59] To establish collusion it must be shown that the creditor was "participant in a fraudulent design."[60]

Transactions in the ordinary course of business
The second exception is transactions in the ordinary course of business. **22.7** This operates "wherever the transaction is in the ordinary course of dealing, and requisite or suitable to the fair purpose of the debtor proceeding with his trade, and unaccompanied by indications of collusion or notice of insolvency."[61] The transaction must be "the natural and ordinary course"[62] for the debtor to pursue and "incident to transactions in which the parties are ordinarily engaged."[63] Accordingly, if a debtor enters into such a transaction with his creditor, any security which the creditor obtains as an incidental result is not struck at. So, where goods were sent to bleachers in the ordinary course of trade and the bleachers thereby acquired a lien on the goods for prior debts, the security was not affected.[64] A similar result followed where a farmer sent goods to an auctioneer to be sold and the auctioneers thereby acquired a right to withhold part of the proceeds against a prior debt due to them[65]; where a merchant indorsed a bill to his bankers[66]; and where a purchaser returned an article for which he had not paid to the seller on the ground that he no longer required it.[67] Cash payment of a debt which is not yet due may be a transaction in the ordinary course of business.[68]

A transaction is obviously not in the ordinary course of business where its main object is to give the creditor a security, as where the debtor sells goods to the creditor to set off a prior debt,[69] or where the debtor hands

---

[56] *Speir* v. *Dunlop* (1827) 5 S. 729; *Blincow's Tr.* v. *Allan & Co., supra*.

[57] per L. P. McNeill, *Guild* v. *Orr Ewing & Co.* (1858) 20 D. 392 at 397; any such cases can be regarded as falling under the next exception—transactions in the ordinary course of business.

[58] *Whatmough's Tr.* v. *British Linen Bank, supra; Jones' Tr.* v. *Jones* (1888) 15 R. 328; *Neil's Tr.* v. *British Linen Co.* (1898) 36 S.L.R. 139; *Angus' Tr.* v. *Angus* (1901) 4 F. 181; *Newton & Sons' Tr.* v. *Finlayson & Co.*, 1928 S.C. 637.

[59] *Coutts' Tr. and Doe* v. *Webster, supra; Pringle's Tr.* v. *Wright* (1903) 5 F. 522; *Nordic Travel Ltd.* v. *Scotprint Ltd.*, 1980 S.C. 1.

[60] Bell, *Comm.*, II, 226; *Whatmough's Tr.* v. *British Linen Bank, supra*.

[61] Bell, *Comm.*, II, 205.

[62] per Lord Guthrie, *Crockart's Tr.* v. *Hay & Co. Ltd.*, 1913 S.C. 509 at 521.

[63] per L. P. Inglis, *Loudon Bros.* v. *Reid & Lauder's Tr.* (1877) 5 R. 293 at 301.

[64] *Anderson's Trs.* v. *Fleming* (1871) 9 M. 718.

[65] *Crockart's Tr.* v. *Hay & Co. Ltd., supra*.

[66] *Stein's Crs.* v. *Forbes Hunter & Co.* (1791) Mor. 1142.

[67] *Loudon Bros.* v. *Reid & Lauder's Tr., supra*; Goudy, p. 87, considers this decision open to criticism on its facts. See also *Watson & Sons Ltd.* v. *Veritys Ltd.* (1907) 24 Sh.Ct. Rep. 148.

[68] *McLaren's Tr.* v. *National Bank* (1897) 24 R. 920; *cf. McFarlane* v. *Robb & Co.* (1870) 9 M. 370.

[69] *Stewart* v. *Scott* (1832) 11 S. 171; *Dawson* v. *Lauder* (1840) 2 D. 525.

over goods to the creditor to be sold for payment of the debt.[70] A transaction is not in the ordinary course of business only because it has become the debtor's habitual method of conducting business in a prolonged state of insolvency.[71] A transaction which took place after the debtor's notour bankruptcy was not in the ordinary course of business.[72]

Nova debita

22.8 The third exception is *nova debita:* "all those cases in which a fair and present value is given for the conveyance or other deed executed by the bankrupt."[73] Obviously, the creditors are not prejudiced if the bankrupt transfers property in return for a fair consideration because the consideration becomes part of the assets available to the creditors. Accordingly, a conveyance of property which has been sold for a fair price is not struck at.[74] Similarly, where money has been advanced to the bankrupt in reliance upon a security to be granted by him, the granting of the security is not affected.[75] On the same principle the substitution of one security for another security is not affected[76]; and where a security had been granted for a prior debt which was subsequently paid, and a further advance was then made on the strength of the security, it was held that the security was valid.[77]

Considerable difficulties arise where there is an interval of time between the making of the advance and the granting of the security. To come within the exception, the advance must be made in reliance upon the security[78] which is to be granted and the whole transaction must be carried out *unico contextu.*[79]

Unfair preferences—1985 Act

22.9 Under the statute an unfair preference is a transaction entered into by the debtor which has the effect of creating a preference in favour of a creditor to the prejudice of the general body of creditors and which became completely effectual not earlier than six months before the date of sequestration.[80] This would cover the granting of a security, the transfer of property, the discharge or renunciation of rights and the abandonment of a competent defence. A circuitous device might be included.

---

[70] *Morton's Tr.* v. *Fifeshire Auction Co. Ltd.*, 1911 1 S.L.T. 405.
[71] *Horsbrugh* v. *Ramsay & Co.* (1885) 12 R. 1171.
[72] *Jackson* v. *Fenwick's Tr.* (1899) 6 S.L.T. 319.
[73] Bell, *Comm.*, II, 205.
[74] *Brugh* v. *Gray* (1717) Mor. 1125; *Cranstoun* v. *Bontine* (1830) 8 S. 425; (1832) 6 W. & S. 79; *Taylor* v. *Farrie* (1855) 17 D. 639; *Miller's Tr.* v. *Shield* (1862) 24 D. 821.
[75] *Bank of Scotland* v. *Stewart & Ross*, Feb. 7, 1811, F.C.; *Renton & Gray's Tr.* v. *Dickison* (1880) 7 R. 951.
[76] *Roy's Tr.* v. *Colville & Drysdale* (1903) 5 F. 769.
[77] *Robertson* v. *Ogilvie* (1798) Mor. *s.v.* "Bills of Exchange" App. No. 6; *Robertson's Tr.* v. *Union Bank of Scotland*, 1917 S.C. 549; *Thomas Montgomery & Sons* v. *Gallacher*, 1982 S.L.T. 138.
[78] *White* v. *Briggs* (1843) 5 D. 1148, *per* Lord Fullerton at p. 1164; *MacArthur* v. *Campbell's Tr.*, 1953 S.L.T. (Notes) 81.
[79] *Cowdenbeath Coal Co. Ltd.* v. *Clydesdale Bank Ltd.* (1895) 22 R. 682.
[80] s.36(1). There may not be a challenge where the financial markets régime applies; C.A. 1989, s.165(2)(*a*). See para. 20.9.

There are the following exceptions[81]:
(1) a transaction in the ordinary course of trade or business; the prior case law would appear to be relevant here.
(2) a payment in cash for a debt which when it was paid had become payable unless the transaction was collusive with the purpose of prejudicing the general body of creditors; this will cover payments by cash, cheque, bank draft, bill drawn on a bank, but not cheques or bills indorsed to parties other than the debtor's bank.
(3) a transaction whereby the parties undertake reciprocal obligations (whether the performance by the parties of their respective obligations occurs at the same time or different times) unless the transaction was collusive with the purpose of prejudicing the general body of creditors; this is obviously based on the idea of the *novum debitum* but it is rather wider as the *unico contextu* requirement seems to have gone; a security granted for a contemporaneous loan is the paradigm case but an undertaking to grant a security at a future date would now seem to be within the exception.
(4) the granting of a mandate by the debtor authorising an arrestee to pay over the arrested funds or part thereof to the arrester where there has been a decree for payment or a warrant for summary diligence preceded by an arrestment on the dependence or followed by an arrestment in execution.

The challenge may be brought by the trustee or by a creditor whose debt was incurred on or before the date of sequestration.[82] The court, if satisfied that the statutory provision applies to the transaction, grants decree of reduction or for such restoration of property to the debtor's estate or other redress as may be appropriate.[83] There is protection for rights and interests acquired in good faith and for value from or through the creditor in whose favour the preference was created. Equitable considerations cannot be taken into account in applying the provisions.[84] The creditor cannot set off his claim against the estate against the trustee's claim.[84]

Trusts and donations

The funds of an *inter vivos* trust constituted by the bankrupt may be available to creditors if the trust is revocable in character.[85] Where a trust has been constituted under the Married Women's Policies of Assurance (Scotland) Act 1880, if it is proved that the policy was effected and the premiums paid thereon with intent to defraud the creditors, or if the bankruptcy occurs within two years of the date of the policy, the creditors may claim repayment of the premiums so paid from the trustee of the policy out of the proceeds thereof.[86] A trust deed for creditors is superseded, or, at least, suspended, by the grantor's sequestration (or

22.10

---

[81] s.36(2). As to cash payments, see *Bob Gray (Access) Ltd.* v. *T.M. Standard Scaffolding Ltd.*, 1987 S.C.L.R. 720.
[82] s.36(4).
[83] s.36(5).
[84] *Raymond Harrison & Co.'s Tr.* v. *North West Securities*, 1989 S.L.T. 718.
[85] *Scott* v. *Scott*, 1930 S.C. 903; *Lawrence* v. *Lawrence's Trs.*, 1974 S.L.T. 174.
[86] s.2; *Stewart* v. *Hodge* (1901) 8 S.L.T. 436; *Chrystal's Tr.* v. *Chrystal*, 1912 S.C. 1003.

English bankruptcy) and the trustee under the deed must denude in favour of the trustee in the sequestration.[87]

Divorce orders

22.11 Where there has been a court order against the debtor for payment of a capital sum or the transfer of property on divorce and the debtor was absolutely insolvent at the date of the order or was rendered so by implementation of the order, then, if the debtor's estate is sequestrated within five years of the order, the trustee can apply to have the order recalled and for repayment in whole or in part to the trustee of any sum paid or for the return in whole or in part of the property transferred or for payment in whole or in part of the proceeds of sale of the property.[88] Before making an order the court must have regard to all the circumstances including the financial and other circumstances in so far as made known to the court of the person against whom the order would be made.

Extortionate credit transactions

22.12 Where the debtor entered into a credit transaction not more than three years before the date of sequestration the trustee may apply to the court for an order to be made with respect to the transaction on the ground that it was extortionate.[89] A transaction is extortionate if, having regard to the risk accepted by the person providing the credit, the terms required grossly exorbitant payments to be made, whether conditionally or in certain contingencies, or it otherwise grossly contravened ordinary principles of fair dealing.[90] A transaction is presumed to be extortionate unless the contrary is proved.

The provision thus resembles closely the provisions of the Consumer Credit Act 1974 although there is here no list of matters which have to be taken into account in deciding whether the bargain is extortionate. The case law under the 1974 Act is relevant.[91] The order of the court may set aside obligations, vary the terms of the transaction, require the payment to the trustee of any sum paid by the debtor by virtue of the transaction, require the surrender of any security or direct the taking of accounts between any persons.[92] Any sums paid or property surrendered vests in the trustee.[93] The power may be exercised concurrently with the powers relating to gratuitous alienations and unfair preferences. Neither the trustee nor the debtor while undischarged can apply to re-open an agreement under the 1974 Act.[94]

---

[87] Bell, *Comm.*, II, 391; *Salaman* v. *Rosslyn's Trs.* (1900) 3 F. 298.
[88] B.A., s.35.
[89] s.61(2).
[90] s.61(3).
[91] See para. 3.2.
[92] s.61(4).
[93] s.61(5).
[94] s.61(6).

Chapter 23

THE CLAIM

Procedure

In general, a creditor must proceed by lodging a claim in the sequestration.[1] After sequestration, an action against the debtor for recovery of a debt due at the date of sequestration is not incompetent but it is of small practical value as there are no assets which can be attached by diligence on the decree. As a general rule, it is not proper to bring an action for recovery of a debt due by the debtor against the trustee in his sequestration although there may be exceptional cases where it is a correct procedure in order to obtain a decree of constitution of the debt.[2] Where a decree for payment has been granted against the trustee in a sequestration, as such trustee, it can be enforced only if it is in respect of a matter for which the trustee has come under a personal obligation to pay. If the decree is in respect of a prior debt due by the debtor at the date of sequestration, it cannot be enforced against the trustee and the holder is entitled only to rank for a dividend in the sequestration.[3] A judicial factor who has been appointed on the estate of a solicitor under the Solicitors (Scotland) Act 1980, s.41, is not in the position of a trustee in a sequestration and can be sued for a debt due by the solicitor.[4]

23.1

Claim for ranking

The trustee makes up accounts of his intromissions with the estate in respect of accounting periods of 26 weeks, the first such period commencing with the date of sequestration, and pays a dividend to creditors in respect of each accounting period.[5] To obtain a dividend a creditor must submit a claim not later than 8 weeks before the end of the accounting period.[6] The claim is submitted by producing to the trustee a statement of claim in the prescribed form and an account or voucher (according to the nature of the debt) which constitutes prima facie evidence of the debt.[7] The statement of claim contains the name and address of the creditor, the nature of the debt, when it was incurred and when payment became due. The amount of principal and interest to the date of sequestration must be shown separately; VAT is shown separately and it must be indicated whether it is being claimed back from the Customs and Excise. A claim may be stated in foreign currency where it is constituted by a court decree ordering payment in the foreign

23.2

---

[1] Goudy, p. 373. The permanent trustee may have a duty to write to a foreign creditor: B.A., ss.22(3), 48(3).

[2] *Crichton's Tr.* v. *Stewart* (1866) 4 M. 689; *Adam & Winchester* v. *White's Tr.* (1884) 11 R. 863; *Martin's Tr.* v. *Wilson* (1904) 12 S.L.T. 112; *Legal and General Assurance Society Ltd.* v. *Carter*, 1926 S.L.T. 63; *Dow* v. *Pennell's Tr.*, 1929 S.L.T. 674.

[3] *Thomson & Co.* v. *Friese-Greene's Tr.*, 1944 S.C. 336.

[4] *Ross* v. *Gordon's J.F.*, 1973 S.L.T. (Notes) 91.

[5] B.A., s.52.

[6] B.A., s.48(1). Once submitted the claim is deemed to have been re-submitted in respect of subsequent accounting periods but a further claim specifying a different amount may be submitted (s.48(2), (4)).

[7] ss.22(2), 48(2); B.Regs. Form 5.

currency or it arises from a contract or bill of exchange in terms of which payment is or may be required in foreign currency.[8] The statement of claim must also specify the nature of any security held for the debt including the subjects covered, the date when it was given and its value; the creditor must also state whether he is surrendering or undertakes to surrender the security. If the security is not surrendered, its value must be deducted from the total amount of the debt.

The only interest which can be claimed is that due on the debt as at the date of sequestration[9]; however, after all ordinary debts have been paid in full, if the estate is sufficient interest is paid on ordinary debts between the date of sequestration and the date of payment at whichever is the greater of 15 per cent. and the rate applicable to the debt apart from the sequestration.[10]

In the case of a future debt which but for the sequestration would not have been payable until after the date of the sequestration, the claim is calculated as if it were payable at the date of sequestration but under deduction of interest from the date of sequestration to the date when payment was due at the rate of whichever is the greater of 15 per cent. and the rate applicable to the debt apart from the sequestration.[11]

Where the existence or amount of a debt depends upon a contingency, the creditor must apply to the trustee or the sheriff who will put a value on the debt in so far as it is contingent and the creditor can then claim that amount; where the contingent debt is an annuity, a cautioner may not then be sued for more than that value.[12]

A creditor must deduct any discount (other than any discount for payment in cash) which is allowable by contract or course of dealing between the creditor and the debtor or by the usage of trade.[13]

Aliment or periodical allowance payable on divorce cannot be claimed for any period after the date of sequestration nor for any period before that date unless it has been quantified by a court decree or a legally binding obligation supported by evidence in writing and in the case of spouses (or, where the sum is payable to a divorced person in respect of a child, former spouses) they were living apart during that period.[14]

Adjudication of claims

23.3   To satisfy himself as to the validity or amount of a claim the trustee may require a creditor to produce further evidence or any other person to produce relevant evidence and can force the creditor or other person to appear for private examination before the sheriff if they refuse or delay to do so.[15] Not later than 4 weeks before the end of each accounting period he must accept or reject each claim submitted to him and record in the sederunt book the amount of each claim accepted by him, the category of debt and the value of any security as decided by him and his reasons for

---

[8] Reg. 6.
[9] Sched. 1, para. 1(1).
[10] s.51(1)(g), (7); reg. 8.
[11] Sched. 1, para. 1(2). Estimated future calls on a contributory may be proved: I.A., s.82(4).
[12] Sched. 1, para. 3.
[13] Sched. 1, para. 1(3).
[14] Sched. 1, para. 2.
[15] s.48(5).

rejecting any claim.[16] Reasons for a rejection must be given to the creditor forthwith.[17] Claims stated in foreign currency have to be converted into sterling at the rate of exchange prevailing at the close of business on the date of sequestration.[18] The debtor or any creditor dissatisfied with the trustee's adjudication can appeal to the sheriff not later than two weeks before the end of the accounting period.[19]

"The trustee is expected to take all reasonable means of obtaining satisfactory information, and to exercise the powers conferred on him so far as necessary. If he is satisfied that the debt claimed is due, he is entitled to admit it, and rank the creditor accordingly. If not satisfied, it is his duty to reject the claim, and refuse to rank the claimant."[20]

Secured creditors

A creditor whose security[21] has been realised must deduct from his claim the amount which he has received, or is entitled to receive, from the realisation, less the expenses of realisation. If the security has not been realised, the creditor must deduct from his claim the value of the security as estimated by him. The trustee can, at any time after the expiry of 12 weeks from the date of sequestration, require the creditor at the expense of the estate to discharge the security or convey or assign it to the trustee on payment of the value specified by the creditor; the creditor's claim is then restricted to the balance of the debt remaining after receipt of such payment.[22] The security cannot be revalued by the creditor after the trustee has made the requirement.[23]

23.4

If the trustee intimates that he wishes to take over the security, the creditor cannot defeat this by withdrawing his claim.[24] If the trustee does not offer to take over the security the creditor is free to realise it.[25] If he recovers less than the specified value he may substitute the sum realised for the specified value and rank for the balance. If he recovers more than the specified value the trustee is entitled to substitute the sum realised for the specified value and rank the creditor only for the balance of his claim so far as subsequent dividends are concerned but the trustee cannot restrict the subsequent dividends to the creditor so as to take into account the over-payment in the earlier dividends.[26] The creditor in a question with the trustee must apply the sum realised *primo loco* towards the principal debt and not towards the interest accrued thereon from the date of sequestration.[27] If the sum realised is more than the creditor's claim, he must account to the trustee or the debtor for the balance.[28]

---

[16] s.49(2), (5).
[17] s.49(4).
[18] s.49(3).
[19] s.49(6).
[20] *per* L. P. Inglis, *Phosphate Sewage Co.* v. *Molleson* (1874) 1 R. 840 at 846.
[21] A "security" means "any security, heritable or moveable, or any right of lien, retention or preference": B.A., s.73(1). A deposit is a security: *British Marine Mutual Insurance Association Ltd.* v. *Adamson* (1932) 48 Sh.Ct.Rep. 3.
[22] B.A., Sched. 1, para. 5.
[23] B.A., s.48(4).
[24] *Macdougall's Tr.* v. *Lockhart* (1903) 5 F. 905.
[25] *Henderson's Tr.* v. *Auld and Guild* (1872) 10 M. 946; *Maclachlan* v. *Maxwell, supra.*
[26] *Union Bank of Scotland* v. *Calder's Tr.*, 1937 S.C. 850.
[27] *Ibid.*
[28] *Kinmond Luke & Co.* v. *James Finlay & Co.* (1904) 6 F. 564; *Clydesdale Bank Ltd.* v. *McIntyre*, 1909 S.C. 1405.

Ineffectual diligence does not create a security for purposes of these provisions.[29] Bills indorsed to a bank for collection are securities and their value must be deducted.[30]

The foregoing provisions apply only where the security subjects form part of the bankrupt's estate[31]—where the subject "were it not for the creditor's nexus, would go to increase the divisible fund."[32] They do not apply to a collateral security. The creditor can realise them and receive a dividend on the full amount of the debt so long as he does not receive more than 100p in the pound.

Effect of inhibition

23.5 An inhibition against the debtor does not affect the trustee's power to sell the heritable estate but the inhibiting creditor may be entitled to a preference in ranking.[33]

Where a creditor has used an inhibition more than 60 days before the date of sequestration, he is entitled to a preference in the ranking on the heritable estate.[34] The mode of giving this preference is regulated by Professor Bell's five canons of ranking.[35] The general principle is that the inhibitor obtains a preference over creditors whose debts were contracted after the inhibition (posterior creditors), but does not obtain a preference over creditors whose debts were contracted before the inhibition (anterior creditors) and the anterior creditors obtain no preference over the posterior creditors.[36] The procedure is that the proceeds of the heritable estate are firstly divided among all the creditors *pari passu*; the anterior creditors receive a dividend on this basis; the ranking is then calculated on the basis that the posterior debts did not exist; the inhibitor then draws back from the posterior creditors the difference between what he would receive on the first basis and what he would receive on the second. For example, if the debts of each of the three classes are equal in amount and the dividend on a *pari passu* ranking is 50p per pound, the anterior creditors receive 50p. If there had been no posterior debts the *pari passu* dividend would have been 75p. The inhibitor therefore draws 25p from the posterior creditors so that he obtains 75p and they receive 25p.

It has been held that where the debtor entered into a lease prior to the inhibition, the rent payable for a period after the inhibition, and damages for breach of the lease arising when the trustee in the sequestration failed to adopt it, were anterior debts.[37]

In the ranking on the moveable estate the inhibitor is not obliged to deduct what he has drawn from the heritable estate affected by the

---

[29] *Dow & Co.* v. *Union Bank* (1875) 2 R. 459.
[30] *Clydesdale Bank* v. *Liqrs. of James Allan Senior & Son*, 1926 S.C. 235.
[31] See the definition of "secured creditor," B.A., s.73(1).
[32] Goudy, p. 319. See *McClelland* v. *Bank of Scotland* (1857) 19 D. 574; *British Linen Bank* v. *Gourlay* (1877) 4 R. 651; *Royal Bank* v. *Purdom* (1877) 15 S.L.R. 13; *University of Glasgow* v. *Yuill's Tr.* (1882) 9 R. 643; *Royal Bank of Scotland* v. *Millar & Co.'s Tr.* (1882) 9 R. 679.
[33] B.A., s.31(2).
[34] B.A., s.37(2).
[35] Bell, *Comm.*, II, 413.
[36] *Baird & Brown* v. *Stirrat's Tr.* (1872) 10 M. 414.
[37] *Scottish Waggon Co. Ltd.* v. *James Hamilton's Tr.* (1906) 13 S.L.T. 779.

inhibition.[38] An inhibition within the period of 60 days before the date of sequestration is not effectual to create a preference for the inhibitor and any relevant right of challenge vests in the trustee as does any right of the inhibitor to receive payment for discharge of the inhibition; this, however, does not entitle the trustee to receive any payment made to the inhibitor before the date of sequestration or affect the validity of anything done before that date in consideration of such payment.[39]

Co-obligants

Obviously the creditor must deduct from his claim any payments made to him by any co-obligant and any dividends received from the estates of co-obligants prior to the sequestration.[40] The co-obligant is not freed or discharged from his liability for the debt by reason of the debtor's discharge or by virtue of the creditor's voting or drawing a dividend or assenting to or not opposing the discharge of the debtor or any composition.[41] If the co-obligant pays the debt, he may require and obtain at his own expense from the creditor an assignation of the debt and may then submit a claim, and vote and draw a dividend if otherwise legally entitled to do so.[42] If, however, the creditor draws a dividend from the bankrupt's estate and then obtains payment of the deficiency from a co-obligant, the latter cannot rank on the estate because of the rule against double ranking.[43]

23.6

There is a special statutory provision dealing with the case in which the co-obligant holds a security over part of the debtor's estate. Section 60(2) provides: "Where (a) a creditor has had a claim accepted in whole or in part; and (b) a co-obligant holds a security over any part of the debtor's estate, the co-obligant shall account to the permanent trustee so as to put the estate in the same position as if the co-obligant had paid the debt to the creditor and thereafter had had his claim accepted in whole or in part in the sequestration after deduction of the value of the security." There are two possible ways of proceeding; if the creditor (X) ranks on the estate of the debtor (Y) for the whole debt (d), gets a dividend thereon (kd) and then recovers the balance of his debt ($d-kd$) from the co-obligant (Z), Z's loss on the transaction after recouping himself from the security (s) will be $d-kd-s$; if X recovers the full debt d from Z who recovers s from the security and then ranks for the debt minus the value of the security ($d-s$) on Y's estate, receiving a dividend $k(d-s)$, then Z's loss will be $d-s-kd+ks$ which exceeds the loss on the alternative method by ks; the effect of s.60(2) is to produce the second result in all cases. If all the obligants are bankrupt, the creditor can rank on each of the estates so long as he recovers no more than 100p in the pound in all. There can then be no relief between the estates because of the double ranking rule.

---

[38] *Scottish Waggon Co. Ltd.* v. *James Hamilton's Tr., supra; cf. Baird & Brown* v. *Stirrat's Tr., supra.*

[39] B.A., s.37(2). For the difficulties of this subsection see Gretton, pp. 120–122. The provision applies to liquidations: I.A., s.185(1).

[40] *Hamilton* v. *Cuthbertson* (1841) 3 D. 494; *Royal Bank of Scotland* v. *Commercial Bank of Scotland* (1881) 8 R. 805.

[41] B.A., s.60(1).

[42] B.A., s.60(2).

[43] Bell, *Comm.*, II, 420. See *Mackinnon* v. *Monkhouse* (1881) 9 R. 393, *per* L. P. Inglis at p. 401.

Cautionary obligations

23.7 Where there is a cautionary obligation the position is complicated because the creditor usually has alternative courses of action. One general point to be made *in limine* is that the creditor's claim against any estate must be made under deduction of securities held from the principal debtor and of all payments or dividends received from the debtor or cautioners or their estates prior to the date of sequestration of the estate against which the claim is being made but no adjustment is required in respect of payments and dividends subsequently received.[44]

Three cases can be distinguished:

(1) Where the debtor is bankrupt and the cautioners solvent. The creditor may (a) claim in the debtor's sequestration and then require the cautioners to pay the deficiency, or, (b) simply demand payment from the cautioners without resorting to the debtor's estate.

In (a) if the cautionary obligation is proper (*i.e.* appears *ex facie* of the instrument), each cautioner is liable only for a *pro rata* share,[45] but in the case of improper cautionry, each is liable for the full amount of the deficiency. Any cautioner who pays more than his *pro rata* share has a right of relief against his co-cautioners for the excess. The cautioners cannot claim against the debtor's estate because of the rule against double ranking but they may be able to rank in respect of payments made before the sequestration.

In (b) the distinction between proper and improper cautionry determines the nature of the cautioner's liability as in (a). The cautioners have a *pro rata* right of relief *inter se* and have a right of relief against the debtor's estate as they stand in the position of the creditor. The right of relief is not dependent upon an assignation by the creditor to them but in some circumstances it may be advantageous to have such an assignation.[46] Where the limit of the cautioner's liability is less than the debtor's liability to the creditor, it is a question of construction of the cautionary obligation whether the cautioner has guaranteed a part of the total debt and is thus entitled to rank on the debtor's estate in respect of the proportion which he has paid, or whether he has guaranteed the whole debt and placed a limitation on his liability and is thus not entitled to rank on the debtor's estate.[47]

(2) Where the debtor and some of the cautioners are bankrupt and some of the cautioners solvent.

The creditor may (a) claim for the whole amount of the debt on each of the estates of the debtor and the insolvent cautioners and then require payment of the deficiency from the solvent cautioners, or (b) simply demand payment from the solvent cautioners.

  (a) The solvent cautioners are liable *pro rata inter se* and have no right of relief against the estates of the debtor and insolvent cautioners because of the rule against double ranking. If the

---

[44] *Royal Bank of Scotland v. Commercial Bank of Scotland* (1881) 8 R. 805, *per* L. P. Inglis at p. 817.
[45] Bell, *Prin.*, § 267.
[46] Gloag & Irvine, p. 806.
[47] *Harvie's Trs. v. Bank of Scotland* (1885) 12 R. 1141; *Veitch v. National Bank of Scotland*, 1907 S.C. 554.

creditor has received in dividends (not in ranking) from the estate of an insolvent cautioner more than the cautioner's *pro rata* share, the estate has a right of relief against the solvent cautioners for the excess.[48]

(b) The solvent cautioners are again liable *pro rata inter se*. They have a right of relief against the debtor's estate. They also have jointly a right of relief against the estate of each insolvent cautioner for the excess of what they have paid over their original *pro rata* share.[49]

(3) Where the debtor and all the cautioners are insolvent the creditor can rank for the full amount of his debt on each estate although he cannot obtain more than 100p in the pound in all. Because of the double ranking rule the estates of the cautioners have no right of relief *inter se* or against the debtor's estate. If the creditor obtains more than 100p in the pound, an estate which has paid more than its share of the debt is entitled to the benefit of the creditor's ranking on the other estates.[50]

Cautioner's securities

Section 60(2) of the Bankruptcy Act applies to cautioners.[51]   23.8

A cautioner must share the benefit of his security with his co-cautioners.[52]

Where there are two bankrupt co-obligants, one of whom is cautioner for the other and holds a security from the other, the security is applied first to indemnifying the cautioner's estate in respect of the dividends paid to the creditor. The sum obtained by this is then used to pay a further dividend to all the cautioner's creditors, including the creditor in the cautionary obligation. The process is repeated until the security is exhausted.[53]

Bills of exchange

If the bankrupt has given a creditor a bill for an amount larger than the   23.9
debt, the creditor cannot rank for more than the amount of the debt either on the estate of the bankrupt or on the estate of a cautioner but if the bill has been negotiated a holder in due course can rank for the full amount.[54] Similarly, if the bankrupt has negotiated bills to his creditor in security of the debt, the creditor can rank for the full amount on the estates of the parties liable thereon. An accommodation party is treated as a cautioner and so, while on the one hand he may rank on the debtor's estate for relief if he has paid the bill, on the other hand, if he and the debtor are bankrupt, the creditor can rank for the full amount on both estates but the trustee of the accommodation party cannot rank for relief on the debtor's estate.[55] Where the accommodation party holds funds or

---

[48] Bell, *Comm.*, I, 373.
[49] *Ibid.*
[50] Gloag & Irvine, p. 841.
[51] See para. 23.6.
[52] Gloag & Irvine, pp. 819–824.
[53] *Royal Bank of Scotland* v. *Saunders & Sons' Trs.* (1882) 9 R. (H.L.) 67.
[54] *Jackson* v. *McIver* (1875) 2 R. 882.
[55] *Anderson* v. *Mackinnon* (1876) 3 R. 608; For the position as to cross-accommodation bills see Goudy, pp. 574–576 and *Encyclopaedia of the Laws of Scotland*, Vol. II, p. 253.

property of the debtor and both parties are bankrupt it seems that the trustee on the estate of the accommodation party cannot plead retention or compensation if the funds or property were not appropriated as security for the liability on the bill.[56] If there is such a specific appropriation the trustee can plead retention or compensation.

Distribution

23.10   The funds are distributed in the following order[57]:
(1) the outlays and remuneration of the interim trustee;
(2) the outlays and remuneration of the permanent trustee;
(3) the expenses of the petitioning and the concurring creditors;
(4) the preferred debts,[58] excluding interest thereon to the date of sequestration (such interest is, it is thought, on ordinary debt)[59];
(5) ordinary debts, *i.e.*, debts which are neither secured nor mentioned under another heading;
(6) interest on (i) the preferred debts, (ii) the ordinary debts, between the date of sequestration and the date of payment of the debt at a rate which is whichever is the greater of 15 per cent. and the rate applicable to the debt apart from the sequestration;
(7) postponed debts, *i.e.*, loans made to the debtor in consideration of a share in the profits of his business postponed under the Partnership Act 1890, s.3, loans made to the debtor by the debtor's spouse and a creditor's right to anything vesting in the trustee by virtue of a successful challenge as a gratuitous alienation or to the proceeds of sale of such a thing;
(8) any surplus is made over to the debtor or his successors or assignees.

Debts falling under the same heading have the same priority and if the estate is insufficient to pay them they abate in equal proportions.

The foregoing distribution is of course subject to the rights of creditors who hold a lien over documents or a valid security.

Preferred debts

23.11   The preferred debts are[60]:
(1) Sums due at the date of sequestration on account of deductions of income tax from emoluments paid during the twelve months next before that date under the pay as you earn scheme less the amount of any repayments of tax the debtor was liable to make during that period.
(2) Sums due in respect of deductions required to be made under the provisions applying to sub-contractors in the construction industry.
(3) Value added tax due to the Customs and Excise referable to the period of six months before the date of sequestration.
(4) Car tax due at the date of sequestration which became due within the 12 months before that date.
(5) Amounts due in respect of general betting duty, bingo duty, pool

---

[56] *Royal Bank of Scotland* v. *Saunders & Sons' Trs., supra.*
[57] B.A., s.51.
[58] See para. 23.11. Certain claims arising under the financial markets régime have priority to preferred debts: C.A. 1989, ss.163(4), 164(6), 175(6). See para. 20.9.
[59] For an alternative view, see McBryde, p. 194.
[60] B.A., Sched. 3.

betting duty and gaming licence duty at the date of sequestration which became due in the 12 months before that date.
(6) Sums due in respect of Class 1 or Class 2 social security contributions which became due in the 12 months before the date of sequestration.
(7) Sums assessed on and due from the debtor on account of Class 4 social security contributions, being sums due to the Inland Revenue and assessed on the debtor up to April 5 before the date of sequestration but not exceeding, in the whole, any one year's assessment.
(8) Contributions to occupational pension schemes and state scheme premiums owed by the debtor, being sums to which Schedule 3 to the Social Security Pensions Act 1975 applies.
(9) Any amount owed to a present or former employee of the debtor as remuneration in respect of the whole or any part of the four months next before the date of sequestration, not exceeding £800.[61] Remuneration includes wages or salary payable for time or piece work or earned wholly or partly by commission in respect of services rendered to the debtor in the period. It also includes remuneration under a protective award under the Employment Protection Act 1975 and payments under the Employment Protection (Consolidation) Act 1978 for guarantees, suspension on medical grounds, trade union duties, looking for work and ante-natal care. Where the Secretary of State has made payments of sums in this category (or holiday pay—see (10)) he is entitled to assert the preference which the employee would have had and his claim has priority over any preferred claim of the employee in respect of debts of this kind.[62]
(10) Any amount owed by way of accrued holiday remuneration, in respect of any period of employment before the date of sequestration to a person whose employment by the debtor has been terminated, whether before, on, or after, that date.[63]
(11) So much of any sum owed in respect of money advanced for the purpose as has been applied for the payment of a debt which, if it had not been paid, would have been a debt falling within (9) or (10).[64] This covers, for example, a bank overdraft made for the payment of wages.
(12) Certain sums to be paid by the debtor under the Reserve Forces (Safeguard of Employment) Act 1985.[65]
(13) Coal and steel levies and surcharges under the European Coal and Steel Community Treaty.[66]

Ancestor's creditors
The creditors of the bankrupt's ancestor have a preferential right in respect of items of the ancestor's estate which can be distinguished and

23.12

---

[61] B.Regs. 14 (added by S.I. 1986 No. 1914).
[62] Employment Protection (Consolidation) Act 1978, s.125(2), subst. by Employment Act 1989, s.19.
[63] B.A., Sched. 3, para. 5(2).
[64] para. 5(3). Previously this was a preferential debt only in liquidation; for the case law on the earlier provision see para. 25.12.
[65] para. 6.
[66] para. 6A, added by the Insolvency (E.C.S.C. Levy Debts) Regulations 1987 (S.I. 1987 No. 2093).

identified. The trustee in the bankrupt's estate is trustee also for the ancestor's creditors and it is unnecessary and incompetent to sequestrate the ancestor's estates to effectuate this preference.[67]

---

[67] *Menzies* v. *Pontz*, 1916 S.C. 143.

CHAPTER 24

ALTERNATIVES TO SEQUESTRATION

Offer of composition

At any time after the issue of the Act and Warrant, an offer of composition may be made by or on behalf of the debtor to the trustee specifying the caution or other security to be provided for its implementation.[1] The trustee submits it to the commissioners, or, if there are no commissioners, to the Accountant in Bankruptcy, who, if they think that the offer will be timeously implemented, that a distribution in accordance with the sequestration rules would secure a dividend of at least 25p in the pound for the ordinary creditors and that the security is satisfactory, recommend that the offer be placed before the creditors.[2] The trustee advertises the offer and invites every creditor known to him to accept or reject it by completing a prescribed form[3]; with the form he sends to the creditors a report summarising the offer and the present state of the debtor's affairs and the progress in realising his estate and estimating, if the offer is accepted, the expenses to be met in concluding the sequestration proceedings and the dividend which would be payable.[4] If the trustee determines that a majority in number and not less than two-thirds in value of the creditors known to him have accepted the offer, he submits to the sheriff a statement that he has so determined, a copy of the report and a declaration by the debtor that he has made a full surrender and disclosure of his estate and that he has delivered to the trustee every document under his control relating to his estate or his business or financial affairs.[5] After a hearing the sheriff may make an order approving the offer if he is satisfied that the requisite majority has accepted it and that the terms are reasonable; he may approve the offer even although there has been a failure to comply with any provision of Schedule 4 to the Act.[6] After the trustee has had his accounts audited he lodges with the sheriff clerk a declaration that all necessary charges in the sequestration have been paid and when the bond of caution or other security has also been lodged the sheriff makes an order discharging the debtor and the trustee.[7] The sequestration thereupon ceases, the debtor is re-invested in his estate as existing at the date of the order, the debtor is discharged of all debts for which he was liable at the date of the sequestration (other than the debts from which he would not have been discharged in the sequestration) and the claims of the creditors in the sequestration are converted into claims for their respective shares in the composition.[8]

The Court of Session, on the application of any creditor, may recall the

24.1

---

[1] s.56; Sched. 4, para. 1.
[2] paras. 2, 3.
[3] B. Regs., Sched., Form 9.
[4] Sched. 4, para. 4.
[5] para. 6.
[6] para. 8.
[7] para. 1.1.
[8] paras. 13, 16.

order approving the composition and discharging the debtor if it is satisfied that there has been, or is likely to be, a default in payment of the composition or an instalment thereof or that for any reason the composition cannot be proceeded with or cannot be proceeded with without undue delay or without injustice to the creditors; the effect of the decree of recall is to revive the sequestration but this does not affect the validity of a transaction entered into by the debtor since his discharge with a person who has given value and has acted in good faith; a judicial factor may be appointed to administer the estate.[9] The Court of Session may reduce an order approving a composition if a payment or preference was made or promised to facilitate the debtor's discharge.[10]

A debtor may make two, but no more than two, offers of composition in the course of a sequestration.[11]

It is possible to have an extra-judicial composition contract.[12] This is a purely contractual arrangement in which the debtor offers a composition on the debts in exchange for a discharge. It is not binding on a creditor who has not assented to it. Accession is a matter of fact and no obligatory writing is necessary.[13] If the composition is not paid, the original debt revives.[14]

Trust deeds

24.2 A trust deed may be adopted as a quick and cheap alternative to sequestration. This is a voluntary extra-judicial arrangement in which the insolvent grants in favour of a trustee a deed transferring his property to the trustee for behoof of his creditors for their several rights and preferences. The deed usually provides that the trustee shall be judge of the creditors' claims; that the trustee shall have power to reduce voluntary dispositions and illegal or fraudulent preferences[15]; that the estate shall be distributed in accordance with the rules pertaining in a sequestration[16]; and that acceptance of a dividend by a creditor is to import a discharge.[17] The trustee completes title to the estate and realises it; he may record a notice in the register of inhibitions and adjudications which has the same effect as letters of inhibition[18]; he can require the supply of utilities.[19] The creditors lodge claims which are adjudged by the trustee[20]; the trustee distributes the estate among the creditors in

---

[9] para. 17. As to the amount of a creditor's claim in the sequestration, see B.A., Sched. 1, para. 4.

[10] para. 18.

[11] para. 15.

[12] See Goudy, Chap. XXXVI.

[13] *Henry* v. *Strachan & Spence* (1897) 24 R. 1045.

[14] *Woods Parker & Co.* v. *Ainslie* (1860) 22 D. 723.

[15] But the trustee's power is derived from the accession of creditors with a title to reduce: *Fleming's Trs.* v. *McHardy* (1892) 19 R. 542.

[16] Unless the deed provides otherwise, B.A., Sched. 1 applies to the valuation of claims with some minor modifications: B.A., Sched. 5, para. 3.

[17] *Larkin* v. *Morrow* (1932) 48 Sh.Ct.Rep. 59.

[18] B.A., Sched. 5, para. 2.

[19] B.A., s.70. See para. 20.5.

[20] An affidavit is not required; a statement suffices. The lodging of a claim interrupts prescription: Prescription and Limitation (Scotland) Act 1973, s.9(1)(c) (inserted by B.A., Sched. 7, para 11). It bars the effect of limitation in any part of the United Kingdom: B.A., Sched. 5, para. 3.

accordance with their rights and preferences; and any surplus is returned to the insolvent. The trustee must complete title to shares by obtaining and registering a transfer in the ordinary form.[21]

The insolvent may revoke the deed at any time before the creditors are aware of it.[22] A creditor who accedes to the trust deed cannot do diligence against the estate or petition for the sequestration of the insolvent unless a non-acceding creditor is obtaining a preference by doing diligence.[23] If, however, the trustee rejects his claim, he can raise an action against the truster and the trustee to constitute his claim.[24] A non-acceding creditor can execute effectual diligence against the assets of the estate until the trustee has completed his title thereto; after completion the assets are not liable to diligence.[25] A non-acceding creditor cannot reduce the trust deed as a fraudulent preference at common law[26] but he can petition for sequestration.[27] Sequestration, at any subsequent time, supersedes the trust deed and the trust estate must be handed over to the trustee in the sequestration.[28] The trustee under the trust deed can petition for sequestration.[29] A non-acceding creditor is entitled to a dividend from the trust estate without giving a discharge and he can sue the trustee for his dividend.[30] A creditor cannot bring an action against the trustee for declarator that he is entitled to a ranking.[31]

The insolvent retains a radical right in the estate and, when the creditors are satisfied, he can call on the trustee to account for and to reconvey the surplus.[32] He is not, however, entitled to a retrocession of the estate unless full satisfaction has been made or the creditors consent to abandon some portion of it or a discharge on composition is given.[33] Whether the discharge is in effect a discharge on composition depends on its terms and on the provisions of the trust deed.

Protected trust deeds

A trust deed is a protected trust deed if (1) the trustee would not be disqualified from acting as permanent trustee in the debtor's sequestration, (2) the trustee forthwith after the trust deed has been delivered to

24.3

---

[21] *Walker* v. *Hunter* (1933) 49 Sh.Ct.Rep. 139.

[22] *per* Lord Cranworth, *Synnot* v. *Simpson* (1854) 5 H.L.C. 121 at 133; *per* Lord Dunedin, *Carmichael* v. *Carmichael's Exix.*, 1920 S.C. (H.L.) 195 at 201.

[23] *Jopp* v. *Hay* (1844) 7 D. 260; *Campbell & Beck* v. *Macfarlane* (1862) 24 D. 1097.

[24] *Crerar* v. *Dow* (1906) 22 Sh.Ct.Rep. 311.

[25] *Gibson* v. *May* (1841) 3 D. 974; *Ogilvie & Son* v. *Taylor* (1887) 14 R. 399, *per* Lord Young at p. 401; *Doughty* v. *Wells* (1906) 14 S.L.T. 299.

[26] Bell, *Comm.*, II, 388; *Snodgrass* v. *Trs. and Crs. of Bent* (1744) M. 1209; Goudy, p. 485.

[27] *per* Lord Gifford, *Kyd* v. *Waterson* (1880) 7 R. 884 at 886.

[28] Bell, *Comm.*, II, 391; *Nicolson* v. *Johnstone & Wright, supra*; *Salaman* v. *Rosslyn's Trs.* (1900) 3 F. 298. As to the position of the trustee under the trust deed where no creditor has acceded, see *Mess* v. *Hay* (1898) 1 F. H.L. 22; *McAlister* v. *Swinburne & Co.* (1874) 1 R. 958 (sequestration on debtor's petition).

[29] B.A., s.5(2)(c).

[30] *Ogilvie & Son* v. *Taylor* (1887) 14 R. 399; *Athya* v. *Clydesdale Bank* (1881) 18 S.L.R. 287; *Davidson* v. *Union Bank of Scotland* (1881) 19 S.L.R. 15; *Heritable Securities Investment Association Ltd.* v. *Wingate & Co.* (1891) 29 S.L.R. 904.

[31] *Mackie* v. *McMillan* (1925) 41 Sh.Ct.Rep. 339.

[32] *Gilmour* v. *Gilmours* (1873) 11 M. 853; *Edmond* v. *Dingwall's Trs.* (1860) 23 D. 21; *Buttercase & Geddie's Tr.* v. *Geddie* (1897) 24 R. 1128.

[33] *Flett* v. *Mustard*, 1936 S.C. 269.

him publishes in the Gazette and sends to every known creditor a notice[34] stating that the trust deed has been granted and inviting creditors to accede within four weeks, (3) within four weeks a majority in number and not less than two-thirds in value of the creditors accede to the trust deed, (4) the trustee immediately after the expiry of the four week period sends to the Accountant in Bankruptcy a copy of the trust deed with a certificate indorsed thereon that it is a true copy and that the necessary accession of creditors has been obtained.[35] It would seem that the majority required is of all the creditors and not only of those known to the trustee.[36]

The "protection" is that a creditor who has not acceded to the trust deed has no higher right to recover his debt than a creditor who has acceded and the debtor may not petition for sequestration of his estate while the trust deed subsists.[37] However, a qualified creditor who has not acceded may petition for sequestration not later than 6 weeks after the publication of the Gazette notice and the court may award sequestration if it considers that to do so would be in the best interests of the creditors.[38] A non-acceding creditor may petition for the debtor's sequestration at any time within four months of apparent insolvency if he avers that the provision for distribution of the estate is or is likely to be unduly prejudicial to a creditor or to a class of creditors and the court must award sequestration if it is satisfied that the averment is correct.[39]

The trustee under a protected trust deed can challenge gratuitous alienations, unfair preferences and divorce settlements.[40] Where the trustee has obtained a discharge from the creditors who acceded to the trust deed he must forthwith give notice of the discharge by notice to every non-acceding creditor known to him and to the Accountant in Bankruptcy. That makes the discharge binding on the non-acceding creditor unless within 28 days he applies to the court for an order that he is not bound by the discharge.[41] The order will be granted if the court is satisfied on grounds other than those on which the creditor could have petitioned for the debtor's sequestration, that the intromissions of the trustee have been so unduly prejudicial to the creditor's claim that he should not be bound by the discharge.[42]

Once the final distribution to creditors has been made the trustee must send to the Accountant in Bankruptcy a statement[43] indicating how the estate was realised and distributed and a certificate that the distribution was in accordance with the trust deed.[44]

---

[34] B. Regs., Sched., Form 10.
[35] s.59; Sched. 5, para. 5.
[36] McBryde, p. 252.
[37] para. 6.
[38] para. 7(1)(a), (2).
[39] para. 7(1)(b), (3).
[40] B.A., ss.34(2)(b)(ii), 34(8), 35(2), 36(4)(b), 36(6).
[41] para. 10.
[42] para. 12.
[43] B.Regs., Sched., Form 11.
[44] B.A., Sched. 5, para. 9.

CHAPTER 25

LIQUIDATION

The process

A company registered under the Companies Acts cannot be sequestrated.[1] The legal process corresponding to sequestration in the case of companies is winding up or, as it is more usually known in Scotland, liquidation.[2] An official known as a liquidator is appointed to distribute the assets of the company to the creditors in accordance with their rights and to distribute any balance among the contributories. A liquidator, however, differs from the trustee in a sequestration in that there is no transfer of the company's property to him; he is not vested in the estate to the exclusion of the company; he has no new or independent title; he is a mere administrator for the statutory purposes and the doctrine of *tantum et tale* has no application in relation to him.[3]

25.1

The petition

A creditor of the company may petition for its liquidation if the company is unable to pay its debts.[4] The company is deemed to be unable to pay its debts if (a) a creditor for a sum exceeding £750 then due has served on the company at its registered office a written demand in the prescribed form[5] requiring payment of the sum and the company has for three weeks thereafter neglected to pay the sum or to secure or compound for it to the creditor's reasonable satisfaction[6]; there must be 21 clear days between the presenting of the demand and the presenting of the petition[7]; postal service is not competent[8] but service by a sheriff officer is not necessary[9]; or (b) the induciae of a charge for payment on an extract decree, an extract registered bond or an extract registered protest have expired without payment being made[10]; it has been suggested[11] that the debt should be for at least £750 (that being the English practice) but this seems contrary to earlier Scottish authority[12]; or (c) it is proved to the satisfaction of the court that the company is unable to pay its debts as they fall due.[13]

25.2

---

[1] B.A., s.6(2).

[2] *Haig and Others* v. *Lord Advocate*, 1976 S.L.T. (Notes) 16.

[3] *Gray's Trs.* v. *Benhar Coal Co. Ltd.* (1881) 9 R. 225; *Clark* v. *West Calder Oil Co.* (1882) 9 R. 1017; *Bank of Scotland* v. *Liquidators of Hutchison Main & Co. Ltd.*, 1914 S.C. (H.L.) 1. See also *Smith* v. *Lord Advocate*, 1978 S.C. 259; *Re International Tin Council* [1987] Ch. 419 at p. 446.

[4] I.A., s.122(1)(*f*). As to procedure, see McBryde and Dowie, *Petition Procedure in the Court of Session* (2nd. ed.), pp. 100–105.

[5] Ins. Rules, Form. 4.1. (Amendment Rules).

[6] I.A., s.123(1)(*a*).

[7] *Re Lympne Investments Ltd.* [1972] 1 W.L.R. 523.

[8] *Craig* v. *Iona Hotels Ltd.*, 1988 S.C.L.R. 130.

[9] *Lord Advocate* v. *Blairwest Investments Ltd.* (Sh.Ct.) 1989 S.C.L.R. 352.

[10] I.A., s.123(1)(*c*).

[11] *Palmer's Company Law* (24th ed.), paras. 88–06, 90–07.

[12] *J. Speirs & Co.* v. *Central Building Co. Ltd.*, 1911 S.C. 330.

[13] I.A., s.123(1)(*e*); *Taylor's Industrial Flooring Ltd.* v. *M. & H. Plant Hire (Manchester) Ltd.* [1990] B.C.L.C. 216.

A company is also deemed unable to pay its debts if the value of its assets is less than the amount of its liabilities, taking into account contingent and prospective liabilities.[14]

The creditor may be a prospective or contingent creditor[15] but a debt claimed in a court action which is disputed is not a contingent debt for this purpose.[16] A creditor who holds a floating charge over property comprised in the company's property and undertaking may petition for liquidation if his security is in jeopardy, *i.e.* if events have occurred or are about to occur which render it unreasonable in the interests of the creditor that the company should retain power to dispose of the property subject to the floating charge.[17]

The Court of Session has jurisdiction to wind up any company registered in Scotland.[18] If the share capital paid up or credited as paid up does not exceed £120,000 the petition may be presented to the sheriff court in whose jurisdiction the registered office is situated.[19]

Presentation of the petition

25.3 The liquidation is deemed to commence at the time of the presentation of the petition for winding up unless the company has previously passed a resolution for voluntary liquidation in which case the liquidation commences at the time of the passing of the resolution.[20] If the company, a debenture holder, holder of a floating charge, receiver, shareholder or other person claiming an interest has lodged a caveat, no order is pronounced without the person lodging the caveat having been given an opportunity to be heard by the court.[21] Otherwise the court orders intimation service and advertisement.[22] There must be advertisement in The *Edinburgh Gazette* and as the court directs in one or more newspapers for ensuring that the petition comes to the notice of the creditors of the company.[23]

The court may also, on presentation, or at any time before the first appointment of liquidators, appoint a provisional liquidator.[24] Whether such an appointment should be made is in the discretion of court.[25] The provisional liquidator has to take into his custody and control all the property and things in action to which the company is, or appears to be, entitled.[26] His powers may be limited or restricted by the order appointing him and he may be granted further powers.[27] Where a provisional liquidator has been appointed, no action or proceeding

---

[14] I.A., s.123(2); see *Re a Company* [1986] B.C.L.C. 261.
[15] I.A., s.124(1).
[16] *Walter L. Jacob & Co. Ltd.* v. *FIMBRA,* 1988 S.C.L.R. 184.
[17] I.A., s.122(2).
[18] I.A., s.120(1).
[19] I.A., s.120(3). As to the petition, see R.C. 217; Sh.Ct. Ins. Rule 18.
[20] I.A., s.129; *Haig and Others* v. *Lord Advocate,* 1976 S.L.T. (Notes) 16. In relation to diligence note, however, I.A., s.185(3); see paras. 16.12, 17.13.
[21] R.C., 218A; Sh.Ct. Ins. Rule 20.
[22] R.C., 218; Sh.Ct. Ins. Rule 19.
[23] R.C., 218 (6); Sh.Ct. Ins. Rule 19.
[24] I.A., s.135; R.C. 218E; Ins. Rules 4.1–4.6; Sh.Ct. Ins. Rule 23.
[25] *Levy* v. *Napier,* 1962 S.L.T. 264; *McCabe* v. *Andrew Middleton (Enterprises) Ltd.,* 1969 S.L.T. (Sh.Ct.) 29.
[26] I.A., s.144.
[27] I.A., s.135(5).

against the company or its property can be commenced or proceeded with unless with leave of the court.[28]

At any time after presentation of the petition and before the winding-up order is made, the company, a creditor or a contributory can apply to a court in England and Wales or Northern Ireland to stay proceedings against the company there and to the court having jurisdiction in the liquidation to sist other proceedings against the company.[29]

Generally, a petitioning creditor whose debt is unpaid is entitled to a winding-up order *ex debito justitiae*.[30] A letter from the company's solicitors stating that the company had no assets on which execution could be levied is evidence that the company is unable to pay its debts.[31] If the company shows that the debt is bona fide disputed the petition will be dismissed because the purpose of the petition is not to constitute a debt.[32] If the matter is in doubt, the petition will be sisted to allow constitution.[33] The dispute, however, must be as to the existence of the debt and not merely as to its precise amount.[34] If the company was in bona fide doubt as to the party from whom a valid discharge could be obtained, liquidation is not an appropriate procedure.[35] It may be an answer for the company to show that the petitioner has security for his debt if it is clear that the security commands in the market the amount of the debt.[36] The petition may be refused if the general voice of the creditors is against the application or if it is shown that refusal of the order would not prejudice the petitioner.[37] If the petitioner has been paid the petition must fail.[38] If a petitioner is found not entitled to present the petition or if he fails to proceed with the petition, another creditor can be sisted in his place.[39]

The liquidator

When the winding-up order is made the court appoints a liquidator,[40] known as the "interim liquidator," who may be ordered to advertise his appointment[41] and who then calls a meeting of creditors to choose a liquidator (who may be the same person as the interim liquidator).[42] The functions of the liquidator are to secure that the assets of the company are got in, realised and distributed to the company's creditors and, if there is a surplus, to the persons entitled to it.[43] As soon as may be after his

25.4

---

[28] I.A., s.130(2).
[29] I.A., s.126; see *Re Dynamics Corporation of America* [1973] 1 W.L.R. 63.
[30] *Smyth & Co.* v. *Salem Flour Mills Co. Ltd.* (1887) 14 R. 441.
[31] *Re Douglas Griggs Engineering Ltd.* [1963] Ch. 19.
[32] *Cuninghame* v. *Walkinshaw Oil Co. Ltd.* (1886) 14 R. 87; *W. & J. C. Pollok* v. *The Gaeta Pioneer Mining Co.*, 1907 S.C. 182; *Mann* v. *Goldstein* [1968] 1 W.L.R. 1091; *Holt Southey Ltd.* v. *Catnic Components Ltd.* [1978] 1 W.L.R. 630; *Re a Company (No. 003729 of 1982)* [1984] 1 W.L.R. 1090.
[33] *Landauer & Co.* v. *Alexander & Co.*, 1919 S.C. 492.
[34] *Re Tweeds Garages Ltd.* [1962] Ch. 406.
[35] *Craig* v. *Iona Hotels Ltd.*, 1988 S.C.L.R. 130.
[36] *Commercial Bank of Scotland Ltd.* v. *Lanark Oil Co. Ltd.* (1886) 14 R. 147.
[37] *Smyth & Co.* v. *Salem Flour Mills Co. Ltd., supra*; *Bouboulis* v. *Mann Macneal & Co.*, 1926 S.C. 637. See also *Foxhall & Gyle (Nurseries) Ltd., Ptrs.*, 1978 S.L.T. (Notes) 29.
[38] *Furmston, Petr.*, 1987 S.L.T. (Sh.Ct.) 10.
[39] R.C., 218C; Sh.Ct. Ins. Rule 2.
[40] I.A., s.138(1).
[41] R.C., 218D; Sh.Ct. Ins. Rule 22.
[42] I.A., s.138(3).
[43] I.A., s.143(1).

appointment, he must take possession of the whole assets of the company and any property, books, papers or records in the possession or control of the company or to which the company appears to be entitled.[44] He has a wide range of powers—*e.g.* to pay debts, compromise claims, institute and defend proceedings and carry on the business of the company; the exercise of some of these powers requires the sanction of the liquidation committee or of the court.[45] In addition, he has the same powers as a trustee in sequestration, including powers to deal with heritage subject to a security.[46] The meeting at which the liquidator is elected, or a subsequent meeting of creditors, may elect a liquidation committee of not less than three and not more than five creditors.[47] The liquidator has a right to the supply of public utilities similar to that of a trustee in a sequestration.[48]

The effect of the order

25.5 Any disposition of the company's property, and any transfer of shares, or alteration of the status of the company's members, made after the commencement of winding up—the time of presentation of the petition—is unless the court otherwise orders, void.[49] Payments by the company into its overdrawn bank account after the presentation of the petition are accordingly void unless validated by the court.[50] The granting of a security is a disposition of the company's property.[51] After the winding-up order no action or proceeding can be proceeded with or commenced against the company or its property except by leave of the court.[52]

Conspectus of further procedure

25.6 The liquidator may apply to the court for the public examination of the officers of the company and certain other persons.[53] He ingathers the assets of the company. He advertises for claims by creditors and adjudicates upon them. The court may make calls.[54] He distributes the funds in the prescribed order.[55] When it appears to him that the winding up is for practical purposes complete he summons a final meeting of the creditors to receive his report and determine whether he should have his release. The liquidator is released when he has given notice of the result of the meeting to the court and the registrar; the registrar registers the

---

[44] I.A., s.144; Ins. Rule 4.22. His functions may be restricted by the drugs legislation: Drug Trafficking Offences Act 1986, s.17; Criminal Justice (Scotland) Act 1987, s.35; Criminal Justice Act 1988, s.86.
[45] I.A., s.167; Sched. 4.
[46] I.A., s.169(2); Ins. Rule 4.22(5).
[47] I.A., s.142; Ins. Rules 4.40–4.59.
[48] I.A., s.233. See para. 20.5.
[49] I.A., s.127.
[50] *Re Gray's Inn Construction Co.* [1980] 1 W.L.R. 711. See also *Millar* v. *National Bank* (1891) 28 S.L.R. 884.
[51] *Site Preparations Ltd.* v. *Buchan Development Co. Ltd.*, 1983 S.L.T. 317.
[52] I.A., s.130(2). Proceedings outside the United Kingdom can be restrained: *California Redwood Co.* v. *Merchant Banking Co. of London* (1886) 13 R. 1202. As to a counterclaim, see *G. & A. (Hotels) Ltd.* v. *T.H.B. Marketing Services Ltd.*, 1983 S.L.T. 497.
[53] I.A., s.133.
[54] I.A., s.150. An order may be enforced by summary diligence: I.A., s.161.
[55] See para. 25.11.

notice and at the end of three months from the date of registration the company is dissolved.[56]

Effect on property

As has already been mentioned, there is no transference of the property of the company to the liquidator[57] but liquidation has an effect on property similar to that of sequestration. The basis of this has not been the subject of much discussion but it seems to be founded on the liquidator's duty to administer the property for distribution among the creditors *pari passu*[58] and on the cumulative effect of a number of the sections of the Insolvency Act.[59]

25.7

Unfortunately, the effect of the statutory provisions has recently become more obscure. The Companies Act 1985, s.623(2), and its predecessors, provided that winding up was ". . . equivalent, as at the date of its commencement, to an arrestment in execution and decree of furthcoming, and to an executed or completed poinding . . .;" that could obviously be used, among other purposes, to give the liquidator priority over the holder of an assignation granted by the company which had not been intimated at the date of commencement of the liquidation. However, the Insolvency Act 1986, s.185, replaces that provision with one which incorporates s.37 of the Bankruptcy (Scotland) Act 1985, a section which, as altered to apply to liquidations, gives the liquidation the effect of an arrestment and poinding but is qualified by the words ". . . in relation to diligence done . . . in respect of any part of the company's estate . . .;" the section cannot therefore be used to obtain a preference over an unintimated assignation; this does not cause any difficulty in a sequestration because the trustee obtains priority over an unintimated assignation by virtue of s.31(4) of the Bankruptcy Act which vests the estate in him. In England it has been held that s.127 of the 1986 Act, which makes void any disposition of the company's property after winding up, prevents the honouring after winding up of a cheque drawn by the company[60] but it is not clear that this section could be used to give liquidation the effect of an intimated assignation. The result seems to be that in the case of all incorporeal moveable property including debts subject to an unintimated assignation there is something resembling the "race to the register."[61]

Corporeal moveable property is treated as if the liquidator took possession of it at the commencement of liquidation and matters such as retention of title are treated as in sequestration.[62] The liquidation does transfer the company's rights against a liability insurer to the third party.[63]

---

[56] I.A., ss.146, 172(8), 205.

[57] *Gray's Trs.* v. *Benhar Coal Co. Ltd.* (1881) 9 R. 225; *Clark* v. *West Calder Oil Co.*, (1882) 9 R. 1017; *Bank of Scotland* v. *Liqrs. of Hutchison Main & Co. Ltd.*, 1914 S.C. (H.L.) 1; *Liqr. of Style & Mantle Ltd.* v. *Prices Tailors Ltd.*, 1934 S.C. 548. See also *Ayerst* v. *C. & K. (Construction) Ltd.* [1976] A.C. 167; *John Mackintosh & Sons Ltd.* v. *Baker's Bargain Stores (Seaford) Ltd.* [1965] 1 W.L.R. 1182.

[58] *Clark* v. *West Calder Oil Co.*, *supra.*, per L. P. Inglis at p. 1025.

[59] *Ibid.*, per Lord Shand at p. 1031.

[60] *Re Gray's Inn Construction Co.* [1980] 1 W.L.R. 711.

[61] See para. 21.13; *Liqr. of Union Club Ltd.* v. *Edinburgh Life Assurance Co.* (1906) 8 F. 1143.

[62] See para. 21.7.

[63] Third Parties (Rights Against Insurers) Act 1930, s.1(1)(*b*).

Where missives of sale have been concluded by the company and the price has been received but no disposition delivered, on liquidation the heritage is still the company's property and the buyer's only remedy is to claim in the liquidation.[64] The grantee of a disposition or standard security may be defeated if the liquidator completes title first[65]; it is thought that the liquidator can complete title by notice of title.[66] It is thought that the liquidator's power to sell heritage is not affected by the existence of an inhibition.[67] Where the inhibition is within 60 days of the winding-up order (or the date of the winding-up resolution) the relevant provision of the Bankruptcy (Scotland) Act is applicable.[68]

It is clear that property held by the company on trust must be delivered up by the liquidator if it can be identified.[69]

The liquidator may adopt or abandon a contract made by the company. If he is to adopt it he must intimate his intention to do so within a reasonable time. If he abandons it, the other party can claim damages for breach of contract in the liquidation.[70] The court, on the application of the other party to a contract with the company may make an order rescinding the contract on such terms as to payments by or to either party of damages for the non-performance of the contract, or otherwise as the court thinks just; any damages payable to the other party may be proved as a debt in the liquidation.[71]

The financial markets régime[72] applies to liquidations.

Antecedent transactions

25.8   Certain antecedent transactions can be attacked by the liquidator.[73] The law now closely resembles that applicable in sequestrations.

(a) Gratuitous Alienations: the liquidator can challenge a gratuitous alienation by the company to an associate of the company within the previous five years or to any other person within the previous two years.[74] The principle and the exceptions thereto are the same as those applicable in sequestration of an individual.[75] It should be noted, however, that the definition of "associate" to be used here is the definition given in the Bankruptcy (Scotland) Act 1985[76] and not that given in the Insolvency Act 1986. The date for calculation of the

---

[64] *Gibson and Hunter Home Designs Ltd.*, 1976 S.C. 23.
[65] *Ibid.*, per Lord Cameron at p. 30. Gretton (1984) 29 J.L.S. 357, 400; Gretton & Reid (1985) 30 J.L.S. 109. *Cf.* McDonald (1985) 30 J.L.S. 20.
[66] Titles to Land Consolidation (Scotland) Act 1868, s.25.
[67] Gretton, pp. 132–133.
[68] I.A., s.185. See para. 23.5.
[69] *Turnbull* v. *Scottish County Investment Co.*, 1939 S.C. 5; *Smith* v. *Liqr. of James Birrell Ltd.*, 1967 S.L.T. (Notes) 116; *Lord Advocate* v. *McInnes Textiles Ltd.*, 1978 S.L.T. (Notes) 84; *Re Eastern Capital Futures Ltd.* [1989] B.C.L.C. 371. As to the client bank account of an incorporated solicitors' practice, see Solicitors (Scotland) Act 1980, s.42 (2A).
[70] *Crown Estate Commissioners* v. *Liqrs. of Highland Engineering Ltd.*, 1975 S.L.T. 58.
[71] I.A., s.186.
[72] See para. 20.9.
[73] Gratuitous alienations and unfair and fraudulent preferences cannot be challenged where the financial markets regime applies: C.A. 1989, s.165. See para. 20.9.
[74] I.A., s.242.
[75] See para. 22.2.
[76] B.A., s.74; see para. 22.3.

five and two year periods is the date of commencement of the liquidation.[77]
(b) Gratuitous Alienations at Common Law: the right to challenge gratuitous alienations at common law is preserved.[78]
(c) Unfair Preferences: there is a statutory provision for the challenge of unfair preferences which closely follows the rules in sequestration.[79] The six month period is calculated from the date of commencement of the liquidation.[80]
(d) Fraudulent Preferences at Common Law: again a right is preserved.[81]
(e) Extortionate Credit Transactions: the provision again follows that found in the Bankruptcy Act.[82] The three-year period is calculated from the date the company went into liquidation.
(f) Floating Charges: certain floating charges may be avoided.[83]
(g) Diligence: this has been treated earlier.[84]

If there has been fraudulent or wrongful trading, the persons responsible may be ordered to make a contribution to the company's assets. Fraudulent trading is where the company's business has been carried on with intent to defraud creditors of the company or of any other person, or for any fraudulent purpose; the court, on the application of the liquidator, may declare that persons who were knowingly parties to the carrying on of the business in this way are to be liable to make such contributions to the company's assets as the court thinks proper.[85] A director of the company is guilty of wrongful trading if at some time before the commencement of the liquidation he knew or ought to have concluded that there was no reasonable prospect that the company would avoid going into insolvent liquidation; the court may declare that he is liable to make such contribution to the company's assets as the court thinks proper; it is a defence that he took every step with a view to minimising the potential loss to the company's creditors that he ought to have taken.[86] Liability for debts of a company may be incurred if a person who was a director of a company in the 12 months before it went into insolvent liquidation becomes a director or participates in the management of a company which has the same name as the liquidated company or a similar name within a period of five years from the date of the liquidation.[87]

Contributories

In a liquidation, past and present members of the company may be liable to contribute to the assets of the company to an amount sufficient to

25.9

---

[77] I.A., s.242(3).
[78] I.A., s.242(7); *Bank of Scotland, Petrs.*, 1988 S.L.T. 690. See para. 22.1.
[79] I.A., s.243; see para. 22.9.
[80] I.A., s.243(1).
[81] I.A., s.243(6); see para. 22.4.
[82] I.A., s.244; see para. 22.12.
[83] I.A., s.245; see para. 9.12.
[84] I.A., s.185; see para. 16.12 (poinding); para. 17.13 (arrestment); para. 23.5 (inhibition).
[85] I.A., s.213.
[86] I.A., s.214; *Re Produce Marketing Consortium* [1989] 1 W.L.R. 745.
[87] I.A., ss.216–217.

pay its debts and liabilities and the expenses of winding up and for adjustments of the rights of contributories *inter se*.[88] No member, past or present, of a company limited by shares can be liable for more than the amount unpaid on the share in respect of which he is liable.[89] A past member is liable only if the present members cannot satisfy their contributions[90] and he is not liable for debts contracted after he ceased to be a member.[91] He is not liable if he ceased to be a member for a year or more before the commencement of the winding up.[92] The liability of a contributory creates a debt accruing due from him at the time his liability commenced but payable at the times when calls are made enforcing the liability.[93] The court makes orders enforcing the calls and such an order is conclusive evidence that the money ordered to be paid is due.[94]

If a company carries on business for more than six months with a number of members below the legal minimum of two everyone who is a member during the period after the six months and is cognisant of the illegality is jointly and severally liable for the debts contracted during the period.[95]

A member of a company whose liability to pay calls is decreased by a reduction of capital may be liable to a creditor who because of ignorance of the proceedings was not entered on the list of creditors in the reduction proceedings, if the company is later unable to pay the debt.[96] The liability is to the extent to which he would have been liable to contribute if there had been a winding up commenced on the day before registration of the reduction minute and seems to be in addition to his liability to the company.

In the case of a company limited by guarantee, a member may be liable to pay a sum not exceeding the amount he undertook to contribute on winding up together with any sum unpaid on his shares.[97]

In the case of an unlimited company, the contributories are liable to the full extent of their means. Persons registered as trustees are liable as contributories.[98]

Creditor's claim

25.10 The creditor's remedy is to claim for his debt in the liquidation. A creditor must submit his claim not later than eight weeks before the end of the accounting period.[99] The statement of claim must be in the prescribed form and accompanied by an account or voucher constituting prima facie evidence of the debt.[1] Certain provisions of the Bankruptcy Act are adapted *mutatis mutandis* to claims in a liquidation.[2] So the

---

[88] I.A., ss.74(1), 79. See *Barbor* v. *Middleton*, 1988 S.C.L.R. 178.
[89] I.A., s.74(2)(*d*).
[90] I.A., s.74(2)(*c*).
[91] I.A., s.74(2)(*b*).
[92] I.A., s.74(2)(*a*).
[93] I.A., s.80.
[94] I.A., s.152.
[95] C.A., s.24.
[96] C.A., s.140.
[97] I.A., s.74(3).
[98] *Muir* v. *City of Glasgow Bank* (1879) 6 R. (H.L.) 21.
[99] Ins. Rule 4.15(1).
[1] Ins. Rule 4.15(2); Form 4.7.
[2] Ins. Rule 4.16. These include B.A., s.60, dealing with co-obligants: see para. 23.6.

provisions of Schedule 1 of the Bankruptcy Act relating to interest, discount, future and contingent debts and securities apply to liquidation claims. Where a creditor holds a decree ordering payment in a foreign currency or has a claim arising from a contract or bill of exchange in terms of which payment is or may be required to be made in foreign currency, the claim may be stated in foreign currency and is converted into sterling at the rate of exchange for the foreign currency at the mean of the buying and selling spot rates prevailing in the London market at the close of business on the date of commencement of winding up.[3] A creditor who has submitted a claim may at any time submit a further claim specifying a different amount but a secured creditor cannot put a different value on his security after the liquidator has required him to transfer it to him.[4] The liquidator may require the creditor or any other person to produce evidence relating to the claim.[5] The liquidator eventually adjudicates upon the claims.[6] There is an appeal to the court against the adjudication.[7]

Distribution of assets
Subject to the rights of secured creditors which are preferable to those of the liquidator and to the preference of any lien holder,[8] the funds are distributed in the following order[9]:

(a) the expenses of the liquidation including the outlays and remuneration of the liquidators and the expenses of the petitioner[10]; this also includes the amount of any corporation tax on chargeable gains accruing on the realisation of any asset of the company, whether effected by the liquidator, a secured creditor or otherwise;
(b) the administration expenses of any voluntary arrangement which was in force when the liquidation petition was presented;
(c) the preferential debts,[11] excluding interest thereon to the date of commencement of liquidation; it is thought that such interest is recoverable as an ordinary debt;
(d) ordinary debts;
(e) interest at 15 per cent. on the preferential debts and the ordinary debts between the commencement of the winding-up and payment of the debt;[12] all interest ranks equally whether or not the debts on which it is payable rank equally;
(f) postponed debts, *i.e.*, creditor's rights to any alienation which has

25.11

---

[3] Ins. Rule 4.17.
[4] Ins. Rule 4.15(4).
[5] Ins. Rule 4.16; B.A., s.48.
[6] B.A., s.49.
[7] B.A., s.49(6).
[8] Ins. Rule 4.66(6). As to the landlord's hypothec, see *Scottish Metropolitan Co.* v. *Sutherlands Ltd.*, 1934 S.L.T. (Sh.Ct.) 62.
[9] Ins. Rule 4.66(1).
[10] Ins. Rule 4.67.
[11] I.A., s.175; Ins. Rule 4.66(1)(*b*). Certain claims arising under the financial markets régime have priority to preferential debts: C.A. 1989, ss.163(4), 164(6), 175(6). See para. 20.9. Where the liquidation follows upon an administration, it is thought that the claims given priority in the administration (see para. 26.9) rank before the preferential debts.
[12] Ins. Rule 4.66(1)(*d*), (2)(*b*).

been reduced or restored to the company's assets or to the proceeds of sale of such alienation.

There is a specified priority for the expenses of liquidation.[10] Any debt falling within one of (c) to (f) has the same priority as any other debt falling into the same category and if the assets are insufficient to meet them in full they abate in equal proportions.[13] Any surplus remaining after all these debts have been paid in full is distributed among the members according to their rights and interests in the company unless the articles otherwise provide.[14]

Preferential debts

25.12   The preferential debts are[15]:

(1) Sums due at the relevant date on account of deductions of income tax from emoluments paid during the 12 months next before that date under the pay as you earn scheme less the amount of any repayments of income tax the company was liable to make during that period.

(2) Sums due in respect of deductions required to be made under the provisions for deduction of tax from sums due to sub-contractors in the construction industry.

(3) Value added tax due to the Customs and Excise referable to the period of six months before the relevant date.

(4) Car tax due at the relevant date which became due within the 12 months before that date.

(5) Amounts due in respect of general betting duty, bingo duty, pool betting duty and gaming licence duty at the relevant date which became due in the 12 months before that date.

(6) Sums due in respect of Class 1 or Class 2 social security contributions which became due in the 12 months before the relevant date.

(7) Sums assessed on and due from the company on account of Class 4 social security contributions, being sums due to the Inland Revenue and assessed on the company up to April 5 before the relevant date but not exceeding, in the whole, any one year's assessment.

(8) Contributions to occupational pension schemes and state scheme premiums owed by the company being sums to which Schedule 3 to the Social Security Pension Act 1975 applies.

(9) Any amount owed to a present or former employee of the company as remuneration in respect of the whole or any part of the four months next before the relevant date, not exceeding £800.[16] Remuneration includes wages or salary payable for time or piece work or earned wholly or partly by commission in respect of services rendered to the company in the period. It also includes statutory sick pay, remuneration under a protective award under the Employment Protection Act 1975 and payments under the Employment Protec-

---

[13] Ins. Rule 4.66(4).

[14] Ins. Rule 4.66(5).

[15] I.A., ss.175, 386, Sched. 6. As amended by Insolvency (E.C.S.C. Levy Debts) Regulations 1987 (S.I. 1987 No. 2093). Where the Secretary of State for Employment has paid sums to an employee in respect of some of these categories of debt he has the preference which the employee would have had and his claim has priority over a claim by the employee: Employment Protection Act 1978, s.125(2) subst. by Employment Act 1989, s.19.

[16] Insolvency Proceedings (Monetary Limits) Order 1986 (S.I. 1986 No. 1996), Art. 4.

tion (Consolidation) Act 1978 for guaranteed remuneration, suspension on medical grounds, trade union duties, looking for work and ante-natal care.

(10) Any amount owed by way of accrued holiday remuneration, in respect of any period of employment before the relevant date, to a person whose employment by the company has been terminated, whether before, on, or after, that date.

(11) So much of any sum owed in respect of money advanced for the purpose as has been applied for the payment of a debt which, if it had not been paid, would have been a debt falling within (9) or (10). This covers, for example, a bank overdraft made for the payment of wages. A bank usually requires the opening of a special wages account to make advances for payment of wages but the preference can be obtained without such a special arrangement if the advances were in fact made to enable the company to meet its commitments including the payment of wages.[17] Where there was a wages account in debit and a current account kept in credit so that the credit always exceeded the debit it was held that the two accounts had to be regarded as one account which was in credit even although there was a larger debit on a third account which was "frozen."[18] On the other hand a preference can be obtained for sums transferred to the wages account by debiting an overdrawn current account.[19] Sums paid to a "labour-only" sub-contractor are not remuneration of an employee.[20]

(12) Certain sums to be paid by the company under the Reserve Forces (Safeguard of Employment) Act 1985.

(13) Coal and steel levies and surcharges under the European Coal and Steel Community Treaty.

The relevant date for determining the amount and existence of a preferential debt if the winding up is by the court and a voluntary winding up had not commenced before the winding-up order, is the date of appointment, or first appointment, of a provisional liquidator, or, if no such appointment has been made, the date of the winding-up order. However, if the liquidation by the court occurred immediately upon the discharge of an administration order, the relevant date is the date of the administration order. Otherwise, the relevant date is the date of the passing of the winding-up resolution.[21]

A secured creditor whose debt is preferential only in part can apply the proceeds of his security to the non-preferential part.[22] Where a creditor had a preferential and a non-preferential claim and also owed a sum to the company, it was held in England that as a matter of equity the sum due to the company had to be set off rateably against the two claims.[23] Preferential claims have to be construed strictly.[24]

---

[17] *Re Primrose (Builders) Ltd.* [1950] Ch. 561; *Re Rampgill Mill Ltd.* [1967] Ch. 1138.
[18] *Re E. J. Morel (1934) Ltd.* [1962] Ch. 21.
[19] *Re James R. Rutherford & Sons Ltd.* [1964] 3 All E.R. 137.
[20] *Re C. W. & A. L. Hughes Ltd.* [1966] 2 All E.R. 702.
[21] I.A., s.387.
[22] *Re William Hall (Contractors) Ltd.* [1967] 1 W.L.R. 948.
[23] *Re Unit 2 Windows Ltd.* [1985] 1 W.L.R. 1383.
[24] *per* Danckwerts J., *Re Baker* [1954] 1 W.L.R. 1144 at p. 1148.

Subordinated debt

25.13 In England it was at one time doubted whether a creditor could agree that his debt would rank after all other debts. The view now is that the doubt was unfounded.[25] No other creditor is prejudiced by such an agreement. In Scotland, there is the dictum of Lord Dunedin already cited.[26]

Voluntary liquidation

25.14 A company can be wound up by a voluntary liquidation. This is initiated by a resolution of the company and notice of the passing of the resolution must be given in the *Edinburgh Gazette*.[27] The date of commencement of the liquidation is the time of the passing of the resolution.[28] Within the five weeks preceding the passing of the resolution, the directors may make a statutory declaration of solvency to the effect that they have made a full inquiry into the affairs of the company and have formed the opinion that the company will be able to pay its debts in full with interest within such period not exceeding 12 months from the commencement of the winding up as may be specified in the declaration. The declaration must embody a statement of the company's assets and liabilities as at the latest practicable date before the making of the declaration. If such a declaration is made the winding-up is a "members' voluntary winding up"; and if such a declaration is not made the winding up is a "creditors' voluntary winding up."[29] In the former, the liquidator is appointed by the company; in the latter, the company must summon a meeting of creditors not later than the 14th day after the day on which the winding-up resolution is to be proposed. The directors must lay a full statement of the company's affairs before the meeting of creditors.[30] The creditors and the company at their respective meetings may nominate a person to be liquidator; the creditors' nominee becomes the liquidator.[31] If no person is nominated by the creditors, the company's nominee becomes liquidator.[32] The creditors' meeting may also appoint a liquidation committee.[33]

A members' voluntary liquidation may have to be converted into a creditors' one. If the liquidator is of the opinion that the company will be unable to pay its debts within the period stated in the directors' declaration he must summon a meeting of creditors within 28 days by sending notices to creditors and advertising in the *Gazette* and in two newspapers circulating in the locality in which the company's principal place of business is situated[34]; as from the day of the meeting the liquidation becomes a creditors' voluntary one.[35] The meeting may

---

[25] Goode, *Legal Problems of Credit and Security* (2nd ed., 1988), pp. 24, 95–97; Penn, Shea & Arora, *Law Relating to Domestic Banking*, paras. 14.12–14.15; Dyer (1990) J.I.B.L. 154; Wood, *The Law relating to Subordinated Debt* (1990), pp. 23–26.
[26] See para. 1.1.
[27] I.A., s.85.
[28] I.A., s.86.
[29] I.A., ss.89, 90.
[30] ss.98, 99.
[31] I.A., s.100.
[32] I.A., s.100(2).
[33] I.A., s.101.
[34] I.A., s.95.
[35] I.A., s.96.

nominate a liquidator and appoint a liquidation committee.[36] In a creditors' voluntary liquidation, on the appointment of the liquidator, all the powers of the directors cease except in so far as the liquidation committee sanctions their continuance.[37] The liquidation committee has the powers and duties of commissioners on a bankrupt estate.[38]

In both types of voluntary liquidation the company ceases to carry on business from the commencement of winding up except insofar as may be required for its beneficial winding up but its corporate state and its corporate powers continue until the company is dissolved.[39] Any transfer of shares, not being to or with the sanction of the liquidator, and any alteration in the status of the members, is void.[40] The court, on the application of the liquidator, may direct that no action or proceeding shall be commenced or proceeded with except by leave of the court and subject to such terms as the court may impose.[41] The liquidator has some powers which he can exercise without sanction and others which require the sanction of an extraordinary resolution of the company in the case of a members' voluntary liquidation or of the court or the liquidation committee or the creditors in the case of the creditors' liquidation.[42] However, if a liquidator has been nominated by the company in a creditors' voluntary liquidation he cannot exercise any powers other than those necessary for the protection of the company's assets[43] in the period before the holding of the creditors' meeting except with the sanction of the court[44]; this is to prevent what is known as "centre-binding," in which the liquidator nominated by the company disposes of the assets to associates of the directors at an undervalue before the creditors know about it or are in a position to stop him.[45]

After the company is in voluntary liquidation there may be a petition for a winding up by the court.[46] The court has a discretion as to the making of the order.[47] There must be some good reason for making it. The views of creditors must be taken into account but the views of creditors who are also shareholders or former managers of the company may be given less weight. A creditor should not be left with a grievance because he has been denied an investigation of the company's affairs by an independent liquidator. The making of an order is not necessarily a reflection on the probity or competence of the existing liquidator.

The liquidator must pay the debts of the company and adjust the rights of contributories among themselves.[48] The expenses of winding up, including the liquidator's remuneration, are payable in priority to all

---

[36] I.A., s.102.
[37] I.A., s.103.
[38] Ins. Rules 4.40–4.59.
[39] I.A., s.87.
[40] I.A., s.88.
[41] I.A., s.113.
[42] I.A., s.165; Sched. 4.
[43] I.A., s.166(3).
[44] I.A., s.166(2).
[45] *Re Centrebind Ltd.* [1966] 3 All E.R. 889.
[46] I.A., s.116.
[47] *Re J. D. Swain* [1965] 1 W.L.R. 909; *Re M.C.H. Services Ltd.* [1987] B.C.L.C. 535; *Re H. J. Tomkins & Sons Ltd.* [1990] B.C.L.C. 71.
[48] I.A., s.165(5).

other claims.[49] Thereafter, subject to the preferential payments, the property of the company is applied in satisfaction of its liabilities *pari passu* and, subject to such application, shall, unless the articles otherwise provide, be distributed among the members according to their rights and interests in the company.[50]

When the liquidation appears to be complete, the liquidator submits accounts and a return to the registrar and the company is dissolved three months from the date of registration of the return.[51] The court may defer the dissolution on the application of the liquidator or other person interested.

Dissolved companies

25.15   After a company has been dissolved, previously unknown assets or debts may come to light.

If the company has been dissolved, the liquidator or other person interested may apply to the court to declare the dissolution void and thereupon such proceedings might be taken as might have been taken if the company had not been dissolved.[52] This must be done within two years of the dissolution date but an application for the purpose of bringing proceedings against the company in respect of personal injuries or death may be made at any time. This cannot be done to enable the company to receive a legacy to the prejudice of the heirs on intestacy.[53]

The registrar may strike a company off the register if the company is not carrying on business or in operation or if the affairs of the company are fully wound up. A member or creditor who feels aggrieved may apply within 20 years to have the company restored to the register. The court may give such directions or make such provision as seems just for placing the company and all other persons in the same position as nearly as may be as if the company had not been struck off.[54] An application may be made by a contingent creditor[55] but not by an assignee who acquired right to a debt after the dissolution.[56]

---

[49] I.A., s.115.
[50] I.A., s.107; Ins. Rules 4.66, Sched. 1, para. 29. If there is a surplus after payment of debts interest from the commencement of liquidation is payable at the higher of the contractual rate and 15 per cent. If the contractual rate is the lower, it will benefit shareholders to discharge liabilities if possible before the commencement of liquidation: Wilkinson (1989) 4 I.L. & P. 111.
[51] I.A., ss.94, 106, 201. See *Re Cornish Manures Ltd.* [1967] 1 W.L.R. 807.
[52] C.A., s.651 (amended by C.A. 1989, s.141).
[53] *Re Servers of the Blind League* [1960] 1 W.L.R. 564.
[54] C.A., ss.652, 653.
[55] *Re Harvest Lane Bodies Ltd.* [1969] 1 Ch. 457.
[56] *Re New Timbiqui Gold Mines Ltd.* [1961] Ch. 319.

CHAPTER 26

VOLUNTARY ARRANGEMENTS AND ADMINISTRATION ORDERS

Voluntary arrangements

26.1 The directors of the company may make a proposal to the company and its creditors for a composition in satisfaction of its debts or a scheme of arrangement of its affairs which is known as a "voluntary arrangement."[1] The proposal should give a short explanation why, in the opinion of the directors, the arrangement is desirable and give reasons why the company's creditors may be expected to concur with the arrangements; specified information must be given.[2] The proposal must provide for a "nominee" to act in relation to the voluntary arrangement either as a trustee or otherwise for the supervising of its implementation and that nominee must be a person qualified to act as an insolvency practitioner.[3] The directors must give the intended nominee notice of the proposal and, within seven days after delivery of the proposal to him, deliver to him a statement of the company's affairs. The nominee must within 28 days after he is given notice of the proposal report to the court as to whether in his opinion meetings of the company and its creditors should be summoned to consider the proposal.[4] The nominee then summons the meetings of the company and creditors which decide whether to approve the proposed arrangement with or without modifications.[5] 14 days' notice of the meeting must be given and with the notice must be sent a copy of the proposal and a copy or summary of the statement of affairs.[6] A creditor is entitled to vote if his claim has been submitted in writing and accepted.[7] The rules as to claims in a liquidation[8] apply with the date of the meeting being substituted for the date of liquidation.[9] Some rules as to secured creditors do not apply.[10]

At the creditors' meeting, for approval, there must be in favour at least three-quarters in value of the creditors present or represented and voting, in person or by proxy.[11] At the company meeting, a resolution is passed when a majority in value of those voting, in person or by proxy, have voted in favour of it.[12] A proposal which affects the rights of a secured creditor to enforce his security cannot be approved unless the

---

[1] I.A., s.1(1). The company must not be in liquidation or under an administration order. See para. 26.3. See also Hill, "Company Voluntary Arrangements" (1990) 6 I.L. & P. 47.
[2] Ins. Rule 1.3.
[3] I.A., s.1(2).
[4] I.A., s.2(2); Ins. Rule 1.7; R.C. 203, 204; Sh.Ct. Ins. Rules 4, 5.
[5] ss.3, 4; Ins. Rules 1.9, 1.13–1.17.
[6] Ins. Rule 1.9.
[7] Ins. Rule 7.9(2).
[8] Ins. Rules 4.15–4.17. See para. 25.10.
[9] Ins. Rule 7.9(4).
[10] Ins. Rule 7.9(5).
[11] Ins. Rule 7.12(2).
[12] Ins. Rule 7.12(1).

creditor concurs.[13] Unless the preferential creditor[14] concurs, the meeting cannot approve a proposal under which a preferential debt is not paid in priority to other debts or one preferential debt is paid to a smaller proportionate amount than another.[15] A proposal can be modified to some extent by the meetings. The functions proposed to be conferred on the nominee may be conferred on another insolvency practitioner.[16] If each of the meetings approves the proposed arrangement it takes effect as if made by the company at the creditors' meeting and binds every person who had notice of and was entitled to vote at that meeting, whether or not he was present or represented at it, as if he were a party to the voluntary arrangement.[17] Application may be made to the court to challenge the decisions made at the meetings.[18] Once the arrangements have been approved by the meetings the nominee becomes known as the "supervisor" of the voluntary arrangement.[19] The directors of the company must do all that is necessary to put the supervisor into possession of the assets included in the arrangement.[20] The supervisor can be given directions by the court on the application of creditors or any other person dissatisfied by any act, omission or decision of the supervisor.[21]

A proposal for a voluntary arrangement may be made by an administrator or liquidator of the company[22] in which case there is no report to the court and the administrator or liquidator summons the meetings of the company and creditors.[23] The making of a voluntary arrangement is a possible purpose of an administration order. The administrator or liquidator may be the nominee. If the proposal is approved, the court may sist the winding up or discharge the administration order or give appropriate directions as to the conduct of the winding up or administration.[24].

ADMINISTRATION ORDERS

The idea

26.2 The idea of an administration order is that a company in financial difficulties is put under the control of an independent insolvency practitioner to ascertain whether a more advantageous solution to its difficulties than a winding up can be found. From the time of the presentation of the petition for the making of the administration order the company is given protection from its creditors in that actions and diligence against it cannot proceed and securities over its property cannot

---

[13] I.A., s.4(3).
[14] If the company is not being wound up the date for calculation of the preferential debts is the date of the administration order, if there is one; otherwise it is the date of approval of the voluntary arrangement (I.A., s.387(2)).
[15] I.A., s.4(4).
[16] s.4(2).
[17] I.A., s.5(2).
[18] I.A., s.6; Ins. Rule 1.20; R.C. 208; Sh.Ct. Ins. Rule 9.
[19] I.A., s.7(2).
[20] Ins. Rule 1.19.
[21] I.A., s.7(3); R.C. 208; Sh.Ct. Ins. Rule 9.
[22] s.1(3).
[23] s.3(2); Ins. Rules 1.10–1.12.
[24] s.5(3).

be enforced. The protection, and the powers of the administrator, are to some extent qualified where the financial markets régime applies.[25]

The petition

If a company[26] is not in liquidation, the company, its directors or a creditor, may apply by petition to the court for an administration order to be made in relation to the company.[27] There may be prepared in support of the petition a report by an independent person to the effect that the appointment of an administrator is expedient.[28]

26.3

When the petition is presented notice of it must be given forthwith to any person who has appointed or is entitled to appoint a receiver under a floating charge which is over the whole, or substantially the whole, of the company's property (an "administrative receiver")[29] and also to any administrative receiver already appointed, anyone who has petitioned for a liquidation, any provisional liquidator, the proposed administrator, the registrar of companies, the Keeper of the Register of Inhibitions and Adjudications and to the company if the petition was presented by the directors or by creditors.[30] In the period between the presentation of the petition and the making of the order or the dismissal of the petition, no resolution may be passed or order made for the winding-up of the company, securities over the company's property cannot be enforced, goods under a hire-purchase agreement[31] cannot be repossessed except with the leave of the court and no proceedings or diligence may be commenced or continued against the company or its property without the leave of the court.[32] However, a liquidation petition can be presented and an administrative receiver can be appointed and an administrative receiver, whenever appointed, can carry out his functions.[33] Where there is an administrative receiver in office when the petition is presented the "freeze" period does not begin to run until the person by or on whose behalf the receiver was appointed consents to the making of the administration order.[34] The court has power to make an interim order on hearing a petition[35] and it has been suggested in England that, while there is no power to appoint an interim administrator, the court could appoint a person to take control of the company until the petition is disposed of[36]; in Scotland an interim administrator has been appointed.[37]

---

[25] See para. 20.9.
[26] Other than an insurance company; s.8(4). An order can now be made in respect of a bank: Banks (Administration Proceedings) Order 1989 (S.I. 1989 No. 1276). The first Scottish order was made on January 19, 1987 in respect of John McMillan (Gleniffer Bakery) Ltd.: Hughes (1987) 3 I.L. & P. 66.
[27] s.9(1). As to the content of the petition, see R.C. 209(1): Sh.Ct. Ins. Rule 10.
[28] Ins. Rule 2.1.
[29] ss.9(2), 251. The English definition of an administrative receiver is slightly wider: s.29(2).
[30] Ins. Rule 2.2; R.C. 210; Sh.Ct. Ins. Rule 11.
[31] A hire-purchase agreement includes a conditional sale agreement, a sale of goods agreement with retention of title, and a hire of goods which is capable of subsisting for more than three months: ss.10(4), 251.
[32] s.10(1). This is affected by the financial markets régime: C.A. 1989, s.175; para. 20.9.
[33] s.10(2).
[34] s.10(3).
[35] s.9(4).
[36] *Re a Company (No. 00175 of 1987)* [1987] B.C.L.C. 467.
[37] St. Clair & Drummond Young, pp. 92, 98.

The order
26.4 If an administrative receiver has already been appointed the court must dismiss the petition unless the person who appointed the receiver has consented to the making of the order or the security under which the receiver was appointed would be liable to be avoided as a gratuitous alienation, an unfair or fraudulent preference at common law, under s.245 of the 1986 Act, or because the security has not been registered.[38] Otherwise the court may make the order if it is satisfied that the company is or is likely to become unable to pay its debts[39] and it considers that the making of an order would be likely to achieve one or more of the following purposes:

(a) the survival of the company, and the whole or any part of its undertaking, as a going concern[40];
(b) the approval of a voluntary arrangement;
(c) the sanctioning of a compromise or arrangement between the company, its members or creditors;
(d) a more advantageous realisation of the company's assets than would be effected on a winding up.[41]

It need not be more probable than not that the purpose would be achieved.[42] In deciding whether an order should be made the interests of secured creditors are of less weight than those of unsecured creditors.[43]

Effect of order
26.5 The administration order directs that during the period for which the order is in force the affairs, business and property of the company shall be managed by an administrator appointed by the court.[44] On the making of the order any petition for the winding up of the company must be dismissed and any administrative receiver vacates office.[45] No resolution may be passed or order made for the winding up of the company, no administrative receiver under a floating charge can be appointed, securities over the company's property[46] cannot be enforced nor can any step be taken to re-possess goods in the company's possession under a hire-purchase agreement except with the consent of the administrator or the court. No proceedings or execution of diligence may be commenced or continued except with the consent of the administrator or the court.[47] Proceedings before the Civil Aviation Authority for revocation of the company's air transport licence are not affected.[48]

Invoices, orders and business letters of the company must disclose the

---

[38] s.9(3). Amended C.A. 1989, Sched. 16, para. 3(2).
[39] ss.8(1), 123.
[40] A "hive-down" is not the survival of the company: *Re Rowbotham Baxter Ltd.* [1990] 3 C.L.C. 397.
[41] s.8(3).
[42] *Re Harris Simons Constructions Ltd.* [1989] 1 W.L.R. 368; *Re Primlaks (U.K.) Ltd.* [1989] B.C.L.C. 734; cf. *Re Consumer and Industrial Press Ltd.* [1988] B.C.L.C. 177.
[43] *Re Imperial Motors (U.K.) Ltd.* [1990] B.C.L.C. 29.
[44] s.8(2).
[45] s.11(1).
[46] Aircraft leased to the company were held to be the company's "property": *Bristol Airport plc* v. *Powdrill* [1990] 2 W.L.R. 1362.
[47] s.11(3). As to "proceedings", see *Bristol Airport plc* v. *Powdrill, supra*, at p. 1377.
[48] *Air Ecosse Ltd.* v. *Civil Aviation Authority*, 1987 S.L.T. 751.

existence of the administration order.[49] Notice of the making of the order must be forthwith published in the *Edinburgh Gazette* and in a newspaper circulating in the company's business area, and sent within 28 days to the known creditors.[50]

Course of the administration

The administrator, who must be a qualified insolvency practitioner,[51] may do all such things as may be necessary for the management of the affairs, business and property of the company and has a number of specified powers.[52] Any power of the company or its officers under statute, the memorandum or the articles to interfere with the exercise of the administrator's powers is not exercisable except with the administrator's consent.[53] In exercising his powers the administrator is deemed to act as the company's agent.[54] A person dealing with the administrator in good faith and for value is not concerned to inquire whether the administrator is acting within his powers.[55] The administrator may remove and appoint directors of the company and call any meeting of the members or creditors.[56] He may remove a receiver of part of the company's property.[57] He must take into his custody or under his control all the property to which the company is or appears to be entitled.[58] He may utilise the provisions of the Act dealing with gratuitous alienations[59] unfair preferences[60] extortionate credit transactions,[61] the avoidance of floating charges,[62] supplies by public utilities,[63] and the ingathering of the company's property.[64] The officers and other persons concerned with the company may be required to submit to him statements as to the affairs of the company.[65] Within three months of the making of the order the administrator must send to the Registrar of Companies and to all creditors a statement of his proposals for achieving the purpose or purposes specified in the order and lay a copy of the statement before a meeting of creditors.[66] Entitlement to vote is determined as it is for claims in a liquidation[67] with the date of the administration order substituted for the date of liquidation and with some modification of the rules as to secured creditors.[68] Approval requires a majority in value of those voting,

26.6

---

[49] s.12.
[50] s.21; Ins. Rule 2.3.
[51] ss.388–389.
[52] s.14(1), Sched. 1.
[53] s.14(4).
[54] s.14(5).
[55] s.14(6).
[56] s.14(2).
[57] s.11(2).
[58] s.17(1). See also s.234.
[59] See para. 25.8(*a*). He has power to reduce alienations under the common law: s.242(7).
[60] See para. 25.8(*c*). He has power to challenge fraudulent preferences under the common law rule: s.243(6).
[61] See para. 25.8(*e*).
[62] See para. 9.12.
[63] See para. 25.4 n. 48.
[64] s.14.
[65] s.22; Ins. Rules 2.4–2.6.
[66] s.23; Ins. Rule 2.7.
[67] Ins. Rules 4.15–4.17.
[68] Ins. Rule 7.9.

in person or by proxy.[69] If the meeting of creditors approves of the administrator's proposals the administrator must manage the affairs, business and the property of the company in accordance with those proposals.[70] If the proposals are not approved, the court may discharge the order.[71] The meeting may approve the proposals with modifications but only if the administrator consents to each modification.[72] The meeting may elect a creditors' committee.[73] The administrator must summon a meeting of creditors if one-tenth of them in value so request or if he is directed to do so by the court.[74]

Revision of proposals

26.7 There is provision for substantial revisions of the administrator's proposals.[75] Any creditor or member of the company may apply to the court by petition for relief on the ground that the company's affairs, business and property are being managed by the administrator in a manner which is unfairly prejudicial to the interests of its creditors or members generally or some part of the members or creditors.[76] The administrator may at any time apply to the court for the administration order to be discharged and shall do so if it appears to him that the purposes of the order have been achieved or are incapable of achievement or if he is required to do so by a meeting of the company's creditors.[77]

Provision is made for the vacation of office by, and discharge or release of, the administrator.[78]

Creditors with fixed securities

26.8 The effect of the order is that no steps can be taken to enforce any security over the company's property except with the consent of the administrator or the leave of the court.[79] "Security" is defined to include any right of lien or preference and any right of retention (other than a right of compensation or set off) so securities arising by operation of law including the landlord's hypothec are affected.[80] An airport operator's statutory right of detention of aircraft is a "security."[81] Where the security is not one which as created was a floating charge, the administrator can apply to the court for an order authorising him to dispose of the property subject to the security as if it were not so subject and the court may authorise the disposal if it is satisfied that the disposal would be likely to

---

[69] Ins. Rule 7.12(1).
[70] s.17(2).
[71] s.24(5).
[72] s.24(2).
[73] s.26(1).
[74] s.17(3).
[75] s.25. See *Re Smallman Construction Ltd.* [1989] B.C.L.C. 420.
[76] s.27.
[77] s.18.
[78] ss.19–20.
[79] ss.10(1)(*b*), 11(3)(*c*); *Royal Trust Bank* v. *Buchler* [1989] B.C.L.C. 130. It would seem from *Re Atlantic Computers plc* [1990] 6 I.L. & P. 66 (discussed in para. 26.11) that the court may quite readily give leave.
[80] s.248(*b*)(ii).
[81] *Bristol Airport plc* v. *Powdrill* [1990] 2 W.L.R. 1362.

promote the purposes of the administration order.[82] It is, however, a condition of such an order that the administrator shall apply towards discharging the sums secured by the security the net proceeds of the disposal and, where those proceeds are less than such amount as may be determined by the court to be the net amount which would be realised on the sale of the property in the open market by a willing vendor, such sums as may be required to make good the deficiency[83]; the source of the funds from which this deficiency payment is made will be discussed *infra*.[84] If there are two securities over the property these sums are applied in discharging the securities in the order of their priorities.[85] On making the disposal, the administrator must grant to the disponee an appropriate document of transfer or conveyance and that document, or where any recording, intimation or registration of the document is a legal requirement for completion of title to the property, that recording, intimation or registration, has the effect of freeing the property from the security.[86]

A slight problem arises where a creditor has a possessory lien, as in the case of a carrier. The effect of the administration order is that he cannot take steps to enforce his lien and he must therefore deliver the goods to the company. It would seem that the goods are then no longer "subject to a security" and the administrator need not obtain authorisation from the court if he wishes to dispose of them. It has been suggested in England[87] that the court might preserve the rights of the holder of the lien. The same kind of problem may arise in relation to goods held under a pledge but it is thought that for the pledgee to retain possession of the goods and to refuse to deliver them up to the administrator is not an "enforcing" of the security. The statutory machinery does not seem to be adapted to deal with a security in an *ex facie* absolute form, for example, a registered transfer of shares; can the administrator grant a transfer of shares which are registered in the name of the creditor? Or is such an arrangement not a "security"? It would seem that the landlord cannot take any steps to enforce or protect his hypothec so the administrator is free to reduce the scope of the hypothec by removing *invecta et illata* from the premises. Only securities over the company's property are affected so the making of an administration order does not prevent the operation of a cautionary obligation.

Property subject to a floating charge

Where there is property subject to a security which, as created, was a floating charge, the administrator can dispose of or otherwise exercise his powers in relation to that property as if it were not subject to the security.[88] However, where such property is disposed of by the administrator, the holder of the security is given the same priority in respect of any property representing directly or indirectly the property

26.9

---

[82] s.15(2). See *Re ARV Aviation Ltd.* [1989] B.C.L.C. 664. As to securities over debts, see Paget, p. 281.
[83] s.15(5).
[84] See para. 26.9.
[85] s.15(6).
[86] s.16(1).
[87] *Bristol Airport plc v. Powdrill, supra.*
[88] s.15(1), (3).

disposed of, as he would have had in respect of the property subject to the security.[89] This would not appear to be a particularly satisfactory situation from the point of view of the holder of the security as it may be difficult to identify his surrogate security once it is in the form of cash. Moreover, certain payments can be made out of the assets subject to his security in priority to his security; these are, first any sums payable in respect of debts or liabilities incurred under contracts entered into or contracts of employment adopted by the admininstrator in the carrying out of his functions,[90] and, secondly, the administrator's remuneration and expenses.[91] Then, in addition to these payments which are expressly given priority over the floating charge, there are the "deficiency payments" which have to be made when the administrator disposes of property subject to a fixed security[92]; it would seem that these payments may well have to come out of the assets subject to the floating charge. The result of the administration order will often be the erosion of the floating charge holder's security and that is no doubt why he is given a veto on the making of the order if his security extends over the whole, or substantially the whole, of the company's property.

Unsecured creditors

26.10 The effect of the order is that a creditor cannot commence an action against the company except with the consent of the administrator or the leave of the court.[93] As the making of the administration order does not have the effect of interrupting prescription, the court will presumably be prepared to grant leave to raise an action where the prescriptive period is about to expire. The making of the offer does not have the effect of transferring the company's rights against an insurer to the third party under the Third Parties (Rights against Insurers) Act 1930.[94] Creditors whose debts would have been preferential in a liquidation are not in any privileged position during the administration but if a winding-up order is made immediately upon the discharge of the administration order the relevant date for calculation of the preferential debts is the date of the making of the administration order so that the preference is not lost because of the running of time during the subsistence of the administration order[95] Similarly if a voluntary arrangement is proposed while the administration order is in force the relevant date for calculation of the preferential debts is again the date of the making of the administration order.[96] The definition of "security" excludes a right of compensation or set-off so the administration order has no effect on the right of a debtor of the company to plead compensation or set-off.[97]

---

[89] s.15(4).
[90] s.19(5).
[91] s.19(4).
[92] See para. 26.8.
[93] I.A., s.11(3)(*d*). As to the client bank account of an incorporated solicitors' practice, see Solicitors (Scotland) Act 1980, s.42(2A).
[94] Insolvency Act 1985, Sched. 8, para. 7(2).
[95] I.A., s.387(3)(*a*).
[96] I.A., s.387(2)(*a*).
[97] I.A., s.248(*b*).

Goods on hire purchase, etc.

Where goods are in the possession of the company under a hire **26.11** purchase, conditional sale, leasing or retention of title agreement, the administrator can, as in the case of property subject to a fixed security, apply to the court for authority to dispose of the goods as if all rights of the owner under the agreement were vested in the company[98]; authority is given if the disposal would be likely to promote the purposes of the administration order. As in the case of the property subject to a fixed security, the net proceeds and a sum to make up any deficiency in value have to be applied towards discharging the sums payable under the agreement.[99] The disposal has the effect of extinguishing, as against the disponee, all rights of the owner of the goods under the agreement. What happens if the administrator, instead of selling the goods subject to the agreement, uses them in a manufacturing process or incorporates them in other goods? The answer seems to be that he cannot do this; section 15(1) allows him to exercise his powers in relation to property which is subject to a floating charge but section 15(2) pointedly refrains from conferring this facility in relation to property subject to fixed securities or hire purchase and similar agreements. Section 15(5) implies that a "disposal" must be a sale.

If the administrator sells goods held under a "chattel leasing agreement," *i.e.*, an agreement for the hiring of goods which is capable of existing for more than three months,[1] he must apply the proceeds towards "discharging the sums . . . payable under the hire-purchase agreement." In the case of an operating lease, what sums will be payable under the agreement? The balance of rent for the current period of the lease? Can the administrator keep the balance of the capital value of the asset?

Of course, the owner of the goods can apply for leave to recover them under s.11 and the decision of the Court of Appeal in *Re Atlantic Computers plc*[2] indicates that leave may be granted fairly readily. The factors which the court will consider include the extent to which the purposes of the administration order would be impeded if leave were given; the point that an administration for the benefit of the unsecured creditors should not be conducted at the expense of those who have proprietary rights; whether significant loss would be caused to the owner by refusal of leave; the financial position of the company. In the same case it was held that, if goods are retained by the company, the rentals do not rank as administration expenses and are not payable in priority to the claims of the pre-administration creditors.

Incomplete diligence

A major obscurity of the provisions as to administration orders is **26.12** encountered where diligence has been begun before the date of the order but the subjects affected are still part of the property of the company: a poinding not yet followed by a sale; an arrestment not followed by a furthcoming. The effect of the order is that diligence cannot be

---

[98] s.15(2)(*b*). Articles leased by the company and then sub-leased are in the possession of the company; *Re Atlantic Computers plc.* [1990] 6 I.L. & P. 66.
[99] s.15(3).
[1] I.A., s.251.
[2] s.251.

"continued" but it is thought that this does not annul any nexus which the diligence already done has placed on property. If such property can be said to be subject to a security there is no problem and the provisions of para. 26.8 *supra* can largely be applied, although where there is an arrestment on the dependence there could not be immediate payment of the proceeds to the creditor in every case.[3] There is no doubt that in some statutory contexts diligence has been held to create a "security" but it would seem that that cannot be the result under the Insolvency Act; the definition of "security"[4] would not seem to extend to the effect of diligence unless it is "any . . . preference"; section 11(3) deals in separate paragraphs with securities and execution; the diligence may subsequently be rendered ineffectual if the administration order is discharged and liquidation follows. If diligence does not create a security the result would seem to be that the administrator cannot dispose of goods which have been poinded and he cannot obtain payment of funds which have been arrested; an inhibition prevents the alienation of heritage; where there has been an adjudication the legal continues to run. It has been suggested[5] that an administration order constitutes apparent insolvency and therefore brings about equalisation of diligence but it is difficult to bring the making of the order within the statutory definition of apparent insolvency.[6]

---

[3] s.15(5).
[4] s.248(*b*).
[5] St. Clair & Drummond Young, p. 177.
[6] B.A., s.7(1), (4); see para. 20.1.

CHAPTER 27

ASSIGNATION OF DEBTS

Assignability

A debt is, in general, transferable by assignation.[1] 27.1
In particular the following are assignable: a *spes successionis*[2]; uncalled capital[3]; a shareholder's interest in the surplus assets of a company in liquidation[4]; a claim for damages (including *solatium*) in respect of personal injuries[5]; damages for breach of contract[6]; the share of a limited partner[7] (with the consent of the general partners); a participation in a European Economic Interest Grouping (with the unanimous authorisation of the other members)[8]; a floating charge.[9] Rights to damages for patrimonial loss and loss of society awards under the Damages (Scotland) Act 1976, are probably assignable but the right to the loss of society award is extinguished by the cedent's death.[10]

The following are not assignable: uncalled capital of a limited company where a resolution under s.120 of the Companies Act 1985 has been passed[11]; an amount payable under letters of guarantee by members of a limited company operative only on liquidation[12] (except where the guarantees are by non-members[13]); social security benefits,[14] the wages of a seaman.[15] A policy under the Married Women's Policies of Assurance (Scotland) Act 1880 is now assignable.[16]

Alimentary liferents and other periodical payments of an alimentary character are not assignable[17] but: (i) each term's payment when it falls due and is reduced into possession can be paid as the beneficiary directs,[18] (ii) arrears of payments can be assigned,[19] (iii) the provision can be

---

[1] Bell, *Comm.*, II, 15.
[2] *Wood* v. *Begbie* (1850) 12 D. 963; *Trappes* v. *Meredith* (1871) 10 M. 38. But see *McEwan's Trs.* v. *Macdonald*, 1909 S.C. 57.
[3] *Liqr. of Union Club Ltd.* v. *Edinburgh Life Assurance Co.* (1906) 8 F. 1143; *Ballachulish Slate Quarries* v. *Menzies* (1908) 45 S.L.R. 667.
[4] *Jackson* v. *Elphick* (1902) 10 S.L.T. 146.
[5] *Cole-Hamilton* v. *Boyd*, 1963 S.C. (H.L.) 1.
[6] *Constant* v. *Kincaid & Co.* (1902) 4 F. 901.
[7] Limited Partnership Act 1907, s.6(5)(*b*).
[8] Reg. 2137/85/EEC Art. 22.
[9] *Libertas-Kommerz GmbH* v. *Johnson*, 1977 S.C. 191.
[10] Damages (Scotland) Act 1976, s.3. See *Traill* v. *Actieselskabat Dalbeattie Ltd.* (1904) 6 F. 798.
[11] *Re Mayfair Property Company* [1898] 2 Ch. 28.
[12] *Robertson* v. *British Linen Co.* (1891) 18 R. 1225.
[13] *Lloyds Bank* v. *Morrison & Son*, 1927 S.C. 571.
[14] Social Security Act 1975, s.87(1). An award under the statutory Criminal Injuries Compensation Scheme, when it is in force, will not be assignable: Criminal Justice Act 1988, s.117.
[15] Merchant Shipping Act 1970, s.11.
[16] Married Women's Policies of Assurance (Scotland) (Amendment) Act 1980, s.3.
[17] *Rennie* v. *Ritchie* (1845) 4 Bell's App. 221.
[18] *Hewats* v. *Robertson* (1881) 9 R. 175.
[19] *Drew* v. *Drew* (1870) 9 M. 163.

assigned in so far as it is excessive as aliment[20] but the court will not determine the excess for the future.[21]

There is little authority as to the effect of an express contractual provision that a debt will be non-assignable.[22] An assignation may carry future or contingent debts.[23]

Form of assignation

27.2   Mere delivery of the document of debt is not sufficient.[24] Although it has been said that writing is necessary to prove the transaction but not to constitute it, it is doubtful whether a verbal assignation is possible.[25] A form of assignation is given in the Transmission of Moveable Property (Scotland) Act 1862, which can be used for bonds, personal property or effects of every kind.[26] There is also a special statutory form for policies of assurance.[27] But it is clearly established that no special form is essential: "no words directly importing conveyance are necessary to constitute an assignation, but any words giving authority or directions, which if fairly carried out will operate a transference, are sufficient to make an assignation."[28] Accordingly, the following have been held valid: a letter containing the words "I. . . . hand over my life policy to my daughter" delivered with a certified copy of the policy[29]; a letter containing the words "I hand you two policies of insurance. . . . which I give you as an added security for the loan" which was delivered with the policies.[30] However, the wording must be capable of being construed as effecting an immediate transference of the cedent's right.[31] Presentment of a bill of exchange or cheque operates as an intimated assignation of the sum for which it is drawn in favour of the holder.[32] Presentment of a bill of exchange accepted "payable at" a bank operates as an intimated assignation of the funds of the acceptor in the bank.[33]

It seems now to be established that a mandate by the creditor authorising the debtor to pay to a third party or authorising the third party to receive payment from the debtor may be equivalent to an assignation.[34] If the creditor is indebted to the third party it is a mandate *in rem suam* and cannot be unilaterally revoked by the creditor. The *tempus inspiciendi* is the time of intimation of the mandate and if the creditor was not indebted to the third party at that time the mandate does

---

[20] *Claremont's Trs.* v. *Claremont* (1896) 4 S.L.T. 144.

[21] *Cuthbert* v. *Cuthbert's Trs.*, 1908 S.C. 967; *Coles, Petr.*, 1951 S.C. 608.

[22] Gloag, p. 413.

[23] *Flowerdew* v. *Buchan* (1835) 13 S. 615; *Carter* v. *McIntosh* (1862) 24 D. 925; *Allan & Son* v. *Brown and Lightbody* (1890) 6 Sh.Ct.Rep. 278.

[24] *UK Life Assurance Co.* v. *Dixon* (1838) 16 S. 1277.

[25] Gloag, p. 180; see *McCracken* v. *McCracken* (1928) 44 Sh.Ct.Rep. 11.

[26] Scheds. A and B.

[27] Policies of Assurance Act 1867.

[28] per L. J.-C. Inglis, *Carter* v. *McIntosh* (1862) 24 D. 925 at 933; see also *McCutcheon* v. *McWilliam* (1876) 3 R. 565; *International Fibre Syndicate Ltd.* v. *Dawson* (1901) 3 F. (H.L.) 32.

[29] *Brownlee* v. *Robb*, 1907 S.C. 1302.

[30] *Caledonian Insurance Co.* v. *Beattie* (1898) 5 S.L.T. 349.

[31] *Gallemos Ltd. (in receivership)* v. *Barratt (Falkirk) Ltd.*, 1990 S.L.T. 98.

[32] Bills of Exchange Act 1882, s.53(2). See para. 66.

[33] *British Linen Co.* v. *Rainey's Tr.* (1885) 12 R. 825.

[34] *Carter* v. *McIntosh, supra*; *Executive Council for the City of Glasgow* v. *T. Sutherland Henderson Ltd.*, 1955 S.L.T. (Sh.Ct.) 33.

not become irrevocable by reason only of the subsequent creation of indebtedness. The intention of the granter must be determined from the terms of the document and the circumstances in which it was granted.[35]

A mere mandate which does not amount to an assignation is revocable by the granter and falls by his sequestration.[36]

Intimation: form

Intimation of an assignation is necessary to complete the assignee's title and to put the debtor in bad faith to pay to anyone other than the assignee.[37] It is usually made by the assignee but can be made by the assignor on his behalf.[38] The Act of 1862 provides two methods of intimation.[39] The first is by a notary public delivering to the debtor a copy of the assignation certified as correct; a certificate by the notary in the form of Schedule C to the Act is sufficient evidence of intimation. The second is by transmitting a copy of the assignation, certified as correct, to the debtor by post; a written acknowledgement by the debtor is sufficient evidence of intimation. The Policies of Assurance Act 1867 provides that an assignee shall have no right to sue on the policy unless a written notice of the date and purport of the assignation is given to the assurance company at its principal place of business and the date of receipt of this notice regulates the priority of the claims.[40] Upon request and payment of a 25p fee, the company must give an acknowledgement of receipt signed by a principal officer which is conclusive evidence against the company.[41]

27.3

Generally, however, intimation can be proved *rebus ipsis et factis*.[42] The terms must be such as to convey to the debtor that the debt has been transferred and that the transferee is asserting his claim to the debt from the debtor; the amount of the debt being assigned must be stated; general statements may not suffice; letters from the debtor to the intimator can be looked at.[43] It seems that intimation to the law agents of a trust is sufficient intimation to the trustees[44] although the general rule is that intimation to the debtor's factor is not sufficient.[45] Where one of two trustees was ill, intimation to the other who held the funds and administered the trust, was held sufficient.[46] Intimation to one of several co-obligants completes the assignee's right but it does not interpel the others from paying to the cedent.[47] Intimation to the principal debtor operates against the cautioner.[48] Intimation to a corporation is made at

---

[35] *National Commercial Bank of Scotland Ltd.* v. *Millar's Tr.*, 1964 S.L.T. (Notes) 57.
[36] *McKenzie* v. *Campbell* (1894) 21 R. 904.
[37] *per* Lord Young, *Grigor Allan* v. *Urquhart* (1887) 15 R. 56 at 61.
[38] *Libertas-Kommerz GmbH* v. *Johnson*, 1977 S.C. 191.
[39] Transmission of Moveable Property (Scotland) Act 1862, s.2.
[40] s.3.
[41] s.6.
[42] *Hill* v. *Lindsay* (1847) 10 D. 78.
[43] *Wallace* v. *Davies* (1853) 15 D. 688; *Donaldson* v. *Ord* (1855) 17 D. 1053; *Libertas-Kommerz GmbH, supra*; *Gallemos Ltd. (in receivership)* v. *Barratt (Falkirk) Ltd., supra*.
[44] *Browne's Tr.* v. *Anderson* (1901) 4 F. 305.
[45] Bell, *Lects.*, i, 318; *E. of Aberdeen* v. *Merchiston's Crs.* (1729) Mor. 867, seems to be an exceptional case.
[46] *Jameson* v. *Sharp* (1887) 14 R. 643.
[47] Ersk., III, 1, 10.
[48] *Mosman* v. *Bells* (1670) 2 Br.Sup. 457.

common law to the treasurer[49] but documents may be served on a limited company by leaving them at, or sending them by post to, the registered office.[50]

It should be noted that, where a debt has been assigned *ex facie* absolutely but truly in security, a further assignation of the reversionary interest should be intimated to the prior assignee and not to the original debtor.[51]

Intimation: equivalents

27.4 The following are equivalent to intimation: the raising of an action by the assignee for recovery of the debt[52]; the production of the assignation (not the lodging of a claim[53]) in a multiplepoinding for distribution of the fund assigned[54]; diligence by the assignee[55]; recording the assignation in the General Register of Sasines[56]; the presentation of a bill of exchange for acceptance or payment.[57]

The following are *not* equivalent to intimation: registration of the assignation in the Books of Council and Session[58]; in the case of an assignation of uncalled capital, the reading of a report mentioning the assignation at a meeting attended by some of the shareholders.[59]

Intimation is unnecessary where the debtor is a party[60] (not a witness[61]) to the assignation as cedent[62] or assignee.[63] But where an assignation of his shares in a friendly investment society was granted by the society's manager it was held that his private knowledge did not make intimation to the society unnecessary.[64]

Otherwise the effect of the debtor's private knowledge of an unintimated assignation is doubtful. It is clear that it is of no effect in a competition with other creditors[65]; but it is not clear whether it even puts the debtor *in mala fide* to pay the cedent.[66] Certain actings on the part of the debtor, however, make intimation unnecessary—a promise to pay to the assignee proved *scripto*[67]; a written acknowledgment of indebtedness

---

[49] *Keir* v. *Menzies* (1739) Mor. 850.
[50] Companies Act 1985, s.725.
[51] *Whittall* v. *Christie* (1894) 22 R. 91; *Ayton* v. *Romanes* (1895) 3 S.L.T. 203; in practice intimation will be made to both (Burns, *Conveyancing Practice* (4th ed.), p. 679).
[52] *Elphingston* v. *Ord* (1624) Mor. 858; Ersk., III, 5, 4; *Watt's Trs.* v. *Pinkney* (1853) 16 D. 279 at 288.
[53] *M.P.-Mounsey* (1896) 4 S.L.T. 46.
[54] *Dougal* v. *Gordon* (1795) Mor. 851; *Carter* v. *McIntosh* (1862) 24 D. 925.
[55] *Whyte* v. *Neish* (1622) Mor. 854; Ersk., III, 5, 4.
[56] *Paul* v. *Boyd's Trs.* (1835) 13 S. 818; *Edmond* v. *Gordon* (1858) 3 Macq. 116.
[57] Bills of Exchange Act 1882, s.53(2).
[58] *Tod's Trs.* v. *Wilson* (1869) 7 M. 1100.
[59] *Liqr. of Union Club Ltd.* v. *Edinburgh Life Assurance Co.* (1906) 8 F. 1143.
[60] *Turnbull* v. *Stewart & Inglis* (1751) Mor. 868; see also *Crs. of L. Ballenden* v. *Countess of Dalhousie* (1707) Mor. 865, where the assignation was *in gremio* of the bond constituting the debt.
[61] *Murray* v. *Durham* (1622) Mor. 855.
[62] *Paul* v. *Boyd's Trs.* (1835) 13 S. 818; *Browne's Tr.* v. *Anderson* (1901) 4 F. 305.
[63] *Miller* v. *Learmonth* (1870) 42 J. 418; *Ayton* v. *Romanes* (1895) 3 S.L.T. 203.
[64] *Grigor Allan* v. *Urquhart* (1887) 15 R. 56.
[65] *L. Rollo* v. *Laird of Niddrie* (1665) 1 Br.Sup. 510; *Dickson* v. *Trotter* (1776) Mor. 873.
[66] *Adamson* v. *McMitchell* (1624) Mor. 859; *L. Westraw* v. *Williamson & Carmichael* (1626) Mor. 859; *cf. Leith* v. *Garden* (1703) Mor. 865.
[67] *Home* v. *Murray* (1674) Mor. 863.

to the assignee[68]; payment of interest or of part of the debt to the assignee[69]; entering into a submission to arbitration relating to the debt with the assignee.[70] Mere "communings" with the assignee are not sufficient.[71]

Intimation: importance

Intimation is not necessary to make the assignation effectual in a question with the cedent or his executors.[72] The executors are bound to warrant the assignation. The importance of intimation appears in questions with third parties:

(a) If the cedent is sequestrated before intimation the trustee in the sequestration is preferred to the debt.[73] Except in the case of registered titles,[74] the trustee does not require to intimate his title in order to obtain his preference because the sequestration itself is equivalent to an intimated assignation as at the date of sequestration.[75] The same principle holds in liquidations.[76]

(b) The debtor can safely pay to the cedent prior to intimation[77] and the cedent can treat with him and give him an effectual discharge.[78]

(c) If the cedent, after granting the assignation, assigns the same debt to a third party who takes in good faith and for value and whose assignation is intimated before that of the first assignee, the third party is preferred to the debt.[79]

(d) If a creditor of the cedent executes an arrestment in the hands of the debtor after the granting of the assignation but before intimation, the arrester is preferred.[80]

(e) The debtor can plead against the assignee any defence which he could have pleaded against the cedent provided that the defence was available to him prior to intimation. So, if the debtor acquired, prior to intimation, a debt due by the cedent, he can plead compensation on it against the assignee.[81] If, however, the debt was acquired by an assignation, this assignation must have been intimated to the cedent before intimation of the assignation granted by the cedent.[82] If the

27.5

---

[68] *Wallace v. Davies* (1853) 15 D. 688.
[69] *Livingston v. Lindsay* (1626) Mor. 860.
[70] *Ritchie v. McLachlan* (1870) 8 M. 815.
[71] *Faculty of Advocates v. Dickson* (1718) Mor. 866; cf. *L. of Dunipace v. Sandis* (1624) Mor. 859.
[72] *Grant v. Gray* (1828) 6 S. 489; *Brownlee v. Robb*, 1907 S.C. 1302; *Strawbridge's Trs. v. Bank of Scotland*, 1935 S.L.T. 568.
[73] *Tod's Trs. v. Wilson* (1869) 7 M. 1100.
[74] *Morrison v. Harrison* (1876) 3 R. 406.
[75] B.A. 1985, s.31(4).
[76] *Liqr. of Union Club Ltd. v. Edinburgh Life Assurance Co.* (1906) 8 F. 1143; I.A. 1986, ss.86, 129. But see para. 25.7.
[77] *McDowal v. Fullertoun* (1714) Mor. 840.
[78] *McGill v. Laurestoun* (1558) Mor. 843.
[79] *Campbell's Trs. v. Whyte* (1884) 11 R. 1078.
[80] *Strachan v. McDougle* (1835) 13 S. 954; for competition with an executor-creditor, see para. 29.7.
[81] *Shiells v. Ferguson, Davidson & Co.* (1876) 4 R. 250.
[82] *Wallace v. Edgar* (1663) Mor. 837; *Alison v. Duncan* (1711) Mor. 2657.

defence became available to the debtor after intimation it cannot be taken against the assignee.[83]

A person seeking to rely on a failure to intimate may be personally barred from doing so if, for example, he himself in another capacity was responsible, or partially responsible, for the failure. The trustee in his sequestration may be similarly barred.[84]

Title to sue

27.6   If at the date of raising an action the pursuer has no title to sue, the defect cannot be cured by a subsequent assignation or retrocession.[85] It was thought at one time[86] that where a party granted an assignation and then raised an action he had a good title to sue if he obtained a retrocession during the course of the action, but this is not correct.[87] Apparently, the position is different where the pursuer's title to sue has been affirmed although it is not complete or is subject to some qualification. So, where the assignation of his interest granted by the pursuer before the raising of the action was rescinded in the English courts on the ground of misrepresentation during the course of the action it was held that the pursuer had a good title to sue.[88]

An assignee can sue in the name of the cedent or in his own name; normally there is no objection to the assignee's suing in the name of the cedent and concluding for payment to himself.[89]

Assignee's right

27.7   *Assignatus utitur jure auctoris.* The assignee has no better right than the cedent had and the debtor can take any defence against the assignee which he could have taken against the cedent and which was available to him prior to intimation. So the insurers can reduce a policy against an onerous assignee on the ground of the false statements made by the cedent in the proposal form[90]; there may be a duty on the insurers to communicate to the assignee any objection to the validity of the policy which comes to their knowledge.[91] Similarly, where a superior had not fulfilled his obligation to build streets and sewers, the vassal could retain the feuduty in a question with the superior's assignee.[92] The assignee of a gratuitous allowance cannot sue the donor.[93] A plea of compensation

---

[83] *Chambers' J.F.* v. *Vertue* (1893) 20 R. 257; *Macpherson's J.F.* v. *Mackay*, 1915 S.C. 1011.
[84] *Graeme's Tr.* v. *Giersberg* (1888) 15 R. 691.
[85] *Symington* v. *Campbell* (1894) 21 R. 434; Maclaren, *Court of Session Practice*, p. 189. See also *Microwave Systems (Scotland) Ltd.* v. *Electro-Physiological Instruments Ltd.*, 1971 S.L.T. (Notes) 38.
[86] Maclaren, *op. cit.*, p. 219.
[87] *Bentley* v. *MacFarlane*, 1964 S.C. 76; *Cobham* v. *Minter*, 1986 S.L.T. 336.
[88] *Westville Shipping Co. Ltd.* v. *Abram S.S. Co.*, 1923 S.C. (H.L.) 68—distinguished in *Bentley* v. *MacFarlane, supra, per* L.P. Clyde at p. 80, Lord Guthrie at p. 82; *Lanarkshire Health Board* v. *Banafa*, 1987 S.L.T. 229.
[89] *Blyth Dry Docks & Shipbuilding Co. Ltd.* v. *Commissioners for Port of Calcutta*, 1972 S.L.T. (Notes) 7.
[90] *Scottish Widows' Fund* v. *Buist* (1876) 3 R. 1078; *Scottish Equitable Life Assurance Society* v. *Buist* (1877) 4 R. 1076; affd. (1878) 5 R. (H.L.) 64.
[91] *per* L. P. Inglis, *Scottish Equitable Life Assurance Society* v. *Buist, supra,* at p. 1081.
[92] *Arnott's Trs.* v. *Forbes* (1881) 9 R. 89.
[93] *Robertson* v. *Wright* (1873) 1 R. 237.

which could have been taken against the cedent can be taken against the assignee if it arose before intimation.[94] In this connection, it should be noted that the expenses of an action are deemed to arise at its commencement so that where an action was assigned the defender could set off against the assignee an amount awarded to him in respect of expenses.[95]

The nature of the right assigned, however, can be such that it is affected by the actings of the cedent or of other parties after the date of intimation. Where a husband assigned a sum which was to be paid to him by his antenuptial marriage contract trustees on the death of his wife's father if the marriage then subsisted, and the husband was later divorced on the ground of adultery, the assignee obtained nothing.[96] If trustees have a discretion to restrict the cedent's interest to a liferent, or to reduce the amount of revenue payments, the exercise of the discretion—even after intimation—can affect the assignee's right.[97]

Warrandice

Where the assignation is for an onerous cause, there is an implied warrandice that the debt subsists.[98] In the case of a bond, this applies to the obligation of any cautioners as well as to that of the principal debtor. It is also implied that the cedent confers on the assignee everything necessary to make the assignation effectual.[99] There is, however, no implied warrandice as to the debtor's ability to pay. In assignations to a cautioner or co-obligant the implied warrandice is from fact and deed only.[1]

27.8

Bill as transfer

Obviously, if the drawee accepts a bill presented to him there is, in the normal case, a transfer of a debt from the drawer to the holder but it is not clear that a drawee, even if he is indebted to the drawer, is bound to accept a bill presented to him.[2] The transfer of the debt is not dependent upon his acceptance, however, because, by s.53(2) of the Bills of Exchange Act 1882, in Scotland, where the drawee of a bill has in his hands funds available for the payment thereof, the bill operates as an assignation of the sum for which it is drawn in favour of the holder, from the time when the bill is presented to the drawee.[3] Where a bill is accepted "payable at" a bank, presentment to the bank operates as an assignation of the acceptor's funds in the banker's hands to the extent of the sum in the bill.[4]

27.9

---

[94] *Shiells* v. *Ferguson, Davidson & Co.* (1876) 4 R. 250; but obviously not a counter-claim—*J. E. Binstock Miller & Co.* v. *E. Coia & Co. Ltd.* (1957) 73 Sh.Ct.Rep. 178. (Professor McBryde (*Law of Contract in Scotland*, p. 392) criticises this decision but it seems to be right.)
[95] *Livingston* v. *Reid* (1833) 11 S. 878.
[96] *Johnstone-Beattie* v. *Dalzell and Others* (1868) 6 M. 333.
[97] *Weller* v. *Ker* (1866) 4 M. (H.L.) 8; *Train* v. *Buchanan's Trs.*, 1907 S.C. 517; affd. 1908 S.C. (H.L.) 26.
[98] Ersk., II, iii, 27; *Reid* v. *Barclay* (1879) 6 R. 1007.
[99] *Miller* v. *Muirhead* (1894) 21 R. 658.
[1] *Russell* v. *Mudie* (1857) 20 D. 125.
[2] Thomson, *Bills of Exchange* (3rd ed.), p. 228; *Encyclopaedia of the Laws of Scotland*, Vol. II, p. 217.
[3] See, however, as to countermanded cheques, para. 6.8.
[4] *British Linen Co.* v. *Rainey's Tr.* (1885) 12 R. 825.

CHAPTER 28

JOINT AND SEVERAL OBLIGATIONS

Kinds of liability

28.1   Where an obligation is assumed by two or more parties, the liability may be *in solidum* or *pro rata*. If the liability is *in solidum*, any one party is liable, in a question with the creditor, for the whole amount of the debt. If the liability is *pro rata*, any one party is liable only for a *pro rata* (*i.e.* equal) share. Where liability is *in solidum*, the bankruptcy of one obligant does not affect the liability of each of the others for the whole debt. Where liability is *pro rata*, the bankruptcy of the co-debtor does not increase the liability of the others except in cautionary obligations.[1]

There is a presumption in favour of *pro rata* liability[2] but the liability is *in solidum* if the parties are bound "jointly and severally,"[3] "conjunctly and severally,"[4] "severally,"[5] "as co-principals and full debtors,"[6] "as full debtors."[7] The following prima facie indicate *pro rata* liability: "jointly,"[8] "conjunctly,"[9] "each for his own part."[10] *Pro rata* liability was inferred where A bound himself "along with B"[11] and also where the expression was "conjunctly and severally ilk one for his own part."[12]

In certain circumstances joint and several liability is implied. In partnership, each partner is liable jointly and severally for all debts and obligations of the firm incurred while he is a partner.[13] Co-acceptors and co-drawers of bills of exchange and co-makers of a promissory note are liable jointly and severally.[14] That is the position at common law apart altogether from the statutory provision that if a promissory note in the form "I promise to pay . . . ." is signed by two or more persons they are deemed to have incurred joint and several liability.[15] Liability *in solidum* is also implied where several persons contract with an individual for a common object[16] and in particular where a number of persons grant a mandate to the same agent to appear in the same suit in a matter of common interest.[17] There can, of course, be a contrary agreement.[18] Joint

---

[1] *Duke of Montrose* v. *Edmonstone* (1845) 7 D. 759.
[2] Stair, I, 17, 20; Ersk., III, iii, 374; Bell, *Comm.*, I, 361; *Prin.*, § 51.
[3] Bell, *Comm.*, I, 361; *Fleming* v. *Gemmill*, 1908 S.C. 340.
[4] *Dundee Police Commissioners* v. *Straton* (1884) 11 R. 586; *Burns* v. *Martin* (1887) 14 R. (H.L.) 20.
[5] Montgomerie Bell, *Lectures*, I, p. 262.
[6] *Cleghorn* v. *Yorston* (1707) Mor. 14624.
[7] *Cloberhill* v. *Ladyland* (1631) Mor. 14623.
[8] *Coats* v. *Union Bank of Scotland*, 1928 S.C. 711; the point seems to have been conceded in the House of Lords (1929 S.C. (H.L.) 114); Bell, *Comm.*, I, 362, *Prin.*, § 57, is in error here.
[9] *Campbell* v. *Farquhar* (1724) Mor. 14626.
[10] Bell, *Comm.*, I, 362.
[11] *Alexander* v. *Scott* (1827) 6 S. 150.
[12] *Farquhar* v. *McKain* (1638) Mor. 2282.
[13] Partnership Act 1890, s.9.
[14] Bell, *Comm.*, I, 363; *Prin.*, § 61.
[15] Bills of Exchange Act 1882, s.85(2).
[16] *French* v. *Earl of Galloway* (1730) Mor. 14706.
[17] *Walker* v. *Brown* (1803) Mor. App. "Solidum et pro rata," No. 1; *Smith* v. *Harding* (1877) 5 R. 147.
[18] McBryde, *Law of Contract in Scotland*, p. 360.

Right of Relief

wrong-doers[19] and, in certain circumstances, joint purchasers,[20] are liable *in solidum*. Co-obligants in an obligation *ad factum praestandum* incur joint and several liability[21] and this applies also to a claim for damages for failure to perform such an obligation unless the original obligation was clearly alternative.[22] The position of co-cautioners is dealt with elsewhere.[23]

If a joint and several obligation *ex contractu* has not been constituted by writing or decree, the pursuer in an action to enforce the obligation must call all the co-obligants as defenders if that is possible.[24] He need not call those outwith the jurisdiction.[25] If the obligation is constituted by writing the pursuer can bring his action against any one co-obligant; he need not call all the co-obligants.[26] The same holds with regard to joint wrongdoers including trustees sued for breach of trust.[27] In an action on a bond against two obligants bound jointly and severally, where only one remained in the process, it was held that the other could not in that process reduce the bond *ope exceptionis* on the ground of misrepresentation.[28]

On the other hand, where the obligation is *pro rata*, all the obligants must be called if possible[29] although where there were three co-cautioners liable *pro rata* it was held that the creditor could sue two of them for their shares without calling the representatives of the third.[30]

If two co-obligants are bound jointly and severally and decree in absence for the sum sued for is granted against one, the pursuer can continue the action against the other unless it is shown that the decree has been fully satisfied.[31] This does not apply where the taking of decree is an election between principal and agent.[32]

Right of relief

Where there is a contractual liability *in solidum*, an obligant who had paid more than his *pro rata* share of the debt is entitled to recover the excess from the co-obligants;[33] but where the obligants are bound jointly and severally to the creditor but are in fact principal and cautioner, the cautioner is, of course, entitled to total relief from the principal and he may prove the true relationship *prout de jure*.[34] In a question of relief where all the co-obligants are solvent, each is liable only for his *pro rata*

28.2

---

[19] Ersk., III, i, 15.
[20] *Mushet* v. *Harvey* (1710) Mor. 14636; *Reid* v. *Lamond* (1857) 19 D. 265.
[21] Gloag, p. 200.
[22] *Darlington* v. *Gray* (1836) 15 S. 197; *Rankine* v. *Logie Den Land Co.* (1902) 4 F. 1074.
[23] See para. 10.1.
[24] *Neilson* v. *Wilson* (1890) 17 R. 608.
[25] *Muir* v. *Collett* (1862) 24 D. 1119.
[26] *Richmond* v. *Grahame* (1847) 9 D. 633.
[27] *Western Bank* v. *Douglas* (1860) 22 D. 447; *Croskery* v. *Gilmour's Trs.* (1890) 17 R. 697; *Allen* v. *McCombie's Trs.* 1909 S.C. 710.
[28] *Lucarelli* v. *Buchanan*, 1954 S.L.T. (Sh.Ct.) 46.
[29] Mackay, *Manual of Court of Session Practice*, p. 172.
[30] *McArthur* v. *Scott* (1836) 15 S. 270.
[31] *Royal Bank* v. *McKerracher*, 1968 S.L.T. (Sh.Ct.) 77; *Hamilton Leasing Ltd.* v. *Clark*, 1974 S.L.T. (Sh.Ct.) 95.
[32] *Lamont & Co.* v. *Reid* (1926) 42 Sh.Ct.Rep. 262.
[33] Bell, *Prin.*, § 62.
[34] Bell, *Prin.*, § 245; *Thow's Tr.* v. *Young*, 1910 S.C. 588.

share and this is so even where the obligant seeking relief has obtained an assignation of the debt from the creditor.[35] In calculating the number of *pro rata* shares, it is a question of construction of the obligatory document whether or not a firm is to be treated as a co-obligant separate from its partners.[36] Where some of the co-obligants are insolvent, they are ignored in the calculation of the shares.[37] It seems that the obligant seeking relief need not prove the insolvency so long as there is a doubt as to solvency.[38] An obligant seeking relief may rank on the estate of a bankrupt co-obligant for the *pro rata* share unless the creditor has ranked for the same portion of the debt.[39]

Right to assignation

28.3 A co-obligant who has made payment in full is entitled to an assignation of the debt from the creditor.[40] He is also entitled to an assignation of any securities held by the creditor. This, however, applies only where there has been actual payment and not where the creditor has received only a dividend from the obligant's estate.[41] The creditor is entitled to refuse the assignation if he is prejudiced by granting it.[42] He is entitled to refuse to assign a security if another debt is due to him by the co-obligant who granted the security and that other debt was incurred prior to the debt paid by the co-obligant.[43] The co-obligant does not require an assignation in order to seek relief from his co-obligants and he cannot use the assignation to alter the right of equalisation *inter se* of all the obligants.[44] The assignation is, however, of advantage if there is a security for the debt, or if the debt has a preference, or if the debt is constituted by a document on which summary diligence can be commenced.

Co-obligants: prescription

28.4 Where, by a probative writ, two or more persons are bound jointly and severally by an obligation to pay money to another party, the obligation as respects the liability of each of the co-obligants, is subject to the quinquennial prescription.[45] However, this does not apply to a co-obligant if the creditor establishes that he is truly a principal debtor or that, although he is not truly a principal debtor, the original creditor was not aware of that fact at the time when the writ was delivered.

Joint delinquents

28.5 Where there are joint delinquents, the injured party may sue them all jointly and severally or recover all the damages from one if he so

---

[35] *Gilmour* v. *Finnie* (1832) 11 S. 193; *Anderson* v. *Dayton* (1884) 21 S.L.R. 787.
[36] *Macbride* v. *Clark Grierson & Co.* (1865) 4 M. 73; *Hamilton & Co.* v. *Freeth* (1889) 16 R. 1022.
[37] Bell, *Prin.*, § 62.
[38] *Buchanan* v. *Main* (1900) 3 F. 215; Gloag, p. 208.
[39] *Anderson* v. *Mackinnon* (1876) 3 R. 608.
[40] Bell, *Prin.*, § 255.
[41] *Ewart* v. *Latta* (1865) 3 M. (H.L.) 36.
[42] *Russell* v. *Mudie* (1857) 20 D. 125; *Bruce* v. *Scottish Amicable Life Assurance Society*, 1907 S.C. 637.
[43] *Sligo* v. *Menzies* (1840) 2 D. 1478.
[44] Gloag, p. 213.
[45] Prescription and Limitation (Scotland) Act 1973, Sched. 1, para. 3.

pleases.[46] If he sues one and obtains a decree against him upon which no satisfaction[47] or less than full satisfaction[48] is obtained, he can sue the others whose right of relief against the discharged delinquent is not affected.[49] But where he has obtained a decree against one in respect of the full damage and that award has been obtempered, he cannot proceed against the others.[50]

It has been held that it is competent to sue two defenders jointly and severally where the pursuer has suffered a loss to which each defender, by breach of his separate contract with the pursuer, has contributed.[51]

Where it is sought to make two defenders liable for the wrong but it is possible that in the end of the day liability will be established against only one of them, the conclusion should be "jointly and severally, or severally."[52]

Relief between joint delinquents

If the wrongdoers are sued in the same action and both are found liable, the pursuer will be given a joint and several decree against them but the court will apportion their liability for damages and expenses *inter se* and if one pays to the pursuer more than the sum thus apportioned to him he may obtain relief from the other.[53]

28.6

Where only one wrongdoer is sued and has been found liable in damages or expenses, he is entitled to recover from any other person who "if sued, might also have been held liable"[54] in respect of the loss or damage on which the action was founded, such contribution, if any, as the court may deem just. The liability must have been established by a decree of the Scottish courts.[55] A decree giving effect to an agreed settlement will suffice; there need not have been a judicial decision on a contested issue of liability.[55] The right to relief prescribes in two years after the date on which the right to recover the contribution became enforceable.[56] The right of relief is not prejudiced by the pursuer abandoning an action against another delinquent.[57] The words "if sued" mean "relevantly, competently and timeously" sued; so where the pursuer's attempt to bring in a delinquent by third party notice has failed because of a time bar, the defender's right of relief is not affected.[58]

A difficulty arises where one wrongdoer has made an extra-judicial

---

[46] *Croskery* v. *Gilmour's Trs.* (1890) 17 R. 697.
[47] *Steven* v. *Broady Norman & Co.*, 1928 S.C. 351; *Arrow Chemicals Ltd.* v. *Guild*, 1978 S.L.T. 206.
[48] *Dillon* v. *Napier, Shanks & Bell* (1893) 20 S.L.R. 685; *Douglas* v. *Hogarth* (1901) 4 F. 148; *McNair* v. *Dunfermline Corporation*, 1953 S.C. 183; *Carrigan* v. *Duncan*, 1971 S.L.T. (Sh.Ct.) 33.
[49] *Corvi* v. *Ellis*, 1969 S.L.T. 350.
[50] *Balfour* v. *Baird & Sons*, 1959 S.C. 64.
[51] *Grunwald* v. *Hughes*, 1964 S.L.T. 94.
[52] *Ellerman Lines Ltd.* v. *Clyde Navigation Trustees*, 1909 S.C. 690; *Arrow Chemicals Ltd.* v. *Guild*, 1978 S.L.T. 206.
[53] Law Reform (Miscellaneous Provisions) (Scotland) Act 1940, s.3(1).
[54] s.3(2). The liability may arise from breach of contract: *Engdiv Ltd.* v. *G. Percy Trentham Ltd.*, 1990 S.L.T. 617.
[55] *Comex Houlder Diving Ltd.* v. *Colne Fishing Co. Ltd.*, 1987 S.L.T. 443.
[56] Prescription and Limitation (Scotland) Act 1973, s.8A.
[57] *Singer* v. *Gray Tool Co. (Europe) Ltd.*, 1984 S.L.T. 149.
[58] *Dormer* v. *Melville Dundas & Whitson Ltd.*, 1990 S.L.T. 186.

settlement with the injured party and wishes to obtain a contribution from a joint delinquent. He has, it seems, no statutory or common law right of relief.[59] His only remedy seems to be to obtain an assignation of the injured party's right against the joint delinquent and sue him on the assignation for the full amount of the damages.[60] The second delinquent can then, presumably, recover a proportion from the first under s.3(2) of the Act of 1940.

Discharge of co-obligants

28.7 Where the creditor obtains partial payment from one co-obligant, a distinction is made between a *pactum de non petendo* and a discharge. The effect of a *pactum de non petendo* is that the creditor can make no further claim on the co-obligant who has paid but can recover the balance from the other co-obligants who in turn can still obtain *pro rata* relief from the first co-obligant. A document will be construed as a *pactum de non petendo* if the creditor expressly reserves his rights against the other obligants[61] and even where there is no such reservation it seems that this effect is presumed if the payment is a composition.[62] The effect of a discharge is to release the other obligants from any liability beyond their *pro rata* share.[63]

The position is different in the case of co-cautioners. The discharge of one without the consent of the others, discharges all.[64] The discharge of the debtor discharges the cautioner.[65]

Where one co-obligant or co-cautioner is sequestrated the others are not freed or discharged from liability by reason of the discharge of the debtor or by virtue of the creditor's voting or drawing a dividend or assenting to, or not opposing, the discharge of the debtor or any composition.[66]

Discharge of co-delinquents

28.8 If a discharge is granted to one delinquent which appears to discharge the claims against all or which is given in return for a sum of money which is accepted as complete satisfaction for the wrong, the injured party cannot subsequently proceed against co-delinquents.[67] On the other hand, if the discharge is granted for a sum which is not accepted in full satisfaction for the wrong, the injured party can proceed against the co-delinquents. The sum received must, however, be taken into account in assessing the liability of the co-delinquents and, it seems, their right of relief is not prejudiced.[68]

---

[59] *National Coal Board* v. *Thomson*, 1959 S.C. 353; but see *Corvi* v. *Ellis, supra, per* Lord Guthrie at p. 354.
[60] *Cole-Hamilton* v. *Boyd*, 1963 S.C. (H.L.) 1.
[61] *Secretary of State for Scotland* v. *Coltness Industries Ltd.*, 1979 S.L.T. (Sh.Ct.) 56.
[62] Gloag, p. 215; *cf. Delaney* v. *Stirling* (1892) 20 R. 506, *per* Lord McLaren at p. 509.
[63] *Muir* v. *Crawford* (1875) 2 R. (H.L.) 148; *Smith* v. *Harding* (1877) 5 R. 147; *Morton's Trs.* v. *Robertson's J.F.* (1892) 20 R.72.
[64] Mercantile Law Amendment Act (Scotland) 1856, s.9. See para. 10.3.
[65] *Aitken's Trs.* v. *Bank of Scotland*, 1944 S.C. 270.
[66] B.A., s.60(1).
[67] *Delaney* v. *Stirling, supra.*
[68] *Western Bank* v. *Bairds* (1862) 24 D. 859; *Dillon* v. *Napier, Shanks & Bell* (1893) 30 S.L.R. 685; *Douglas* v. *Hogarth* (1901) 4 F. 148; *McNair* v. *Dunfermline Corporation*, 1953 S.C. 183; *Cole-Hamilton* v. *Boyd*, 1963 S.C. (H.L.) 1.

CHAPTER 29

DEATH

CREDITOR'S DEATH

Transmissibility
As a general rule, debts transmit in the creditor's succession and on his death form part of his estate.[1] A right to damages in respect of personal injuries sustained by the deceased does not transmit to his executor in so far as it consists of *solatium* or compensation for patrimonial loss attributable to any period after the deceased's death; a claim in respect of patrimonial loss for a period prior to death, *e.g.* wage loss between injury and death, does transmit and the executor's claim for this is not excluded by the fact that a relative of the deceased is claiming damages in respect of the death.[2] Where the deceased died vested in a right to claim damages in respect of the death of another person, the claim in so far as it is for a loss of society award does not transmit but a claim for loss of support up to the death of the deceased does transmit.[3] An order for payment of periodical allowance to a divorced spouse terminates on the spouse's death except in relation to arrears.[4]

An annuity is prima facie for the life of the annuitant but the terms of the deed may show a different intention, as, for example, where the annuity was said by the grantor to be payable "during my lifetime."[5]

29.1

Heritable and moveable
As the whole estate, heritable and moveable, now vests in the executor on confirmation,[6] the distinction between heritable and moveable debts is, in relation to the creditor's succession, of importance only with regard to legal rights. Most debts are moveable. In particular the following are moveable: personal bonds (unless executors are expressly excluded by the terms of the deed)[7]; heritable securities in the form of a standard security or bond and disposition in security[8]; ground annuals[9]; an interest in a partnership[10] or joint adventure[11] even if heritage forms part of the

29.2

---

[1] Stair, III, v, 5.
[2] Damages (Scotland) Act 1976, ss.2, 4.
[3] *Ibid.*, s.3.
[4] Family Law (Scotland) Act 1985, s.13(7)(*b*).
[5] *Reid's Exx.* v. *Reid*, 1944 S.C. (H.L.) 25.
[6] Succession (Scotland) Act 1964, s.14.
[7] Bonds Act 1661 (c.32); Conveyancing (Scotland) Act 1924, s.22. See Meston, *The Succession (Scotland) Act 1964* (3rd ed.), p. 47.
[8] Titles to Land Consolidation (Scotland) Act 1868, s.117; Conveyancing and Feudal Reform (Scotland) Act 1970, s.32; They remain heritable *quoad fiscum* and *quoad* legal rights.
[9] Titles to Land Consolidation (Scotland) Act 1868, s.117; Conveyancing (Scotland) Act 1874, s.30; Succession (Scotland) Act 1964, Sched. 3; they remain heritable *quoad fiscum* and *quoad* legal rights.
[10] Partnership Act 1890, s.22.
[11] *Lord Advocate* v. *Macfarlane's Trs.* (1893) 31 S.L.R. 357.

partnership property; company shares[12]; an assignation in security of a lease.[13]

The following debts are heritable in the creditor's succession: feuduties and rents[14] (but arrears are moveable)[15]; securities in the form of an *ex facie* absolute disposition[16]; an assigned *spes successionis* relating to heritage.[17] Rights having a tract over future time and not having a relation to any capital sum or stock are heritable.[18] So an annuity is heritable although each term's payment as it falls due is moveable.[19] Similarly, an assigned liferent is heritable,[20] as is a pension. The right to the annual interest of a capital sum is, however, moveable because the right has relation to a principal sum.[21]

The nature of an interest in a trust estate depends upon the nature of the property held by the trust and, possibly, upon the operation of the doctrine of constructive conversion.[22]

The doctrine of constructive conversion is also of importance in regard to sales of heritage. Where the deceased has contracted to sell heritage and the conveyance has not been effected at his death, the executor is bound to execute the conveyance but the price forms part of the moveable estate.[23]

Recovery

29.3 The only person entitled to collect debts due to the deceased's estate is the executor[24] and, in general, payment can be made to him only if he has confirmed to the debt; payment should not be made of an amount larger than that appearing in the confirmation.[25] However, under various statutes, there are certain small payments which can be made without the necessity of confirmation.[26] A person or corporation who, in reliance on any instrument purporting to be a confirmation (or any instrument purporting to be a probate or letters of administration issued by any court in England and Wales or Northern Ireland, as the case may be) has made or has permitted to be made a payment or transfer bona fide upon such document, is indemnified and protected in so doing, notwithstanding any defect or circumstance whatsoever affecting the validity of the document.[27] A debtor who has paid the executor is not concerned with the

---

[12] Companies Act 1985, s.182(1).
[13] *Stroyan* v. *Murray* (1890) 17 R. 1170.
[14] Bell, *Prin.*, § 1484.
[15] *Logan's Trs.* v. *Logan* (1896) 23 R. 848; *Watson's Trs.* v. *Brown*, 1923 S.C. 228.
[16] Gloag & Irvine, p. 162.
[17] *Thain* v. *Thain* (1891) 18 R. 1196.
[18] Ersk., II, ii, 6.
[19] *Reid* v. *McWalter* (1878) 5 R. 630.
[20] *Allan* v. *Williamson* (1741) Elchies' Heritable, No. 12; *Drummond* v. *Ewing* (1752) Elchies' Heritable, No. 16.
[21] *Hill* v. *Hill* (1872) 11 M. 247.
[22] McLaren, *Wills and Succession*, I, p. 223.
[23] *Chiesley* v. *His Sisters* (1704) Mor. 5531; *McArthur's Exrs.* v. *Guild*, 1908 S.C. 743.
[24] *Barnet* v. *Duncan* (1831) 10 S. 128. See, as to a sole solicitor's client account, Solicitors (Scotland) Act 1980, s.46.
[25] *Buchanan* v. *Royal Bank* (1842) 5 D. 211.
[26] The present limit is £5000: Administration of Estates (Small Payments) (Increase of Limit) Order 1984 (S.I. 1984 No. 539).
[27] Confirmation and Probate Amendment Act 1859, s.1.

application of the money unless he knows of the executor's intention to misapply it.[28]

If the deceased has not pursued the debt and if it is transmissible, his executors may raise an action for its recovery. This may be done before they have confirmed to the debt but confirmation must be obtained before decree is granted.[29] A summons which was served by the deceased but had not been called, can be called in the name of his representatives.[30] If the deceased had raised an action for recovery of the debt which is in dependence, his executors are entitled to be sisted in his place,[31] even after judgment has been given.[32] If the deceased had obtained decree authorisation for diligence can be obtained by producing the confirmation.[33] If a poinding had been executed, the executors can obtain a warrant for sale on production of the confirmation[34] If the warrant had been obtained prior to death the executors may carry out the sale without further procedure.[35] Where an arrestment had been executed before death, the executors can raise a furthcoming.[36] An inhibition which has been served transmits to the executors if they sist themselves as pursuers in the relevant action.[37]

DEBTOR'S DEATH

Diligence commenced before death

29.4 Where the common debtor dies after execution of the arrestment, it is competent to bring an action of furthcoming against the representatives.[38] Similarly, where the debtor dies after execution of a poinding, the creditor can proceed with the sale.[39] These diligences may, however, be affected by (a) confirmation to the asset by an executor-creditor,[40] (b) sequestration of the deceased's estate within 12 months of death[41]; (c) appointment of a judicial factor on the deceased's estate within 12 months of the death, where the estate was absolutely insolvent at the date of death.[41]

It is not competent to commence diligence on a decree against the debtor after his death, although if another creditor has poinded or arrested, the decree can be produced in the process to obtain equalisation.[42]

Transmission: debtor's estate

29.5 The general rule is that debts transmit against the debtor's estate. The

---

[28] *Taylor* v. *Forbes* (1830) 4 W. & S. 444.
[29] *Mackay* v. *Mackay*, 1914 S.C. 200.
[30] *Gallie* v. *Lockhart* (1840) 2 D. 445; Maclaren, *Court of Session Practice*, p. 350.
[31] *Martin's Exrx.* v. *McGhee*, 1914 S.C. 628.
[32] *Scott* v. *Mills's Trs.*, 1923 S.C. 726; *Cumming* v. *Stewart*, 1928 S.C. 709.
[33] See para. 15.3.
[34] Graham Stewart, p. 363.
[35] Graham Stewart, p. 363.
[36] Ersk., III, vi, 11; Graham Stewart, p. 134.
[37] Bankton, I, vii, 140; Graham Stewart, p. 552.
[38] Stair, III, i, 26; Ersk., III, ix, 34; *Earl of Wemyss* v. *May* (1679) Mor. 782.
[39] Bell, *Comm.*, II, 80; Graham Stewart, p. 363.
[40] See *infra*, para. 7.
[41] See B.A., s.37(7).
[42] Graham Stewart, Chap. XXXV.

rights of creditors are not affected by any testamentary dispositions which the deceased may have made and the rights of beneficiaries do not open except to the free estate of the deceased *debitis deductis*.[43] In particular, the following transmit: claims *ex delicto*,[44] an order for payment of a periodical allowance to a divorced spouse (although the executor can apply for variation or recall).[45]

The children of the deceased have no claim for aliment against his estate if he had made provision for them.[46]

The executor may be liable in damages to the landlord if he does not take up a lease.[47]

On the death of a contributory before or after he has been placed on the list of contributories, his personal representatives and the heirs or legatees of his heritable estate are liable to pay calls in his stead,[48] where the personal representatives are placed on the list of contributories, the heirs or legatees of heritage need not be added but they may be added as and when the court thinks fit.

It is possible for a man to contract in such a way that the obligation is prestable from him during his life but does not bind his representatives; but the intention must be made clear.[49]

The personal obligation contained in any deed constituting a heritable security transmits against any person taking the security subjects by succession or bequest but the obligation is limited to the value of the estate to which the person succeeds and cannot be enforced by summary diligence unless an agreement to the transmission of the obligation has been executed by the person.[50]

Where a husband has gifted to his wife heritage which is burdened by a bond, the presumption is that the gift is taken *cum onere* and the husband's estate is not liable for the amount of the bond in a question with the wife even although the personal obligation in the bond has transmitted against the husband and wife jointly and severally.[51]

Certain property *in bonis* of the deceased may not pass to the executor as such and is not confirmed to. This occurs where property is disposed of by special assignation,[52] special destination,[53] nomination[54] or *donatio mortis causa*.[55] In principle, property subject to a special destination should be available for payment of the debts of the deceased and it is unfortunate that the wording of the Succession (Scotland) Act 1964,

---

[43] *Heritable Securities Investment Association Ltd.* v. *Miller's Trs.* (1893) 20 R. 675.
[44] *Evans* v. *Stool* (1885) 12 R. 1295.
[45] Family Law (Scotland) Act 1985, s.13(7)(*a*).
[46] *Strathmore* v. *Strathmore's Trs.* (1825) 1 W. & S. 402; *Ferguson* v. *Ferguson* (1899) 15 Sh.Ct.Rep. 20.
[47] *Bethune* v. *Morgan* (1874) 2 R. 186; Paton & Cameron, *Landlord and Tenant*, p. 187.
[48] I.A., s.81.; *Galletly's Trs.* v. *Lord Advocate* (1880) 8 R. 74.
[49] *Gardiner* v. *Stewart's Trs.*, 1908 S.C. 985.
[50] Conveyancing (Scotland) Act 1874, s.47; Conveyancing (Scotland) Act 1924, s.15; *Welch's Exrs.* v. *Edinburgh Life Assurance Co.* (1896) 23 R. 772.
[51] *Ballantyne's Trs.* v. *Ballantyne's Trs.*, 1941 S.C. 35.
[52] Confirmation Act 1690.
[53] A deposit receipt has no testamentary effect: *Dinwoodie's Exrx.* v. *Carruther's Exr.* (1895) 23 R. 234.
[54] *Gill* v. *Gill*, 1938 S.C. 65; *Ford's Trs.* v. *Ford*, 1940 S.C. 426.
[55] *Morris* v. *Riddick* (1867) 5 M. 1036.

s.18(2), has led to a decision to the contrary.[56] The funds of an *inter vivos* trust constituted by the deceased may be available to creditors if the trust is revocable.[57]

Recovery

Where an executor has been confirmed to the estate of the deceased, the creditor's remedy is to intimate a claim to him. The executor is *eadem persona cum defuncto* and in relation to the deceased's creditors is a debtor with a liability limited to the amount of the deceased's estate.[58] The executor is not entitled, and cannot be obliged, to make payment of a debt until the expiry of six months from the date of death.[59] An action to constitute the debt can be brought within that period[60] but an action of accounting cannot be.[61] Payment can be made before the six months of privileged debts—deathbed and funeral (including cremation) expenses, the widow's mourning allowance[62] (which need not be claimed before the funeral[63]) the current term's rent of the house occupied by the deceased and domestic servants' wages for the current term.[64] By universal practice aliment for the family of the deceased is provided from the date of death from all estates not manifestly insolvent.[65] If the executor does not petition for sequestration or the appointment of a judicial factor within a reasonable period after he knew or ought to have known that the estate was absolutely insolvent and likely to remain so, any intromission by him with the estate after the expiry of that period is deemed to be an intromission without a title.[66]

29.6

After the expiry of the six months period the executor is bound to pay any just debt *primo venienti*.[67] He is not obliged to make provision for contingent debts. If it appears that the estate may be insolvent, he should not make any payment and should merely give notice of the possible insolvency. The creditors must then proceed by sequestration of the estate.[68] If the executor pays ordinary debts without providing for privileged debts, or pays the beneficiaries without providing for debts, he is personally liable.[69] An executor can make payment of a claim in safety even although he has not been made to pay by legal process but if the estate is small, and the amount of claims uncertain and the existence or amount of the alleged debt doubtful, he is entitled to protect himself and the estate by requiring formal constitution.[70] The rule that the creditor

---

[56] *Barclay's Bank Ltd.* v. *McGreish*, 1983 S.L.T. 344; cf. *Renouf's Trs.* v. *Haining*, 1919 S.C. 497, *per* Lord Dundas at p. 507.
[57] See *Scott* v. *Scott*, 1930 S.C. 903; *Ross* v. *Ross's Trs.* (*sub nom. Rose* v. *Rose's Trs.*), 1967 S.L.T. 12.
[58] *Stewart's Tr.* v. *Stewart's Exrx.* (1896) 23 R. 739.
[59] Bell, *Prin.*, § 1900; *Sanderson* v. *Lockhart-Mure*, 1946 S.C. 298.
[60] *McPherson* v. *Cameron* (1941) 57 Sh.Ct.Rep. 64.
[61] *Brown* v. *Wallace* (1894) 10 Sh.Ct.Rep. 142.
[62] *Griffith's Trs.* v. *Griffiths*, 1912 S.C. 626.
[63] *Morrison* v. *Cornfoot* (1930) 46 Sh.Ct.Rep. 74.
[64] Bell, *Prin.*, §§ 1402–1405.
[65] *Barlass* v. *Barlass's Trs.*, 1916 S.C. 741.
[66] B.A., s.8(4).
[67] *Taylor & Ferguson Ltd.* v. *Glass's Trs.*, 1912 S.C. 165.
[68] See *infra*, para. 12.
[69] *Lamond's Trs.* v. *Croom* (1871) 9 M. 662; *Heritable Securities Investment Association Ltd.* v. *Miller's Trs.* (1893) 20 R. 675.
[70] *McGaan* v. *McGaan's Trs.* (1883) 11 R. 249.

constitutes the debt at his own expense is not absolute.[71] If the executor puts forward an unreasonable defence he may be held personally liable in expenses with a right of relief against the estate.[72] Where an action for payment has been raised against the executor a formal action of constitution is not necessary.[73] In some circumstances he may be justified in raising an action of multiplepoinding.[74] The executor can be sued even although he has not been confirmed.[75] The executor is entitled to make payment of sums due to himself, as an individual, unless the estate is apparently insolvent or there is a serious dispute about the validity of the claim.[76] A creditor who has received payment of his debt in good faith is not obliged to refund it if it subsequently transpires that the estate is insolvent.[77]

If, after the expiry of the six months, the executor, in the reasonable belief that all debts have been satisfied, makes payment of the balance of the estate to the beneficiaries he is not personally liable to a creditor who has not intimated a claim before the payment.[78]

The assets in the possession of the executor may be attached by the completion of diligence commenced before the debtor's death.[79] Where the executor dies in the course of the administration of the estate, the creditor's ultimate remedy is to sequestrate the original debtor's estate; he cannot proceed against the executor's executor unless he has intromitted with the debtor's executry estate.[80]

Where the creditor proceeds against the executor or the beneficiary and the estate of the executor or beneficiary is sequestrated, the creditor has, it seems, in competition with the creditors of the bankrupt, a preference over the assets of the deceased which can be distinguished and identified. As regards heritable estate, this preference was conferred by the Act 1661, c.24 but, as that statute has now been repealed,[81] the preference as regards the whole assets now depends on the common law,[82] as the Confirmation Act 1695 applies only where an executor has not been confirmed. This preferential right was subject to the long negative prescription and may be extinguished in a shorter period by personal bar or acquiescence.[83] Where the executor has properly paid over the funds to the legatees or beneficiaries the creditor's remedy is to sue them.[84] It seems that the claim must be constituted against the

---

[71] *Barclay's Bank Ltd.* v. *Lawton's Trs.*, 1928 S.L.T. 298.
[72] *Law* v. *Humphrey* (1876) 3 R. 1192; *cf. Harper* v. *Connor's Trs.* (1927) 43 Sh.Ct.Rep. 138.
[73] *Galloway* v. *MacKinnon* (1936) 52 Sh.Ct.Rep. 135.
[74] *Jamieson* v. *Robertson* (1888) 16 R. 15; *cf. Mackenzie's Trs.* v. *Sutherland* (1895) 22 R. 233.
[75] *Emslie* v. *Tognarelli's Exrs.*, 1967 S.L.T. (Notes) 66.
[76] *Salaman* v. *Sinclair's Trs.*, 1916 S.C. 698; *Watson* v. *British Linen Bank*, 1941 S.C. 43.
[77] *Cathcart* v. *Moodie* (1804) Mor. "Heir & Executor," App. 1, No. 2.
[78] *Stewart's Trs.* v. *Evans* (1871) 9 M. 810; *Beith* v. *Mackenzie* (1875) 3 R. 185.
[79] See *supra*, para. 4.
[80] *Hutcheson & Co.'s Administrator* v. *Taylor's Exrx.*, 1931 S.C. 484.
[81] Succession (Scotland) Act 1964, Sched. 3.
[82] Bell, *Comm.*, II, 85; McLaren, *Wills and Succession*, II, pp. 866, 1299; Graham Stewart, p. 681; *Menzies* v. *Poutz*, 1916 S.C. 143.
[83] *Traill's Trs.* v. *Free Church of Scotland*, 1915 S.C. 655.
[84] *Poole* v. *Anderson* (1834) 12 S. 481; *Stewart's Trs.* v. *Evans* (1871) 9 M. 810; *Beith* v. *Mackenzie* (1875) 3 R. 185.

executor first.[85] The beneficiary is not liable if at the time the payment was made to him there remained sufficient funds in the hands of the executor to meet all claims.[86]

Where testamentary trustees have carried on a business and thereby contracted debt, they can be sequestrated as trustees.[87]

Confirmation as executor-creditor

If no executors have been confirmed, there has been no vitious intromission,[88] and no third party has obtained possession of the estate,[89] the creditor's remedy is to confirm to the deceased's estate as executor-creditor. This is a species of diligence by which the creditor satisfies his debt out of the estate to which he confirms.[90] Formerly, this had to be moveable estate but it seems that the effect of s.14 of the Succession (Scotland) Act 1964, is to allow an executor-creditor to confirm to heritable estate of the deceased. The creditor must hold a decree or a liquid document of debt.[91] An appointment as executor-creditor is null if executors *qua* next of kin have already been confirmed.[92] A foreign title does not exclude an executor-creditor.[93] It is possible to confirm as executor-creditor to estate which has not been confirmed to by an executor *qua* next of kin. The procedure is to apply for decerniture and then obtain confirmation. The domicile of the deceased is immaterial.[93] Notice of the application must be inserted in the *Edinburgh Gazette* immediately after its presentation.[94] The inventory must include the whole estate of the deceased but the confirmation may be restricted to certain assets.[94] The effect of confirmation is to create a *nexus* on these assets which is limited by (a) the amount of the debt, and (b) the value in the confirmation.[95] The executor-creditor must use due diligence to ingather the assets in the confirmation and must account for any surplus.[96] If there are two successive confirmations to the same asset and the asset is included at a higher value in the second confirmation, the creditor first confirming has no preference beyond the value in his confirmation.[97] The confirmation gives a complete title to the creditor.[98] He may sist himself as a party to an action begun by the deceased to recover an asset included in the confirmation.[99] If an executor-creditor dies without having received payment of his debt, his representatives can proceed with its recovery.[1]

It is necessary that the assets to which the executor-creditor confirms should be *in bonis defuncti*. So if an *inter vivos* assignation granted by the

---

[85] *Clelland* v. *Baillie* (1845) 7 D. 461.
[86] *Magistrates of St Andrews* v. *Forbes* (1893) 31 S.L.R. 225.
[87] *J. & W. Campbell & Co.* (1899) 6 S.L.T. 406; B.A., s.6(1)(*a*).
[88] See Wilson & Duncan, *Trusts, Trustees and Executors*, p. 448.
[89] *Irvine* v. *King's and Lord Treasurer's Remembrancer* (1949) 65 Sh.Ct.Rep. 53.
[90] *Smith's Trs.* v. *Grant* (1862) 24 D. 1142.
[91] For the procedure where the debt is not liquid see next paragraph.
[92] *Lees* v. *Dinwidie* (1706) 5 Brown's Sup. 35.
[93] *Smith's Trs.* v. *Grant, supra.*
[94] Confirmation of Executors (Scotland) Act 1823, s.4.
[95] per Lord Curriehill, *Smith's Trs.* v. *Grant, supra*, at p. 1169.
[96] *Lee* v. *Donald*, 17 May 1816, F.C.
[97] *Smith's Trs.* v. *Grant, supra.*
[98] *Dickson* v. *Barbour* (1828) 6 S. 856.
[99] *Mein* v. *McCall* (1844) 6 D. 1112.
[1] *Mitchel* v. *Mitchel* (1737) Mor. 3935.

deceased has been intimated prior to confirmation, the assignee is preferred.[2] Similarly, if a special assignation or disposition falling under the Confirmation Act 1690 has been made by the deceased and intimation or possession has followed thereon, confirmation is incompetent.[3] A decree of preference in a multiplepoinding,[4] or consignation,[5] does not take assets *ex bonis defuncti*.

The position as to competition is as follows:
(a) *Privileged Debts*: the right of the executor-creditor is postponed to these.[6]
(b) *Other Creditors*: any other creditor holding a liquid document of debt or a decree may apply to be conjoined in the application for decerniture and thereafter ranks *pari passu* with the original applicant.[7] Moreover, any creditor who cites the executor-creditor within six months of the death is ranked *pari passu* but he must bear a proportion of the expense of confirmation.[8] After the expiry of the six months, an executor-creditor who has confirmed within the six months is preferred to other creditors who have not cited him by that time. Similarly, if no creditor has confirmed within the six months, the first to do so thereafter obtains a preference. Creditors who cite the executor-creditor after the six months are ranked *pari passu inter se* if the one has not obtained decree before citation by the other.[9] If one has already obtained decree he is preferred.

If an executor-nominate or executor-dative *qua* next of kin is also a creditor he obtains the same preference as an executor-creditor after the six months period.[10]
(c) *Diligence commenced before Death*: the executor-creditor is preferred if his confirmation is prior to the date of sale[11] or the decree in the furthcoming.[12]
(d) *Sequestration*: it is not competent for a creditor to be confirmed as executor-creditor after the date of the sequestration.[13] If the deceased's estate is sequestrated or a judicial factor is appointed to administer the estate within 12 months of the death, no confirmation as executor-creditor is effectual in a question with the trustee or judicial factor but the creditor is entitled out of the estate confirmed to, or the proceeds of sale thereof, to the expenses incurred by him in obtaining the confirmation.[14]

Decree cognitionis causa tantum

29.8 In the case where the debt is not liquid, the creditor must proceed

---

[2] *Sinclair v. Sinclair* (1726) Mor. 2793; *Cust v. Garbet & Co.* (1775) Mor. 2795.
[3] *Bell v. Willison* (1831) 9 S. 266.
[4] *Anderson v. Stewart* (1831) 10 S. 49.
[5] *Smith's Trs. v. Grant, supra*.
[6] Stair, III, viii, 64; *Crawford v. Hutton* (1680) Mor. 11832.
[7] *Willison v. Dewar* (1840) 3 D. 273.
[8] Act of Sederunt, 28 February 1662; *Ramsay v. Nairn* (1708) Mor. 3139.
[9] *Graeme v. Murray* (1738) Mor. 3141.
[10] *Macleod v. Wilson* (1837) 15 S. 1043.
[11] Graham Stewart, p. 452.
[12] *Wilson v. Fleming* (1823) 2 S. 430.
[13] B.A., s.37(8).
[14] B.A., s.37(9).

against the *hereditas jacens* by raising an action against the deceased's next-of-kin for a decree *cognitionis causa tantum*.[15] It is not now necessary to charge the next-of-kin before raising the action.[16] All the known next-of-kin must be called for their interests whether or not they are subject to the jurisdiction of the Scottish courts.[17] An action against "the representatives of the late X" was held to be incompetent.[18] Executors who have not confirmed need not be called.[19] It is competent to bring an action against two defenders jointly and severally and to restrict the decree sought against one to a decree *cognitionis causa tantum*.[20] Once decree *cognitionis causa tantum* has been obtained, the debt, being now liquid, can be the basis of an application for confirmation as executor-creditor.

Creditors of next-of-kin

If there has been no confirmation, the creditors of the deceased's next-of-kin may confirm as executors-creditors.[21] The deceased's creditors doing diligence within a year and a day of the death are, however, preferred to the diligence of the creditors of the next-of-kin.

29.9

Heritable and moveable debt

Although a creditor is entitled to payment of his debt from any part of the debtor's estate, in questions between the debtor's representatives heritable debts must be paid from the heritable estate and moveable debts from the moveable estate.[22] As a general rule debts resting *in obligatione* are moveable *quoad debitorem*. The following moveable debts require special mention: the unpaid price of heritage[23]; arrears of feuduty[24] and rent[25]; and obligations of warrandice.[26]

The following are heritable—debts secured over heritage and real burdens.[27]

Where the security subjects are insufficient in value to satisfy the heritable debt secured, the other heritable estate is liable for the balance.[28]

29.10

Judicial factors

If the deceased left no settlement appointing trustees or other parties having power to manage his estate or part thereof, or if such parties do not accept or act, one or more creditors or persons interested in the

29.11

---

[15] Confirmation Act 1695.
[16] *Forrest* v. *Forrest* (1863) 1 M. 806; *Ferrier* v. *Crockhart*, 1937 S.L.T. 205.
[17] *Smith* v. *Tasker*, 1955 S.L.T. 347. See *Davidson Pirie & Co.* v. *Dihle's Reps.* (1900) 2 F. 640; *Stevens* v. *Thomson*, 1971 S.L.T. 136.
[18] *Kay* v. *Morrison's Reps.*, 1984 S.L.T. 175.
[19] *Smith's Trs.* v. *Grant* (1862) 24 D. 1142; *cf. Emslie* v. *Tognarelli's Exrs.*, 1967 S.L.T. (Notes) 66.
[20] *Smith* v. *Tasker*, *supra*.
[21] Confirmation Act 1695.
[22] McLaren, *Wills and Succession*, II, p. 1305; Succession (Scotland) Act 1964, s.14(3). The distinction is still important where there are legal rights and in cases of partial intestacy.
[23] *Clayton* v. *Lowthian* (1826) 2 W. & S. 40; *Ramsay* v. *Ramsay* (1887) 15 R. 25.
[24] *Johnston* v. *Cochran* (1829) 7 S. 226.
[25] *Kinloch's Exrs.* v. *Kinloch* (1811) Hume 178.
[26] *Duchess of Montrose* v. *Stuart* (1887) 15 R. (H.L.) 19.
[27] *Breadalbane's Trs.* v. *Jamieson* (1873) 11 M. 912.
[28] *Bell's Tr.* v. *Bell* (1884) 12 R. 85.

succession may petition the court to appoint a judicial factor on the estate.[29] The procedure is not competent where the deceased left no assets[30] nor where nominated but unconfirmed executors are acting.[31] The application is to the Court of Session or to the sheriff court where the deceased resided or carried on business during the year immediately preceding the date of the petition or where heritage belonging to the deceased at his death was situate.[32] In the Court of Session, procedure is regulated by Rule of Court 201. Intimation is made to the creditors and other persons interested in the estate and in the *Edinburgh Gazette*. The court's power to appoint is discretionary.[33] The factor advertises for claims within 14 days of the issue of the first certified interlocutor of his appointment.[34] He examines the claims and may call for further evidence thereof or require the creditor to constitute the debt.[35] For purposes of ranking and payment the date of his appointment is equivalent to the date of sequestration.[36] He administers the estate subject to the Judicial Factors Acts and under the supervision of the Accountant of Court.[37] Where the judicial factor has been appointed within 12 months after the death, and the estate was absolutely insolvent at the death gratuitous alienations, unfair preferences, and diligence can be challenged, the relevant date for calculation of the periods being the date of death.[38] Gratuitous alienations and fraudulent preferences can be challenged at common law.[39] There is no title to challenge extortionate credit bargains. A divorce order can be challenged.[40] The appointment of a factor on the insolvent estate of a deceased person brings the Third Parties (Rights against Insurers) Act 1930, into operation.[41] Within six months of the issue of the first certified interlocutor of his appointment he must prepare an inventory of the estate, a state of the debts, a state of funds and a scheme of division amongst the creditors which is laid before the Accountant of Court who reports thereon to the court.[42] If the estate is insolvent, it is to be divided among the creditors in accordance with the rules as to ranking obtaining in sequestrations.[43] Notice of the scheme must be given to the creditors who may lodge a note of objections thereto which is disposed of by the court.[44] If the scheme is approved payment is made to the creditors in accordance therewith. Out of the first funds realised the factor reserves the estimated cost of administration of the

---

[29] Judicial Factors (Scotland) Act 1889, s.11A (added by B.A., Sched. 7, para. 4).
[30] *Dunn* v. *Britannic Assurance Co. Ltd.*, 1932 S.L.T. 244.
[31] *Emslie* v. *Tognarelli's Exrs.*, 1967 S.L.T. (Notes) 66.
[32] It seems that, if there is no heritage, the petition is competent only within a year of death: Lewis, *Sheriff Court Practice* (8th ed.), p. 298; Dobie, *Sheriff Court Practice*, p. 394.
[33] *Masterton* v. *Erskine's Trs.* (1887) 14 R. 712; *Youngson, Petrs.*, 1911 2 S.L.T. 448; *London & Brazilian Bank* v. *Lumsden's Trs.*, 1913 1 S.L.T. 262.
[34] R.C., 201(*d*).
[35] R.C., 201(*e*).
[36] R.C., 201(*e*).
[37] 1889 Act, s.11A(2).
[38] B.A., ss.34(2)(*b*)(iv), 36(1)(*c*)(ii), 37(7)(*b*).
[39] B.A., ss.34(8), 36(6).
[40] B.A., s.35(1)(*c*)(iv).
[41] 1930 Act, s.4 (amended B.A., Sched. 7, para. 6).
[42] R.C., 201(*f*), (*g*).
[43] 1889 Act, s.11A(2).
[44] R.C., 201(*h*)–(*k*).

estate and he may, without waiting for the expiry of six months from the date of death, pay the deathbed and funeral expenses, rent, taxes, such servants' wages as are privileged debts and interest becoming due or past due to creditors having preferences over the estate.[45] If there is a residue after payment of the creditors the factor submits a statement of the amount, the parties claiming and the grounds of claim. He then pays over the residue to the parties found entitled thereto by the court.[46] In the sheriff court, the procedure is regulated by the Court of Session Rules.[47] The appointment of the factor has the effect of an intimated assignation of the deceased's rights.[48] It does not prevent a subsequent sequestration.[49]

Sequestration of estate of a deceased debtor

It is possible to sequestrate the estate of a deceased debtor. The petition must be at the instance of the executor, a person entitled to be appointed executor, the trustee acting under a trust deed granted by the deceased, or one or more creditors qualified as in the case of a living debtor.[50] The Court of Session has jurisdiction in respect of the sequestration of a deceased debtor if he had an established place of business in Scotland, or was habitually resident there, at any time in the year immediately preceding the date of death.[51] A sheriff court has jurisdiction if the business or residence was within the sheriffdom.[52] An executor or a person entitled to be appointed as executor on the estate or the trustee acting under a trust deed can petition at any time. Creditors qualified as in the case of a living debtor can petition at any time if the apparent insolvency[53] of the debtor was constituted within four months before his death; in any other case they can petition not earlier than six months after the debtor's death.[54]

29.12

Where a successor of the debtor has made up title to, or has taken possession of, any part of the estate, the court, on the application of the trustee, may order the successor to convey such estate to him.[55] Where the estate has been sequestrated within 12 months after the debtor's death gratuitous alienations, unfair preferences, divorce orders and diligence can be challenged, the relevant date for calculation of the periods being the date of death. Gratuitous alienations and unfair preferences can be challenged at common law.[56] In the case of extortionate credit bargains it would seem that the period is calculated from the date of sequestration. Deathbed and funeral expenses and the

---

[45] R.C., 201(*n*). The wording of the rule does not seem to have been related to the general insolvency law.
[46] R.C., 201(*o*).
[47] Judicial Factors (Scotland) Act 1880, s.4(4) and 4(6).
[48] *Campbell's J.F.* v. *National Bank*, 1944 S.C. 495 (*ex concessione*).
[49] *Arthur* (1903) 10 S.L.T. 550.
[50] B.A., s.5(3).
[51] B.A., s.9(1), (5).
[52] B.A., s.9(4).
[53] See para. 20.1.
[54] B.A., ss.5(3), 8(3).
[55] B.A., s.31(7).
[56] B.A., ss.34(1)(*b*)(iii), 36(1)(*c*)(i), 35(1)(*c*)(iii), 37(7)(*a*).

expenses of administering the estate rank immediately after the trustees' outlays and remuneration.[57]

The subsequent course of the sequestration of a deceased debtor does not differ in its general features from that of a living debtor.

It is not competent for any creditor, after the date of the first deliverance on the petition for sequestration, to be confirmed executor-creditor.[58] Sequestration within 12 months of death makes any confirmation of an executor-creditor ineffectual.[59] The sequestration of a deceased debtor is merely a process for the distribution of the estate and the court will not recall the sequestration on the application of the executor unless he shows that he has sufficient funds to pay the creditors or that there would be some advantage in having the estate administered by him.[60]

---

[57] B.A., s.51(1)(c).
[58] B.A., s.37(8).
[59] B.A., s.37(7).
[60] *McLetchie* v. *Angus Brothers* (1899) 1 F. 946.

CHAPTER 30

SPECIAL PARTIES

AGENTS

Agency

30.1 A contract may be entered into through an agent. This may be done in three ways: (a) where the agent enters the contract expressly as agent for a named principal; (b) where he enters expressly as agent for a principal whose name is not disclosed; (c) where he enters the contract nominally as principal without the existence of the agency being disclosed.

In general, in all three cases the principal can sue on the contract[1] but there are certain exceptions: (i) where the principal's title to sue is expressly excluded,[2] (ii) where evidence of the existence of an undisclosed principal would contradict the terms of a written contract,[3] (iii) where the other party to the contract entered the contract "with reference to the known personal capabilities or character" of the agent acting on behalf of an undisclosed principal.[4]

In general the agent can sue on the contract only if he is liable thereon but there are exceptions: (i) where there is an express term of a contract that the agent has a title to sue although he is not liable on the contract,[5] (ii) where the agent has a lien for his charges and commission.[6]

Liability of agent

30.2 As a general rule, the principal is liable on a contract made by the agent when acting within his actual or ostensible authority. The onus of proving the authority is on the third party attempting to enforce the contract.[7] There may be exceptions to the general rule where it is clear that the parties entering the contract did not intend that the principal would be liable.[8] Where the agent has contracted ostensibly as a principal without disclosing the existence of the agency, the agent is liable on the contract but, once the principal's name is disclosed, the third party may elect to hold liable either the principal or the agent.[9] In these circumstances the liability of the principal and the agent is alternative and not joint and several; once the third party has elected to hold the one liable he cannot proceed against the other. The obtaining of a decree against one,[10] or the acceptance of a dividend in his bankruptcy,[11] constitutes election; in other

---

[1] Bell, *Comm.*, I, 526; *Bennett* v. *Inveresk Paper Co.* (1891) 18 R. 975.
[2] *Ransohoff & Wissler* v. *Burrell* (1897) 25 R. 284.
[3] *Drughorn Ltd.* v. *Rederiaktiebolaget Transatlantic* [1919] A.C. 203.
[4] Bell, *Comm.*, I, 527.
[5] *Bonar* v. *Liddell* (1841) 3 D. 830; *Levy & Co.* v. *Thomsons* (1883) 10 R. 1134.
[6] *Mackenzie* v. *Cormack*, 1950 S.C. 183.
[7] *Wylie & Lochhead Ltd.* v. *Hornsby* (1889) 16 R. 907.
[8] *Lamont, Nisbett & Co.* v. *Hamilton*, 1907 S.C. 628.
[9] *Bennett* v. *Inveresk Paper Co.* (1891) 18 R. 975.
[10] *Meier & Co.* v. *Küchenmeister* (1881) 8 R. 642.
[11] *David Logan & Son Ltd. & Liquidator* v. *Schuldt* (1903) 10 S.L.T. 598; a claim for ranking may be sufficient: Gloag, p. 141.

cases election is a question of fact.[12] Even where the third party does not become aware of the existence of the agency until after he has obtained decree against the agent he cannot proceed against the principal.[13] If the third party elects to sue the agent, the agent can enforce a counterclaim due to the principal.[14]

Where an agent has expressly contracted on behalf of a named principal, as a general rule he incurs no liability under the contract.[15] There may, however, be circumstances showing that the parties intended that the agent would be personally liable on the contract,[16] and the general rule is also affected by a custom of trade.[17] There seems to be no absolute rule that an agent contracting on behalf of a foreign principal is personally liable.[18]

Where the agent has contracted expressly as agent for a principal whose name is not disclosed, the position is not altogether clear but it seems that the agent may be liable.[19] It seems that it is not competent for the agent to prove by parole evidence that he is in fact the principal.[20]

Where the agent contracts ostensibly as a principal without disclosing the existence of the agency, he is, as has already been explained, liable on the contract and, once the principal's name is disclosed, the third party may elect to hold liable either the principal or the agent.[21] This, however, does not apply, and the agent is not liable, where the third party knew of the agency at the time the contract was made,[22] but it is incompetent to prove such knowledge by extrinsic evidence if the contract is in writing.[23]

Where the agent has entered a contract outwith his authority, he is not personally liable thereon but he may be liable in damages for delict or misrepresentation.[24]

---

[12] Gloag, p. 141.

[13] *Ingram Clothing Mfg. Co. (Glasgow) Ltd.* v. *Lewis* (1960) 76 Sh.Ct.Rep. 165.

[14] *Craig & Co.* v. *Blackater*, 1923 S.C. 472; *James Laidlaw & Sons Ltd.* v. *Griffin*, 1968 S.L.T. 278.

[15] Bell, *Comm.*, I, 536; *Millar* v. *Mitchell* (1860) 22 D. 833; *Livesey* v. *Purdom & Sons* (1894) 21 R. 911; *Armour* v. *Duff*, 1912 S.C. 120; see, as to the relationship between the terms of the contract and the form of the signature, *Universal Steam Navigation Co. Ltd.* v. *James McKelvie & Co.* [1923] A.C. 492; *Stone & Rolfe* v. *Kimber Coal Co.*, 1926 S.C. (H.L.) 45. An agent who has opened a bank account for a named principal is not liable for an overdraft: *Royal Bank of Scotland* v. *Skinner*, 1931 S.L.T. 382. Contrast *Bank of Scotland* v. *McNeill*, 1977 S.L.T. (Sh.Ct.) 2, where the agency was not fully divulged.

[16] *Lamont, Nisbett & Co.* v. *Hamilton*, 1907 S.C. 628; Gloag, p. 136.

[17] *Meier & Co.* v. *Küchenmeister*, supra.

[18] Gloag, p. 139.

[19] Gloag, p. 138; Gloag & Henderson, p. 323. See *P. & M. Sinclair* v. *Bamber Gray Partnership*, 1987 S.L.T. 674.

[20] *Hill Steam Shipping Co.* v. *Hugo Stinnes Ltd.*, 1941 S.C. 324.

[21] Bell, *Comm.*, I, 536; if the agent signs the contract in his own name without qualification he is deemed to be contracting personally unless it appears from other parts of the document that he did not intend to bind himself as principal: *Stewart* v. *Shannessy* (1900) 2 F. 1288; where a firm of brokers gave an order to supply a named ship it was held that they made the contract as agents for a disclosed principal, the owner of the ship: *Armour* v. *Duff & Co.*, 1912 S.C. 120.

[22] *Bank of Scotland* v. *Rorie* (1908) 16 S.L.T. 21.

[23] *Lindsay* v. *Craig*, 1919 S.C. 139.

[24] Gloag, p. 155; *Anderson* v. *Croall & Sons Ltd.* (1903) 6 F. 153; *Scott* v. *J. B. Livingston & Nicol*, 1990 S.L.T. 305.

Ostensible authority

There may be circumstances in which a general agent has an implied **30.3** power to borrow money.[25]

The onus is on the other party to prove the agent's authority.[26]

SOLE TRADERS

The sole trader

An individual may carry on business under a name which is not his **30.4** own. Such an individual is sometimes erroneously called a "sole partner." On his sequestration, no distinction is made between the assets of the business and his other assets.[27] On the sale of such a business to another individual, the purchaser incurs no liability for the debts of the business in the absence of any special agreement.[28] Where the "sole partner" assumes a partner, however, the new partner may incur liability for the business debts.[29]

Business names

Where an individual is carrying on a business or profession under a **30.5** name which does not consist of his surname[30] without any addition other than his forename or his initial or a recognised abbreviation of a name or an indication that the business is carried on in succession to a former owner of the business, he is obliged to do three things.[31] First, he must state in legible characters on all business letters, written orders for goods or services to be supplied to the business, invoices and receipts issued in the course of the business and written demands for payment of debts arising in the course of the business, his name and an address in Great Britain at which service of any document relating in any way to the business will be effective. Secondly, in any premises where the business is carried on and to which the customers of the business or suppliers of any goods or services to the business have access, he must display in a prominent position so that it may easily be read by such customers or suppliers a notice containing his name and address. Thirdly, he must secure that the name and address are immediately given by written notice to any person with whom anything is done or discussed in the course of the business and who asks for such name and address. Failure in any of these duties is a criminal offence[32] and there may also be civil consequences. Where the individual brings legal proceedings to enforce a right arising out of a contract made in the course of a business in respect of which he was, at the time the contract was made, in breach of any of these duties, the action shall be dismissed if the defender shows that he has a claim against the pursuer arising out of that contract which he has been unable to pursue by reason of the breach or that he has suffered some

---

[25] *Paterson v. Banks*, 1958 S.L.T. (Sh.Ct.) 33.
[26] *Blackwood & Tinto Ltd. v. Gascoines Ltd.*, 1950 S.L.T. (Sh.Ct.) 5.
[27] *Reid v. Chalmers* (1828) 6 S. 1120.
[28] *Turnbull & Kay v. Chisholm & Co. and Blair* (1887) 3 Sh.Ct.Rep. 379.
[29] *Miller v. Thorburn* (1861) 23 D. 359. See para. 30.8.
[30] In relation to a peer or person usually known by a British title different from his surname, this means the title by which he is known.
[31] Business Names Act 1985, s.4.
[32] ss.4(6),7.

Partnership

Authority of partners

30.6 Partnership is the relation which subsists between persons carrying on a business in common with a view of profit.[35] If the business is limited in purpose and duration the partnership is sometimes known as a joint adventure.[36] A partner is an agent of the firm and his acts for carrying on in the usual way business of the kind carried on by the firm bind the firm, unless he has in fact no authority to act for the firm in that particular matter and the person with whom he is dealing either knows that he has no authority, or does not know or believe him to be a partner.[37] Consequently, if there is an agreement between the partners restricting the power of one or more of them to bind the firm, an act done in contravention of that agreement does not bind the firm in a question with a person having notice of the agreement.[38] If a partner pledges the credit of the firm for a purpose apparently not connected with the firm's ordinary course of business, the firm is not bound unless he was in fact specially authorised by the other partners.[39] If a contract is not binding on the firm, it binds the partner personally even if he signed the firm name.[40] An act or instrument relating to the firm's business and done or executed in the firm's name or in any other manner showing an intention to bind the firm, by any person thereto authorised, whether a partner or not, is binding on the firm and all the partners.[41]

Liability of firm

30.7 The firm is liable for any wrongful act or omission of a partner acting in the ordinary course of the firm's business which causes loss or injury to a person who is not a partner in the firm.[42] The firm is also liable to make good the loss where a partner acting within the scope of his apparent authority receives money or property of a third person and misapplies it and where a partner misapplies the money or property of a third person which has been received by the firm in the course of its business and is in its custody.[43] If a partner who is a trustee improperly employs trust property in the business or on the account of the partnership no other partner who has no notice of the breach of trust is liable for the property but the trust money can be followed and recovered from the firm if still in its possession or under its control.[44]

---

[33] s.5(1).
[34] s.5(2).
[35] Partnership Act 1890, s.1(1).
[36] *Mair* v. *Wood*, 1948 S.C. 83.
[37] 1890 Act, s.5.
[38] 1890 Act, s.8.
[39] 1890 Act, s.7.
[40] *Fortune* v. *Young*, 1918 S.C. 1.
[41] 1890 Act, s.6.
[42] 1890 Act, s.10.
[43] 1890 Act, s.11.
[44] 1890 Act, s.13.

Liability for firm debts

30.8 A partner is liable jointly and severally with the other partners for all debts and obligations incurred by the firm while he is a partner.[45] The estate of a partner who dies, or is sequestrated, is not liable for firm debts contracted after the date of death or sequestration but it is liable for debts contracted before that date.[46] A retiring partner remains liable for firm debts contracted before his retirement unless he is discharged by an express or implied agreement between himself, the members of the firm as newly constituted and the creditors.[47] Moreover, the retiring partner may, in certain circumstances, be liable for firm debts contracted after his retirement because a person dealing with a firm after a change in its constitution is entitled to treat all apparent members of the old firm as still being members of the firm until he has notice of the change.[48] It seems that the creditor need not elect to hold liable either the old firm including the retired partner or the newly constituted firm; the liability is joint and several.[49] An advertisement in the *Edinburgh Gazette* is sufficient notice to persons who had no dealings with the old firm. In other cases individual notice is required but it is always competent to show that the creditor knew of the change although he was not given formal notice thereof.

A person who is admitted as a partner does not thereby become liable for debts contracted before he became a partner.[50] Whether liability exists depends on the facts. If the whole assets of a going concern are transferred to the new firm there is a presumption that the new firm, including the new partner, has assumed the liabilities of the old. This presumption may be rebutted if the new partner has paid in a large sum of capital and the other partners have put in the going concern as their shares and also if the basis is that the new firm is not liable for the debts of the old and has no right to collect debts due to the old firm.[51] These principles apply equally where an individual carrying on a business has taken in a partner.

A person who is not a partner may render himself liable for firm debts by "holding out," *i.e.* representing himself by words or conduct, or knowingly suffering himself to be represented, as a partner in the firm. He is liable as a partner to any one who has on the faith of the representation given credit to the firm, whether or not the representation was communicated to the person giving credit by or with the knowledge of the person holding out.[52]

Enforcement of liability

30.9 If the debt has to be constituted, the action must be brought against the firm and not against one partner alone.[53] If the firm debt has been

---

[45] 1890 Act, ss.9 and 12.
[46] 1890 Act, s.36(3).
[47] 1890 Act, s.17. As to liability for delict, see *Welsh* v. *Knarston*, 1973 S.L.T. 66.
[48] 1890 Act, s.36.
[49] *Blacks* v. *Girdwood* (1885) 13 R. 243; Gloag & Henderson, p. 338.
[50] 1890 Act, s.17(1).
[51] *McKeand* v. *Laird* (1861) 23 D. 846; *Miller* v. *Thorburn* (1861) 23 D. 359; *Heddle's Exrx.* v. *Marwick & Hourston's Tr.* (1888) 15 R. 698; *Thomson & Balfour* v. *Boag & Son*, 1936 S.C. 2; *Miller* v. *John Finlay MacLeod & Parker*, 1974 S.L.T. 99.
[52] 1890 Act, s.14(1).
[53] Kilkerran, *s.v.* "Society," No. III, Feb. 26, 1741; *Reid & McCall* v. *Douglas*, 11 June 1814, F.C.

constituted by bill, bond or decree, any partner may be sued alone or charged.[54] A decree against the firm is a warrant for diligence against the partners whether they are named in the decree or not[55] but it is not a warrant for diligence against a person liable for the firm debts in respect of "holding out."[56] The remedy of a person who is not a partner is to suspend the charge. When an obligation is granted by all the partners without mention of the firm, there is a rebuttable presumption that it was granted for the firm's purposes and the firm's property can be poinded even if only the partners have been charged.[57] The prescriptive period runs against the liability of the partner from the date of decree against the firm.[58]

Instance

30.10 Where the firm name consists of personal names—whether these are the names of the partners or not—the firm can sue and can be sued in the firm name in the Court of Session and the sheriff court.[59] If the firm name is descriptive, (*e.g.* "Antermony Coal Company") the firm can sue or be sued in that name in the sheriff court but in the Court of Session it is necessary to add the names of three of the partners (or of two, if there are only two).[60] In all cases, however, the firm can sue in the names of the whole partners provided that words are added to show that the action is for a partnership debt.[61] An action cannot proceed in the name of the partnership if a majority of the partners disclaim it.[62] If the firm has been dissolved, the former partners can sue and be sued together as such former partners or individuals but in an action against the dissolved firm all the former partners within the jurisdiction must be called.[63]

Partnership-business names

30.11 The Business Names Act 1985 applies to partnerships which carry on a business or profession under a name which does not consist of the surnames of all the partners who are individuals and the corporate names of all partners who are bodies corporate without an addition other than the forenames of individual partners or their initials or abbreviated names or where two or more partners have the same surname, the addition of "s" at the end of that surname or an addition indicating that the business is carried on in succession to a former owner.[64] The names and addresses of all the partners must be on the business letters and other documents unless (i) there are more than 20 persons in the partnership, (ii) there is maintained at the principal place of business a list of the

---

[54] *Wallace* v. *Plock* (1841) 3 D. 1047.
[55] Partnership Act 1890, s.4(2); O.C.R. 14; *Ewing & Co.* v. *McClelland* (1860) 22 D. 1347.
[56] *Brember* v. *Rutherford* (1901) 4 F. 62.
[57] *Rosslund Cycle Co.* v. *McCreadie*, 1907 S.C. 1208.
[58] *Highland Engineering Ltd.* v. *Anderson*, 1979 S.L.T. 122.
[59] *Forsyth* v. *Hare & Co.* (1834) 13 S. 42.
[60] O.C.R. 14; *Antermony Coal Co.* v. *Wingate* (1866) 4 M. 1017.
[61] *Plotzker* v. *Lucas*, 1907 S.C. 315.
[62] *Hutcheon and Partners* v. *Hutcheon*, 1979 S.L.T. (Sh.Ct.) 61.
[63] *Muir* v. *Collett*, (1862) 24 D. 1119; *McNaught* v. *Milligan* (1885) 13 R. 366; *D. Forbes Smith & Johnston* v. *Kaye*, 1975 S.L.T. (Sh.Ct.) 33.
[64] Business Names Act 1985 s.1. See para. 30.5.

names of all the partners, (iii) none of the names of the partners appears in the document otherwise than in the text or as a signatory, and (iv) the document states in legible characters the address of the principal place of business and that the list of partners is open to inspection at that place[65]; any person may inspect the list during office hours. The other two duties under the Act apply without qualification.[66]

Compensation

Questions of compensation arising from the existence of a partnership are regulated by the principle that a partner is a debtor in debts due by the firm but is not a creditor in debts due to the firm.[67] So, where a creditor of a firm is also a debtor of a partner, either the creditor or the firm can plead compensation.[68] But where a debtor of the firm is also a creditor of a partner neither the firm's debtor nor the partner can plead compensation[69] unless the firm has been dissolved when solvent in which event the partner's share of the debt due to the firm can be set-off against the private debt.[70] If a former partner is sued for a debt due by a dissolved firm he can set-off a debt due to him personally by the pursuer.[71] It has not been decided whether, if two separate firms have the same partners, a debt due to one firm can be set-off against a debt due by the other.[72]

30.12

Sequestration of firm

Sequestration may be awarded of the estates of a firm, either with or without sequestration of the individual estates of the partners.[73]

If two firms, although consisting of the same partners, carry on separate and distinct businesses—having a real and perceptible distinction of trade and establishment—they cannot be treated as one firm for bankruptcy purposes.[74] A dissolved firm is not a "deceased debtor" for bankruptcy purposes.[75]

The partnership must be apparently insolvent, apparent insolvency being constituted either in one of the ways applicable to an individual or by any of the partners being rendered apparently insolvent for a firm debt: "one which the company as a company have to pay."[76] The petition may be at the instance of the partnership with the concurrence of qualified creditors. It seems that citation of the firm does not warrant

30.13

---

[65] s.4(3).
[66] See para. 30.5.
[67] Gloag & Irvine, p. 325.
[68] *Russell* v. *McNab* (1824) 3 S. 63; *Christie* v. *Keith* (1838) 16 S. 1224; *Scott* v. *Hall & Bissett*, June 13, 1809, F.C.; *Salmon* v. *Padon & Vannan* (1824) 3 S. 406; *Hill* v. *Lindsay* (1847) 10 D. 78; *Thomson* v. *Stevenson* (1855) 17 D. 739.
[69] *Mackie* v. *McDowal* (1774) Mor. 2575; *Morrison* v. *Hunter* (1822) 2 S. 68.
[70] *Oswald's Trs.* v. *Dickson* (1833) 12 S. 156; *Heggie* v. *Heggie* (1858) 21 D. 31; Bell, *Comm.*, II, 553.
[71] *Lockhart* v. *Ferrier* (1842) 4 D. 1253.
[72] See *Mitchell* v. *Canal Basin Co.* (1869) 7 M. 480.
[73] B.A., s.6. The estates of the firm and the individual partners cannot be sequestrated jointly: *J. & J. Messenger's Tr.*, 1990 G.W.D. 26–1432.
[74] *Commercial Bank of Scotland* v. *Tod's Tr.* (1895) 33 S.L.R. 161.
[75] *Stewart & McDonald* v. *Brown* (1898) 25 R. 1042.
[76] B.A., s.7; *Mullen Ltd.* v. *Campbell*, 1923 S.L.T. 497. As to the difficulties of serving a "three-week demand" on a partnership, see McBryde, p. 25.

sequestration of the estates of the partners as well as those of the firm if citation of the individual partners has not been effected.[77]

Where the firm is sequestrated but the partners remain solvent, the partners are liable jointly and severally for the debts of the firm. It has been doubted whether the trustee on the estate of the firm can sue a solvent partner for payment of debts by the firm; it seems that any action against the solvent partners must be at the instance of the creditors individually.[78] A partner who pays a debt is entitled to a proportionate relief from the other partners.

Where the firm and the individual partners are sequestrated, the primary rule is that the creditors of the firm rank on the estate of the firm to the full amount of their debts to the exclusion of the private creditors of the partners.[79] The firm creditors can also claim on the estates of a partner but a firm creditor must estimate the value of his claim against the firm's estate and deduct that value from his claim against the partner's estate and rank only for the balance.[80] The ranking here is of course *pari passu* with the partner's private creditors. Moreover, the firm's trustee can also rank on the partner's estate for debts due by the partner to the firm on capital account but the dividend drawn on this claim is taken into account in estimating the value of the firm's estate for purposes of the deduction from the creditors' claims on the partner's estate.[81]

A wife of a partner who has lent money to the firm is not a postponed creditor.[82]

Limited partnerships

30.14 A limited partnership must be registered under the Limited Partnerships Act 1907 and if it is not so registered it is deemed to be a general partnership.[83] It consists of one or more general partners and one or more limited partners. A body corporate may be a limited partner.[84] The total number of partners cannot exceed 20 except in the case of solicitors, accountants, stockbrokers and other types of business specified by regulations.[85] General partners are liable for all debts and obligations of the firm. Limited partners contribute to the partnership a sum of money as capital or property valued at a stated amount and are not liable for the firm's debts beyond the amount of that contribution. If he directly or indirectly draws out or receives back any part of his contribution during the continuance of the partnership, the limited partner becomes liable for the firm's debts to the amount taken back.[86] A limited partner cannot take part in the management of the business and if he does so he becomes liable for the debts incurred while he is taking such part.[87] He has no

---

[77] *Central Motor Engineering Co.* v. *Galbraith*, 1918 S.C. 755.
[78] *Laing Brothers & Co.'s Tr.* v. *Low* (1896) 23 R. 1105; *cf.* Goudy, p. 578, n. (c).
[79] Bell, *Comm.*, II, 550.
[80] B.A., Sched. 1, para. 6. See *Clydesdale Bank Ltd.* v. *Morison's Tr.*, 1982 S.C. 26.
[81] Goudy, p. 578; *Dunlop* v. *Spiers* (1776) Mor. 14610, affirmed 1777 (H.L.) Mor., *s.v.* "Society," App. No. 2.
[82] *Lumsden* v. *Sym* (1912) 28 Sh.Ct.Rep. 168.
[83] s.5; See *Reed* v. *Young* [1986] 1 W.L.R. 649.
[84] s.4(4).
[85] C.A., 1985, s.717.
[86] 1907 Act, s.4(3).
[87] 1907 Act, s.6(1).

power to bind the firm. The Business Names Act 1985 applies to a limited partnership. The rules of the Partnership Act 1890, and the general law relating to partnerships apply to limited partnerships subject to the provisions of the Act of 1907.[88]

When the limited partnership is dissolved its affairs are wound up by the general partners unless the court orders otherwise.[89] The court may order a winding up by a judicial factor.[90] A limited partnership can be sequestrated.[91] The Court of Session has jurisdiction if the partnership is registered in Scotland and the sheriff if it has an established place of business within the sheriffdom.[92] The petition may be presented by a qualified creditor or creditors only if the apparent insolvency founded on was constituted within four months from the presentation of the petition or at any time by any other person.[93]

OTHER BODIES

The European Economic Interest Grouping

The preamble to the EEC Regulation[94] declares that the EEIG is being set up to allow persons, companies and firms to co-operate effectively across frontiers in the single market and remove the legal, fiscal and psychological difficulties which were being encountered in such co-operation. The purposes of an EEIG are restricted; the purpose is not to make profits for the EEIG itself but to facilitate or develop the economic activities of its members and to improve or increase the results of these activities; its activity must be related to the economic activities of its members and must be not more than ancillary to these activities.[95] An EEIG may not manage the activities of its members or of another undertaking, hold shares in its members, employ more than 500 persons, or be a member of another EEIG.[96]

30.15

The members of an EEIG must be companies, firms or other legal bodies formed under the law of a member state and having their registered office and central administration within the EEC or be natural persons who carry on any industrial, commercial, craft or agricultural activity or provide professional or other services in the EEC. An EEIG must comprise at least two legal or natural persons who are located in different member states.[97] In the United Kingdom, but not necessarily in all member states, an EEIG is to be a body corporate.[98] However, the members of the EEIG have unlimited joint and several liability for its

---

[88] 1907 Act, s.7.
[89] 1907 Act, s.6(3).
[90] *Muirhead* v. *Borland*, 1925 S.C. 474.
[91] B.A., s.6(1)(*d*); B. Regs., reg.12(1)(2).
[92] Reg. 12(3).
[93] Reg. 12(4).
[94] Council Regulation (EEC) No. 2137/85 of July 25, 1985 on the European Economic Interest Grouping (EEIG). That Regulation is supplemented by the European Economic Interest Grouping Regulations 1989 (S.I. 1989 No. 638). In this paragraph "Art." refers to Articles of the EEC Regulations and "Reg." to Regulations of the Statutory Instrument.
[95] Art. 3.1.
[96] Art. 3.2.
[97] Art. 4.
[98] Reg. 3.

debts and other liabilities, the consequences of such liability being determined by the national law.[99]

The EEIG is founded by concluding a contract followed by registration. The contract must include the name of the EEIG, its official address, its objects, its duration unless that is indefinite and the names and addresses of the members.[1] The official address must be in the EEC and be where the EEIG has its central administration or where one of the members has its central administration or, in the case of a natural person, his principal activity, provided that the EEIG carries on an activity there.[2] The law applicable to the contract except as regards the status or capacity of natural persons and the capacity of legal persons and the law applicable to the internal organisation of the EEIG is the internal law of the state in which the official address is situated.[3] Registration must be made in the state in which the official address is situated.[4] Where the official address is in Scotland, registration must be with the Companies Office in Scotland. The contract must be filed along with Form EEIG 1; the registrar issues a certificate which is conclusive evidence that the requirements have been complied with.[5] A "grouping establishment" situated in a state other than the one in which the official address is located must be registered in that state; a certified translation of the contract must be filed along with Form EEIG 2.[6] Notice of the formation of the EEIG must be published in the *Edinburgh Gazette* and the Official Journal of the EEC.[7]

Once registered, an EEIG has capacity in its own name to have rights and obligations of all kinds, to make contracts or accomplish other legal acts, and to sue and be sued.[8] The two organs of the EEIG are the members acting collectively and the managers.[9] Certain decisions, for example, alteration of the objects, require unanimity of the members; the contract may provide that other decisions can be taken by a majority.[10] The managers represent the EEIG in dealings with third parties and their acts bind the EEIG.[11] Profits from EEIG activities are deemed to be the profits of the members and are apportioned in accordance with the contract.[12] Profits are taxable only in the hands of the members.[13]

There is machinery for the introduction of new members,[14] and for the withdrawal of a member.[15] The Business Names Act 1985 and certain provisions of the Companies Act 1985, the Insolvency Act 1986 and the

---

[99] Art. 24.1.
[1] Art. 5.
[2] Art. 12.
[3] Art. 2.1.
[4] Art. 6.
[5] Reg. 9.
[6] Art. 10; Reg. 12.
[7] Arts. 8, 11; Reg. 15.
[8] Art. 2.
[9] Art. 16.
[10] Art. 17.
[11] Art. 20.
[12] Art. 21.
[13] Art. 40.
[14] Art. 26.
[15] Art. 27.

Company Directors Disqualification Act 1986 are applied to the EEIG. The provisions of the Companies Act 1985 as to registration of charges apply to an EEIG. An EEIG can create a floating charge.

Members of a grouping have unlimited joint and several liability for its debts and liabilities of whatever nature.[16] A new member becomes liable for the EEIG's debts including those arising out of activities before his admission but he may be exempted from liability for pre-admission debts by a clause in the EEIG contract or in the instrument of admission but such a clause can be relied on as against third parties only if it is published in accordance with Article 8.[17] A member who ceases to belong to an EEIG remains answerable for the debts and liabilities arising out of its activities before he ceased to be a member but actions against the member in connection with such debts and liabilities are subject to a five year limitation period dating from the publication in the *Gazette* of notice of his ceasing to belong to the EEIG. A similar five year limitation period running from publication of notice of the conclusion of liquidation of the EEIG applies to actions against any member in connection with debts and other liabilities arising out of the EEIG's activities.[18]

Creditors cannot proceed against a member for payment of debt before the conclusion of the liquidation of the EEIG unless they have first requested the EEIG to pay and payment has not been made within "an appropriate period."[19] The EEIG is wound up as an unregistered company under Part V of the Insolvency Act 1986. For purposes of jurisdiction the EEIG is treated as a company with a capital not exceeding £120,000. A member may assign his participation in the EEIG but the unanimous authorisation of the other members is required.[20] It would seem that the interest of a member can be arrested in the hands of the EEIG.

Clubs and associations

An unincorporated association is not a legal person.

30.16

A member of a club or association does not, in the absence of a special provision in the constitution, become liable for the debts of the body and is liable only for his subscription.[21]

The liability for debts is a question of circumstances.[22] There may be personal liability on the part of a manager but as a rule he contracts as an agent for the committee or for the whole membership. Individual committee members may be personally liable if they personally gave orders or signed cheques for specific accounts. Where the system of orders and payments was such that members of the committee had general knowledge that supplies were being obtained from a particular tradesman and his accounts were passed for payment by the committee as

---

[16] Art. 24.
[17] Art. 26.
[18] Art. 37.
[19] Art. 24.
[20] Art. 22.
[21] *Wise* v. *Perpetual Trustee Co. Ltd.* [1903] A.C. 139.
[22] *Thomson & Gillespie* v. *Victoria Eighty Club* (1905) 13 S.L.T. 399. See also *Bryson & Co. Ltd.* v. *Glasgow Civil Service & Mercantile Guild* (1916) 32 Sh.Ct.Rep. 23; *James McVey Ltd.* v. *Budhill Social and Recreation Club*, 1932 S.L.T. (Sh.Ct.) 27; *Cromarty Leasing Ltd.* v. *Turnbull*, 1988 S.L.T. (Sh.Ct.) 62.

part of its ordinary business, the members of the committee were held jointly and severally liable. The whole membership of the club may be liable if they gave the committee a mandate to pledge the credit of the general body of members.

In the Court of Session the association should sue or be sued in its own name with the addition of the office-bearers[23]; in the sheriff court the association can sue and be sued in its name alone but the addition of the names of the office-bearers is desirable.[24] However, if the constitution prescribes a mode of suing, that should be used.[25]

An extract decree against the association is a warrant for diligence against the association but not against office-bearers or members not called in the action.[26]

An unincorporated association can be made apparently insolvent if a person representing the association is apparently insolvent, or a person holding property of the body in a fiduciary capacity is apparently insolvent, for a debt of the body.[27] An unincorporated association can be sequestrated[28] on the petition of a person authorised to act on behalf of the body with the concurrence of a qualified creditor or creditors or, of a qualified creditor or creditors if it is apparently insolvent.[29]

English debtor

30.17　A petition for sequestration may be sisted or dismissed if bankruptcy proceedings are in train in England and Wales.[30] A sequestration may be recalled if a majority in value of creditors reside in a country other than Scotland and it is more appropriate for the debtor's estate to be administered in that other country. It is also a ground of recall that a bankruptcy or administration order has been made in England.[31]

Subordinate legislation is to be made to provide that a trustee appointed under the insolvency law of one part of the United Kingdom will have the same rights over property situated in another part as he would have if he were a trustee in that other part.[32] It would appear that discharge in an English bankruptcy is recognised in respect of a Scottish debt.[33]

Scottish companies

30.18　Securities granted by companies[34] and the liquidation of companies[35] are dealt with elsewhere. A company is not liable for a debt incurred prior to the date of its incorporation; so a company is not liable for a debt

---

[23] *Bridge v. South Portland St. Synagogue*, 1907 S.C. 1351; *Pagan & Osborne v. Haig*, 1910 S.C. 341.
[24] O.C.R. 14; *Whitecraigs Golf Club v. Ker*, 1923 S.L.T. (Sh.Ct.) 23; *Borland v. Lochwinnoch Golf Club*, 1986 S.L.T. (Sh.Ct.) 13.
[25] *Whitecraigs Golf Club v. Ker, supra*.
[26] O.C.R. 14; *Aitchison v. McDonald*, 1911 S.C. 174.
[27] B.A., s.7(3)(*b*).
[28] B.A., s.6(1)(*c*).
[29] B.A., s.6(6).
[30] B.A., s.10.
[31] B.A., s.17.
[32] I.A., s.426(3). See para. 21.21.
[33] I.A., ss.281, 382(1).
[34] Chap. 9.
[35] Chap. 25.

incurred prior to its incorporation by another company, later dissolved, which had the same name, some of the same directors, and carried on the same type of business.[36] A contract binds the company if it is signed by any person acting under its authority.[37] Where a document is signed by a person "as director" it is a question of circumstances as to whether he is personally bound or is to be treated as an agent. A document is validly subscribed by the company if it is signed on its behalf by a director or the secretary or by a person authorised to sign the document on its behalf. A document is validly executed by the company and is probative if it is subscribed on behalf of the company by two directors or a director and the secretary or two persons authorised to subscribe on behalf of the company notwithstanding that it is not attested or sealed.[38]

English company

Charges created by a company registered in England are registered with the registrar of companies for England and Wales even if the security subjects are situated in Scotland.[39] A floating charge created by an English company is given effect in Scotland. An English receiver may exercise his powers in Scotland so far as their exercise is not inconsistent with the law applicable there.[40]

In the liquidation of an English company the English court can restrain proceedings against the company in Scotland.[41]

30.19

Oversea company

When a company incorporated outside Great Britain establishes a place of business in Great Britain, it must within one month deliver to the registrar for registration a number of documents including a certified copy of the charter, statutes or memorandum and articles of the company and a return containing, *inter alia*, a list of the names and addresses of some one or more persons resident in Great Britain authorised to accept on the company's behalf service of process and any notices required to be served on it.[42] Registration is effected in England and Wales or Scotland according to where the place of business has been established; if there is a place of business in both jurisdictions there must be registration in both.[43] Any process can be served on any person whose name has been delivered to the registrar as the name of a person on whom process can be served; if there is no such name available a document may be served on the

30.20

---

[36] *F. J. Neale (Glasgow) Ltd.* v. *Vickery*, 1973 S.L.T. (Sh.Ct.) 88. See, however, I.A., ss.216–217.

[37] C.A., 1985, s.36. As to the secretary's authority, see *Panorama Developments (Guildford) Ltd.* v. *Fidelis Furnishing Fabrics Ltd.* [1971] 2 Q.B. 711; *McLean* v. *Stuart*, 1970 S.L.T. (Notes) 77. See, as to bills, para. 5.13.

[38] C.A., s.36B, subst. by Law Reform (Miscellaneous Provisions) (S.) Act 1990, s.72.

[39] C.A., s.395(3), (4).

[40] I.A., s.725; *Gordon Anderson (Plant) Ltd.* v. *Campsie Construction Ltd. and Anglo Scottish Plant Ltd.*, 1977 S.L.T. 7. As to recall of an inhibition, see *Taymech Ltd.* v. *Rush & Tompkins Ltd.*, 1990 G.W.D. 21-1198.

[41] I.A., s.126; *Re Dynamics Corporation* [1973] 1 W.L.R. 63. As to the effect of Scottish diligence in the liquidation of an English company, see I.A., s.185(4).

[42] C.A., s.691. See *Lord Advocate* v. *Huron and Erie Loan and Savings Co.*, 1911 S.C. 612; *Re Oriel Ltd.* [1986] 1 W.L.R. 180.

[43] C.A., s.696.

company by leaving it at, or sending it by post to, any place of business established by the company.[44] When a registered overseas company creates a charge over property situated in Great Britain which would require registration if created by a company registered in Great Britain it must register the charge within 21 days in the part of Great Britain in which it is registered[45]; if the company is registered in both parts but the charged property is situate in one part only, the charge is registered in that one part; in any other case, the charge is registered in both parts.[46] There must similarly be registration if the company acquires property in Great Britain which is subject to a charge and when the charge is in existence at the time when the company is first registered. A ship, aircraft or hovercraft is regarded as situate in Great Britain if, and only if, it is registered there and other vehicles are so regarded on a day, if and only if, at any time on that day the management of the vehicle is directed from a place of business of the company in Great Britain; a vehicle shall not be regarded as situate in one part of Great Britain only.[47] Future property is regarded as situate in Great Britain unless the property is of a kind which cannot, after being acquired or coming into existence, be situated in Great Britain.[48] An oversea company may be wound up as an unregistered company, notwithstanding that it has been dissolved or otherwise ceased to exist under the laws of the country in which it was incorporated.[49]

Married persons

30.21 One spouse is not in general liable for the debts of the other. Where the spouses are living apart, if the husband is not adequately supporting the wife and if the wife has no means of her own, the husband is liable on the principle of recompense to those who have supplied necessaries to the wife.[50] This liability cannot be terminated by notice to traders. A husband is not liable, by reason only of being her husband, for any debts incurred by his wife before marriage.[51]

Foreign insolvencies

30.22 The provisions of s.426 of the Insolvency Act have already been explained[52] and trustees or assignees acting under the law of another part of the UK can seek the assistance of the Scottish courts by virtue of them. These provisions can also be used by those acting under the law of any "relevant territory," which is defined to include, *inter alia*, the Republic of Ireland, the Channel Islands and the Isle of Man.[53]

---

[44] C.A., s.695; *Punjab National Bank* v. *Rome* [1989] F.S.R. 380.
[45] C.A., s.703D (C.A. 1989 Sched. 15).
[46] C.A., s.703E.
[47] C.A., s.703L(1).
[48] C.A., s.703L(2).
[49] I.A., s.225; *Inland Revenue* v. *Highland Engineering Ltd.*, 1975 S.L.T. 203.
[50] *Neilson* v. *Guthrie & Gairn* (1672) Mor. 5878; *Moore Taggart & Co.* v. *Kerr* (1897) 14 Sh.Ct.Rep. 10; *Buie* v. *Gordon* (1827) 5 S. 464; (1831) 9 S. 923.
[51] Law Reform (Husband and Wife) (Scotland) Act 1985, s.6.
[52] See para. 21.21.
[53] Co-operation of Insolvency Courts (Designation of Relevant Countries and Territories) Order (S.I. 1986 No. 2123).

INDEX

ACCEPTANCE,
  bill, 5.3
ACCEPTOR, 5.3
ACCOMMODATION BILL, 5.7
ACCOMMODATION PARTY, 5.7, 23.9
  cautioner, as, 23.9
ACCOUNT,
  continuing, 14.5
  fitted, 12.14
  money of, 1.5
  open, 12.14
  running, 13.1
  settled, 12.14
ACCOUNT-CURRENT, 12.5, 13.1
  duty of banker, 6.2
"ACCOUNT PAYEE", 6.11
ACCOUNTANT,
  lien, 7.9
ACCOUNTANT IN BANKRUPTCY, 20.6
ACCOUNTING,
  action, 11.4
ACQUIRENDA,
  sequestration, 21.20
ACT AND WARRANT, 20.4, 21.1
ACTIO QUANTI MINORIS, 2.11
ACTION,
  accounting, 11.4
  count, reckoning and payment, 11.4
  Court of Session, 11.18
  furthcoming, 11.10
  multiplepoinding, 11.5
  payment, of, 11.3
  relief, 1.6
ACTION FOR PAYMENT,
  partial admission, 11.13
  tender, 11.14
AD FACTUM PRAESTANDUM,
  co-obligants, 28.1
ADJUDICATION, 8.2, 15.1
  debitum fundi, 1.7
  defined, 19.4
  liquidation, 19.4
  procedure, 19.4
  redemption, 19.4
  sequestration, 19.4
  subjects, 19.4
  time to pay direction, 11.20
ADMINISTRATION,
  apparent insolvency, 26.12

ADMINISTRATION—*continued*
  bank account, 6.10
  cautionary obligation, 26.8
  defined, 26.2
  directions, 26.1
  discharge, 26.7
  equalisation of diligence, 26.12
  extortionate credit transaction, 26.6
  financial markets régime, 26.2
  fixed security, 26.8
  floating charge, 26.6, 26.9
  gratuitous alienation, 26.6
  hire-purchase, 26.11
    sale, 26.11
  hypothec, 26.8
  incomplete diligence, 26.12
  insolvency practitioner, 26.2
  interim administrator, 26.3
  interim order, 26.3
  meeting of creditors, 26.6
  notice, 26.3
  order, 26.4
    effect of, 26.5
  petition, 26.3
  pledge, 26.8
  possessory lien, 26.8
  preferential debt,
    relevant date, 26.10
  prescription, 26.10
  purposes, 26.4
  secured creditor, 26.4
  set-off, 26.10
  sist, 26.1
  statement of proposals, 26.6
    revision, 26.7
  unfair preference, 26.6
  unsecured creditor, 26.4, 26.10
ADMINISTRATION ORDER, 9.23
ADMINISTRATIVE RECEIVER, 9.23, 26.3, 26.4
ADMINISTRATOR,
  discharge, 26.7
  functions, 26.5, 26.6
  interim, 26.3
  nominee, as, 26.1
  powers, 26.6
  public utilities' supply, 26.6
  release, 26.7
  voluntary arrangement, 26.1
ADMISSION,
  partial, 11.13
ADVERTISEMENT,
  credit, 3.11

321

AGENCY, 21.2
  bill of exchange, 5.13
  foreign principal, 30.2
  prescription, 14.4, 14.5

AGENT, 3.14
  administrator, 26.6
  authority, 30.2
    ostensible, 30.3
  banker, 6.13
  del credere, 13.4
  liability, 30.2
    on bill, 5.13, 5.14
  oath of, 4.6
  partner, 30.6
  payment to, 12.6
  principal,
    liability, 30.2
    title to sue, 30.1
    undisclosed, 30.2
  proof, 30.2
  title to sue, 30.1
  undisclosed principal, 30.2

AGREEMENT,
  cancellation, 3.13
  content, 3.12
  copy of, 3.12
  legibility, 3.12
  termination, 3.15

AGRICULTURAL CHARGE, 7.3

AIRCRAFT,
  mortgage, 7.3, 7.6
  security over, 7.6

ALIMENT, 29.5
  adopted child, 1.6
  civil imprisonment, 19.8
  deceased debtor, 29.5, 29.6
  sequestration, 21.19, 23.2

ALIMENTARY LIFERENT,
  assignation, 27.1

ALIMENTARY PAYMENT,
  arrestment, 17.3
  assignation, 27.1
  compensation, 13.8

ALIMENTARY PROVISION,
  sequestration, 21.9

ANCILLARY CREDIT BUSINESS, 3.10

ANNUAL FLAT RATE, 3.9

ANNUAL PERCENTAGE RATE OF CHARGE, 3.8

ANNUITY,
  arrestment, 18.2
  heritable, 29.2
  heritably secured, 1.7
  prescription, 14.4
  transmissibility, 29.1

ANTECEDENT NEGOTIATIONS, 3.13, 3.14

ANTERIOR CREDITOR, 23.5

APOCHA TRIUM ANNORUM, 12.10

APPARENT INSOLVENCY,
  administration, 26.12
  defined, 20.1
  equalisation of diligence, 15.5
  multiple, 15.5
  partnership, 30.13
  proof of, 20.2
  unincorporated association, 30.16

APPEAL,
  Court of Session, 11.18
  ordinary action, 11.17
  small claim, 11.15
  summary cause, 11.16

ARBITRATION, 14.7

ARBITRATION AWARD,
  prescription, 14.4

ARREARS,
  feu-duty, 29.2, 29.10
  interest on, 11.7
  rent, 29.2, 29.10

ARRESTEE,
  agent, 17.2
  auctioneer, 17.2
  bank, 17.6
  blacksmith, 17.4
  carrier, 17.4
  commissioner, 17.2
  company, 17.6
  consignee, 17.4
  corporation, 17.6
  curator bonis, 17.6
  debtor's wife, 17.2
  depositary, 17.4
  executor, 17.6
  factor, 17.2
    loco absentis, 17.2
  furth of Scotland, 17.5
  incapax, 17.6
  innkeeper, 17.4
  judicial factor, 17.6
  liquidator, 17.6
  minor, 17.6
  partnership, 17.6
  pupil, 17.6
  purchaser, 17.2
  servant, 17.2
  shipbroker, 17.6
  shipowner, 17.4, 17.6
  solicitor, 17.2
  tenant, 17.4
  trustee, 17.2, 17.6
  tutor, 17.6

ARRESTER, 17.1

ARRESTMENT, 15.1
  alimentary payment, 17.3
  appointment of receiver, 17.14
  arrestee. *See* ARRESTEE.

Index

ARRESTMENT—*continued*
arrester, 17.1
bank account, 6.8n.
bill, 17.4
bond, 17.3
books, 17.4
calls on shares, 17.3
common debtor, 17.1
competition, 17.9
  with adjudication, 17.10
  with arrestment, 17.9
  with assignation, 17.11, 27.5
  with confirmation, 17.10
contract payment, 17.3
corporeal moveables, 11.9, 17.4
damages, 17.3
death of creditor, 29.3
death of debtor, 29.4
definition, 17.1
deposit receipt, 17.3
earnings, 17.3
effect, 17.7
  of liquidation, 17.13
  of sequestration, 17.12
"effectually executed diligence", 17.14
execution, 11.10
execution, in, 11.9, 17.1 *et seq.*
exempt articles, 17.4
expenses, 17.3
furthcoming, 17.8
in rem, 17.16
insurance policy, 17.3
interdict, 11.10, 17.15
legitim, 17.3
liability to account, 17.3
obligation to account, 11.9
on the dependence, 11.10
partnership interest, 17.3
periodical payment, 17.7
prescription, 1.10, 11.10, 17.7
prevention, 17.15
prior assignation, 27.5
recall, 11.10, 11.20, 17.15
rent, 17.3
restriction, 17.15
schedule, 11.8, 17.5
security, in, 11.12
service, 17.4
shares, 17.3
ship, 11.8, 17.16
spes successionis, 17.3
stolen property, 17.4
subjects, 11.9, 11.10, 17.3
time to pay direction, 11.20
to found jurisdiction, 11.8
trust fund, 1.10
trust interest, 17.3
validity, 11.10
warrant, 11.8, 11.10, 17.5

ARRESTMENT ON THE DEPENDENCE, 11.10
effect of sequestration, 17.12

ARRESTMENT ON THE DEPENDENCE—*continued*
prescription, 17.7

ASCRIPTION OF PAYMENT, 12.5

ASSIGNATION, 8.1
alimentary payment, 27.1
appointment of judicial factor, 29.11
assignee's right, 27.7
assurance policy, 27.1, 27.2
bill of exchange, 27.2, 27.9
cedent, 27.5
cheque, 27.2
compensation, 13.6
competition with arrestment, 27.5
contingent debt, 27.1
co-obligants, 28.2 *et seq.*
damages, 27.1
executor, 27.5
floating charge, 27.1
form, 27.2
future debt, 27.1
inter vivos, 29.7
intimation. See INTIMATION OF ASSIGNATION
joint delinquents, 28.6
limited partner's share, 27.1
mandate, 27.2
reversionary interest, 27.3
seaman's wages, 27.1
sequestration, 27.5
social security benefit, 27.1
special, 29.5, 29.7
spes successionis, 27.1
standard security, 8.2
third party, 27.5
title to sue, 27.6
uncalled capital, 27.1
warrandice, 27.8
warrant for diligence, 15.3

ASSIGNEE,
oath of, 4.6

ASSIGNATUS UTITUR JURE AUCTORIS, 5.2, 27.7

ASSOCIATE, 22.3

ASSUMPTION,
as to credit, 3.6

ASSURANCE POLICY, 3.17
assignation, 27.1, 27.2

ASSURED TENANCY,
diligence, 15.6
sequestration, 21.15

AUCTIONEER,
arrestee, 17.2
lien, 7.10

BALANCING ACCOUNTS IN BANKRUPTCY, 13.10

BANK,
    administration, 26.3n.
    arrestee, 17.6
    compensation, 13.4, 13.8
    creditor, 3.4
    overdraft, 3.3

BANK ACCOUNT,
    arrestment, 6.8n.

BANK DRAFT, 3.15
    fraudulent preference, 22.6
    sequestration, 21.8

BANK NOTE, 3.20
    poinding, 16.2
    prescription, 14.4
    Scottish, 1.2n.

BANK OF ENGLAND NOTES, 1.2

BANKER,
    agent, 6.13
    collecting, 6.1, 6.13
    duty to customer, 6.2
    lien, 7.10
    paying, 6.1, 6.12

BANKING TRANSACTION, 14.5

BANKRUPT,
    oath of, 4.6

BANKRUPTCY,
    balancing accounts, 13.10
    compensation, 13.4

BEARER, 5.2

BEARER BOND,
    pledge of, 7.4

BENEFICIARY,
    liability for debt, 29.6
    right in trust, 1.11
    sequestration, 29.6

BENEFICIUM DIVISIONIS, 10.1

BETTING AND GAMING DUTY,
    poinding, 19.7
    preferential debt, 25.12
    preferred debt, 23.11

BILL OF EXCHANGE,
    acceptance, 5.3
    acceptor, 5.3
    accommodation, 5.7
    accommodation party, 5.7, 23.9
    agency, 5.13
    arrestment of corpus, 17.4
    assignation, 27.2
    capacity, 5.17
    cheque, 6.1
    consideration, 5.18
    co-acceptors, 28.1
    co-drawers, 28.1
    defences, 5.16 et seq.
    defined, 5.3

BILL OF EXCHANGE—continued
    delivery, 5.15
    dishonour, 5.5
    drawee, 5.3
    drawer, 5.3
    enforcement, 5.8
    force and fear, 5.16
    forgery, 5.10, 5.21
    fraud, 5.16
    fraudulent preference, 22.6
    holder for value, 5.7
    holder in due course, 5.9
    illegality, 5.20
    in a set, 5.9n.
    indorsee, 5.4
    interest, 11.7
    joint and several liability, 28.1
    liability, 5.6
    lien, 5.9
    lost, 5.8
    negotiation, 5.4
    notice of dishonour, 5.26
    payee, 5.3
    payment, 5.3, 5.22
    prescription, 5.23
    presentment, 5.24, 5.25
        for acceptance, 5.24
        for payment, 5.24
    proof, 5.19
    qualifying agreement, 5.18
    sequestration, 23.9
    summary diligence, 19.6
    transfer of debt, 27.9
    transferee for value, 5.8
    ultra vires, 5.11
    unauthorised signature, 5.12
    value, 5.9

BILL OF LADING, 5.2, 7.3

BOND,
    arrestment, 17.3
    defined, 5.1
    liquid, 1.9
    moveable, 29.2

BOND OF CAUTION, 24.1

BOND OF CORROBORATION, 14.8

BONUS,
    arrestment, 18.2

BOOK DEBT,
    security over, 9.1

BOTTOMRY BOND, 7.5

BREACH OF CONTRACT, 1.6
    interest on damages, 11.7
    prescription, 14.4
    sale of goods, 2.4, 2.5
    sale of heritage, 2.11

BREACH OF TRUST,
    prescription, 14.4

Index 325

BUILDING CONTRACT, 2.10, 14.5
   retention, 13.9
   sequestration, 21.12

BUILDING SOCIETY,
   banking services, 6.1
   creditor, 3.4
   compensation, 13.8

BUSINESS DAY, 5.3

BUSINESS NAME, 30.5, 30.11

BUSINESS PREMISES, 3.13

CALLS ON SHARES,
   arrestment, 17.3
   security over, 4.1
   set-off, 13.10

CANCELLATION,
   regulated agreement, 3.13
   right of, 3.12

CAR TAX,
   preferential debt, 25.12
   preferred debt, 23.11
   summary warrant procedure, 19.7

CARRIER,
   arrestee, 17.4

CATHOLIC SECURITY, 8.6

CAUTIONARY OBLIGATION. *See* CAUTIONRY.

CAUTIONER'S SECURITY, 23.8

CAUTIONRY, 145 *et seq.*
   accessory, 10.1
   accommodation party, 23.9
   administration, 26.8
   co-cautioners, 10.1, 23.7, 23.8
   composition, 24.1
   confusio, 14.3
   Consumer Credit Act 1974, 10.1
   defined, 10.1
   discharge, 10.3, 28.7
   form, 10.1
   improper, 10.1, 23.7
   interest, 11.7
   intimation of assignation, 27.3
   liability of cautioner, 10.1
   performance bond, 10.2
   prescription, 10.2
   proper, 10.1, 23.7
   right of relief, 28.2
   security, 23.8
   sequestration, 23.7

CEDENT,
   assignation, 27.5
   oath, 4.6

CHARGE,
   agricultural, 7.3
   book debt, 9.1

CHARGE—*continued*
   debenture issue, 9.1
   defined, 9.1
   floating, 7.3, 9.1. *See also* FLOATING CHARGE.
   goods, 9.1
   goodwill, 9.1
   Inland Revenue, 7.3
   intellectual property, 9.1
   land, 9.1
   registrable, 9.1
   share capital, 9.1
   solicitor, 7.3
   void, 9.7

CHARGE FOR CREDIT. *See* TOTAL CHARGE FOR CREDIT.

CHARGE FOR PAYMENT,
   time to pay direction, 11.20

CHARGE PER POUND LENT, 3.9

CHARITY,
   creditor, 3.4

CHATTEL LEASING AGREEMENT, 26.11

CHEQUE, 3.15, 3.20
   acceptance, 6.1
   "account payee", 6.11
   assignation, 27.2
   certification, 6.1
   countermand, 6.1, 6.8
   crossing, 6.11
   death of customer, 6.9
   defined, 6.1
   forgery, 6.11
   fraudulent preference, 22.6
   indorsement, 6.4, 6.5
   insolvency of customer, 6.10
   insufficient funds, 6.7
   loan proved by, 4.5
   marking, 6.1n.
   "not negotiable", 6.11
   payment, as, 12.2
   post-dated, 6.2
   precautions against theft, 6.1
   presumption of value, 6.1
   stale, 6.3
   theft, 6.11
   transfer of funds, 6.6
   undated, 6.9n.

CHEQUE CARD, 3.3, 6.2
   countermand, 6.8n.

CHIROGRAPHUM, 4.5, 12.9

CIVIL IMPRISONMENT, 19.8

CLAIM,
   partial, 11.6

CLAIM EX DELICTO,
   transmission, 29.5

CLUB, 30.16

COAL LEVY,
  preferential debt, 25.12
  preferred debt, 23.11

CO-CAUTIONERS,
  discharge, 28.7
  sequestration, 28.7

COGNITIONIS CAUSA TANTUM, 29.8

COINS, 1.2

COLLATERAL OBLIGATION, 2.11

COLLATERAL SECURITY, 23.4

COLLECTING BANKER, 6.1
  protection, 6.13

COLLUSION, 22.6

COMMISSION,
  arrestment, 18.2

COMMISSIONERS, 20.4

COMMON DEBTOR, 17.1
  arrestment, 11.10

COMMUNITY CHARGE,
  summary warrant procedure, 19.7

COMPANY,
  administration, 26.2
  arrestee, 17.6
  bill, signing of, 5.13
  dissolution, 25.15
  English, 30.19
  floating charge, 9.9 et seq. See also
    FLOATING CHARGE.
  fraudulent trading, 25.8
  intimation of assignation, 27.3
  liability, 30.18
  limited, 25.9
    by guarantee, 25.9
  overseas, 30.20
  register of charges, 9.8
  Scottish, 30.18
  securities, 9.1 et seq.
    registration, 9.2
  unlimited, 25.9
  voluntary arrangement, 26.1
  wrongful trading, 25.8

COMPENSATION, 13.1 et seq.
  agent, 13.4
  agreement, 13.6
  aliment, 13.8
  arrestment, 18.2
  bank, 13.4, 13.8
  bankruptcy, 13.4
  building society, 13.8
  client account, 13.8
  contributory, 13.8
  co-obligants, 13.4
  deposit, 13.8
  executor, 13.4

COMPENSATION—continued
  liquidation, 13.4
  prescription, 13.6
  sequestration, 13.4
  suspension, 13.7
  trust deed, 13.4
  tutor, 13.4

COMPOSITION,
  extra-judicial, 24.1
  voluntary arrangement, 26.1

CONCURSUS DEBITI ET CREDITI, 13.3, 13.10

CONDICTIO CAUSA DATA CAUSA NON
  SECUTA, 1.6

CONDICTIO INDEBITI, 1.6, 12.7

CONDITIONAL SALE, 2.3n.
  floating charge, 9.18
  prescription, 14.5

CONDITIONAL SALE AGREEMENT, 4.10
  land, of, 4.12

CONDITIONAL OBLIGATION, 1.11

CONFIDENT PERSON, 22.3

CONFIRMATION, 29.3
  executor-creditor, 29.4, 29.7
  need for, 29.3

CONFIRMATION AS EXECUTOR-CREDITOR, 29.7

CONFUSIO, 14.3

CONJOINED ARRESTMENT ORDER, 17.7, 18.1
  debt, 18.13
  deduction from earnings, 18.16
  disbursement, 18.17
  duration, 18.5
  effect, 18.14
  of sequestration, 18.12
  procedure, 18.12
  variation, 18.18

CONJUNCT PERSON, 22.3

CONNECTED LENDER LIABILITY, 4.8

CONSIDERATION,
  bill, 5.18

CONSIGNATION, 29.7
  fraudulent preference, 22.6

CONSIGNEE,
  arrestee, 17.4

CONSTANT PERIOD RATE OF CHARGE, 3.8, 3.9

CONSTITUTION OF DEBT,
  executor, against, 29.6
  partnership, against, 30.9

CONSTRUCTIVE CONVERSION, 29.2

CONSUMER CREDIT ACT 1974,
  advertising, 3.11
  antecedent negotiations, 3.13, 3.14

Index

CONSUMER CREDIT ACT—*continued*
ascription of payment, 12.5
cancellation, 3.13
cautionary obligation, 10.1
charge for credit, 3.6
conditional sale agreement, 4.10
conditional sale of land, 4.12
connected lender liability, 4.8
consumer credit agreement, 3.3
consumer hire agreement, 3.3, 3.5, 4.11
credit bargain, 3.2
credit card agreement, 3.3
credit limit, 3.3
credit token, 4.13
  agreement, 4.13
death of debtor, 3.17
debtor-creditor agreement, 3.3, 4.7
debtor-creditor-supplier agreement, 3.3
default, 3.16, 3.21
  notice, 3.16, 3.21
enforcement order, 3.18
exempt agreement, 3.2, 3.3, 3.4
extortionate credit bargain, 3.2
extortionate credit transaction, 22.12
fixed-sum credit, 3.3, 3.8
heritable security, 8.4
hire-purchase agreement, 3.3, 4.10
land mortgage, 8.4
licensing, 3.10
linked transaction, 3.2, 3.4, 3.5, 3.15
loan, 4.7
modifying agreement, 3.5
multiple agreement, 3.5
negotiable instrument, 3.20
non-commercial agreement, 3.5
personal credit agreement, 3.3
pledge, 7.4
principal agreement, 3.5
quotation, 3.11
regulated agreement, 3.2, 3.3, 3.12
reliable lender, 3.4
restricted-use credit agreement, 3.3
running-account credit, 3.3, 3.8
security, 3.20, 3.21, 7.1, 7.2
small agreement, 3.5
summary diligence, 19.5
tables, 3.9
time order, 3.19, 11.20
total charge for credit, 3.6, 3.8, 3.11
unrestricted-use credit agreement, 3.3

CONSUMER CREDIT AGREEMENT, 3.3

CONSUMER CREDIT TABLES, 3.9

CONSUMER HIRE AGREEMENT, 3.3, 3.5, 4.11

CONSUMER PROTECTION ACT 1987,
  prescription, 14.4, 14.9

CONTEMPT OF COURT,
  civil imprisonment, 19.8

CONTINGENT DEBT, 1.9, 1.10, 1.11, 20.2, 25.2

CONTINGENT DEBT—*continued*
  assignation, 27.1
  liquidation, 25.10
  payment by executor, 29.6
  sequestration, 23.2

CONTINGENT LIABILITY, 1.11

CONTINUING ACCOUNT, 14.5

CONTRACT, 1.6
  building. *See* BUILDING CONTRACT.
  liquidation, 25.7

CONTRACT PAYMENT,
  arrestment, 17.3

CONTRIBUTORY,
  compensation, 13.8
  death of, 29.5
  liability, 25.9
    company limited by guarantee, 25.9
    limited company, 25.9
    unlimited company, 25.9
  liquidation, 25.8, 25.9

CONVERSION, 6.13

CO-OBLIGANTS, 23.6
  assignation, 28.3
  discharge, 28.7
  intimation of assignation, 27.3
  oath of, 4.6
  pactum de non petendo, 28.7
  prescription, 28.4
  right of relief, 28.2
  security, 28.3
  sequestration, 23.6, 23.8, 28.2, 28.7

COPYRIGHT,
  security over, 9.1

CORPORATION,
  arrestee, 17.6

CORPOREAL MOVEABLES,
  arrestment, 11.9, 17.4
  floating charge, 9.18
  liquidation, 25.7
  security over, 7.3

COUNSEL'S FEES, 12.8

COUNT, RECKONING AND PAYMENT,
  action, 11.4

COUNTER CLAIM,
  competency, 13.2
  Crown, 13.8

COURT OF SESSION,
  action for payment, 11.18

COURTESY,
  prescription, 14.4

CREDIT,
  amount assumed, 3.6
  date of provision, 3.6
  definition, 3.1, 3.3

CREDIT—*continued*
 period of provision, 3.6
 total charge for, 3.6, 3.8. *See also* TOTAL CHARGE FOR CREDIT.

CREDIT AGREEMENT, 3.2

CREDIT BARGAIN, 3.2

CREDIT-BROKER, 3.5, 3.10

CREDIT-BROKERAGE, 3.10

CREDIT CARD, 4.8
 payment, 12.3

CREDIT CARD AGREEMENT, 3.3

CREDIT LIMIT, 3.3, 3.6

CREDIT REFERENCE AGENCY, 3.10

CREDIT SALE,
 prescription, 14.5

CREDIT-SALE AGREEMENT,
 defined, 4.9

CREDIT-TOKEN, 4.13

CREDIT-TOKEN AGREEMENT, 4.13

CREDITOR,
 ancestor's, 23.12
 anterior, 23.5
 claim,
  composition, 24.1
  liquidation, 25.10
  sequestration, 23.1 *et seq.*
 contingent, 25.2
 death, 29.1 *et seq.*
 prospective, 25.2
 secured, 23.4
 unsecured, 26.10
 voluntary arrangement, 26.1

CREDITORS' MEETING,
 administration, 26.6
 voluntary arrangement, 26.1

CREDITORS' VOLUNTARY WINDING UP, 25.14

CREMATION EXPENSES, 29.6

CROSSED CHEQUE, 6.11

CROWN,
 compensation, 13.8
 counter claim, 13.8

CURATOR,
 oath of, 4.6

CURATOR BONIS,
 arrestee, 17.6

CURRENCY,
 foreign, 1.5
 United Kingdom, 1.2

CURRENT MAINTENANCE ARRESTMENT, 17.7, 18.1
 competency, 18.7

CURRENT MAINTENANCE ARRESTMENT—*continued*
 competition with earnings arrestment, 18.11
 daily rate of maintenance, 18.7
 deduction from earnings, 18.8, 18.9
 defined, 18.1
 duration, 18.10
 effect, 18.8
 employer, 18.7, 18.8
 expenses, 18.10
 maintenance order, 18.7
 orders, 18.10
 ranking, 18.11
 schedule, 18.7

CUSTOMS AND EXCISE,
 poinding, 19.7

DAMAGES,
 arrestment, 17.3
 assignation, 27.1
 breach of contract, 1.6, 2.4
 interest on, 11.7
 liquid claim, 1.6
 transmissibility, 29.1

DAY, 14.6

DAY CERTAIN, 2.2

DE LIQUIDO IN LIQUIDUM, 13.3

DEATH,
 bank account, 6.10
 Consumer Credit Act 1974, 3.17
 contributory, 29.5
 creditor, 29.1 *et seq.*
 debtor, 29.1 *et seq.*
 diligence, 29.4
 executor, 29.6
 executor-creditor, 29.7
 partner, 30.8

DEATHBED EXPENSES, 29.6

DEBENTURE BOND, 5.2

DEBENTURE ISSUE,
 charge on, 9.1

DEBITUM FUNDI, 1.7, 1.8, 19.4

DEBITUM IN PRAESENTI SOLVENDUM IN FUTURO, 1.10

DEBT,
 constitution, 25.3, 29.6
 contingent, 1.9, 1.10, 1.11, 25.2, 25.10, 29.6
 current maintenance, 18.1
 definition, 1.1
 discharge, 12.13
 foreign, 1.5
 future, 25.10
 heritable, 29.10
 interest on, 11.7
 liquid, 1.9, 13.1, 13.5, 13.10

DEBT—*continued*
  moveable, 29.2, 29.10
  ordinary, 1.1, 18.1, 23.10, 25.11, 29.6
  postponed, 23.10, 25.11
  preferential, 25.11, 25.12
  preferred, 23.10, 23.11
  privileged, 29.6
  pure, 1.10
  source, 1.6
  subordinated, 25.13
  to a day, 1.10
  transmission, 29.1, 29.5

DEBT-ADJUSTING, 3.10

DEBT-COLLECTING, 3.10

DEBT-COUNSELLING, 3.10

DEBTOR,
  common, 11.10
  death, 29.1 *et seq.*
  English, 30.17
  joint, 14.8

DEBTOR-CREDITOR AGREEMENT, 3.3

DEBTOR-CREDITOR-SUPPLIER AGREEMENT, 3.3

DECIMALISATION, 1.2

DECREE,
  cognitionis causa tantum, 29.8
  in foreign currency, 1.5
  liquid claim, 1.9
  prescription, 14.4

DEDUCTION OF TAX, 12.7
  preferred debt, 23.11

DEFAMATION,
  prescription, 14.4

DEFAULT,
  by debtor, 3.16

DEFAULT NOTICE, 3.16, 3.21, 7.2

DEL CREDERE AGENCY, 13.4

DELEGATION, 10.1, 14.2

DELICT, 1.6

DELIVERY,
  actual, 7.3
  bill, of, 5.15
  constructive, 7.3
  symbolic, 7.3

DEMAND FOR PAYMENT, 11.1

DEMURRAGE,
  interest on, 11.7

DEPENDENCE,
  arrestment on the, 11.10
  inhibition on the, 11.11

DEPOSIT,
  compensation, 13.8

DEPOSIT ACCOUNT, 6.2

DEPOSIT OF MONEY,
  prescription, 14.5

DEPOSIT RECEIPT, 5.2
  arrestment, 17.3
  defined, 6.15

DEPOSITARY,
  arrestee, 17.4

DILIGENCE, 9.10
  adjudication, 19.4
  administration, 26.3, 26.5, 26.12
  apparent insolvency, 15.5
  arrestment, 17.1 *et seq.*
  charge, 15.4
  club, 30.16
  confirmation as executor-creditor, 29.7
  death of creditor, 29.3
  death of debtor, 29.4, 29.12
    confirmation by executor-creditor, 29.4
    sequestration, 29.4
  defined, 15.1
  earnings. *See* DILIGENCE AGAINST EARNINGS.
  effect of sequestration, 15.5
  "effectually executed diligence", 17.13
  equalisation of, 15.5, 17.13, 26.12, 29.4
  hire-purchase goods, 2.6
  in security, 11.12
  incomplete, 26.12
  inhibition, 19.1 *et seq.*
  liquidation, 25.8
  multiple apparent insolvencies, 15.5
  partnership, 30.9
  period for payment, 15.4
  poinding, 16.1 *et seq.*
  prior claims, 15.2
  restrictions, 15.6
  ship, 17.16
  summary, 8.2, 19.5
  summary warrant procedure, 19.7
  suspension of, 11.5
  time to pay order, 15.7
  unincorporated association, 30.16
  warrant, 15.3

DILIGENCE AGAINST EARNINGS,
  amount of deduction, 18.5
  arrestment schedule, 18.5
  charge, 18.3
  conjoined arrestment order. *See* CONJOINED ARRESTMENT ORDER.
  creditor's duty, 18.6
  current maintenance, 18.1
  current maintenance arrestment. *See* CURRENT MAINTENANCE ARRESTMENT.
  daily rate of maintenance, 18.7
  deduction from earnings, 18.4
  defined, 18.1

DILIGENCE AGAINST EARNINGS—*continued*
  duration, 18.6
  earnings, 18.2
  effect, 18.4, 18.8
    sequestration, 18.6
  employer's fee, 18.4
  equalisation, 18.6
  execution, 18.7
  maintenance order, 18.7
  method of payment, 18.4
  net earnings, 18.2
  orders, 18.6
  ordinary debt, 18.1
  prescription, 18.6
  procedure, 18.3, 18.7
  schedule, 18.7

DIRECTOR,
  "associate", 9.12
  fraudulent trading, 25.8
  oath of, 4.6
  shadow director, 9.12
  wrongful trading, 25.8

DISCHARGE,
  construction, 12.13
  on composition, 12.13

DISSOLVED COMPANY, 25.15

DIVORCE ORDER,
  protected trust deed, 24.3
  sequestration, 22.11

DONATIO MORTIS CAUSA, 29.5

DOUBLE RANKING, 13.10, 23.6

DRAWEE, 5.3
  fictitious, 5.3

DRAWER, 5.3

"DUE", 1.10

EADEM PERSONA CUM DEFUNCTO, 13.4

EARNINGS ARRESTMENT, 17.3, 17.7, 18.1
  charge, 18.3
  competition with current maintenance arrestment, 18.11
  deduction from wages, 18.4, 18.5
  duration, 18.6
  effect of sequestration, 18.6
  employer, 18.4
  equalisation of diligence, 18.6
  orders, 18.6
  prescription, 18.6
  procedure, 18.3
  ranking, 18.11
  schedule, 18.3, 18.4

"EFFECTUALLY EXECUTED DILIGENCE", 17.13, 17.14

ELECTRICITY,
  account, 2.12

ELECTRONIC TRANSFER OF FUNDS, 3.3n.

ENFORCEMENT ORDER, 3.18

ENGLISH COMPANY,
  floating charge, 30.19
  liquidation, 30.19
  securities, 30.19

EQUALISATION OF DILIGENCE, 15.5, 17.13, 29.4
  administration, 26.12

ERROR,
  payment in, 1.6

EUROPEAN CURRENCY UNIT (ECU), 1.3

EUROPEAN ECONOMIC INTEREST GROUPING (EEIG), 30.15

EUROPEAN UNIT OF ACCOUNT, 1.3

EX FACIE ABSOLUTE DISPOSITION,
  heritable, 29.2

EXCESS CHARGE, 1.6

EXECUTOR,
  assignation, 27.5
  confirmation, 29.3
  contingent debt, 29.6
  dative, 29.7
  death of, 29.6
  diligence, 29.3
  insolvent estate, 29.6
  intromission, 29.6, 29.7
  lease, 29.5
  liability, 29.6
  nominate, 29.7
  oath of, 4.6
  recovery of debt, 29.3
  sequestration, 29.6
    of deceased's estate, 29.12
  sist of, 29.3

EXECUTOR-CREDITOR,
  competition with,
    creditor, 29.7
  diligence, 29.7
  privileged debt, 29.7
  sequestration, 29.7
  confirmation, 29.4, 29.7
  death, 29.7
  deceased's next-of-kin, 29.9
  diligence, 29.7
  judicial factor, 29.7
  sequestration of deceased's estate, 29.12

EXECUTOR-DATIVE, 29.7

EXECUTOR-NOMINATE, 29.7

EXEMPT AGREEMENT, 3.3, 3.4
  defined, 3.2

EXPENSES, 11.14
  action of furthcoming, 17.8
  arrestment, 17.3
  recovery of debt, 11.19

EXTORTIONATE CREDIT BARGAIN, 3.2

EXTORTIONATE CREDIT TRANSACTION, 22.12
  administration, 26.6
  death of debtor, 29.12
  liquidation, 25.8

EXTRA COMMERCIUM,
  property, 14.4

FACTOR,
  lien, 7.10
  oath, 4.6

FAIR DEALING, 3.2

FAMILY HOME,
  sequestration, 21.16

FEES,
  arrestment, 18.2
  medical, 2.7
  professional scale, 2.7
  solicitor, 2.7
  usage, 2.7

FEUDUTY, 1.7
  arrears, 29.2, 29.10
  heritable, 29.2
  interest on, 11.7
  prescription, 14.4

FICTITIOUS DRAWEE, 5.3

FICTITIOUS PAYEE, 5.3

FICTITIOUS SALE, 7.3

FINANCIAL MARKETS RÉGIME, 20.9
  administration, 26.2
  claim, 25.11n.
  liquidation, 25.7

FINANCIAL PROVISION ON DIVORCE,
  death of debtor, 29.12
  judicial factor, 29.11
  periodical allowance,
    transmission, 29.5
  transmissibility, 29.1

FINE,
  civil imprisonment, 19.8

FIRST CALLING DAY, 11.17

FITTED ACCOUNT, 12.14

FIXED SECURITY, 9.10
  administration, 26.8

FIXED-SUM CREDIT, 3.3, 3.8

FLOATING CHARGE, 7.3, 9.1
  administration, 26.3, 26.4, 26.6, 26.9
  administration order, 9.23
  administrative receiver, 9.23
  assignation, 27.1
  attachment, 9.10, 9.18
  avoidance, 9.12
  conditional sale, 9.18

FLOATING CHARGE—*continued*
  corporeal moveables, 9.18
  creation, 9.9
  English company, 30.19
  fraudulent preference, 9.12, 9.18
  goods, 9.18
  gratuitous alienation, 9.12
  heritage, 9.18
  hire-purchase goods, 9.18
  incorporeal moveables, 9.18
  liquidation, 9.10, 9.21, 9.22, 25.8
  operation, 9.10
  partial, 9.23
  ranking, 9.10, 9.11
  receiver. *See* RECEIVER.
  registration, 9.9
  set off, 9.19
  trust, 9.18
  unfair preference, 9.12
  wrongful trading, 9.18

FORCE AND FEAR,
  bill, 5.16

FORECLOSURE, 8.2

FOREIGN CURRENCY,
  decree in, 25.10

FORGERY,
  bill of exchange, 5.10, 5.21
  cheque, 6.11

FRANC, 1.3

FRAUD,
  bill, 5.16

FRAUDULENT PREFERENCE, 12.13
  anticipatory payment, 22.6
  arrested funds, 22.9
  bank draft, 22.6
  bill of exchange, 22.6
  cash payment, 22.6
  challenge, 22.4
  cheque, 22.6
  collusion, 22.6
  consignation, 22.6
  defined, 22.4
  floating charge, 9.12, 9.18
  judicial factor, 29.11
  liquidation, 25.8
  nova debita, 22.8
  ordinary course of business, 22.7
  transactions affected, 22.5

FRAUDULENT TRADING,
  liquidation, 25.8

FREIGHT,
  retention, 13.9

FRIENDLY SOCIETY,
  creditor, 3.4

FRIENDLY SOCIETY CONTRACTS, 1.2

FUNERAL EXPENSES, 29.6

FURTHCOMING, 17.8
    action of, 11.10
    time to pay direction, 11.20

FUTURE DEBT,
    assignation, 27.1
    liquidation, 25.10
    sequestration, 23.2

GAS,
    account, 2.12

GENERAL AVERAGE, 1.6

GENERAL LIEN, 7.10

GIVING TIME, 10.3

GOLD,
    franc, 1.3
    sterling, 1.3

GOLD CLAUSE, 1.4

GOODS,
    acceptance of, 2.5
    charge, 9.1
    floating charge, 9.18
    protected, 4.10
    rejection of, 2.5

GOODWILL,
    charge, 9.1

GRATUITOUS ALIENATION, 22.1, 22.2
    administration, 26.6
    associate, 22.3
    challenge, 22.1, 22.2
    confident person, 22.3
    conjunct person, 22.3
    death of debtor, 29.12
    floating charge, 9.12
    judicial factor, 29.11
    liquidation, 25.8
    protected trust deed, 24.3

GROUND ANNUAL, 1.7
    moveable, 29.2

GROWING CROPS,
    poinding, 16.2

GUARANTEE, 3.5

GUARANTEE PAYMENT,
    preferential debt, 25.12

HERITABLE SECURITY, 8.1 *et seq.*, 9.10
    heritable, 29.10
    inhibition, effect of, 19.3
    moveable, 29.2
    summary diligence, 19.5
    transmission, 29.5

HERITAGE. See also SALE OF HERITAGE.
    adjudication, 19.4
    annuity, 29.2
    ex facie absolute disposition, 29.2

HERITAGE—*continued*
    feuduty, 29.2
    floating charge, 9.18
    heritable security, 29.10
    liferent, 29.2
    pension, 29.2
    real burden, 29.10
    rent, 29.2
    security over, 8.1 *et seq.*
    sequestration, 21.15
    spes successionis, 29.2

HIRE,
    landlord's hypothec, 7.12
    prescription, 14.5

HIRE-PURCHASE,
    agreement, 3.3, 4.10, 26.3n.
    administration, 26.3, 26.5, 26.11
    arrears, 2.6
    chattel leasing agreement, 26.11
    damages, 2.6
    diligence, 2.6
    floating charge, 9.18
    hypothec, 7.12
    implied terms, 2.6
    landlord's hypothec, 2.6
    lien, 7.8
    motor vehicle, 2.6
    passing of property, 2.6
    prescription, 14.4
    sequestration, 21.7
        of hirer, 2.6
    title, 2.6

HIRE-PURCHASE AGREEMENT, 26.3n.
    as credit, 3.3
    defined, 4.10

HOLDER FOR VALUE, 5.7

HOLDER IN DUE COURSE, 3.20, 5.9

HOLIDAY PAY,
    preferential debt, 25.12
    preferred debt, 23.11

HOTEL BILL, 12.8

HOUSING AUTHORITY,
    creditor, 3.4

HUSBAND,
    oath, 4.6

HYPOTHEC,
    administration, 26.8
    hire-purchase goods, 7.12
    landlord, 7.12
    sequestration, 21.6
    superior, 7.12

IMPLIED TERMS,
    hire-purchase, 2.6
    sale of goods, 2.5

IMPRESCRIPTIBLE OBLIGATION, 14.4

IN MEDITATIONE FUGAE, 11.10, 11.11

IN RE MERCATORIA,
  writ, 5.9

IN SOLIDUM, 28.1

INCAPAX,
  arrestee, 17.6
  oath of, 4.6

INCOME TAX,
  summary warrant procedure, 19.7

INCOMPLETE DILIGENCE,
  administration, 26.12

INCORPOREAL MOVEABLE,
  floating charge, 9.18
  liquidation, 25.7
  security over, 8.1
  sequestration, 21.8

INDEBITI SOLUTIO, 1.6

INDEMNITY, 3.5, 10.1

INDEX, 3.4, 3.6

INDEX-LINKING, 1.4

INDIVIDUAL,
  defined, 3.3

INDORSEE, 5.6

INDORSEMENT,
  bill, of, 5.6
  cheque, 6.4, 6.5
  conditional, 5.4n.
  forged, 6.12
  restrictive, 5.4n.

INDUSTRIAL ASSURANCE CONTRACTS, 1.2

INHIBITION, 15.1
  acquirenda, 19.3
  death of creditor, 29.3
  defined, 19.1
  effect, 19.3
    on sequestration, 19.3
  heritable property, 19.1
  heritable security, 19.3
  in security, 11.12
  Letters of Inhibition, 19.2
  liquidation, 25.7
  on the dependence, 11.11
  prescription, 19.2
  procedure, 19.2
  recall, 11.11
  registration, 19.2
  sequestration, 23.5
  subjects, 19.1
  warrant, 11.11

INNKEEPER,
  arrestee, 17.4

INSOLVENCY,
  apparent, 15.5

INSOLVENCY PRACTITIONER,
  administration, 26.2
  voluntary arrangement, 26.1

INSTALLATION CHARGE, 4.10

INSTALMENTS,
  prescription, 14.5

INSURANCE, 10.1

INSURANCE COMPANY,
  administration, 26.3n.
  creditor, 3.4

INSURANCE POLICY, 9.18
  arrestment, 17.3
  right under, 1.1
  sequestration, 21.8

INSURANCE PREMIUM, 3.4

INSURED,
  right of, 1.11
  right against, 21.11

INSURER,
  liability for repairs, 2.9

INTELLECTUAL PROPERTY,
  charge, 9.1
  security over, 8.1

INTERDICT,
  arrestment, 11.10, 17.15

INTEREST, 3.4, 11.7
  arrears, 11.7
  claim in sequestration, 23.2, 23.10
  compound, 11.7
  debt, 11.7
  deduction of tax, 12.7
  liquidation, 25.10, 25.11
  loan, 4.1
  moveable, 29.2

INTEREST IN POSSESSION, 1.11

INTEREST RATES,
  annual flat rate, 3.9
  annual percentage rate of charge, 3.8
  base rate, 3.4
  constant period rate of charge, 3.8
  percentage rate of charge, 3.8

INTERIM ADMINISTRATOR, 26.3

INTERIM LIQUIDATOR, 25.4

INTERIM TRUSTEE, 20.3
  functions, 20.4
  outlays, 23.10
  remuneration, 20.6, 23.10
  sequestration, 20.4

INTERNATIONAL MONETARY FUND, 1.3

INTIMATED ASSIGNATION,
  appointment of judicial factor, 29.11

INTIMATION,
    action for recovery of debt, 27.4
    appointment of judicial factor, 29.11
    cautioner, 27.3
    company, 27.3
    co-obligant, 27.3
    equivalents, 27.4
    form, 27.3
    importance, 27.5
    multiplepoinding, 27.4
    notarial, 27.3
    postal, 27.3
    proof, 27.3
    registration, 27.4
    trustees, 27.3
    written notice, 27.3

INTROMISSION,
    vitious, 29.7

INVECTA ET ILLATA, 7.12

IOU,
    as security, 7.1
    defined, 6.14
    proof, 6.14

JOINT ADVENTURE, 30.6
    interest in, 29.2

JOINT AND SEVERAL LIABILITY, 28.1
    consumer credit, 4.8

JOINT DEBTORS, 14.8

JOINT DELINQUENTS,
    assignation, 28.6
    discharge, 28.8
    extra-judicial settlement, 28.6
    right of relief, 28.5, 28.6

JOINT RECEIVERS, 9.20

JUDICIAL FACTOR,
    appointment, 29.11
    arrestee, 17.6
    confirmation as executor-creditor, 29.7
    deceased debtor, 29.6
    deceased's estate, 29.11
    financial provision on divorce, 29.11
    fraudulent preference, 29.11
    gratuitous alienation, 29.11
    intimation, 29.11

JURISDICTION,
    arrestment to found, 11.8
    liquidation, 25.2
    sequestration, 29.12

JUS CREDITI, 1.1

JUS QUAESITUM, 1.11

JUS RELICTAE,
    prescription, 14.4

JUS RELICTI,
    prescription, 14.4

LAND,
    charge, 9.1
    purchase of, 3.4

LAND MORTGAGE, 8.4

LANDLORD'S HYPOTHEC, 7.12, 9.10
    prior claim, 15.2

LEASE,
    executor, 29.5
    overriding interest, 8.5
    registration, 8.5
    security over, 8.5

LEGACY, 1.6

LEGAL RIGHTS, 1.6, 14.5

LEGAL TENDER, 1.2, 12.1

LEGIBILITY,
    credit agreement, 3.12

LEGITIM,
    arrestment, 17.13
    prescription, 14.4

LETTER OF CREDIT,
    payment, 12.3

LETTERS OF INHIBITION, 11.11, 19.2

LIABILITY,
    agent, 30.2
    bill of exchange, 28.1
    co-cautioners, 28.1
    conjunct and several, 28.1
    co-obligants, 28.1
    executor, 29.6
    in solidum, 28.1
    joint and several, 4.8, 28.1
    joint delinquents, 28.5
    joint purchasers, 28.1
    joint wrong-doers, 28.1
    member of club or association, 30.16
    partner, 30.7
    partnership, 28.1, 30.7
    personal, 1.8
    principal, 30.2
    pro rata, 28.1
    promissory note, 28.1
    receiver, 9.15
    right of relief, 28.2
    several, 28.1
    spouse, 30.21
    trustee, 1.8, 28.1

LIABILITY TO ACCOUNT,
    arrestment, 17.3

LICENSING,
    consumer credit, 3.10

LIEN, 7.7, 9.10
    accountant, 7.9
    auctioneer, 7.10, 22.7
    banker, 7.10
    bill of exchange, 5.9

LIEN—*continued*
　bleacher, 7.8, 22.7
　carrier, 7.8
　engine-builder, 7.8
　factor, 7.10
　general, 7.10
　hirer, 7.8
　hotel proprietor, 7.10
　maritime, 7.3
　papers, 7.9
　possessory, 26.8
　repairer, 7.8
　solicitor, 7.9, 7.11
　special, 7.8
　stockbroker, 7.10
　store-keeper, 7.8

LIFERENT,
　heritable, 29.2

LIMITED PARTNERSHIP, 30.14
　assignation, 27.1

LINKED TRANSACTION, 3.2, 3.4, 3.5, 3.15

LIQUID DEBT, 1.9, 13.1, 13.5, 13.10

LIQUIDATED DAMAGES, 1.6

LIQUIDATION,
　adjudication, 25.10
　administration, 26.3, 26.5
　bank account, 6.10
　caveat, 25.3
　claim, 25.10
　commencement, 25.3
　committee, 25.4, 25.14
　company unable to pay debts, 25.2
　compensation, 13.4
　contract, 25.7
　contributory, 25.8, 25.9
　corporeal moveables, 25.7
　creditors,
　　final meeting, 25.6
　　meeting, 25.4
　declaration of solvency, 25.14
　diligence, 25.8
　directions, 26.1
　director, 25.8
　dissolution, 25.15
　distribution, 25.11
　effect,
　　on adjudication, 19.4
　　on arrestment, 17.13
　　on poinding, 16.12
　　on property, 25.7
　English company, 30.19
　expenses, 25.11
　extortionate credit transaction, 25.8
　financial markets régime, 25.7, 25.11n.
　floating charge, 9.10, 9.21, 9.22, 25.2, 25.8
　fraudulent preference, 25.8
　fraudulent trading, 25.8
　gratuitous alienation, 25.8

LIQUIDATION—*continued*
　heritage, 25.7
　incorporeal moveables, 25.7
　inhibition, 25.7
　interest on debts, 25.11
　interim liquidator, 25.4
　jurisdiction, 25.2
　liquidator, 25.1. *See also* LIQUIDATOR.
　ordinary debt, 25.11
　overseas company, 30.20
　petition, 25.2
　　advertisement, 25.3
　　intimation, 25.3
　　presentation of, 25.3
　postponed debt, 25.11
　preferential debts, 25.11
　　relevant date, 25.12
　provisional liquidator, 25.3
　public examination, 25.6
　secured creditor, 25.10
　set-off, 25.12
　sist, 26.1
　stay of proceedings, 25.3
　subordinated debt, 25.13
　trust property, 25.7
　unfair preference, 25.8
　voluntary, 25.14
　voluntary arrangement, 25.11
　winding-up order, 25.3
　　effect, 25.5
　wrongful trading, 25.8

LIQUIDATOR,
　administration of property, 25.7
　arrestee, 17.6
　challenge of antecedent transaction, 25.8
　contract, 25.7
　functions, 25.4, 25.6
　interim, 25.4
　nominee, 26.1
　powers, 25.4, 25.6
　provisional, 25.3, 26.3
　public utilities' supply, 25.4
　release, 25.6
　remuneration, 25.11
　voluntary arrangement, 26.1
　voluntary liquidation, 25.14

LIQUIDITY, 13.5

LOAN, 4.1
　Consumer Credit Act 1974, 4.7
　interest, 4.1, 11.7
　prescription, 4.1, 14.5
　presumption of, 4.5
　proof, 4.2 *et seq.*
　repayment, 4.1
　series of transactions, 4.3

LOCAL AUTHORITY,
　creditor, 3.4

LUMP SUM,
　repayment, 3.8

LUMP SUM CONTRACT, 2.10

MAILLS AND DUTIES, 15.1

MANDATE,
    assignation, 27.2

MARITIME LIEN, 7.3

MARRIED PERSONS,
    liability, 30.21

MATRIMONIAL HOME,
    sequestration, 21.17

MEASURE AND VALUE CONTRACT, 2.10

MEMBERS' VOLUNTARY WINDING UP, 25.14

MESSENGER-AT-ARMS, 15.1

METERS,
    hire agreements for, 3.4

MINOR,
    arrestee, 17.6

MISSIVES,
    collateral obligation, 2.11
    conditions, 2.11
    date of payment, 2.11

MODIFYING AGREEMENT, 3.5

MONEY OF ACCOUNT, 1.5

MONEY OF PAYMENT, 1.5

MORTGAGE,
    aircraft, 7.3
    land, 8.4
    ship, 7.3, 7.5

MOURNING ALLOWANCE, 29.6

MOVEABLE PROPERTY,
    arrears,
        feuduty, 29.10
        rent, 29.10
    bond, 29.2
    debt, 29.2
    ground annual, 29.2
    heritable security, 29.2
    interest, 29.2
    interest in,
        joint adventure, 29.2
        partnership, 29.2
    price of heritage, 29.2, 29.10
    share, 29.2
    warrandice, 29.10

MULTIPLE AGREEMENT, 3.5

MULTIPLEPOINDING,
    action, 11.5
    decree of preference, 29.7

MUTUUM, 4.1

NEGOTIABLE INSTRUMENT, 5.2
    in consumer credit, 3.20

NEGOTIATION, 5.4
    antecedent, 3.13, 3.14

NEGOTIATOR, 3.5

NEGOTIORUM GESTIO, 1.6
    prescription, 14.4

NET EARNINGS, 18.2

NEXT-OF-KIN,
    creditors of, 29.9

NOMINA DEBITORUM, 1.1

NOMINATION, 29.5

NOMINEE,
    voluntary arrangement, 26.1

NON-BUSINESS DAY, 5.3

NONAGE,
    prescription, 14.6

"NOT NEGOTIABLE", 6.11

NOTICE OF DISHONOUR, 5.26

NOTOUR BANKRUPTCY,
    effect on diligence, 15.5

NOVA DEBITA, 22.8, 22.9

NOVATION, 14.1

OATH,
    agent, 4.6
    assignee, 4.6
    bankrupt, 4.6
    co-obligant, 4.6
    director, 4.6
    executor, 4.6
    husband, 4.6
    incapax, 4.6
    partner, 4.6
    proof of loan by, 4.2, 4.6
    trustee, 4.6
    wife, 4.6

OBLIGATION,
    degrees of, 1.1

OBLIGATION TO ACCOUNT, 1.1
    arrestment, 11.8
    prescription, 14.4

OPEN ACCOUNT, 12.14

ORDINARY ACTION, 11.17

ORDINARY COURSE OF BUSINESS,
    transaction in, 22.7, 22.9

ORDINARY DEBT, 23.10
    arrestment, 18.1
    defined, 18.1
    liquidation, 25.11
    payment by executor, 29.6

OVERDRAFT, 3.3

OVERSEAS COMPANY, 30.20

PACTUM DE NON PETENDO, 28.7
PACTUM DE RETROVENDENDO, 7.3
PARTIAL ADMISSION, 11.13
PARTIAL CLAIM, 11.6
PARTIAL PAYMENT, 11.2
PARTNER,
   authority, 30.6
   death, 30.8
   general, 30.14
   liability, 30.7, 30.8
      prescription, 30.9
   limited, 30.14
   new, 30.8
   oath, 4.6
   retired, 30.8
   sequestration, 30.8, 30.13
   sole, 30.4
   trustee, 30.7
   wife, 30.13

PARTNERSHIP,
   advance for capital, 4.2
   arrestee, 17.6
   arrestment of interest, 17.3
   compensation, 30.12
   constitution of debt, 30.9
   defined, 30.6
   diligence, 30.9
   dissolved, 30.13
   firm name, 30.10, 30.11
   holding out, 30.8
   interest in, 29.2
   joint adventure, 30.6
   joint and several liability, 28.1, 30.8
   liability, 30.7, 30.8
      prescription, 30.9
   limited, 30.14
   limited partner,
      assignation of share, 27.1
   partner. *See* PARTNER.
   prescription, 14.4, 14.5
   sequestration, 30.13
   set-off, 30.12
   title to sue, 30.10

PASS-BOOK,
   entries as proof of loan, 4.5

PATENT,
   security over, 9.1
   sequestration, 21.13

PAWN, 7.4
"PAYABLE", 10.1
PAYEE, 5.3
   fictitious, 5.3
PAYING BANKER, 6.1
   protection of, 6.12

PAYMENT,
   action of, 11.3
   ascription, 12.5
   assumed time of, 3.6
   bill, 5.22
   cheque, 12.2
   credit card, 12.3
   deduction of tax, 12.7
   demand for, 11.1
   error, 1.6
   executor, 29.6
   legal tender, 12.1
   letter of credit, 12.3
   partial, 11.2
   place of, 12.4
   presumption, 12.8 *et seq.*
   proof, 12.8
   punctual, 4.1
   receipt, 12.12
   to third party, 12.6

PENSION,
   arrestment, 18.2
   heritable, 29.2
   sequestration, 21.9

PENSION SCHEME CONTRIBUTION,
   preferential debt, 25.12
   preferred debt, 23.11

PERCENTAGE RATE OF CHARGE, 3.8

PERIODICAL ALLOWANCE,
   transmission, 29.5

PERIODICAL PAYMENT,
   arrestment, 17.7

PERMANENT TRUSTEE, 20.4
   appointment, 20.4
   English property, 30.17
   functions, 20.4
   outlays, 23.10
   powers, 20.4
   powers outwith Scotland, 21.21
   remuneration, 20.6, 23.10
   supplies by utilities, 20.5
   vesting, 21.1

PERSONAL CREDIT AGREEMENT, 3.3
PERSONAL LIABILITY, 1.8
PERSONAL OBLIGATION, 1.7
   heritable security, 29.5
   transmission, 29.5

PHYSICIAN'S FEES, 12.8

PLEDGE,
   administration, 26.8
   Consumer Credit Act 1974, 7.4
   defined, 7.3

POINDING, 15.1
   appointment of receiver, 16.13
   breach, 16.5
   charge, 16.1

Index

POINDING—*continued*
common property, 16.8
competition, 16.10
date of execution, 16.4
death of creditor, 29.3
death of debtor, 29.4
debtor's rights, 16.9
definition, 16.1
effect, 16.5
  of liquidation, 16.12
  of receiving order, 16.14
  of sequestration, 16.11
exempt articles, 16.3
expenses, 16.7
procedure, 16.4
release, 16.5
  of article, 16.8
removal of subject, 16.5
sale, 16.7
schedule, 16.4
sisting order, 16.9
subjects, 16.2
summary warrant, 16.4
  procedure, 19.7
suspension, 16.15
  and interdict, 16.15
third party rights, 16.8
valuation, 16.4
warrant, 15.3, 16.4
  of sale, 16.6

POINDING AND SALE,
time to pay direction, 11.20

POINDING OF THE GROUND, 1.7, 8.2, 15.1

POSSESSORY LIEN,
administration, 26.8

POSTERIOR CREDITOR, 23.5

POSTPONED DEBT, 23.10
liquidation, 25.11

POUND SCOTS, 1.2

POUND STERLING, 1.2

PREFERENTIAL CREDITOR,
voluntary arrangement, 26.1

PREFERENTIAL DEBT, 9.10, 9.16
liquidation, 25.11, 25.12
supervening liquidation, 9.22

PREFERRED DEBT, 23.10, 23.11

PRESCRIPTION,
accounting, 14.4
acknowledgement, 14.8
administration, 26.10
agency, 14.4
annuity, 14.4
arbitration award, 14.4
arrestment, 1.10, 11.10
  in execution, 17.7
  on the dependence, 17.7

PRESCRIPTION—*continued*
bank note, 14.4
bill of exchange, 5.23, 14.4
breach of contract, 14.4
breach of trust, 14.4
cautionry, 10.2
compensation, 13.6
Consumer Protection Act 1987, 14.4, 14.9
contract, 14.4
co-obligants, 28.4
decree, 14.4
defamation, 14.4
earnings arrestment, 18.6
feuduty, 14.4
ground annual, 14.4
inhibition, 19.2
joint debtors, 14.8
jus relictae, 14.4
jus relicti, 14.4
legal disability, 14.6
legitim, 14.4
loan, 4.1
negotiorum gestio, 14.4
nonage, 14.6
obligation of trustee, 14.4
partnership, 14.4, 14.5
  liability, 30.9
period, 14.6
prior right, 14.4
probative writ, 14.4
promise, 14.4
promissory note, 5.27, 14.4
property *extra commercium*, 14.4
quinquennial, 14.4
recompense, 14.4
relevant claim, 14.7
rent, 14.4
reparation, 14.4
repetition, 14.4
res merae facultatis, 14.4
restitution, 14.4
sale of goods, 14.5
service of heir, 14.4
stolen property, 14.4
terce, 14.4
terminus a quo, 14.5
tribunal order, 14.4
trust accounting, 14.4
unjustified enrichment, 14.4
unsoundness of mind, 14.6
vicennial, 14.9

PRESUMPTION OF PAYMENT, 12.8 *et seq.*

PRICE,
action for, 2.2
day certain, 2.2
deposit, 2.1
instalment, 2.1
sale of goods, 2.1

PRIME COST CONTRACT, 2.10

PRINCIPAL AGREEMENT, 3.5

Index

PRIOR RIGHT, 1.6
  prescription, 14.4

PRIVILEGED DEBT, 29.6, 29.7
  cremation expenses, 29.6
  deathbed expenses, 29.6
  funeral expenses, 29.6
  mourning allowance, 29.6
  rent, 29.6
  servant's wages, 29.6

PRO RATA,
  liability, 28.1

PROBATIVE WRIT,
  prescription, 14.4

PRODUCT LIABILITY,
  prescription, 14.4

PROFESSIONAL SERVICES,
  contracts for, 2.7

PROMISE, 1.6
  prescription, 14.4

PROMISSORY NOTE, 5.3, 5.27
  co-makers, 28.1
  defined, 5.27
  interest, 11.7
  liability, 5.27
  prescription, 5.27, 14.4
  presentment, 5.27
  summary diligence, 19.6

PROOF,
  agency, 30.2
  bill, 5.19
  debt, 19.6
  IOU, 6.14
  loan, 4.2
  parole, 4.2, 4.5
  payment of bill, 5.22
  series of transactions, 4.3
  writ or oath, 4.2, 4.5

PROOF OF PAYMENT,
  apocha trium annorum, 12.10
  bill, 5.22
  cheque, 12.16
  lost receipt, 12.15
  mode, 12.11
  onus, 12.8
  parole, 12.11
  passbook, 12.14
  pay-in slip, 12.14
  presumption, 12.8 *et seq.*
  receipt, 12.12
  voucher, 12.9
  writ or oath, 12.14

PROTECTED GOODS, 4.10

PROTECTED TENANCY,
  sequestration, 21.15

PROTECTED TRUST DEED, 24.3

PROTECTIVE AWARD,
  preferential debt, 25.12

PROVISIONAL LIQUIDATOR, 25.3
  administration, 26.3

PUBLIC UTILITIES' SUPPLY,
  administrator, 26.6
  liquidator, 25.4
  trustee in sequestration, 25.4

PUNCTUAL PAYMENT, 4.1

PUPIL,
  arrestee, 17.6

QUANTUM LUCRATUS,
  building contract, 2.10

QUANTUM MERUIT, 2.9, 2.10, 11.7

QUASI-CONTRACT, 1.6

QUASI-OBLIGATION, 1.1, 1.6

QUOTATION,
  credit, 3.11

RATES,
  summary warrant procedure, 19.7

REAL BURDEN, 1.7
  heritable, 29.10

RECEIPT, 12.12
  loan proved by, 4.5

RECEIVER,
  administrative, 9.23, 26.3, 26.4
  appointment, 9.13, 9.14
  arrestment, 17.14
  attachment of floating charge, 9.18
  distribution, 9.17
  English, 30.19
  joint, 9.14, 9.20
  liability, 9.15
  liquidation, 9.21, 9.22
  poinding, 16.13
  powers, 9.15
  preferential debt, 9.16
  set-off, 9.19

RECEIVING ORDER, 20.1
  poinding, 16.14

RECOMPENSE, 1.6
  prescription, 14.4

RECOVERY OF DEBT,
  Court of Session, 11.18
  executor, by, 29.3
  ordinary action, 11.17
  small claim, 11.15
  summary cause, 11.16
  time to pay direction, 11.20

REGISTER OF CHARGES, 9.8

REGISTERED TITLE, 21.13

REGISTRATION,
    adjudication, 19.4
    aircraft mortgage, 7.6
    inhibition, 19.2
    lease, 8.5
    securities. *See* REGISTRATION OF SECURITIES.
    ship mortgage, 7.5
    standard security, 8.2
    summary diligence, 19.5, 19.6

REGISTRATION OF SECURITIES,
    company's duty, 9.2
    defective registration, 9.5
    English company, 30.19
    failure to register, 9.3
    inspection, 9.8
    late registration, 9.4
    memorandum of termination, 9.6
    overseas company, 30.20
    register of charges, 9.8
    registrable charge, 9.1
    subsequent charge, 9.4
    void charge, 9.7

REGULATED AGREEMENT, 3.3
    cancellation, 3.13
    content, 3.12
    copy, 3.12
    default, 3.16
    default notice, 3.16, 3.21
    discharge, 3.15
    information, 3.15
    legibility, 3.12
    requirements, 3.12
    termination, 3.15
    variation, 3.15

RELEVANT CLAIM, 14.7

RELIEF,
    action of, 1.6

RENT,
    arrears, 29.2, 29.10
    arrestment, 17.3
    deceased's estate, 29.6
    heritable, 29.2
    interest on, 11.7
    liquid, 1.9
    prescription, 14.4

REPAIRS,
    contract for, 2.9
    insurer's liability for, 2.9
    quantum meruit, 2.9
    time and materials, 2.9

REPARATION,
    prescription, 14.4

REPETITION, 1.6, 4.8, 6.13
    prescription, 14.4
    price of goods, 2.5

REPRESENTATION, 2.4

RES MERAE FACULTATIS, 14.4

RESERVATION OF TITLE, 2.3

RESTITUTIO IN INTEGRUM, 2.4

RESTITUTION,
    prescription, 14.4

RESTRICTED USE CREDIT AGREEMENT, 3.3

RETENTION, 13.9
    building contract, 13.9
    fraud, 13.9
    freight, 13.9
    store-keeper, 13.9

RETROCESSION, 27.6

RETURN DAY, 11.15, 11.16

RETURN ORDER, 4.10

REVERSIONARY INTEREST, 27.3

"RIGHT", 1.11

RUNNING ACCOUNT, 13.1

RUNNING-ACCOUNT CREDIT, 3.8

SALARY,
    arrestment, 18.2
    preferential debt, 25.12
    preferred debt, 23.11

SALE AND RETURN, 2.3n.

SALE OF GOODS,
    breach of contract, 2.4, 2.5
    condition, 2.5
    conditional sale agreement, 4.10
    fictitious, 7.3
    lien, 2.2
    poinding, 16.10
    prescription, 14.5
    price, 2.1
    re-delivery, 2.2
    rejection of goods, 2.5
    resale, 2.2
    reservation of title, 2.3
    sale and return, 2.3n.
    sequestration, 21.7
    warranty, 2.5

SALE OF HERITAGE,
    breach of contract, 2.11
    constructive conversion, 29.2
    instalments, 2.11
    payment of price, 2.11
    payments on account, 2.11
    rescission, 2.11
    suspensive condition, 2.11
    warrandice, 2.11

SALVAGE, 1.6

SCHEDULE,
    poinding, 16.4

SEAMAN,
  arrestment of wages, 18.2
  assignation of wages, 27.1

SECONDARY SECURITY, 8.6

SECURE TENANCY,
  sequestration, 21.15

SECURED CREDITOR,
  administration, 26.4
  claim in sequestration, 23.4
  liquidation, 25.10, 25.11
  voluntary arrangement, 26.1

SECURITY, 7.1 *et seq.*
  administration, 26.3, 26.5
  agricultural charge, 7.3
  aircraft, 7.6
  cancellation of agreement, 7.2
  catholic, 8.6
  collateral, 23.4
  co-obligants, 28.3
  definition, 7.1
  floating charge. See FLOATING CHARGE.
  form, 3.21
  heritage, 8.2 *et seq.*
  incorporeal moveable, 8.1
  intellectual property, 8.1
  lease, 8.5
  liquidation, 25.10
  pawn, 7.4
  pledge, 7.3
  registration. See REGISTRATION OF SECURITIES.
  regulated agreement, 7.2
  secondary, 8.6
  shares, 8.1
  ship, 7.5
  standard security. See STANDARD SECURITY.
  trust as, 7.3

SEQUESTRATION,
  accommodation party, 23.9
  Accountant in Bankruptcy, 20.6
  accounting period, 23.2
  acquirenda, 21.11, 21.20
  Act and Warrant, 20.4, 21.1
  adjudication, 19.4, 20.3, 23.3
  aliment, 21.19, 23.2
  alimentary provision, 21.9
  ancestor's creditor, 23.12
  anterior creditor, 23.5
  apparent insolvency, 15.5, 20.1
  appeal, 20.6
  arrestment, 17.12
  assignation, 27.5
  associate, 22.3
  assured tenancy, 21.15
  award, 20.3
  balancing of accounts, 13.10
  bank account, 6.10
  bank draft, 21.8

SEQUESTRATION—*continued*
  beneficiary, of, 29.6
  bill of exchange, 23.9
  building contract, 21.12
  cautionary obligation, 23.7
  cautioner's security, 23.8
  claims, 20.4, 23.1 *et seq.*
    adjudication, 23.3
    interest, 23.2
    statement of, 23.2
    submission, 23.2
  club, 30.16
  co-cautioners, 28.7
  collateral security, 23.4
  commissioners, 20.4
  company, 25.1
  compensation, 13.4
  composition, 24.1
  conjoined arrestment order, 18.12
  contingent debt, 23.2
  co-obligants, 23.6, 23.8, 28.2, 28.7
  corporeal moveables, 21.6
  creditor's meeting, 20.4
  date of, 20.2n, 20.3
  debtor, 20.7
    disqualifications, 20.7
    offences, 20.7, 21.20
  debtor's spouse,
    examination of, 20.4
    property of, 21.18
  deceased debtor, 29.4, 29.6, 29.11, 29.12
  diligence, 15.5, 29.12
  discharge, 20.8
    certificate of, 20.8
    composition, 24.1
    deferment, 20.8
    effect of, 20.8
    trust deed, 24.2, 24.3
  discharge of security, 23.4
  disposition in security, 21.15
  distribution, 23.10 *et seq.*
  dividend, 23.2
  divorce order, 22.11
  double ranking, 23.6
  effect on,
    earnings arrestment, 18.6
    executor-creditor, 29.12
    poinding, 16.11
  ejection, 21.15
  English debtor, 30.17
  examination of debtor, 20.4
  excluded property, 21.5
  executor, of, 29.6
  extortionate credit transaction, 22.12, 29.12
  family home, 21.16
  financial markets régime, 20.9
  financial provision on divorce, 29.12
  fraud, acquisitions by, 21.4
  fraudulent preference, 12.13, 22.4
  future debt, 23.2
  gratuitous alienation, 22.1, 22.2, 29.12

SEQUESTRATION—*continued*
    heritable security, 8.3
    heritage, 21.15
    hire-purchase, 21.7
    income, 21.9
    incorporeal moveables, 21.8
    inhibition, 19.3, 20.3, 23.5
    insurance policy, 21.8
    interest, 23.2, 23.10
    interim trustee. *See* INTERIM TRUSTEE.
    judicial factor, 23.1, 29.11
    jurisdiction, 20.2, 21.21, 29.12
    landlord's hypothec, 21.6
    matrimonial home, 21.17
    modified procedure, 20.4
    non-entitled spouse, 21.17
    objections to petition, 20.3
    ordinary debt, 23.10
    partner, 30.8, 30.13
    partnership, 30.13
    patent, 21.13
    patrimonial loss, 21.10
    permanent trustee. *See* PERMANENT TRUSTEE.
    petition, 14.7, 20.2
    posterior creditor, 23.5
    postponed debt, 23.10
    preference, 23.5
    preferred debt, 23.10, 23.11
    procedure, 20.3
    property furth of Scotland, 21.21
    protected tenancy, 21.15
    protected trust deed, 24.3
    protection of debtor, 21.6
    reasons for insolvency, 20.4
    recall, 20.6, 29.12
    recording of title, 21.15
    registered title, 21.13
    registration, 20.3
    right against insurer, 21.11
    sale of goods, 21.7
    secure tenancy, 21.15
    secured creditor, 23.4, 23.10
    security, 20.3
    shares, 21.13
    ship, 21.13
    social security benefit, 21.9
    solatium, 21.10
    sold goods, 2.3
    sole trader, 30.4
    special appropriation, 21.3
    spes successionis, 21.14
    state pension, 21.9
    supplies by utilities, 20.5
    surplus of estate, 23.10
    time to pay direction, 11.20
    trade mark, 21.13
    trust deed for creditors, 22.10, 24.2
    trust property, 21.2
    trustee, of, 29.6
    unfair preference, 22.9, 29.12
    unincorporated association, 30.16

SEQUESTRATION—*continued*
    vesting, 21.1

SEQUESTRATION FOR RENT, 20.1
    hypothec, 7.12

SERVANT,
    wages, 29.6

SERVANT OF HEIR,
    prescription, 14.4

SET-OFF, 13.1
    administration, 26.10
    floating charge, 9.19

SETTLED ACCOUNT, 12.14

SHARE CAPITAL,
    charge, 9.1

SHARES,
    arrestment, 17.3
    moveable, 29.2
    security over, 8.1
    sequestration, 21.13

SHERIFF COURT,
    ordinary action, 11.17
    small claim, 11.15
    summary cause, 11.16

SHERIFF OFFICER, 15.1

SHIP,
    arrestment, 17.16
    mortgage, 7.3, 7.5
    sequestration, 21.13

SHIPBROKER,
    arrestee, 17.6

SHIPOWNER,
    arrestee, 17.4, 17.6

SMALL AGREEMENT, 3.5

SMALL CLAIM, 11.15
    return day, 11.15

SOCIAL SECURITY BENEFIT,
    assignation, 27.1
    sequestration, 21.9

SOCIAL SECURITY CONTRIBUTION,
    preferential debt, 25.12
    preferred debt, 23.11

SOLE TRADER, 30.4

SOLICITOR,
    account, 2.8
    compensation, 13.8
    fees, interest on, 11.7
    judicial factor on estate, 23.1
    lien, 7.9, 7.11

SOVEREIGN,
    gold, 1.3

SPECIAL ASSIGNATION, 29.5, 29.7

SPECIAL DESTINATION, 29.5

SPECIAL DISPOSITION, 29.7

SPECIAL DRAWING RIGHT, 1.3

SPECIAL LIEN, 7.8

SPES SUCCESSIONIS, 1.11, 1.12, 19.4
arrestment, 17.3
assignation, 27.1
heritable, 29.2
sequestration, 21.14

STAMP DUTY, 5.27

STANDARD SECURITY, 1.7, 8.2
adjudication, 8.2
assignation, 8.2
calling-up, 8.2
consent to registration, 8.2
creditor's remedies, 8.2
discharge, 8.2
foreclosure, 8.2
notice of default, 8.2
personal obligation, 8.2
poinding of the ground, 8.2
ranking, 8.2
redemption, 8.2
restriction, 8.2
sale, 8.2
standard conditions, 8.2
summary diligence, 8.2
variation, 8.2

STATUTORY SICK PAY,
arrestment, 18.2
preferential debt, 25.12

STEEL LEVY,
preferential debt, 25.12
preferred debt, 23.11

STOLEN PROPERTY,
prescription, 14.4

STORE-KEEPER,
retention, 13.9

STUDENT LOAN, 20.2n.

SUB-PURCHASER, 4.10

SUBORDINATED DEBT,
liquidation, 25.13

SUCCESSION, 1.6
heritable property, 29.2
legal rights, 1.7
moveable property, 29.2

SUMMARY CAUSE, 11.16
first calling day, 11.16

SUMMARY DILIGENCE,
bill of exchange, 19.6
Consumer Credit Act 1974, 19.5
debtor's death, 19.5
document of debt, 19.5
heritable security, 19.5

SUMMARY DILIGENCE—*continued*
promissory note, 19.6
proof of debt, 19.6
registration, 19.5, 19.6
warrant, 19.5

SUMMARY WARRANT PROCEDURE,
poinding and sale, 19.7

SUPERVISOR,
voluntary arrangement, 26.1

SURETY,
extortionate bargain, 3.2

SUSPENSION,
compensation, 13.7

SUSPENSION ORDER,
4.11

TABLE OF FEES,
Law Society, 2.8

TAX,
deduction of, 12.7
preferential debt, 25.12
preferred debt, 23.11
priority of, 15.2

TAX RELIEF,
assumed, 3.6

TAX RETURN,
loan proved by, 4.5

TAXATION,
solicitor's account, 2.8

TENANT,
arrestee, 17.4

TENDER, 11.14
expenses, 11.14
two defenders, 11.14
withdrawal, 11.14

TENEMENT,
maintenance charges, 1.7

TERCE,
prescription, 14.4

TERMINATION,
agreement, 3.15

TESTAMENTARY TRUSTEE, 29.6

THEFT,
cheque, 6.11

TIME,
calculation of, 3.7

TIME AND MATERIALS BASIS, 2.9, 2.10

TIME ORDER, 3.19, 4.10

TIME TO PAY DIRECTION, 3.19
cessation, 11.20
competency, 11.20

TIME TO PAY DIRECTION—*continued*
  effect, 11.20
    on arrestment, 11.20
    procedure, 11.20
    sequestration, 11.20
TIME TO PAY ORDER, 3.19, 15.7
  cessation, 15.7
  defined, 15.7
  interim order, 15.7
  procedure, 15.7
  variation, 15.7
TITLE,
  reservation, 2.3
TITLE TO SUE,
  assignee, 27.6
TOTAL CHARGE FOR CREDIT,
  annual flat rate, 3.9
  annual percentage rate of charge, 3.8
  assumptions, 3.6
  charge per pound lent, 3.9
  computation, 3.8
  defined, 3.8
  formulae, 3.8
  tables, 3.9
TOTAL PRICE, 4.10
TRADE MARK,
  security over, 9.1
  sequestration, 21.13
TRANSFER ORDER, 4.10
TRANSFEREE FOR VALUE, 5.8
TRANSMISSIBILITY,
  annuity, 29.1
  claim *ex delicto*, 29.5
  damages, 29.1
  debtor's estate, 29.5
  financial provision on divorce, 29.1
  periodical allowance, 29.5
  personal obligation, 29.5
  prescription, 14.4
TRUST,
  arrestment of interest, 17.3
  beneficiary's right in, 1.11
  discretionary, 1.11
  floating charge, 9.18
  inter vivos, 29.5
  interest in, 29.2
  revocable, 29.5
TRUST DEED FOR CREDITORS, 24.2
  compensation, 13.4
  protected, 24.3
  sequestration, 22.10, 24.2
TRUST FUND,
  prescription, 14.4
TRUST PROPERTY,
  sequestration, 21.2

TRUSTEE,
  acknowledgement by, 14.8
  arrestee, 17.6
  contributory, 25.9
  intimation, 27.3
  liability, 30.7
  oath, 4.6
  partner, 30.7
  personal liability, 1.8
  sequestration, 29.6
  testamentary, 29.6
TUTOR,
  arrestee, 17.6

ULTRA VIRES,
  cheque, 5.11
UNCALLED CAPITAL,
  assignation, 27.1
UNFAIR PREFERENCE,
  administration, 26.6
  cash payment, 22.9
  challenge, 22.9
  death of debtor, 29.12
  defined, 22.9
  floating charge, 9.12
  liquidation, 25.8
  nova debita, 22.9
  ordinary course of business, 22.9
  protected trust deed, 24.3
UNINCORPORATED ASSOCIATION, 30.16
UNIT OF ACCOUNT, 1.3
UNJUSTIFIED ENRICHMENT, 1.6, 6.13
  prescription, 14.4
UNRESTRICTED-USE CREDIT AGREEMENT, 3.3
UNSECURED CREDITOR,
  administration, 26.4, 26.10

VALUE ADDED TAX,
  preferential debt, 25.12
  preferred debt, 23.11
  summary warrant procedure, 19.7
VERBA JACTANTIA, 2.4
VERGENS AD INOPIAM, 11.10, 11.11, 13.5
VESTING, 1.12
VITIOUS INTROMISSION, 29.7
VOLUNTARY ARRANGEMENT,
  nominee, 26.1
  preferential debt,
    relevant date, 26.1n.
  proposal, 26.1
  supervisor, 26.1
VOLUNTARY LIQUIDATION, 25.14

WAGES,
  arrestment, 18.2
  preferential debt, 25.12
  preferred debt, 23.11
  seaman, 18.2, 27.1
  servant, 29.6

WARRANDICE,
  assignation, 27.8
  moveable, 29.10
  sale of heritage, 2.11

WARRANT,
  arrestment, 17.5
  sale, 16.6
  summary diligence, 19.5

WARRANT FOR DILIGENCE, 15.3
  assignation, 15.3

WARRANT OF SALE, 2.6

WARRANTY, 2.4

WEEK, 3.7

WIDOW,
  mourning allowance, 29.6

WIFE,
  debtor's, 20.4, 21.18
  oath, 4.6
  partner's, 30.13

WINDING UP. *See* LIQUIDATION.

WRIT,
  proof of loan by, 4.2, 4.5

WRONGFUL TRADING,
  floating charge, 9.18
  liquidation, 25.8